JOURNAL FOR THE STUDY OF THE OLD TESTAMENT SUPPLEMENT SERIES
333

Editors
David J.A. Clines
Philip R. Davies

Executive Editor
Andrew Mein

Editorial Board
Richard J. Coggins, Alan Cooper, J. Cheryl Exum, John Goldingay,
Robert P. Gordon, Norman K. Gottwald, John Jarick,
Andrew D.H. Mayes, Carol Meyers, Patrick D. Miller

THE HEBREW BIBLE AND ITS VERSIONS
2

Sheffield Academic Press
A Continuum imprint

Michael P. Weitzman
1946–1998

Biblical Hebrews, Biblical Texts

Essays in Memory of Michael P. Weitzman

edited by
**Ada Rapoport-Albert and
Gillian Greenberg**

Journal for the Study of the Old Testament
Supplement Series 333

The Hebrew Bible and its Versions 2

Copyright © 2001 Sheffield Academic Press

Published by
Sheffield Academic Press Ltd
The Tower Building, 11 York Road, London SE1 7NX
71 Lexington Avenue, New York, NY 10017-653

www.SheffieldAcademicPress.com
www.continuum-books.com

British Library Cataloguing-in-Publication Data

A catalogue record for this book is available from the British Library

Typeset by Sheffield Academic Press
Printed on acid-free paper in Great Britain by MPG Books Ltd, Bodmin, Cornwall

ISBN 1 84127 235 3

CONTENTS

PREFACE

Michael Weitzman, Reader in Hebrew and Jewish Studies at University College London, died suddenly and prematurely in March 1998. His death at the age of 51 deprived the world of biblical studies of one of its most distinguished and versatile scholars. For 26 years he taught and supervised research in Hebrew language, the Hebrew Bible and its literary history, other Semitic languages and rabbinic texts. His research interests included Semitic philology, Hebrew liturgy, and above all the Peshitta—the Syriac version of the Hebrew Bible, a field in which his work enjoyed an international reputation. At the time of his death he was putting the finishing touches to a major book which appeared posthumously as *The Syriac Version of the Old Testament: An Introduction* (Cambridge: Cambridge University Press, 1999). Shortly afterwards, a collection of his essays, which had previously appeared in various scholarly journals and collective volumes, was assembled by the present editors and published under the title *From Judaism to Christianity: Studies in the Hebrew and Syriac Bibles* (Oxford: Oxford University Press, 1999). While these two volumes witness to his own great learning, many who had worked with Michael Weitzman wished to pay tribute to him. The present volume is the result.

The range and balance of the disciplines represented reflect Michael's own scholarly concerns. Parts 1, on the Hebrew Bible, and 2, on the Versions, are therefore by far the largest, and they include contributions from some of the most distinguished scholars in these fields as well as from a number of Michael's recent research students. Parts 3 and 4, which deal with intertestamental texts and the Eastern Church tradition respectively, engage with the wider contexts in which the impact of the Hebrew and Syriac Bibles was felt. Part 5 is a personal tribute by one of the most eminent Semitic scholars of our time, whose account of Goethe as a young Hebraist evokes something of the linguistic virtuosity of Michael Weitzman himself.

The publication of this volume has been greatly facilitated by the help we have received from Sebastian Brock, Philippa Claiden, Anthony Gelston, David Jacobson, Morris Greenberg, Michael Teper and Hugh Williamson. We would also like to thank our publishers, Sheffield Academic Press, and in particular Philip Davies, who has advised and guided us at various stages of the project, as well as Jeremy Schonfield and Martin Goodman who first connected us with the Press. Finally, thanks are due to our contributors; it was a pleasure to work with all of them.

Ada Rapoport-Albert and Gillian Greenberg
September 2000

ABBREVIATIONS

AAAbo.H	Acta Academiae Aboensis. Ser. A., Humaniora
AAWG	Abhandlungen der Akademie der Wissenschaft in Göttingen
ABD	David Noel Freeman (ed.), *The Anchor Bible Dictionary* (New York: Doubleday, 1992)
AGJU	Arbeiten zur Geschichte des antiken Judentums und des Urchristentums
AB	Anchor Bible
AOAT	Alter Orient und Altes Testament
APOT	R.H. Charles (ed.), *Apocrypha and Pseudepigrapha of the Old Testament in English* (2 vols.; Oxford: Clarendon Press, 1913)
ATD	Das Alte Testament Deutsch
ATDan	Acta Theologica Danica
AV	Authorized Version
BA	*Biblical Archaeologist*
BDB	F. Brown, S.R. Driver and C.A. Briggs, *A Hebrew and English Lexicon of the Old Testament* (Oxford: Clarendon Press, 1907)
BETL	Bibliotheca ephemeridum theologicarum lovaniensium
BEvT	Beiträge zur evangelischen Theologie
BFCT	Beiträge zur Förderung christlicher Theologie
BH	Biblical Hebrew
BHBib	Bibliotheca hispana biblica
BHK	R. Kittel (ed.), *Biblia hebraica* (Stuttgart: Württembergische Bibelanstalt, 1937)
BHS	*Biblia hebraica stuttgartensia*
BHT	Beiträge zur historischen Theologie
Bib	*Biblica*
BibSac	*Bibliotheca Sacra*
BJRL	*Bulletin of the John Rylands Library*
BKAT	Biblischer Kommentar Altes Testament
BN	*Biblische Notizen*
BWANT	Beiträge zur Wissenschaft vom Alten und Neuen Testament
BZ	*Biblische Zeitschrift*
BZAW	Beihefte zur *ZAW*
CAT	Commentaire de l'Ancien Testament
CBQ	*Catholic Biblical Quarterly*

CBQMS	*CBQ* Monograph Series
CCSG	Corpus christianorum series graeca
CCSL	Corpus christianorum series latina
CPJ	V. Tcherikover (ed.), *Corpus papyrorum judaicorum*
CSCO	Corpus scriptorum christianorum orientalium
	Syr = Scriptores Syriaci; Subs = Subsidia
CTA	*Corpus des tablettes en cunéiformes alphabétiques*
DBSup	*Dictionnaire de la Bible, Supplément*
DJD	Discoveries in the Judaean Desert
DSD	*Dead Sea Discoveries*
EBib	Etudes bibliques
EMML	Ethiopian Manuscript Microfilm Library
EncJud	*Encyclopedia Judaica*
ExpTim	*Expository Times*
FJB	*Frankfurter judaistische Beiträge*
FOTL	The Forms of the Old Testament Literature
FzB	Forschung zur Bibel
GCS	Die griechischen christlichen Schriftsteller der ersten drei Jahrhunderte
HALAT	Ludwig Koehler *et al.* (eds.), *Hebräisches und aramäisches Lexicon zum Alten Testament* (5 vols.; New York: Charles Scribner's Sons, 1898–1904)
HAR	*Hebrew Annual Review*
HeyJ	*Heythrop Journal*
HKAT	Handkommentar zum Alten Testament
HSM	Harvard Semitic Monographs
HSS	Harvard Semitic Studies
HTR	*Harvard Theological Review*
HUCA	*Hebrew Union College Annual*
ICC	International Critical Commentary
IDB	George Arthur Buttrick (ed.), *The Interpreter's Dictionary of the Bible* (4 vols.; Nashville: Abingdon Press, 1962)
Int	*Interpretation*
JA	*Journal Asiatique*
JAB	*Journal for the Aramaic Bible*
JAOS	*Journal of the American Oriental Society*
JBL	*Journal of Biblical Literature*
JJS	*Journal of Jewish Studies*
JNES	*Journal of Near Eastern Studies*
JPSV	*Jewish Publication Society Version*
JTS	*Journal of Theological Studies*
JQR	*Jewish Quarterly Review*
JSHRZ	Jüdische Schriften aus hellenistisch-römischer Zeit
JSJ	*Journal for the Study of Judaism*
JSOTSup	*Journal for the Study of the Old Testament*, Supplement Series

JSP	*Journal for the Study of the Pseudepigrapha*
JSS	*Journal of Semitic Studies*
JTS	*Journal of Theological Studies*
KAT	Kommentar zum Alten Testament
KB	Ludwig Koehler and Walter Baumgartner (eds.), *Lexicon in Veteris Testamenti libros* (Leiden: E.J. Brill, 1953)
KHAT	Kurzer Handkommentar zum Alten Testament
LD	Lectio Divina
LSJ	H.G. Liddell, Robert Scott, H. Stuart Jones, *Greek–English Lexicon* (Oxford: Clarendon Press, 9th edn, 1968)
MPIL	Monographs of the Peshitta Institute, Leiden
MSU	Mitteilungen des Septuaginta-Unternehmens
Mus	*Muséon: Revue d'études orientales*
NCB	New Century Bible
NEB	*New English Bible*
NGG	*Nachrichten von der königlichen Gesellschaft der Wissenschaften zu Göttingen*
NICOT	New International Commentary on the Old Testament
NIV	New International Version
NRSV	New Revised Standard Version
NTS	*New Testament Studies*
OBO	Orbis biblicus et orientalis
OBT	Overtures in Biblical Theology
OCA	*Orientalia christiana analecta*
OCP	*Orientalia christiana periodica*
OGIS	Orientis graeci inscriptiones selectae
OrChr	*Oriens christianus*
OTG	Old Testament Guides
OTL	Old Testament Library
OTS	*Oudtestamentische Studiën*
PGL	*Patrologia graeca latina*
PL	J.P. Migne (ed.), *Patrologia cursus completus...Series prima [latina]* (221 vols.; Paris: J.-P. Migne, 1844–65)
PO	Patrologia Orientalis
PW	August Friedrich von Pauly and Georg Wissowa (eds.), *Real-Encyclopädie der classischen Altertumswissenschaft* (Stuttgart: Metzler, 1894–)
RB	*Revue biblique*
REB	*Revised English Bible*
RevQ	*Revue de Qumran*
RHPR	*Revue d'histoire et de philosophie religieuses*
SANT	Studien zum Alten und Neuen Testament
SBL	Society of Biblical Literature
SBLDS	SBL Dissertation Series
SBLSCS	SBL Septuagint and Cognate Studies

SBS	Stuttgarter Bibelstudien
SBT	Studies in Biblical Theology
SEL	*Studi epigrafici e linguistici sul vicino oriente antico*
SJT	*Scottish Journal of Theology*
SPB	Studia post-biblica
STDJ	Studies on the Texts of the Desert of Judah
SVTP	Studia in Veteris Testamenti pseudepigrapha
TBü	Theologische Bücherei
TEG	Traditio exegetica graeca
TLOT	*Theological Lexicon of the Old Testament*
TSAJ	Texte und Studien zum Antiken Judentum
TU	Texte und Untersuchungen
UBL	Ugaritisch-biblische Literatur
UF	*Ugarit-Forschungen*
VT	*Vetus Testamentum*
VTSup	*Vetus Testamentum*, Supplements
WBC	Word Biblical Commentary
WMANT	Wissenschaftliche Monographien zum Alten und Neuen Testament
WO	*Die Welt des Orients*
ZA	*Zeitschrift für Assyriologie*
ZAW	*Zeitschrift für die alttestamentliche Wissenschaft*
ZDMG	*Zeitschrift der deutschen morgenländischen Gesellschaft*

BIOGRAPHICAL NOTES

Philip S. Alexander is Professor of Post-Biblical Jewish Literature in the Department of Religions and Theology at the University of Manchester, and co-director of the Centre for Jewish Studies at the University of Manchester. His main research interests are Jewish history and literature in the Second Temple and Talmudic periods. His publications include the edition of Cave 4 fragments of the Community Rule published in the Discoveries in the Judaean Desert Series 26 (1999) and *Textual Sources for the Study of Judaism* (1984, 1992).

Siam Bhayro received his doctorate from University College London in June 2000 for a thesis on the descent of the Watchers in *1 Enoch* 6–11, part of which is reproduced in the present volume. His interests are Semitic languages, the Bible, and the ancient Near East.

Sebastian P. Brock is Reader in Syriac Studies in the University of Oxford, Professorial Fellow of Wolfson College, Oxford, and a Fellow of the British Academy. His main research interest is Syriac literature; his recent publications include *A Brief Outline of Syriac Literature* (1997) and *From Ephrem to Romanos: Interactions between Syriac and Greek in Late Antiquity* (1999).

George J. Brooke is Rylands Professor of Biblical Criticism and Exegesis in the Department of Religions and Theology at the University of Manchester. He is a member of the international team of editors of the Dead Sea Scrolls and has authored many studies on the scrolls including *Exegesis at Qumran: 4Q Florilegium in its Jewish Context* (1985) and *The Allegro Qumran Collection* (1996). He has edited or co-edited and contributed to various collective volumes including, most recently, *Narrativity in Biblical and Related Texts* (2000), and *Jewish Ways of Reading the Bible* (2000).

John A. Emerton is Emeritus Regius Professor of Hebrew at the University of Cambridge, a Fellow of St John's College, Cambridge, an Honorary Canon of St George's Cathedral, Jerusalem, and a Fellow of the British Academy. From 1975 until 1997 he was the editor of *Vetus Testamentum*. His main research interests are Hebrew and other North-West Semitic languages, especially Syriac and Ugaritic, and the religion and literature of ancient Israel. His publications include *The Peshitta of the Wisdom of Solomon* (1959) and numerous articles in journals and *Festschriften*.

Anthony Gelston is Emeritus Reader in Theology at the University of Durham. In retirement he is editing the Twelve Prophets for the fifth edition of *Biblia Hebraica*. His publications include *The Peshitta of the Twelve Prophets* (1987) and 'Was the Peshitta of Isaiah of Christian Origin?', in Craig C. Broyles and Craig A. Evans (eds.), *Writing and reading the Scroll of Isaiah: Studies of an Interpretive Tradition* (1997).

Robert P. Gordon is Regius Professor of Hebrew at the University of Cambridge, and a Fellow of St Catharine's College. His main research interest is the Hebrew Bible and its ancient Versions; his publications include *Studies in the Targum to the Twelve Prophets* (1994); *The Old Testament in Syriac: Chronicles* (1998); and *Hebrews: A Commentary* (2000).

Sally L. Gold teaches Biblical Hebrew at University College London, and Biblical Hebrew, Aramaic, and Targum Studies at Leo Baeck College London, where she is a doctoral student. Her main research interest is the Aramaic translations of the book of Job, which form the subject of her doctoral thesis. Her publications include various articles in J. Bowker (ed.), *The Complete Bible Handbook* (1998).

Gillian Greenberg has recently entered the field of biblical studies, after retirement from a first career in clinical medical research. Her main research interest is the Peshitta, particularly the books of Jeremiah, Isaiah, and the Psalms. Her PhD thesis, 'Translation Technique in the Peshitta to Jeremiah', which was supervised by the late Michael Weitzman, will be published in the series of monographs of the Peshitta Institute, Leiden. Other publications include 'The Peshitta to 2 Samuel

22 and Psalm 18: One Translation or Two?', *JAB* 2 (2000). She now teaches Syriac language and literature at University College London.

Coralie A. Gutridge is a teacher of Classical Hebrew at University College London. Her main research interests include the ethics of power and control in Hebrew and Greek Wisdom, their influence on other genres, and the language, art, and ethics of the Hebrew Bible. Her PhD thesis, supervised by the late Michael Weitzman, was on 'Wisdom, Anti-wisdom and the Ethical Function of Uncertainty: The Book of Qoheleth/Ecclesiastes in the Context of Biblical and Greek Wisdom Theory'.

Konrad D. Jenner is Head of the Peshitta Institute, Leiden, Director of the Peshitta Projects co-ordinated by that Institute, and Senior Lecturer (University Docent) at Leiden University. His main research interests are the comparative history of religions, the empirical and applied study of religion, and Old Testament Studies, especially Text-Criticism, Textual and Reception History. He has recently edited, jointly with P.G. Borbone, *The Old Testament in Syriac According to the Peshitta Version*. Part 5. *Concordance*. I. *Pentateuch* (1997); his other publications include 'Syrohexaplarische und proto-syrohexaplarische Zitate in syrischen Quellen außer den individuellen Examplaren des syrohexaplarischen Psalters', in A. Aejmaleus und U. Quast (eds.), *Der Septuaginta-Psalter und seine Tochterübersetzungen: Symposium in Göttingen, 1997* (2000).

Jan Joosten is Professor of Biblical Philology at the Protestant Faculty of the Marc Bloch University, Strasbourg. His main research interests include Hebrew grammar, and the textual history of both the Hebrew Bible and the New Testament. His recent publications include *The Syriac Language of the Peshitta and Old Syriac Versions of Matthew* (1996) and 'La Peshitta de l'Ancien Testament dans la recherche recente', *RHPR* 76 (1996).

Michael A. Knibb was most recently Samuel Davidson Professor of Old Testament Studies (now Emeritus) and Head of the School of Humanities at King's College London. He is a Fellow of the British Academy. His main research interests are Jewish writings from the Second Temple period, and Ethiopic Bible translations. His recent publications include *Translating the Bible: The Ethiopic Version of the Old Testament* (1999); 'The Ethiopic Translation of the Psalms', in A. Aejmaleus and U. Quast (eds.), *Der Septuaginta-Psalter und seine Tochterübersetzungen: Symposium in Göttingen, 1997* (2000); and articles in L.H. Schiffman and J.C. VanderKam (eds.), *Encyclopedia of the Dead Sea Scrolls* (2000).

David J. Lane is now retired. He has taught in the Universities of Oxford and Toronto, and prepared material for the Leiden Edition of the Peshitta. His research interests include the early seventh-century Syriac writer Shubhalmaran, whose work *The Book of Gifts* he is preparing for publication.

Dan Levene is a lecturer in Jewish History and Civilisation at Southampton University. His main research interests are Jewish Aramaic dialects, Jewish magic in late antiquity, and Talmudic realia. His doctoral thesis is entitled 'Incantation Texts in Jewish Aramaic from Late Antiquity—A Corpus of Magic Bowls'. Recent publications include ' "…and by the name of Jesus". An Unpublished Magic Bowl in Jewish Aramaic', *Jewish Studies Quarterly* 6 (1999), and, with B. Rothenberg, 'באשׁי אבי—A Fundamental Aspect of the Nature of Metal', *JAB* 2.1 (2000).

Raphael Loewe is Emeritus Goldsmid Professor of Hebrew at University College London. His publications include *Gilguley merubba'im* (Hebrew translation of Fitzgerald's *Omar Khayyam*) (1982), *The Rylands Haggadah* (1988), and *Ibn Gabirol* (1989); his edition and translation of Isaac ibn Sahula, *Meshal haqadmoni*, will appear in 2002.

Andrew A. Macintosh is a Fellow and Dean of St John's College, Cambridge, where he also served as President. He is the author of *Isaiah xxi: A Palimpsest* (1980) and of a Commentary on Hosea in the International Critical Commentary series (1997).

Ada Rapoport-Albert is Reader in Jewish History at the department of Hebrew and Jewish Studies, University College London. Her main research interests are the history of Jewish spirituality, especially Hasidism and Sabbateanism. Her publications include, as editor, *Essays in Jewish Historiography* (1988), *Hasidism Reappraised* (1996), and, as

author, various studies on the history of Hasidism, a Hebrew monograph on the position of women in Sabbateanism (2001), and *Female
Bodies—Male Souls* (forthcoming).

R. Bas ter Haar Romeny is a Royal Netherlands Academy Research
Fellow at the Peshitta Institute in the Faculty of Theology at the Uni-
versity of Leiden. His research interests include the Hebrew Bible and
the ancient Versions, Syriac language and literature, and the history of
Jewish and Christian exegesis. His current research project is entitled
'Text and Context: The Syriac Bible (Old Testament) in the Period
between the 8th and the 13th Centuries'. Recent publications include *A
Syrian in Greek Dress: The Use of Greek, Hebrew, and Syriac Biblical
Texts in Eusebius of Emesa's Commentary on Genesis* (1997).

Beno Rothenberg is Professor of Archaeo-Metallurgy and Director of
the Institute for Archaeo-Metallurgical Studies at University College
London. His main research interest is the history and archaeology of
metallurgy. His main excavations have been in the Timna Valley, the
Sinai Desert, the Arabah, and the South of Spain. His publications
include *The Egyptian Mining Temple at Timna* (1988) and *The Ancient
Metallurgy of Copper* (1990).

Alison Salvesen is a Fellow of the Oxford Centre for Hebrew and Jewish Studies, Research Fellow of Wolfson College Oxford, and Hebrew
Centre Lecturer at the Oriental Institute Oxford. Her main research
interests are the ancient translations and interpretations of the Hebrew
Bible, especially those in Greek and Syriac. Recent publications include
I–II Samuel in the Syriac Version of Jacob of Edessa (1999) and, as
editor, *Origen's Hexapla and Fragments: Papers Presented at the Rich
Seminar on the Hexapla, Oxford Centre for Hebrew and Jewish Studies*
(1998), to which she has contributed 'Symmachus Readings in the
Pentateuch'.

Marian Smelik is assistant editor of *A Bilingual Concordance to the
Targum of the Prophets* (1995–), prepared by a team at the Theologische Universiteit Kampen, The Netherlands.

Willem Smelik is a lecturer in Biblical Hebrew at University College
London, and editor of the *Journal for the Aramaic Bible*. His research

interests range from the Hebrew Bible to Rabbinic Judaism, with a particular interest in the Targums. He is currently working on a monograph on the rabbinic views of translations of the Bible, and his publications include *The Targum of Judges* (1995).

Edward Ullendorff is Emeritus Professor of Semitic Languages and of Ethiopian Studies in the University of London. He is a Fellow of the British Academy and of the Accademia Nazionale dei Lincei, Rome. His publications include *The Semitic Languages of Ethiopia* (1956), *Ethiopia and the Bible* (1968), *Is Biblical Hebrew a Language? Studies in Semitic Languages and Literatures* (1977) and *The Two Zions* (1988).

Donald Walter is Professor of Religion at Davis and Elkins College in West Virginia, USA. His main research interest is the Peshitta. He is an editor of several works in this field, including the Concordance to the Pentateuch, Psalms, Jeremiah, and Kings, all published or awaiting publication by the Peshitta Institute, Leiden, and of the article on the Peshitta in the Abingdon Press *Dictionary of Biblical Interpretation* (1999).

H.G.M. Williamson is Regius Professor of Hebrew at the University of Oxford, a Student of Christ Church, and a Fellow of the British Academy. His main research field is the Hebrew Bible, particularly the book of Isaiah, and post-exilic history and literature. Recent publications include *The Book Called Isaiah: Deutero-Isaiah's Role in Composition and Redaction* (1994) and *Variations on a Theme: King, Messiah and Servant in the Book of Isaiah* (1998).

Michael M. Winter was Dean of St Edmund's College, Cambridge, and has taught Syriac at University College London. His main research interest is Ben Sira, which was the subject of his doctoral thesis. His publications include a *Concordance to the Peshitta Version of Ben Sira* (1975) and articles in *Vetus Testamentum* in which he has argued that Ben Sira was translated from Hebrew into Syriac by the Ebionites.

Part I
THE HEBREW BIBLE

ISAIAH AND THE HOLY ONE OF ISRAEL

H.G.M. Williamson

The divine title 'The Holy One of Israel' has long been recognized as peculiarly characteristic of the book of Isaiah, and indeed has frequently been cited by conservative scholars, both Jewish and Christian, as a major reason why unity of authorship of the whole book should be upheld.[1] Similarly, among those who accept plurality of authorship but who, in increasing numbers, nevertheless believe that the association of the various parts within a single work is due to more than the vagaries of chance alone, this expression is usually mentioned as a particularly strong argument in their favour. In what is often now regarded as a pioneering contribution to this modern phase of the study of Isaiah, for instance, John Eaton wrote that 'the persistence of the divine title "The Holy One of Israel" throughout the book of Isaiah to an extent quite without parallel in the rest of the Old Testament is a striking indication of a solidarity existing between the various authors'.[2] Similarly,

---

1.   E.g. J. Kennedy, *A Popular Argument for the Unity of Isaiah* (London: James Clarke, 1891), pp. 115-18; J.J. Lias, 'The Unity of Isaiah', *BibSac* 72 (1915), pp. 560-91 (572); W.A. Wordsworth, *Sawn Asunder: A Study of the Mystery of the Gospel of Isaiah* (London: Alexander Moring, 1927), p. 95; G.L. Robinson, *The Book of Isaiah* (Grand Rapids: Baker Book House, rev. edn, 1954), p. 14; E.J. Young, *Who Wrote Isaiah?* (Grand Rapids: Eerdmans, 1958), p. 57; R. Margalioth, *The Indivisible Isaiah: Evidence for the Single Authorship of the Prophetic Book* (New York: Yeshiva University, 1964), pp. 43-48; R.K. Harrison, *Introduction to the Old Testament* (London: The Tyndale Press, 1970), p. 796; J.N. Oswalt, *The Book of Isaiah, Chapters 1–39* (NICOT; Grand Rapids: Eerdmans, 1986), p. 19; J.A. Motyer, *The Prophecy of Isaiah* (London: Inter-Varsity Press, 1993), pp. 17-18 and 29.

2.   J.H. Eaton, 'The Origin of the Book of Isaiah', *VT* 9 (1959), pp. 138-57. The citation given above (from p. 153) continues 'surely exceeding the relationship of literary dependence'. This relates to Eaton's hypothesis of a continuing school of disciples of Isaiah, a theory which is now less commonly accepted.

Douglas Jones, who not long before had written an equally influential early article on the connections between the various parts of the book,[3] could later say of this title that it 'becomes one of the common themes of the whole Isaianic corpus'.[4] The same observation has been repeatedly made in more recent years,[5] and indeed at least once it has been used as the basis for an attempt to outline a theology of the book as a whole.[6]

At first sight the facts seem to bear out these conclusions. However, as soon as they are examined in more detail, they raise interesting questions which have not generally been commented upon but which nevertheless appear deserving of further reflection. First, then, what are the facts? Since those who have previously discussed the matter differ among themselves over the precise figures, I here set out the position in full.

The phrase 'The Holy One of Israel (קְדוֹשׁ יִשְׂרָאֵל)' itself occurs 25

3.   D.R. Jones, 'The Traditio of the Oracles of Isaiah of Jerusalem', *ZAW* 67 (1955), pp. 226-46.

4.   D.R. Jones, 'Exposition of Isaiah Chapter One Verses One to Nine', *SJT* 17 (1964), pp. 463-77.

5.   Among many examples that could be cited, see J. Schreiner, 'Das Buch jesajanischer Schule', in J. Schreiner (ed.), *Wort und Botschaft: Eine theologische und kritische Einführung in die Probleme des Alten Testaments* (Würzburg: Echter Verlag, 1967), pp. 143-62; W.L. Holladay, *Isaiah: Scroll of a Prophetic Heritage* (Grand Rapids: Eerdmans, 1978), p. 17; R. Rendtorff, 'Zur Komposition des Buches Jesaja', *VT* 34 (1984), pp. 295-320 (310-12) (ET, 'The Composition of the Book of Isaiah', in M. Kohl [ed.], *Canon and Theology: Overtures to an Old Testament Theology* [Edinburgh: T. & T. Clark, 1994], pp. 146-69 [160-62]); D.G. Meade, *Pseudonymity and Canon: An Investigation into the Relationship of Authorship and Authority in Jewish and Earliest Christian Tradition* (Grand Rapids: Eerdmans, 1987), pp. 32-33; R. Albertz, 'Das Deuterojesaja-Buch als Fortschreibung der Jesaja-Prophetie', in E. Blum *et al.* (eds.), *Die hebräische Bibel und ihre zweifache Nachgeschichte: Festschrift für Rolf Rendtorff zum 65. Geburtstag* (Neukirchen–Vluyn: Neukirchener Verlag, 1990), pp. 241-56. I have myself previously given some attention to this matter, of which the present article may be seen as both a refinement and an extension; cf. *The Book Called Isaiah: Deutero-Isaiah's Role in Composition and Redaction* (Oxford: Clarendon Press, 1994), pp. 41-45.

6.   J.J.M. Roberts, 'Isaiah in Old Testament Theology', *Int* 36 (1982), pp. 130-43; see too J.G. Gammie, *Holiness in Israel* (OBT; Minneapolis: Fortress Press, 1989), ch. 3.

times in the book, 12 times in chs. 1–39,[7] 11 times in 40–55,[8] and twice in 56–66.[9] In addition, however, there are some very closely related expressions, and it is usual to include these in the discussion as well. Thus, 'his Holy One (קדושו)', with Israel as its antecedent, occurs twice (10.17; 49.7), 'the Holy One of Jacob (קדוש יעקב)' occurs once (29.23) in parallel with 'the God of Israel', and 'your Holy One (קדושכם)', followed by the appositional 'the creator of Israel' also occurs once (43.15). Finally, there is one use of the absolute קדוש in 40.25,[10] while in 5.16 he is called האל הקדוש and in 57.15 his name is said to be קדוש. Though these absolute uses are clearly related to a certain extent, they are nevertheless distinguished in that they lack the explicit association with Israel[11] which characterizes all the other examples mentioned, and so they will not be discussed further here. If we therefore revise our statistics to take account of all this, we arrive at 14 occurrences in chs. 1–39, 13 in 40–55 and 2 in 56–66.

The first point that immediately strikes us in considering these figures is the relative paucity of occurrences in chs. 56–66, where the title is found only twice, and that in a single passage. Moreover, it is widely agreed that of all the material in Trito-Isaiah, chs. 60–62, within which our occurrences fall, is the part most closely related to the work of Deutero-Isaiah,[12] and indeed a few have argued that they are the work of the same author.[13] Without necessarily going as far as that, we may

7.   1.4; 5.19, 24; 10.20; 12.6; 17.7; 29.19; 30.11, 12, 15; 31.1; 37.23.
8.   41.14, 16, 20; 43.3, 14; 45.11; 47.4; 48.17; 49.7; 54.5; 55.5.
9.   60.9, 14.
10.   The same title, used absolutely, also occurs in Hab. 3.3 and Job 6.10.
11.   The conjecture of J. Morgenstern, 'The Loss of Words at the Ends of Lines in Manuscripts of Biblical Poetry', *HUCA* 25 (1954), pp. 41-83 (54), that ישראל should be restored in 40.25 has been rightly rejected by subsequent commentators; cf. C.R. North, *The Second Isaiah: Introduction, Translation and Commentary to Chapters xl-lv* (Oxford: Clarendon Press, 1964), p. 88; K. Elliger, *Deuterojesaja. I. Jesaja 40,1–45,7* (BKAT 11/1; Neukirchen–Vluyn: Neukirchener Verlag, 1978), p. 87.
12.   See, for instance, the summaries of recent research in P.A. Smith, *Rhetoric and Redaction in Trito-Isaiah: The Structure, Growth and Authorship of Isaiah 56–66* (VTSup, 62; Leiden: E.J. Brill, 1995), and G.I. Emmerson, *Isaiah 56–66* (OTG; Sheffield: Sheffield Academic Press, 1992). The particular importance of Westermann's commentary in this regard should not be overlooked; cf. C. Westermann, *Das Buch Jesaja, 40–66* (ATD, 19; Göttingen: Vandenhoeck & Ruprecht, 1966) (ET, *Isaiah 40–66: A Commentary* [OTL; London: SCM Press, 1969]).
13.   See especially N.H. Snaith, 'Isaiah 40–66: A Study of the Teaching of the

certainly observe that, in the case of 60.9, not only is the substance of the verse reflective of one of Deutero-Isaiah's familiar themes (see, for example, 43.6; 51.5), but the occurrence of the title itself seems to be due to what amounts to a citation of 55.5; compare 'for the name of the Lord your God, and for the Holy One of Israel, because he has glorified you' (60.9b) with 'because of the Lord your God, the Holy One of Israel, for he has glorified you' (55.5b).[14] It is on this basis, we may note in passing, that Koenen relegates the line to the status of a redactional addition.[15] Whether or not he is justified in this conclusion,[16] it certainly seems to be the case that the occurrence in this verse owes more to the accident of imitation than to substance; the surrounding context points to the likelihood that it was the use of 'glorify (פאר)' which attracted the author to 55.5 rather than the divine title (cf. vv. 7 and 13[17]).

With regard to 60.14, the case is slightly different. Certainly, the substance of the verse again echoes parts of Deutero-Isaiah (e.g. 45.14 and 49.23),[18] but it is then followed by an apparently unparalleled expression, 'they shall call you the City of the Lord, the Zion of the Holy One of Israel'. That Jerusalem should be given new names is common enough in the prophets, not least in Isaiah,[19] but 'the Zion of the Holy

---

Second Isaiah and its Consequences', in H.M. Orlinsky and N.H. Snaith, *Studies on the Second Part of the Book of Isaiah* (VTSup, 14; Leiden: E.J. Brill, 1967), pp. 139-46.

14. לשם יהוה אלהיך ולקדוש ישראל כי פארך (60.9b), and למען יהוה אלהיך ולקדוש ישראל כי פארך (55.5b).

15. K. Koenen, *Ethik und Eschatologie: Eine literarkritische und redaktionsgeschichtliche Studie* (WMANT, 62; Neukirchen–Vluyn: Neukirchener Verlag, 1990), pp. 148-49.

16. His arguments are rejected by O.H. Steck, *Studien zu Tritojesaja* (BZAW, 203; Berlin: W. de Gruyter, 1991), p. 122.

17. *Mutatis mutandis*, this conclusion stands, of course, regardless of whether or not we follow Koenen in seeing these references also as redactional.

18. Cf. W. Zimmerli, 'Zur Sprache Tritojesajas', in *Gottes Offenbarung: Gesammelte Aufsätze zum Alten Testament* (TBü, 19; Munich: Chr. Kaiser Verlag, 1963), pp. 217-33 (222).

19. See the list in P.-E. Bonnard, *Le second Isaïe, son disciple et leurs éditeurs: Isaïe 40–66* (Paris: J. Gabalda, 1972), p. 409 n. 5. Whether we should see a specific echo here of the formulation of Isa. 1.26 is uncertain, contra J. Vermeylen, *Du prophète Isaïe à l'apocalyptique: Isaïe, I–XXXV, miroir d'un demi-millénaire d'expérience religieuse en Israël*, II (Paris: J. Gabalda, 1978), p. 476.

One of Israel' is not attested elsewhere.[20] Nonetheless, as suggested by Fishbane,[21] it is possible that the expression echoes Isa. 12.6, where the two elements of the new name occur in parallel halves of the same line: 'Shout aloud and sing for joy, O inhabitant of Zion, for great in your midst is the Holy One of Israel'. Certainly this is the only passage in the Hebrew Bible where Zion and the Holy One of Israel are mentioned in close proximity with one another, and the fact that it has recently been shown that Isa. 60 draws heavily not just on Deutero-Isaiah but on the first part of the book as well[22] makes the proposal appealing.

Even without this, however, it is clear that our divine title was not of great significance for Trito-Isaiah. In one case certainly, and possibly in both, it enters his work in the form of a citation or allusion selected for the sake of other elements in the parent text, and so cannot be held to be in any way central to his thought. Furthermore, it appears to be attested only in what is generally regarded as the earliest stratum in these chapters. It does not occur in the work of the later hand or hands which scholars generally identify. This conclusion stands in marked contrast with the recent assertion of Lau that the thought of 'The Holy One of Israel' has played an important role in the work of the authors of chs. 56–66.[23] Closer inspection of the evidence that he cites in support of this assertion shows, however, that he is thinking rather of such clear allusions to Isa. 6 as those in 57.15 and in the 'high and lofty mountain' of 57.7. Without wishing for a moment to deny the influence of Isa. 6 and related passages on such formulations, it seems to be straining the evidence too far to run all this together into what becomes virtually an

20. That does not, however, seem to be sufficient ground for revocalizing the Masoretic Text, as has sometimes been proposed; cf. *BHS*.

21. M. Fishbane, *Biblical Interpretation in Ancient Israel* (Oxford: Clarendon Press, 1985), p. 498. This is regarded as 'doubtful', however, by B.D. Sommer, *A Prophet Reads Scripture: Allusion in Isaiah 40–66* (Stanford: Stanford University Press, 1998), p. 259.

22. Cf. R.E. Clements, ' "Arise, Shine; for your Light has Come": A Basic Theme of the Isaianic Tradition', in C.C. Broyles and C.A. Evans (eds.), *Writing and Reading the Scroll of Isaiah: Studies of an Interpretive Tradition*, I (VTSup, 50, 1; Leiden: E.J. Brill, 1997), pp. 441-54; see too Fishbane, *Biblical Interpretation*, pp. 497-98.

23. W. Lau, *Schriftgelehrte Prophetie in Jes 56–66: Eine Untersuchung zu den literarischen Bezügen in den letzten elf Kapiteln des Jesajabuches* (BZAW, 225; Berlin: W. de Gruyter, 1994), p. 322: 'Eine wichtige Rolle für die Autoren in Jes 56–66 spielt auch der jesajanische Gedanke an den "*Heiligen Israels*" '.

abstract concept, especially as the title in question appears neither in ch. 57 and the other passages he refers to, nor even, as we shall see, in ch. 6 itself.

Following on from this conclusion, it is interesting to observe next the generally unnoticed fact that the title does not occur even once in the 'Isaiah Apocalypse' of chs. 24–27 or in the so-called 'little apocalypse' of chs. 34–35, both significant sections of the first part of the book which scholars generally agree should be dated relatively late. It therefore begins to look as though the title is not after all characteristic of the Isaiah tradition as a whole, but that it fell away from use at least in the later stages of the book's composition.

Let us turn now from endings to beginnings and consider in more detail the situation with regard to Isa. 1–39. And here two points require discussion, namely the much debated issue of whether Isaiah was himself responsible for coining the title and secondly the frequency with which he may have used it.

To take the second point first, there is a wide diversity of opinion about how many of the passages in 1–39 where the title occurs should be ascribed to the eighth-century prophet himself. At one end of the scale, more conservative scholars attribute all, or virtually all, occurrences to him, while at the other end Loretz has argued that not a single one goes back to him.[24] Most critical scholars, of course, come somewhere in between. Thus Wildberger, who is generally regarded as on the conservative side of moderate, ascribes the following seven occurrences to Isaiah himself: 1.4; 5.19, 24; 30.11, 12, 15; 31.1.[25]

24. O. Loretz, *Der Prolog des Jesaja Buches (1,1–2,5): Ugaritologische und kolometrische Studien zum Jesaja-Buch*, I (UBL, 1; Altenberge: CIS-Verlag, 1984), pp. 97-110. As is well known, O. Kaiser became increasingly uncertain through the course of writing and later rewriting his commentary about how much of the present book could be ascribed to the eighth-century prophet. Loretz is incorrect, however, in claiming his support even for 31.1; cf. O. Kaiser, *Der Prophet Jesaja: Kapitel 13–39* (ATD, 18; Göttingen: Vandenhoeck & Ruprecht, 1973), p. 248 (ET, *Isaiah 13–39: A Commentary* [OTL; London: SCM Press, 1974], pp. 311-12). Admittedly, when Kaiser later undertook the major revision of his first volume he seems to have become less certain; cf. *Das Buch des Propheten Jesaja: Kapitel 1–12* (ATD, 17; Göttingen: Vandenhoeck & Ruprecht, 5th edn, 1981), p. 20 (ET, *Isaiah 1–12: A Commentary* [OTL; London: SCM Press, 1983], pp. 1-2).

25. H. Wildberger, *Jesaja*. I. *Jesaja 1–12* (BKAT, 10/1; Neukirchen–Vluyn: Neukirchener Verlag, 2nd edn, 1980), p. 23 (ET, *Isaiah 1–12: A Commentary* [Minneapolis: Fortress Press, 1991], p. 24).

It is highly unlikely, of course, that agreement will ever be reached on an issue such as this, and many nowadays find even the discussion of the topic tedious, if not irrelevant. Nevertheless, in the present context it cannot be wholly sidestepped, even if space precludes examination of every passage.

In my opinion, Wildberger's list needs to be reduced further. The occurrences in 1.4b and 5.24b are closely related in theme and vocabulary: 'They have abandoned the Lord, they have spurned the Holy One of Israel' (1.4), and 'They have rejected the law of the Lord of Hosts, and they have spurned the word of the Holy One of Israel' (5.24). In both cases the lines give a general explanation for a woe saying, and they share the use of the verb נאץ, the divine title we are examining, and a twofold use of the accusative marker את. Partly on this basis, and in the light of a wider hypothesis concerning the nature of the composition, or better compilation, of the first chapter of Isaiah, I have speculated that this may all be due to 1.4 having been given its present position by the chapter's redactor who moved the verse from its original setting preceding 5.8, where it will have served to introduce the series of woe sayings in 5.8-24, just as 5.24b serves to conclude it.[26] The suggestion that both lines are the work of the redactor who grouped the series of woe sayings follows naturally, and it may help explain the presence of what a number of scholars regard as Deuteronomic vocabulary,[27] as well as the use of the prose particles. Even without an appeal to my admittedly speculative hypothesis, however, it is noteworthy that many commentators have concluded that 5.24b is redactional,[28] and if so the close similarities with 1.4b would point to a similar origin for

26. H.G.M. Williamson, 'Relocating Isaiah 1:2-9', in Broyles and Evans (eds.), *Writing and Reading the Scroll of Isaiah*, pp. 263-77.

27. E.g. Vermeylen, *Du prophète Isaïe à l'apocalyptique*, pp. 55-56 and 174-75; Kaiser, *Jesaja*, p. 34 (ET, *Isaiah 1–12*, p. 18). Jer. 23.17 (cf. LXX) should be added to their already extensive lists of parallels.

28. E.g. K. Marti, *Das Buch Jesaja* (HKAT, 10; Tübingen: J.C.B. Mohr [Paul Siebeck], 1900), pp. 59-60; O. Procksch, *Jesaia I* (KAT, 9; Leipzig: A. Deichert, 1930), p. 97; H. Barth, *Die Jesaja-Worte in der Josiazeit: Israel und Assur als Thema einer produktiven Neuinterpretation der Jesajaüberlieferung* (WMANT, 48; Neukirchen–Vluyn: Neukirchener Verlag, 1977), pp. 115-16; R.E. Clements, *Isaiah 1–39* (NCB; Grand Rapids: Eerdmans; London: Marshall, Morgan & Scott, 1980), p. 66; R. Porath, *Die Sozialkritik im Jesajabuch: Redaktionsgeschichtliche Analyse* (Frankfurt: Peter Lang, 1994), pp. 134-37.

that line too.[29] Either way, there is a strong probability that these two occurrences should be attributed to the hand of a later, though still pre-exilic, redactor.[30]

If this conclusion is correct, then it should be noted that the only possible use of the divine title 'The Holy One of Israel' which could conceivably come from the first part of Isaiah's ministry would be 5.19. Not even that conclusion can be regarded as certain, however, not so much because of doubts about authenticity[31] as because of difficulties of knowing when to set the saying within Isaiah's lifetime. It is generally assumed that it is early simply on the ground that many, if not all, the other woe sayings in ch. 5 are. On the other hand, however, it could equally well be observed that Isaiah certainly used this form later on as well (cf. 28.1; 29.1; 30.1; 31.1), and that the mocking speech here condemned finds its closest parallels in ch. 28 (note the אנשי לצון in 28.14) and in 30.10-11, where it is again linked specifically with rejection of 'The Holy One of Israel'. Indeed, Høgenhaven has made a strong case for dating the whole series of woe sayings to this later period.[32] The fact of the matter is that we simply do not know when to date this verse. All we can say, on the basis of the evidence available to

29. So correctly L. Rost, *Israel bei den Propheten* (BWANT, 71; Stuttgart: Kohlhammer, 1937), pp. 37-38.

30. Probably the fullest attempt to defend Isaianic authorship is J. Jensen, *The Use of tôrâ by Isaiah: His Debate with the Wisdom Tradition* (CBQMS, 3; Washington: The Catholic Biblical Association of America, 1973), pp. 95-104. Wildberger himself (*Jesaja*, I, p. 197 [ET, *Isaiah 1–12*, p. 212]) adopts a middle position, which almost gives the game away: he accepts that the verse was given its present position by a later redactor in order to round off the series of woe oracles, but maintains that it nevertheless originated with Isaiah. His main arguments are the use of some characteristically Isaianic terminology and especially the use of אמרה, which occurs elsewhere in Isaiah but which is not, he claims, Deuteronomic. However, it occurs in Deut. 32.2 and 33.9, as Wildberger himself admits, so that it is not clear how much weight should be put upon this point; that a later redactor should borrow Isaianic phraseology (such as the divine title) is not only to be expected, but well established from elsewhere.

31. W. Werner, *Studien zur alttestamentlichen Vorstellung vom Plan Jahwes* (BZAW, 173; Berlin: W. de Gruyter, 1988), pp. 14-20, is possibly the strongest advocate of a date long after the time of Isaiah for this verse.

32. J. Høgenhaven, *Gott und Volk bei Jesaja: Eine Untersuchung zur biblischen Theologie* (ATDan, 24; Leiden: E.J. Brill, 1988), pp. 169-77; in addition, W. Dietrich, *Jesaja und die Politik* (BEvT, 74; Munich: Chr. Kaiser Verlag, 1976), pp. 168-70, has argued that specifically 5.18-19 derives from the later period.

us, is that our divine title does not seem to have been of particular importance for Isaiah in the first part of his ministry and that conceivably he did not use it then at all. If he had, we might certainly have expected to find it more widely attested, not least in ch. 6, where the *trisagion* of v. 3 would have been an obvious trigger to bring it to his mind.[33]

The relatively few occurrences that can be dated with some degree of certainty thus all seem to come from Isaiah's role in the events leading up to Sennacherib's invasion in 701 BCE. The authenticity of 31.1, for instance, has hardly ever been doubted, but in order to ensure that we are building on a solid foundation, a brief response to the counterarguments of Loretz ought to be added.

In his analysis of this verse,[34] Loretz argues that the second two lines (which include the divine title in question) have been added secondarily. Two of his arguments relate directly to the third line, which is of most immediate concern to us. First, he asserts that the accusative particle את could not have been used in poetry as early as the time of Isaiah. While that principle may have some validity in general terms, its application is misguided in the present instance, where the particle follows the verb דרש. For whatever reason, it seems that the accusative particle was regularly used with this particular verb in eighth-century poetry, including by Isaiah himself (cf. Isa. 9.12; Hos. 10.12; Amos 5.6);[35] the explanation may have something to do with the expression as a whole being a technical religious term, and so fixed. In addition, the rather rigid parallelism displayed by these lines may also have called for a balance for the preposition על in the first half of the line. Loretz's second argument against this line relates to his idiosyncratic colometric analysis (i.e. the counting of consonants). However, even if we work with his system for the sake of argument, it is not clear that there is a problem. By his own count, the line is reckoned as 17/13, which compares closely with the 16/12 of the first line of the

---

33. It may be noted in passing that there is no reference to holiness in the poem in 2.9-21, which shows considerable influence from ch. 6, but that when part of that poem is cited in the intrusive passage 5.15-16, 'the holy God (האל הקדוש)' makes his appearance, no doubt reflecting the growing importance of ch. 6 for the later tradents of Isaiah.

34. Loretz, *Prolog*, pp. 107-109.

35. Cf. F.J. Gonçalves, *L'expédition de Sennachérib en Palestine dans la littérature hébraïque ancienne* (EBib NS, 7; Paris: J. Gabalda, 1986), pp. 162-63.

verse.[36] More positively, there is good reason, in fact, to want to retain the line in its present position. The negative point that it makes, contrasting the Judaeans' dependence on Egypt with their lack of trust in the Lord, seems to be demanded in context by the development of the argument in v. 3,[37] and it is also supported by the parallel in thought with 30.1-5.[38] Whether Loretz's arguments are sufficient to cast doubt on the authenticity of the second line of this verse need not detain us here, though they seem equally improbable.[39] It is sufficient to observe that no sound reason has been advanced for denying the widespread view that this reference to 'The Holy One of Israel', at least, goes back to Isaiah's own usage.

The result of our analysis so far, then, is that Isaiah himself made only occasional use of this divine title, and that mainly, if not entirely, in the final stages of his long ministry. This at once has a bearing on the second point that needs consideration with regard to Isa. 1–39, namely whether Isaiah was personally responsible for coining the term.

That Isaiah was so responsible has been frequently asserted, usually, of course, on the basis of the cry of the seraphim in Isa. 6.3.[40] Along-side this, however, it needs to be recalled that the title is found not only

36. In arriving at this figure, I have discounted the extra-metrical הוי, as Loretz does in common with most other metrical systems, but I have retained לעזרה, whose deletion he neither explains nor justifies.

37. Cf. F. Huber, *Jahwe, Juda und die anderen Völker beim Propheten Jesaja* (BZAW, 137; Berlin: W. de Gruyter, 1976), pp. 122-30.

38. Cf. B.S. Childs, *Isaiah and the Assyrian Crisis* (SBT, 2nd series, 3; London: SCM Press, 1967), p. 35.

39. On a conventional analysis, the poetic parallelism and length of the line are entirely satisfactory; cf. H. Donner, *Israel unter den Völkern* (VTSup, 11; Leiden: E.J. Brill, 1964), p. 135. Indeed, it is not even clear that its slightly greater length from a 'colometric' point of view (15/17) is a real problem. The use of a waw-consecutive at the start of the line (Loretz's only other argument) is admittedly unusual, but not therefore necessarily inexplicable; cf. Dietrich, *Jesaja und die Politik*, p. 145 n. 67; M.A. Sweeney, *Isaiah 1–39, with an Introduction to the Prophetic Literature* (FOTL, 16; Grand Rapids: Eerdmans, 1996), pp. 402-403.

40. See, for instance, Procksch, *Jesaia*, p. 32; Rost, *Israel bei den Propheten*, p. 41; G. Bettenzoli, *Geist der Heiligkeit: Traditionsgeschichtliche Untersuchung des QDŠ-Begriffes im Buch Ezechiel* (Quaderni di Semitistica, 8; Florence: Università di Firenze, 1979), p. 44; W. Kornfeld, 'QDŠ und Gottesrecht im Alten Testament', in J.A. Emerton (ed.), *Congress Volume: Vienna 1980* (VTSup, 32; Leiden: E.J. Brill, 1981), pp. 1-9.

in the book of Isaiah, but in six other passages as well, and this is the appropriate point at which to consider them.

Three of these passages may be quickly dealt with, because they seem certainly to be dependent upon the Isaianic tradition itself in some way. This is most obvious with regard to 2 Kgs 19.22, which comes in the long narrative about Hezekiah and Isaiah which has a close parallel in Isa. 36–39 (cf. Isa. 37.23). The explanation of the literary relationship between these two blocks of material has been much discussed of late, but need not detain us now.[41] It is sufficient to accept the point on which there would be widespread agreement that the Kings passage is closely related to the Isaianic tradition. Indeed, the use of the divine title 'The Holy One of Israel' in this context fits extremely well with the results of our analysis of its distribution within the authentic sayings of Isaiah himself.

The case is probably similar with regard to two occurrences in the closing chapters of the book of Jeremiah (50.29; 51.5). Obviously these chapters are sufficiently late to allow that the title may have been picked up from Isaiah, but in fact the connection is rather stronger than that. The use of this title is only one of a number of striking connections between Jer. 50–51 and the book of Isaiah, so that recognition of some particularly close association seems to be demanded.[42] That being so, we cannot safely draw any conclusions from these two occurrences.

More problematic are the three remaining uses of the title, which all come in the Psalms: 71.22; 78.41; 89.19. While there are notorious difficulties over the dating of individual psalms, there seems to be widespread agreement that Ps. 71 is post-exilic, and for what it is worth the use of our title as an object of praise ('I will sing praises to you with the lyre, O Holy One of Israel') would seem to fit that date best. The other

41. I have treated this issue at length in *The Book Called Isaiah*, pp. 189-211, with reference to a wide variety of secondary literature. To this may now be added J. Vermeylen, 'Hypothèses sur l'origine d'Isaïe 36–39', in J. van Ruiten and M. Vervenne (eds.), *Studies in the Book of Isaiah: Festschrift Willem A.M. Beuken* (BETL, 132; Leuven: Leuven University Press/Peeters, 1997), pp. 95-118.

42. See recently, for instance, B.M. Zapff, *Schriftgelehrte Prophetie—Jes 13 und die Komposition des Jesajabuches: Ein Beitrag zur Erforschung der Redaktionsgeschichte des Jesajabuches* (FzB, 74; Würzburg: Echter Verlag, 1995); E. Bosshard-Nepustil, *Rezeptionen von Jesaia 1–39 im Zwölfprophetenbuch: Untersuchungen zur literarischen Verbindung von Prophetenbüchern in babylonischer und persischer Zeit* (OBO, 154; Freiburg: Universitätsverlag; Göttingen: Vandenhoeck & Ruprecht, 1997), esp. pp. 225-28.

two psalms are less easily dated, however, but in both cases significant arguments have sometimes been brought for regarding them as relatively early.[43] The issue is further complicated in the case of Ps. 89 by the view of a number of commentators that it is composite; those who take this approach generally include v. 19 with what they regard as the older material.

Two conclusions seem to be justified in the face of these unavoidable uncertainties. First, on any showing 'The Holy One of Israel' was not a widely used divine title in the Israelite cult. And secondly, whatever their date, it seems unlikely that these two psalms should have been influenced by Isaiah on this one matter; the view that they drew on the cult tradition in Jerusalem as they knew it is inherently more plausible.

This latter conclusion may be further supported by the evidence that holiness was attributed to God in the Jerusalem cult under originally Canaanite influence. There is some dispute about the details of this: while there is no doubt that in Ugaritic, as in Hebrew, members of the heavenly court could be designated as 'the holy ones' or the like,[44] it is less clear whether El himself was entitled *qdš*,[45] though he probably

43. There is a full survey and balanced discussion in M.E. Tate, *Psalms 51–100* (WBC, 20; Dallas: Word Books, 1990), pp. 284-87 and 413-18. To his bibliography we should add J. Day, 'Pre-Deuteronomic Allusions to the Covenant in Hosea and Psalm lxxviii', *VT* 36 (1986), pp. 1-12, and P. Stern, 'The Eighth Century Dating of Psalm 78 Re-argued', *HUCA* 66 (1995), pp. 41-65, both of whom argue strongly that Ps. 78 should be dated earlier than 722 BCE.

44. E.g. Exod. 15.11(?); Deut. 33.2-3; Zech. 14.5; Ps. 89.6, 8; Job 5.1; 15.15, etc.; cf. H.-P. Müller, *TLOT*, III, pp. 1112-13.

45. The relevant passages are CTA 16.1.10-11, 21-22; 16.2.111, where Krt is called not only a son of El, but also a *šph . ltpn . wqdš*. There are three principal views on this: (1) usually, it is rendered 'the offspring of the Gracious and Holy One' or the like, so that *qdš* refers to El; see most recently D. Pardee in W.W. Hallo (ed.), *The Context of Scripture*. I. *Canonical Compositions from the Biblical World* (Leiden: E.J. Brill, 1997), pp. 339b and 341a. This approach is adopted in particular by W.H. Schmidt in relation to our present discussion; cf. 'Wo hat die Aussage: Jahwe "der Heilige" ihren Ursprung?', *ZAW* 74 (1962), pp. 62-66; sec too H. Niehr, 'Bedeutung und Funktion kanaanäischer Traditionselemente in der Sozialkritik Jesajas', *BZ* NF 28 (1984), pp. 69-81; (2) alternatively, A. van Selms follows Ginsberg in rendering 'an offspring of the Kindly One, and a holy being', thus attributing the title to Krt himself as 'a minor god', and proposing that our title was coined by Jebusite priests after David's capture of Jerusalem with the meaning 'the divine being adored by Israel'; cf. 'The Expression "The Holy One of Israel" ', in W.C. Delsman *et al.* (eds.), *Von Kanaan bis Kerala: Festschrift für Prof. Mag. Dr.*

was. Either way, holiness is brought into the closest possible proximity with El Elyon of Jerusalem in Ps. 46.5, and Schmidt may be right in suggesting that through this route the title 'Holy One of Israel' came to be applied by a natural extension to Yahweh.[46] That such an association would have been congenial may be further suggested by the association of the ark with the holiness of God (cf. 1 Sam. 6.20) and the fact that the title parallels such expressions as אביר ישראל/יעקב[47] (and note too אלהי יעקב twice in Ps. 46.8, 12).

I conclude, therefore, that the title was probably used already before the time of Isaiah in the Jerusalem cult, with which he will have been familiar, and that this was the source from which he appropriated it. However, it was not, apparently, commonly used, nor, as we have seen, did he himself use it very frequently. Nor need the threefold ascription of holiness to God in 6.3 be narrowly linked to this title, though of course it moves in the same circle of ideas. In this connection, the interesting possibility seems previously to have been overlooked that our title may be associated with divine kingship in Ps. 89.19,[48] but it would

---

Dr. J.P.M. van der Ploeg O.P. zur Vollendung des siebzigsten Lebensjahres am 4. Juli 1979 (AOAT, 211; Kevelaer: Butzon & Bercker; Neukirchen–Vluyn: Neukirchener Verlag, 1982), pp. 257-69; (3) finally, it is occasionally suggested that the reference is to Krt's divine mother: 'the offspring of Kindly One ('El) and Qudšu ('Aṯirat)'; cf. E.T. Mullen, *The Divine Council in Canaanite and Early Hebrew Literature* (HSM, 24; Chico, CA: Scholars Press, 1980), p. 250.

46. W.H. Schmidt, *Alttestamentliche Glaube und seine Umwelt: Zur Geschichte des alttestamentlichen Gottesverständnisses* (Neukirchen–Vluyn: Neukirchener Verlag, 1968), p. 136-37 (ET, *The Faith of the Old Testament: A History* [Oxford: Basil Blackwell, 1983], p. 154). He also notes the frequency with which Zion and Jerusalem are called holy.

47. Cf. H. Wildberger, 'Gottesnamen und Gottesepitheta bei Jesaja', in *Jahwe und sein Volk: Gesammelte Aufsätze zum Alten Testament* (TBü, 66; Munich: Chr. Kaiser Verlag, 1979), pp. 219-48 (esp. 241-44); *Jesaja*, I, pp. 23-25 (ET, pp. 24-26). Høgenhaven, *Gott und Volk bei Jesaja*, p. 197, however, warns against some of the more extreme theological conclusions that Wildberger draws from this possible association of the two major sources of the Jerusalem cult tradition, as he does against some similar proposals by M. Garcia Cordero, 'El Santo de Israel', in *Mélanges bibliques rédigés en l'honneur de André Robert* (Paris: Bloud & Gay, 1957), pp. 165-73.

48. כי ליהוה מגננו ולקדוש ישראל מלכנו. The issue turns, of course, on the rendering of the ל. Usually, it has been taken in its commonest sense as a possessive dative, so that מלכנו refers to the Davidic king; cf. NRSV, 'our shield belongs to the Lord, our king to the Holy One of Israel'. Alternatively, however, it is thought

be pressing speculation too far to see any direct influence from this verse on Isaiah's vision report. More likely, the *trisagion* was itself part of the Jerusalem liturgy,[49] and the absence of the divine title either in ch. 6 or in most, if not all, of the early sayings of Isaiah points firmly away from any great impression made on Isaiah by this relatively obscure name for God at the start of his ministry. And finally on this point, if Ps. 78 is indeed early, or at any rate independent of Isaiah, then even the proposal[50] that Isaiah filled the title with new meaning by making it a basis of judgment rather than protection seems wide of the mark: 'They tested God again and again, and provoked the Holy One of Israel' (v. 41). Comparison of this verse with Ps. 89.19 (however translated; see n. 48 above) suggests that the title could apply equally to judgment or to protection from the earliest times.

If the argument so far is broadly along the right lines, then clearly interest focuses next on the use of the title by Isaiah's later redactors, and in the context of the present discussion we shall need to distinguish as far as possible those occurrences that predate the time of Deutero-Isaiah from those that follow him. That this is a much disputed issue hardly needs emphasizing, and space requirements dictate that a somewhat cavalier approach be adopted. Nevertheless, there is fortunately widespread agreement in the majority of the cases, so that the areas of dispute are not likely to distort the general picture too much.

I have already indicated that the uses of our title in 1.4, 5.24 and

by others to be emphatic, so that the king is God himself: cf., for example, G.R. Driver, 'Hebrew Notes on "Song of Songs" and "Lamentations" ', in W. Baumgartner *et al.* (eds.), *Festschrift Alfred Bertholet zum 80. Geburtstag* (Tübingen: J.C.B. Mohr [Paul Siebeck], 1950), pp. 134-46 (134); D. Winton Thomas, *The Text of the Revised Psalter* (London: SPCK, 1963), p. 37; A.A. Anderson, *The Book of Psalms* (NCB; London: Oliphants, 1972), p. 639; Tate, *Psalms 51–100*, p. 410; hence NEB: 'The Lord, he is our shield; the Holy One of Israel, he is our king' (REB has reverted, however, to 'To the Lord belongs our shield, to the Holy One of Israel our king'). An argument either way can be made from the context, so that certainty seems unattainable.

49. In this connection, it should be noted that Ps. 99, the only other passage to include a threefold use of 'holy', albeit as part of a refrain rather than in close juxtaposition, has been shown to be almost certainly dependent upon Isaiah, not the other way round; cf. R. Scoralick, *Trishagion und Gottesherrschaft: Psalm 99 als Neuinterpretation von Tora und Propheten* (SBS, 138; Stuttgart: Katholisches Bibelwerk, 1989).

50. E.g. Schmidt, *Alttestamentliche Glaube*, pp. 138-39 (ET, p. 155).

37.23 are most probably to be associated with the development of the
Isaianic tradition in pre-exilic times, and that in the case of the first two
passages mentioned they will originally have been part of the earliest
collection of and reflection on his own sayings. Isa. 10.17 ('his Holy
One') is similar. It comes in a short passage (10.16-19) which is
generally now agreed to draw its inspiration from a combination of
9.17-18 and 17.4-6.[51] It cannot, therefore, be earlier than the latest stage
of Isaiah's ministry, if Nielsen is right in her cautiously expressed
suggestion that it may reflect a redactional (anti-Assyrian) re-use of an
originally Isaianic anti-Judaean saying, though most would put it later,
whether as part of the Josianic redaction of Isaiah,[52] or even later.

While 10.17 uses the title as part of a judgment saying, 10.20 does
the opposite (they 'will lean on the Lord, the Holy One of Israel, in
truth'). Isa. 10.20-23 has been joined redactionally to 10.16-19, and is
therefore later than it. While Clements claims that it too is a part of the
Josianic redaction of Isaiah,[53] with primary reference to the remnant of
the northern kingdom, most commentators regard it as post-exilic.

There would be little disagreement nowadays that none of the
remaining uses of our title in Isa. 1–39 (namely 12.6; 17.7 and 29.19,
23) can be dated earlier than the time of Deutero-Isaiah. Putting all this
together in the form of crude statistics, we may conclude that Isaiah
himself used the title a maximum of five times in his recorded sayings,
that it was used four (or possibly five) times by those who extended his
work in the late pre-exilic or early exilic period, and that the remaining
five (or four) occurrences are later. Needless to say, all the latter share
the same positive outlook as Deutero-Isaiah, and in some cases there is
a close similarity of theme or expression (e.g. compare 17.7 with 41.20,
though cf. 31.1, and 29.19 with 41.16).

The situation with regard to Deutero-Isaiah himself is straightforward, and may be quickly summarized. That 'the Holy One of Israel'
is a God of salvation is clear from the fact that on six occasions it is

---

51. See, for instance, Wildberger, *Jesaja*, I, pp. 407-408 (ET, p. 430); Vermeylen, *Du prophète Isaïe à l'apocalyptique*, pp. 259-60; Barth, *Die Jesaja-Worte
in der Josiazeit*, pp. 28-34 (with earlier literature), and especially K. Nielsen, *There
is Hope for a Tree: The Tree as Metaphor in Isaiah* (JSOTSup, 65; JSOT Press,
1989), pp. 190-201.

52. So Barth, *Die Jesaja-Worte in der Josiazeit*, p. 34; Clements, *Isaiah 1–39*,
p. 113.

53. Clements, *Isaiah 1–39*, pp. 114-15.

associated with גואל (which, incidentally, always precedes it) and once with מושיעך. Elsewhere, he has 'created' Israel, 'formed' her, 'chosen' her and 'glorified' her. In one passage he has created the transformation of the wilderness, and in the remaining one Israel will glory in him (הלל ב). In four of these 13 occurrences the title occurs in an introductory speech formula, something paralleled elsewhere only at 30.12 and 15 (the latter being the only passage in earlier material to hint at the way of salvation, even though it is there rejected).

The analysis presented above gives a somewhat different pattern of distribution of the use of the divine title 'The Holy One of Israel' in the book of Isaiah from that which might be inferred from the kinds of summary statement cited at the start of this article, and some explanation is called for. Obviously, in the light of the fact that we have so little evidence on which to base any hypothesis, the following suggestions can only be tentative in the extreme.

First, why did Isaiah, late in his ministry, seize on this relatively obscure title from the Jerusalem cult? Our findings have suggested that it had little or nothing directly to do with his vision as recorded in ch. 6, so we must seek some other motivation. One possibility is that it had something to do with the fact that in the meantime the northern kingdom of Israel had come to an end, that the books of Amos and Hosea (to go no further) had been brought south to Jerusalem and were there being read, and, it is generally agreed, edited with renewed eyes in the light of their initial fulfilment in the events surrounding the fall of Samaria. That Isaiah may have known some form of both these prophetic books has been maintained, for instance, by Blenkinsopp.[54] In this connection, it may be worth recalling the suggestion of Gammie that 'the Holy One in your midst' of Hos. 11.9 was the inspiration behind Isaiah's coining of the phrase 'The Holy One of Israel'.[55] Put

54. J. Blenkinsopp, *A History of Prophecy in Israel: From the Settlement in the Land to the Hellenistic Period* (London: SPCK, 1984), pp. 112-13 and 116-17. The links between Amos and Isaiah have been studied in particular by R. Fey, *Amos und Jesaja: Abhängigkeit und Eigenständigkeit des Jesaja* (WMANT, 12; Neukirchen–Vluyn: Neukirchener Verlag, 1963), but I am not aware of any full study of those between Hosea and Isaiah.

55. Gammie, *Holiness in Israel*, pp. 74-76. In formulating his view, Gammie expresses disagreement with J.J. Schmitt, 'The God of Israel and the Holy One', *Hebrew Studies* 24 (1983), pp. 27-31, but I regret that I have not been able to gain access to this article. He also reminds us of the, surely untenable, view of S. Terrien, *The Elusive Presence: Toward a New Biblical Theology* (Religious

like that, our findings have pointed in a different direction, but the possibility that interest in Hosea in Jerusalem prompted Isaiah during the course of his ministry to give greater weight to the title is worth consideration. The impossibly difficult Hos. 12.1 (English versions 11.12) at least indicates that Hosea's Judaean redactors worked in particular with this text, and the use of the name Israel in this connection would also have been attractive at this time[56] (note how Isaiah alone uses the name אביר ישראל, 1.24, for אביר יעקב elsewhere; Gen. 49.24; Isa. 49.26; 60.16; Ps. 132.2, 5).

Secondly, why did Isaiah's later editors, and then in particular Deutero-Isaiah, pick up this title, so making it a characteristic of the book? Here, we are, in my opinion, on firmer ground in suggesting that Isa. 6 comes into its own, for whereas we have found little to support the view that the *trisagion* had much influence on Isaiah himself in this particular connection, with regard to those who followed him the situation is completely different. The echoes of this chapter in many of the later parts of the book are pervasive, as many recent studies have shown. It would be only natural that, as part of that reflection, an association should have been made, and then accentuated, between the praise of God as holy and the title for him which most closely reflected that.

Finally, we have seen that Deutero-Isaiah is in reality the writer to have made most intensive use of the title, and that as part of the way in which he emphasized God's new work of salvation in reversal of the older message of judgment. But for the most part this was not continued in the substantial parts of the work that followed on from him (e.g. Trito-Isaiah and the Isaiah apocalypse). By contrast, the late passages in Isa. 1–39 which use the title are all closely associated with the thought-world of Deutero-Isaiah, however that is to be explained. Once again, therefore, the role of this unnamed prophet of the exile stands out as central to the forging of a sense of identifiable unity in the book.

Perspectives, 26; San Francisco: Harper & Row, 1978), p. 246, that Isaiah was a disciple of Hosea.

    56. So Rost, *Israel bei den Propheten*, pp. 43-48.

SOME DIFFICULT WORDS IN ISAIAH 28.10 AND 13

John A. Emerton

After a condemnation of the drunkards of Ephraim in Isa. 28.1-6, vv. 7-13 are concerned with prophets and priests probably in Jerusalem. They too are accused of drunkenness, and their tables are said to be covered with the vomit caused by their excesses. In v. 9 it appears that they mock Isaiah, asking whom he thinks he is teaching. Does he suppose that he is addressing tiny children? The obscure v. 10 may contain their words (in which case, it may contain their imitation of what Isaiah has said to them), or it may contain a criticism of them by Isaiah. Verse 11 announces that someone—presumably God—will speak to the people with stammering lips and in another (presumably a foreign) language; and this is usually, and doubtless rightly, thought to be a reference to the Assyrians. Verse 12 says that God offered rest to the people (of Judah), but they were not willing to listen. Verse 13 (which some scholars believe to be secondary) announces what the word of the Lord will be to the people: it repeats the obscure words of v. 10, apart from the opening conjunction כִּי.

The MT of v. 10 is as follows: כִּי צַו לָצָו צַו לָצָו קַו לָקָו קַו לָקָו זְעֵיר שָׁם זְעֵיר שָׁם. 1QIsaᵃ differs from the MT by reading צֵי instead of צַו. A possible significance of this variant will be considered below in the discussion of the Greek versions.

The purpose of the present article is to discuss the interpretation of these difficult verses. It is dedicated to the memory of my friend Michael Weitzman, whose untimely death was such a loss to scholarship.

I

The first stage in the study of the passage is a consideration of the principal ancient versions.

1. *The Greek Versions*

The LXX of v. 13 says that 'the oracle of the Lord God to them will be' and continues: θλῖψις ἐπὶ θλῖψιν ἐλπὶς ἐπ᾽ ἐλπὶδι ἔτι μικρὸν ἔτι μιμρὸν, 'affliction upon affliction, hope upon hope, yet a little, yet a little'.[1] There is no repetition of the first two phrases in the Greek, and the translator perhaps thought that the repetition in the Hebrew added nothing to the meaning. The Greek noun θλῖψις has been thought to represent *ṣar* rather than *ṣaw*. That is possible, but it is also possible that the *Vorlage* had *ṣw* but that it was misread as *ṣr*; or perhaps the translator was puzzled and translated it as if it were *ṣr*, which is similar in appearance. The rendering of *qw* by ἐλπίς suggests the Hebrew verb *qwh*, piel 'to expect', and the noun *tiqwâ* 'hope'. Similarly, the LXX translates *gôy qaw-qaw* by ἔθνος ἀνέλπιστον in Isa. 18.2, and by ἔθνος ἐλπίζον in 18.7. In the latter verse, Aquila has a participle of ὑπομένω, a verb often used in the LXX to translate *qwh*.

Isaiah 28.10 differs from 28.13 in having no introduction apart from *kî*; and so a different construction is needed in the LXX. It begins with θλῖψιν ἐπὶ θλιψῖν and then has προσδέχου, a verb in the imperative singular, followed by ἐλπίδα ἐπ᾽ ἐλπίδι. The verb is added to make a translation possible, but it also recalls the Hebrew verb *qwh*, which may have been suggested by *qw*; there may even be a double translation of *qw*. Ottley suggests as an alternative that the verb is taken from *lqḥ* ' "receive" for *lqw*'. The alternative is, however, improbable: if ἐπ᾽ ἐλπίδι represents *lqw*, then *lqḥ* was not read.

Symmachus translates *ṣw lṣw* ἐντολὴ οὐκ ἐντολή 'a commandment not a commandment'. The negative presumably represents *l* understood as if it were *l'*. The translation of *ṣw* relates it to the verb *ṣwh*, piel 'to command', and the noun *miṣwâ* 'command'. Theodotion renders *ṣw* as δεισαλία 'filth' and *qw lqw* as ἐμετὸν εἰς ἐμετόν 'vomit to vomit'. These renderings recall Theodotion's translation of *qî' ṣō'â* in v. 8 as ἐμετοῦ δεισαλίας 'of filth of vomit'. Aquila there has ἐμετοῦ ῥύπου 'of uncleanness of vomit'. Kutscher's discussion of 1QIsa[a]'s reading *ṣy* in Isa. 28.10 compares it to Theodotion's translation and also to Syriac *ṣ'î* 'to be filthy', and to the Peshitta's *tbt'*.[2]

1.   R.R. Ottley, *The Book of Isaiah According to the Septuagint (Codex Alexandrinus)*, I and II (Cambridge: Cambridge University Press, 1904 and 1906).

2.   Y. Kutscher, *The Language and Linguistic Background of the Isaiah Scroll (1Qisa^a)* (Leiden: E.J. Brill, 1974; Hebrew Edition, Jerusalem: Magnes Press, 1959), p. 278; Hebrew, p. 211.

Isa. 30.22 uses the following words of idols: *tizrēm kᵉmô dāweh ṣēʾ tōʾmar lô*. The word *ṣēʾ* looks like the masculine singular imperative qal of the verb *yāṣāʾ* 'to go out', although it is strange if addressed to idols in the plural. Theodotion has for it and the preceding word (ὡς) ὀδυνηρὰν δεισαλίας '(as) painful filth', which recalls the use of δεισαλία to translate *ṣw* in 28.13 and *ṣʾh* in 28.8. Aquila has in 30.22 ταλαιπώρου ῥύπου 'of filth of one in distress', and the second Greek word is also used to translate *ṣʾh* in 28.8. Corresponding to the words in 30.22 quoted above from the MT, the LXX has λεπτὰ ποιήσεις καὶ λικμήσεις ὡς ὕδωρ ἀποκαθημένης καὶ ὡς κόπρον ὥσεις αὐτά 'thou shalt make them small, and shalt scatter them away as the water of her that sitteth apart, and as dung shalt thou remove them' (Ottley). The verb *tzrm* appears to be translated twice; *kmw* of the MT has been read as *kmy* 'as the water of'; and *dwh* has been read as feminine. It is not clear what has happened to the verb that appears as *tʾmr* in the MT. Ottley suggests that it was read as *timʾas*, but it and *tʾmr* are not so similar as to make the suggestion probable. Perhaps *ṣʾ* was understood to be an imperative, and 'thou shalt say to it "Go out"' was paraphrased by ὥσεις. If so, then κόπρον 'dung' is either a translator's gloss or an example of a double rendering of *ṣʾ*, as a noun meaning 'dung' and as a form of the verb *yāṣāʾ*.

2. *The Vulgate*

Jerome's commentary on Isaiah contains a transliteration of the relevant words in 28.10, 13, which shows that he read them in a way agreeing with the traditional vocalization: *sau lasau sau lasau cau lacau cau lacau zer sam zer sam*.[3] The Vulgate has *manda remanda manda remanda expecta reexpecta expecta reexpecta modicum ibi modicum ibi*, 'Command, command again, command, command again, expect, expect again, expect, expect again, a little there, a little there'. Jerome thus understands *ṣaw* and *qaw* to be the imperative singular piel of the verbs *ṣwh* and *qwh*. Similarly, *gwy qw-qw* in Isa. 18.2, 7 is translated *gentem expectantem expectantem*.

---

3. This transliteration (in Greek) is also found in Epiphanius, *Panarion haer.* 25.4 (ed. K. Holl, p. 271); cf. F. Field, *Origenis hexaplorum quae supersunt; sive veterum interpretum graecorum in totum Vetus Testamentum fragmenta* (Oxford: Clarendon Press, 1875), p. 479.

3. *The Peshitta*

The relevant words in Isa. 28.10, 13 are *tbt' 'l tbt' wtbt' 'l tbt' wtywb' 'l tywb' wtywb' 'l tywb' ltmn qlyl ltmn qlyl*, 'dung upon dung and dung upon dung, and vomit upon vomit and vomit upon vomit, a little there, a little there'.

As Weitzman points out,[4] the translation of *ṣw* as 'dung', and of *qw* as 'vomit' identifies them with *ṣ'h* and *qy'* in v. 8, where *qy' ṣ'h* is translated by the Peshitta as *tywb' wtbt'*. In Isa. 30.22, the last six words of the MT, which were quoted above, have as their counterpart in the Peshitta *wtdrwn 'nwn 'yk my' dkpsnyt' w'yk npt' tpqwn 'nwn*, 'you shall scatter them as the waters of a menstruous woman, and as dung you shall cast them out'. The problem of the relation of these words to the MT is essentially the same as that of the LXX, which was discussed above. Weitzman has found parallels between the LXX and the Peshitta of Isaiah, which he describes as 'sporadic',[5] and this verse can be added to their number.

4. *The Targum*

The Targum offers a long, homiletical paraphrase of Isa. 28.10, 13. Verse 10 tells of the past disobedience of the Israelites, who would not do what they had been commanded (*'tpqdw*); they 'hoped (*bsrw*) that the service of idols would be established for them, and did not hope for the service of my [God's] sanctuary': the service of the sanctuary was a small thing in their eyes, as was God's Shekinah. The reference to being commanded suggests that *ṣw* in the MT was interpreted from *ṣwh* and *miṣwâ*, and the reference to hoping suggests that *qw* was derived from the verb *qwh* and the noun *tiqwâ* 'hope'. The paraphrase in v. 13 differs from v. 10, but it too refers to the Israelites being commanded (*'tpqdw*) and it speaks of their hoping (*ysbrwn*). In v. 13 too the sanctuary is said to have been a small thing in their eyes; therefore they will be left a small thing among the nations. It seems unnecessary for the present purpose to discuss further details.

---

4.   M.P. Weitzman, *The Syriac Version of the Old Testament: An Introduction* (University of Cambridge Oriental Publications, 56; Cambridge: Cambridge University Press, 1999), p. 228.

5.   Weitzman, *Syriac Version of the Old Testament*, p. 181.

II

To survey the whole range of later Jewish interpretation of Isa. 28.10, 13 would be an undertaking far beyond the limits of the present article. I shall confine myself here to a consideration of the interpretations offered in the *Haketer* edition of *Miqra'ot Gedolot*. Moreover, my enquiry will be focused on the interpretation of the words *ṣaw* and *qaw*, not on the exegesis of the passage as a whole. I shall briefly consider the explanations given by Rashi, David Qimḥi and Abraham Ibn Ezra, for it does not appear that the other commentators quoted add anything to their definitions.

Rashi and Qimḥi understand *ṣaw* to be a synonym of *miṣwâ* 'command', and the latter comments that this meaning is found only in this passage and that the word is a 'little' (*qᵉṭannâ*) *miṣwâ*. His comments on Isa. 30.22 note that some exegetes understand *ṣē'* in that verse to have the same meaning as *ṣō'â*. Rashi and Qimḥi both take *qaw* to be a measuring-line, as in v. 19. In v. 13, however, Rashi's comments also allow for an allusion to the verb *qwh* 'to expect, look for', and he compares Job 3.9, where the reference is to disappointed hope. Ibn Ezra understands *ṣaw lāṣāw* to refer to a way of teaching, as a father teaches his little son 'commandment (*miṣwâ*) after commandment' or 'commandment joined [or related] to commandment', step by step. His understanding of *qaw* is that one teaches writing (*hktybh*) gradually, line by line.

III

In examining various ways of explaining vv. 10 and 13, I have come across seven types of interpretation, some of which exist in more than one variant.

1. *'Precept upon precept, precept upon precept, line upon line, line upon line; here a little and there a little'*
The above rendering of the relevant words in v. 13 is found in the AV of 1611. Verse 10 differs in that it has 'For precept must be upon precept...' This translation is clearly dependent on the interpretation of the words found in Jewish commentaries. Given the accuracy of the translation, it is not difficult to make sense of the passage in its context. For example, the eighteenth-century scholar Robert Lowth suggests that

Isaiah's opponents 'treat God's methods of dealing with them, and warning them by his prophets, with contempt and derision…imitating at the same time, and ridiculing, in verse 10 the concise prophetical manner'.[6] This offers an intelligible interpretation of part of v. 10. The difficulty remains, however, that, as Qimḥi pointed out, ṣaw has the meaning of 'precept' in no other passage. The objection is not that it would have been impossible to have two nouns—ṣaw and miṣwâ—with similar meanings from the same root, but that we should have expected to find the alleged noun ṣaw somewhere else. In Ps. 119, for instance, the poet uses various synonyms, or near-synonyms, for 'law', and he would have been expected to use ṣaw as well, if he had known it as a noun denoting 'precept'. Despite the long history of this kind of interpretation of the passage, it therefore seems better to look elsewhere for a more satisfactory interpretation of the verse.

2. An Unintelligible Jumble of Sounds

A different suggestion is that ṣaw lāṣāw and qaw lāqāw have no meaning as words. Perhaps they imitate the babbling of children or drunkards[7] or the patter of children's feet.[8] Perhaps Bishop Lowth's supposition that Isaiah's words are being mocked is to be modified so that the words represent a nonsensical imitation of his exhortation. As one might put it, what the prophet has said is something like 'Blah, blah, blah, gabble, gabble, gabble!' Thus, a footnote to these Hebrew words in the NIV says 'possibly meaningless sounds; perhaps a mimicking of the prophet's words'.

The view that the words are unintelligible appears to be presupposed by Michael Weitzman's comment on v. 13:

> The preceding verses seem to identify the Hebrew words צו and קו with incomprehensible speech (לעגי שפה), though their exact meaning remains uncertain.[9]

Weitzman's suggestion must be taken seriously. Verse 11 says that the Lord will speak to his people in a foreign language, presumably the language spoken by the Assyrian invaders. The incomprehensible

6. R. Lowth, *Isaiah* (London: J. Dodsley and T. Cadell, 1778), p. 148.

7. A. Dillmann and R. Kittel, *Der Prophet Jesaja* (Leipzig: S. Hirzel, 6th edn, 1898).

8. B. Duhm, *Das Buch Jesaia* (Göttingen: Vandenhoeck & Ruprecht, 1892).

9. Weitzman, *Syriac Version of the Old Testament*, p. 228.

words used to mimic Isaiah's teaching will find a grim realization in the Assyrian words used by the enemy.

This interpretation of the relation of v. 11 to vv. 10 and 13 is possible, but it is not the only possibility. Verse 9 asks whether Isaiah is seeking to teach tiny children; and the implication is perhaps that his teaching is too elementary for adults. So God will provide more advanced teaching—in a foreign language. They have rejected the simple language that would have brought rest (v. 12), and now they must face the consequences.

The strength of the case for regarding the relevant words as unintelligible lies in the difficulty of attaching any meaning to them. Individually, they may make sense: *ṣaw* may be an imperative (though *la-* scarcely fits an imperative), and *qaw* may be a noun meaning 'line', and both *z^{e}êr* and *šām* have meanings. But, taken together, the words yield no sense. On the other hand, it is necessary to consider other explanations of the passage to see whether, after all, they can make sense of it.

3. *Harsh Cries and Raucous Shouts*

In the first edition (1948) of *Semitic Writing*,[10] G.R. Driver found in Isa. 28.10, 13 a comparison of Isaiah to a teacher of the alphabet to small boys (see section 5 below). In the third edition,[11] as in his article of 1968,[12] however, he abandons his earlier interpretation and argues instead that the passage refers to 'the fuddled ramblings of a party of drunken revellers' described in the preceding verses. The words *ṣaw* and *qaw* 'designate nothing but meaningless sounds'.[13] Driver's view is not, however, identical with that described above in section 2. Although the words 'reflect the shouts and cries of drunken revellers, they may well have recalled, if not actually been, real words'. This interpretation is reflected in the NEB:

> It is all harsh cries and raucous shouts,
> 'A little more here, a little there!'

10. G.R. Driver, *Semitic Writing from Pictograph to Alphabet* (The Schweich Lectures, 1944; London: Oxford University Press, 1948; 3rd edn, 1976), pp. 89-90.

11. Driver, *Semitic Writing*, 3rd edn, pp. 242-43.

12. G.R. Driver, ' "Another Little Drink"—Isaiah 28: 1-22', in P.R. Ackroyd and B. Lindars (eds.), *Words and Meanings* (Festschrift D.W. Thomas; Cambridge: Cambridge University Press, 1968), pp. 47-67.

13. Driver, 'Another Little Drink', p. 53.

Driver compares *ṣaw* and *qaw* with what look like the same words in other Hebrew passages, and also with possible cognates in other Semitic languages.[14] They are, he believes, both onomatopoeic in character.

First, Hebrew *ṣaw* is compared with Arabic *ṣawwun* 'empty', and *ṣawwatun* 'echoing sound', 'which suggests the notion of some mere empty sound, void of meaning'; and also Arabic *ḍawwatun* 'clamour' and *ḍawātun* 'uproar', which 'may be taken as cognate, if strengthened, forms of these words'.[15] The word 'strengthened' draws attention to the difference in meaning between the Arabic words (and the difference between *ṣ* and *ḍ* is also to be noted, though it is not fatal to the theory) and serves to underline the need for caution even beyond the caution that is always needed in evaluating attempts to explain Hebrew words with the help of Arabic.

Caution is also needed in evaluating Driver's examples in Hebrew. One of them is הואיל הלך אחרי צו in Hos. 5.11, which he translates 'he [Ephraim] was content to pursue vain follies' (the LXX here has τὰ μάταια), though 'vain follies' is not the meaning that he suggests for Isa. 28.10, 13. The other example is CD 4.19 (7.1 in his system of reference): אשר הלכו אחרי צו הצו הוא מטיף. Driver translates these words 'those who have gone after *ṣāw*' followed by '*ṣaw*: that is the babbler'. He thinks that, although this is based on the passage in Isaiah, it 'shows knowledge of' a noun *ṣaw* meaning 'babble, chatter'[16] or, as he puts it, 'they went after *ṣāw*' and '*ṣāw*: that is a driveller'.[17] It is, however, more likely that the last three words of the Hebrew are not defining the meaning of *ṣaw*, but saying that the reference in Isaiah is to a contemporary of the Qumran sect called the 'babbler' or 'driveller'. 1QpHab 10.9 refers to the מטיף הכזב as one of the enemies of the sect.[18] With this may be compared מטיף כזב in CD 8.13; and CD 1.14: איש הלצון אשר הטיף לישראל. In the latter passage, הלצון may echo לצו in Isa. 28.10, 13, and explain how the interpretation מטיף was derived in CD 4.19 from צו (which is followed by לצו) in Isaiah.

Second, Driver compares *qaw* with Aramaic *qawqaw* 'croaking of frogs', Syriac *qawqî* 'hooted' ('to caw, croak', according to Payne

14. Driver, 'Another Little Drink', pp. 55-57; *idem, Semitic Writing*, 3rd edn, pp. 242-43.

15. Driver, 'Another Little Drink', p. 55.

16. Driver, *Semitic Writing*, 3rd edn, p. 242.

17. Driver, 'Another Little Drink', p. 55.

18. G.R. Driver, *The Judaean Scrolls* (Oxford: Basil Blackwell, 1965), p. 309.

Smith),[19] and Arabic *qawqa'a*, *qawqā* 'cacked, clicked' (used of a hen), which are probably onomatopoeic in character. The Driver claims that Hebrew *qaw* 'can without hesitation be taken as a confused medley of senseless shouts'.[20] While the sounds made by frogs and birds may be comparable to the noise made by intoxicated revellers, at least to some extent, the difference is such that perhaps some hesitation is appropriate after all.

Driver also adduces as evidence the meaning 'chord, note, sound' for *qaw* in addition to 'line' (cf. Greek χορδή, whose meanings include both the string of a lyre or harp and a musical note).[21] Driver had suggested that this meaning is found in *qawwām* in Ps. 19.5, that the LXX's φθόγγος and Symmachus's ἦχος are to be thus explained, and that there is no need to adopt the widely accepted emendation to *qôlām*.[22] Driver claims that the meaning '(musical) note, notation' is also found in Sir. 44.5, 1QH 1 (otherwise known as 1QHᵃ 9).28-29, and 1QS 10.9. In the first passage, MS B has חקרי מזמור על קו, but MS M has חוק in place of קו. In the second, the phrase על קו appears parallel to מדה; and in the third, בקו משפטו is found. The contexts of the two Qumran texts suggest a meaning other than 'note' or 'sound', and Vermes's translations 'metre' and 'measure' seem preferable.[23] Further, Driver derives *qaw* from the root *qwh*,[24] and that does not easily fit the claim that it is an onomatopoeic noun. Driver rightly does not advance this interpretation of *qaw* to explain Isa. 28.10, 13.[25]

Driver's interpretation of *zᵉ'êr šām* seems as uncertain as that of *ṣaw* and *qaw*. He understands it to be 'the tippler's call for another glass of beer or wine': 'another drop here, another drop there!'.[26] He compares the words of the song 'Another little drink won't do us any harm'. The use of the phrase 'another little drink', in which 'little' is not intended

19. Jessie Payne Smith, *A Compendious Syriac Dictionary* (Oxford: Clarendon Press, 1903).

20. Driver, 'Another Little Drink', p. 56.

21. Driver, *Semitic Writing*, 3rd edn, p. 243.

22. G.R. Driver, 'Notes on the Psalms', *JTS* 36 (1935), pp. 147-56 (148). J.D. Michaelis, *Supplementa ad lexica hebraica* (Göttingen: J.G. Rosenbusch, 1792), p. 2242, had earlier thought of '*chorda* psalterii' in Ps. 19.5. Cf. also BDB, p. 876.

23. G. Vermes, *The Complete Dead Sea Scrolls in English* (London: Allen Lane, The Penguin Press, 1997), pp. 255, 112.

24. Driver, 'Another Little Drink', p. 55.

25. Driver, 'Another Little Drink', pp. 54, 57.

26. Driver, 'Another Little Drink', pp. 57, 62.

to be taken literally makes sense in accordance with English idiom. Whether we may assume that the idiom in ancient Jerusalem was the same, and whether a drunken reveller would have been content to ask for only 'a little more', may be doubted. Certainly, a very different way of speaking is found in Isa. 56.12. We must not retroject an English way of speaking on to an ancient Israelite. The same objection stands against Driver's alternative theory that *śîm* should be read for *šām* in the sense of 'lay on (the table)'.

Driver's revised interpretation of Isa. 28.10 and 13 lacks adequate evidence. It is better to look elsewhere for a solution to the problem.

4. *Assyrian Orders to Prisoners*

An ingenious and original solution to the problem is A. van Selms's suggestion that the relevant words are orders given in the Assyrian language to prisoners: *ṣī lūṣī, ṣī lūṣī, qî luqqi/u, qî luqqi/u, ṣeḥēru šeme, ṣeḥēru šeme*, 'Go out! Let him go out! Go out! Let him go out! Wait! Let him wait! Wait! Let him wait! Servant, listen! Servant, listen!'

The difficulty with this hypothesis is that it presupposes a knowledge of Assyrian in Jerusalem, not only in Isaiah but also in his hearers, that is improbable. According to 2 Kgs 8.16-17 = Isa. 36.11-12, the ordinary people of Jerusalem did not understand Aramaic. How much less likely are they to have understood the more distantly related Assyrian language!

Van Selms suggests that 'Isaiah and his contemporaries would have heard from fugitives that the Assyrians used these phrases when exiling the population of Samaria in 722'.[27] The theory is unconvincing. First, few if any of the Israelites close enough to hear the words spoken by the Assyrians to those going into exile are likely to have escaped the same fate. Second, it may be doubted whether the Assyrians would have given orders to their prisoners in a language that they could not understand. Third, it is also unlikely that Israelite fugitives would have understood and remembered these foreign sentences and passed them on reasonably accurately to the people in Jerusalem, or that the latter would have understood and remembered them. Van Selms's theory must be rejected.

---

27. A. van Selms, 'Isaiah 28 9-13: An Attempt to give a New Interpretation', *ZAW* 85 (1973), pp. 332-39 (334).

5. *Letters of the Alphabet*

In v. 9 it is asked, probably by Isaiah's enemies, whether he thinks he is teaching tiny children. It is not surprising that v. 10 has also been thought to speak of the prophet as a teacher, and we have seen that Ibn Ezra suggests that the prophet is likened to a father teaching writing to his little son. Recently, it has been questioned whether there were schools in ancient Israel, but someone, whether or not the father, must have taught others how to read.

In the late eighteenth century, C.F. Houbigant[28] interpreted v. 10 in terms of teaching the alphabet—and the letter *ṣ* is followed by *q*. He writes of the difficulty of pronouncing some of the consonants, though it seems unlikely that Israelite children, brought up from infancy to speak Hebrew, would have experienced the same difficulties as Europeans accustomed to speaking non-Semitic languages.

A. Klostermann's view that v. 10 refers to a schoolmaster teaching writing was mentioned in 1886 by C.J. Bredenkamp, who thought, however, that *ṣaw* and *qaw* were not the names of letters but were concerned with writing them: *ṣaw* denoted a small hook on some letters, and the meaning of *qaw* had developed from 'cord' to 'line'. Klostermann's own discussion of the question was published in 1908 (where he says that one of his pupils was the source of Bredenkamp's information).[29] He regards *ṣaw* and *qaw* as simplified names of successive letters of the alphabet used when teaching children to pronounce, read and write them. The words 'here a little' refer to details in writing the letters.

Similarly, J.A. Montgomery suggested in 1912, apparently independently, that *ṣaw* and *qaw* correspond to the letters otherwise known as *ṣadhe* and *qoph*.[30] R.H. Kennett's Schweich Lectures for 1931 suppose that the passage refers to a spelling lesson.[31]

28. K.F. Houbigant, *Biblia Hebraica cum Notis criticis et Versione Latina ad notas criticas facta*, IV (Paris: C. Briasson & L. Durand, 1753), pp. 71-74. C.J. Bredenkamp, *Der Prophet Jesaia* (Erlangen: A. Deichert, 1886), pp. 167-68.

29. A. Klostermann, 'Schulwesen im alten Israel', in N. Bonwetsch *et al.*, *Theologische Studien* (Festschrift T. Zahn; Leipzig: A. Deichert, 1908), pp. 214-18.

30. J.A. Montgomery, 'Notes on the Old Testament', *JBL* 31 (1912), pp. 140-49.

31. R.H. Kennett, *Ancient Hebrew Social Life and Custom as Indicated in Law, Narrative and Metaphor* (The Schweich Lectures, 1931; London: Oxford University Press, 1933).

The first edition (1948) of Driver's Schweich Lectures, supposes that 'the drunkards of Ephraim, mocking the prophet, liken him to a dull drone of a schoolmaster...teaching the letters of the alphabet'.[32] Driver understands *z"êr šām z"êr šām* to be words addressed to pupils in the class: '(you) boy, there, (you) boy there!'

It was seen in section 3 above that in 1968 and in the third edition of his Schweich Lectures, Driver adopted a different interpretation of the passage.[33] First, vv. 10 and 13 do not suggest the coherent teaching of the alphabet, but 'the fuddled ramblings of...drunken revellers', and 'no master is likely to be teaching' newly weaned children. This argument has no force against the view that the verses represent the drunkards' mocking comparison of Isaiah to a teacher, rather than describing the actual words of a teacher. Further, the consistency of their words should not be pressed too far. It is possible to move in thought from tiny children to boys a few years older. Second, Driver asks, 'how can learning the alphabet have resulted in the drunkards' downfall?' But the point is a mocking comparison of Isaiah to a teacher, not that teaching the alphabet leads to downfall. Third, if the reference is to the alphabet, Driver expects 'from *'aleph* to *beth*, and so on' or 'from *'aleph* to *taw*', not 'from *ṣ* to *q*', 'two letters chosen arbitrarily from the middle of the alphabet'. But the choice is not arbitrary. Driver himself holds that *ṣaw* and *qaw* 'were chosen...partly...as echoing' *ṣō'â* and *qî'* in v. 8 (albeit in the opposite order).[34] Further, Driver, who had originally held[35] that the masculine *z"êr* ' "lad" echoes the last clause of the preceding verse', later insisted[36] that it 'is used only of things' and that it is so translated in the versions. The word *z"êr* is, however, found in only one other place (Job 36.2), and so the argument from usage carries no weight.

Driver's reasons for changing his mind are not compelling, but that does not prove that his earlier interpretation was correct. He says that his new interpretation does not mean that the letters *ṣadhe* and *qoph* 'may not originally have been called respectively *ṣaw* and *qaw*, but only that such names cannot be proved from the present passage'.[37] Here he has put his finger on the difficulty. Unless evidence can be

---

32. Driver, *Semitic Writing*, 1st edn, pp. 89-90.
33. Driver, *Semitic Writing*, 3rd edn, pp. 142-43.
34. Driver, *Semitic Writing*, 3rd edn, p. 273.
35. Driver, *Semitic Writing*, 1st edn, p. 90.
36. Driver, 'Another Little Drink', pp. 90-91.
37. Driver, *Semitic Writing*, 3rd edn, p. 243.

found for the use of these names for the relevant letters of the alphabet, this theory cannot be raised from a possibility to a probability.

W.W. Hallo refers to a Ugaritic text which lists the signs for the letters of the Ugaritic alphabet 'in their, by now, familiar order, and next to them, in a second column a set of Akkadian syllabograms which are evidently intended to explain their value'.[38] He thinks that 'what the Ugaritic scribe had in mind was the rendering of the Ugaritic signs by one each of their possible Akkadian equivalents, in short, the naming of the Ugaritic signs'.[39] We find, for example, that the Ugaritic signs for *p*, *ṣ*, *q* and *r* are represented by *pu*, *ṣa*, *qu* and *ra*.[40] He does not, however, think that every name of a letter consisted of a consonant plus a vowel, but that another pattern was consonant plus *-aw*, as in *waw* and *taw*, and he compares *gaw* 'back' and conjectures that it was once the name of *gimel*. He applies this hypothesis to Isa. 28.10, 13.

Hallo's hypothesis is interesting and may be correct, but it is no more than a hypothesis. That is the difficulty facing the theory that Isa. 28.10, 13 refers to letters of the alphabet. It makes sense and it is attractive, but it lacks firm evidence.

6. *Stench (or Dung) and Vomit*

It was seen above in part I, section 1 that *ṣaw* in Isa. 28.13 is understood by Theodotion to mean 'filth', and *qaw* to mean 'vomit'; similarly, *qî' ṣō'â* in 28.8 is rendered 'vomit of filth' by Theodotion (and Aquila). In 30.22, *ṣē'* is translated 'dung' by the LXX, and 'filth' by Theodotion and Aquila (cf. part II above on Qimḥi). The Peshitta also understands *ṣaw* and *qaw* in Isa. 28.10, 13 to mean 'dung' and 'vomit'.

The German translation of Isaiah by J.D. Michaelis (1779) renders *ṣaw* and *qaw* in 28.10, 13 as 'Stank' and 'Gespieenes'.[41] He does not mention the versions, but he vocalizes the words as *ṣô* and *qô*, regards them as related to *ṣō'â* and *qî'* in v. 8, and suggests that the aleph has been lost after the vowel.[42]

---

38. W.W. Hallo, 'Isaiah 28 9-13 and the Ugaritic Abecedaries', *JBL* 77 (1958), pp. 324-38 (334).

39. Hallo, 'Isaiah 28', pp. 334-35.

40. Hallo, 'Isaiah 28', p. 333.

41. J.D. Michaelis, *Die Weissagungen Jesaia* (Deutsche Uebersetzung des Alten Testaments, VIII; Göttingen: Vandenhoeck & Ruprecht, 1779), pp. 50-51.

42. The words are discussed in Michaelis, 'Vorzügliche Varianten in Propheten Jesaia', *Orientalische und Exegetische Bibliothek* 14 (1779), Anhang, pp. 3-229

Abraham Geiger understands *ṣaw* and *qaw* to have the same meaning as the relevant words in v. 8, namely, 'Unrath' and 'Auswerf'.[43] He thinks that Theodotion and the Peshitta read the words as *ṣô* and *qô*. In 30.22, *ṣ'* was read as *ṣō'* 'Koth' by the LXX; and the versions other than the Targum read *ṣô* 'Unrath' in Hos. 5.11. Similarly, Hans Schmidt's commentary on Isaiah follows the Peshitta and translates *ṣaw* and *qaw* as 'Unflat' and 'Gespei', regarding them as synonyms of *ṣō'â* and *qî'* in v. 8.[44]

If the above understanding of *ṣaw* and *qaw* is accepted, then v. 10 may be interpreted in either of two ways. It may be Isaiah's comment on the filth of the place where the prophets and and priests of v. 7 are assembled. Alternatively, it may continue their complaints about him in v. 9 and express their mocking imitation of his condemnation of their intoxication and its resulting filth and vomit all over the place, a little here and a little there. But would Isaiah have described the mess as 'a little' (*zeʿêr*)? It is possible: the point may be not that the total amount was little, but that it was scattered all over the place. On the other hand, such a description is perhaps more likely in a mimicking of Isaiah's words. Verse 13 then says that the Lord takes up the mocking words and adapts them to the chaotic scene of carnage after the Assyrian attack (cf. 29.2).

Ex hypothesi, vv. 10 and 13 use *ṣaw* and *qaw* as synonyms, probably by-forms, of *ṣō'â* and *qî'* in v. 8. Did Theodotion, Aquila and the author of the Peshitta know, independently of this context, *ṣaw* and *qaw* as words with those meanings, or did they derive their renderings solely from the words beginning with the same consonants in v. 8? It is impossible to be certain, but let us consider the possibility that the nouns used in vv. 10 and 13 were already in use as synonyms of those in v. 8.

Nouns with different formations but from the same root certainly exist in Hebrew. There are, for example, masculine and feminine forms of the same root, such as *ṣedeq* and *ṣedāqâ*, and *ḥōq* and *ḥuqqâ*, or other variant formations, such as *ḥēṭ'* and *ḥaṭṭā't*. Is there any evidence

(84-85), and in his *Supplementa ad lexica hebraica* (Göttingen: J.G. Rosenbusch, 1792), pp. 1140-41, 2169.

43. A. Geiger, *Urschrift und Uebersetzungen der Bibel* (Breslau: Julius Hainauer, 1857), pp. 410-13.

44. H. Schmidt, *Die grossen Propheten* (Göttingen: Vandenhoeck & Ruprecht, 2nd edn, 1923).

outside this context for *ṣaw* and *qaw* as by-forms of *ṣō'â* and *qî'*?

As we have seen, the LXX, Theodotion, Aquila and the Peshitta all take *ṣē'* in Isa. 30.22 to be a noun denoting 'dung' or 'filth' (an inter-pretation known to Qimḥi). Driver has argued persuasively for the correctness of this translation, in contrast to the view that the word is a masculine singular imperative of *yāṣā'* 'to go out' which, as we have seen, would be strange if addressed to idols in the plural.[45] He under-stands *ṣē' tō'mar lô* to mean 'You will...call them ordure' (NEB). The suffix in *lô* is explained as singular by attraction to the singular noun *ṣē'*. Geiger notes that *'aḥᵃrê-ṣaw* in Hos. 5.11 is rendered *post sordem* in the Vulgate.[46] Similarly, *lᵉšimṣâ* in Exod. 32.25 is treated in several versions as *lᵉšēm* plus *šh* or perhaps *ṣw*, for the Samaritan text reads *lšmṣw*. Aquila has εἰς ὄνομα ῥύπου, the Vulgate *propter ignominiam sordis*, and the Peshitta *šmā' saryā'* ('a foul, or stinking, name'). The same understanding is implied by κακονυμία 'a bad name' in Sym-machus, and *šûm bîš* in *Targum Onqelos*. Such renderings suggest that the translators knew of a noun *ṣ'*, *ṣh* or *ṣw* meaning 'filth' or 'dung'. The root postulated for *ṣw* is, of course, the same as that suggested for *ṣō'â*. Driver compares Ethiopic *ṣō'* and Akkadian *zu-u* 'dung, filth'.[47] BDB notes the Hebrew noun *ṣē'â* 'filth' and the adjective *ṣō'î* 'filthy', and Aramaic and Syriac *ṣātā'* 'filth', and the Syriac verb *ṣ'î* 'to be filthy'. To this may be added the Sabaic verb *ṣyw* 'be contaminated with'.[48] The Semitic cognates are clear, whether or not Görg is justified in suggesting an Egyptian cognate.[49]

There is less evidence for *qw* as an independent word. Geiger draws attention to *qîqālôn* in the MT of Hab. 2.16, which is treated as two words in the Vulgate and translated *vomitus ignominiae*; this shows that Jerome or his source thought of a noun *qî* meaning 'vomit'.[50] Thus, if not *qw*, at least *qy*, is regarded as a form of *qy'*. Further, if the evidence

45. G.R. Driver, 'Hebrew Notes', *ZAW* 52 (1934), pp. 51-56 (53), and his 'Notes on Isaiah', in J. Hempel and L. Rost (eds.), *Von Ugarit nach Qumran* (Festschrift O. Eissfeldt; BZAW, 77; Berlin: Alfred Töpelmann, 1958), pp. 42-48 (45-46).

46. Geiger, *Urschrift und Uebersetzungen*, p. 41.

47. Driver, 'Hebrew Notes', p. 52.

48. A.F.L. Beeston, M.A. Ghul, W.W. Müller and J. Ryckmans, *Sabaic Diction-ary* (Louvain-la-Neuve: Editions Peeters; Beirut: Librairie du Liban, 1982), p. 147.

49. M. Görg, 'Jesaja als "Kinderlehrer"? Beobachtungen zur Sprache und Semantik in Jes 28,10 (13)', *Biblische Notizen* 29 (1985), pp. 12-16 (15-16).

50. Geiger, *Urschrift und Uebersetzungen*, p. 412.

for the existence of *ṣw* is found convincing, it implies that the same is probably true of *qw*.

Geiger further suggests that *ṣw* and *qw* were originally read as *ṣô* and *qô* (and *ṣ'* as *ṣō'* in Isa. 30.22) in order to sound less offensive[51] (whereas in v. 8 the words 'in ihrer vollen Schreibart…nicht so leicht beseitigt werden konnten'). Without necessarily following him in this further hypothesis, however, one may recognize the possibility of different traditions of vocalization (cp. also *ṣy* in 1QIsaᵃ).

If *ṣw* and *qw* are synonyms, or by-forms, of *ṣō'â* and *qî'*, why do vv. 10 and 13 use them, whereas v. 8 uses the other form? The answer may lie in the fact that v. 8 gives Isaiah's words, but the other verses the mocking imitation of them by his enemies. Tur-Sinai suggests that v. 10 reflects the language in which people spoke to children.[52] It is also possible that *ṣaw* and *qaw* are vulgar and offensive forms, such as might be use in crude abuse. Yet another possibility, namely, that the words in v. 10 reflect the slurred speech of drunkards, seems less likely, if *ṣē'* in Isa. 30.22 is a noun, and if the renderings of the Vulgate in Hos. 5.11, and of Aquila, Symmachus and the Vulgate, Peshitta and Targum in Exod. 32.25 attest knowledge of a noun *ṣ'*, *ṣh* or *ṣw* as a by-form of *ṣō'â* meaning 'filth' or 'dung'.

This theory offers a coherent interpretation of the passage, and it is based on some of the ancient versions. There is uncertainty about the vocalization of *ṣw* and *qw*, but the view that they mean 'filth' or 'dung'

---

51. Geiger, *Urschrift und Uebersetzungen*, p. 411.

52. N.H. Tur-Sinai, '*ṣaw*', in E. Ben Yehuda, *A Complete Dictionary of Ancient and Modern Hebrew*, VI (repr.; New York and London: Thomas Yoseloff, 1960), p. 5407. Edward Ullendorff, 'C'est de l'hébreu pour moi!', *JSS* 13 (1968), pp. 125-35 (131), refers to Tur-Sinai's discussion of the passage in הלשון והספר, vol. הלשון (Jerusalem: Bialik Institute, 2nd edn, 1954), pp. 371-73. The second edition was not originally available to me, but Professor S.C. Reif kindly supplied me with a copy of the relevant pages after I had completed the present article. Tur-Sinai refers to Theodotion and the Peshitta. He compares *ṣaw* (= *ṣō'â* to *ṣē'* in Isa. 30.22, to *haṣṣe'ᵉṣā'îm* (followed by *wᵉhaṣṣᵉpī'ôt*) in Isa. 22.24, and to Shimei's words to David in 2 Sam. 16.7: *ṣē' ṣē'*. Similarly, he compares *qaw* (= *qî'*) to *gôy qaw-qāw* in Isa. 18.2, 7, and (with loss of *aleph*) to *ûqᵉyû* (for which there is a variant *wqww*), which he believes to be equivalent to *wᵉqî'û* in Jer. 25.7. B. Halpern's article on this passage in Isaiah, ' "The Excremental Vision": The Doomed Priests of Doom in Isaiah 28', *Hebrew Annual Review* 10 (1986), pp. 109-21, is influenced by Tur-Sinai.

and 'vomit' is plausible. This is a possible understanding of the relevant words.

7. A Rock and a Snare or Net

V. Tanghye argues that the key to understanding Isa. 28.10, 13 is to be found in Isa. 8.14-15.[53] His reason is that several of the same verbs are used in both passages. In Isa. 28.13 we find *wᵉkāšᵉlû*, *wᵉnišbᵉrû*, *wᵉnôqᵉšû*, and *wᵉnilkādû*, and 8.15 has *wᵉkāšᵉrû*, *wᵉnāpᵉlû*, *wᵉnišbārû*, *wᵉnôqᵉšû* and *wᵉnilkādû*. He concludes that 'Es ist offensichtlich der gleiche Vorgang, der an beiden Stellen beschrieben wird'.[54] In 8.14, the causes of the disaster are said to be a 'stone of offence' (*'eben negep*) and a 'rock of stumbling' (*ṣûr mikšôl*) on the one hand, and a 'trap' (*paḥ*) and a 'snare' (*môqēš*) on the other. Tahghye therefore argues that corresponding meanings are to be found in Isa. 28.10, 13, namely, something like 'snare' and 'rock' for *ṣaw* and *qaw*, respectively.

He suggests that *qaw*, which sometimes means 'cord' has here developed the meaning 'snare' (*Schlinge*) or 'hunting net' (*Fangnetz*). This meaning is also found, he argues, in 2 Kgs 21.13, where God says that he will stretch out (*wᵉnāṭîtî*) over Jerusalem the *qāw* of Samaria in punishing the former city. The corresponding meaning for *ṣaw* in Isa. 28 would be 'stone' or 'rock', and he compares Arabic *ṣuwwatun* 'A sign for the guidance of travellers, consisting of stones,…set up…in the way', etc.[55]

Tanghye's theory is open to objection. First, the use of similar language in Isa. 8.14 and 28.13 does not necessarily imply that other details must correspond. It is possible that the same words are used to describe the coming disaster, without the precise causes being the same. Second, the hypothesis of a semantic development from 'cord' to 'snare' or 'net' lacks convincing evidence. 2 Kings 21.13 speaks of stretching out a line, but Tanghye gives no reasons for rejecting the view that the reference is to an act of measuring before a building is destroyed. Nor does he discuss *mišqōlet*, which is a further object of *wᵉnāṭîtî* and may be supposed to have a related meaning. It is usually thought to mean 'plummet', and that suggests that *qāw* is something

53. V. Tanghye, 'Dichtung und Ekel in Jesaha xxviii 7-13', *VT* 43 (1953), pp. 235-60 (252-55).

54. Tanghye, 'Dichtung und Ekel', p. 254.

55. E.W. Lane, *An Arabic-English Lexicon* (London: Williams & Norgate, 1863–1893), p. 1739.

concerned with measuring, not a snare or net. Similarly, Isa. 28.17 says *wᵉśamtî mišpāṭ lᵉqāw ûṣᵉdāqâ lᵉmišqālet*, using *misqālet* as a parallel to *qāw*. Further, *qāw* is used as the object of *nāṭâ* in Job 38.5 (cf. Zech. 1.16) in a context referring to building. The same expression is thus used of the preparations both for building and for demolition (cf. Isa. 34.11; Lam. 2.8), and that scarcely fits the meaning 'snare'. Third, if Tanghye's argument that *qaw* means 'snare' or 'net' breaks down, his main argument that *ṣaw* means 'stone' or 'rock' disappears. It would be rash to build too much on the alleged Arabic cognate without supporting evidence. Tanghye's interpretation of Isa. 28.10, 13 must be rejected.

IV

What conclusion may be drawn from this examination of different interpretations of Isa. 28.10 and 13? I have argued that interpretations 1, 3, 4 and 7 should be rejected and that, although interpretation 5 is plausible, it lacks corroborative evidence. Interpretation 2—that the verses contain an unintelligible jumble of words—is possible. However, the fact that *ṣaw* and *qaw* begin with the same letters as *ṣō'â* and *qî'* only two verses before v. 10 leads us to suspect that there may be a relationship between Isaiah's words in v. 8 and what is probably the mocking imitation of them in v. 10. Such a relationship is postulated in more than one interpretation, but most clearly in interpretation 6. That interpretation has very early support in Theodotion, Aquila and the Peshitta. There is a hypothetical aspect to this interpretation: the words used in v. 8 are not identical with those in vv. 10 and 13, but the hypothesis that the latter are vulgar words, unsurprising in mocking abuse, or words used in speaking to children, is plausible. Interpretation 6 offers a coherent interpretation of the passage and has the strongest claim to acceptance. Isa. 28.10, 13 probably contains a mocking imitation of Isaiah's words condemning the filth or dung and vomit mentioned in v. 8; and v. 13 uses the same words to compare the devastation after the Assyrian invasion.[56]

56. I am grateful to Professor R.P. Gordon for reading and commenting on a draft of this article, to Professor S.C. Reif for help in interpreting mediaeval Jewish commentaries, to Dr J. Day and Professor H.G.M. Williamson for giving me photocopies of parts of publications to which I should not otherwise have had access, to Ms Ora Lipschitz and Professor Rudolf Smend for allowing me to consult them on particular questions, and to Dr G.I. Davies for his help.

THE LEGACY OF LOWTH: ROBERT LOWTH AND THE BOOK OF ISAIAH IN PARTICULAR*

Robert P. Gordon

Robert Lowth was born on 27 November 1710, in Winchester where his father William had been appointed a canon of the cathedral in 1696. William Lowth was himself a theologian of some accomplishment whose interests included the Old Testament prophets, Josephus and Clement of Alexandria. It was ordained, therefore, that the young Robert should study at the school founded by William of Wykeham several centuries earlier for the preparation of young men for the service of church and state. The régime under which Lowth began his learning was exacting and consisted almost entirely of the study of classical authors in the original languages. A Winchester alumnus writing several decades before Lowth records how in his day school began at six o'clock each morning, with the first exercise of the day a verse composition on a set theme.[1] At Winchester Lowth developed a rare facility for verse-making that is represented by two compositions subsequently published: *The Genealogy of Christ*, inspired by the Old Testament characters depicted on the east window in the college chapel, and *Katherine-Hill Near Winchester*, apostrophizing the spot where the boys of Winchester disported themselves during their limited free time away from their desks ('When to thy pleasures joyful I repair / To draw in health, and breathe a purer air').

It was a precocious talent such that when the poet and Olney hymnist Wiliam Cowper was shown some of Lowth's schoolboy verses he declared that, had he been present when Lowth declaimed them,

---

*   The first draft of this study was written in the private library of Ora Lipschitz and Simcha Friedman in Ein Kerem, Jerusalem, in September 1999. Their generous hospitality greatly assisted its production.

1.   See A.K. Cook, *About Winchester College* (London: Macmillan, 1917), pp. 14-17.

> I should have trembled for the boy, lest the man should disappoint the
> hopes such early genius had given birth to. It is not common to see so
> lively a fancy so correctly managed, and so free from irregular exuber-
> ances, at so unexperienced an age; fruitful, yet not wanton, and gay
> without being tawdry.[2]

If Lowth acquired classical learning at Winchester it was 'Orientalism'
and primitivism that captured his imagination when he went up to New
College, Oxford, in 1729. In Oxford he established credentials as the
foremost theorist among a group of Wykehamist 'pre-Romantics' who,
in keeping with the prevailing doctrine, traced the origins of poetry as
the purest and most ancient expression of the human imagination to 'the
Orient', and more particularly to the poetry of the Hebrews.

Lowth's views on Hebrew poetry are set out in *De sacra poesi
hebraeorum*,[3] which was published in 1753 and which gives the text of
34 lectures delivered in Oxford during his tenure as Professor of Poetry
from 1741 to 1750. Here we are told, not only that poetry originated in
the ancient east, but that it was a gift from the creator to the first
humans; and so, following Milton, Lowth can attribute Ps. 148 to
Adam.[4] Most famously, in these lectures Lowth argues for the essentially poetic character of Hebrew prophecy and highlights parallelism as
the defining feature of Hebrew poetry. However, when he surmises that
there were colleges of trainee prophets where the tiros were taught the
skill of composing to music,[5] we may detect the influence of his own
schooling at Winchester. Already the importance of Isaiah is becoming
evident in the *Praelectiones*. After the Psalms, Isaiah is the book most
frequently quoted, while Lowth's translation of Isa. 14, containing the
ode on the downfall of the king of Babylon, won him special praise
from such admirers as Christopher Smart and Joseph Warton.[6] According to Lowth, Isaiah represented 'the first of all the prophets both in
order and in dignity'.[7] While his primitive anthology was contained

2.   See J.G. Frazer (ed.), *Letters of William Cowper*, I (London: Macmillan,
1912), p. 182 (Letter LXXIX, dated 9 February 1782).

3.   *De sacra poesi hebraeorum: Praelectiones academicae oxonii habitae*
(Oxford: Clarendon Press, 1753).

4.   *Praelectio* XXV (p. 334).

5.   *Praelectio* XVIII (p. 230).

6.   Cf. B. Hepworth, *Robert Lowth* (Boston: Twayne Publishers, 1978), pp. 37,
165-67. The poem is translated into Latin at the end of *Praelectio* XXVIII (pp. 376-
79).

7.   *Praelectio* XXI (p. 281).

within the Hebrew Bible, Orientalism as promoted by him and his contemporaries tended to play down distinctions between the Hebraic and the non-Hebraic, and between the ancient and the modern.[8] So the observations of 'modern' travellers like Sir John Chardin, Edward Pococke and Thomas Harmer in 'the east' are cited regularly in illustration of points of detail in the biblical text. Moreover, the poetical book of Job, which Lowth regarded as the oldest of the biblical books, is also viewed as the least specifically Israelite of them.[9] At the same time, Lowth's intensive classical education at Winchester could not be denied, and—although it was hardly expressive of Orientalism or primitivism—in the commentary he frequently adverts to classical sources for illustrative purposes.

Lowth's preoccupation with the forms of Hebrew poetry and, indeed, his explicit eschewing of theological discussion have resulted in his being classed as more humanist than Christian,[10] but this is to misread him. Theological comment is by no means absent from his notes on Isaiah (see below), and when it occurs it is orthodoxly Christian in assuming revelation in history and through Scripture, prefiguration and incarnation. As John Milbank observes, it is wrong 'to conclude that because Lowth is not concerned to expound the *truth* of the scriptures, nor to establish their factual veracity, the work is theologically neutral'.[11] Lowth is rightly lauded for his contribution to the study of the forms of Hebrew poetry, and indeed for giving classic expression to the view that the prophetic books of the Hebrew Bible largely consist of what may be described as 'poetry'. This all came to a heady climax in *Isaiah: A New Translation*, published in 1778, in which Lowth presented not only a translation but also extensive notes on the Hebrew text.[12] In the 'Preliminary Dissertation' he states his position on a number of basic issues relating to the practice of textual criticism. He recognized that the Masoretic vocalization of the received Hebrew text was a secondary development: 'in effect an Interpretation of the

---

8. Cf. Hepworth, *Robert Lowth*, pp. 51, 94-95.

9. *Praelectio* XXXII (pp. 420-21).

10. Cf. Hepworth, *Robert Lowth*, pp. 36, 94, 98, 154 on Lowth's 'materialistic', 'humanistic', 'secular' outlook.

11. J. Milbank, *The Word Made Strange: Theology, Language, Culture* (Oxford: Basil Blackwell, 1997), p. 63.

12. *Isaiah: A New Translation. With a Preliminary Dissertation, and Notes Critical, Philological, and Explanatory* (London: J. Dodsley & T. Cadell, 1778).

Hebrew Text made by the Jews of later ages, probably not earlier than the Eighth Century; and may be considered as their Translation of the Old Testament' (p. liv). He was aware that the Septuagint translation of Isaiah has many flaws, opining that it is as bad as for any book in the Hebrew Bible (p. lxvi), though that does not prevent him from frequently quoting it or occasionally retroverting on the basis of it. He was less objective, and certainly less accurate, in his estimation of the work of his friend Benjamin Kennicott—'a Work the greatest and most important that has been undertaken and accomplished since the Revival of letters' (p. lxii). Kennicott made his collation of mediaeval manuscripts of Isaiah available to Lowth pre-publication, and Lowth frequently cites Kennicott variants as pointing to more pristine readings of the Hebrew.[13]

When Lowth does emend the MT towards a presumed original reading he sometimes has precedent among the commentators whom he consults, and very often the support of the ancient versions which, not surprisingly, he uses without too much regard for their general characteristics, or for the necessity often enough laid upon the ancient translators of making the best sense out of a text that was problematic already in antiquity. Thus, to take some instances from the early chapters of Isaiah, the emendations at 1.7 and 2.6 are representative in already having been advocated by earlier scholars. Lowth's positive evaluation of the ancient versions is illustrated at 6.11, where he accepts the presumed *Vorlage* of the LXX (cf. Vulgate), while at 1.3 he expresses high regard for the text underlying Aquila's version. At 3.8 he follows the Syriac and emends the text, and similarly at 9.8 on the basis of the Targum ('Chaldee'). The writers whom Lowth most frequently quotes are K.F. Houbigant, Thomas Secker, who was archbishop of Canterbury from 1758 to 1768, and the Jewish rabbinical commentator Kimchi. Houbigant's critical notes on Isaiah were published in 1753.[14] In the 'Preliminary Dissertation' Lowth notes that he was given permission by Archbishop Secker's successor to consult the archbishop's marginal notes written in, respectively, a folio English Bible and a Hebrew Bible in the edition of J.H. Michaelis (Halle, 1720),

---

13. Kennicott's collations were published as *Vetus Testamentum hebraicum cum variis lectionibus* (2 vols.; Oxford: Clarendon Press, 1776).

14. In *Biblia hebraica cum notis criticis et versione latina*, IV (Paris: C. Briasson & L. Durand, 1753).

which had been deposited by order of Secker in the Lambeth Library (p. lxix).

And so to the main purpose of this study, which is to consider two examples of Lowth the textual critic at work and to note how, in his emendations of the Hebrew text—in which his views on parallelism were a contributory factor—he anticipated later scholarship by deferring to the doubtful evidence of the ancient versions.

Isaiah 57.17

The second half of Isa. 57, beginning with v. 14, marks a change in tone from the preceding verses in that now God in all his majesty extends the hope of healing and restoration to his people in spite of their defection from him. This is the setting within which God declares in v. 17: בעון בצעו קצפתי. This clause is most often translated as if בצעו derives from the familiar BH בצע, '(unlawful) gain',[15] as in NRSV 'Because of their wicked covetousness I was angry'. The verse continues with the assertion that those whom God 'struck' had persisted in their contrariness. The LXX, however, has βραχύ τι for בצעו and so represents God as having been angry 'a little' or 'for a little while'. *BHS* notes the Greek and proposes an emendation of the MT on the basis of it, viz. *בצע, without the suffix, now glossed with the Latin 'paululum' ('for a little while'). No doubt the prior proposal to replace בעון, the first word in the verse, by בעונו (i.e. with 3 m.s. suffix) is an emendation consequential on the decision about *בצע, since בעון would no longer be in construct relationship with the following word, and 'I was angry for a little while because of *their* sin' reads a little more easily than would a text with an unsuffixed form.[16] The *BHS* editor may even have reckoned that the 3 m.s. suffix had crossed from one noun to the other through a simple scribal lapse at some point in the early transmission of the MT. For all that, whatever the LXX had in its *Vorlage* corresponding to בצעו, it appears to have read בעון unsuffixed as in the MT, hence its rendering by δι᾽ ἁμαρτίαν.

The main sponsors in the modern period of what we may for the moment dub the LXX-*BHS* approach have been NEB and REB, the

---

15. I am grateful to Peter Harland for letting me consult an advance copy of his paper 'בצע: Bribe, Extortion or Profit?' (see now *VT* 50 [2000], pp. 310-22), in which he argues that the term generally has a negative connotation.

16. Cf. the MT's suffixing of בצעו.

former translating our clause by 'For a time I was angry at the guilt of Israel' and the latter revising to 'For a *brief* time...' The revised Gesenius lexicon also accepts the meaning that appears to be supported by the LXX and refers its readers to C.C. Torrey's commentary on Isaiah for further explanation.[17] Torrey claims, without further comment, that בצע has its 'etymological' meaning of 'bit, morceau, Bisschen' and compares BH רגע ('moment'). He thinks that the LXX rendering has a more solid basis than mere guesswork, and that it may well represent a *Vorlage* with an MT-type reading.[18] The dictionary references to Torrey notwithstanding,[19] the first to propose this explanation of בצע in the modern period appears to have been Robert Lowth in *Isaiah: A New Translation*. In his notes on Isa. 57.17 Lowth remarks:

> For בצעו, I read בצע, paululum, à בצע, abscidit; as LXX read and render it βραχυ τι. 'Propter iniquitatem *avaritiae ejus*,' the rendering of Vulg. which our translators, and I believe all others follow, is surely quite beside the purpose.[20]

Lowth therefore translates the first line of the verse by 'Because of his iniquity for a short time I was wroth'. He clearly believed that he was the first to follow the lead of the LXX in his treatment of בצעו. The verb meant basically 'cut', and the LXX translator assumed a noun denoting something cut off, or of short duration.[21] Basically, then, the issue is whether there is evidence in Biblical Hebrew for a noun derived from the root בצע, meaning '(small) portion, piece' and capable of being used adverbially with the sense 'for a short time'. *HALAT*, which cites the (Lowth)/Torrey explanation without giving it approval, does

17. R. Meyer and H. Donner (eds.), *Wilhelm Gesenius: Hebräisches und aramäisches Handwörterbuch über das Alte Testament*, I (Berlin: Springer-Verlag, 18th edn, 1987), p. 167.

18. C.C. Torrey, *The Second Isaiah: A New Interpretation* (Edinburgh: T. & T. Clark, 1928), p. 436. Cf. also J. Fischer, *In welcher Schrift lag das Buch Isaias den LXX vor? Eine textkritische Studie* (BZAW, 56; Giessen: Alfred Töpelmann, 1930), pp. 63-64.

19. As well as the revised Gesenius lexicon, see also *HALAT*.

20. *Isaiah*, Notes, p. 251. The punctuation is reproduced as in Lowth.

21. At Isa. 38.12 בצע (piel) is translated in the LXX by the verb ἐκτέμνειν, according to D. Barthélemy, *Critique textuelle de l'Ancien Testament. II. Isaïe, Jérémie, Lamentations* (OBO, 50/2; Fribourg: Editions universitaires; Göttingen: Vandenhoeck & Ruprecht, 1986), p. 415, but the Hebrew and the Greek are not that closely related in this verse and too much should not be made of the possible equation.

suggest, coincidentally in the same entry, two possible occurrences of בצע with something like the required meaning.[22] Its explanation of the occurrence of בצעך in Jer. 51.13 by 'abgeschnittenes Stück' is based upon the presumed root meaning of 'cut' for BH בצע, but Jer. 51.13b is a very difficult text; the LXX (= 28.13) certainly represents a root other than בצע in this case.[23] The expression בצע כסף in Judg. 5.19 is also cited in *HALAT* as illustrating a similar meaning for בצע, but there are no special grounds for seeing anything here other than the more usual sense of 'gain', now extended in the direction of 'plunder'. Now if the biblical support for Lowth's explanation at Isa. 57.17 is doubtful, there is not much in post-biblical usage that would sustain it. Saadia may reflect awareness of such an explanation of בצע in his Arabic translation of Isa. 57.17 where, at the same time as he represents the more usual sense associated with this noun, he speaks of God's wrath being directed against *a section of the community*.[24] Ben Yehuda notes a couple of instances of בצע meaning 'piece', but this does not amount to much and still falls short of the temporal significance proposed for Isa. 57.17.[25]

Since it is difficult to buttress Lowth's proposal with philological support, the same must, of course, apply to the LXX—if we are to assume that the LXX's treatment of בצע/בצעו is to be explained philologically. There are, however, other potentially viable ways of explaining the difference between the MT and the LXX. Houbigant, whom Lowth regularly cites, though not on this particular point, suggests that the LXX reflects a text with פתע ('immediately').[26] R. Kittel, who edited Isaiah for *BHK*, cites the Greek in support of the emendation רגע ('[for] a moment'), reading also בעונו for בעון. This suggestion had, however, already been dismissed by Bernhard Duhm as 'ein verdientes Unglück des Konjekturensports'.[27] Duhm himself assumed that the LXX *Vorlage*

22. *HALAT*, pp. 141-42.

23. εἰς τὰ σπλάγχνα σου probably assumes במעיך with *BHS*.

24. See J. Derenbourg, *Oeuvres complètes de R. Saadia ben Iosef Al-Fayyoûmî*. III. *Version arabe d'Isaïe* (Paris: Ernest Leroux, 1896), pp. 86 (Arabic), 101 (French).

25. E. Ben Yehuda, *Thesaurus totius hebraitatis*, II (Berlin: Schoeneberg, n.d.), p. 585.

26. *BHK*, IV, p. 160.

27. B. Duhm, *Das Buch Jesaia* (Göttinger Handkommentar zum Alten Testament; Göttingen: Vandenhoeck & Ruprecht, 3rd edn, 1914), p. 404.

had מצער, with which we may compare Ziegler's subsequent proposal of מזער.[28] מצער occurs with prefixed lamedh in Isa. 63.18, apparently with the meaning 'for a little while', rendered in the LXX by μικρὸν (+ τι S* Or. V 214 Cyr.).

If we were to pursue this possibility of an alternative *Vorlage* at 57.17, we could, for that matter, suppose that the Greek translator thought that he saw בצער—with only the final letter differing from what we have in the MT—and so translated by βραχύ τι. In that case the variant would consist of the adjective צעיר ('small'), written defectively, and the inseparable preposition ב. Here, however, we run into a procedural issue, since it is a good question whether the textual critic should be obliged to reconstruct readings using a precise lexical form or idiomatic phrasing in order to explain every versional divergence from the MT. In other words, is he or she required to proceed in cases of variant readings as if what an ancient translator thought he saw in his *Vorlage* was necessarily grammatical or idiomatic? If the textual critic favours an ancient version with a 'best possible' retroversion into Hebrew he or she may actually complicate the task of adjudication between competing readings by creating a more viable alternative to the MT than ever actually existed. In the case of Isa. 57.17 it is perfectly conceivable that the translator read בצער (= בצעיר)—which is nearer to the MT than the מצער or מזער proposed by others—and translated as he did.[29] However, having thus set up the possible Greek *Vorlage*, we might then proceed to question its suitability in respect of idiomacy and contextual appropriateness; and, despite the inherent circularity in all this, the procedure is legitimate, even if liable to misfire. At any rate, since Lowth's explanation of the MT lacks support, the possibility of relating LXX βραχύ τι to MT בצעו suffers with it, and the attraction of the explanation from the Hebrew root צער gains in appeal. We should note, too, that if the LXX could be shown to represent מצער/בצער this would confirm that its *Vorlage* had a fourth radical after בצע, corresponding to the waw in MT בצעו.

28. J. Ziegler, *Untersuchungen zur Septuaginta des Buches Isaias* (Alttestamentliche Abhandlungen, 12/3; Münster: Aschendorffsche Verlagsbuchhandlung, 1934), pp. 165-66.

29. In view of the speculative nature of the discussion, it seems unnecessary to appeal to the graphic similarity between beth and mem in the old Hebrew script, or to the possibility of aural confusion between these two labial consonants.

So far the discussion has been in terms of possible variant readings, but it is necessary also to consider the interpretative factor that is so often involved in the translational equivalences of the ancient versions, and from which no translation can be completely free. The two approaches are not mutually contradictory, since sometimes the translator's interpretative preference or ideological tendency will have inclined him to read a difficult, or not so legible, text in a certain way, or to choose a particular option where more than one possibility existed. The first colon of Isa. 57.17 has to be examined in this light before any final decision about *Vorlage* is reached. In the first place, we should note that, whereas the idea of God being wrathful against his people is widely represented in the Old Testament, there are a few texts where it is suggested that this divine anger is not interminable, as perhaps classically expressed in Ps. 30.6(5):

> For his anger is but for a moment;
> his favour is for a lifetime.

This idea is expressed a couple of times in Isaiah, and more so in LXX Isaiah. According to 10.25 the divine wrath that used Assyria as its agent of punishment against Israel would end 'very soon' (עור מעט מזער). At 26.16 the LXX is innovative in this respect, representing the difficult צקון לחש מוסרך למו of the MT by '*with small affliction* do you correct us'. There is no strikingly obvious explanation of the Greek in relation to the Hebrew;[30] what is important for the present discussion is the Greek translator's inclination to think in terms of the limited intensity, or even duration, of the chastisement meted out by God to his people. As regards the MT, Isa. 54.7-8 is the text closest to 57.17: 'For a brief moment I forsook you, but in great compassion I will gather you together' (v. 7), where the LXX has χρόνον μικρὸν for ברגע קטן. While it is hardly necessary to attribute the LXX plus (ἀπέστρεψα) τὸ πρόσωπόν μου ἀπ' αὐτοῦ in 57.17 to 54.8 in view of the obviously elliptical nature of the MT at 57.17,[31] the LXX translator cannot have been unaware of the close verbal connexion between the two verses—a

---

30. Cf. R.R. Ottley, *The Book of Isaiah According to the Septuagint (Codex Alexandrinus). II. Text and Notes* (Cambridge: Cambridge University Press, 1906), pp. 231-32.

31. *pace* M.H. Goshen-Gottstein (ed.), *The Book of Isaiah* (The Hebrew University Bible Project; Jerusalem: Magnes Press, The Hebrew University, 1995), p. 258.

connexion that he has cemented by his introduction of βραχύ τι into his translation of 57.17.

Most obviously, the immediate context may also have influenced the Septuagintal rendering of Isa. 57.17. The preceding verse has God declare that his accusations and his anger do not last forever. Considerations of context can, of course, work in either of two ways, whether by confirming the originality of a reading that is appropriate to its wider setting or by giving grounds for suspecting that a contextually compatible reading has been influenced secondarily by the context. Perhaps, therefore, the Greek translator of 57.17 (or his *Vorlage*) was influenced by the immediate context, possibly with assistance from such a text as 54.7-8, into emphasizing the finiteness of the divine wrath when directed against Israel. If the translator (or copyist-editor) was already predisposed by theological *Tendenz* into amelioration of the biblical text in favour of Israel–Judah (cf. above on Isa. 26.16) he will have been all the more susceptible to the pull of the immediate context in this case.

Bergmeier[32] introduces another factor when he notes how the Greek translators of the Hebrew Bible had difficulty in handling BH בצע ('gain'). He claims that, whereas the word is correctly rendered in eight of its occurrences, there are ten that are incorrectly translated. More particularly, in Isaiah MT אִישׁ לבצעו מקצהו at 56.11 is translated very freely by ἕκαστος κατὰ αὐτό, which is contextually appropriate— 'shepherds' going their own way, in ironic reversal of the sheep motif of 53.6, according to which the 'we' of the passage had gone astray 'like sheep'—but it scarcely reflects a proper understanding of the Hebrew term. Bergmeier concludes that LXX 57.17 had בצעו in its *Vorlage* and that the translator opted for a free rendering out of simple ignorance of the true meaning.

Other indications of actual *Tendenz* may be present in LXX 57.17. The Hebrew verb קצף is translated by λυπεῖν, which at first sight looks like an attempt to evacuate קצף of the idea of divine anger, except that the קצף/λυπεῖν equation operates elsewhere (cf. 1 Sam. 29.4; 2 Kgs 13.19; Isa. 8.21).[33] At the same time, the equation of קצף with ὀργίζεσθαι is tolerated in v. 16. There is, however, the difference that,

32. R. Bergmeier, 'Das Streben nach Gewinn—des Volkes עֲוֹן', *ZAW* 81 (1969), pp. 93-97 (95).

33. It is therefore unnecessary to assume that the Greek represents the verb עצב ('grieve') instead of MT בצע[ו] (cf. Goshen-Gottstein, *The Book of Isaiah*, p. 258).

whereas in v. 17 the intransitive qal of קָצַף is represented by a transitive verb and object in ἐλύπησα αὐτὸν ('I grieved him'), אֶקְצוֹף in v. 16 is translated by ὀργίζεσθαι in a statement that God would *not* be angry forever. In the third colon of v. 17 the differences are more substantial and may be credited with more obvious intention to ameliorate this address to Judah. Where the MT says that God's people 'went stubbornly in the way of their heart', the Greek says that they 'went gloomily (or 'sullenly'[?]) in their ways'. στυγνὸς for שׁוֹבָב has the appearance of mitigation, and the same may be said of the absence of an equivalent of לִבּוֹ (in בְּדֶרֶךְ לִבּוֹ), since with the omission goes the idea of wilfulness, just as happened with the neutralization of שׁוֹבָב in στυγνὸς. A softer focus on Judah in the hands of its God is clearly the intention of the Greek translator.

So where does this survey of options leave us? We have seen that MT Isa. 57.17 and, quite probably, the LXX attest to a form with a radical after the 'ayin in בֶּצַע; that, even if we were to read בֶּצַע instead of בִּצְעוֹ, there is no substantial basis for translating by 'paululum'; that the Septuagintal βραχύ τι probably reflects a reading (whether actual or imagined by a translator) derived from the root צָעַר; that the immediate context could have influenced the Greek translator into emphasizing the limited duration of God's wrath vis-à-vis his people; that the LXX is otherwise and evidently in the business of ameliorating the text and thus may come under suspicion for its rendering of בֶּצַע by βραχύ τι; that the LXX in general is less than sure-footed when dealing with BH בֶּצַע ('gain'). Two further considerations may be briefly introduced. First, in Isa. 56.11 the leaders of the community have been accused of turning aside 'each to their unjust gain (לְבִצְעוֹ)', and such straying is the subject of 57.17-18 ('went stubbornly in the way of their heart' [v. 17], 'I have seen their ways' [v. 18])'. Just as בֶּצַע makes perfect sense in 56.11, so its occurrence in 57.17 in a similar setting occasions no difficulty. Secondly, we may have some sympathy with Bergmeier's point that the idea of God's being 'angry' with Judah for only a moment is very appropriate to 54.7, which falls within chs. 40–55 with their message of imminent salvation for the Judaean exiles, but may not so obviously reflect the viewpoint of chs. 56–66 and 57.17 in particular.

It seems, therefore, that Robert Lowth's venture into textual criticism at Isa. 57.17 was ill-founded, and that those texts, editions, translations and commentaries that have followed him—they include *BHK*, *BHS*,

J.B. Moffatt's translation,[34] NEB, REB, the German 1980 *Einheitsüber-setzung*[35] and the new Gesenius lexicon—have done so ill-advisedly.

Isaiah 59.18

In his treatment of this verse Lowth again displays his reserve for the MT, which he declares to be 'very imperfect, and absolutely unintel-ligible',[36] and he shows his willingness to retrovert towards an osten-sibly superior Hebrew text on the basis of versional evidence—in this case the Targum to Isaiah. He comments on 'the learned Vitringa' (as he is wont to call him) and his unavailing efforts to explain the MT, adding that those who regard the Hebrew text as absolutely infallible 'ought surely to give us somewhat that has at least the appearance of sense'. He then introduces the Targum which, retroverted, points to what he believes to be the original form of the text. For the Hebrew כעל גמלות כעל ישלם ('According to their deeds, so will he repay', NRSV) the Targum has מרי גמליא הוא גמלא ישלם, which Lowth renders in Latin by 'Dominus retributionum ipse retributionem reddet' ('The Lord of retributions himself will render retribution'). In other words, the Targum represents כעל at the beginning of the verse by the equi-valent of בעל ('Lord').

Now we may think that Lowth has exaggerated the difficulties in this colon, especially since כעל, the word that he is anxious to emend, occurs in 63.7, again in the context of recompense, though without any of the syntactical awkwardness attaching to the second occurrence of כעל in 59.18. The MT has, at any rate, exercised the minds of both ancient and modern interpreters, and the LXX translator plainly was uncomfortable. He joins the colon to the preceding verse with its description of God putting on his armour before intervening on behalf of truth and justice: 'as one about to pay recompense, reproach to the enemy'. In defence of his reconstruction Lowth compares the resultant expression 'lord of retribution' with בעל אף (lit. 'lord of anger') in Prov. 22.24.[37] As he notes, the same Targumic expression מרי גמליא

---

34. *A New Translation of the Bible* (London: Hodder & Stoughton, 1928).

35. *Die Bibel: Einheitsübersetzung* (Freiburg: Herder, 1980) ('Kurze Zeit zürnte ich wegen der Sünde [des Volkes]').

36. *Isaiah*, Notes, p. 255.

37. Cf. also בעל חמה in Nah. 1.2.

also appears in Isa. 35.4, there as the equivalent of MT גמול אלהים ('with terrible recompense', NRSV). This, of course, still leaves the second occurrence of כעל in Isa. 59.18 requiring explanation. Lowth says that the word has been omitted in the Targum, but claims that it too should be read as בעל, and so he assumes an original Hebrew text that ran: בעל גמולות הוא/בעל גמולות ישלם. However, it is more likely that the Targum was doing its best with a text that was closer to the MT and that, even with the modification of כעל 2° to בעל, was still problematical. For if we were to suppose for the sake of argument that בעל did indeed stand in place of כעל 2° in the Targumist's *Vorlage*, it would be a fair question what the Targumist would be likely to do with it. This is probably why the Targum, while representing neither כעל 2° nor בעל in strict literalness, translates כעל ישלם by הוא גמלא ישלם. Lowth, at any rate, translates his reconstructed text, with בעל twice for כעל, as follows:

> He is mighty to recompence [*sic*];
> He that is mighty to recompence [*sic*] will requite:

This Targum-driven emendation of the MT was picked up by Rudolf Kittel in *BHK* where it is proposed that כעל 1° should be emended with the Targum to בעל and that כעל 2° should be changed to גמול, again (supposedly) in line with the Targum. Since it is the second occurrence of כעל—with no noun to govern, as Skinner notes[38]—that is specially difficult, *BHS* retains only the second emendation, again to גמול and purportedly on the basis of the Targum. We have already noted, however, the difficulty facing the Targumist as he sought to render the Hebrew text. If he had indeed been faced by a text that ran כעל גמלות גמול ישלם (or similar) it is doubtful that he would have included the pronoun הוא in his translation. The presence of the pronoun might actually suggest that the Targumist thought that he was reading בעל and paraphrased in order to gloss over the slight problem of having בעל on its own. Moreover, suspicion that the Targum does not reflect a *Vorlage* with גמול for כעל is confirmed by Jer. 51.56 where, in a reference to divine retribution, the statement that God will 'requite' (שלם ישלם) is expanded to say that God will requite 'their recompense to them'. In

---

38. J. Skinner, *The Book of the Prophet Isaiah: Chapters XL–LXVI* (Cambridge Bible for Schools and Colleges; Cambridge: Cambridge University Press, 1917), p. 193.

other words, the root גמל supplies a translational object to ישלם, just as we may suspect that it has at Isa. 59.18.

The Targum to Jer. 51.56 is also important for our discussion in that it has another occurrence of the term מרי גמליא. The underlying Hebrew in this case is אל גמלות ('a God of recompense'), which becomes in the Targum אלהא מרי גמליא ('a God the Lord of recompense'). This could be interpreted to mean that מרי, as additional, is simply exegetical. Nevertheless it is probably better—and not quite the same thing—to receive מרי גמליא as a set piece paralleled in Isa. 35.4, where it stands for MT גמול אלהים, and in Isa. 59.18 where it corresponds to MT כעל גמלות.

Now when a word or phrase recurs in the Targums in other than a straight word-for-word equivalence it is prudent to consider whether the Targum is simply a witness to the Hebrew text or has been rendering in accordance with the interpretative principle of *gezerah shavah*, according to which similar phrasings in otherwise unrelated texts may be translated in more or less identical fashion. Even if not consciously invoking a hermeneutical principle such as *gezerah shavah*, a translator of a biblical text might easily translate one passage in the light of another, and especially when confronted by a textual crux. The Targums for their part regularly have the same renderings for words and phrases that are not identical but that nevertheless were thought to correspond in one way or another, and this creates hazards for any textual critic who is inclined to retrovert without making proper allowance for this Targumic trait. In his 'Preliminary Dissertation' to *Isaiah* Lowth's comments on the Targum are exceptionally brief. He appears to accept the ascription to Jonathan ben Uzziel and thinks that the translation was made not later than the first century CE. He acknowledges the closeness of the Targum to the MT, and its occasional usefulness for 'ascertaining the true reading of the Hebrew Text'—in spite of its tendency towards 'wordy allegorical explanation'.[39] Elsewhere in the 'Preliminary Dissertation' Lowth finds the Targum already witnessing to the conjectured reading ותפר for MT וכפר at Isa. 28.18. However, even though he correctly notes that the Targum's use of בטל parallels its translation of the verb פרר in the expression הפיר ברית, he does not discuss the possibility that it is not the Targumic *Vorlage* but its translation method that accounts for its reading here (p. xxxix). This uncritical approach to

39. Lowth, *Isaiah*, p. lxviii.

the Targum as textual witness is also evident in the commentary, for example at Isa. 16.9. Here Lowth happily emends the text in the light of the parallel at Jer. 48.32 and cites the Targumic agreements with the Jeremiah text as if they constitute independent textual evidence.

So Lowth fails to pay attention to the significance of parallel renderings in the Targum. At the same time, it may be possible to go beyond simply identifying 'parallel translation' as a feature of the Targum at Isa. 35.4, 59.18 and Jer. 51.56, since there may be an identifiable starting-point for the parallelism that occurs in these references. It is reasonable to test the supposition that one text may have influenced the others. In the case of Isa. 35.4, however, it is not so likely that the Targumic מרי גמליא was minted here in the process of translating the MT of the verse. For MT גמול אלהים הוא the Targum has הוא מרי גמליא יוי. Since the Targum to Isaiah habitually represents אלהים, when referring to the God of Israel, by the tetragrammaton (cf. 13.19; 37.4, 16, 17; 53.4; 58.2), the same may be assumed to apply in 35.4. This almost certainly means that the expression מרי גמליא was triggered off by the occurrence of גמול in the MT. That this is probably the case is indicated by Jer. 51.56, where on a strict word-for-word basis the Targumic ארי אלהא corresponds to כי אל in the MT, leaving גמלות to generate our set-piece expression מרי גמליא. It therefore appears as if the assumed *Vorlage* of the Targum at Isa. 59.18 may have been responsible for the coining of the expression מרי גמליא. And if מרי גמליא is original to the Targum to Isa. 59.18, this at least means that we cannot dismiss the Targumic expression as a mere standard translation that is irrelevant to the reconstruction of the Targumic *Vorlage*.[40] Moreover, the supposition that, of the three texts cited, Isa. 59.18 is more likely to have generated the expression may be confirmed by the occurrence of בעל גמולות in a marginal reading in MS B of Ecclesiasticus at 35.13, which runs: מלוה ייי נותן לאביון ומי בעל גמולות כי אם הוא. The origin of the marginal reading is uncertain, though it cannot be later than the Peshitta version of Ecclesiasticus, since it appears there.[41] There is nothing else in the reading that would support a direct reference to Isa. 59.18, while

---

40. *pace* J. Reider, 'Substantival 'AL in Biblical Hebrew', *JQR* NS 30 (1940), pp. 263-70 (267 n. 9).

41. See F. Vattioni (ed.), *Ecclesiastico* (Naples: Istituto Orientale di Napoli, 1968), p. 185. For this and for other helpful observations on Ben Sira I am most grateful to my colleague James K. Aitken.

on the other hand there is obvious affinity with Prov. 19.17. It could be
that בעל גמולות was simply a current expression or even an ad hoc
coinage; nevertheless, the correspondence with the assumed *Vorlage* of
the Targum at Isa. 59.18 is noteworthy.

As already noted, it is possible to exaggerate the difficulties in the
first colon of Isa. 59.18. The expression כעל גמלות, for correction of
which Lowth turned to the Targum, presents no problems when taken
by itself. Not only is כעל גמלות good Hebrew, we have already noted
that there is a strikingly similar expression also involving the use of
כעל in Isa. 63.7: כעל כל אשר גמלנו יהוה. It would be cause for comment if originally 59.18 had בעל and 63.7 had כעל, even if the referents
in the two texts are quite distinct.[42]

Both *BHK* and *BHS*, and especially the former, have been beholden
to the Targum for their reconstruction of the text of Isa. 59.18, though
whether through the mediation of Lowth or independently it is not
possible to say. At first sight NEB also seems to be in agreement with
the Targum:

> High God of retribution that he is,
>   he pays in full measure...

However, NEB assumes that the MT contains an occurrence of על meaning 'High One', in reference to God.[43] REB reverts to the more traditional interpretation: 'According to their deeds he will repay...'[44]

The legacy of Lowth is substantial, if it is assessed in terms of the
influence that his views on Hebrew poetry exercised on his contemporaries and on later scholarship. In England poets and writers of the
eighteenth century took up his insights; in Germany Johann David
Michaelis published his own edition of Lowth's *Praelectiones* in two
volumes in 1758 and 1761, and Johann von Herder's *Vom Geist der
ebräischen Poesie* (1782–83) famously betrays its indebtedness to

---

42. Cf. S. Sekine, *Die Tritojesajanische Sammlung (Jes 56–66) redaktionsgeschichtlich untersucht* (BZAW, 175; Berlin: W. de Gruyter, 1989), pp. 132-33, 273.

43. See G.R. Driver, 'Hebrew *'al* ('high one') as a Divine Title', *ExpTim* 50
(1938), pp. 92-93 ('like the high one will He pay full recompense').

44. The emendation of the first occurrence of בעל to כי אל, on the basis of Jer.
51.56, is favoured by A.B. Ehrlich, *Randglossen zur hebräischen Bibel*. IV. *Jesaia,
Jeremia* (Leipzig: J.C. Hinrichs, 1912), pp. 212-13.

Lowth in its enthusiasm for poetic parallelism.[45] However, the acclaim has not been universal or unqualified. That Lowth's views on poetic parallelism in the prophets did not persuade the revisers of the AV is quite ironical. Lowth expresses more than once in his writings the hope that there would be a revision of the AV in view of its manifest failings. Referring to the numerous marginal annotations in Archbishop Secker's Bibles, he says that '[t]hese valuable remains of that great and good man will be of infinite service, whenever that necessary work, a New Translation, or a Revision of the present Translation, of the Holy Scriptures, for the use of our Church, shall be undertaken'.[46] Again, having paid generous tribute to 'our Vulgar Translation' as having an excellent style that has 'taken possession of our ear', and having noted the way in which the AV had pre-empted most of '[t]he most obvious, the properest, and perhaps the only terms, which the language affords', Lowth goes on to suggest that when it is thought desirable to set forth the Scriptures 'to better advantage…the expediency of which grows every day more and more evident…a Revision or Correction of that Translation may perhaps be more adviseable [*sic*], than to attempt an entirely new one'.[47] The revision did come, just over a hundred years later, but without affirming Lowth's discovery of poetic form in the prophets. The 1885 revisers note in their preface:

> In the poetical portions, besides the division into paragraphs, the Revisers have adopted an arrangement in lines, so as to exhibit the parallelism which is characteristic of Hebrew Poetry. But they have not extended this arrangement to the prophetical books, the language of which although frequently marked by parallelism is, except in purely lyrical passages, rather of the nature of lofty and impassioned prose.[48]

45. On Lowth, Herder and others, see further C. Bultmann, *Die biblische Urgeschichte in der Aufklärung* (BHT, 110; Tübingen: Mohr Siebeck, 1999), pp. 75-85.

46. *Isaiah*, p. lxix.

47. *Isaiah*, pp. lxxii-lxxiii. Cf. also his remarks, in a sermon preached in Durham in 1758, to the effect that nothing would confirm and illustrate the teachings of the Bible better than 'the exhibiting of the Holy Scriptures themselves to the people in a more advantageous and just light, by an accurate revisal of our vulgar translation by public authority' (*Sermons, and Other Remains of Robert Lowth* [repr.; London: Routledge/Thoemmes Press, 1995], pp. 85-87 [85]).

48. 'Revisers' Preface to the Old Testament', *The Holy Bible. The Revised Version* (Oxford: Oxford University Press, 1885); cf. R.P. Gordon, ' "Isaiah's Wild Measure": R.M. McCheyne', *ExpTim* 103 (1992), pp. 235-37.

While Wilhelm Gesenius followed Lowth's lead in his commentary on Isaiah published in 1820–21, in Britain T.K. Cheyne, whose commentary came out just a few years before the RV Old Testament, anticipated the revisers in his avoidance of poetic form in his translation of Isaiah.[49] The 1980s saw further reassessment of Lowth on parallelism, by James Kugel in *The Idea of Biblical Poetry*.[50] Kugel upholds the idea of parallelism in the prophets, but rejects Lowth's division of it into categories such as synonymous, synthetic and antithetic. There is much more variability at both the formal and functional levels, and purely synonymous parallelism is scarcely allowed to exist. Kugel is particularly effective in his attack on this category, as in his discussion of Isa. 1.3 where he rejects the idea of mere restatement in 'An ox knows its owner/and an ass its master's trough'.[51] Instead there is progression here:

> The animal of the first [clause] was hardly considered the most praiseworthy of beasts: nevertheless 'ox' is in several significant respects considered superior to its frequent pair, 'ass.' More important, parallel to the 'owner' of the first is 'master's trough' in the second.[52]

—for even an ass knows where to get its food. Kugel rightly makes the point that, strictly speaking, Lowth was not the first to 'discover' parallelism. Nor indeed was it the centrepiece of the *Praelectiones*, though by the time of the commentary on Isaiah it had an enhanced status in Lowth's thinking. Even here, however, he enumerates a list of other important criteria for distinguishing poetry from non-poetry.[53]

Part of the problem is that parallelism is a tendency in Hebrew writing of various types, and it is precarious to talk of poetical form simply on this basis. Most recently, Mary Douglas comments on the presence of parallelism in the laws of Leviticus as a product of the book's delight in craftsmanship and design, and she cites Lev. 22.10 in illustration.

---

49. Cf. G.B. Gray, *The Book of Isaiah I–XXXIX (XXVII)* (ICC; Edinburgh: T. & T. Clark, 1912), p. lx.

50. J.L. Kugel, *The Idea of Biblical Poetry: Parallelism and its History* (New Haven: Yale University Press, 1981). For criticism of Kugel, see A. Berlin, *The Dynamics of Biblical Parallelism* (Bloomington: Indiana University Press, 1985), pp. 4-6.

51. Lowth cites Isa. 1.3 in his section on 'synonymous parallelism' in *Isaiah*, 'Preliminary Dissertation', p. xvi.

52. Kugel, *The Idea*, p. 9.

53. *Isaiah*, p. li, with cross-reference to *Praelectiones* III, XIV, XV.

Echoing Kugel's scepticism, she claims that '[t]he good bishop did not make a discovery that had been missed for two millennia, he invented a word'.[54] It seems that 'the good bishop' contributed to the problem by telescoping—probably in all innocence—the history of previous scholarship. Others such as Marc Meibom and Christian Schoettgen had discussed parallelism in all but name.[55] Schoettgen addressed the subject in an essay in his *Horae hebraicae et talmudicae*, published in 1733, in which he divided Hebrew writing into the ordinary-historical ('pedestris sive historicus') and the rhetorical-poetic ('oratorius sive poëticus').[56] His examples of 'exergasia', taken principally from the Psalms, also include Isa. 1.18 and 53.5, Jer. 8.22, and even Dan. 12.3; but one finds no mention of Meibom or Schoettgen in the index of Lowth's Isaiah commentary.

Lowth's contribution to biblical scholarship consisted in part in his recognition that parallelism is intrinsic to biblical poetry and that it is a feature in its own right rather than a colouring agent of figurative-tropical language. For him parallelism implied metre, but Hebrew metre was unrecoverable. The Masoretic tradition, late and interpretative, could offer no help towards recovery: the different system of *te'amim* for Job, Psalms and Proverbs was not even extended to obvious poetry like Song of Songs and Lamentations.[57] By the time of the Isaiah commentary Lowth was commending parallelism as an aid to the restoration of the Hebrew text:

> Thus [two] inveterate mistakes, which have disgraced the Text above two thousand years, (for they are prior to the Version of the Seventy,) are happily corrected, and that, I think, beyond a doubt, by the Parallelism, supported by the example of similar passages'.[58]

---

54. M. Douglas, *Leviticus as Literature* (Oxford: Oxford University Press, 1999), pp. 46-47.

55. Cf. Kugel, *The Idea*, pp. 258, 267.

56. C. Schoettgen, 'Dissertatio VI, de Exergasia Sacra', in *Horae hebraicae et talmudicae*, I (Dresden: C. Hekel, 1733), pp. 1249-63; cf. the appendix 'Christian Schoettgen's *Exergasia Sacra*', in J. Lundbom, *Jeremiah: A Study in Ancient Hebrew Rhetoric* (SBLDS, 18; Missoula, MT: Scholars Press, 1975), pp. 121-27 (2nd edn; Winona Lake: Eisenbrauns, 1997).

57. *Praelectio* XVIII (p. 227).

58. *Isaiah*, p. xl.

So too had Meibom and Schoettgen suggested the restorative potential in parallelism.[59]

Since we need not restrict the force of Lowth's comment to straight binary relationships, in the case of Isa. 57.17 the parallel suggested by the LXX with the first bicolon of the previous verse may well have been instrumental in Lowth's coinage of *בצע 'paululum', which has so misled a number of later scholars. So too at 59.18 Lowth is to be found constructing synthetic parallelism out of what is a mere colon in the MT—admittedly with internal parallelism—now purportedly with the support of the Targum. While there are, no doubt, better examples of parallelism helping towards probable reconstructions of the Hebrew text, Lowth's legacy was never going to be substantial on the textual, linguistic or philological fronts.

It is a special privilege to contribute this discussion of Robert Lowth to a volume that honours the memory of a scholar who both enjoyed and excelled in the practice of textual criticism.[60]

59. Cf. Kugel, *The Idea*, pp. 267, 272-73.

60. The following studies have been encountered since this article was written: G. Stansell, 'Lowth's Isaiah Commentary and Romanticism', and P.K. Tull, 'What's New in Lowth? Synchronic Reading in the Eighteenth and Twenty-First Centuries', in *Society of Biblical Literature, 2000 Seminar Papers* (SBLSP, 39; Atlanta: Society of Biblical Literature, 2000), pp. 148-82 and 183-217, respectively; D. Norton, *A History of the English Bible as Literature* (Cambridge: Cambridge University Press, 2000), pp. 219-29, 245-47.

HOSEA: THE RABBINIC COMMENTATORS AND THE ANCIENT VERSIONS

Andrew A. Macintosh*

Examination of the interpretations by rabbinic commentators of a number of verses in Hosea's prophecies prompts the conclusion that they contain material that sheds light not only upon the meaning of Hosea's words but sometimes also on the renderings of the ancient versions. The finding is significant in that it suggests the possibility, in some instances, of tracing back to an earlier stage traditions of interpretation recorded by these commentators. And, secondly, it suggests that the procedure, adopted over the past century or so, whereby versional renderings often prompted scholars to emend the Hebrew text was unnecessarily hazardous. Rather, the rabbinical material is capable of illuminating some of the traditions of interpretation upon which the ancient versions are based and thus of providing a useful check upon the nature of their renderings.

In the five examples that follow, I restrict myself to the particular words that illustrate the concern of this paper as just described. The translations of Hosea's words are my own and, for further and wider elucidation of them, reference should be made to my commentary on the prophecy.

Hosea 9.2

Threshing-floor and vat will not *give attention to them*, and the new wine will disappoint them.

* The author of this paper, a Fellow of St John's College, Cambridge, for over thirty years, was privileged to witness Michael Weitzman's distinguished undergraduate career at the College and, with great pleasure, notes that his daughter, Gail Margalit, was admitted to St John's in October 1999 to read English.

Ibn Ezra understands ירעם לא to mean 'will not recognize them' (לא
יכירם). Ibn Janaḥ, commenting on what is likely to be the same word in
Hos. 12.2, gives it the meaning 'thought, review, attention' (Arabic
'lfkr w'ltfqd w'lr''yh. The third of these synonyms makes use of the
Arabic cognate root √*r'y* which is clearly attested with the meaning
'attention' (Lane III, p. 1108, col 3), and ibn Janaḥ's rendering may be
held to agree with ibn Ezra's view of ירעם in this verse.[1]

The Vulgate has *non pascet eos* 'will not feed them', where √ רעה is
clearly interpreted by reference to the meanings 'tend, pasture'. Whether
that is likely when predicated of threshing-floor and (especially) wine-
vat is, however, questionable, and it is preferable to detect in ירעם the
meaning suggested by ibn Janaḥ and ibn Ezra. The Peshiṭta and the
Targum have *l' nsb'wn* / יתזנון לא 'they will not be satisfied/they will
not be nourished from threshing-floor and wine-vat'. These renderings
appear to be of a sort with that of the Vulgate and differ only in that
they use passive verbs which necessitate the introduction of the preposition *mn* 'from'. The LXX, with οὐκ ἔγνω αὐτούς 'did not know them',
may well have seen in the Hebrew ירעם a form of the root ידע. On
the other hand, it is just possible that this version did indeed translate
ירעם, and in a way that coincides with the views of ibn Janaḥ and ibn
Ezra, since 'knowledge' is not so far removed from 'attention' and
'recognition'.

The proposal (e.g., Wellhausen, Marti, Harper, cf. *BHS*) to emend the
MT to read ירעם (pointed as a perfect or imperfect) on the basis of the
LXX is thus not so well founded as might appear at first sight, and particularly when the satisfactory understanding of ירעם by ibn Janaḥ and
ibn Ezra is taken into account.

Hosea 10.7

As for Samaria, its king will fade away *like foam* on the surface of the
water.

The word קצף is a hapax legomenon. Rabbinic tradition suggests two
accounts of the word. First, ibn Ezra and Kimchi refer to Joel 1.7
where, as Kimchi explains, the phrase לקצפה תאנתי means that the fig-

---

1.   BDB identifies three homonymous roots of which √ I means 'to pasture,
tend, graze' and √ III coincides with ibn Janaḥ's account noted above. The Syriac
cognate there cited is also telling evidence in favour of ibn Janaḥ's assessment.

tree's fate is to be stripped of its bark (קְלִיפַת הָעֵץ) by locusts who devour it. In Hos. 10.7, then, Kimchi presumably understands the word קֶצֶף to denote a piece of bark that has been stripped from a tree (again, קְלִיפַת הָעֵץ) and is now floating away on water. It is possible that some such explanation lies behind the renderings of the LXX (and Theodotion) ὡς φρύγανον; cf. the Peshiṭta *'yk gl'* 'like dry stick(s)' 'twigs' (>'firewood'). Secondly, ibn Janaḥ relates the noun קֶצֶף to the familiar √ קצף 'was angry', and he explains that the fundamental meaning is 'boiling (with rage)'. In Hos 10.7 that fundamental meaning comes to the fore and the noun means here the 'agitation or boiling of water through the force of the wind'. This view appears to parallel the renderings of Aquila ὡς ἀφρόν (cf. the Vulgate *quasi spumam*) 'like foam', and Symmachus ὡς ἐπίζεμα 'like boiling'; on this latter rendering Jerome comments *volens ostendere ferventis ollae superiores aquas* 'he seeks to depict the water at the top of a boiling pot'. The Targum כרתחא (see Jastrow, p. 1464, col. 2) appears to take this view of the word in question as does Rashi, who renders it by (French) *écume*.

BDB ad loc., cf. Blau VT (1955), p. 343, draws attention to the Arabic cognate *qṣf* 'to break off' and *qṣyf* 'broken' and this has prompted a number of modern scholars (e.g. Rudolph, Borbone) to translate קֶצֶף with meanings such as 'chip of wood', 'twig'. It is possible that this particular (philological) account of the word accords with the tradition reported by Kimchi, that is, that קֶצֶף in both Hosea and Joel means 'bark (stripped from a tree)'. Lane *Supplement*, ad loc., confirms that the Arabic cognate has the meanings indicated above, but, on the other hand, it is perhaps striking that appeal to this root is not made by the Arabic-speaking rabbinic authorities such as ibn Janaḥ and (especially) ibn Barun. Some doubt, then, attaches to the explanation.

Ibn Janaḥ, in his account of the forms of קֶצֶף in Hosea and Joel, offers a view that may be said to fit both occurrences more convincingly. He cites the Arabic verb *šyṭ* as providing an accurate parallel to the semantic range of קֶצֶף displayed in the two verses. Thus, the word has the meanings 'singeing', 'scorching' as well as 'boiling', 'agitation'. Ibn Janaḥ detects the former sense in Joel 1.7, where the fate of the fig-tree is to be scorched by fire; the latter sense he detects in Hos. 10.7 as indicated above.

Hosea 11.6

The sword will fall upon his (sc. Ephraim's) cities, it will consume his *villages*...

Kimchi and ibn Ezra compare Ezek. 17.6 and suggest that the word means 'his branches'. Kimchi explains that the usage is figurative and denotes 'villages' since villages are to cities what branches are to trees. Earlier, but without reference to this verse, ibn Janaḥ (a medical man) had explained the word בד 'branch' in terms of the nerves and sinews of the body spreading out as branches from the brain. The verse, on this view of בדיו, means that the cities of Ephraim will fall to the sword, as well as the smaller dependent communities, the villages and outlying suburbs.

The LXX has ἐν ταῖς χερσὶν αὐτοῦ '(the sword came to an end) in his hands' (cf. the Peshiṭta *mn 'ydyhwn* and Gelston, pp. 167f). If these versions saw or read in the Hebrew *Vorlage* a form of יד 'hand' (with the preposition ב prefixed), the resulting sense is scarcely satisfactory. Symmachus, by contrast, has a direct object: τοὺς βραχίονας αὐτοῦ '(it will bring to an end) his arms'. It is possible that the rendering implies a (mis)understanding of the tradition that בדיו meant extremities/limbs of the body.[2] Jerome is aware of Symmachus's rendering, and his own translation in the Vulgate, *electos eius* (cf. the Targum גיברוהי 'his warriors'[3]), is, he says in his commentary, merely a metaphorical extension of the meaning 'arms'. Of the many emendations of בדיו that have been proposed, mention may be made here of that suggested by Grätz and Oettli who propose בחריו 'his choice men' on the basis of the Vulgate and of the Targum. Investigation of the tradition recounted by ibn Janaḥ and Kimchi is likely to expose the proposed emendation as unnecessary.

Hosea 13.15

Since he is the one who *behaves wilfully* among brothers, an east wind shall come, a mighty wind...

---

2.   For another instance of בדים with the sense 'members, limbs', cf. Job 18.13 and BDB ad loc.

3.   A semantic parallel to this rendering may be found in the Targum of Amos 1.5 where בריח 'bar' is rendered תקוף 'strength'.

While Rashi, ibn Ezra and Kimchi understand the hapax legomenon יפריא to be a by-form of √ פרה 'be fruitful', ibn Janaḥ (and Rashi, as an alternative) thinks that it is related to the well-attested noun פרא 'wild ass'. The noun is found in Gen. 16.12 and Hos. 8.9 (cf. Jer 2.24) and denotes, by reference to this animal, wilful, arbitrary behaviour. Hosea, in word-play, clearly makes use of the verb to deprecate Ephraim and (cf. Gen. 41.52) his erstwhile characteristic fruitfulness. At all events, on ibn Janaḥ's view, the internal hiphil of the denominative verb conveys a pejorative description of the nation's disruptive behaviour: Ephraim has behaved with gross selfishness and has damaged what Rashi terms 'the brotherhood of Israel'.[4]

The Targum's rendering ועובדין מקלקלין אסגיאו 'they have multiplied corrupt deeds' has the characteristics of a 'standard translation', the same phrase occurring, for example, in the Targum to Isa. 17.10, where it answers to the (obscure) Hebrew 'striking cuttings for a foreign god' (so NEB). The use of אסגיאו implies identification of √ פרה 'be fruitful, multiplied'. The other versions, however, do not seem to have detected this root in the Hebrew *Vorlage*. The LXX has διαστελεῖ, 'tears asunder (between brothers)'; cf. the Vulgate *dividet* (*inter fratres*) and the Peshiṭta *byt 'ḥ' nprwš*. The sense of these renderings is not inconsistent with that advocated by ibn Janaḥ and Rashi (the latter suggesting it as a possibility). A number of modern commentators, however, have, on the basis of these three versions, suggested the emendation יפריד 'divides' (so, e.g., Sebök, Grätz; cf. *BHS*). However, in view of ibn Janaḥ's and Rashi's account of the word יפריא, the emendation may be regarded as unnecessary.

Hosea 14.6

I will be like the dew to Israel, that he may flower like the lily and that he may *strike root* like the trees of Lebanon.

4. For 'the brotherhood of Israel', see Zech. 11.14. Rashi does not otherwise refer to this verse or to the hiphil form of √ פרר which occurs there; nor, on Zech. 11.14, does he refer to Hos. 13.15. While he explicitly identifies √ פרא for Hos. 13.15, it is possible that Zech. 11.14 prompted his comment that it was Jeroboam who הפריא אחוותו של ישראל, i.e. it was he who was 'responsible for the division of the kingdom'. His use of הפריא as a transitive verb (with the 'brotherhood of Israel' as its object) suggests that he is investing it with the same sense as the transitive hiphil of √ פרר in Zech. 11.14, notwithstanding his reference to √ פרא and its occurrence in Gen. 16.12.

וַיֵּךְ שָׁרָשָׁיו. The use of the √ נכה 'strike' in connection with the roots of a plant is unique to this verse. (The usage seems to be mirrored precisely by that of English.) Ibn Janaḥ and Kimchi refer to Num. 34.11 and compare the use of the verb מחה there in the sense 'extend far off'. For ibn Janaḥ the roots 'spread under the earth' and for Kimchi 'the roots will strike (יכו השרשים) all over the place'. If these commentators seem to suggest that the roots are the subject of the verb, that is because they are comparing Num. 34.11 and the parallel use of מחה. What they say in no way precludes the understanding of Hosea's metaphor in the sense that Israel will strike (his) root(s) (where roots are the object of the verb).

The LXX has καὶ βαλεῖ (τὰς ῥίζας αὐτοῦ) 'he will throw, push out (his roots)'; cf. the Peshiṭta *wnrm'*. These renderings may constitute evidence that an apocopated hiphil form of √ ידה or of √ ירה was read or perceived in the Hebrew *Vorlage*. On the other hand, the renderings are not inconsistent with the explanation of the two rabbinic commentators quoted above. The same may be said of the Vulgate *et erumpet (radix eius)* 'his root will break forth', for this differs from the other versions only in that the 'root' is construed as the subject and the difference may be merely translational.[5] Examples of emendations proposed for וַיֵּךְ in MT include: וילכו 'shall go/spread' (Wellhausen, Nowack); ויר (√ ירה), cf. βαλεῖ in the LXX and *nrm'* in the Peshiṭta, 'shall throw out/ extend (his roots)' (Borbone, cf. *BHS*); ויט 'extend' (cf. *BHS*). Again, the evidence of ibn Janaḥ and Kimchi cited above forms a satisfactory explanation of the MT and goes some way to explain the versional renderings cited. Thus the use of them as a basis for emendation of the MT is questionable.

---

5.   The Targum, characteristically free, speaks of branches rather than roots, and so does not provide clear evidence.

THE SACRIFICE OF FOOLS AND THE WISDOM OF SILENCE: QOHELETH, JOB AND THE PRESENCE OF GOD

Coralie A. Gutridge

The cautionary (if not pessimistic) tone of Qoh. 5.1-7 lays this passage open to misinterpretation as a radical statement that God is literally unapproachable, and that the Temple cult is of little worth. To Blenkinsopp, for example, it seems to indicate that

> Qoheleth's relationship to the traditional and ancestral religion is tenuous to say the least, and his attitude to the external expressions of that religion—animal sacrifice, prayer, vows etc.—is critical and detached.[1]

On closer inspection, however, these verses offer no real evidence that the author distances himself at all from the traditional pietist ideal of cultivating God's presence, both in general and more specifically through the Temple cult.

Although the expression 'sacrifice of fools' is indeed critical, of someone or of something, this derisive language would seem to indicate that our author's attitude is a little too heated to be called 'detached'. Furthermore, the object of his criticism does not appear to be the cult as such. In 5.1[2] he says, 'Guard your steps *when*[3] you go to the house of God'. He recommends that we 'draw near to *listen*', not that we refrain from drawing near; and when he reminds those who have made a vow to God to pay it,[4] his point is unmistakably identical to that of Deut. 23.21-23. In fact, the evocative quality of his references to Deuteronomic thinking in general[5] makes it implausible that his relationship to

---

1.   J. Blenkinsopp, *Wisdom and Law in the Old Testament: The Ordering of Life in Israel and Early Judaism* (Oxford: Oxford University Press, 1983), p. 68.

2.   4.17 in the Hebrew Bible, but 5.1 in the English translations. The English numeration remains one verse ahead of the Hebrew throughout ch. 5.

3.   Not *if*.

4.   5.4-6.

5.   This is the view maintained in my PhD thesis, 'Wisdom, Anti-wisdom and

the ancestral religion is as tenuous as Blenkinsopp suggests.

A coherent and forceful message emerges from Qoh. 5.1-7, however, if the passage is interpreted as a conscious and emphatic re-statement of the traditional standards (whether or not the traditional type) of piety. Its pregnant allusions to 1 Sam. 15.22 and Deut. 23.21-23 make this very clear. Although this message may well reflect negatively on the actual state of the Jerusalem cult in the author's own day, it is not an ironic and hostile rejection of the cult as such, nor of the ideal of cultivating God's presence with Man, whether through the cult or otherwise.[6] Qoheleth is not here denouncing all attempts of Man to approach God in any way.[7] What he *is* denouncing is actual irreverence, and probably of a type urgently familiar to him in his own experience.

Qoheleth has, admittedly, the reputation of seeming more aloof from God, and of presenting God as more remote from Man, than most biblical authors; and it is perfectly possible that he has no perception of God's presence, nor any experience of approaching Him, in the more individualistic sense of a personal closeness to God. It is impossible to infer from his book, however, either that he has or that he has not. Moreover, even if he has not, there is no indication that this has undermined his endorsement of approaching God and cultivating His presence in the more formal sense of adhering to the Temple cult.

If he has a more private experience of approaching God, Qoheleth never unambiguously refers to it; he speaks of God as if He were a remote subject of his discourse, rather than the centre of his personal life. But this does not in itself indicate any lack of pious zeal. Indeed, it could, on the contrary, reflect the view that acceptance of God's remoteness, in the sense of reverent awareness that God is not to be approached brashly,[8] is essential to piety, not a contradiction of it. If so,

the Ethical Function of Uncertainty: The Book of Qoheleth / Ecclesiastes in the Context of Biblical and Greek Wisdom Theory' (unpublished, University College London, 1998), esp. pp. 269-323 and 326-31.

6.   See Gutridge, 'Wisdom, Anti-wisdom', pp. 53-56 and 620-47, for the possibility that he is deeply committed to the cult, and concerned about it as a critical insider (perhaps as a member of the priestly class) rather than as a hostile outsider.

7.   On the contrary, Man's artificial, egocentric remoteness from God cannot be acceptable to him, or he would not say in 5.1, '*Draw near* to listen'. See also Gutridge, 'Wisdom, Anti-wisdom', pp. 48-49 and 60-61.

8.   Emphasizing not only the desirability of approaching God but also the necessity for restricting access to Him is profoundly characteristic of the Temple tradition. The very structure of the Temple—including its distinctions between

then 5.1-7 warns us not that the traditional piety of the Temple cult is wrong, but rather that a man who is presumptuous in approaching God and rash in what he says to God is not pious at all, either by traditional / cultic criteria or otherwise. Eagerness to perform religious acts and to make religious vows is not in itself any evidence of being devout. This is a theme already well familiar from the prophets,[9] and its reiteration by Qoheleth here certainly cannot be taken to indicate his rejection of the cult as such, or of any kind of worship, public or private, but only as expressing his disapproval of their abuse.

The abuse in question is described in 5.1 as 'the sacrifice of fools'. Qoheleth's 'Go near to listen (לשמע) rather than to offer the sacrifice (זבח) of fools' recalls 1 Sam. 15.22, 'To obey (שמע) is better than sacrifice (מזבח טוב)'.[10]

The extraordinary foolishness of Saul in this chapter stems from his insincerity and preoccupation with mere appearances. He wants Samuel to believe that he has obeyed the Lord, and insists that he has done so (1 Sam. 15.13, 20), even though he all too obviously has not. Sacrificing to the Lord is the very issue he then decides to make into an excuse (v. 21) for having kept alive the animals that the Lord had ordered him to kill (v. 3). Even when, after much denial, he finally admits that he has sinned (v. 24), he then, in his very next breath (v. 25), glibly requests that Samuel now accompanies him in an act of worship; and that only to keep up appearances, so that he will still appear estimable to the elders of the people (v. 30).

outer area, Holy Place and Holy of Holies, with the varying levels of restricted access corresponding to them—constitutes in itself a warning to 'Guard your steps when you go to the House of God'. Similarly, the ritual requirements for the priests, such as washing before entering to minister, etc., all reflect exactly the same double-edged requirement: not only to approach God, but also to exercise caution in approaching Him. Qoheleth is here expressing in verbal form exactly the attitude of reverence which the very Temple cult itself expresses in architectural and ritual form.

9. E.g. Isa. 1.10-18.

10. This allusion is rarely acknowledged; and even when it is acknowledged, its key importance for grasping Qoheleth's meaning here is still not recognized. Gordis, for example, claims that '(Qoheleth) is using the traditional passage in a spirit far removed from that of classic Hebrew prophecy' (R. Gordis, *Koheleth: The Man and his World* [Texts and Studies of the Jewish Theological Seminary of America, 19; New York: Bloch Publishing Co., 2nd augmented edn, 1955], p. 237). This misleading comment masks the force of the allusion entirely.

Even though God has just announced His disapproval of Saul by rejecting him as King, Saul's next comment after the announcement is an ultra-brief admission of guilt followed by his proposal to perform a public religious act in order to look admirable in the sight of men. He makes it painfully clear that he is not moved at all by God's disapproval of him; but he is very concerned indeed about men's opinion of him, and that is why he is going to sacrifice to the Lord.

Evidently, then, this sacrifice of Saul's is what Qoheleth means when he refers to 'the sacrifice of fools' in 5.1.[11] His point here is that it is not those most forward in outward acts of worship who are necessarily the most spiritual. Better to be backward in approaching God than to mock Him with an outward show of superficial worship. The irony of 1 Sam. 15 is that Samuel explains this quite clearly in v. 22; but Saul, as he still insists on his empty sacrifice, presumably does not get the point. Qoheleth, however, evidently *does* get the point, and refers to it here in 5.1. It is also significant to the allusion that the 'fools' of 5.1 '*do not know* that they are doing wrong'. This too is reminiscent of Saul, whose personality seems to disintegrate, becoming erratically violent under the influence of an 'evil spirit'. Saul loses his integrity even to the point of consulting a witch, despite the fact that he himself had previously conducted a purge of witches. It seems that he no longer knows what is right at all, even on matters in which he once had strong convictions and once unflinchingly acted on those convictions. He also has delusions of being supported by God, despite the fact that God's favour has definitely departed from him and now rests with David. In 1 Sam. 23.7, for example, he says, 'God has handed (David) over to me', even though God is in fact supporting David against him. Saul is thus an unusually pointed example of one who loses not only his integrity, but also his grip on reality; not only is he doing wrong, but he also '*does not know* that he is doing wrong'.

Similarly, Qoheleth's warning in the following verses against careless vows to the Lord is well in line with traditional standards of piety, echoing exactly the sentiments of Deut. 23.21-23, even to the fact that not making a religious vow at all is perfectly acceptable (Deut. 23.22), and definitely preferable to making one but failing to keep it (Deut. 23.21, 23). The comparison in Qoh. 5.3, 7 of dreaming with talking too much seems to imply that false (and even merely superfluous) words

11. However, for the probability of a *double* intertextuality here, with Job 42.8 as well as with 1 Sam. 15.22, see below, this article.

are as odious and as potentially dangerous as the false dreams of Deut. 13.1-5.[12]

This is especially likely since Qoheleth concludes 5.7 with an exhortation to 'Fear God', instead of paying any attention to empty dreams and idle words; and this is exactly the message of Deut. 13.4: not to be led astray by false dreams, but to fear God. These false dreams of Deut. 13, although spoken with great confidence, and with every appearance of divine inspiration,[13] are nevertheless lying revelations. For they are designed to entice the people into idolatry, an evil so opposed to the very core of the divine commandments that even genuinely supernatural manifestations like accurate prediction cannot possibly endorse their objective. Similarly, the airy dreams and idle words that Qoheleth refers to in 5.2-7 can all too easily constitute an arrogant 'anti-wisdom'[14] based on false certainty, which leads to dangerous delusions. Job's 'words without knowledge' would have continued to 'darken counsel', had he not humbled himself before God in the end; and the dream-visions of Eliphaz (Job 4.12-21) only confirm the dreamer in his wrong opinion of Job's moral standing, namely that Job's sins must in some way be responsible for his calamities.

False wisdom, then, can be just as dangerous as false prophecy; and this 'revelation' of Eliphaz suggests that such false wisdom is sometimes phenomenologically related to false prophecy as well. Compare Elihu, another of Job's deluded 'comforters', in his endorsement of such dream-revelations as a genuine source of wisdom (Job 33.15). It would seem, then, that there is not such a clear dividing line as is usually assumed between wisdom (false as well as true) and the supernatural realm associated more often with prophecy. Evidently Solomon's dream in 1 Kgs 3.5 was not the last of the wisdom-dreams, true or false.

---

12. For dreams as a vehicle of false prophecy, see also Jer. 23.25-32.

13. Since the miraculous signs the dreamer promises actually come to pass.

14. I.e. pseudo-wisdom, based on an anthropocentric world-view which trusts in human ingenuity as self-sufficient. Opposed to this 'anti-wisdom' is the pietist concept of a true wisdom based on the fear of God and on a realistic recognition of Man's limitations, as in Ps. 111.10, Prov. 1.7, etc. The influence of the latter, pietist wisdom tradition on Qoheleth (who focuses far more on Man's limitations than on his ingenuity) is far from superficial. See Gutridge, 'Wisdom, Anti-wisdom', *passim*.

It is only to be expected, therefore, that the true wisdom teacher should pay serious attention to refuting and rebuking false wisdom, just as true prophets make denunciation of false prophecy a high priority.[15] It is also natural that in executing this duty, Qoheleth should employ allusions to the piety of the Deuteronomists. For the motivation behind his teaching is entirely devout. It would not even be true to say that his emphasis on wariness in approaching God is demonstrably stronger[16] than that of the traditional pietists. No warning to be careful in approaching God could be clearer than, for example, 2 Sam. 6.6-10, where Uzzah is supernaturally killed for presumptuously steadying the Ark.[17]

However, despite David's alarm at the incident, this story is not meant to signify that God's presence is undesirable, nor that having or desiring this presence is by definition presumptuous. For in v. 11 the man whose house receives the Ark is particularly blessed because of it. Similarly, far from dissuading men from drawing near to God, Qoheleth simply says in 5.1, 'Draw near to *listen*'.

Rather than approaching God to *assert*, by word or by deed, one's own standing, intentions, vows or opinions, one should rather approach Him in readiness to obey Him and to respond to Him. Better not to approach God at all than to approach Him in arrogant assertiveness, instead of in humble receptivity. A truthful and reverent remoteness is far preferable to a false and presumptuous show of intimacy.

This attitude suggests that Qoheleth is unusually open to the numinous. Willingness to keep quiet before God indicates a high level of faith in God's external reality. If Qoheleth were a lesser pietist, he would not be so emphatic about the importance of listening in God's presence rather than speaking; for he would not have such faith in

15. See, e.g., Elijah, 1 Kgs 18.22-40; Micaiah ben Imlah, 1 Kgs 22.13-28, esp. vv. 19-25; Isa. 56.10-12; Jer. 2.8; 5.31; 14.14-16; 23.13-32, etc.

16. Moreover, even if it were stronger, this might well be construed simply as evidence of exceptional zeal on Qoheleth's part. It would not necessarily be symptomatic of a radically different and more negative attitude toward God from that of earlier biblical writers, such as a desire to stand aloof from Him through mistrust or indifference. Even though such an attitude often has been attributed to Qoheleth, it is highly questionable as to whether this view can be reconciled with the in-depth implications of his text.

17. The Ark symbolizes God's *presence*, and so is a pre-eminent focus of faith in evoking God's literal presence.

God's ability to communicate something for the worshipper to listen *to*. It is not necessarily the case that the Temple cult, for all its possible musical aspects, offered organized teaching or reading and exposition of Scripture by human agents, in the way the synagogue ultimately did. For the synagogue was presumably established as an attempt to supply something in public worship that previously had been lacking. So when Qoheleth exhorts drawing near in the house of God to listen, he probably means literally listen to *God* rather than merely listen to Man teaching about God. For the prime significance of the Temple is as the place of God's literal presence and manifestation.[18] This interpretation would also be in harmony with the echo of 1 Sam. 15.22 here, since it is God that Saul should have been concerned to listen to and to obey, rather than seeking merely to win the good opinion of men by making a public show of sacrificing to the Lord.

Despite the fact that we are accustomed to consider direct, supernatural contact with God (so necessary for the prophet's ministry) as not required for that of the wisdom teacher, the grounds for this distinction are far from solid. Qoheleth's belief in *listening to/obeying* God as opposed to making rash utterances before Him certainly sounds like a more realistic setting for experiencing a genuine mystical encounter, whether in the form of revelation or otherwise, than the 'sacrifice of fools' scenario he repudiates in 5.1. It would be interesting indeed to know if our author had a closer sense of God's personal presence after all than he directly reveals in his book.[19]

In rejecting the anthropocentric pseudo-piety based on making assertions to or about God, instead of more properly cultivating His presence to listen and to obey, Qoheleth is fully in harmony with the book of Job. The climactic[20] place given to the theophany in Job shows a further and much later development from even the relatively God-friendly wisdom of Proverbs. Proverbs, although a very Man-centred book in its subject-matter, already reflects the possibility of God and wisdom as partners,

18. See 1 Kgs 8.10-13, Isa. 6.1, etc.

19. See also Gutridge, 'Wisdom, Anti-wisdom', pp. 229-53.

20. That God's eventual direct confrontation with Job *is* climactic, not merely cosmetic as some might argue, is underlined with particular force by Alter's demonstration of the key antitheses between the wording of Job's poem in ch. 3 and that of God's answers in 38.2-38. See R. Alter, *The Art of Biblical Poetry* (Edinburgh: T. & T. Clark, 1990), pp. 94-102.

rather than wisdom as Humanity's chief weapon in its bid to be independent of God and a 'god' in its own right.[21] Job, however, preaches not just God-friendly wisdom, but God-centred wisdom, Terrien's 'dénuement du moi'.[22] Job is perhaps the first example of the Wisdom genre directly positing the objective presence of and encounter with God as the only force capable of silencing anthropocentric 'wisdom'. Already in Job this egotistical human 'wisdom' is perceived (and later in Qoheleth, 5.3b and 10.14, it is explicitly described) as the 'much-speaking' that characterizes the fool. Such 'words without knowledge'—which is all the human 'wisdom' that asserts itself independently of God's presence really amounts to—is said to '(darken) counsel' (Job 38.2). Job's anguished sarcasm in 13.5 is far more profound and central to the issue of the book than he himself realizes:

מי־יתן החרש תחרישון;
ותהי לכם לחכמה.

If only you would be altogether silent!
For you, that would be wisdom.[23]

As wisdom-writing, Job reflects the fact that the polarity between the two wisdoms is now complete. There are two distinct and opposite wisdoms: the anthropocentric anti-wisdom and the theocentric wisdom, at war with each other. As in their different ways both Terrien[24] and

21. As in Gen. 3.5-8. For the anti-pietist image of wisdom in general, including the prophetic books, see Gutridge, 'Wisdom, Anti-wisdom', *passim*.

22. S. Terrien, *Job* (CAT, 13; Neuchâtel: Delachaux et Niestlé, 1963), p. 48.

23. So the NIV translation; but Job's literal wording here is not irrelevant to the issue. His exasperated מי ('Who?')—a word used rarely of things, but more often where persons are understood or implied—suggests that no-one (rather than merely nothing) is capable of damming the flow of his friends' loquacity. From the standpoint of the author, this is gross theological incorrectness on the part of the friends, even if his protagonist's verbal reflection of the fact here is unwitting. Their reverence for God, and for the inscrutability of His workings, should render the friends silent. They should not be so quick or so persistent in making pronouncements on these matters, which are too high for them to understand. God Himself, and their awe of Him, should suffice to render them silent. In that sense, God is the מי implied here.

24. See Terrien, *Job*, p. 47 for his point that when Job speaks of repentance in 42.6 he is repenting not of a single and specific wrong act, but rather of an overall attitude of egocentricity as opposed to one of theocentricity. Terrien sees God's willingness to manifest himself to Man as giving Man the ability to become God-centred instead of Man-centred; and he posits the central importance of God's

Alter[25] perceive, the human quality most under attack in Job is ego-centricity. When God appears, Job's 'words without knowledge' cease; he says (40.4, 5) that he no longer has anything to say.[26] Instead of speaking, he now listens (42.3, 4). Only God's personal appearance could have brought him to this state; otherwise, he and his 'friends' would have wrangled on, at loggerheads with each other forever, each unassailable in their conviction of being right, and each inexhaustible in their eloquence. Only the objective and recognized presence of God can return Mankind to its proper status as a reacting and responsive creature rather than a groundlessly but endlessly assertive one.

Even when God does appear, however, there is a noticeable difference between Job's own level of response and that of his companions. Job, the man who has particularly pinned his hopes on God appearing in person (as in 19.25-27), is also the one who reacts wisely to the

---

presence and of Man's quest for God's presence as the key to an overall theological unity of the Bible.

Regarding God's self-revelatory initiative in this 'Hebraic theology of presence', he says in an unpublished article quoted by James Sanders, 'The entire literature of the Bible portrays the Deity as coming to Man... [The earlier attempt to centre Biblical theology in the idea of Covenant] ignored the diversity of its meaning in Israel... [and tended] also to confuse the means with the end, for the idea of Covenant was in any case subservient to the prior reality of Presence' (J.A. Sanders, 'Comparative Wisdom: L'Oeuvre Terrien', in J.G. Gammie *et al.* [eds.], *Israelite Wisdom: Theological and Literary Essays in Honour of Samuel Terrien* [New York: Scholars Press for Union Theological Seminary, 1978], pp. 3-14 [11]).

On Man's side of the initiative, Terrien similarly sees the main distinguishing feature of Israel's faith as 'A determined and even obstinate will to live in the presence of the Holy God' (S. Terrien, 'The Religion of Israel', in C.M. Laymon [ed.], *The Interpreter's One-Volume Commentary on the Bible* [Nashville: Abingdon Press, 1971], pp. 1150-58 [1158]). Also on the central importance of the divine presence, see S. Terrien, *The Elusive Presence: Toward a New Biblical Theology* (Religious Perspectives, 26; San Francisco: Harper and Row, 1978), *passim.*

25. See Alter, *Biblical Poetry*, p. 96, where he calls 'Job's first poem—a powerful, evocative, authentic expression of Man's essential, virtually ineluctable egotism'. He sees ch. 3 as conveying an egocentric narrowness that contrasts starkly with the 'panoramic vision' of God's reply. See *Biblical Poetry*, p. 104 for what Alter sees as the uniqueness, even in the Bible, of the standpoint of chs. 38–41, in not making Man's perspective on the total Creation the focus of its importance.

26. Now himself adopting the very policy he has previously recommended to his 'friends' at 13.5: a genuine wisdom, consisting of a reverent silence in recognition of his own limited understanding.

theophany, by '(Speaking) of (God) what is right' in 40.3-5 and 42.2-6. His friends, however, as God notices in 42.7, do not respond this way. The implication here is that however wrong Job may have been to have thought he would be able to justify himself before God at His eventual appearance, nevertheless he is *not* wrong to have made the literal arrival of God's presence the focus of his hopes. Job's raw spirituality in desiring, however angrily, God's personal appearance, is represented as being far wiser than the opinionated and humanly self-contained ethical eloquence of his friends.

However superficially and verbally defensive of God their speeches may have been in the safely limited context of that self-containment, and however impious and hostile Job's attack on God may have sounded (e.g. 19.6, 7), it is ardent desire for God's presence like Job's that is the real key both to wisdom and to piety. It is Job to whom God openly shows His favour, at the end of his life (42.7-16) as at the beginning (1.2-5, 8-10; cf. 42.12a). God's preference for Job's attitude over that of his companions in vv. 7-9 is unmistakably pointed, and is intended to commend to us Job's unusual zeal in seeing the manifestation of God's presence as the answer to his dire problems. It also indicates God's approval of Job's realism and honesty about his creaturely status, which he demonstrates by humbling himself before God when God eventually comes. In this respect, the Epilogue's appearance of naïveté is misleading, since it is completely consistent with, and an effective reinforcement of, the central standpoint of the book overall.[27]

The contents of Qoh. 5.1-7 affirm this standpoint of Job, by reflecting that alert attentiveness to God and devout contemplation of Him constitute the only source of wisdom; whereas over-confident assertion of one's own human viewpoint leads only to confusion and distortion of

27. However, that central standpoint, in Job as in Qoheleth, should be understood as a strong warning against the moral danger of false certainty. The ill-founded assurance of Job's friends that his standing with God is low is a prime example of such false certainty. The central issue of Job is often mistakenly thought to be the problem of human suffering, or of the suffering of the righteous. If the book's prime issue really were suffering as such, the Epilogue would indeed be naïve: at best irrelevant to the issue, and at worst grossly insensitive to it. However, for the importance of recognizing both Job and Qoheleth as denunciations of false certainty, and of the anthropocentric 'wisdom' that fosters it, see Gutridge, 'Wisdom, Anti-wisdom', p. 198 n. 44 and p. 200 n. 48.

the facts: the 'words without knowledge' of Job himself (Job 38.2; 42.3) and those of his accusing 'comforters' (42.7).

Qoheleth writes in 5.1 of coming into the presence of God and listening, and he contrasts it vehemently with egocentric loquacity in vv. 2, 3. Then in v. 6b, even though the immediate context concerns keeping vows, he seems to be recalling Job's opinionated friends when he says,

> Why should God be *angry* at what you *say*?
> Much dreaming and *many words* are meaningless (5.6b, 7).

This is apparently echoing Job 42.7,

> I am *angry* with you and your two friends, because you have not *spoken of Me* what is right as My servant Job has.

Certainly the friends have uttered 'many words'; in fact, they have said 'many words without knowledge', like Job. Unlike Job, however, as noted above, they have not subsequently renounced their egocentricity by despising themselves and repenting in dust and ashes, as Job has in 42.6 when God appears.

Speech is traditionally regarded as a major focus of Man's rebellion against God; hence, for example, the curse of Babel in Gen. 11.1-9. This seems to be because the tongue is the focus of the human ego, as in, for example, Ps. 12.4's boastful

> We will triumph with our tongues;
> We own our lips—who is our master?

Such is the boasters' pride in their tongues, it leads them to believe that even God is not their master. This is because there is no God on their narrow horizon; all they can see or hear is themselves articulating their own ambitions. In Qoh. 5.2, which begins and ends with a warning against too much talk, heavily reinforced by vv. 3b, 6a and 7, we are reminded in between the two warnings that 'God is in heaven and you are on earth'.[28] This is not primarily, however, to emphasize God's absence or distance, as is sometimes thought. Rather, it is to remind us of the Job-scenario, and particularly of how it highlights how dangerously self-opinionated and narrow-minded are human beings specifically *when they forget* that God is in heaven but that they are only on earth.

28. A point which would not have found much favour with the Babel-builders of Gen. 11, since they intended their tower to reach 'to the heavens' (v. 4) anyway.

The keynote of that scenario is that God is at first conspicuous by His absence, and Job longs for Him to come (e.g. in 19.27); but this initial absence, which left the wrangling, negative eloquence of Job and his 'friends' disproportionately in the foreground, only makes His eventual appearance all the more startling by contrast. It seems that Qoh. 5.6b's 'Why should God be angry at what you *say*?' is deliberately reminiscent of Job 42.7, even though 'what you say' in Qoh. 5.6b also refers back to the unfulfilled vow. For what Eliphaz and his friends have *said* and what they have failed to *say* are so exactly what God is angry *about* in Job 42.7. Like Job, the friends should be humbled once they actually see God and realize how small they and their opinions really are. They should be awestruck at God's greatness and repent of their false and presumptuous wisdom; but they fail to do so. They betray no sign of awe or even of recognition at God's presence; they do not respond to Him at all. Only Job interacts with God when He appears. His friends are only forgiven because Job prays for them. They do not take the initiative of seeking forgiveness for themselves by expressing repentance as Job did. For unlike Job—the true pietist, whose hopes are pinned on God Himself and on His literal presence—the friends perceive no sin in themselves to repent of; they fit exactly the description of Qoh. 5.1:

> Fools, who *do not know* that they are doing wrong.

In Qoh. 5.2, then, it is as though God's distance away ('in heaven') is not laying the stress on His absence as such at all, but is only mentioning His absence in anticipation of His coming presence before long, as a warning to self-absorbed would-be sages whose 'wisdom' does not extend beyond the blinkered false certainties of anthropocentrism. Qoheleth's device for hinting at this imminent appearance of God is his allusion to the book of Job, with its climactic theophany. Qoheleth's point here is a moral one. God's apparent distance away ('in heaven') gives those 'on earth' an exaggerated sense of their own wisdom and greatness. Those who, before God's appearance, are (like Job and his friends) very eloquent and opinionated in their judgments on matters beyond their understanding, may well find that when He eventually does appear, He will be angry at what they have said.[29]

---

29. The idea that Qoheleth contains allusions to Job may, of course, be contested. The similarity, for example, between Job 1.21a and Qoh. 5.14 (5.15 in

To underline that Qoheleth is evoking here the idea of a theophany or literal manifestation of God's presence, it should be added that there are further indications[30] of allusion to Job in Qoh. 5.1-7. In 5.1's reference to 'The sacrifice of fools, who do not know that they are doing wrong', the intertextuality is double: that is, not only with 1 Sam. 15.22,[31] but also with Job 42.7-9. For the very reparation God demands from Job's friends for having so angered him is a sacrifice (Job 42.8).

Moreover, the friends have already demonstrated that they are too complacent to 'Know—that they are doing wrong'. For Job's apology to God (40.4, 5) is so emphatic and uncompromising, and, moreover, later repeated and enlarged upon (42.2-6), that the absence of any comparable remarks from the friends makes a deafening silence by contrast;

English translations) has provoked speculation as to whether the Qoheleth-passage is echoing Job, or whether both passages reflect an independent proverb known to the authors of both books. Gordis, *Koheleth*, p. 45, inclines to the latter view.

However, it may well be significant that this echo of Job 1.21a occurs in the *same* chapter of Qoheleth as the apparent allusions to Job discussed here. This tilts the balance of probabilities somewhat away from Gordis's opinion toward the probability of direct intertextuality between Job and Qoheleth. Similarly, most of the apparent references to the *Wisdom of Amenemope* in Proverbs are grouped closely together in the same section, between Prov. 22.17 and 23.10-11. E.g., the 'thirty chapters' of Prov. 22.20 (cf. *Amenemope* XXX.1); the skilled man worthy to serve at court in Prov. 22.29 (cf. *Amenemope* XXX.10); and the riches that sprout wings and fly off to the sky in Prov. 23.4, 5 (cf. *Amenemope* VII.1, 15).

It seems, then, to be not unusual for wisdom-writers who, like Qoheleth, quote or allude to other sages' proverbs in their own work, to concentrate several sayings or ideas of the same teacher into the same passage of their own work. In view of this practice, therefore, when in doubt as to whether one really has detected in Qoheleth an echo of some other particular author, it is worth looking to see if there are any other echoes of that same author nearby in the same passage of Qoheleth. If there are, then one's initial identification of that author's work in the Qoheleth passage seems somewhat likelier to be correct than if there are not.

Also, the fact that Qoheleth is said to have made collections of proverbs (Qoh. 12.9, 10) makes it seem likely that it is he who is echoing someone else's work; and allusion works best with a book that is well known and well liked, which makes Job a fairly likely choice. For the probability of Job being the earlier work and Qoheleth the borrower, rather than vice versa, see also Gutridge, 'Wisdom, Anti-wisdom', pp. 200-201 n. 48.

30. Apart from the words of Job's friends having occasioned God's anger.

31. See above, this article, for the folly of Saul's proposed sacrifice in 1 Sam. 15.21.

they have not 'Spoken of (God) what is right, as (His) servant Job has'
(42.7). Inevitably, therefore, the 'sacrifice of fools' in Qoh. 5.1 recalls
the sacrifice of Job's friends in Job 42.8, 9.

Similarly, in 5.3, Qoheleth speaks of a dream that comes 'When there
are many cares (ברב ענין)'. This is not unlike the disquieting night-
vision of Eliphaz in Job 4.12-21, בשעפים מחזינות לילה (v. 13), which is
described in lurid supernatural detail, grating uneasily against the commandments of the Torah against contact with familiar spirits.[32] Qoheleth
compares the 'dream—when there are many cares' with 'many words',
which are characteristic both of the fool (as he himself says in v. 3b)
and of Job's friends (as we know from the inordinate length of their
speeches). Then, straight after v. 6c's reference to God being angry at
one's words, Qoheleth returns in v. 7 to the negative association
between 'much dreaming' and 'many words' (both of which he
describes as הבל). He recommends instead the fear of God.

Eliphaz, however, in sharp contrast, sets great store by his dream-
vision, which contributes, among his other credentials as a wise man, to
the misguided confidence he expresses in Job 5.27. Also, Elihu (33.15-
18) ratifies such night-visions as a genuine source of wisdom. He calls
them 'dreams' in v. 15, as do Job himself (7.14) and Zophar (20.8). In
view of this, the pointed attack in Qoh. 5.3, 7 on dreams as something
opposed to the fear of God[33] points again to Job's friends, whose
wisdom is empty because it is centred on Man and on his spectacular
experiences, on his words and on his dreams, instead of centred on
fearing God and keeping His commandments. This 'wisdom', therefore,
is not unlike the empty, boasted pomp of the wicked in Ps. 73.19, 20,
which is also compared to a dream. God will despise it as mere fantasy,
so swiftly will it be swept away at their sudden judgment.

There is, then, in Qoh. 5.1-7, a dense interweaving of motifs reminiscent of Job: the 'sacrifice of fools'; 'many words' and 'not (knowing)
that they are doing wrong' as the salient characteristics of the fool;

32. See Lev. 19.31; 20.6, 27; Deut. 18.11. Cf. 1 Sam. 28.3, 7-9; 2 Kgs. 21.6;
23.24; 1 Chron. 10.13; 2 Chron. 33.6; Isa. 8.19; 19.3. Saul's compromise in 1 Sam.
28.5-25 on these very same commandments is intrinsically bound up with losing his
true identity and his grasp of reality, a disintegration of character which is the complete opposite of wisdom.

33. I.e. in rivalry with the fear of God in their claim to be the source or the hallmark of true wisdom.

God's anger at people's words; and the worthlessness of dreams, in parallel twice (5.3, 7) with the equal worthlessness of many words. This seems to confirm that the fools of 5.1 should be identified with Job's friends, and hence also, by implication, with all misguided counsellors of like kind, who wrongly insist that they have certainty about the ways of God.

In Qoh. 5.1-7, the intertextuality with Job, which is both penetrating and organic, underlines how both Qoheleth and Job tend to fuse into one issue the desirability of recognizing and cultivating God's presence on the one hand and on the other the ethical necessity for the humbling and silencing of Man. However, although both books merge these two issues of piety into one, their exact emphasis varies slightly. For Job is an exotic illustration of the conviction that only the direct impact of God's literal appearance is *capable* of bringing about this humbling process; whereas Qoheleth insists that the reality and realization of God's presence *must* bring it about, for it is Man's solemn obligation to recognize this presence and to cultivate the humility of silence before it.

Job gives us a mocking description of anti-wisdom. It tells us that nothing less startling than God's formidable and unexpected challenge out of a whirlwind could shock a human being out of its self-opinion-ated complacency. The book exposes the stupidity of egocentric human pretensions to wisdom in the form of a burlesque. The exaggerated elo-quence and stubborn persistence of Job's misguided would-be counsel-lors sit ill-at-ease both with Job's own sarcastic and impassioned denials and with the wrathfulness of God's eventual appearance. Job's hyperbolic and bitter rejection of their viewpoint shows how insensitive and how useless to him the comments of his 'friends' really are; and God's awesome appearance shows how over-inflated a view of them-selves and of their own perspectives all the human characters have, even Job himself, let alone his ineffectual 'comforters'. Job, then, makes a colourful display of the folly of anthropocentricity; but Qoh. 5.1-7 is not, like Job, a *demonstration* of folly, but rather an *exhortation* to wisdom.

The injunction of Qoh. 5.2 not to be 'Hasty in your heart to utter any-thing before God', coupled with the fact that Job ultimately recognizes he *has* been hasty in his utterances before God, gives the impression that the writers of both books see the contemplative silence appropriate to Man before God as a central Wisdom issue. Because this receptive approach to God can only be cultivated by renouncing anthropocentricity and embracing a God-centred world-view,[34] it makes sense to the writers of both books to posit an actual presence of God to startle Humanity out of its self-absorption. In Job, therefore, a suitable theophany is dramatically presented as literally taking place; and in Qoh. 5.1-7, God is represented as an aware and listening numen, of whose objective, external presence the worshipper must keep himself in mind in order to avoid offence. This presence is not startling and unmistakable like the God of Job, speaking out of a whirlwind;[35] but this absence of dramatic manifestations is all the more reason for worshippers to need *reminding* of their duty to stand in awe of God until He does make His presence manifest. The passage is a stern warning to Mankind to remember its obligation to cultivate God's presence, and not to permit the distance between God and Man and the predominance of Man's own ego to mask God's reality.

Qoheleth's God is not a God who is absent, but rather a God whose presence human beings must strive to remember by not allowing their own words—the prime outflow of the human ego—to swarm into the foreground and blot out their awareness of that presence. Man's words are equated in 5.3, 7 with dreaming, a universal symbol of insubstantiality. Although words are the choicest fruit of Man's egocentric creativity, and hence often seem to human creatures to be their proudest and 'weightiest' achievement, Qoheleth warns that 'much dreaming and many words' are not substantial after all; they are actually הבל, mere 'breath', which is the complete opposite of substantial.

The 'fear of God' in 5.7b, however, provides the key contrast to v. 7a's 'much dreaming and many words', the typical hallmark of Man. For God is *not* הבל, but a substantial and definite Presence, as in Isa. 40.6b-8:

> All men are like grass,
> And all their glory is like the flowers of the field.
> The grass withers and the flowers fall,
> Because the breath of the Lord blows upon them.
> Surely the people are grass.
> The grass withers and the flowers fall;
> But the word of our God stands forever.

---

34. As noted above, a favourite theme of Samuel Terrien.

35. Or at least, not until the appointed time for judgment referred to in 3.17; at this stage God is still seen as 'in heaven', by contrast with the worshipper 'on earth'.

In the editorial summary which constitutes the closing verses of Qoheleth (12.9-14), this solid, lasting 'word of our God', in the form of the commandments (12.13b), is contrasted with the typical words of Man, the 'many books' of 12.12, like the insubstantial 'many words' of 5.7. In 12.13, the obligation to obey God's commandments is stated, and the warning of 5.7 to fear God is restated,[36] so that, at the end of the book, the word of God is left as the dominant assertion. Man, however, is left silent as the recipient, with the duty of obedience: an essentially listening, responsive and non-assertive rôle.

---

36. The combination of 'fearing God' and 'keeping His commandments' is a familiar Deuteronomic formula. See, e.g., Deut. 5.29; 6.2, 24; 8.6; 10.12, 13; 13.4; 17.19; 28.58; 31.12. For the importance of 'fearing God' and other Deuteronomic expressions in Qoheleth, see Gutridge, 'Wisdom, Anti-wisdom', pp. 308-13.

TIN AND TIN-LEAD ALLOYS IN HEBREW AND JEWISH ARAMAIC*

Dan Levene and Beno Rothenberg

There is a wide variety of evidence that there was trade in, and use of, tin in its metallic, unalloyed form, from as early as the middle of the third millennium BCE.[1] Particularly important is the archival material from the Anatolian Kültepe which recorded a flourishing trade in tin ingots and ore between the Assyrians and Karum Kanesh in the second millennium BCE.[2] According to Larsen's conservative estimate, on the basis of this archive, some 100 tons of tin were traded during a period of 40–50 years over this route alone.[3]

The first part of this essay deals with the meaning of the Biblical Hebrew term בדיל, for which there are a number of good reasons to assume the meaning of 'tin'. This part of the paper also examines some of the biblical evidence concerning the use of this metal and its trade. The second part of this paper deals with post-biblical metallurgical terms that occur in the Mishnah, Tosefta, Talmuds and Targums, the principal ones being בעץ and קסטרון.

The Bible

G.R. Driver states that the meaning of the Hebrew term בדיל 'which occurs in four or five passages of the Old Testament, has long been a puzzle'. He adds, 'The ancient Vss. almost unanimously suggest tin',

---

*   This research was sponsored by Dr Felix Posen, London.

1.   P.R.S. Moorey, *Ancient Mesopotamian Minerals and Industries: The Archaeological Evidence* (Oxford: Clarendon Press, 1994), p. 298. For an extensive review see pp. 297-301.

2.   K.R. Veenhof, *Aspects of Old Assyrian Trade and its Terminology* (Leiden: E.J. Brill, 1972).

3.   M.T. Larsen, *Old Assyrian Caravan Procedures* (Istanbul: Nederlands-historisch-archaeologisch instituut in het Nabije Oosten, 1967).

but this 'by no means suits all the passages where it occurs'.[4] The four passages for which, according to Driver, this meaning is less problematic are:[5]

	MT	LXX	Peshitta	Vulgate
Num. 31.22	בדיל	κασστέρον	*'nk'*	stagnum
Ezek. 22.18-22	בדיל	κασστέροφ	*'nk'*	stagnum
Ezek. 22.20	בדיל	κασσίτερος	*'nk'*	stagni
Ezek. 27.12	בדיל	κασσίτερον	*'nk'*	stagno

Numbers 31.22
The text and a standard translation (JPSV) are as follows:

אַך אֶת הזהב ואֶת הכסף אֶת הנחשת אֶת הברזל אֶת הבדיל ואֶת העפרת
Gold and silver, copper, iron, tin and lead

The verse includes a list of the six main metallic materials: gold, silver, copper,[6] iron, בדיל, and lead, which may be viewed as a part of a lexical definition of the generic term 'metals'.[7] An understanding of בדיל in the sense of 'tin', as in the LXX, Peshitta and Vulgate is in agreement with current archaeometallurgical research in as much as tin was amongst the six most commonly used metals in antiquity.

Ezekiel 22.18-22
This unit of verses comprises a rather lengthy and complicated description of metallurgical processes that requires some explanation before the presence of בדיל within it can be assessed. The text and a standard translation (JPSV) are as follows:

---

4. G.R. Driver, 'Babylonian and Hebrew Notes', *WO* 2 (1954–1959), pp. 21-24 (21).

5. *Pace* S. Abramsky, 'סיגים ובדילים בישעיהו פרק א', *Eretz-Israel* 5 (1958), pp. 106-107, who concluded that בדיל means a type of lead, possibly that which is discharged in the process of silver refining.

6. The term נחשת is used indiscriminately in pre-modern Hebrew as a designation for copper and a variety of its alloys. We have therefore decided that it would be easier for the purposes of this article to translate it in all cases simply as 'copper' and thus avoid an issue that is rather complex. Copper and its alloys in the biblical and rabbinic sources is the main topic of a forthcoming study by the same authors.

7. See D. Levene and B. Rothenberg, 'יבא באש—A Fundamental Aspect of the Nature of Metal', *JAB* 2.1 (2000), pp. 75-87.

(יח) בֶּן אָדָם הָיוּ לִי בֵית יִשְׂרָאֵל לְסִיג כֻּלָּם נְחֹשֶׁת וּבְדִיל וּבַרְזֶל וְעוֹפֶרֶת בְּתוֹךְ
כּוּר סִגִים כֶּסֶף הָיוּ: (יט) לָכֵן כֹּה אָמַר אֲדֹנָי יְהוָה יַעַן הֱיוֹת כֻּלְּכֶם לְסִגִים לָכֵן
הִנְנִי קֹבֵץ אֶתְכֶם אֶל תּוֹךְ יְרוּשָׁלָ͏ִם: (כ) קְבֻצַת כֶּסֶף וּנְחֹשֶׁת וּבַרְזֶל וְעוֹפֶרֶת
וּבְדִיל אֶל תּוֹךְ כּוּר לָפַחַת עָלָיו אֵשׁ לְהַנְתִּיךְ כֵּן אֶקְבֹּץ בְּאַפִּי וּבַחֲמָתִי וְהִנַּחְתִּי
וְהִתַּכְתִּי אֶתְכֶם: (כא) וְכִנַּסְתִּי אֶתְכֶם וְנָפַחְתִּי עֲלֵיכֶם בְּאֵשׁ עֶבְרָתִי וְנִתַּכְתֶּם
בְּתוֹכָהּ: (כב) כְּהִתּוּךְ כֶּסֶף בְּתוֹךְ כּוּר כֵּן תֻּתְּכוּ בְתוֹכָהּ וִידַעְתֶּם כִּי אֲנִי יְהוָה
שָׁפַכְתִּי חֲמָתִי עֲלֵיכֶם:

(18) O Mortal, the House of Israel has become dross to me; they are all
copper, tin, iron, and lead. But in a crucible, the dross shall turn to silver.
(19) Assuredly, thus said the Lord God: Because you have all become
dross, I will gather you into Jerusalem. (20) As silver, copper, iron, lead,
and tin are gathered into the crucible to blow the fire upon them, so as to
melt them, so will I gather you in My fierce anger and cast you [into the
fire] and melt you. (21) I will gather you and I will blow upon you the
fire of My fury, and you shall be melted in it. (22) As silver is melted in
a crucible, so shall you be melted in it. And you shall know that I the
Lord have poured out My fury upon you.

The passage could be understood to describe the process of silver smelting and cupellation,[8] but contains a number of lexical difficulties as
well as possible corruptions. This has led commentators such as Cooke,[9]

---

8.   Depending on the type of lead ore used in the process, the production of
silver could be either more or less complex. Galena, a sulphur-lead compound—the
most common lead ore used in our region—practically always contained silver, and
was its major source. Silver was the final product of a three step process: (1) After
roasting, i.e. desulphurization, the ore was smelted or in other words the oxidized
ore was reduced in a furnace producing 'crude lead' which contained silver and
much of the impurities of the ore (arsenic, antimony, copper and other minerals).
(2) The 'crude lead', that is the lead containing the silver, was remelted so that it
(the soft lead containing the silver) separated and flowed away, leaving behind, as
waste product, the 'dross', i.e. a slaggy mixture of the by now oxidized metallic
impurities listed above. (3) The final stage of silver production was the 'cupellation': the lead/silver was melted in a crucible ('cupel') and air was blown over the
molten metal in order to oxidize and separate the lead oxide ('litharge'), leaving the
now separated silver in the cupel. This was the principal method of silver production in antiquity. Other types of ore, such as massive complex ores and jarosite
ores from pyritic ore deposits, which were also exploited for silver production in
the ancient Mediterranean world, employed locally adapted variants of the same
method, such as the addition of lead to the ore of Rio Tinto (a huge Phoenician
mine in south-west Spain) which did not contain enough lead to serve as the
'collector' of the silver.
9.   G.A. Cooke, *A Critical and Exegetical Commentary on the Book of Ezekiel*
(Edinburgh: T. & T. Clark, 1936), pp. 242-44, suggests, as do Abramsky and the

Driver[10] and Abramsky[11] to propose various emendations, all of which are only partially successful in providing a version that makes sense. Some of the statements are incompatible with the realities of silver smelting and refining. First, there is no evidence for the assumption that the lists of metals named in vv. 18 and 20 refer to metal ores, from which the metals would be extracted via smelting. Even if the ores and fluxes[12] that were used did contain metallic elements such as tin, iron or copper, it is far from certain that the smelter in antiquity would have been aware of this. Even less likely is the possibility that he would have referred to them by the names of metals. Another difficulty is the inclusion of iron among the metals listed in the passage. This is incompatible with the fact that iron could not be melted by the heating methods used in antiquity.

In view of these difficulties, the metallurgical processes described in this passage may be explained as follows: The list of metals in vv. 18 and 20 may be schematic and used, as in Num. 31.22, simply to evoke the sense of 'metal' for which there is no specific term in Biblical Hebrew. Verses 18-19 and 20-22 would then comprise descriptions of two quite different processes. Verses 18-19 are a rough metaphor for metal smelting and working that have gone wrong. Poor smelting conditions, such as lack of reducing atmosphere and excessive oxidation in the furnace, result in excessive quantities of useless by-products and

BHS, that in v. 18 silver might have been misplaced and should appear before copper rather than at the end of the verse. He also proposes that vv. 21 and 22 are not part of the original text but a repetition that was 'inserted by an annotator who wished to give further emphasis' to God's threat. In support of this he points out the similarity between עברתי באש עליכם ונפחתי and Ezek. 21.36, from which he claims it could have been taken, noting that the verb כוס in v. 21 'belongs to later literature'. Cooke was, however, baffled by v. 22 which describes the melting of silver, presumably the last stage of silver smelting, and comments that 'the writer is no doubt thinking of the process described in vv. 18-20, but his allusion is not quite exact' as the extraction of the pure metallic product could hardly be the correct simile for God's wrath.

10. Driver's ('Babylonian', pp. 22-24) emendation consists of changing the end of v. 18 to היו מכסף סיג 'they are dross "from" or "without" silver'.

11. Abramsky, 'סיגים', p. 105.

12. Flux. Smelting processes need the addition of iron ore or siliceous matter to slag off unwanted minerals in the smelting charge and also reduce the temperature needed. Iron flux often contains various metallic trace elements which will combine with the silica of the ore to form iron-silica slag.

waste (slag or dross); over-forging[13] produces too much scale. In vv. 20-22 the necessary intense heat is used as a simile for God's fury. There is thus no evidence that בדיל was a term for anything other than 'tin', listed among those metals in most common use.[14]

Ezekiel 27.12

Ezekiel's reference to the many materials traded through Tarshish includes tin. The Huelva Project,[15] which excavated the silver mines in Rio-Tinto in south-west Spain, found extensive evidence of Phoenician workings at the mining sites covering a period probably beginning at the tenth century BCE and lasting for 1000 years. Their findings suggested cooperation and trade, and led them to identify the Iberian Tartessos with the biblical Tarshish and to conclude that Ezek. 27.12 is 'the first mention of Tartessos providing tin for the eastern Mediterranean'.[16]

Isaiah 1.25

The unusual form בדיליך occurs in Isa. 1.25. Driver translates this as 'separated', meaning 'dross'[17] in this particular context. Driver argues that בדיל is used as a parallel to סיג. As the latter means 'dross' the former—literally 'the separated'—must mean 'slag'. Driver goes on to

---

13. Too often repeated heating and forging (hammering) iron will produce excessive hammer scale (mainly oxide of iron), badly damaging the iron objects.

14. *Pace* Driver ('Babylonian', p. 23) who argued on the basis that these verses refer to silver smelting and refining, that because tin and silver do not occur together in ore, antimony must be the 'sole claimant of the name' בדיל.

15. Conducted by the Institute of Archaeo-Metallurgical Studies, Institute of Archaeology, University College London, 1974–86. B. Rothenberg and A. Blanco-Freijeiro, *Studies in Ancient Mining and Metallurgy in South-West Spain* (London: The Institute for Archaeo-Metallurgical Studies, 1981).

16. B. Rothenberg and A. Blanco-Freijeiro, *Studies in Ancient Mining and Metallurgy in South-West Spain* (London: The Institute for Archaeo-Metallurgical Studies, 1981), pp. 171-73.

17. 'Dross' is a thin layer or crust of metal oxides (as impurities), which forms at the top of molten metal, and is skimmed off as a useless by-product of a secondary process, like melting/casting or refining. In silver production from complex ore, 'drossing' is an intermediate refining stage of the 'lead bullion', the first crude lead/silver product, and is performed before the final cupellation. In contrast, 'slag' is a siliceous residue containing impurities from the smelting charge (ore and flux), a by-product of all primary metallurgical processes. I.e. smelting ore to metal.

say that בדיל, *separatum*, can mean 'dross' and 'slag' as well as 'tin' and 'antimony', since, like the waste products of smelting, these two metals (tin and antimony) are 'obtained by separation from other metals'.[18] However, this is not accurate, since pure tin was only obtained by smelting tin ore and could not be obtained from other metals at the time.[19] As tin was primarily used to produce bronze by alloying with copper, or as solders[20] and pewters when alloyed with lead, it might equally well have meant 'alloy', for this would have been its most frequent use,[21] and the refining process referred to in Isa. 1.25 would have included removal of 'alloys' (בדיליך) as well as of the 'dross'.

Post-Biblical

Archaeological finds from the Classical period show evidence of a marked growth in the use of domestic vessels and tools made of metal, including tin and, to an even greater extent, the versatile alloys that can be produced by mixing it with different proportions of lead. The main uses of tin-lead alloys were: (1) The manufacture of a wide variety of pewter-ware. (2) The production of soft solders used in the manufacture of jewellery, for attaching handles, bases, rims and spouts to various metal vessels, and the joining of lead water pipes. (3) For tinning,[22] which was a relatively easy and effective way of coating copper and iron utensils so as to prevent corrosion and provide a silver-like surface finish. All these techniques are documented in the sources cited below.

18. Driver, 'Babylonian', pp. 23-24.

19. On the basis of his assumption that בדיל essentially means *separatum*, Driver ('Babylonian', p. 24) quotes Köhler's novel etymology that בדיל was assimilated from the Sanskrit word for 'tin'—*pāṭīra*.

20. 'Solder' is an alloy of tin and lead: 50% tin to 50% lead is a common solder. Joining metal pieces through the fusion of heated alloys, the solders, is called 'soldering' from Latin *solidare* = to make solid. 'Soft solder' is based on tin-lead, 'hard solder' is silver based.

21. BDB, p. 95b.

22. 'Tinning' is the coating of a metal vessel or tool with pure tin or a tin-lead alloy by dipping the object into liquid tin or rubbing ('wiping') sticks of tin onto a heated metal object, mainly bronze or iron.

Tin

κασσίτερος

קיסטרון and גיסטרון are variant spellings of a loanword derived from the
Greek term for 'tin' κασσίτερος. In the Babylonian Talmud[23] the latter
is used, in the Tosefta and the Yerushalmi Talmud[24] the former occurs.
It is clear from parallel texts[25] that these variant spellings are due
simply to an interchange between the palatals ק and ג.

This term also occurs in *Sepher Ha-Razim* (First Heaven l. 144) in
connection with a prescription for the making of a love charm which
instructs the writing of certain angelic names 'upon a foil of tin
(קסיטרון)...'[26]

In most of the places where קסיטרון is mentioned it occurs together
with another metal called בעץ. For the sake of brevity these have been
dealt with together in the sections that follow.

בעץ *Tin-Lead Alloy*

In *y. Sanh.* 7.2, 24b a definition of בעץ is given in the name of the
'Cesarean rabbis', according to whom it is 'lead and tin mixed
together'.[27] This term occurs primarily in the Hebrew of the Mishnah,
Tosefta and Baraitot and the Talmuds, although in *Targum Jonathan* it
occurs in Aramaic as the preferred translation of the Biblical Hebrew

---

23. As well as a single attestation in *Sifre Zuṭṭa* 19.15.

24. קסטיטריון.

25. *t. Men.* 9.20 = *b. Men.* 28b, *t. Bat.* 5.9 = *b. Bat.* 89b.

t. Men. 9.20	נמצאת אומר פסול במנורה כשר בחצוצרות פסול בחצוצרות כשר
	במנורה של בעץ ושל אבר ושל קסטרון ושל מתכות רבי פוסל ורי
	יוסי בר׳ יהודה מכשיר
b. Men. 28b	תני רב פפא בריה דרב חנין קמיה דרב יוסף מנורה היתה באה מן
	העשת מן הזהב עשאה של כסף כשרה של בעץ ושל אבר ושל
	גיסטרון רבי פוסל ור׳ יוסי ברבי יהודה מכשיר
t. B. Bat. 5.9	ולא יעשה משקלותיו של בעץ של אבר ושל קיסטרון ושל מתכת אלא
	של זכוכית
b. B. Bat. 89b	ת׳׳ר: אין עושין משקלות לא של בעץ ולא של אבר ולא של גיסטרון
	ולא של שאר מיני מתכות, אבל עושה הוא של צונמא ושל זכוכית

26. M. Margalioth, *Sepher Ha-Razim: A Newly Recovered Book of Magic from
the Talmudic Period* (Jerusalem: The Louis M. and Minnie Epstein Fund of the
American Academy for Jewish Research, 1966), p. 74. See also his comments on
p. 3.

27. מהו בפתילה של בעץ רבנין דקיסרין אמרין אבר וקסטיטריון מעורבין.

בדיל. Kohut[28] suggests that בעץ derives from the Arabic *b'ḍ* in the sense of 'to make white', from which the name *mubayyiḍ* for a 'tinner' was derived.[29] Similarly, the expression 'white tin' occurs in Akkadian. Muhly suggests that this designates 'a special quality of tin'.[30] The Arabic *b'ḍ* and Akkadian *peṣû*[31] are similar to the root *b'ṣ*, but both these words more usually refer to the colour white rather than tin.

Whereas *Targum Pseudo-Jonathan* and *Targum Yerushalmi* use the Greek loan word קסטרא and *Targum Onqelos* uses the hapax legomenon אבצא, *Targum Neb.* and *Neophiti* render the Biblical Hebrew בדיל with what are perhaps Aramaized forms of the Hebrew בעץ (see table below). Surprisingly, the later Targums use neither אנכא nor קסטרא, terms that have cognates in a variety of Aramaic dialects and mean simply 'tin', rather than בעץ which clearly means 'tin-lead alloy'.

Aramaic					Hebrew	
Targ. Neof.	*Targ. Yer.*	*Targ. Neb.*	*Targ. Ps-J.*	*Targ. Onq.*	*MT*	
בעצה	קיסטרא		קסטירא	עבצא[32]/אבצא	בדיל	Num. 31.22
		בעיץ			בדיל	Ezek. 22.18
		בעיץ			בדיל	Ezek. 22.20
		בעיץ/עבי[33]ץ			בדיל	Ezek. 27.12

Sealing the Lid of a Jar

m. Kel. 10.2 expands the ruling in Num. 19.15 which states that 'every open vessel, with no lid fastened down, shall be unclean' with a list of materials that can be used to stop up such vessels. These include 'lyme or gypsum, pitch or wax, mud or excrement, crude clay or potter's clay, or material used for plastering'. The use of ' בעץ or lead is prohibited, for although they serve as a covering they cannot serve as a cover that

28. A. Kohut, *Aruch Completum*, I (New York: Pardes, 1955), p. 15b.

29. S.D. Goitein, *A Mediterranean Society, The Jewish Communities of the Arab World as Portrayed in the Documents of the Cairo Genizah*. IV. *Daily Life* (Berkeley: University of California Press, 1983), p. 408 n. 205.

30. J.D. Muhly, *Copper and Tin: The Distribution of Mineral Resources and the Nature of the Metals Trade in the Bronze Age* (New Haven: The Connecticut Academy of Arts and Sciences, 1973), pp. 246 and 411 n. 78.

31. Though *e* in Akkadian could represent an *'ayin* in Hebrew or Aramaic one would expect the *û* in *peṣû* to represent a final weak consonant (personal communication with M.J. Geller).

32. Manuscript variants.

33. Manuscript variants.

is tightly stopped up'.[34] In any case, lead and בעץ could not act as barriers against impurity.[35] In *t. Kel. b. Qam.* 7.7 another opinion is given: 'They do not stop up with tin (קסטרון), for [though] it is a covering it is not tightly stopped up. And if one used it for reinforcing [the cover], it provides protection'.[36] 'Tin' (קסטרון) rather than 'tin-lead alloy' and 'lead' (בעץ ועופרת) is used here. It is not clear how tin, a tin-lead alloy or lead could function as a seal for the lid of a jar. Brand[37] suggests that this may refer to a technique in which tin or lead wire is threaded through holes provided in the lid and the vessel in such a way as to fasten them together.[38] Another possibility is that thin sheets, or even foil, were pressed over the lid and part of the vessel. As both the Mishnah and the Tosefta state, neither of these methods would seal the lid properly.

Fixing a Hole

m. Kel. 30.3[39] refers to the use of בעץ to repair a hole in a glass cup; the method is probably that which is described in *b. Roš Haš.* 19a: 'a glass

---

34. במה מקיפים בסיד ובגסיס בזפת ובשעוה בטיט ובצואה בחומר ובחרסית ובכל דבר המתמרח אין מקיפים לא בבעץ ולא בעופרת מפני שהוא פתיל ואינו צמיד אין מקיפין לא בדבילה שמינה ולא בבצק שנילוש במי פירות שלא יביאנו לידי פסול ואם הקיף הציל

35. In *t. Ḥul.* 1.20, also discussed in *b. Ḥul.* 24b, is the rule that earthenware vessels are unique in that if they are sealed and come into contact with impurity on the outside it is not conducted through the wall of the vessel into its inside, thus preserving the purity of their contents. Metal, and other vessels, do communicate impurity through to the inside rendering their cargo impure. The Mishna mentioned above extends the discussion of this rule to include the sealant which also has to be of at least a clay-like material in order to prevent the impurity from passing through to the inside of the vessel and thereby contaminating its contents.

36. אין מקיפין בקסטרון מפני שהוא פתיל ואינו צמיד ואם עשאו לחיזוק הרי זה מציל.

37. Y. Brand, *Klei haheres besifrut hatalmud (Ceramics in Talmudic Literature)* (Jerusalem: Mosad Harav Kook, 1953), pp. 134-35. See Brand for some references to actual archaeological finds as well as classical literary references.

38. Mediaeval 'Moorish' ceramic from Andalusia was often repaired by a wire threaded through holes especially drilled for this purpose. One such plate is in my private collection (B.R.). There is a 'Moorish' jug showing the same technique for attaching the lid in the Huelva Museum. These wires have not been analysed; both look like lead or tin-lead alloy. The author of *t. Kel. b. Qam.* 7.7 specifically used the word קסטרון, which strictly speaking means 'tin'. As pure tin wire is very weak, the term may be inaccurate: an alloy containing lead might have been used.

39. כוס שנפגם...ניקב ועשאו...בבעץ

utensil which he perforated and into which he dripped lead'.[40] This is true too of the wine jug, probably made from earthenware,[41] mentioned in *t. Kel. b. Qam.* 3.4,[42] which could be repaired either with the 'tin-lead alloy' or 'tin'.

Tinning

In the Babylonian Talmud there are three references (*b. Roš Haš.* 24b, *b. 'Abod Zar.* 43a and *b. Men.* 28b) to the Hasmonaeans explaining that, when they first recaptured the temple from the Syrians, as they were too poor to make golden candlesticks for the candelabra, they made these from iron and 'overlaid them with בעץ'.[43] The tinning referred to here is with a tin-lead alloy rather than pure tin.

Soldering

In *t. Sot.* 4.7[44] there is a clear reference to the use of soft solder: שפודין של מתכת וחברום בבעץ 'spits of metal joined with *soft solder*'.

Pewter[45]

Two objects of pewter and of tin are mentioned: the weights in *t. b. Bat.* 5.9 and *b. b. Bat.* 89b (see n. 25),[45] and the temple candelabra in *t. Men.* 9.20 and *b. Men.* 28b.

---

40. כלי זכוכית שניקבו והטיף לתוכן אבר. Such a lead section filling a hole would stay firm in its place by virtue of undercuts in the glass edge; this would ensure that once the lead was cast into the hole that it would lock firmly into place. Undercuts would either occur naturally on the broken edge of the glass or could be formed by the artisan. ('Undercut': to cut under or beneath; cut away material so as to leave a portion overhanging.)

41. Brand, *Klei*, p. 114.

42. חבית שניקבה ועשאה בבעץ ובקנטרין. S. Lieberman (*Tosefeth Rishonim: A Commentary Based on the Manuscripts of the Tosefta and Works of the Rishonim and Midrashim in Manuscripts and Rare Editions* [Jerusalem: Bamberger & Wahrmann, 1939], pp. 10, 11) explains the corruption of קסטרא to קנטרין.

43. *b. Roš Haš.* 24b, שפודין של ברזל היו וחיפום בבעץ; *b. 'Abod Zar.* 43a, שפודין של ברזל היו וחיפום בבעץ; *b. Men.* 28b, שפודים של ברזל היו וחיפין בבעץ.

44. Lieberman, *Tosefeth.*

45. 'Pewter' is a tin-lead alloy, which was commonly used in the time of the Mishna and Talmud, especially for household vessels. In Classical times the pewter alloy was tin-lead, in a ratio of 2.5 tin to 1.0 lead (by weight).

46. Maimonides (*Mishne Torah Gneba* 8.4) explains this restriction on the manufacture of weights from tin or lead with the fact that with these metals there is loss of material in time through oxidation which might encourage fraud. Rather

The Pin of the Adjustable Lamp

In *t. Kel. b. Meṣ* 1.8 there is a discussion concerning a type of lamp that was made of two parts. Of particular interest in the present context is the pin that joins these two parts and allows the height of the lamp to be adjusted.[47]

מסמר שהוא מעלה ומוריד בו קנה לבסיס טהור ורבן שמעון בן גמליאל
מטהר עשאו בבעץ ובקסטרון חיבור לטומאה ולהזאה תקעו חיבור לטומאה
ואין חיבור להזאה ניטל (נוטל) ונותן אינו חיבור לא לטומאה ולא להזאה:

(1) A pin for raising and lowering a rod for a base is [susceptible to] impurity,[48] (2) but, Raban Shimon ben Gamliel decrees that it is pure (not susceptible to impurity). (3) If it was made from 'tin-lead alloy' and/ or 'tin' it conducts the impurity as well as the sprinkling (which would purify it).[49] (4) If stuck in, (the pin) conducts the impurity but not the purity reinstated by sprinkling. (5) [If it is a pin capable of being] removed and put back then it is neither a conductor for impurity or sprinkling.

than listing בעץ, אבר and קיסטרון, Maimonides mentions only two of the three, using the Biblical Hebrew terminology עופרת and בדיל.

47. D. Sperber, *Material Culture in Eretz-Israel during the Talmudic Period* (Jerusalem: Bar Ilan, 1993), pp. 100-101, mentions this section and presents an illustration. According to Sperber, the Tosefta refers to a type of lamp which is fixed on the top of a rod that slots into another rod, like a telescope. The height of the lamp can thus be adjusted and fixed with a pin that is put through any one of a set of holes fixed along the rods.

48. Lieberman (*Tosefeth*, p. 35) amends according to the Vilna Gaon from 'pure' (טהור) to 'impure' (טמא).

49. Rules concerning metals: חיבור לטומאה—'a joining for impurity', i.e. 'conducting impurity'. If one part of an object (which is composed of a number) comes in contact with impurity then the whole object (the composite of all its parts), by default, contracts that impurity.

חיבור להזאה—'a joining for sprinkling' for purposes of purification by sprinkling (sprinkling for purification is done with water mixed with the ashes of the red heifer [Num. 19]). If two objects are joined and one of them acquires impurity, the other contracts it via the rules implied in חיבור לטומאה. The rules implied in the term חיבור להזאה concern such questions as: if one of a group of objects was then sprinkled and purified (even if it is a part of a group of objects which together constitute a whole) will the other linked object/s regain a status of purity by default? Or will the whole of the group, which combine to make a single unit, have to be sprinkled all over? One of the parameters that affects the difference in such rulings is the material from which the object is made.

In this halakhah an exception is made in the case of the pin that is made of either a tin-lead alloy or plain tin. The statement in section (1) is equivalent to that in section (4) which describes the behaviour of a metal utensil that is susceptible to impurity. That is, it will become impure by physical contact with an impure thing, but only regain the status of purity by the appropriate ritual process (*m. Kel.* 14.7). Section (2), the statement of Raban Shimon ben Gamliel, is equivalent to section (5), which describes an object or material that has the status of being unsusceptible to impurity, and can function as a barrier conducting neither impurity or purity. The exceptional situation that is described for the tin-lead alloy or tin pin in section (3) applies to only one other case, namely when a metal utensil is made of one solid piece. A possible explanation of this anomaly may be that, being either tin-lead alloy or tin, the pin is no different from solder with which different metal sections become one integral object. As such, the pin is regarded in the same light as a soldered joint, and so the lamp is considered as one integral object. A similar situation applying to tin is referred to in *t. Kel. b. Meṣ* 1.3: 'pure utensils that are tinned with impure tin are pure', that is, once the tin is applied it becomes an inseparable part of the object and its status of purity is entirely determined by that of the object which it covers.

Conclusions

Tin is a metal that is not usually used on its own in the manufacture of objects owing to the poor combinations of properties of the pure metal. Its most frequent use is in the production of bronze: copper alloyed with tin has greatly enhanced properties. However, as shown above, tin was used for tinning, soldering and, on occasion, for making objects, when it was desired to achieve, cheaply, the appearance of silver; sometimes deliberate dishonesty was the motive. As tin would mostly be found only as an ingredient of an alloy or in a soldered joint, it was in effect invisible to the end user; it is probably safe to say that pure tin was generally known only to traders and artisans.

The first biblical occurrence of the term בדיל, in Num. 31.22, is in association with the names of the other five main metals (gold, silver, copper, iron, בדיל and lead). Since these names apparently constitute the Biblical Hebrew definition of the class of materials that we call 'metals', it seems probable that בדיל means 'tin'. Some support is provided by the identification of the Iberian Tartessos, a major supplier of tin in antiquity, with the biblical Tarshish from which Ezekiel (27.12) tells us בדיל was imported. Admittedly, the meaning of בדילין in Isa. 1.25 is uncertain: notably, such a plural form is unattested for any other metal. Part of the problem of identifying the meaning of בדיל is the fact that, though the other five names of metals in Biblical Hebrew have cognates in one or another of the Semitic languages, בדיל has none.

The post-biblical literature provides more information about the practical use of tin and tin-lead alloys. There are references to the manufacture of objects from tin as well as pewter, tinning with either tin or a tin-lead alloy, and to the use of soft solder. For 'tin', both the terms קסטרון, loaned from Greek, and אנך, which has cognates in a variety of Semitic languages are used, but for the tin-lead alloys a new term of unknown origin occurs—בעץ. This expansion of terminology coincides with the approach of the Graeco-Roman sphere of influence, accompanied by the extended use of tin-lead alloys. The rendering of the authors of the *Targ. Neb.* of the Biblical Hebrew בדיל (tin) with בעיץ (tin-lead alloy), rather than one of the other words for tin (קסטרון or אנך), is puzzling and one can only wonder whether either of these two terms lost its meaning by that time.

A late Aggadah (*Otsar ha-Midrashim*, p. 526) illustrates the use-lessness of tin on its own. The story concerns a scheme which King Solomon devised to prove that women are less merciful than men. For this purpose he sought out a married couple, known to be particularly devoted, and offered the husband fortune and rank if he would murder his wife. Although tempted, the man could not bring himself to murder his beautiful wife, the loving mother of his children. The King praised the man and commanded him not to reveal the story to his wife. After some time, the King approached the wife with a similar proposition. As he suspected, the woman failed to resist temptation; however, wishing to avoid the murder of the man, the King had provided a useless weapon—a tin knife so soft and weak that it could not cut human flesh. The woman was fooled by its glint, and mistaking it for silver, she attempted to kill her spouse but was unsuccessful as her weapon failed her.

ARK, ARCHAISM AND MISAPPROPRIATION

Raphael Loewe

ולי מה יקרו רעיך

Michael Weitzman shared with me an interest, in his case perhaps indulgent, in mine somewhat more cynical, in the vicissitudes of Hebrew terms for institutions, cultic objects, values and ideals as these have been subjected to pressures from within and without—pressures that have left their clearest mark in semantic shifts, sometimes in modern Hebrew, but more especially in the choice of translation 'equivalents' in other languages, Semitic and western, in both Gentile and Jewish use, Jews sometimes incongruously ingesting a translation whose implications are incompatible with Judaism. I have myself examined[1] this phenomenon in connection with ישועה = deliverance, especially military deliverance, which cannot be rendered 'salvation' without introducing Christian overtones, and with the introduction into Hebrew of σχολή[2] as the equivalent of בית המדרש, only to find itself successfully extradited by the early rabbis. The following pages consider the ark of the covenant, the capture of which by the Philistines at the battle of 'Eben 'Ezer (1 Sam. 4.11) was perhaps ominous of its fate, down the ages, at the hand of both Jewish and Christian translators.

In order to gain a perspective, it may be helpful to begin by glancing at an Islamic institution which constitutes, at least architecturally, a parallel—not, indeed, to the biblical ark, but to its synagogal counterpart: that is to say, the *miḥrāb* which marks the direction of Mecca (the *qibla*) towards which prayer is to be directed.[3] One of the meanings in

---

1. ' "Salvation" is not of the Jews', *JTS* 32 (1981), pp. 341-68.
2. 'Rabbi Joshua b. Ḥananiah: Ll. D. or D. Litt.?', *JJS* (25) 1974, pp. 135-54.
3. See G. Fehérvári, 'Miḥrab', in *Encyclopaedia of Islam*, VII (Leiden: E.J. Brill, 2nd edn, 1993), pp. 7-14; 'Masdjid, 2, c', in *Shorter Encyclopedia of Islam* (Leiden: E.J. Brill, 1961), p. 343. Franz Landsberger, 'The Sacred Direction in Synagogue and Church', *HUCA* 28 (1957), pp. 181-203 (188), assumed that the

Arabic of the root *ḥ-r-b* is fight, whence *ḥarba* = lance, *miḥrab* = warrior. The niche was not an original feature of the mosque, in which the *qibla* was probably indicated by a lance or pole. As churches were converted into mosques a niche in whichever wall was appropriate, previously the location of the statue or ikon of a saint, or which had formed the recess for the bishop's throne, or else the door at the east end, would be chosen as the focal point where the imam would stand during the prayers, and the term *miḥrāb* was applied to it; without prejudice, however, to the continued use of *miḥrāb* in other senses, including the king's private apartments in the palace,[4] a place of prayer (within the Jerusalem temple[5]), or even a synagogue,[6] for which, as might be expected, the usual term is *kanīs*. Whilst the *miḥrāb* shows us islamicization of an architectural feature of the church that had been taken over from the synagogue but then extended, there is here no transfer from Judaism or Christianity of the term for the cultic feature which determines the architectural ensemble; nor did Jewish speakers of Arabic, insofar as I have been able to check, adopt the term *miḥrāb* into their own synagogal terminology. *Miḥrāb aljāmi'* (i.e. of the place of worship) is recorded[7] as the equivalent of the altar (sc. in a church), but the very fact that it is thus qualified suggests that the expression did not originate amongst Christian Arabs.

Before examining the versional equivalences of the Hebrew word for

Muslim *miḥrāb* was adopted from the synagogal niche for the container of torah-scrolls (see below, p. 133) referring to his *History of Jewish Art* (Cincinnati: Hebrew Union College, 1946), pp. 169-70, as confirmed by Elie Lambert, 'La synagogue de Douro-Europos et les origines de la mosquée', *Semitica* 3 (1950), p. 67. While it may be allowed that it was from Judaism that early Islam took over the institution of the *qibla*, in view of what here follows it seems far more probable that churches converted into mosques, rather than synagogues in continuing Jewish use, determined the architectural form which the *miḥrāb* took.

4. Qur'an, sura 38.21.

5. 3.38; 19.11.

6. E.W. Lane, *Arabic–English Lexicon* (London: Williams & Norgate, 1863–93), s.v., cites *maḥārib bani isrā'il* in this sense from the *Tahdhib*, the *Qamus*, and the *Taj al-arus*.

7. E.A. Elias, *Elias' Modern Dictionary English–Arabic* (Cairo: Elias' Modern Press, 3rd edn, 1929), p. 35. Similar reservations apply to the equivalent *haykal alkanīsa* offered by N.S. Doniach, *Oxford English–Arabic Dictionary of Current Usage* (Oxford: Oxford University Press, 1972), p. 38. Regarding *haykal*, see below, pp. 135-36.

what is called in the English bible the ark, it will be necessary to consider the meaning of the Hebrew term itself (as well as of two other words; one of which has caused some interference). But such examination must itself be preceded by consideration of the form, function and fate of the artefact to which it refers, insofar as these may be determined. From analysis of the biblical evidence Morgenstern[8] recognized in the earliest strata an analogy between the function of the ark and that of the pre-islamic *qubba*, or rather more particularly with the two developments from the latter, viz. the *'utfa* or *'atfa* and the *mahmal* or *mihmal* which have survived, at any rate until very recent times, amongst the Arabs. Both are camel-borne structures, necessarily erected on an approximately rectangular wooden framework. The *'utfa* when fully erected was roughly oval in shape; it was kept in the close custody of the tribal chief, who, acting as *kāhin*, would identify and communicate oracular information. It was taken into battle, but in critical situations only, when it would be occupied by a bare-breasted battle-maiden whose exhortations and objurgations would urge the troops to ever greater effort; and, should it be captured, this would spell disaster. The *mahmal*, surmounted by a textile cone or pyramid into the textiles of which qoranic texts are woven, shelters no human passenger but contains, suspended within, two manuscript copies of the Qur'an. The camel bearing it leads the pilgrimage-caravan (*hujāj*) to Mecca and on the return; the route which it takes, and its halts to rest, determine the movement of the caravan, being regarded as not spontaneous on the part of the animal, but divinely intimated because of the *mahmal* with which it has been saddled.

Some of the information preserved regarding the ark[9] is strongly suggestive of the *'utfa*, whilst its function as described in Num. 10.33 is precisely that of the *mahmal*. Morgenstern surmised that the two copies

---

8. J. Morgenstern, 'The Book of the Covenant', *HUCA* 5 (1928), pp. 1-151; *idem*, 'The Ark, the Ephod, and the Tent of Meeting', *HUCA* 17 (1942–43), pp. 153-265, 18 (1943–44), pp. 1-52. In spite of its repetitiousness and the self-assurance of, e.g., its dating, this study is of fundamental importance. See also N.H. Tur-Sinai, 'אֲרוֹן', *'Ensiqlopediah miqra'ith* (Jerusalem: Mosad Bialik, 1950), I, pp. 538-50; R. de Vaux, *Ancient Israel: Its Life and Institutions* (trans. J. McHugh; London: Darton, Longman & Todd, 1961), pp. 297-302; G. Henton Davies, 'Ark of the Covenant', *IDB* (1962), I, pp. 222-26; Y.M. Grintz, 'Ark of the Covenant', *EncJud* (1971), III, pp. 459-66; C.L. Seow, 'Ark of the Covenant', *ABD* (1992), I, pp. 386-93.

9. Num. 14.41-42, especially 44; 1 Sam. 4.3-4, 17-18; 6.1–7.2; 2 Sam. 6.3-4.

of the Qur'an (or occasionally some other religious work) which the latter carries are distant echoes of the betyls, that is, sacred stones in which deities were believed to inhere, that were borne in the *qubba*; and that in early Israel, too, such stones were carried, albeit with their sanctity transformed through transference to the divine words inscribed upon them that were kept in the ark.[10] Possibly before the destruction of the first temple, the ark had already disappeared or disintegrated;[11] if constructed, like the *'utfa*, out of thin poles and wicker-work, it could not have survived for centuries without periodic repair. Certainly, if the *'utfa* model is assumed, those priestly circles in and after the exile to which modern biblical scholarship credits the directions for the ark's construction[12] can have had no idea of the historical reality of the original artefact constructed by Moses. In point of fact, as rabbinical tradition itself testifies,[13] there was no ark, as such, in the restored temple, even though the כפרת prescribed[14] as its superstructure was erected in the holy of holies. This lacked any recess for a receptacle, its purpose being merely that of providing a 'throne' for the invisible divine presence.

The Hebrew word ארון, when referring to this object, is nearly always in the construct, being followed by a qualifying noun, for example הברית, details of which need not concern us.[15] In the sense of (various types of) receptacle, it is found in the cognate languages: Phoenician ארן = sarcophagus, Nabataean ארנא, Syriac ܐܪܘܢܐ (for money or books), Arabic *irān* = bier, litter, Akkadian *erenu* = container,[16] conceivably by extension from the word for the commonest material used (*erinnu* = a kind of wood, perhaps compare Hebrew ארז, fir, Isa. 44.14[17]); if, as seems reasonable to suppose, such a link was meaningless to speakers of the languages other than Akkadian, that could

10. Exod. 32.16; 34.1; Deut. 10.1-5; 1 Kgs 8.9.
11. Cf. Jer. 3.16.
12. Exod. 25.10-11, 37.1-2.
13. *m. Yom.* 5.2, *b. Yom.* 53b.
14. Exod. 25.17-18, 37.6-7.
15. See BDB, p. 75; D.J.A. Clines (ed.), *Dictionary of Classical Hebrew*, I (Sheffield: Sheffield Academic Press, 1993), pp. 372-73.
16. According to N. Tur-Sinai (Torczyner) in E. Ben Yehuda, *Hebrew Thesaurus* (repr. New York: Thomas Yoseloff, 1959), I, p. 383, footnote, such (בית קבול) is the basic meaning.
17. KB, p. 85. However, according to I. Löw, *Flora der Juden* (4 vols.; repr.; Hildesheim: Olms, 1967 [1928]), II, pp. 119-21, ארז = laurel.

account for the use of the word for stone sarcophagi. Within biblical Hebrew the specific meanings, other than ark (of the covenant) are: (1) mummy-case (possibly including also the outer sarcophagus), Gen. 50.26,[18] and (2) a chest, suitable—once a hole had been made in its lid—for collecting (fragments of) silver ingots used as currency, 1 Kgs 12.10, 11, cf. 2 Chron. 24.8, 10, 11. For brevity, in what follows I symbolize (1) by *sarc.* (i.e. corpse-container, without regard to the material) and (2) by *ch.[est]*, particularizing as necessary.

Since at least some of the bible-translators may have been influenced by knowledge of post-biblical Hebrew, we should first take note of the usage of ארון in the late-antique, mediaeval and so into the modern period of the language. It scarcely needs to be said that awareness of the meaning ark (of the covenant) survives throughout.

Late antiquity	Dead Sea Scrolls and inscriptions[19]	[Qumranic use of ארון is with reference to the ark of the covenant[20]]
		sarc. common in inscriptions[21]
	Talmudic etc.	*sarc.*,[22] including (*y. Kil.* 9.3, end) coffins for transport of dead
		ch., including a corn-chandler's bin with lid[23]
Middle ages +		*sarc.*, e.g. Maimonides, *Hilkhoth 'ebel* 4.4 (ארון של עץ); *Shulḥan 'Arukh, Yoreh de'ah*, 362.1, 4.

It would appear that ארון = *ch.* (in general) fell out of use in mediaeval Hebrew; for the specific meaning *synagogal ark* see below, pp. 131-32.

18. Cf. an inscription from Beth She'arim, ארונות הפנימיות והחיצונות, N. Avigad, *Beth She'arim. Report on the Excavations, 3, Cacatombs 12-23* (Jerusalem: Masada Press, 1976), Catacomb 20, Room III, no. 17, p. 244, Plate xxxviii 3; for other occurences of ארון in these catacombs, see index, p. 295.

19. Qumranic and epigraphical occurrences are as recorded in the Sheffield *Dictionary of Classical Hebrew* (see n. 15), the 4 volumes of which so far published reach to the end of lamedh.

20. CD 5.3, C. Rabin, *The Zadokite Documents* (Oxford: Oxford University Press, 1954), p. 19 n. 3; 11QT (Temple Scroll) 7.12, Y. Yadin (ed.), מגילת המקדש, II, *The Temple Scroll* (Jerusalem: Israel Exploration Society, 1983), p. 21, 3, pl. 22; 4Q375 (Moses Apocryphon), J. Strugnell (ed.), *Qumran Cave XIV* (DJD, 19; Oxford: Oxford University Press, 1995), p. 115.

21. See, e.g., n. 18.

22. *m. Ohol.* 9.15; *y. Kil.* 9.3 = *Gen. R.* 100.2; *b. m. Qaṭ.* 25a; *b. Sanh.* 98b, etc.

23. *m. Kel.* 12.5.

Contemporary
usage

sarc. (But it is to be observed that while the Efros, 1929, renders *coffin* by ארון (של מת), M. Segal and M.B. Dagut, 1977, and N.S. Doniach and A. Kahane, 1996, have ארון מתים)[24]

ch. Whilst Efros–Kaufman include ארון alongside synonyms to render chest (i.e. a receptacle intended for mobile use), but for *cupboard* (i.e. a [semi-]permanent fixture) offer ארון כלים alongside מגדל etc., neither Segal–Dagut nor Doniach–Kahane include ארון for *chest* (except for *chest of drawers*, Doniach–Kahane ארון מגרות); both equate ארון with *cupboard* (Doniach–Kahane + alternative שדה). It is probable that the progressive entrenchment of ארון = *cupboard* [not moved, even if movable] reflects the semantic secularization of ארון = *synagogal ark*, for which see p. 132.

It is appropriate to take note of the rare word ארגז, which, at its occurrence at 1 Sam. 6.8-15, refers to a container used by the Philistines for the golden objects that were placed on a waggon together with the captured ark of the Israelites. Since in the context the latter is termed, as one would expect, '' ארון, a different word for this receptacle had to be chosen in order to avoid confusion: but that need not mean that the container was itself also a box. Citing the philological evidence, the *Oxford Hebrew Lexicon* notes that Syriac *rāgōztā* = sack;[25] and that the Arabic *rijāza* includes within its meanings a container for a stone, a pair of which, suspended, balance the *haudāj*[26] within which women are borne on camel-back, conceivably linking up with רגז = *be in a state of motion*, on the strength of which Koehler-Baumgartner[27] make bold to

24. I. Efros, *English-Hebrew Dictionary* (ed. J. Kaufman; Tel Aviv: Dvir, 1929); M. Segal and M. Dagut, *English-Hebrew Dictionary* (Jerusalem: Kiriath Sepher, 1977); N. Doniach and A. Kahane, *The Oxford English Hebrew Dictionary* (Oxford: Oxford University Press, 1996).

25. BDB *in loc*. add 'cf. HPS' (? slip for R[obert] P[ayne] S[mith], *Thesaurus Syriacus*); but neither the *Compendious Syriac Dictionary* abbreviated from it by his daughter J. Payne Smith (Margoliouth), 1902, nor its *Supplement*, 1927, include this.

26. Lane, *Arabic–English Lexicon*, p. 2885.

27. KB, p. 83.

render the biblical occurrence by *saddlebag*. Their confidence is perhaps unjustified in view of the circumstance that although אֲרֹן is indeed rare in post-biblical Hebrew, it occurs meaning *sarcophagus*[28] and, more generally, *chest*(s) for household effects.[29] Presumably it is this that led the editors of the Sheffield *Hebrew Dictionary* to render it, more cautiously, by *box* (perhaps *saddlebag*).

At this point it is necessary to take account of interference through identification with what may conveniently be termed the wrong box, since in some biblical versions one word is used to translate both אָרן and תבה: thus, English biblical tradition renders them indifferently by *ark*. Apart from the flood story (Gen. 6.14–9.18), the only biblical occurrence of תבה is at Exod. 2.3, where Moses' waterproof carry-cot is called תבת גמא (NEB *rush basket*). The *Oxford Hebrew Lexicon* regards it as 'probably' an Egyptian loan-word from *T-b-t = chest, coffin*.[30] In the context of the flood-story, which seems to assume a human race as yet incapable of navigation, the choice of 'chest' to describe the vessel which Noah built is not implausible dramatically speaking; but it is incongruous in the Egyptian setting of Moses' infancy narrative, unless תבת גמא was there deliberately chosen to describe a water-proofed carry-cot improvised by a housewife, as opposed to the papyrus-made products of the Nile shipwrights (אניות אבה Job 9.26, כלי גמא Isa. 18.2).

28. J. Levy, *Neuhebräisches und chaldäisches Wörterbuch* (4 vols.; Leipzig: Brockhaus, 1876–89), I, p. 159, points out that at *b. Sanh.* 46b for דליעבד ליה ארון (i.e. coffin) Hai Ga'on (died 1038) read אֲרֹן.

29. Judah Ibn Tibbon (died c. 1190) in his צוואה (moral testament) encouraged his son to treat his library as his companions and his book-cases as the equivalent of real property, שים ספריך חבריך וארגזיך ותיבותיך פרדסיך וגנותיך, in I. Abrahams (ed. and trans.), *Hebrew Ethical Wills* (Philadelphia: Jewish Publication Society of America, 1926), I, p. 63. In contemporary Hebrew אֲרֹן, is fairly common.

30. BDB refer to J.P.A. Erman, *ZDMG*, 46 (1892), p. 123, rejecting a Babylonian origin proposed by P. Jensen in *ZA* 4 (1889), pp. 272-73, and J. Halevy, *Journal Asiatique* (1888), p. 517. KB, p. 1017, distinguish תבה at Exod. 2.3, for which they endorse the Egyptian etymology, from Noah's תבה which they render palace, ark, under the influence of *Epic of Gilgamesh* 11.96 where the hero's boat is compared to an *ekallu* (i.e. = היכל, for which see below, p. 136); but this was subsequently withdrawn (*Supplementum*, p. 192). Tur-Sinai (?), in a note in Ben Yehuda, *Hebrew Thesaurus*, VIII, p. 7646, likewise dismissed it, and suggested that the underlying Egyptian word may be that for the wooden material, cf. אֲרֹן ? = Akkadian *erinnu*, see above, n. 17.

Late Antiquity	Dead Sea Scrolls	[Qumranic תבותא = Noah's ark[31]]
	Talmudic etc.	*ch.*, generally;[32] specifically, of a *bathtub*;[33] for תבה = the synagogal ark, see pp. 131-32. By *semantic extension*, = (1) [military] *square*,[34] as opposed to [rectangular] column; (2) [written] word.[35]
Middle ages +		(1) *ch.*, generally; specifically, of a communal money-chest or fund[36] (corresponding to rabbinic קפה, *charity collection-box* or *fund.* (2) *word.*)
Contemporary usage		*ch.* The *Oxford English–Hebrew Dictionary* of Doniach–Kahane propose תבה as the first equivalent for *case* [i.e. for storage or transit], and as the second for box and chest. Conjoined phrases include תבת מכתבים = *letter-box*, תבת דואר = *P.O. Box (poste restante).*
		[Except for the rabbinic ראשי תבות = *initial letters*, which is still current, תבה in the sense of *word* would no longer be recognized by vernacular speakers except for those possessed of a Jewish education worthy of the name].

I now tabulate the versional treatment of the words discussed above, with brief comments where appropriate, and must point out that for the word ארון itself, the renderings of a few significant occurrences only have been examined. Comprehensive treatment would probably have added little or nothing, and, if its results were recorded, might have blurred the emergent pattern. For similar reasons internal textual variation has generally been disregarded, since the present study is multiversionally orientated. That means, however, that if individual versional history is the reader's prime object of interest, the results here set forth must be used with circumspection, as is highlighted by the case of the

31. E.g. N. Avigad and Y. Yadin, *Genesis Apocryphon*, X.2 (Jerusalem: Magnes Press, 1956), p. 20 (but the text itself is not there reproduced).

32. E.g. *t. Kel.*, *b. Meṣ.* 10.1, 2.

33. תיבת הבלנים (i.e. pl. of βαλανεύς), *Siphra, Meṣoraʿ, pereq zabim*, I, ii, 5, f. 85b. col. ii.

34. *y. ʿErub.* 5.1, end, *y. Ṣoṭ.* 8.3, *b. Men.* 94b.

35. E.g. *b. Šab.* 104a, *Sop.* 2,2.

36. Examples cited in Ben Yehuda, *Thesaurus*, VIII, p. 7647, col. ii, infra.

Peshitta (see p. 124 n. 51). The order in which the versional material is here rehearsed is approximately chronological.

The final stage of this contribution will consider the extent to which the original Hebrew, or its versional renderings, have been adopted as, or have impinged upon the various post-biblical Jewish terms used for the synagogal ark, whether they are still current or obsolete. Secondary versions, late antique and mediaeval, have been excluded from scrutiny here except for the Syriac, which seems to have been translated from the Hebrew except for the gaps in the *Vorlage* supplied from the Greek, and the Old Latin which, although basically derived from the Greek, can scarcely be excluded, since its renderings were carefully considered and frequently retained by Jerome. And since the terms used for the synagogal ark are part of our concern, it has been judged appropriate to include a few mediaeval and early modern Jewish versions up to the eighteenth century. I have felt it right also to include Luther's German, both because it was made direct from the Hebrew, and because its literary (and linguistic) significance makes it relevant at least in regard to Mendelssohn's German Bible.

In summary, the key biblical texts (including the Greek of the New Testament passages[37]) are the following:

1. אֲרוֹן (a) Gen. 50.26 (b) Exod. 25.10 (c) Num. 10.25 (d) 2 Kgs 12.10 (e) 2 Chron. 24.8, 10, 11 (*bis*) (f) Heb. 9.3-4 κιβωτὸν τῆς διαθήκης, similarly (g) Rev. 11.19.
2. תֵּבָה (a) Gen. 6.14 (b) Exod. 2.3 (c) Mt. 24.38 κιβωτόν = (d) Lk. 17.27, similarly (e) 1 Pet. 3.20.
3. אֲרוֹנוֹ (a) 1 Sam. 6.8 (b), (c) 1 Sam. 11.15.

Where no references (a)–(g) are indicated, the rendering for all the passages here listed is identical, ignoring any such elaborations as τῆς διαθήκης in the version concerned.

a. *Greek* (LXX and Hexapla: the vocabulary, including that of Philo, Josephus, and patristic Greek, is more fully set out by M. Harl.)[38]

---

37. Until this paper was substantially complete, I was not aware of Marguerite Harl's article 'Le nom de "l'arche" de Noé dans la septante. Les choix lexicaux des traducteurs alexandrins, indices d'interpretations théologiques?', in *ΑΛΕΞΑΝΔΡΙΝΑ: Mélanges Claude Mondésert, S.J.* (Paris: Cerf, 1987), pp. 15-43.

38. Harl, 'Le nom de "l'arche" ', p. 41.

1. אֲרוֹן (a) σορῷ, Ἀ γλωσσοκόμῳ. (b) κιβωτόν, Ἀ γλωσσόκομον. (c), (d) κιβωτόν, (e) γλωσσόκομον (Hex. unassigned κιβωτόν).

2. תֵּבָה (a) κιβωτόν, = ᾽ΑΣ, (b) θῖβιν, (c) (d) (e) all referring to Noah's ark, κιβωτόν, -τοῦ. (Wis. 14.6 σχεδίᾳ).

3. אֲרוֹנִ (a) θέματι βερεχθάν (B^ab βερσεχθαν); Ἀ λάρνακι, ἀγγείῳ apparently added by glossator.[39] (b) (c) τὸ θέμα ἐργάβ (A αργοζ); (b) Hex. unassigned λαρνάκιον, σκεῦος.

σορός, attested from Homer onwards, = *funerary urn*, later *coffin* (so modern Greek). In patristic Greek = *tomb, reliquary.*

κιβωτός in pre-septuagintal Greek means *chest, coffer* (5th–6th cent. onwards). LSJ quote ἱερὰ κιβωτός (for money) from an inscription (2nd cent. BCE) from Delos.[40] Patristic usage follows LXX.[41] In modern Greek = the biblical *ark* only.

γλωσσόκομον (neuter), in the sense of *case, casket*, is attested from the Hellenistic period; at Jn 12.6 it means *purse*. As a masculine noun = *sarcophagus* it is confidently restored in an inscription of the late

---

39. See F. Field, *Origenis Hexaplorum quae supersunt* (2 vols.; Oxford: Clarendon Press, 1875), in loc.

40. F. Dürrbach *et al.* (eds.), *Académie des Inscriptions et Belles Lettres* (Paris: Champion, 1926, 1929), 442A, l. 2 (l. 75 δημοσίᾳ κ. pp. 129, 132).

41. G.W.H. Lampe (ed.), *Patristic Greek Lexicon* (Oxford: Clarendon Press, 1961), s.v., also records the meaning [mathematical] *cube*, from Procopius of Gaza, d. 538 CE. Harl, 'Le nom de "l'arche" ', asserts that κιβωτός is a loan-word, either Semitic (citing H. Lewy, *Die semitischen Fremdwörter im Griechischen* (Berlin, 1895), and P. Chantraine, *Dictionnaire étymologique de la langue grecque*. Her reference to BDB as allegedly supporting an Egyptian etymology for κιβωτός is confused; it is advanced for תֵּבָה, see above, p. 119. Evidence that familiarity with κιβωτός referring specifically to Noah's ark extended to pagans also is afforded by a coin-type from Apamea Kibotus in ancient Pisidia, now Turkey (modern Dinar, between L. Aci and L. Egridir), where in the second to third century, from the reign of Septimius Severus (193–211) onwards, coins were being struck figuring Noah and his wife leaving the ark, this reflecting local legend that the city lay beneath Mt Ararat. For a hitherto unpublished specimen dating from the reign of Trebonianus Gallus (251–53), see the illustration in J.G. Westerholz, *Images of Inspiration: The Old Testament in Early Christian Art* (Jerusalem: Bible Lands Museum, 2000), p. 45. For the type, see B.V. Head, *Historia Numorum: A Manual of Greek Numismatics* (Oxford: Clarendon Press, 2nd edn, 1911 [1887]), p. 666; *idem, Catalogue of the Greek Coins of Phrygia* (London: British Museum, 1906), pp. xxxix, 101, no. 181; E.R. Goodenough, *Jewish Symbols in the Greco-Roman Period* (New York: Pantheon, 1953–68), II, pp. 119-20, III, fig. 700.

Roman period from Pamphylia,[42] and rabbinic Hebrew evinces both the
general senses and that of a receptacle for removing a corpse for inter-
ment in the loan-word גלוסקום.[43]

θῖβις, meaning a *basket made of papyrus*, occurs in papyri from the
3rd cent. BCE. J.R. Forster first proposed an Egyptian etymology
through Coptic (= *boat of palm-leaves*[44]). The Hebrew תבה, with wider
reference than the sense in which it is rendered by θῖβις, is reckoned[45]
to ascend to Egyptian *T-b-t* = *chest, coffin*, whence presumably also
Arabic *tābūt, coffin*, > Spanish *ataúd*.

(σχεδία, *raft*, at Wis. 14.6 is a contextually determined paraphrase,
the argument underscoring the fragility of sea-going vessels; v. 5,
ἐλαχίστῳ ξύλῳ, 'the merest chip of wood').

θέμα, *deposit*; for the meaning *coffer* LSJ cite LXX to 1 Sam. 6.8-9
only. Other Greek biblical equivalences, and patristic developments,
have no relevance here. The appended βερ(σ)εχθαν is apparently a corrupt transliteration of בארגז.[46]

λάρναξ, λαρνάκιον a general term for *box* attested from Homer, is
used of a *coffin* or *cinerary urn* (*Iliad* 24.795); it was also applied to
Deucalion's ark, and, by Josephus, to Noah's and (presumably thence)
in a Christian context included in the *Palatine Anthology*;[47] both senses
survive into patristic usage.[48] Of the other hexaplaric renderings σκεῦος
is a wide term applied to *vessels* or *utensils*; ἀγγεῖον = *bucket* or similar
type of container.

It is natural enough that the septuagintal translators, working as they
did in Egypt, should render תבה where it refers to Moses' basket by the
local term which they transliterated as θῖβις: but one might have

42. H.A. Ormerod and E.S.G. Robinson, 'Notes and Inscriptions from Pamphylia', *Annual of the British School of Archaeology at Athens* 17 (1910–11),
p. 235. See also Harl, 'Le nom de "l'arche" ', pp. 19-20 n. 6.

43. S. Krauss, *Griechische und lateinische Lehnwörter im Talmud, Midrasch
und Targum*, II (Berlin: Calvary, 1899), pp. 175-76.

44. *Liber singularis de Bysso antiquorum* (London, 1776), p. 113, reported by
J.F. Schleusner, *Novus Thesaurus...in LXX...* (Glasgow, 1822), II, p. 61.

45. See above, n. 30.

46. Cf. Schleusner, *Novus Thesaurus*, I, p. 453.

47. Josephus, *Ant.* 1, iii, (2) 77–(6), 93; *Anthology* 1, 6; F. Dübner (ed.), *Epi-
grammatum anthologia palatina* (Paris: Didot, 1864–90). Other references in H.E.
Liddell, R. Scott and H. Jones, *Greek-English Lexicon* (Oxford: Oxford University
Press, 1940, henceforth LSJ), s.v. cf. Harl, 'Le nom de "l'arche" ', p. 27 n. 15.

48. See Lampe, *Patristic Greek Lexicon*, s.v.

expected Aquila and whichever of the remaining hexaplaric translators is referred to, who presumably were not exposed to Egyptian Greek, to have opted at Exod. 2.3 for λάρναξ, since that is the word that describes the container in which the infant Perseus was placed at the mercy of the sea, in circumstances reminiscent of Moses' own.[49] Possibly they avoided it precisely because one of its specific meanings is a vessel in which unwanted infants were exposed to die.

b. *Syriac (Peshitta)*[50]

1. ארון (a) ܪܘܦܢܐ (b) (c) ܐܪܟܒܘܬܐ (d) ܐܪܩܐ (e) (f) (g) ܩ[ܐ]ܒܘܬܐ
2. תבה (a) (b) (e) ܐܪܟܒܘܬܐ (c) (d) (of Noah's ark) ܟܘܠܐ (At Wis. 14.6 the Syriac omits reference to the ark).
3. אַרֹן (a) (b) ܓܠܘܣܩ

ܪܘܦܢܐ (דופנא) = *mummy-case, wooden coffin*, cf. Arabic *dafana* = *hide, bury*, rabbinic Hebrew דופן = *side, wall*.

ܩ[ܐ]ܒܘܬܐ and ܐܪܩܐ take over the Greek κιβωτός and Hebrew ארון. M. Weitzman showed[51] that the distribution of the two renderings in Peshitta Samuel, combined with other evidence, points to two translators, the second taking over at 2 Sam. 6.18.

ܟܘܠܐ (*kewela*), not listed in Payne Smith, which refers to Noah's ark at Mt. 24.38 = Lk. 17.27, is presumably to be explained from the Palestinian Aramaic כילתא ,כילה which is used of the draping placed over the *synagogal* ark,[52] cf. Syriac ܟܠܬܐ (*keltā*) Arabic *killa = mosquito net*.

49. So *scholion* to Homer, *Iliad* 14.319, W. Dindorf (ed.), *Scholia Graeca in Homeri Iliadem* (Oxford, 1877, 4, p. 62). For a full list of sources dealing with this episode in the Perseus legend, see PW, XIX, part 1, col. 983.

50. For convenience, the edition of S. Lee (London, 1823), has been used. Any closer study should be based on the critical edition now in progress (University of Leiden, Peshitta Institute; Leiden: E.J. Brill).

51. M. Weitzman, *The Syriac Version of the Old Testament* (Cambridge Oriental Publications, 56; Cambridge: Cambridge University Press, 1999), pp. 176, 182-83.

52. *y. Meg.*, 3.1, כילה דעל ארונא כארונא. Syriac ܓܠܬܐ (canopy, bed-curtain) was also used as a term for the covering placed over the eucharist (possibly significant as a borrowing from Judaism?). It is to be noted that the veil in the temple is not thus designated in the Synoptic Gospels (Mt. 27.51; Mk 15.38; Lk. 23.45 ܐܪ ܬܠܐ).

ܪܓܘܙܬܐ (רגוזתא) is stated by Jessie Payne Smith[53] to mean 'a wallet of hair cloth or wool, a fodder bag, nosebag; a plaited basket'. See also above, pp. 118-19.

c. *Latin* (Vulgate,[54] and where different, Vetus Latina [OL];[55] Vulgate occurrences where surviving citations from the OL have not yet been assembled are marked [ ])

1. ארון (a) *loculo*, OL *sarcophagum, -go* (b) (c) *arcam, -ca* [ ] (d) *gazofilacium* [ ] (e) *arcam* [ ] (f) *arcam* (g) *arca*
2. תבה (a) *arcam* (b) *scirpeam* [ ] (c) (d) (e) *arcam, -ca* (Wis. 14.6 *ratem*)
3. ארגז (a) *capsella, -am* [ ]

Loculus, the diminutive of *locus*, includes amongst its specific meanings in classical Latin that of *coffin*[56] (cf. Lk. 7.14).

Sarcophagus was naturalized in Latin at least by the time of Pliny the Elder.[57]

Arca in Latin is a general term for a receptacle in which objects are placed for safe keeping (cf. *arx*, < *arcere*); specialized meanings include *money-box* and *coffin*.[58] Of interest in connection with its rendering of ארון (הברית) in the Latin Bible is Cicero's reference to an *arca* made out of olive-wood in order to contain objects for casting lots (*sortes*),[59] although it is not here contended that that particular instance necessarily prompted the first Latin translator of Exodus to select it. In view of what will be discussed below (p. 137), two applications found in later

---

53. See n. 25; *Compendious Syriac Dictionary*, p. 528.

54. I cite from R. Weber's edition, with major textual variants only (*Biblia Sacra...* [Stuttgart: Württembergische Bibelanstalt, 1969).

55. Cited from the Beuron critical edition begun by B. Fischer (Freiburg, 1949–), insofar as it is yet published; otherwise from that of P. Sabatier, *Bibliorum Sacrorum Latinae Versiones antiquae* (Rheims, 1743–[49]).

56. E.g. Pliny, *Nat. Hist.* 7.16, §75.

57. Pliny, *Nat. Hist.* 2.96, 98, §211; the reference is, however, not to the container but to its optimal material, viz. a kind of stone, the mineral content of which accelerates disappearance of the flesh (circa Asson Troadis lapis nascitur quo consumuntur omnia corpora; *sarcophagus* vocatur).

58. E.g. Horace, *Sat.* 1.8.9.

59. *De Divinatione* 2.41.86: *ex illa olea arcam esse factam eoque conditas sortes.*

Latin should be noted. The combination *arca libraria*, a box for keeping books, is recorded from 690 CE,[60] and in ecclesiastical Latin *arca* standing alone may be used in the same sense as *ciborium*, that is, the container in which the holy sacrament is placed.[61]

Scirpeus is an adjective formed from *scirpus = (bul)rush*; as a noun, *scirpea* means a *basket-work container*, especially the *body of a* light (farm-)*waggon*.

Capsella, the diminutive of *capsa = book-case, satchel*, is attested in Petronius,[62] who uses it when referring to an outsize golden locket worn round the neck, but is otherwise post-classical. The rabbinic Hebrew loanword קופסא[63] = *small box* is derived from the (probably discrete) Greek κάμψα, κάψα = *basket* (cf. κάμπτειν = *bend*: *capsa < capere = contain*).

Gazofilacium is attested in Greek in an inscription from Didyma, 3rd cent. BCE.[64] In LXX γαζοφυλάκιον renders גנזים (Ezra 3.9), לשכה (2 Kgs 23.11, etc., cf. Neh. 13.7); γαζοφύλακι = הגזבר Ezra 1.8 (1 Esd. 2.10[11]). In patristic usage, = *offertory box*,[65] *genizah*.[66]

---

60. J.H. Baxter *et al.* (eds.), *Medieval Latin Word List from British and Irish Sources* (Oxford: Oxford University Press, 1934), p. 26.

61. W.-H. Maigne d'Arnis, *Lexicon manuale ad Scriptores mediae et infimae latinitatis* (Paris: Migne, 1866), col. 191, 'apud quosdam scriptores ecclesiasticos', no references being cited. No such usage is recorded either in the *Thesaurus Linguae Latinae*, II, col. 433, VII, the paragraph which deals with specifically Christian use of the word, or in D. du Cange, *Glossarium mediae et infimae Latinitatis* (Paris, 1766), s.v. For present concerns, it would be helpful to know whether *arca* in the sense of *ciborium* has left any echoes in the Romance languages; superficial investigation as regards French and Spanish has proved negative. Should *arca* (or a Romance derivative thereof) in this sense be authenticated, one might suspect a borrowing from Judaism (cf. n. 52).

62. *Satiricon* 69.

63. Krauss, *Lehnwörter*, II, p. 517.

64. W. Dittenberger, *Orientis Graeci Inscriptiones Selectae*, I (Leipzig, 1903), no. 225, l. 16, p. 358.

65. Origen, *In Johann.* 19.7.

66. Epiphanius, *Adv. haereses* 30.3, *PGL* 41, 409C. For early ecclesiastical Latin, see references in A. Souter, *A Glossary of Later Latin to 600 AD* (Oxford: Oxford University Press, 1949), p. 158.

d. *Aramaic Targums*

O = *Onqelos*,[67] J = *Jonathan*,[68] Ps.-J. = *Pseudo-Jonathan* to Penta-teuch,[69] fr. T. = fragmentary Pentateuch Targum,[70] N = MS Vatican, *Neofiti* 1,[71] T. Sam. = Samaritan Targum.[72]

Targumic fragments in the Genizah that include the passages here considered are noted by reference to M.L. Klein's Catalogue[73] (= Kl.), but I have not collated them. Except where indicated, all are identified by Klein as *Onqelos*.

1. ארון (a) O, T. Sam. (א)בארונ, Ps.-J., fr. T. בגלוסקמא, N בארינא (*sic*), + *marg.* בגלוסקמא. Genizah, T-S NS 221.68 (Kl. 709), + Arabic (b) ארונא, N, T. Sam. ארון. [Genizah ?T-S D1, 100 (Kl. 422), *masorah* to *Onqelos*]. (c) O, Ps. J. ארונא, N, T. Sam. נה-. Genizah T-S B11.92 (Kl. 297), NS 53.66 (Kl. 565). (d), (e) J ארונא

2. תבה (a) O, Ps.-J תיבותא, = Genesis Apocryphon (see n. 31), N תבו (i.e. construct), T. Sam. ספינה. Genizah, T-S A40.25 (Kl. 15), B1.3 (Kl. 26), + Arabic, B10.5 (Kl. 194), B11.70 (Kl. 275), B11.105 (Kl. 310), F8.81 (Kl. 424), NS 173.67 (Kl. 664), NS 189.24 (Kl. 695), AS 58.13 (Kl. 932), AS 71.99 (Kl. 1384) (b) O, Ps.-J. תיבותא, N תיבי, T. Sam. תבת (construct). Genizah T-S B11.114 (Kl. 319), B11. 116 (Kl. 321), + Arabic

3. ארגז (a) J (ב)תיבותא) Genizah 1 Sam. 6.11(?) T-S AS 20.49 (Kl. 891), described as *Onqelos* (? *sic*).

    גלוסקמא = Greek γλωσσόκομον, see above, nn. 42, 43.

67. A. Berliner (ed.), *Targum Onkelos* (2 parts; Berlin, 1884).

68. P. de Lagarde (ed.), *Prophetae Chaldaice* (Leipzig, 1872); R. Le Déaut and J. Robert, *Targum des Chroniques* (*Cod. Vat. Urb. Ebr. 1*) (2 vols.; Analecta Biblica, 51; Rome: Pontificio Istituto Biblico, 1971).

69. M. Ginsburger, *Pseudo-Jonathan* (Berlin: Calvary, 1903).

70. M. Ginsburger, *Das Fragmententhargum (Thargum jeruschalmi zum Penta-teuch)* (Berlin: Calvary, 1899).

71. *The Palestinian Targum to the Pentateuch...Neofiti*, I (2 vols.; Jerusalem: Maqor [facsimile], 1970).

72. A. Brüll, *Das samaritanische Targum zum Pentateuch* (Frankfurt am Main, 1874–75).

73. Michael L. Klein, *Targumic Manuscripts in the Cambridge Genizah Col-lections* (Cambridge University Library Genizah Series, 8; Cambridge: Cambridge University Press, 1992).

e. *Arabic*

The version here cited is cited from Walton's *Polyglot*, where it is stated to be that of Sa'adyah; for the Pentateuch it has been checked against Derenbourg's edition,[74] with which it agrees except where stated. It is desirable that it should be collated with whatever alternatives, rabbanite and karaite, can be traced in the *Genizah* or in print.

1. ארון (a) *tābūt*, ed. Derenbourg צנדוק. (b)–(e) *ṣundūq*.
2. תבה (a), (b) *tābūt*.
3. ארגז (a) *miḥlād*.

Regarding *tābūt* see above, p. 119 n. 30, p. 123.

ṣundūq = chest.

miḥlād I have failed to trace in the Arabic *lexica*, and its root meaning *endure* (cf. Hebrew חלד) does not obviously connect with anything to do with a container. It is, however, possible to state that the translator must have envisaged the Hebrew ארגז as being the same as the Arabic cognate *rijāza* = *container suspended* from a camel's *haudāj*, cf. Syriac ܬܘܠܩܐ = *sack*.[75] That this is so is clear from the fact that in 1 Sam. 6.8 the Hebrew מצדו is paraphrased by *wa-'uqlu almiḥlād fi jānib al'ajal*, 'and hang the *miḥlād* on the side of the waggon', and similarly, v. 11 before *al-miḥlād* + *wa'alaqu* ('they hung').

f. *Spanish*

Ar. = Moses Arragel[76] (1433), Fe. = Ferrara Bible,[77] M.b.I. = Menasseh b. Israel.[78]

1., 2. ארון and תבה are both translated by *arca* in all recensions throughout (no M.b.I. for 2 Chron. 24.8-9 ארון) except at 1. (a) = *coffin*, where Ar. has *ataúd* (< Arabic, see p. 123).

3. ארגז (a) Ar. (*pequeña*) *arqueta*, Fe. *caxeta* (no M.b.I.)

74. *Biblia Sacra Polyglotta* (ed. B. Walton; London, 1657), I, Prolegomena, p. 95, §15. J. (= Naphtali) Derenbourg, *Version arabe de Pentateuque de R. Saadia…* (Paris, 1893).

75. See on both above, pp. 118-19.

76. Moses Arragel's version was commissioned by Luiz de Guzmán in 1422. Facsimile edn, *La Biblia de Alba: An Illustrated Manuscript Bible in Castilian* (Fundación de Amigos de Sefarad, Madrid, Facsimile Editions, London, 1992).

77. Ed. Jeronimo de Vargas and Duarte Pinel [= Abraham Usque], Ferrara, 1553.

78. *Humas o cinco libros de la Ley Divina…juntas las Aphtarot* (Amsterdam, 5415 [1655]).

g. *German*
L. = Luther,[79] Y. =Judaeo-German,[80] M. = Mendelssohn.[81]

1. ארון (a) L.,M. *Lade*, Y. קישט (*Kiste*) (b) L.,M. *Lade*, Y. שריין
   (*Schrein*) (c) L.,M. *Lade*, Y. (ארון). (d) L. *Lade*, M. קאסטען
   (*Kasten*), Y. v. 9 שריין , 10 קישט. (e) L. *Lade*, M. קאסטען, Y.
   שריין. (f) L. *Lade*. (g) L. *Arche*.
2. תבה (a) L. *Kasten*, M. ארכע (*Arche*), Y. קישטין (*Kisten*) (b) L.
   Kästlein, M. קאסטכען (*Kästchen*), Y. קעשטכין (c), (d) L.
   Arche, (e) *Archa* (sic). (Wis. 14.6. L. *Schiff*).
3. ארגז (a) L. *Kästlin*, M. קאסטכען, Y. קישט

We may now summarize the effect of reductionist equivalence on the
various recensions of the biblical version in the eight languages here
examined; but for the sake of clarity the detail assembled above will
have to be presented somewhat arbitrarily, and in any case the *caveat*
sounded above (pp. 120-21) must be borne in mind. Renderings of ארגז
may be left aside. With regard to ארון and תבה it will be best to begin at
the bottom, and address the following series of questions:

A (1) which versions (a) attempt to distinguish, and which (b)
   make no distinction between rendering ארון = *coffin* (Gen. 50.26)
   and ארון הברית?
   (2) which versions (a) attempt to distinguish, and which (b)
   make no distinction between rendering תבה = Noah's ark (Gen.
   6.14) and = Moses' carry-cot (Exod. 2.3)?
B which versions (a) use different terms to render ארון and תבה,
   and (b) which do not?

With regard to תבה, it is fair to point out that in each of the two occurrences it stands in the construct followed by a noun indicating material,

79. New Testament 1522, Old Testament and Apocrypha, 1523–34; complete
Bible, Wittenberg, 1534, thereafter repeatedly revised during Luther's lifetime. I
have used edn Strasburg, 1630.

80. See 'Ze'enah u-re'enah', *EncJud* XVI, col. 1987, on the background to the
emergence of a Judaeo-German Bible version in print by the early seventeenth
century. I have used the edition printed by Uri Phaibush(/Faibush etc.), Amsterdam,
5439 (1679).

81. The preparation of this version, printed in Hebrew characters but in High
German, not Judaeo-German, was shared by Mendelssohn with a team of collaborators; his own Pentateuch appeared in 1783, the first complete Bible edition in
1805. I have used edn Basle, 1822.

Gen. 6.14 עצי גפר, Exod. 2.3. גמא, and translators may have felt that this limitation was sufficient to dispense them from seeking for different words to render תבה itself. The siglum ( ) indicates that differentiation has been indicated by resort to a diminutive form.

Differentiated	Recensions vacillate	Undifferentiated
	A (1) ארון = *coffin* and ארון הברית	
	Greek	
Syriac		
Latin		
	Targums	
Arabic (Sa'adyah) →		
Spanish (Arragel)		Spanish (Ferrara, M. ben I.)
Judaeo-German		German (Luther, Mendels.)
	(2) תבה = Noah's ark or Moses' carry-cot	
Greek		
		Syriac
Latin		
Samaritan Targum		Other Targums
		Arabic (Sa'adyah)
		Spanish
German ( )		
	B ארון and תבה (ignoring Gen. 50.26 = *coffin* and Exod. 2.3, Moses' carry-cot)	
		Greek
	Syriac →	
		Latin
Targums		
		Arabic (Sa'adyah)
		Spanish
German (Luther Mendelssohn)	←Judaeo-German	

For the purposes of the present study, the most significant feature is what is subsumed under B. Mainly under the powerful influence of the Greek and Latin versions, the respective meanings of ארון and תבה have been identified except in regard to the coffin and the carry-cot, whilst the Targums, Sa'adyah and the Yiddish versions struggle to preserve the distinction. It is thus the more surprising to find that the Spanish versions, the translators of which (apart from Arragel) were emerging from crypto-Judaism and consciously endeavouring to turn their back on their Catholic background, could not shake themselves free from the Latin Bible, and carried over *arca* = ארון and = תבה indifferently.

We may now revert to our starting-point and consider the history and, more particularly, the nomenclature of the feature that constitutes the focal point of the interior architecture of any synagogue,[82] namely the piece of furniture containing the pentateuchal scrolls which, in order to avoid confusion with the biblical artefact, I shall henceforth distinguish by inverted commas as the 'ark'. One may well ask why these two disparate articles have come to be known by the same term in the languages of the west, and even in Ashkenazic usage ascending to late antiquity (see below, pp. 132, 136), and so on into modern Hebrew, as ארון (הקדש). True, the contents of each bear some mutual analogy: the biblical ark held the two tablets of stone, to which whatever was intended by ספר התורה הזה was, according to Deut. 31.26, to be added,[83] and the synagogal 'ark' houses scrolls of the Pentateuch. However, not only does the Mishnah record[84] that in the furniture of the second temple there was no ark of the covenant at all, but the mishnaic term for the receptacle in which pentateuchal scrolls are kept for synagogal worship is not ארון but invariably תבה.[85] This 'ark' was originally not a permanent fixture but, as the word תבה most naturally means, a

---

82. The standard works are those of S. Krauss, *Synagogale Altertümer* (Berlin: Harz, 1922), pp. 364-76; Lee I. Levine (ed.) *The Synagogue in Late Antiquity* (Philadelphia: American Schools of Oriental Research, 1987); see, most recently, Hanswulf Bloedhorn and Gil Hüttenmeister, 'The Synagogue', in W. Horbury *et al.* (eds.), *The Cambridge History of Judaism*, III (Cambridge: Cambridge University Press, 1999), pp. 267-97. Material regarding the ancient iconography of ark and 'ark' is conveniently brought together by P. Prigent, *Le Judaïsme et l'image* (TSAJ, 24; Tübingen: Mohr, 1990), pp. 47-58; R. Wischnitzer, 'Ark', *EncJud*, III, cols. 450-58, Y.M. Grintz, 'Ark of the Covenant', cols. 459-65.

83. Exod. 40.20 (העדות), explicitly Deut. 10.1-2, 5; 31.26 directs that the book of the Torah was to be placed 'in', or strictly at the side of (מצד) the ark. The Talmud (*b. b. Bat.* 14b, more briefly *Ber.* 8b) infers from these texts that the ark likewise contained the first tablets, broken by Moses.

84. *m. Yom.* 5.2, cf. *m. Šeq.* 6.1-2.

85. *m. Meg.* 3.1, *b. Meg.* 26b. Since the series there rehearsed makes it clear that in the context תבה must mean 'ark', it is puzzling that Yom Ṭob Lippmann Heller (17th cent., תוספות יום טוב, in loc.) should assert that it here means *reading-desk*, for which application of the term see below, pp. 134-35.

moveable object, brought into the synagogue as required, and on Fridays before the onset of the sabbath[86]—this arrangement clearly being a practical one, perhaps with security particularly in mind.[87] There is no reason at all to suppose that a transportable 'ark' was intended to imply that the peripatetic ark of the Bible constituted its immediate prototype. But that the 'ark' had, already in talmudic times, attracted to itself the designation ארונא is made clear by the censure of such nomenclature in a *baraita* cited in the Babylonian Talmud,[88] even though in the Palestinian Talmud[89] it passes without comment, and it seems to have established itself sufficiently in Babylonia also for protests against it to disappear. Thus, when R. Huna asserted that in default of a tenth adult male to complete a quorum for congregational worship, the 'ark' may be counted in (תשעה וארון מצטרפין), the only objection that he elicited was that the 'ark' is not a person.[90]

That the terminological nonchalance of Palestine was, in this respect, paralleled by (and, we may suspect, was regarded as good enough authority for) laxity in the Greek-speaking diaspora, is made clear by the use of κιβωτός in the sense of 'ark' by patristic writers in anti-Jewish controversial contexts—a turn of language that would be meaningless if it did not reflect the vernacular usage of the Jews themselves: and that is, as it happens, attested in the inscription (late second to early third century) in the Ostia synagogue recording Mindius Faustus's installation of the κειβωτον.[91] Challenging the alleged sanctity of the synagogal 'ark', Dio Chrysostom (347–407 CE)[92] writing in Antioch

86. *b. ʿErub.* 86b infra, parallel *b. Suk.* 16b; *b. Soṭ* 39b.

87. One may compare the apophthegm, not traceable before the thirteenth century, attributed to R. ʾElʿazar in the *Zohar, Nasoʾ* 134a, that 'everything depends on luck—even a scroll in the 'ark'' (הכל תלוי במזל אפילו ספר תורה שבהיכל).

88. *b. Šab.* 32a infra. Krauss, *Altertümer*, pp. 366-67. The *baraita* is credited to an otherwise unknown Ishmael b. ʾElʿazar: if the son of ʾElʿazar b. Azariah (so, tentatively, C.G. Montefiore and H. Loewe, *A Rabbinic Anthology* (London: Macmillan, 1938), p. 702; positively, *EncJud*, XV, cols. 801-802, chart) he would fall within the fourth tannaitic generation, i.e. mid-second century and thus approximately contemporary with Tertullian (see below, p. 137).

89. E.g. *y. Meg.* 3.1 כילה דעל ארונא כארונא etc.

90. *b. Ber.* 47b.

91. D. Noy, *Jewish Inscriptions of Western Europe*, I (Cambridge: Cambridge University Press, 1993), no. 13; briefly (without Greek and Latin texts), L.I. Levine, in *The Cambridge History of Judaism*, III (n. 81), p. 1003.

92. *Adversus Judaeos* 1.5, 6.7 *PGL* 48, (850), 914: ποία κιβωτὸς νῦν παρὰ

soon after 386, declared that the fact that the 'ark' contains the law and the prophets does not in itself render it holy, and [the ones of which he has knowledge are], in his view, of poorer quality than the small boxes (κιβώτια) on sale in the market; in any case, what sort of 'ark' is it that the Jews now have, with no mercy-seat, tablets of stone, and so on? A Latin term for the 'ark', albeit one that is unlikely to reflect Jewish vernacular use, will be considered below (p. 137).

In regard to the impermanence of the location of the 'ark', the Talmud and archaeology speak with one voice; it was not until the late third century CE that it became a fixture in Palestinian synagogues.[93] Originally it had been placed, when brought in, either on a pedestal[94] or in an apsidal niche, the best preserved example of which is that of the Dura Europos synagogue[95] (destroyed 256 CE), these niches being eventually filled with a built-in cupboard.[96] The circumstance that they are apsidal in form rather than square may not be due to aesthetic considerations only, but seems to tell us something about the shape of the moveable תבה in which the scrolls were kept: the Roman *capsa* or

---

Ἰουδαίοις, ὅπου ἱλαστήριον οὖκ ἔστιν; ὅπου οὐ χρησμός, οὐ διαθήκης πλάκες; The diatribe is summarized by A. Lukyn Williams, *Adversus Judaeos* (Cambridge: Cambridge University Press, 1935), pp. 133-35. Regarding Chrysostom and the Jews, see R.L. Wilken, *John Chrysostom and the Jews* (Berkeley, 1983), and the succinct summary in S. Krauss and W. Horbury, *The Jewish–Christian Controversy* (Tübingen: Mohr, 1995), pp. 37-38, and W. Horbury, *Jews and Christians in Contact and Controversy* (Edinburgh: T. & T. Clark, 1998), p. 234, who notes that the similar disparagement of the contemporary 'ark' by Aphraates in his Twelfth Homily has been discussed, with precisely the mobile nature of the תבה = 'ark' in mind, by Z. Safrai in R. Hachlili (ed.), *Ancient Synagogues in Israel, Third–Seventh Century C.E.* (British Archaeological Reports, 499; Oxford: B.A.R., 1989), p. 76.

93. Bloedhorn and Hüttenmeister, 'The Synagogue', pp. 273, 280, 291. Eric M. Meyers, James F. Strange, Carol L. Meyers, 'The Ark of Nabratein—A First Glance', *BA* 44 (1981), pp. 237-43.

94. So at Chorazin (late third to fourth century); plan in Bloedhorn and Hüttenmeister, 'The Synagogue', p. 277.

95. The best illustration is in A.R. Bellinger, C.H. Kraeling *et al.* (eds.), *The Excavations at Dura-Europos, Final Report*, VIII, 1 (New Haven: Yale University Press, 1956), plate 51, pp. 54-55; smaller photograph in *EncJud* VI, facing col. 301.

96. The rock-cut representation in the Beth She'arim catacombs (second to fourth centuries) apparently represents the 'ark' as a fixture; illustrated in B. Mazar (Maisler), *Beth She'arim, Report on the Excavations, 1, Catacombs 1-4* (Jerusalem, 1957; repr. New Brunswick: Rutgers University Press, 1972), pp. 110-11, plates XXXII, XXXIV; a reduced photograph in *EncJud*, IV, col. 769, fig. 5.

scrinium, in which small sets of papyrus rolls were stored standing vertically, was commonly circular in form.[97]

The circumstance that another Hebrew term for the 'ark'—to be considered shortly—is found perhaps underlines the fact that its being called ארון gave rise to objections. That the leader of communal prayer in the early synagogue stood in front of the 'ark' is clear from the formula by which he is described in the Mishnah, העובר (יורד) לפני התבה[98]—the arrangement maintained in many Ashkenazi synagogues today. His podium was styled בימה, that is, the Greek βῆμα,[99] which, translated into Arabic as *al-minbar*, = *stage, pulpit, throne*, has survived, curiously enough in Ashkenazi but never in Sephardi usage, as *almemar*. In the exceptionally spacious synagogue of late-antique Alexandria the בימה was placed centrally,[100] a position which became the norm in Sephardi synagogues by the middle ages and similarly (from an undetermined period) in oriental ones, to be frequently adopted, in more recent centuries, in Ashkenazi synagogues as well. Whereas Maimonides[101] still refers to the podium as בימה, the term which has come to replace it regularly in Sephardi parlance is, somewhat confusingly, תבה. Since a centrally positioned railed platform has, since mediaeval times, been rectangular or approximately so,[102] תבה = *box* is a natural enough term to describe it. Regrettably, it is not yet

---

97. See M.R. James, 'Books and Writing', in L. Whibley (ed.), *A Companion to Greek Studies* 4 (Cambridge: Cambridge University Press, 1931), p. 610; *idem*, 'Books and Writing', in J.E. Sandys (ed.), *A Companion to Latin Studies* 3 (Cambridge: Cambridge University Press, 1921), p. 239; T. Birt, *Die Buchrolle in der Kunst* (Leipzig: Teubner, 1907), pp. 162, 251. The wall paintings at Pompeii (house of the Vettii, peristyle) figure just such a round container, as does also the mosaic in San Vitale, Ravenna, dated 547, of St Matthew writing (the latter reproduced by C. Sirat, *Du Scribe au Livre* [Paris: CNRS, 1994], p. 111, pl. 67).

98. E.g. *m. Ber.* 5.3.

99. Krauss, *Lehnwörter*, II, p. 150, rightly dismisses Jastrow's contention that בימה, like במה, is Hebrew. The fact that the heading of the article 'Bimah' in *EncJud*, IV, col. 1002, asserts its hebraicity tells us more about the *Zeitgeist* than about scholarship.

100. *b. Suk.* 51b.

101. Maimonides, *Mishneh Torah, Hilkhoth tephillah* 11.3. *EncJud*, IV, p. 1004, lists and summarizes subsequent halakhic rulings.

102. Illustrations in *EncJud, loc. cit.*

possible to establish when this re-application of תבה began and when it established itself as the norm.[103]

The alternative term to ארון = 'ark' is היכל. Elbogen[104] pointed to a tannaitic passage[105] in which the place (perhaps already an apsidal

103. Ben Yehuda, *Hebrew Thesaurus*, in his entry for תבה, VIII, pp. 7646-47, fails to record this meaning of the word. The language in which the following halakhic authorities express themselves is perhaps significant:

(i) Jacob b. Asher (1270?–1340, born in the Rhineland, from 1303 in Toledo), *'Arba'ah Turim, 'Oraḥ ḥayyim*, §150: ובונין בה היכל להניח בו ספר תורה ומעמידין בימה באמצע בית הכנסת לעמוד עליה הקורא בתורה וכו'. This closely follows Maimonides, 1135–1204 (see n. 101).

(ii) Joseph Karo (1488–1575), born in Toledo, subsequently lived in Istanbul, Salonike, Adrianople and Safed, in his digest, the *Shulḥan 'arukh, 'Oraḥ ḥayyim*, §150, 7 essentially follows Maimonides and Jacob b. Asher, retaining their term בימה באמצע and referring to the 'ark' as ארון; but earlier, commenting in his *Beth Yoseph* on Jacob b. Asher's above-mentioned code, the *'Arba'ah Turim*, in loc., he had expatiated as follows: בכאן מפורש דהיכל אינה תיבה ותיבה בימה אינה בימה אלא היכל הוא הנקרא ארון הקודש שבונין בכותל להניח בו ס"ת ותיבה היא והוא ז"ל מפרש דתיבה דקתני היינו היכל שמניחין בו ס"ת וכו'. It would seem that there may be here a tacit demurrer against the improper use of בימה = תבה. That impression is perhaps supported by the fact that in what follows, Karo points out that Jacob Ibn Ḥabib (?1445–1515/6), from Salamanca, who settled at Salonike, in a halakhic work now lost did not in fact equate בימה and תבה, even though from a cursory reading it might seem as if he had done so. Sephardi responsa *ad rem*, particularly those between Jacob b. Asher and Joseph Karo (i.e. mid-fourteenth to mid-fifteenth century) might yield further evidence as to when the use of תבה for reading-desk first begins; and, as Prof. S.C. Reif has pointed out to me, rubrics included in Sephardic liturgical manuscripts, especially dated ones, would constitute valuable source-material.

104. I. Elbogen, *Der jüdische Gottesdienst* (Frankfurt: Kauffmann, 2nd edn, 1924), p. 470.

105. *t. Meg.* 4.21. This passage shows that the conventional Ashkenazi ארון הקדש ascends to antiquity. It occurs in *b. Šab.* 32a, touched on above (p. 132 n. 88), where Rashi gives it as his view that the reason for the discountenance of ארונא (*tout simple*) was that without the appended הקדש the 'ark' was downgraded to a mere cupboard. This seems to imply that in his time ארון הקדש was conventional. Similarly, Joseph Karo on the *'Arba'ah ṭurim*, quoted in n. 102. The combination occurs in the Bible, at 2 Chron. 35.3 (no parallel in 2 Kgs 22–23), in connection with Josiah's religious reform; and the fact that it is cited in *b. Yom.* 52b (= *b. Hor.* 12a, *Ker.* 5b, *y. Šeq.* 6.1, *y. Soṭ* 8.3) no doubt promoted its familiarity. *b. Ket.* 104a, recording Bar Kappara's announcement, in figurative language, of the death of R. Judah the Patriarch (אראלים ומצוקים אחזו בארון הקדש וכו'), is evidence that the phrase had become common currency by the end of the tannaitic period.

niche) where the תבה = 'ark' was deposited is called קודש (without the article), surmising that this was abbreviated from the conventional ארון הקדש current amongst modern Ashkenazim. Discoveries since he wrote provide a simpler explanation. Such niches, normally orientated towards Jerusalem,[106] were sometimes—perhaps regularly—surmounted by a representation of the temple's facade, as at Dura Europos (see n. 95). The regular rabbinic term for the temple is (בית ה)מקדש). It would seem that the representation of the temple at the focal point of the ancient synagogue—corresponding to the position occupied by the initial words of the Ten Commandments in the modern—also accounts for the use of היכל, which would become the exclusive designation for the 'ark' in Sephardi usage.[107] A loan-word from Assyrian *ekallu* = *palace, temple*,[108] in turn < Sumerian *e-gal* = *great house*, היכל is used in the Bible both of the sanctuary at Shiloh (1 Sam. 1.9) and commonly of a part or the whole of either temple.[109] But its adoption in place of בית המקדש for this purpose is distinctly odd. Conceivably it was a device intended to distinguish the pictorial representation of the temple from the real thing; or did the apsidal form of the niche, perhaps thought to have been characteristic of Herod's temple, attract a more 'poetic' biblical term to replace that in everyday use?[110]

(The context excludes understanding ארון as referring to R. Judah's sarcophagus). Their approximate contemporary Clement of Alexandria (c. 150–c. 215) likewise uses the words ἐπὶ τῆς ἁγίας κιβωτοῦ, referring, of course, not to the 'ark' but the ark: *Stromata* 5.84, 85 *PGL* 9,61 (references from Harl, 'Le nom de "l'arche" ', pp. 19 n. 5, 29 n. 19).

  106. Bloedhorn-Hüttenmeister, 'The Synagogue', pp. 278, 280.

  107. Of the occurrences of היכל in talmudic and midrashic Hebrew discussed by Krauss (*Altertümer*, pp. 367-78) the only one in which the context requires that it be understood as 'ark' is *y. Ta'an.* 3.11(13), linked to the name of Yoḥanan b. Zakkai (קומי לך קומי היכלא). Even assuming that the incident is historical and that it preceded 70 CE, the preposition קומי precludes understanding היכלא of the temple. In *Tanḥ.*, ויחי, ed. Buber, f. 109a regarding the legendary deposit, in the time of Nehemiah, of a document בהיכל, the parallel in *Midr. Ruth rabbathi* 4.5 (on 2.4) reads בעזרה (i.e. in the *temple court*). For היכל in mediaeval sources, see n. 103.

  108. See n. 30.

  109. Passages assembled and analysed in BDB, p. 225, 2. e. -d.

  110. Krauss, *Altertümer*, p. 367 n. 1, referring to his *Studien zur byzantinisch-jüdische Geschichte*, p. 124, records *haikal* as the term used in Coptic for frescoes (*Bilderwand*) in monastic buildings; and J.B. Belot, *Vocabulaire Arabe–Français* (Beirut, 1899), includes under *haykal* the meaning *altar*. Krauss assumes that the Coptic is dependent on Jewish use of היכל = 'ark', and the Arabic must surely do

It remains to take note of one other term. The Latin-speaking church father Tertullian (c. 160–c. 225), who lived in Carthage, knew that the furnishings of a synagogue included an 'ark', which he calls *armarium judaicum*.[111] *Armarium* means a *closet, chest,* or *strongbox* for clothing, money, and so on, later also *library,* and would thus be a reasonable translation of the Hebrew תבה; but even taking into account Tertullian's specific labelling of it as *judaicum,* his remark does not in itself afford adequate grounds for supposing either that the Latin word had become part of the religious vocabulary of North African Jewish communities, or even that they maintained the Hebrew תבה itself in the sense of 'ark' as current in contemporary tannaitic Palestine. On the contrary: Horbury argues[112] that patristic insistence on downgrading the 'ark' is prompted by remonstrance at Christians sharing in response to the numinous mystique inspired by the Jewish quasi-identification of 'ark' and ark. By implication, this would support the probability that the Jews themselves either called the 'ark' ארון (a practice for which their brethren in Babylonia were being rebuked), or—more probably—were already using the Latin *arca* or perhaps, for old times' sake, its immediate Greek forbear κιβωτός.

Neither of the two main questions to which this investigation has been directed has yielded a satisfactory answer. To take the second one first—Why was the rabbinic תבה for 'ark' displaced by ארון?—one may

so. A curiosity noted by Krauss, *Altertümer,* p. 369, 1, referring to T. Nöldeke, *ZDMG* 25 (1871), p. 129, is the Aramaic היכלא referring to languages after the flood; Krauss, by confusion, took it to refer to Noah's ark (cf. above, n. 30), an application which he stated is also found in Arabic (including Karaite) texts. Although היכל = 'ark' is now virtually unknown amongst Ashkenazim, traces of its survival are to be found. Moses Isserlis of Cracow (?1525–72) in his *additamenta* to the *Shulḥan ‘arukh, loc. cit.,* n. 103, (ii), refers to the space בין הבימה להיכל; and היכל still figured, as an alternate of (הקדש) ארון, in the rubrics of printed Ashkenazi prayer-books as late as the nineteenth century. So Isaac Baer, עבודת ישראל (Rödelheim, 1868), pp. 122 and 125, similarly Michael Sachs, *Festgebete der Israeliten* (New Year vol.; Breslau, 23rd edn, 1898), pp. 157 and 181.

111. *De Cultu feminarum* 1.3, *PL* 1,1421. Discussed by W. Horbury, 'Early Christians on Synagogue Prayer and Imprecation', in G.N. Stanton and G. Stroumsa (eds.), *Tolerance and Intolerance in Ancient Judaism and Christianity* (Cambridge: Cambridge University Press, 1998), p. 303, = W. Horbury, *Jews and Christians in Contact and Controversy* (Edinburgh: T. & T. Clark, 1998), pp. 233-34.

112. op. cit., p. 235, cf. above, n. 92.

perhaps be justified in supposing that the very choice of תבה, chest, as
the term for the 'ark' was in itself intended to assert the distinction,
both practical and in regard to degree of sanctity, between 'ark' and ark.
Niches for the originally moveable תבה were often, perhaps regularly,
surmounted by a picture of the temple facade, frequently so designed as
to lead the eye up to the representation of the original ark (even though
it was not in fact present in the second temple), figured in the form of a
synagogal 'ark';[113] but to take note of this is not to answer our question,
merely to move it back a stage. Although Harl is prepared to recognize[114] an 'essential analogy' between ark and 'ark', the explanation,
has, I fear, to be sought in the general proclivity of humanity to casualness in the use of language—a casualness the more reprehensible in the
case of Jewry, in view of its recognition in Hebrew of an especial quality and significance. What we are faced with in this instance is a
(quasi)-identification of two discrete artefacts, prompted by the desire
to assert and to inspire awareness of continuity, an object in itself
perfectly legitimate, and indeed praiseworthy, but one which, if it is to
be responsibly pursued, requires historical scrupulousness and terminological accuracy. A comparison that seems particularly appropriate in
this instance is heraldry, the rules and practice of which are safeguarded
with scholarly nicety in England by the College of Arms and by
analogous bodies elsewhere. All too often, however, those concerned to
promote a national or other sentiment of continuity have scant patience
with accuracy, to say nothing of the circumstance that any spoken
language is at the mercy of its native speakers who take it for granted,
so that it lies naked before enthusiasts bent on exploiting its resources
for their own purposes. Thus, already in middle English 'holy day' was
being used in the sense of 'holiday', and Israeli Hebrew has spawned,
as a formula for festival greetings, חג שמח—a phrase that flouts the
essential meaning of its first word, and betrays grammatical incom-
petence in the handling of the second.[115] Those who, like R. Ishmael

113. See Prigent, *Le Judaïsme*, pp. 50-51.
114. 'Le nom de "l'arche" ', p. 20.
115. חג (cf. Arabic *ḥaj*) means a pilgrim-festival, and is consequently inapplicable to the season of New Year, *ḥanukkah*, etc. A festival, being an occasion as
distinct from those who celebrate it, is itself incapable of emotional reaction, so that
one cannot predicate of it anything derived from the stem שמח in the *qal*. Since,
however, it is capable of inspiring with joy those who observe the occasion, it could
be defensibly described, in the *pi'el*, as משמח. The phrase appears to be a calque,

b. 'El'azar,[116] feel in conscience bound to protest, realize well enough that they are fighting a losing battle, and face with equanimity being pilloried as (mere) pedants, since to concede would imply abdication of responsibility for the use of human speech—not forgetting its resources of poetical metaphor—as the medium of the logically articulated communication of facts, ideas and values. Human-kind were distinguished by Aristotle from animals in virtue of their possession of a 'rational' soul (ψυχὴ νοητικός, Hebrew, נפש משכלת, מדברת); and whoso knowingly sells the pass, aligns himself with one, or possibly both of the following positions. (1) By endorsing a laissez-faire attitude, one disavows all assertion that language may have a significance that transcends utilitarian human concerns, and declares oneself a scientific recorder of what the human race, or some particular section of it, has made of the faculty of speech—an approach that is proper, and indeed essential, in an anthropologist or a lexicographer. (2) By taking any given language as it is, including its manifold abuse by those who speak it, one may exploit the linguistic situation by slight-of-hand, that is, fallacies of equivocation, and so forth, for some particular purpose, be it wholesome or otherwise (e.g. mass murder > 'ethnic cleansing'). Such is the stock-in-trade of politicians, (self-)publicists, and peddlers of enthusiasm. Those who would claim that speech, ideology and conviction are substantially interdependent should be on their guard.

Our other problem has to be left unresolved. The vocabulary of Hebrew, though richly expressive, is economical in regard to assigning different terms to manifold aspects of an idea or concrete object. This is particularly so in regard to that small fraction of the language that has been preserved from the biblical period containing תבה and ארון—the first certainly, and the second possibly a loan-word.[117] ארגז apparently means a *bag* rather than a *box*,[118] and the only other word preserved in Biblical Hebrew for various kinds of rigid case (as distinct from sacks and bags) is בית.[119] What it is important to note is that תבה and ארון both preserve their respective identities unblurred, and that what is

---

compounded of the Yiddish *gut yomtov* and its westernized derivatives and such non-Jewish formulae as the English *merry Christmas*.

116. See n. 88.

117. See nn. 17, 30.

118. See nn. 26, 27.

119. E.g. Isa. 3.20, בתי הנפש. A few other examples occur, see BDB, p. 109, 3, *Dictionary of Classical Hebrew*, II, p. 151, infra, *container*.

specific to any particular ארון can be indicated by the construct state and a following *nomen rectum*, for example ארון העדות. The Targums[120] are careful to preserve the distinction between ארון and תבה. Unlike Hebrew's economy, the western languages evince a proliferation of vocabulary intended to separate specialized forms of a given class (e.g. *hammer*, *sledge-hammer*, *claw-hammer*, *mallet* etc., all, in premodern Hebrew = פטיש); and it is thus the more astonishing that the Greek and Latin Bibles,[121] together with versions translated from or heavily influenced by them, render תבה and ארון by the same word (κιβωτός, *arca*).

Responsibility must be laid, on grounds of anteriority, at the door of the translators of the Pentateuch into Greek, that is the 'Septuagint' in the strict sense of the term, in the third century BCE. Although they distinguished ארון = *coffin* (σορός) from = *ark* (κιβωτός) and the infant Moses' תבה (θίβις) from Noah's, the latter also becomes κιβωτός. Noah's ark was a hexahedron measuring $300 \times 50 \times 30$ cubits,[122] while the ark of the covenant measured $2\frac{1}{2} \times 1\frac{1}{2} \times 1\frac{1}{2}$—a nearer approximation to a cube, for which κιβωτός as well as meaning *box*, is the term.[123] One need not press the mathematics, but why, if κιβωτός had been chosen for תבה, did the translators not avail themselves of another word for ארון? λάρναξ and θήκη suggest themselves as possibilities, and there was doubtless a plethora of other words for different types of box. Alternatively, κιβωτός might have reasonably been kept in reserve to render ארון = *ark of the covenant*, and Noah's תבה translated at Gen. 6.14 by σκάφος (i.e. *hull > ship*), or, if this were felt to be inapposite as anticipating mention of the flood-waters at v. 17, by the wholly unspecific σκεῦος = *vessel*.

Marguerite Harl, in a study[124] of particular value because of its survey of Greek patristic sources, accounts for the situation by appeal to (a) the blandishments of inter-lingual assonance, and (b), superimposed thereon, the theological magnetism of allegory and typology. She suggests[125] that κιβωτός—itself, according to some, a word of Semitic

---

120. See p. 127.
121. See pp. 121, 125.
122. Gen. 6.15; cf. Harl, 'Le nom de "l'arche" ', pp. 17-18.
123. See n. 41.
124. See n. 37.
125. 'Le nom de "l'arche" ', pp. 19, 21.

origin[126]—may have been chosen to render תבה because of its alleged assonance with the Aramaic equivalent of תבה, that is, תיבותא.[127] One has to exclude, first, the possibility of the translators having been philologists before their time, aware of the relationship of *t – q* as between certain Indo-European languages (e.g. Greek τίς, Latin *quis*); and secondly, of their attempting to apply any such rule to Greek and Semitic. An even greater difficulty faces the assumption that in translating from the Hebrew text they substituted for תבה—whether subconsciously, semi-consciously, or deliberately—its Aramaic equivalent. True, תיבותא is found in the Genesis Apocryphon (1QApoc),[128] but even if, as the *Letter of Aristeas* states, the seventy were third-century Palestinian Jews specially summoned to Alexandria to translate the Pentateuch, there is no reason to suppose that Aramaic would then have been their mother-tongue rather than Hebrew, and the likelihood becomes even more remote if they were themselves born in Alexandria as the sons or grandsons of Jews who had settled there. If they were indeed of Egyptian birth, they might perhaps have sensed a link, or identity of meaning, of תבה (even though of the 27 occurrences in the Pentateuch, two only are in the construct form תבת) and Egyptian *t-b-t* = *chest, coffin*;[129] but that would not in itself suggest equation with κιβωτός. I have to say that I find Harl's argument unpersuasive.

Let us now scrutinize her theological reconstruction. The universalist implications of the story of the perpetuation of the human race through Noah after the deluge are obvious enough, even to the least sophisticated reader of Genesis. To what extent do post-biblical Judaism and Christianity integrate and exploit them typologically within their respective schemes of *Heilsgeschichte*? The figures, and the opportunity to allegorize them, virtually threw themselves at the heads of the church fathers: Noah (enclosed in the ark, and party to a divine covenant) prefigures the law (enclosed in the ark of the covenant), prefigures Christ (enclosed within the womb of the virgin, and bearer of a new dispensation). Thus, Noah's ark itself came to prefigure the church, surviving through God's providence although storm-battered by pagan and materialist forces. This is well summarized by Harl,[130] who then

126. But see above, n. 41.
127. See above, pp. 119, 122.
128. See above, n. 31.
129. See pp. 121, 123.
130. 'Le nom de "l'arche" ', pp. 24-25, referring (p. 26 n. 14) to J.P. Lewis, *A*

proceeds to retroject it, *mutatis mutandis*, into the minds of the original Greek translators on the grounds of their equation תבה = κιβωτός = ארון (העדות). What can she adduce to substantiate this alleged continuity? She herself observes[131] that Philo makes nothing, speculatively speaking, of Noah's ark; but neither could she, apparently, find much to support her case in the inter-testamental literature. *4 Maccabees*[132] eulogizes the mother of the seven sons, all martyred, as being 'like Noah's ark, bearing the cosmos (κοσμοφοροῦσα) through the flood... and as keeper of the law (νομοφύλαξ)...though strained by the violent winds of her sons' tortures'.[133] It is the eight survivors of humanity, that is, Noah's family, that constitute the cosmos in question, and there is no hint here of any theological scheme to embrace the whole of reconstituted humankind. A quick examination I have made of two other specimen documents from the inter-testamental period yields equally jejune results. The *Letter of Aristeas* insists throughout on the omnipotence of the one sole God,[134] yet refers once only to his beneficence towards the whole human race.[135] In the account given by *Jubilees* of Noah, the little that is forward-looking focuses on Israel,[136] and its parallel to the rabbinic notion of the Noachide commandments[137] is not developed in universalistic terms; but the writer sees the separation of Israel, consecrated to sabbath-observance, as being envisaged within the very plan of creation.[138]

Study of the Interpretation of Noah and the Flood in Jewish and Christian Literature (Leiden: E.J. Brill, 1968).

131. 'Le nom de "l'arche" ', p. 24 n. 9, end.

132. Dated by R.B. Townshend (*APOT*, II, p. 654) between 63 BCE and 38 CE. L.H. Schiffman (in J.H. Hayes [ed.], *Dictionary of Biblical Interpretation* [Nashville: Abingdon Press, 1999], II, p. 105) summarizes the later datings by Bickermann (20–54 CE) and by Dupont-Sommer and, most recently, Breitenstein (second century CE).

133. 15.31-2 καθάπερ γὰρ ἡ Νῶε κιβωτὸς... κοσμοφοροῦσα καρτεροὺς ὑπήνεγκεν τοὺς κλύδωνας οὕτως σύ, ἡ νομοφύλαξ...καρτεροῖς ἀνέμοις ταῖς τῶν υἱῶν βασάνοις συνεχομένη...

134. E.g. 16, 132, 139, 185, 195.

135. ὡς ὁ θεὸς εὐεργετεῖ τὸ τῶν ἀνθρώπων γένος.

136. See 5.17, 6.11, 19-24.

137. 7.20. See below, nn. 140, 144.

138. 2.19-20. One may compare the discovery of Abraham as an anagram of בהראם, Gen. 2.4, *Gen. R.* 12.9 (R. Joshua b. Qorḥah, mid-second century).

The New Testament references are correspondingly negative. Significantly, in 1 Pet. 3.20 it is the flood waters that prefigure baptism; the ark itself saved as few as eight persons.[139] It seems palpable that the patristic typological scheme would not—indeed, could not—have been constructed without Pauline theology, to which the following two features are integral (and it may be noted that there is no reference to Noah's ark anywhere in the Pauline corpus): (a) the down-grading of the law which, albeit pre-figuring Christ and therefore entitled to some respect, is transcended, and (b) the break with Jewish ethnocentricity. It is consequently futile to attempt to discover the patristic pattern already in the inter-testamental period, unless one is oneself to resort to typology, and to see in the work of the Septuagint translators the figure of St Paul on the road to Damascus.

What do we find if we look at Harl's thesis on the basis of rabbinic source-material? Although, as noted, rabbinic sources are, in regard to *Heilsgeschichte*, largely inward looking, there is present a universalistic motif, albeit one that is necessarily introduced in a minor key.[140] The use made within it of Noah is significant; but I am aware of one text only that focuses on the ark, viz. the preludes credited to Rav ('Abba 'Arekha[141]), second–third century, to the triple anthology of biblical texts recited in the *'amidah* of the additional service on the New Year festival. The prelude to the second series of texts, concerning divine remembrance, includes the following passage:[142]

> Noah, too, didst Thou recall, bearing him in mind in regard to deliverance and freely given love, when Thou didst bring on the waters of the flood to destroy all flesh because of their evil doings: therefore did the

139. κιβωτοῦ εἰς ἣν ὀλίγοι, τοῦτ᾽ ἔστιν ὀκτὼ ψυχαί διεσώθησαν.

140. See, most recently, R. Loewe, 'Gentiles as seen by Jews after 70 CE', in W. Horbury *et al.* (eds.), *The Cambridge History of Judaism*, III (Cambridge: Cambridge University Press, 1999), pp. 250-66, and 'Potentialities and Limitations of Universalism in the *Halakhah*', in R. Loewe (ed.), *Studies...in Memory of Leon Roth* (London: Routledge and Kegal Paul, 1966), pp. 115-50.

141. See *EncJud*, XIII, pp. 1576-77, especially 1578, and 'Teki'ata', 15, 914f.

142. See, e.g., S. Gaon (ed.), *Book of Prayer of the Spanish and Portuguese Jews' Congregation* (London, 1971), II, pp. 119-20: וגם את נח באהבה זכרת
ותפקדהו בדבר ישועה ורחמים בהביאך את מי המבול לשחת כל בשר מפני רע מעלליהם,
על כן זכרונו בא לפניך ה' אלהינו להרבות זרעו כעפרות תבל וצאצאיו כחול הים,
ככתוב בתורתך, ויזכר אלהים את נח וגו'.

memory of him present itself to Thee, O Lord our God, in order to mul-
tiply his seed like the dust of the earth and his offspring like the sand of
the sea. As it is said, *And the Lord remembered Noah…* (Gen. 8.1).

This is a shade more universalistic than *Jubilees*,[143] but still not quite
explicitly ecumenical. Noah's role—a crucial one—in the rabbinic
scheme of somewhat guarded universalism is, it is important to observe,
clearly disassociated from the ark. It is on their emergence therefrom
that he and his sons become party to a divine covenant (Gen. 8.15-16;
9.1-17) on the basis of which the rabbis built the notion of the 'Commandments incumbent on Noah's sons'[144] that made it possible for
them to regard, in a positive light, Gentile political theory and ethics
even though the Gentiles themselves made no claim to such matters
being Torah-based. The concept would generally be handled circum-
spectly, occasionally with substantial openness; and it may be said to
parallel, in some sense, the Pauline reformulation of Christianity as
available to all who believe, whilst safeguarding that ethnic (not racial)
element with which rabbinic Judaism cannot dispense and remain
intact. But it would be as fruitless to attempt, on premisses of historical
scholarship, to carry this back meaningfully to Jewish Alexandria under
Ptolemy II as is the endeavour to read patristic theology into septuagintal choice of vocabulary.

What, then, are we to make of the conflation of תבה and ארון as
κιβωτός? Most speakers of every language take for granted its
resources of grammar, syntax and vocabulary, and handle these with a
nonchalance often amounting to irresponsibility; and the charge lies no
less against those who write (or believe themselves to write) under the
influence of divine inspiration. Our carelessness in such matters—even
when we think that we are taking particular care—is a condition of our
humanity. I am consequently realist enough to find here the source of
this puzzling conflation. But that is, of course, not the whole story.
Canonization of a text, be it original or translated, not only fixes it, but
it also elevates its solecisms to a status which, without such establishment, would probably have remained unnoticed, their sense made clear
by the context. Sometimes, indeed, such things survive in folk memory
long after the document concerned has lost its authority de facto, as in

143. See above, n. 136.
144. See Loewe, 'Universalism in the *Halakhah*', and 'Noachide Laws'
(S. Schwarzschild, S. Berman), *EncJud*, XII, cols. 1189-91.

the case of *mumpsimus*,[145] which goes back to the error of a late mediaeval priest; he used to garble the word when reading the Latin mass (*sumpsimus omnes*), and refused to be corrected, on the grounds of tradition. The Septuagint did their best, and in general made a remarkably good job of their translation. And since we need not take too seriously the legend of the verbal identity of all of their separately prepared drafts,[146] I should like to think that there was at least a lively debate on the Pharos as to equating κιβωτός with both תבה and ארון. But we are as far as ever from understanding why the decision went as it did.

---

145. See *New English Dictionary* ('*The Oxford Eng. Dict*'.), s.v.

146. *y. Meg.* 9a. The septuagintal rendering of Exod. 24.11 ואל אצילי ישראל בני לא שלח ידו by καὶ τῶν ἐπιλέκτων τοῦ Ἰσραὴλ οὐ διεφώνησεν οὐδὲ εἷς appears to reflect the same form of the legend, which is not explicitly stated in *Aristeas*.

Part II
THE VERSIONS

THE ANCIENT VERSIONS OF THE HEBREW BIBLE: THEIR NATURE AND SIGNIFICANCE

Anthony Gelston

The Hebrew Bible is a treasured common inheritance of Judaism and Christianity, and its study has been one of the most fruitful fields of scholarly collaboration between adherents of the two religions. As a Christian scholar I count it a privilege to be invited to contribute to this memorial volume in honour of the late Dr Michael Weitzman, for whom as a person and as a scholar I have the deepest respect. While remaining faithful to his native Judaism and its practice, he developed a wide and informed understanding of Christianity, and was unusually well placed to evaluate the ancient Syriac version of the Hebrew Bible commonly known as the Peshitta. It is fortunate that he lived to complete his magisterial Introduction to that version, to the understanding of which he has made a unique contribution, putting all Peshitta scholars in his debt.

Textual criticism often appears to be a rather esoteric discipline, from which the ordinary reader or even student of the Bible shies away. This is largely due to the constraints of the discipline itself, which require a focus on details of language and textual transmission, which can quickly seem remote from the direct interpretation of the text itself. Yet it needs to be remembered that textual criticism is a necessary prerequisite for the interpretation of any text that originated before the age of printing, and of which we do not possess the original autograph. To put it at its simplest, it is necessary to determine as accurately as possible the precise identity and content of such a text before one is in a position to begin its interpretation. In practice this means evaluating the extant witnesses to the text, and ideally attaining an orderly account of how each of them developed from the original autograph. To put it in another way, it means explaining the differences between the extant witnesses so as to reach a convincing conclusion as to which of the surviving readings is most likely to be that of the original text.

The oldest surviving complete manuscript of the Hebrew Bible, commonly known as the Leningrad Codex, dates from shortly after 1000 CE, that is, at least a millennium after the completion of the original text. We are therefore dependent on at least a millennium of scribal copying in our quest for the original text of the Hebrew Bible. It is not surprising that the ancient translations of this text into Greek, Latin, Aramaic and Syriac should be regarded as important independent lines of witness to the original text, alongside that of the Hebrew manuscript tradition as a whole, since, in the majority of passages, these translations were made at a time anterior to the oldest surviving Hebrew manuscripts, and may therefore be regarded as independent, if necessarily indirect, witnesses to the Hebrew text of an earlier period. The purpose of this article is to stand back from the details of textual criticism in order to consider the broader aspects of this use of the ancient versions as witnesses to the text of the Hebrew Bible itself, and to observe a considerable revolution in the actual use of these ancient versions by textual critics of the Hebrew Bible within the last half-century.

A Quiet Revolution

Until the middle of the twentieth century it would hardly be an exaggeration to say that the ancient versions of the Hebrew Bible were regarded primarily as a quarry from which superior readings could be retroverted in passages where the MT is obscure. One has only to glance at the apparatus of the earlier editions of the *Biblia Hebraica*, including to a large extent the fourth edition known as *Biblia Hebraica Stuttgartensia*, to see the extent of this practice. The underlying assumption was the probability that a number of errors must have crept into the scribal transmission of the Hebrew Bible over such a long period of time, and the expectation that, since the ancient versions were translated from a *Vorlage* much earlier than any manuscripts still extant, in many cases the versions would reflect a Hebrew text free of at least the later corruptions. This method is still practised in the textual criticism of the Hebrew Bible, and will always remain one of the important tools available to the critic. At the end of the twentieth century, however, its practice has become much more circumspect, and the number of passages in which the ancient versions are invoked with confidence as providing the basis for textual emendation is greatly diminished. What are the causes of this revolution?

Undoubtedly the first and by far the most important cause was the discovery of Hebrew Bible texts in the Dead Sea area from 1947 onwards. In particular the early publication of the two major Isaiah scrolls (1QIsa[a] and 1QIsa[b]) made it immediately obvious that the scribal transmission of the text had been far more accurate than had been imagined. Apart from certain orthographic differences, such as the spelling of a second person singular suffix with ה after כ, the text was recognizably the same as that of the traditional MT. One immediate consequence of this was an enhanced respect for the accuracy of the MT.

In fact the matter proved somewhat less simple. It gradually emerged that among the texts from the Dead Sea area there were not only recognizable precursors of the MT, but also texts of a different nature, in not a few cases containing readings that differed from the MT but agreed with readings of the LXX. A well-known example is that of various fragmentary texts of the book of Jeremiah from Qumran Cave 4, some of which were closely aligned to the MT while others agreed in a number of readings with the LXX. This phenomenon gave rise to considerable debate, but one thing that emerged clearly was that around the turn of the era there was not one single tradition of the text; on the contrary several divergent text-forms coexisted, of which one, the proto-Masoretic, was later to become the sole authoritative text, and to be reproduced with great fidelity during the following millennium. At the same time the antiquity and the Hebrew origin of a number of the variants attested in the LXX had been demonstrated, and to this extent the earlier readiness to use the LXX and other ancient versions as a quarry for alternative readings to obscure passages in the MT was vindicated.

The perspective, then, has changed considerably. Instead of envisaging a linear development from a pure archetype through a gradual process of corruption to the extant Masoretic tradition, we are now confronted at the turn of the era with several coexisting parallel forms of text, one of which eventually emerged as the standardized text, and was subsequently transmitted with a far higher degree of accuracy than had previously been thought possible. Indeed it is possible to go even further back and state that, by the time when at least some of the books of the Hebrew Bible received recognition as canonical, they already existed in a plurality of text-forms, including in some cases translations into Greek. An interesting example of this is the book of Esther, which in its Greek form came to include six additional passages in relation to the MT, although four of these are generally considered to have originated in Hebrew.[1] At the same time Esther is one of the books whose canonical status continued to be debated within the first two centuries of the CE. This case indicates that no firm boundary exists between what used to be called the higher and lower criticism of the text. Literary development and modification overlapped for a while the process of scribal transmission, and it can sometimes be difficult to determine whether particular modifications are of a literary or a textual nature. This, however, lies beyond the scope of the present article.

One of the ways in which the biblical text came to be amplified was by the addition of individual words or short phrases to clarify the meaning. This can sometimes be documented in the versions. In Hos. 14, for instance, there are two such additions in the Peshitta: 'and say' is introduced at the beginning of v. 4, to indicate that these are the words the repentant Israel is instructed to use, while 'and Ephraim will say' is introduced for similar reasons at the beginning of v. 9. A similar insertion is made in the Targum at the beginning of v. 9: 'The house of Israel will say'. These clarificatory insertions are helpful to the reader in identifying changes of speaker in the text. In v. 3 there is a similar clause in the Hebrew text itself: 'say to him', which may have originated in a similar way, although at an earlier stage, since it is attested in all the ancient texts and versions. The point is that small clarificatory additions of this kind may have begun to be introduced into the text before it became standardized, but that the same process continued in the versions at a later stage in the transmission.

The evidence of the biblical manuscripts from the Dead Sea region directly attests only the consonantal text, because the several systems for recording the vowels had not yet been devised when they were written. It is often argued, no doubt with justice, that the vocalization of the consonantal text was traditional, and had been handed down faithfully by oral tradition for a long time before it was committed to writing. At the same time it is palpably true that there is much greater safeguard in the transmission of a written text than in that of an oral

---

1. For a succinct review of the possible date and provenance of the Additions to Esther, see C.A. Moore, *Daniel, Esther and Jeremiah: the Additions* (AB, 44; Garden City, NY: Doubleday, 1977), pp. 165-67. It is clear that at least four of the six were in existence by the end of the first century CE.

tradition. It is in fact possible to demonstrate that on occasion manuscripts from the Dead Sea region did reflect a different tradition of
vocalization from what became the traditional Masoretic vocalization.
An interesting and well-known example of this can be seen in Isa.
49.17, where 1QIsa[a] reads בוניך ('your builders'), distinguishing it from
the MT בָּנָיִך ('your sons') by the use of the vocalic ו. There is further
evidence for this vocalization in several of the ancient versions.[2] It is, of
course, only in cases where vocalic letters can be used, as they seem to
have been used more extensively in the Qumran scrolls, that such
potential agreements or disagreements in vocalization in relation to that
of the MT can be detected, but the presence of even a small number of
disagreements indicates that the vocalization had not yet been finally
fixed as that found in the Masoretic tradition.

Before the first of the Qumran discoveries another development had
begun, which was to have a considerable effect on the practice of the
textual criticism of the Hebrew Bible. It is apparent that only a
relatively small literary corpus of Classical Hebrew is extant, not very
much more extensive than the Hebrew Bible itself. In such circum-
stances it is hardly surprising that a considerable number of words
occur only once, and that the meaning of many of these should be
uncertain. Biblical Hebrew belongs to the family of Semitic languages,
and has close affinities with several other north-west Semitic languages.
In particular, the discovery and decipherment of the Ugaritic texts gave
a new impetus to the discipline of comparative Semitic grammar and
philology, whose resources came to be increasingly explored in the
middle of the twentieth century in the quest for solutions to uncertain
words and grammatical forms in the Hebrew Bible. Forms such as
enclitic-mem were invoked to explain otherwise apparently obscure
suffixes in the Hebrew Bible, while considerable efforts were made to
extend the knowledge of Biblical Hebrew lexicography by appeal to
possible cognate words in other Semitic languages. In some cases 'new'
meanings proposed on this basis were supported by appeal to one or
more of the ancient versions, which might be thought to reflect awareness in antiquity of the meaning in question. One of the motivations

---

2. See the concise but interesting discussion of this reading by David Flusser,
'The Text of Isa. xlix, 17 in the DSS', in C. Rabin (ed.), *Textus: Annual of the
Hebrew University Bible Project*, II (Jerusalem: Magnes Press, The Hebrew Uni-
versity, 1962), pp. 140-42.

behind this line of research was to reduce the need to resort to con-
jectural emendation of the text itself. When faced with an obscurity in
the Hebrew Bible, critics began to think in terms of the limitations of
our knowledge of the language, and of how it might be extended, rather
than to assume that there was a textual corruption requiring emendation.
The use of the ancient versions in this approach was less extensive but
more positive, for they were now quarried for new insights into the
meaning of obscure words in the Hebrew Bible rather than as a basis
for emending the text itself.

Unfortunately this new approach was not always characterized by the
restraint and concern for objective evidence that was desirable. The
multiplication of suggestions of new meanings led in some cases to an
improbable number of homonyms, while the philological basis of many
of the suggested meanings was flimsy.[3] There will always be a valuable
contribution from this approach, but its practice has to be much more
disciplined than it was in the middle of the twentieth century, and it is
in any case probable that most of the new insights that can be gained
from this source, subject to the availability of further textual material,
have already been garnered. In recent years there has been a welcome
growth in attention to the work of mediaeval Jewish scholars, who
knew Arabic as well as classical and post-classical Hebrew, and who
were often aware of traditions of meaning that had otherwise been lost.[4]
It is probably primarily from this source that further insights into the
meaning of Biblical Hebrew are to be expected. For our present purpose, however, it is important to notice that for different reasons this
approach has had the same effect as the Dead Sea discoveries, namely
an enhancement of respect for the authenticity of the traditional MT and
for the accuracy of its scribal transmission.

In the meantime a further development had begun, which requires
treatment in a new section.

---

3. For a penetrating critique of this approach, see James Barr, *Comparative
Philology and the Text of the Old Testament* (Oxford: Clarendon Press, 1968). See
also the more recent study by J.A. Emerton, 'Comparative Semitic Philology and
Hebrew Lexicography', in J.A. Emerton (ed.), *Congress Volume Cambridge 1995*
(VTSup, 66; Leiden: E.J. Brill, 1997), pp. 1-24.

4. An example of this renewed attention to the insights of Jewish mediaeval
scholars may be seen in the recent commentary of A.A. Macintosh, *Hosea* (ICC;
Edinburgh: T. & T. Clark, 1997).

The Nature of the Versions

During the last half-century there has been a gradual shift of focus from the ancient versions as witnesses to the Hebrew *Vorlage* from which they were translated to their nature and history as literary texts in their own right. The most obvious aspect of this, which had indeed long been recognized, is that the versions, like the Hebrew Bible itself, originated in the pre-printing era, and were subject to the same kind of accidents in the process of transmission. In one respect they were more exposed to accidental corruption than the Hebrew Bible, because their literal text was rarely regarded as sacrosanct to the degree that that of the Hebrew Bible is shown by the Qumran evidence to have been regarded. The constraints towards precise accuracy of detail in the process of copying were less, and at least some scribes felt at liberty to modernize or improve the style of the translation they were copying, or to insert small additions to clarify its interpretation.

Like the Hebrew Bible itself, the versions were transmitted by a process of copying during many centuries, and in no case do we possess the autograph of an ancient version, Yet their value as witnesses to the Hebrew *Vorlage* from which they were translated lies precisely in their wording at the point when the translation was made. A prerequisite of their use in the textual criticism of the Hebrew Bible is therefore the establishment of as nearly as possible the original text of the versions themselves. This entails a process parallel to that of evaluating the direct evidence for the transmission of the Hebrew Bible. In the case of the LXX in particular the text-history is highly complex, and the quest for the original LXX text, the Ur-LXX, has occupied the minds of LXX scholars for a long time.[5] That text-history is complicated by the text-critical work of Origen in antiquity, and by the existence of recensions such as the Lucianic within the transmission of the LXX. The Göttingen LXX in particular has sought to present in its editions an eclectic text, which approximates as closely as possible in the judgement of the respective editors to that of the Ur-LXX. As a working tool for the textual critic of the Hebrew Bible this is invaluable, but at the same time it has to be remembered that it does not infallibly represent the original text produced by the LXX translators, and in individual

5.   See S. Jellicoe, *The Septuagint and Modern Study* (Oxford: Clarendon Press, 1968) for an account of this and other aspects of LXX study.

passages there is still room for differences of opinion among scholars as to what is most likely to be the Ur-LXX text.

There are similar but different problems with regard to the other ancient versions. In the case of the Targums, for instance, they came to be written down only at a relatively late date, after a long period of oral transmission. In any case there were several Targums in existence, and there was a degree of fluidity in their textual content. It is often much harder to be sure when a Targum reading is to be evaluated as a witness to a Hebrew *Vorlage* distinct from the MT than it is in the case of most of the other versions. In the case of the Peshitta the first critical edition to be produced is the still incomplete Leiden Peshitta, begun in the last half-century. The text printed in this edition is determined by an objective standard: the text of the Ambrosian Codex of Milan is reproduced except (a) for obvious errors and (b) in cases where it lacks the support of at least two of the oldest manuscripts. This rule succeeds in excluding most of the eccentric readings of this particular manuscript, but a comprehensive examination of all the manuscripts suggests that the original Peshitta reading is sometimes to be found in the apparatus rather than in the text of the Leiden edition.[6]

In all the versions there remains some uncertainty as to the identity of their original rendering, and this has to be borne in mind in their use as potential witnesses to the text of the Hebrew Bible. Not least allowance has to be made for the possibility of deliberate correction of the text of a version in the course of its transmission to make it conform with the current MT, as in the case of Origen's text-critical work in antiquity. It was not always appreciated that the current MT was not necessarily identical with the Hebrew text from which the original translation had been made. Any reading in a later manuscript of a version that agrees with the MT against the earlier manuscripts of that version may therefore have to be evaluated as a deliberate correction rather than as a genuine survival of an originally more accurate rendering within the transmission history of the version, and it can sometimes be very difficult to determine which is the true evaluation.

A second major question that has to be addressed is the nature and purpose of the individual versions. What kind of translation were the original translators trying to produce and for what purpose? Clearly the degree of precision and accuracy that can be expected will vary

---

6. See, for instance, A. Gelston, *The Peshitta of the Twelve Prophets* (Oxford: Clarendon Press, 1987), ch. 4, esp. pp. 92-93.

considerably in the light of the answer to these questions. At one extreme stand the Targums, where considerable freedom of inter-pretation was employed, often in conformity to the beliefs of a later age. A notorious example is to be found in *Targum Jonathan* of Isa. 19.25, where the descriptions of Egypt as God's people and Assyria as the work of his hands are modified so that they become merely the places respectively from which God had redeemed his people Israel and to which he had subsequently exiled them. The Targums were never intended to be a substitute for the text of the Hebrew Bible. Indeed for a long time they were not allowed to be written down lest they be thought to possess an equivalent authority with the scriptures themselves. They originated as an oral translation/paraphrase accompanying the public reading of the Torah and Haphtorah in the synagogue, and it is clear from the provisions in *m. Meg.* 4.4 that a greater degree of precision was required in the Targumic rendering of the Torah than in that of the Prophets. In the latter as much as three verses of text might be read out before the Targumist offered an interpretation, but in the Torah only one verse might be read at a time to the interpreter. Where the element of interpretation is as high as this it is clear that we are dealing with a version that can be regarded as a witness to the Hebrew text only with caution, particularly outside the Torah, and readings that are peculiar to a Targum text can rarely be regarded as sufficient evidence for a distinctive Hebrew *Vorlage*.

At the opposite extreme is Aquila's Greek version, which survives only in fragments. His translation method was the most literal to be adopted among the ancient versions of the Hebrew Bible. A famous example is his rendering of the particle אֵת, denoting the definite direct object, by the Greek preposition σύν followed by the accusative case, thus distinguishing it from the preposition אֵת, meaning 'with', which he rendered by σύν followed by the usual dative case. This degree of literalness makes Aquila's translation of particular value to modern textual critics of the Hebrew Bible, not least because he tried as far as possible to be consistent in his choice of lexical equivalents. These characteristics make retroversion into Aquila's Hebrew *Vorlage* a rather more confident enterprise than that with respect to the other ancient versions. The drawback is that by Aquila's time the MT was already largely standardized, and his version can therefore offer little evidence for the crucial earlier period of the transmission of the Hebrew text.

These two examples illustrate the need to assess the nature and intended purpose of the individual versions, as well as their respective dates and possible relation to other versions, before we are in a position to make use of them as witnesses to the text of the Hebrew Bible. Most of the ancient versions seem to have arisen at least in part in response to the need for a vernacular text of the scriptures for use in congregations where Biblical Hebrew was not known, whether such congregations were Jewish or Christian. It is always interesting to observe how the ancient translators handled passages in the current Hebrew biblical text that were already perceived as difficult or obscure. At the end of the day the translators were required to produce a translation that would make some kind of sense when it was read out in the context of an act of worship. Often minor difficulties could be dealt with by discreet emendation or by transliterating a particular Hebrew term such as 'ephod', but on some occasions the translators seem simply to have resorted to a guess. Michael Weitzman has drawn attention to this phenomenon in the Peshitta.[7] In such cases as this the modern textual critic of the Hebrew Bible has to beware of attributing too much value to the evidence of a version, since it is unlikely to reflect a distinct Hebrew *Vorlage*.

This brings us to a third and very important aspect of the question, namely the translation methods and techniques adopted by the respective translators of the different ancient versions of the Hebrew Bible. Already in the second century BCE the grandson and translator of Ben Sira recognized that what was written in Hebrew did not convey precisely the same meaning when it was translated into another language.[8] In other words, no translation from one language to another can ever be a full and exact replica of the original text. Every language has its own idioms, and its vocabulary has overtones which do not correspond with precisely the same semantic field in the nearest available equivalent in the receptor language. Translators such as Aquila may aim to produce a version that is as literal an equivalent of the original text as can be achieved in the receptor language. Such translations are of the most practical use to the modern textual critic of the Hebrew Bible, but it may be doubted how effective they were as translations, when used in antiquity by those with no knowledge of the original language. At the

---

7. *The Syriac Version of the Old Testament: An Introduction* (University of Cambridge Oriental Publications, 56; Cambridge: Cambridge University Press, 1999), pp. 36-48.

8. See the Prologue to Ecclesiasticus.

opposite extreme translators such as Symmachus were concerned to produce a version in good readable Greek, that would convey the essential content and sense of the original text, but in such a way that the reader was not all the time conscious of the artificial constraints of a literal translation. The differences between the two approaches are more apparent in matters of syntax than in those of vocabulary, and of course many translations fall between these two extremes. In spite of the advantages of the more literal approach from the perspective of the modern textual critic, it may readily be seen that the policy of using the same lexical equivalent consistently for a particular Hebrew word, regardless of context, might well prove misleading to the reader of the translation alone, for its use in the receptor language might well suggest in some passages a quite different meaning from that of the original text.

At all events it has become clear that a prerequisite of the critical use of a version as a witness to its Hebrew *Vorlage* is a careful study of the methods and technique of that particular version. Such studies can be carried out in a variety of areas. Lexicography is an obvious one, but syntax is also important, particularly in the study of the Greek and Latin versions, where there are considerable differences from Biblical Hebrew. One has only to think of such idioms as the infinitive absolute, the use of the particle אשר, and the tense system of Biblical Hebrew on the one hand, and of the complex use of subordinate clauses, and a fully developed system of tenses with temporal significance in the classical languages on the other, to appreciate that there is considerable scope for doctoral dissertations on various aspects of translation technique. A great deal of work has indeed already been done in this area, much of it in relation to one particular version of one particular biblical book. Much, however, remains to be done. Gradually a fuller picture of the various translation techniques employed in the versions is being built up, and one of the results of this is a recognition that many renderings that in the past have been thought to reflect a distinctive Hebrew *Vorlage* are rather to be explained in terms of translation technique.

One factor that needs to be taken into account is the extent and limitations of the knowledge of Biblical Hebrew on the part of the ancient translators. This can be quite difficult to assess, as may be seen from James Barr's study of Jerome.[9] It arises particularly in matters of

9.   See his article 'St Jerome's Appreciation of Hebrew', *BJRL* 49 (1966–67), pp. 281-302.

lexicography, which in some cases continue to baffle the modern interpreter of the Hebrew Bible. Sometimes it arises also in passages where the syntax has been misunderstood or misconstrued, and as a consequence the whole development of thought in a passage has been lost. One cannot immediately assume that the translator had actual knowledge of the meaning of a rare or obscure word. The practical necessity of producing an intelligible text to be read in public worship led to a certain amount of 'improvement', some of which might be regarded as hypothetical emendation of a supposedly corrupt Hebrew *Vorlage*, while some was pure guesswork in the light of the context. It is unlikely that we shall ever be in a position fully to evaluate this aspect of the process of translation, but the need to bear it in mind as an important factor in making use of the versions for text-critical purposes is patent.

One element in the process of translation that requires separate consideration is the introduction of interpretative material. The ancient versions were not only translations into a different language, but they also came into being in the context of a different community from that in which the Hebrew scriptures themselves came into being. Even in the case of the Targums, although they clearly originated in a Jewish context, their genesis was occasioned by the fact that a large proportion of the Jewish congregation was no longer familiar with Biblical Hebrew, and needed a version in the Aramaic vernacular to supplement the reading of the Hebrew Bible itself in the synagogue. Judaism, moreover, was by no means a static or monochrome religion, and the Targums bear witness to different layers of interpretation within the Jewish community. It is obvious that when translations were made in the context of other communities, such as Greek-speaking Jews of the Diaspora in the case of the LXX, or Christians in the case of the Old Latin and Vulgate, the influence of the community in which the version arose on the interpretative aspect of the translation was bound to be even greater. This is not to be thought to suggest that the translators deliberately 'rewrote' the text of the scriptures, apart from such particular cases as *Targum Jonathan*'s rendering of Isa. 19.25 mentioned above. It is rather the need to recognize the limitations of their knowledge of Biblical Hebrew, and the inevitable if largely unconscious effect of their own beliefs on their interpretation. The history of interpretation of the biblical text can be traced through pesher, midrash and commentary, and through the use made of citations of biblical passages in the course of other writings. An important strand in the history of interpretation must, however, be traced in the renderings of the ancient versions themselves.

One particularly sharp focus of this process of interpretation may be discerned in the controversies between early Christians and Jews. We may begin with a celebrated example, the rendering of עלמה in Isa. 7.14 by παρθένος ('virgin') in the LXX. This rendering was seen in Mt. 1.23 as a prediction of the birth of Jesus of the Virgin Mary. Had the LXX rendering been made after the emergence of Christianity it might well have been regarded as tendentious. The evidence of Ben Sira's grandson's Prologue to Ecclesiasticus, however, makes it clear that the LXX of the prophets was already in existence by the end of the second century BCE. It is hardly surprising, however, in the light of the Christian use made of this particular rendering, that the later Jewish Greek translators (Aquila, Symmachus and Theodotion) replaced it with the more accurate rendering νεᾶνις ('young woman'). While in the great majority of cases παρθένος is used in the LXX to translate בתולה, and it is used only once more (in Gen. 24.43) to translate עלמה, it is also used to translate נערה five times in Gen. 24 and 34. There is no suggestion, therefore, of a different Hebrew *Vorlage* for the LXX rendering of Isa. 7.14. This is simply a case where the word used in the receptor language has a more precise connotation than that in the *Vorlage*, one which proved significant and contentious in the subsequent history of interpretation.

A less well-known example is to be found in Ps. 96.10, which may be rendered, 'Say among the nations: "the LORD reigned"'. Justin Martyr[10] accuses the Jews of excising the words 'from the tree', quoting the text as, 'Say among the nations: "the LORD reigned from the tree"'. Such a text lent itself readily to an interpretation in which 'the LORD' was identified with Jesus, and 'the tree' was seen as a reference to the cross. The evidence for such a reading is slender, and practically confined to the Old Latin tradition,[11] and 'from the tree' must be regarded as a Christian interpolation, probably originating in a pious gloss. The verse so interpreted lingered in Latin Christianity, as may be seen particularly in its citation in this form in the hymn *Vexilla regis prodeunt*. Justin, however, believed that it was an authentic part of the text, and

10. *Dialogue with Trypho* 73.1.

11. See details in H.B. Swete, *Introduction to the Old Testament in Greek* (Cambridge: Cambridge University Press, 2nd edn, 1914), p. 424 n. 1.

had been wilfully excised by the Jews in view of its relevance for Christian apologetic. This example illustrates the importance of disputes between different religious communities using the same scriptures in the history of interpretation, bearing even in extreme cases on the determination of the text itself.

A third and particularly interesting example is to be found in Amos 9.12. The LXX reads ἐκζητήσωσιν in place of יירשו, presupposing a *Vorlage* ידרשו, differing from the MT by only one letter. It also represents the word אדום by τῶν ἀνθρώπων, presupposing a text without the vocalic ו and vocalized differently as אָדָם ('humanity'), rather than as the proper name 'Edom'. The resultant sense of the clause 'that the remnant of humanity may seek' is very different from that of the MT 'that they may possess the remnant of Edom'. It is hardly surprising that the LXX text is followed in the citation in Acts 15.17, but the universalist perspective it displays would also be congenial to the Diaspora Jewish community in which it arose. While it is possible that the LXX rendering represents a deliberate modification of its *Vorlage*, it seems more probable that the differences between the the Hebrew text it presupposes and the MT are to be regarded as textual.[12] The question of interpretation, however, and of the theological outlook of the Diaspora Jewish community, cannot be ignored in the evaluation of the respective readings.

It is clear from these examples, and from many others that might be cited, that the interpretation of the text in accordance with the religious beliefs of the community in which a translation was made was a factor in the process of translation that cannot be ignored. However desirable it might be in theory to separate the establishment of the text from the history of its interpretation, the attempt to determine the original text cannot be carried out without reference to its subsequent hermeneutical treatment, which in a number of cases has inevitably coloured the actual rendering of the text. This is particularly the case in passages where there is obscurity of one kind or another.[13] It is hardly surprising, then,

---

12. For a full discussion of this passage, see B.A. Jones, *The Formation of the Book of the Twelve* (SBLDS, 149; Atlanta: Scholars Press, 1995), pp. 175-91. My own view is that the LXX rendering arose initially through a misreading of *yodh* as *daleth* in the second word of the verse.

13. The Peshitta of Chronicles is an unusual and particularly interesting example. See the study by Michael Weitzman, 'Is the Peshitta of Chronicles a Targum?', in Paul V.M. Flesher (ed.), *Targum and Peshitta* (Targum Studies, 2,

that there has been a substantial shift in the study of the versions to the environment in which they emerged, and to the effect this had on their interpretation and ultimately on their actual translation of the text. Only when all these factors are taken into account can their evidence be properly evaluated for use by the textual critic of the Hebrew Bible.

Conclusion

The most obvious difference in the practice of the textual criticism of the Hebrew Bible during the last half-century is clearly the much higher evaluation of the MT as an authentic witness to the original text of the Hebrew scriptures. The evidence of some of the Qumran biblical manuscripts demonstrates the high standard of fidelity and accuracy in the copying of the MT, while the study of the ancient versions has enabled many variations to be evaluated as interpretative rather than as witnessing to a distinctive Hebrew *Vorlage*. In the case of Hosea, for instance, A. Macintosh is able to report that 'the ancient versions of Hosea were, in the main, confronted with a Hebrew text which differed little from our received text'.[14] It is probably true of all the later ancient versions of the Hebrew Bible that their *Vorlage*, which was consonantal only, differed little from the consonantal MT. In general it is only the LXX that reflects a Hebrew *Vorlage* appreciably older than that which became the standardized MT.

At the same time, as we have seen, the Qumran biblical manuscripts also demonstrate a plurality of textual traditions that evidently co-existed for a time. Some of these show clear agreement with certain readings of the LXX, which are thereby shown to have a basis in the Hebrew tradition. This plurality of textual traditions raises a fundamental question about the nature and object of the practice of textual criticism of the Hebrew Bible, with which we are still only beginning to engage. Was there a single original text of the Hebrew Bible, from which all extant manuscripts and ancient versions are derived? Or does the plurality of textual traditions extend back to the period of the

South Florida Studies in the History of Judaism, 165; Atlanta: Scholars Press, 1998), pp. 159-93. See also his 'From Judaism to Christianity: The Syriac Version of the Hebrew Bible', in Judith Lieu, John North and Tessa Rajak (eds.), *The Jews among Pagans and Christians: In the Roman Empire* (London: Routledge, 1992), pp. 147-73 (150-58).

   14. *Hosea*, p. lxxv.

archetype(s) from which all the extant witnesses stem? In other words, is it still possible to make a clear distinction between the literary evolution of the text and its textual transmission?

The linear model allows us to posit a point at which a particular text reached its 'final form', in which it was recognized as authoritative, and thereafter was transmitted as faithfully as possible without any further intentional modification. If this decisive point was reached prior to the emergence of the ancient versions, the whole textual process could be seen from a historical perspective and, ideally, the original 'final form' of the text could be reconstructed from the extant witnesses. If, on the other hand, as seems to be the case at least in some books or passages, a period of plurality of text-forms preceded the recognition of one particular form as authoritative and normative, is it still possible to determine which is the original text-form? It is necessary here to distinguish between the question which text is canonical and authoritative, which is not a matter for the textual critic,[15] and the question which of two text-forms is the original from which the other was derived. Even if it is impossible to determine which has the earlier attestation, it is sometimes possible with a strong degree of probability to determine the priority of one of the forms on internal grounds. Arguments of a textual nature, such as the probability of an omission through homoioteleuton, may form at least part of the basis of such a judgement.

All these considerations have led the textual critics of the Hebrew Bible today to adopt a more cautious approach to their task. They still aim to recover the 'original text' of the 'final form' of the scriptures, but recognize that in practice it may only be possible to determine the oldest form of text accessible through actual extant manuscripts and the ancient versions. This is the policy underlying the new edition of the *Biblia Hebraica* (BHQ). The MT is generally recognized as the best overall witness, but this does not preclude the recognition of the readings of other ancient manuscripts or of the versions as superior in particular cases. Retroversion from the versions to a putative Hebrew *Vorlage* is seen as a far more complex and imprecise operation than it used to be thought, and precision can often be found only in such matters as the presence or absence of a pronominal suffix. The ancient

---

15. A similar question arose at a later period. Jerome's defence of the *Hebraica veritas* seems self-evidently right to the modern textual critic of the Hebrew Bible. Yet Augustine, while acknowledging that the Hebrew text was the source, held the LXX to be itself inspired and ultimately the authoritative text.

translators for the most part did their best to produce an accurate rendering of their *Vorlage*, but were impeded to some extent by the limitations of their own knowledge particularly of Biblical Hebrew, and by their unconscious presuppositions. This necessitates a careful evaluation of their evidence before it can properly be used as a witness to the text of the Hebrew Bible. Their testimony is important for the history of exegesis, and still to some extent for the determination of the earliest attainable text of the Hebrew Bible, but they have to be used with far more discrimination than was customary half a century ago.[16]

---

16. No attempt has been made to give a comprehensive bibliography. Readers who wish to pursue the subject further will find extensive treatment and full bibliographies in the following two works: M.J. Mulder (ed.), *Mikra: Text, Translation, Reading and Interpretation of the Hebrew Bible in Ancient Judaism and Early Christianity* (Assen: Van Gorcum; Philadelphia: Fortress Press, 1988); M. Saebø (ed.), *Hebrew Bible / Old Testament: The History of its Interpretation.* I. *From the Beginnings to the Middle Ages (Until 1300); Part 1: Antiquity* (Göttingen: Vandenhoeck & Ruprecht, 1996).

GREEK WORDS SHARED BY THE PESHITTA AND TARGUMS TO THE PENTATEUCH

Jan Joosten

One of Michael Weitzman's qualities as a scholar was his ability to take a complicated and controversial theory and make it appear reasonable and straightforward by the sheer accumulation of converging facts dug out in the course of his wide-ranging researches. An instance of this is the theory of a 'fund of Aramaic renderings', transmitted through the ages and available to different circles of interpreters or translators of the Bible in antiquity.[1] Complementing the less controversial explanations invoking shared linguistic reflexes and accidental agreement, the hypothesis of a fund of Aramaic renderings explains the many similarities between the Peshitta and the Targums, while doing away with the need to postulate a direct family relationship between the two.[2] The materials to be presented in the present paper can well be explained in the framework of Weitzman's approach, which is thus shown to be an effective working hypothesis in dealing with one of the more complicated problems in biblical philology.

Some 16 words of Greek (and, in some cases, ultimately Latin) origin occur in the Peshitta Pentateuch and in one or more of the Targums rendering the same Hebrew word in the same passage. Some of these agreements in the use of a Greek equivalent may be fortuitous, that is,

---

1. Cf. M.P. Weitzman, 'Peshitta, Septuagint and Targum', in R. Lavenant (ed.), *Symposium Syriacum VI 1992* (OCA, 247; Rome: PIB, 1994), pp. 51-84, in particular p. 65; reprinted in *idem.*, *From Judaism to Christianity* (JSS Supplement, 8; Oxford: Oxford University Press, 1999), pp. 181-216.

2. Any theory stipulating a direct genetic relationship between the Peshitta and the Targums—i.e. with the Peshitta depending directly on a Jewish Targum or the Targums depending on the Peshitta or with Peshitta and Targum depending on a Palestinian proto-Targum—runs into insuperable problems, cf. Weitzman, 'Peshitta', pp. 60-79.

they merely indicate that Greek influence was strong on different Aramaic dialects of the Late Aramaic phase. Other agreements, however, cannot be explained in this way. They point to the existence of an exegetical tradition on given passages, providing Greek glosses for certain Hebrew technical terms. This tradition seems to have been known to the Syriac and the Aramaic translators independently.[3]

1. *The Evidence*

A list of the words discussed in this study follows. The Greek donor word is given first, followed by its Syriac and Aramaic forms and an approximate English translation. For each word, the Hebrew equivalent or equivalents are noted, MT chapter and verse references given, and the versions where the word is found are listed.[4] Some doubtful cases will be discussed below.

1. βάσις ܒܣܝܣ בסיס 'base'
   ירך Exod. 25.31; 37.17; Num. 8.4 PN
   כן Exod. 39.39 PON

2. βήρυλλος ܒܘܪܠܐ בורלא 'beryl'
   שהם Gen. 2.12; Exod. 25.7; 28.9, 20; 35.9, 27; 39.6, 13 PO[5]

3. γλύφω ܓܠܦ גלף 'to carve, to sculpture'
   פתח (piel) Exod. 28.9 *et alibi* PON[6]

4. καγκέλλον (< cancelli) ܩܢܩܠ קנקל 'latticed screen'
   מכבר Exod. 27.4; 38.4, 30; 39.39 PN

---

3.   Greek words occurring in the Peshitta and in one of the Targums rendering different words have not been included in the present study. For one example of this phenomenon, cf. J. Joosten, 'χαλκηδών', *RHPR* 79 (1999), pp. 135-43.

4.   Hebrew equivalents are referred to by chapter and verse in the MT. Where this differs from the AV's chapter and verse division, the latter follows in brackets. Peshitta is indicated by P. As far as the Targums are concerned, only *Onqelos* (O), *Neofiti* (N) and the Samaritan Targum (S) have been considered. The Fragment Targum, the Genizah fragments and *Pseudo-Jonathan* have been checked, but were found to provide no independent information on the issue under discussion. The Christian Palestinian Aramaic version has been excluded on methodological grounds. Since it was made from a Greek source text, the Greek words occurring in it require a different approach.

5.   The same Greek word is found in the Septuagint in Exod. 28.20.

6.   The Septuagint too uses this word in rendering this Hebrew verb.

5. κέλλα or κέλλιον (< cella) ܩܠܘܬܐ קהלא 'cell, alcove'
   קבה Num. 25.8 PN

6. κοιτών ܩܝܛܘܢܐ קיטון 'inner room'
   חדר Exod. 7.28 (8.3) PN

7. κρίκος ܩܘܪܟܣܐ קירכס 'ring'
   קרס Exod. 26.6, 11 PS[7]

8. λαμπάς ܠܡܦܕܐ למפד 'lamp, torch'
   לפיד Exod. 20.18 PN[8]

9. λεγιών (< legio) ܠܓܝܘܢܐ לגיון 'legion'
   צים Num. 24.24 PN[9]

10. πεῖσαι ܐܬܦܝܣ אטפס 'to be persuaded'
    אות Gen. 34.15, 22, 23 PO

11. πόρπη ܦܘܪܦ פרך 'clasp, hook'
    קרס Exod. 35.11 PON

12. σειρά ܣܝܪܗ סירה 'cord, lasso (?)'
    תחרא Exod. 28.32; 39.23 PN

13. τήγανον ܛܓܢܐ טיגן 'frying pan'
    מחבת Lev. 2.5; 6.14 (21); 7.9 PS[10]

14. τύπος ܛܘܦܣܐ טופסא 'mold, form'
    חרט Exod. 32.4 PN

15. φιάλη ܦܝܠܘܬܐ פיילי 'dish, bowl'
    קערה Exod. 25.29; Num. 7.13, 19, 25, 31, 37, 43, 49, 55, 61, 67, 73, 79, 84 PN[11]

16. χαράκωμα ܟܪܟܘܡܐ כרכומין 'bulwark, siege works'
    מצור Deut. 20.20 PON

---

7. The Greek word is found in the same passages in the Septuagint, whence it has also penetrated into the Christian Palestinian Aramaic version.

8. The word also occurs in the Septuagint of Exod. 20.18.

9. The first part of this verse is translated doubly in *Targum Neofiti*. The Greek word occurs in the second part of the doublet.

10. The same word occurs in these passages in the Septuagint.

11. The Greek word is frequent in the Septuagint, where, however, it renders Hebrew words other than קערה.

This analysis shows that the Peshitta Pentateuch agrees in the use of a Greek word:

- nine times with *Targum Neofiti* exclusively (nos. 1, 4, 5, 6, 8, 9, 12, 14, 15);
- twice with *Targum Onqelos* exclusively (nos. 2, 10);
- four times with *Onqelos* and *Neofiti* (nos. 1, 3, 11, 16);
- twice with the Samaritan Targum exclusively (nos. 7, 13).[12]

2. *Agreements Due to Independent Borrowing from Greek*

A brief review of the principal features of the use of Greek loanwords in Aramaic will establish the background against which these 16 cases should be viewed. Greek words in Aramaic texts are, in general, an index of Hellenistic influence on the ancient Near East.[13] Such influence goes back a long way,[14] but becomes a dominant factor only from the Hellenistic period onward. Alexander's conquests established the Greek tongue in a dominant position—as the language of administration and warfare, and later of commerce, culture and learning—in much of the Aramaeophone area. As a result, Aramaic assimilated certain Greek elements.[15] A few legal, military and commercial terms were borrowed initially, followed rapidly by words and expressions from other areas. By the Middle Aramaic language period (c. 200 BCE to c. 200 CE),[16]

---

12. The figures add up to 17, because 1 was counted twice, the Greek word corresponding to two different Hebrew equivalents.

13. Cf. A. Tal, *The Language of the Targum of the Former Prophets and its Position within the Aramaic Dialects* [Hebrew] (Tel-Aviv: Tel-Aviv University, 1975), pp. 175-86.

14. For Greek words in early Aramaic, cf. K. Kitchen, 'The Aramaic of Daniel', in D.J. Wiseman *et al.* (eds.), *Notes on Some Problems in the Book of Daniel* (London: Tyndale Press, 1965), pp. 31-79; for Greek words in early Hebrew, cf. J.P. Brown, *Israel and Hellas* (BZAW, 231; Berlin: W. de Gruyter, 1995).

15. Socio-linguistic studies have shown that in a bilingual community, the 'high' or prestige language remains relatively untainted by any systematic influences from the relatively 'low' language, while the 'low' language tends to be heavily influenced by the 'high' language, with particular effect on the lexicon. Cf. the material gathered in M. Silva, 'Bilingualism and the Character of Palestinian Greek', *Bib* 61 (1980), pp. 198-219.

16. For the chronology of the phases of the Aramaic language I have followed J.A. Fitzmyer, 'The Phases of the Aramaic Language', in *idem, A Wandering Aramean: Collected Aramaic Essays* (Missoula, MT: Scholars Press, 1979), pp. 57-84.

when local dialects emerged as a means of written expression, all these dialects, Nabataean, Judaean, Palmyrene, Edessene and Hatran, incorporated Greek loanwords.[17] The process persisted into the Late Aramaic phase (200 CE to 700 CE) where, in the words of J. Fitzmyer, a 'mounting influx of Greek words and constructions into almost all dialects of the language' was evident.[18] For Syriac this increase in Greek loanwords has been described; there is also some literature on the influx into Targumic Aramaic.[19]

Some Greek words may have been borrowed by Aramaic before the dialects branched off into distinct written languages.[20] Many others would naturally have been accepted, even at a later stage, by the different Aramaic dialects. In this light, it is not suprising that many Greek words are attested both in Syriac and in Western Aramaic. Nothing prevents the use of such shared loan-words in the respective Bible versions, and it is to be expected that, when they are so used, they would correspond to the same Hebrew word.

Some at least of the agreements between Peshitta and Targums in the use of Greek words are probably due to this process. Such instances simply show that a given meaning was most naturally expressed, in both Syriac and Western Aramaic,[21] by the Greek word in question. The most obvious example is that of the verb ܓܠܦ/גלף, 'to engrave' (no. 3 in the above list). Although a loan from Greek,[22] this word is, in Syriac

---

17. Cf. J.F. Healey, 'Lexical Loans in Early Syriac: A Comparison with Nabataean Aramaic', *SEL* 12 (1995), pp. 75-84; J. Hoftijzer and K. Jongeling, *Dictionary of the North-West Semitic Inscriptions*, Part 1 and 2 (Handbuch der Orientalistik; Leiden: E.J. Brill, 1995). There is unfortunately no index of Greek words in the latter dictionary.

18. Cf. Fitzmyer, 'Phases', p. 62.

19. For a bibliography of Greek words in Syriac, see J. Joosten, 'Greek and Latin Words in the Peshitta Pentateuch. First Soundings', in R. Lavenant (ed.), *Symposium Syriacum VII 1993* (OCA, 256; Rome: Pontificio Istituto Biblico, 1998), pp. 37-47, in particular p. 37 nn. 3, 4 and 5. For Greek words in the Targums, cf. Tal, *Language*, pp. 175-86, and S. Krauss, *Griechische und lateinische Lehnwörter im Talmud, Midrasch und Targum*, Parts 1 and 2 (repr.; Hildesheim: G. Olms, 1987 [1898]).

20. An example would be the Greek word στατήρ, 'stater', attested as a loan-word in Official Aramaic, in Hatran and in Syriac.

21. There is of course considerable dialectal variety among the different Targums. The term 'Western Aramaic' is used here in a general way.

22. The Greek origin of this word has been contested by A. Schall, but still

as well as in Targumic Aramaic, the normal way to express the relevant meaning. The use of the term in the same passages, to render the same Hebrew word, is no more surprising than the agreement between Peshitta and Targums in the use of many indigenous Aramaic words.[23] The agreement flows from the fact that Syriac and Jewish Aramaic are closely related dialects, and needs no explanation on the basis of mutual influence or dependence on common tradition.

Several other agreements listed in section 1 may confidently be ascribed to the linguistic proximity between Syriac and Targumic Aramaic. These include, for instance, למפד/ܠܡܦܐܕܐ, 'lamp, torch' (no. 8),[24] and קיטון/ܩܝܛܘܢܐ, 'inner room' (no. 6): these words are fairly common in both Syriac[25] and Jewish Palestinian Aramaic.[26] Their occurrence in one and the same passage, rendering the same Hebrew word, is unsurprising.

A similar explanation almost certainly applies to the two examples involving the Samaritan Targum. The words קידרס/ܩܐܝܕܪܘܣ (no. 7)[27] and טינא/ܛܝܢܐ (no. 13)[28] are well attested in both Syriac and Western

seems likely and has been upheld in several more recent publications. For the discussion cf., e.g., Tal, *Language*, p. 177.

23. The high degree of verbal coincidence between Peshitta and Targum is well illustrated by the lists collected in J.C. de Moor and F. Sepmeijer, 'The Peshitta and the Targum of Joshua', in P.B. Dirksen and A. van der Kooij (eds.), *The Peshitta as a Translation* (MPIL, 8; Leiden: E.J. Brill, 1995), pp. 129-76. Note, however, that de Moor and Sepmeijer believe that the data indicate dependence of the Peshitta on the Targum.

24. For this loanword in Syriac, cf. Joosten, 'Greek and Latin', p. 39.

25. Apart from the verses under discussion, ܠܡܦܐܕܐ occurs in the Old Testament Peshitta in Gen. 15.17, Judg. 7.16 and Job 41.10; ܩܝܛܘܢܐ in Judg. 15.1, 1 Kgs 1.15 and 2 Kgs 6.12. For occurrences of these words in other Syriac texts, see R. Payne Smith (ed.), *Thesaurus Syriacus* (Oxford: Clarendon Press, 1879–1897); C. Brockelmann, *Lexicon syriacum* (Halle: M. Niemeyer, 2nd edn, 1928).

26. Cf. M. Sokoloff, *A Dictionary of Jewish Palestinian Aramaic of the Byzantine Period* (Ramat Gan: Bar Ilan Press, 1990).

27. In the Peshitta this word is the regular translation equivalent of Hebrew טבעת. It is well attested in Jewish Palestinian Aramaic (cf. Sokoloff, *Dictionary*) and in Christian Palestinian Aramaic (cf. above, n. 7).

28. This word is used again in the Peshitta of Ezek. 4.3 and Jer. 29.22. Information on Samaritan Aramaic is hard to come by, but the word is well attested in Jewish Palestinian Aramaic (cf. Sokoloff, *Dictionary*) and Mishnaic Hebrew.

Aramaic, and this probably accounts for their use to render the same Hebrew word in the same passage.

The question that naturally arises at this point is: If the occurrence of the Greek loan-words discussed above in both the Peshitta and the Targum is a consequence of the linguistic closeness of Syriac and the Aramaic dialect used in the relevant Targums, does this explanation also account for the remaining agreements between the Peshitta and one or more of the Targums? This approach is attractive because it fits well with the linguistic profile of the Aramaic versions, and dispenses with any complicated theory of mutual dependence on a non-attested source. There are, however, some weighty arguments against this simple solution, as will be demonstrated by the examples given in the following section.

3. *Greek Words Going Back to an Exegetical Tradition*

Two main arguments may be advanced for deriving some of the Greek words of the Peshitta and the Targums from an existing tradition. First, some of the Greek words listed are not obvious equivalents of the Hebrew words they render, thus suggesting that the choice may have been influenced by exegetical tradition. Second, some of the words are rare or even unknown in the Aramaic dialects in which they occur, so that the theory of coincidental use developed in section 2 is inapplicable. A further argument is that some of these words occur in Symmachus's version of the Pentateuch.

3.1. *The Greek Word Is not an Obvious Equivalent*
Provenance from an exegetical tradition may be suggested, first, by the unexpected interpretation of the Hebrew word in question implied by the choice of the Greek term. Several instances have been identified and discussed by Y. Maori.[29] A striking example is that of לגיון/ܠܓܝܘܢܐ, 'legion', in Num. 24.24 (no. 9).[30] The Hebrew of the first part of the verse, וצים מיד כתים, is admittedly oracular; nonetheless, rendering so as to imply a prophecy concerning the coming of (presumably Roman[31])

---

29. Y. Maori, *The Peshitta Version of the Pentateuch and Early Jewish Exegesis* [Hebrew] (Jerusalem: Magnes Press, 1995).
30. Cf. Maori, *Peshitta*, pp. 191-92.
31. Cf. Maori, *Peshitta*, p. 191.

legions indicates a leap in interpretation. The occurrence of this interpretation in both the Peshitta and the Palestinian Targums, where the theme is further developed, cannot be due to chance. An ancient Jewish exegetical tradition has clearly been adopted by both the Syriac translators and the Targumists. The Greek, and ultimately Latin, loan-word ܠܓܝܘܢ/לגיון appears to have been part and parcel of this tradition.

Other words implying a choice which may have been determined by an exegetical tradition include ܛܘܦܣܐ/טופסא, 'mould' (no. 14),[32] and ܐܬܛܦܣ/אטפס, 'to be persuaded' (no. 10),[33] both of which render Hebrew lexemes that proved difficult to early interpreters. The first renders the difficult Hebrew word חרט, to which have been ascribed a variety of meanings including 'stylus',[34] 'cloak',[35] 'mould',[36] and other interpretations.[37] The second corresponds to the Hebrew verb אות, interpreted as 'to become like' in the Septuagint,[38] 'to get involved with' in *Targum Neofiti*,[39] 'to agree, be in agreement with' in a fragment from the Geniza,[40] and 'to be persuaded' in other versions.[41] In the light of this exegetical diversity, it is noteworthy that Peshitta and

32. Cf. Maori, *Peshitta*, pp. 265-66. Maori hesitates to ascribe the agreement of Peshitta and Targum to a common tradition.

33. This word is not treated by Maori, but it is signalled by S.P. Brock, 'Some Aspects of Greek Words in Syriac', in A. Dietrich (ed.), *Synkretismus im syrisch-persischen Kulturgebiet* (AAWG, 96; Göttingen, 1975), pp. 80-108, p. 85.

34. Thus in the Septuagint, γραφίς, on the basis no doubt of Isa. 8.1.

35. Thus in the first rendering of Targum Pseudo-Jonathan and in the Samaritan Targum, cf. 2 Kgs 5.23.

36. Cf. also the rendering in the Vulgate: *formavit opere fusorio*.

37. Ibn Ezra takes the word to mean 'form', with explicit reference to Isa 8.1 where the same interpretation is proposed. Yet another rendering is זיפא in *Targum Onqelos*, a word that is itself difficult to interpret.

38. Cf. below, section 3.3. In 2 Kgs 12.9, however, the Septuagint renders the verb συμφωνέω 'to agree'.

39. *Neofiti* uses the verb אתערב in Gen. 34.15, 22, 23, while a fragment from the Genizah uses it in v. 22 only (for vv. 15 and 23 in this fragment, cf. the following note). It is to be noted that in Qumran Hebrew the verb אות in CD 20.7 is equivalent to the verb התערב in the parallels 1QS 7.24-25 and 8.23.

40. The verb אשתוי is found in vv. 15, 23 in a fragment from the Genizah and in the Samaritan Targum; the Vulgate's rendering in v. 23, *adquiescamus*, also belongs here.

41. Thus the Peshitta and *Targum Onqelos* (but cf. n. 45 below), and Symmachus in v. 22. For the latter cf. section 3.3. below.

Targum arrived at the same interpretation in these passages. That this interpretation was expressed by means of the same Greek word is too striking to be due to chance.

3.2. *The Greek Loan Is Poorly Attested*

A second reason for assuming an exegetical tradition underlying the choice of certain loan-words is that some of these words are not otherwise well attested in Syriac and/or Jewish Aramaic. A good example from Syriac is ܩܘܠܐ (no. 4), unattested except in the biblical passages listed above, and in exegetical comments on these verses. Its etymology is contested: in Payne Smith's *Thesaurus* the word is connected with Latin *craticula*, 'small grate', while Brockelmann ventures a derivation from Greek κλῆθρα, 'bars'. In my opinion, the occurrence of the word קַנְקֵל in the Palestinian Targums, in the same passages, is conclusive evidence of a derivation of both words from καγκέλλον, as already suggested by some native Syriac lexicographers.[42] The formal deterioration is remarkable neither with loan-words in general nor with Greek words in Syriac in particular.[43] Another example of a Greek word poorly attested in Syriac is ܦܘܪܟܐ, 'clasp' (no. 11).[44]

In Jewish Aramaic, the most striking example is certainly סירה, 'cord' (no. 12). This word seems to be unattested in Jewish Aramaic, except for its occurrence in the rendering of Hebrew תחרא in Exod. 28.32 and 39.23 in the Palestinian Targums. The same applies to אטפס (no. 10).[45]

It is very unlikely that ܩܘܠܐ and ܦܘܪܟܐ were used in the Peshitta under the influence of the Targumic tradition while, conversely, סירה and אטפס were taken by the Targumists from the Syriac version, and coincidence is an unlikely explanation of such examples. It would be just plausible to suggest that, for instance, ܩܘܠܐ was a well-established loan-word in early Syriac, and that only by chance is it not attested

42. Cf. Payne Smith (ed.), *Thesaurus Syriacus*, col. 3760.

43. Cf. Joosten, 'Greek and Latin', pp. 38-39.

44. The word is attested also in some manuscripts of 1 Macc. 10.89 where the Greek text has the same word.

45. The form of the verb in *Targum Onqelos* to Gen. 34.15, 22, 23 is, as far as I can see, unique in Targumic Aramaic. It is also noteworthy that the meaning of the loanword in Jewish Aramaic is usually 'to be pacified', or a similar sense. If the meaning in *Onqelos* is 'to be persuaded', as in the Peshitta, the verb is also unique semantically.

elsewhere. Such an explanation, however, is not entirely convincing for any individual example, and becomes even less probable when it needs to be repeatedly invoked. A more likely explanation is that these words are not really loan-words at all, but rather foreign words handed down in an exegetical tradition. Translation into another language was a convenient approach to the interpretation of difficult or rare Hebrew words such as קרס or תחרא.[46] The prestige of the Greek language, and the richness of its vocabulary, may have led, some time before the end of the first century CE, to the compilation of a list of Greek glosses explaining specific Hebrew words in the Pentateuch. If indeed there was such a list, the translators of the Peshitta and the Targumists appear to have made use of it independently, employing the same Greek term to render the same Hebrew word.[47]

This hypothesis would explain the picture in *Targum Neofiti* to Num. 25.8, where a transliterated Greek word has apparently been misunderstood.

MT			ויבא אחר איש ישראל אל הקבה
			And he went after the man of Israel into the alcove.
N			ועל בתר גברא בר ישראל לגו קהלא
			And he went after the man of Israel into the *qhl'*.

Sokoloff does not list this attestation of קהלא in a separate entry, implying that he regards it as an instance of the well-known homograph meaning 'gathering, congregation'.[48] There is no reason to think that earlier readers of the Targum understood the word differently. However, the meaning 'congregation' fits the context poorly, and diverges markedly from the Hebrew. In the light of the Peshitta's *qlyt'*, it is very probable that the Targum, too, reflects the Greek word κέλλα (or κέλλιον). The he in *qhl'* may originally have been intended as a transcription of Greek epsilon;[49] alternatively, it may have been added, or

46. This method is well illustrated by the Fragmentary Targum, manuscript V, to Exod. 27.4, where the Hebrew word מכבר is glossed by means of the Greek (or Latin) loanword קנקל.

47. Some words occurring in this hypothetical list may have been taken up in the Peshitta but not in the Targums, or vice versa. For some other possible examples in the Peshitta, cf. Joosten, 'Greek and Latin', p. 46 n. 48.

48. Cf. Sokoloff, *Dictionary*.

49. As perhaps in סנהדרין < συνέδριον; cf. S.E. Fassberg, 'The Orthography of the Relative Pronoun -שה in the Second Temple and Mishnaic Periods', *Scripta classica israelica* 15 (1996), pp. 240-50.

substituted for another letter, by a scribe who did not correctly identify the word. Be that as it may, the text of the Targum may be accounted for by positing that it incorporated a Greek word in Hebrew characters, which was later misunderstood.[50]

3.3. *The Testimony of Symmachus*

Further support for the view that some of the Greek words contained in Peshitta and Targums derive from an exegetical tradition comes from Symmachus's version of the Pentateuch. Symmachus's version is a Jewish revision of the Septuagint dating from the second century CE.[51] This makes it more or less contemporary with the Peshitta and with *Targum Onqelos*.[52] *Targum Neofiti* represents a later stage in the Targumic tradition, but all authorities agree that it often reflects archaic elements. It is therefore of interest that two of the words discussed above in sections 3.1. and 3.2. also occur in Symmachus.

אות πείθομαι
Gen. 34.22   אך בזאת יאותו לנו האנשים האלה לשבת אתנו
LXX μόνον ἐν τούτῳ **ὁμοιωθήσονται** ἡμῖν οἱ ἄνθρωποι τοῦ κατοικεῖν μεθ᾽ ἡμῶν

The verb אות occurs three times in Gen. 34, in vv. 15, 22, 23. The Septuagint renders with ὁμοιόω, 'to become like', throughout. Symmachus's version has εὐνοήσομεν, 'we will be kindly disposed', instead of ὁμοιωθησόμεθα, in v. 15, while in v. 22 it reads πεισθήσονται, 'they will be persuaded', for the Septuagint's ὁμοιωθήσονται; Symmachus's reading in v. 23 is not known. The rendering in v. 22 clearly agrees with that of the Peshitta and *Targum Onqelos* in all three verses.

---

50. Another possible instance of this phenomenon occurs in *Targum Pseudo-Jonathan* to Exod. 32.4, where we find the word טופרא, 'nail, pencil', corresponding to the Hebrew word חרט. This is probably a simple corruption of the word טופסא as found in *Neofiti*.

51. Cf. A. Salvesen, *Symmachus in the Pentateuch* (JSS Monograph, 15; Manchester: Manchester University Press, 1991).

52. For the date of the Peshitta, cf. M.P. Weitzman, *The Syriac Version of the Old Testament: An Introduction* (University of Cambridge Oriental Publications, 56; Cambridge: Cambridge University Press, 1999); for the date of *Targum Onqelos*, cf. W.F. Smelik, *The Targum of Judges* (OTS, 36; Leiden: E.J. Brill, 1995).

תחרא σειρά/σειρωτόν

Exod. 28.32 והיה פי ראשו בתוכו שפה יהיה לפיו סביב מעשה ארג

כפי תחרא יהיה לו לא יקרע

LXX καὶ ἔσται τὸ περιστόμιον ἐξ αὐτοῦ μέσον, ᾦαν ἔχον κύκλῳ τοῦ περιστόμιου, ἔργον ὑφάντου, τὴν συμβολὴν συνυφασμένην ἐξ αὐτοῦ, ἵνα μὴ ῥαγῇ

The difficult כפי תחרא יהיה לו has been rendered in the Septuagint, apparently rather freely, as 'woven together in the joining of the same piece' (Brenton). For the phrase συμβολὴν συνυφασμένην Symmachus and Theodotion substitute σειρωτόν 'bound (?), twisted (?), hemmed (?)'.[53] Although this Greek word is not otherwise attested, it is clearly related to the Greek word σειρά which is reflected by the rendering in the Peshitta and *Targum Neofiti*.

It is impossible to prove that these suggestions are correct; nonetheless, the most likely explanation for the agreement of Peshitta, Targum and Symmachus in each of these two cases is that the rendering by means of the Greek word in question had been previously established in an exegetical tradition of which translators in each group availed themselves independently. These two examples thus support the hypothesis advanced above.[54]

4. *Conclusions*

The 16 instances where the Peshitta agrees with one or more of the Targums in the use of a Greek word cannot all be similarly explained. Several indicate the close linguistic relationship of Syriac with Western Aramaic dialects. The Greek loan-words involved have been thoroughly assimilated into the Aramaic dialects in question and in fact function as Aramaic words. The agreement between Peshitta and Targums here is no more remarkable than their agreement in the use of many indigenous Aramaic words.

There are, however, a number of agreements between the Peshitta and the Jewish Targums which cannot be explained in this way, but must indicate an established exegetical tradition. It seems probable that this tradition, circulating in a Semitic milieu, listed Greek equivalents

53. The word seems to be a hapax legomenon in Greek, cf. LSJ, p. 1589.

54. Another striking agreement between the Peshitta and Symmachus is the use of the Greek word χρῶμα, 'colour', to render Hebrew עצם in Exod. 24.10. This rendering appears to be unattested in the Targumic tradition.

for a number of difficult words in the Hebrew Pentateuch. The renderings involved are, therefore, not really loan-words in the precise sense of the term, but rather foreign words, that is, Greek words in Semitic transcription employed in an Aramaic text. The occasional misunderstanding of these words during the later course of transmission supports this suggestion.

Thus, the Greek words shared by Peshitta and Targums to the Pentateuch epitomize the relationship of these versions with one another. Because these versions are all more or less contemporary Aramaic translations of the same Hebrew text there is a relatively high degree of coincidental agreement. A number of agreements, however, are due not to chance but to the fact that the Syriac translators and the Jewish Targumists have drawn on the same treasure of traditional Jewish exegesis.

MULTIDIMENSIONAL SCALING (MAPPING) OF PESHITTA
MANUSCRIPTS OF NUMBERS AND DEUTERONOMY

Donald Walter

From his 1974 dissertation at the University of London, 'A Statistical
Approach to Textual Criticism, with Special Reference to the Peshitta
of the Old Testament', to his posthumous *The Syriac Version of the Old
Testament, An Introduction, Appendix III*, M.P. Weitzman was concerned with providing multidimensional maps as a means of examining
the relations among clusters of manuscripts, and as an alternative to the
construction of trees. Articles such as his 'The Tradition of Manuscripts: A New Approach', in 1978, to 'The Analysis of Manuscript
Traditions: Isaiah (Peshitta Version) and the Gospel of Matthew', in
1989, helped to make the application of this important statistical
approach better known. For the dissertation itself he wrote a computer
program in ALGOL which took his basic data and generated the actual
maps. Subsequently, with the ready availability of appropriate statistical
analysis software, he recommended the use of commercial programs.

In his dissertation and in his 1988 'The Originality of Unique Readings in Peshitta Ms. 9a1', delivered initially as a Peshitta Institute Symposium presentation, he gave special attention to the value of the unique
readings of the MS 9a1.

In a monograph on Kings co-authored with Konrad Jenner, Editor-in-
Chief of the Peshitta Institute, awaiting publication in the Peshitta Institute's Monograph Series, I have devoted a great deal of attention to 9a1,
providing as well three-dimensional maps summarizing certain of the
manuscript relations. For this contribution I have chosen to apply mapping to Numbers and Deuteronomy where 9a1 is available, as well as
5b1, which at least for Genesis and Exodus (where 9a1 is not available)
has many of the characteristics associated with 9a1. The text of Genesis
and Exodus in MS 5b1 was copied by the scribe John of Amid in 463/4.
Although his text of 5b1 has been studied a number of times, those

studies lie outside the scope of this investigation.[1] MS 5b1 is not extant for Leviticus, and for Numbers and Deuteronomy it is from a different hand, and, despite its importance as such an early MS, reflects a different text type. For the sake of examining its relationships with 9a1 and the Hebrew, as well as the other MSS, these books are ideal for conducting a multidimensional scaling investigation. The extensive introductions in the Peshitta Institute (of Leiden University) Edition of the Old Testament in Syriac by A.P. Hayman, and W.M. van Vliet, provide comments on the manuscripts that can be checked and modified in the course of this study.

The investigation has been intentionally restricted to shared variants in the published edition of the Peshitta Institute as found in the first and second apparatuses of the 1991 volume.[2] Orthographic variations are not presented there (although they would have been useable for mapping purposes), and so do not belong to this study. Although Weitzman has consistently said that unique readings should be included when they agree with the assumed Hebrew original[3] (since the Hebrew and the manuscript thus constitute a shared reading) this has intentionally not been done here. In Kings, for instance, it would have made arguments for the superiority of the 9a1 text based solely upon shared readings (with other Syriac MSS) circular. Instead 'shared readings' specifically means readings shared with other Syriac MSS. The Edition presents variants in a certain format, but for the purpose of this analysis sometimes a different analysis is better, thus giving a variant count similar to but not identical with that of the Edition. For example, a transposition (1 variant) might occasionally be better treated as an omission and an addition (2 variants). A few cases of variants which only have limited

---

1.   Notable among the more recent are M.D. Koster's *The Peshitta of Exodus: The Development of its Text in the Course of Fifteen Centuries* (Studia Semitica Neerlandica, 19; Assen: Van Gorcum, 1977) and R.B. ter Haar Romeny's 'Techniques of Translation and Transmission of the Earliest Text Forms of the Syriac Version of Genesis', in P.B. Dirksen and A. Van der Kooij (eds.), *The Peshitta as a Translation* (MPIL, 8; Leiden: E.J. Brill, 1995), pp. 177-85.

2.   D.J. Lane, A.P. Hayman, W.M. van Vliet, J.H. Hospers, H.J.W. Drijvers and J.E. Erbes, *The Old Testament in Syriac According to the Peshitta Version*, Part I, fascicle 2; Part II, fascicle 1b (Leiden: E.J. Brill, 1991).

3.   The Hebrew *Vorlage* for the Peshitta of Numbers and Deuteronomy is presumed to be sufficiently close to the Massoretic Text that it can be used for the comparison with the Peshitta variants.

support from some late (eleventh century and later) manuscripts were ignored.

Koster, in his monumental study of the Peshitta of Exodus,[4] distinguished between 'major' and 'minor' variants; 'minor' variants included all alterations in prepositions, alterations in connection with an initial dalath or waw, alterations in the endings or prefixes of words (including nouns and verbs) and matters involving *seyame*—as well as orthographic items. There is a certain arbitrariness to any such distinction; after all, sometimes the addition of a conjunction changes the syntax, and many or most 'major' variants are quite unimportant. Still the initial data was classified as 'minor' or 'major' and indeed provision was made for identifying some of the 'major' variants as being possibly more significant. Substitution of phrases, syntactical changes, transpositions and certain transformations, vocabulary replacements and substitutions were often thought to be less likely to have happened more than once in the transmission of MSS, and might be of a higher level of significance. No nice term like 'minor' or 'major' however suggests itself for that category.

A decision was made in each case whether the Hebrew text was relevant for deciding probable originality between (or among) the variants, and if it was relevant, which text (the lemma or a variant) it supported. Thus, often, but by no means always, the presence or absence of a conjunction in the Hebrew is relevant for deciding which Syriac reading is original. The Hebrew is irrelevant for deciding whether to favor a Syriac reading with an anticipatory pronoun or one without it. Generally the Hebrew is treated as *irrelevant* for cases of vocabulary substitution where one of the equivalent Syriac words has the same root as the Hebrew. The use of the same root as the Hebrew is not good evidence that that is the best Syriac reading, although such an assumption has been unwarrantedly made on occasion in other studies. Indeed there are several cases in this study where a reading found only in eleventh and twelfth century MSS has a root (or makes a vocabulary distinction) corresponding to that of the Hebrew, and against the rest of the tradition, though those cases are not conclusive evidence that the youngest MSS here, alone, preserve original readings.[5] Generally, then, in cases of

---

4.   Koster, *Peshitta.*
5.   E.g. in Deut. 32.27 all the older MSS have 'enemy' and 'enemies' where the Hebrew has 'enemy' and 'adversaries'; 10b1-12b1, however, renders with 'enemy'

doubt, the Hebrew has been regarded as irrelevant for deciding for originality among vocabulary alternatives.

In constructing maps, a ratio of dissimilarities is obtained by counting the number of cases where a given pair of MSS is both present and legible, and the number of times they disagree.[6] For this project the actual counting and calculating of the ratios is done in a computer program written by me; the ratios are then analyzed and maps generated in NCSS (Number Cruncher Statistical System) 2000 by Jerry Hintze.[7] Some of the maps are generated through Metric MDS (Multi-Dimensional Scaling) seeking to minimize *stress*[8] for a map of a certain number of dimensions (here two) defined in terms of observed distances (dissimilarities) and their relationship to the assumed true distances. Other maps are generated through Non-Metric MDS which only uses the rank order of the dissimilarities. All MDS maps will be appropriately labeled as to whether Metric MDS or Non-Metric MDS was used. On all the maps the goodness-of-fit stress statistic is included under the Metric/Non-Metric label. A rule of thumb is that values below 0.05 are acceptable, and below 0.01 are good for either procedure.[9]

and 'adversaries'. A rare case like this is not enough to demonstrate that the late MSS, without any ancient support, have preserved the original vocabulary of the Peshitta. In Deut. 31.28 'elders' in the Hebrew is rendered as 'elders' only by 5b1 and 10b1-12b2. The 'heads' of the other MSS is unlikely to be original, since only one other place in the Torah is Hebrew 'elder' rendered by 'heads'.

6. For the purposes of this analysis 8a1* when marked *l.n.*, when there is only a lemma and a single variant, is assumed to provide support for the reading not supported by its corrector.

7. Jerry L. Hintze, *NCSS 2000: User's Guide* (3 vols.; Kaysville, UT: NCSS, 1998). Chapter 59 (pp. 1221-38) and the extensive bibliography of ch. 120 give an impressive description of the mathematical basis of the procedure, although Weitzman's own treatments are more than adequate.

8. 'Stress' is a measure of 'goodness of fit'; the lower the 'stress' generally the better. If a cartographer tries to represent the location of cities that are far apart on a sphere with a flat map, there is inevitably distortion. In plotting MSS if there are only 4 MSS they can be perfectly fitted onto a 3 dimensional plot; 12 MSS would need 11 dimensions for a perfect fit. Since only 2 or 3 dimensional maps are actually useable, distortion (measured by stress) is inevitable. If the stress is low enough the map is still useable. For the theoretical and mathematical details of how stress is actually computed, see n. 7.

9. For each of the procedures there are some additional measures (for Metric MDS the cumulative percent of the Eigenvalue and the Pseudo R-squared index; for Non-Metric MDS the Percent Rank Maintained and the Dissimilarity Fit Plot);

Maps have been prepared for Numbers and for Deuteronomy based on MSS extensively available for both, and separate maps for all Numbers MSS which are extensively extant, and similarly for Deuteronomy (where the situation turns out to be considerably more complex than for Numbers). Another map is based solely upon information from inscriptions and subscriptions.

No maps are provided for which each pair of MSS shown do not overlap; that is, there are no cases shown where a dissimilarity ratio cannot be calculated for each pair of MSS. Although Weitzman observes there are ways of mapping MSS for which there is incomplete data, a pair of maps involving 6k5 for Deuteronomy suggests that that is potentially very misleading.

Some maps are labeled Hebrew Irrelevant, and some Hebrew Relevant. Maps marked as Hebrew Irrelevant (which necessarily have more available cases of shared variants) include all the appropriate shared variants; of course when the Peshitta MSS on those maps are compared to the Hebrew to get dissimilarity ratios, the Hebrew for that purpose does have to be relevant. It is only when the MSS are compared to each other that the relevance of the Hebrew is ignored. For maps marked Hebrew Relevant only shared variants where the Hebrew is relevant to deciding originality are considered. For instance, a map of all shared variants including the presence of anticipatory pronouns could be made. The Hebrew would never be relevant to those cases, but there would be other cases where it was relevant so the Hebrew could be plotted on the map.

Numbers

12 MSS are common to both Numbers and Deuteronomy. Two maps are shown for them. As usual the maps can be rotated or flipped without making any difference.

The maps generated when the Hebrew is relevant, and for major variants whether the Hebrew is relevant or irrelevant look very similar, although there is no statistical measure for similarity of maps. Maps generated with metric and non-metric procedures are very similar too.

while they have been considered in the preparation of this article, no information from them is included here.

Plot 1

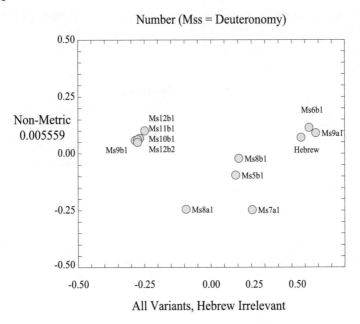

Plot 2

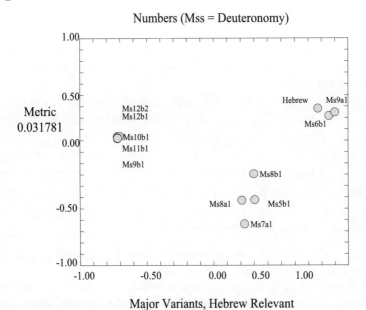

When all the Numbers MSS for which extensive data is available and for which arguments *e silentio* may be made are mapped, Plot 3 is obtained.

Plot 3

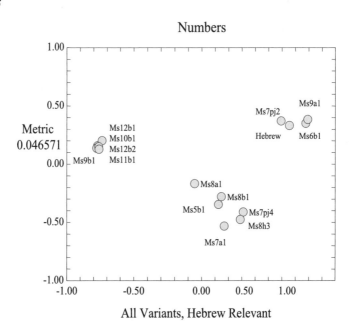

The observations made for Plots 1 and 2 similarly apply here. The relative positions of 8a1 and 5b1 are a little different when a non-metric procedure is used.

Hayman[10] observes that 6b1, 7pj2, and 9a1*fam* share a distinctive form of the text, 7pj2 in an extreme form. MS 8b1 and less often 5b1 share this distinctive form. The map certainly shows the grouping of 7pj2 with 6b1 and 9a1, and also that it is somewhat set apart, although Hayman's legitimate claim of an 'extreme form' rests on its 71 unique readings (48 of which agree with the MT).[11] Plot 1 is more compatible

10. All references are to the appropriate MS descriptions to his Introduction to Numbers in the Leiden edition previously cited.

11. Num. 1.20-42 illustrates this rather well. When other MSS add 'in Israel' to 'all who go out with the host' seven times 7pj2 and 9a1 follow the Hebrew with the shorter text, 6b1 also follows the Hebrew in six of the seven places, and 8b1 twice.

with Hayman's claim regarding 8b1 and 5b1 than Plot 3, although even there they are close together.

Hayman's observation of the close relation of 7a1 and 8h3 is confirmed, and he correctly puts 7pj4 and 8a1 in the same group of MSS. Plot 3 shows 7pj4 right next to 7a1 and 8h3, and 8a1 on the other side of the 5b1/8b1 pair, but does make all of them part of the same larger cluster. For Plot 1 the 5b1/8b1 pair takes an intermediate position.

The map shows that the Nestorian and Western MSS which follow the late 'standard' text are very close together, although maps can be generated from these MSS alone to create a spread.

Deuteronomy

The situation for Deuteronomy is more complex.

Plot 4

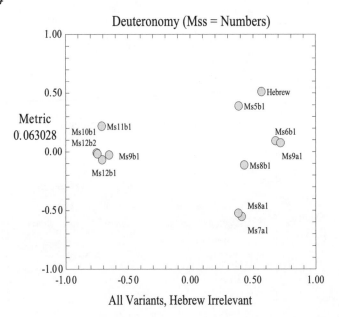

In addition five other times in those verses only 7pj2 retains the shorter reading of the Hebrew.

Plot 5

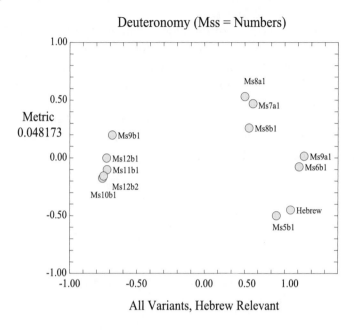

Deuteronomy (Mss = Numbers)

Plot 6

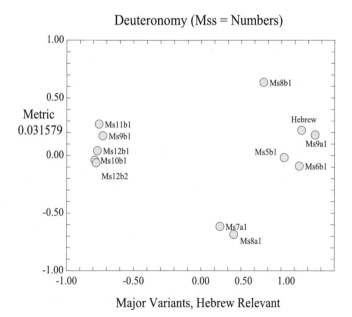

Deuteronomy (Mss = Numbers)

These maps agree in placing 7a1 and 8a1 together, and far from 8b1 (more true of Plot 6 than 4 and 5). The Nestorian and late standard text MSS are more scattered than for Numbers. MS 5b1 is especially close to the Hebrew in Plot 4 where 6b1 and 9a1 are surprisingly far off. Plots 7 and 8, based solely on 'minor' variants, make this much clearer. MS 5b1 is very close to the Hebrew but 6b1 and 9a1 are rather far off. Since 8b1 is clustered with 7a1 and 8a1, it is evidently the agreement on 'minor' variants which explains the relative closeness of 8b1 to the other two in Plots 4 and 5.

Probably Plot 6 is the best general map to use (and it has the lowest stress index) for Deuteronomy. MSS 7a1 and 8a1 are close to each other, and far from 8b1 (which is not really close to anything, but about as far from the Hebrew as it is in Numbers); 5b1 (which is not close to 8b1, unlike the position in Numbers) looks as though it belongs with 6b1 and 9a1, but this may be deceptive and certainly is not the case in Plot 7.

Since there are several ancient MSS partially intact for Deuteronomy, with little overlap (and therefore without reliable dissimilarity ratios) several maps will be required.

Plot 7

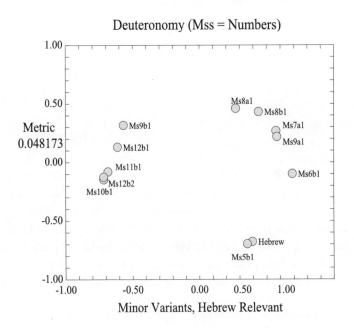

Plot 8

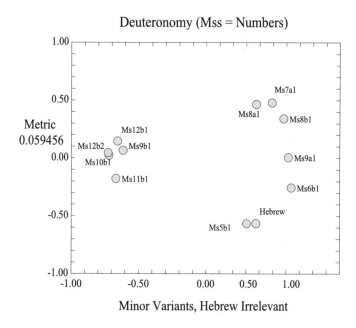

Plot 9

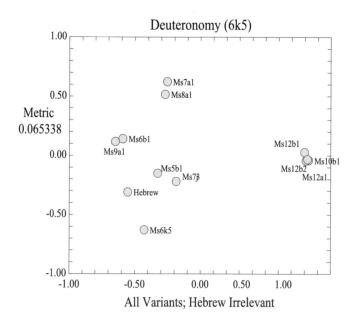

Plot 10

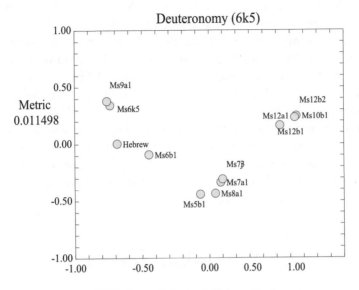

All Variants, 6k5 extant, Hebrew Irrelevant

Plots 9 and 10 have significant differences; MSS 6k5 and 9a1 are in fact extremely close (where 6k5 is extant), yet Plot 9 (with its poor stress index) places them far apart. MSS 7j3 and 5b1 are far from 7a1 and 8a1 in Plot 9. Instead of plotting 6k5 on a map where the other MSS are placed according to their relations with each other across all of Deuteronomy, Plot 10 (with a good stress index) only uses the passages where 6k5 is present (some 25 cases) for its scaling. MS 5b1 is relatively far from the Hebrew, but is part of the group containing 7a1, 7j3, and 8a1.

Probably in plotting MSS that are largely missing, mapping should be restricted to the MSS available for the extant sections. The relations among MSS mapped for a small area need not appear the same as when they are mapped over an extended number of chapters.

Rather than present maps for those places where 6h6 is extant, and then where 7j3 is, and then where 8b1 is (with versions of the maps for all shared variants and for major variants, and with the Hebrew Relevant and for the Hebrew Irrelevant—though all of these have been generated in preparing this study), a few representative maps may suffice, beginning with Plot 11 for those shared major variants, Hebrew

Relevant, where both 6h6 and 7j3 are available simultaneously.[12]

In Plot 11, based on 34 cases, the MSS of the Nestorian and late Western standard text tradition are tightly packed. MS 12a1 in Deuteronomy is simply part of that tradition. (In Numbers no conclusion *e silentio* could be drawn, and so no use of the MS could be made.) MS 8b1 is part of a loose group containing 9a1 and 6b1, and is quite far removed from 8a1. MS 6b1 and 6h6 are far apart, and 5b1 and 7a1 none too close (unlike Plot 10).

When a plot is made of those 35 cases (Plot 12) where 6h6 and 8b1 are present, the variants are major, and the Hebrew is relevant, 5b1 is closest to the Hebrew, 8b1 is to one side, and 9a1 and 6b1 (which are close) are on the other. MS 7j3 stands further off from them, and 8a1, 7a1, and 6h6 further off. Note the distance between 6b1 and 6h6.

Plot 11

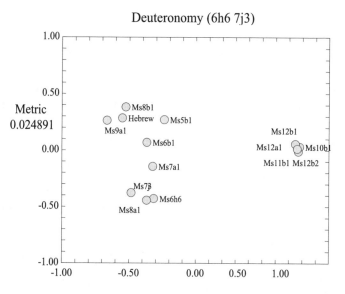

Deuteronomy (6h6 7j3)

Major Variants, 6h6 7j3 intersect; Heb. Relevant

12. A comparison with Plot 13 where 7j3 is extant, the variations are major, and the Hebrew is relevant is informative. It differs from Plot 11 mainly in the relative positions of 6b1 and 6h6!

Plot 12

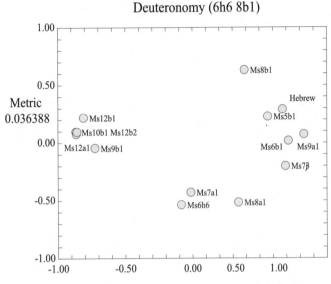

Deuteronomy (6h6 8b1)

6h6 8b1 intersect, Major Variations, Heb. Relevant

When a plot based on the 53 passages where 7j3 is present (Plot 13), the variants are major, and the Hebrew is relevant, the Hebrew and 9a1 (and to the side 8b1) form a group, 6h6 6b1 and 7a1 form another group, with 5b1 to one side, and 7j3 and 8a1 to another side. In Plot 14 6b1 and 6h6 are also members of the same cluster.

While patterns can be seen, the details of the maps vary according to which specific MSS are available, and according to the decisions as to which variants to consider (major, minor, those where the Hebrew irrelevant or where it is relevant).

Van Vliet, in the Introduction to Deuteronomy in the Leiden Edition says that looking at 'the sum total of the variants', 7j3 is closest to 6b1 and 9a1. 'There are some twenty-six variants 7j3 shares with other ancient manuscripts. In half of that number either 6b1 or 9a1 is involved, in a third a variant is found in these three Mss only.'[13] This is misleading, as shown by Plot 14 based on all the passages (148) where 7j3 is present with either 6b1 or 9a1 also extant.

13. Introduction [to Deuteronomy], ix, x.

Plot 13

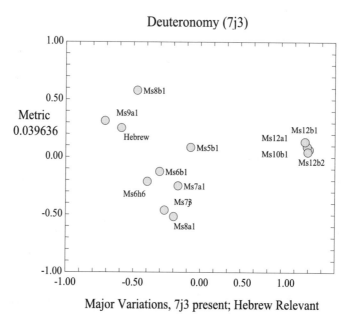

Deuteronomy (7j3)

Major Variations, 7j3 present; Hebrew Relevant

Plot 14

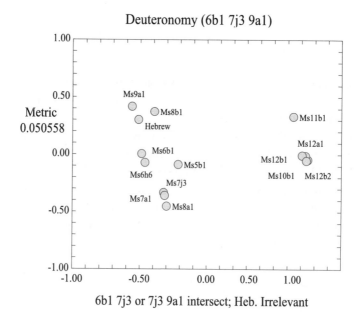

Deuteronomy (6b1 7j3 9a1)

6b1 7j3 or 7j3 9a1 intersect; Heb. Irrelevant

It is not proper to consider only the variants; 7j3 also in other places supports the lemma, together with other ancient MSS (including 6b1 and 9a1). The relation to 6b1 and 9a1 must take all the readings (variants and lemmas) into account, as Plot 14 does. In fact where 7j3 agrees with 6b1 or 9a1 on a variant, it often also agrees with 5b1!

Inscriptions, Subscriptions

Eight of the MSS have a sufficient number of inscriptions and sub-scriptions (when Numbers and Deuteronomy are combined) to warrant generating a map.

The groupings are not surprising. MSS 6b1 and 9a1 are close; the presence of 5b1 with 10b1, 12b1, 2 perhaps is associated with the situation where a reading in the Nestorian and late Western MSS (8a1c 9b1-12b2) has only the support of 5b1 among the ancient MSS! This situation occurs 39 times: 10 times the shared reading supports the Hebrew, 16 times it is against the Hebrew, and 13 times the Hebrew is irrelevant.

Plot 15

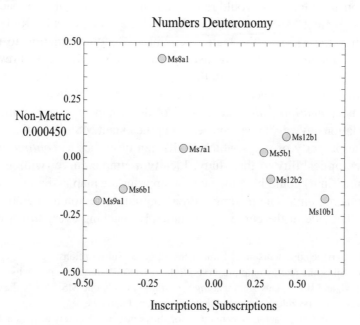

Applications

Weitzman makes use of 'the concept of a team of manuscripts'; in his 'The Tradition of Manuscripts' he describes a set of MSS surrounding the hypothetical original (in this study assumed to be close to although not identical to the Hebrew as represented by the M T), basically independent of each other, and departing from the hypothetical original in different directions. All the original Peshitta readings that have been preserved would be found in one or more of the members of the team. A two-dimensional map typically would have four such extant manuscripts.

It is not clear that such teams can be confidently defined for Numbers and Deuteronomy. Plot 3 shows that the cluster of 7pj2 9a1 6b1 extends nearly a third of the way around the Hebrew. Since 7pj2 has many unique readings that agree with the Hebrew, as does 9a1 (actually 9a1*fam*), both should therefore be members of the team; but they do not seem to be substantially independent of each other. 5b1 would surely be a member of the team,[14] although other MSS are as near the Hebrew. To construct the team would require an analysis of the unique readings of the ancient MSS,[15] which lies beyond the scope of this article. To identify the MSS in the team Weitzman's recommendation to treat unique readings in the manuscripts agreeing with the Hebrew as actually shared (namely, with the Hebrew) might need to be followed, and maps generated accordingly. It is not obvious that there are or have ever been *multiple independent* lines of development from the original translation anyway, to be represented in the extant MSS.[16]

The property of maps which Weitzman describes as *continuity* has more applicability to this study. Ideally a simple curve (without any 'bumps' in it) could be drawn on the appropriate map assigning a continuous region to one reading with a continuous region to the other on the other side of the curve. Systematically checking every fifth variant

14. See the comments on 5b1 under Inscriptions, Subscriptions.

15. Since the team would preserve *all* the original Peshitta readings which have survived, and since many such readings are found in only one MS, clearly the study would need to be enlarged beyond that of the shared variants.

16. On the maps actually generated for this study, the Hebrew always appears near the edge of the map; presumably that is where the hypothetical original Peshitta would also have been. If a team of MSS surrounded the hypothetical original, that hypothetical original ought to be relatively central to the map.

shows that such a curve can be made c. 80% of the time for Numbers, and at most 75% of the time for Deuteronomy. An informal examination, case by case, of a large number (120+ cases) of the more significant variants (whether the Hebrew is relevant or irrelevant) shows that for Deuteronomy more that 80% of the time this could be easily done, and for Numbers a higher percentage of the time. There is no need to provide extensive illustrations, but a few may be informative.

Numbers 22.1. 'Which is on the other side of the Jordan' (lemma: 5b1 7a1 8a1* 8b1c 8h3); 'which is upon the Jordan' (variant: 6b1 9a1 9b1-12b1 plausibly 8b1*); 'at the Jordan' (Hebrew). Probably the reading of the variant is that of the original Peshitta, since the widest spread of MSS on the plots has that reading[17] and it requires only a simple curve to separate off the group of MSS with the reading of the lemma. If that was the original reading of 8b1, the correction would be evidence of 'contamination' of that MS in the course of transmission.

Deuteronomy 2.8. 'To the way of the wilderness of Moab' (lemma: 7a1 8a1, = Hebrew 'the way of the wilderness of Moab'); 'the wilderness to the way of Moab' (5b1); 'to the wilderness in the way of Moab' (6b1 8b1 9a1); 'in the wilderness to the way of Moab' (9b1 10b1 11b1 12a1 12b2); 'to the wilderness to the way of Moab' (12b1). The variants are compatible with Plot 6; 5b1 is distinct from 6b1 8b1 9a1; 7a1 and 8a1 belong together, and the latest MSS form a group, except that 12b1, which often is somewhat independent of the others, has its own variant. Variants in the apparatus and clusters on the plot correspond well. Only 7a1 and 8a1 have the Hebrew order of 'way-wilderness'; their reading might well preserve the original Peshitta text.

Deuteronomy 4.22. 'This good land' (6b1 7a1 8a1* = Hebrew); 'this good land which the Lord your God gave to you' (5b1 6h6 8a1c 8b1 9b1-12b2). The addition of the longer text was made on the basis of v. 21, presumably once. The MSS which expanded the text (except for 6h6 8a1c) also expand it in v. 23 with 'and you became corrupt' on the basis of 4.16, 25.

However there are conspicuous cases where a single continuous region cannot be easily drawn. Manuscripts may have been 'contaminated' by readings from other lines of manuscript transmission. Alterations may have been made independently at more than one point in the transmission; this may well happen when a passage is har-

17. See the comments on angles of separation between MSS appearing later in this paper.

monized with the wording of other passages in the text. It may be that two-dimensional maps are sometimes just too simplifying to correctly represent the MS relationships; sometimes a three-dimensional map might show the desired continuous region. A few examples must suffice.

Numbers 5.6. 'Say to the sons of Israel' (lemma = Hebrew 'Speak to the sons of Israel'); 'Speak with the sons of Israel, and say' (6h1 8a1* 8h3 9a1*fam*). Plot 3 shows that that 6b1 9a1 is not easily joined to 8a1 and 8h3 (which indeed are not shown as close). The variant may be independently made two or more times under the influence of v. 5 'Speak to Moses, and say.'

Deuteronomy 1.41. 'and you stirred yourselves up (ethpael grg) to go up to the hill-country' (5b1mg 7a1 8a1 9b1 10b1 11b1 12a1); 'and you were dragged (ethpalpal gr) to go up to the hill-country' (5b1txt 9a1); 'and you roused yearnings (palpel rg)[18] to go up to the hill-country' (6b1 8b1 12b1.2). The Hebrew (hiphil hwn) is obscure, but the passages deals with Israel's decision to invade the promised land from the south though the Lord said he would not fight for the people (v. 42). The reading of 5b1txt 9a1 appears to be the most difficult; that 5b1 has a marginal reading is some evidence for its being compared with another MS on this difficult passage. The widespread reading of 6b1 8b1 and some of the Nestorian MSS suggests scribes seeking to make sense of the passage, and either independently consulting other MSS or undertaking to 'correct' the text they had received.

Deuteronomy 3.27. The order of directions in 5b1 8b1 is E S[19] W N, but E W N S for the other MSS. The Hebrew runs W N S E. The lemma agrees with the Peshitta of Gen. 28.14 having the sequence E W N S (the Hebrew in Genesis has W E N S). If the variant represents the original Peshitta, the other MSS presumably conformed to the reading of Genesis; if the lemma has the original reading, the reason for the change in 5b1 8b1 is unclear, though it is not obvious that it is a change that would be made twice independently.

Deuteronomy 11.16. 'and you shall turn aside, and you shall serve other gods' (lemma = Hebrew); 'and you shall go astray, and you shall

18. By an oversight this variant is omitted from *The Old Testament in Syriac According to the Peshitta Version*, Part V, *Concordance. I. The Pentateuch* (Leiden: E.J. Brill, 1997), p. 762.

19. In the Concordance to the Pentateuch, previously cited, the South is treated as a Geographical Name (p. 877), whereas the other directions are listed in the main body of the volume.

serve other gods' (6b1 8a1 8b1, with the correction of the misprint in the Leiden Edition of lamadh to teth). This variant could easily be made independently.

Deuteronomy 27.11, 31.18. In Deuteronomy twice the same two MSS, and only they, 5b1 and 9a1, omit the phrase 'in that day'. It is probably relevant to the case of 31.18 that the phrase appeared twice in v. 17, and also once in v. 22. Perhaps 5b1 and 9a1 simplified the text independently there, but it leaves 27.11 unexplained.

Deuteronomy 31.6. 'and do not be shaken' (lemma = Hebrew); 6h6* 10b1 12a1*fam* 12b2 add 'and do not be disquieted.' The longer text corresponds to Deut 20.3, and is likely a case of independent leveling occurring twice.

Another feature of maps to which Weitzman draws attention is the angle between any two MSS made by connecting them to Hebrew (strictly speaking to the original Peshitta, Omega, assumed to have been close to the Hebrew as a translation). The wider the angle the greater the degree of textual independence of the one MS from the other. It is also assumed that MSS of maximum angular separation will not both differ from the original, assuming the original has been preserved at all. The following considerations seem to substantiate the assumption, since the figures of joint disagreement are low and mainly involve 'minor' variants.

For the Deuteronomy maps, the angle 8b1 Hebrew 9a1 would probably be the appropriate one. In Deuteronomy, for cases of shared variants 8b1 and 9a1 agree against the Hebrew eight times, seven of which are 'minor' variants as Koster defined the terms.

If the appropriate angle were 8b1 Hebrew 8a1, there would be 23 cases where 8b1 and 8a1 agree against the Hebrew, 19 of which would be 'minor.'

It must be remembered though that 8b1 is extant for only c. 40% of the text of Deuteronomy, in which case the angle would be between the Nestorian and late Western texts, the Hebrew and 9a1.

For the purposes of this study a value was assigned as a consensus value for the Nestorian and late Western texts (in 361 cases for Deuteronomy), and labeled 'N'. This has not been used previously in this article, but that consensus value was used for the comparison here with 9a1. There are 23 cases where 9a1 and that consensus value are in agreement against the Hebrew, seven of them 'major.'

For Numbers the angle of the consensus value (N) of the Nestorian and late Western texts with Hebrew and 9a1 might be an appropriate one. The consensus value is available for 297 cases of shared readings. There are 24 cases where 9a1 and the consensus value are in agreement against the Hebrew, 12 of them 'major.'

These figures for joint disagreement against the Hebrew are sufficiently low to suggest that the angle subtended from the Hebrew to a pair of MSS is indeed a legitimate device to determine independence between those MSS.

Concluding Comments

No evidence of a systematic revision of the Peshitta text has been found in the ancient MSS in this study; the situation is very different from that of the books of Kings where there is strong evidence[20] of a systematic revision attested as early as the sixth century, and where 9a1 represents an independent development of the unrevised older text. The situation is also different from Exodus where Koster found evidence of what Weitzman would call a virtual edition (represented by the ancient MSS other than 5b1) achieved without any intentional revisionary work, with 5b1 an independent development of an older stage closer to the Hebrew.

Here in Numbers three clusters may be identified: (1) a relatively tight cluster (including 6b1, 9a1, and 7pj2 when extant), (2) a loose clustering of other ancient MSS, members of which sometimes support the readings of the first group, and (3) a tight grouping of Nestorian MSS. The reading of N (the consensus value of the third group) is often found in certain MSS of the second group. In Numbers there are c. 79 cases where 7a1 8a1 (with or without 8h3) and the consensus value of the Nestorian MSS agree against the Hebrew; in 74 of those cases 9a1 agrees with the MT.

In Deuteronomy the membership of the first group is not as clear (and varies according to the map generated); the second group is much more diffuse and not clearly distinct from the first group. In the case of 8b1 the separation from other MSS of the same time period is almost too much to place it in the second group, at least if 'minor' variations are ignored. Plots such as 11 put it with the first group; other plots perhaps in a group of its own. The third group of Nestorian and late Western

20. Note: cf. the monograph on Kings by D.M. Walter and K.D. Jenner awaiting publication by E.J. Brill of Leiden in the Peshitta Institute's Monograph series.

texts (12a1*fam*) is generally more diffuse than in Numbers as well. As in Numbers, the reading of N (the consensus value of the third group) is often found in certain MSS of the second group.

MDS gives a useful visual picture of the clustering of MSS, and helps in representing differences in the transmission character of different books. Instances where contiguous curves are hard to draw between the readings (lemma and variants) suggest further research into the transmission process: for example, the extent of contamination among MSS, and the extent of independent multiple generation of 'shared' variants.

Examining specific variants against the maps not only may help in determining 'originality', but also indicate which MSS are most often associated with the readings of the latest MSS used in the study.

Michael Wietzman has indeed helped to introduce a very useful technique into Peshitta MSS studies.

TEXT DIVISIONS IN THE SYRIAC TRANSLATIONS OF ISAIAH

Sebastian P. Brock

Modern readers of the Hebrew Bible and its various translations are likely to take it for granted that, for any given book, what they read is not presented to them in the indigestible form of a solid mass of continuous text, rather than being broken up into smaller more manageable blocks. The familiar chapter breaks (and numbers) are, however, a comparatively recent phenomenon, having been introduced into the Hebrew Bible in the sixteenth century from the Vulgate, where they are said to have been introduced by Stephen Langton (died 1228). The Hebrew Bible itself has its own system of (unnumbered) text breaks, the *petuḥa* and *setuma*, where spaces denote the sense divisions. These, being much more numerous than the chapter divisions, provide a breaking up of the text into much smaller, and hence more reader-friendly, sense units. Although there is a certain amount of variation between manuscripts of the MT, the basic principle of breaking up the text in this way is now known, thanks to the biblical texts from Qumran, to go back to before the turn of the Common Era.

The way in which a text is broken up can have an important bearing on the way it is understood by the reader. This means that the initial decision how to divide up a given text may have consequences in the subsequent exegetical history of that text. In the case of translations there is a further interest, in that there is a possibility that the earliest text division in a particular translation may also reflect the situation in the Hebrew manuscript from which that translation was originally taken. Where the complete manuscripts of the source text are late (as is the case with the Hebrew Bible), whereas those of the translation are early, this is an aspect of additional importance. In view of this it is unfortunate that most editions of the ancient translations of the Hebrew Bible do not pay any particular attention to this aspect; as a result, for anyone who is interested in discovering how (for example) manuscripts of the Septuagint or Peshitta divided up the text of a particular book, it is necessary to consult photographic editions of individual manuscripts (if they are available) or the manuscripts themselves.

It so happens that a certain amount of attention has been paid to the situation in Isaiah, thanks to the stimulus provided by the remarkably well-preserved 1QIsa, whose text divisions take us back many centuries behind those of the MT. In this context the evidence of the oldest manuscripts of the Syriac Peshitta translation is of considerable interest since the high number of agreements in text breaks with those in 1QIsa and the MT[1] suggests that the system of breaks in the oldest Syriac manuscripts is likely to go back to that of the original translation from Hebrew into Syriac, and that the translator simply took over a system already present in the Hebrew manuscript from which he was working. If this was indeed the case, then there is a corollary: in view of the fact that these Syriac text breaks do not conform exactly either with those in 1QIsa or with those in the MT, this suggests that we have evidence in the Syriac tradition of a distinct third pattern of text division, albeit one that has a great many overlaps with those in 1QIsa and the MT. Since the Peshitta translation of Isaiah is likely to belong to about the second century CE,[2] thus antedating the earliest Hebrew manuscripts by over half a millennium, the evidence provided by this comparatively early witness seems worth giving in full.

The reasoning that lies behind these ancient text divisions has never been properly explored, although their potential significance for literary analysis is now beginning to be realized.[3] A single example may help

---

1. For the divisions in the MT, see especially J. Oesch, *Petucha und Setuma: Untersuchungen zu einer überlieferten Gliederung im hebräischen Text des Alten Testaments* (OBO, 27; Fribourg: Universitätsverlag; Göttingen: Vandenhoeck & Ruprecht, 1979), and for 1QIsa, Y. Maori, 'The Tradition of Pisqa'ot in Ancient Hebrew Manuscripts: The Isaiah Texts and Commentaries from Qumran' [in Hebrew], *Textus* 10 (1982), pp. 1*-50*. For Peshitta Isaiah, see my 'Text History and Text Division in Peshitta Isaiah', in P.B. Dirksen and M.J. Mulder (eds.), *The Peshitta: Its Early Text and History* (Leiden: E.J. Brill, 1988), pp. 49-80, esp. 65-78.

2. See M.P. Weitzman, *The Syriac Version of the Old Testament: An Introduction* (University of Cambridge Oriental Publications, 56; Cambridge: Cambridge University Press, 1999), pp. 248-58.

3. See M.C.A. Korpel and J.C. de Moor, *The Structure of Classical Hebrew Poetry: Isaiah 40–55* (OTS, 41; Leiden: E.J. Brill, 1998), pp. 2-3, and the literature cited there.

indicate the relevance of this neglected evidence. A glance at the Hebrew text and almost any modern translation will indicate a difference in where ch. 9 begins: in the MT it is 'The people who walk in darkness...', but in (for example) the RSV it commences at 8.23 of the Hebrew ('But there will be no gloom for her that was in anguish...'), implying that this goes with what follows rather than with what precedes. The Masoretic tradition offers no help at this point, having no *petuḥa* or *setuma* in the immediate vicinity. On the surface the joining of 8.23 with the following verses might seem just to be due to Christian influence, seeing that 8.23b (concerning Zebulon and Naphtali) is implicitly taken as leading into the quotation of (Hebrew) 9.1 in Mt. 4.15-16. The matter, however, is not so simple, for there is now the pre-Christian evidence of 1QIsa, which turns out to have a break before 8.23b ('In the former time...'), which thus takes the reference to Zebulon and Naphtali as belonging to what follows, as in Matthew, but leaves (Hebrew) 8.23a as part of the previous oracle. As will be seen from the table below, the two earliest Peshitta manuscripts, with some later support, are in full agreement with 1QIsa in providing a text break before 8.23b—in agreement too, it may be noted, with the literary analysis of most modern scholars[4] (who probably did not make use of this ancient evidence, lying ready to hand).

The aim of the present contribution is simply to set out the main evidence for the way in which the text of Isaiah was broken up in the early manuscripts of the Peshitta.[5] For convenience, there is added any supporting evidence in the four early Septuagint uncials, Sinaiticus (S), Vaticanus (B), Alexandrinus (A) and Marchalianus (Q), in the first Isaiah scroll (1QIsa) and in the Masoretic tradition; this is set out in Table 1, Appendix. The evidence for the four Septuagint manuscripts is derived from the photographic editions of these,[6] while that for 1QIsa

4.   E.g. H. Wildberger, *Isaiah 1–12: A Commentary* (Minneapolis: Fortress, 1991), p. 384.

5.   The symbols used for manuscripts are those of the Leiden edition, *The Old Testament in Syriac According to the Peshitta Version*. III.1. *Isaiah* (Leiden: E.J. Brill, 1987), where the first number denotes the century to which the manuscript is dated.

6.   H. Lake and K. Lake, *Codex sinaiticus petropolitanus et Friderico-Augustanus Lipsiensis: The Old Testament...now Reproduced in Facsimile from Photographs* (Oxford: Clarendon Press, 1922); *VT iuxta LXX interpretum versionem e cod. omnium antiquissimo graeco vaticano 1209 phototypice repraesentatum*, III (Rome: Bibliotheca Vaticana, 1890); F.G. Kenyon, *The Codex Alexandrinus in*

and the MT is taken from the tables provided by Maori and Oesch.

In Peshitta manuscripts sense breaks are normally clearly discernible from the presence of four points arranged in a diamond shape (designated D in Table 1; if there is space to fill, the scribe may repeat these, but this is of no practical significance). For reasons of space it has not been possible to include the evidence from all the Peshitta manuscripts earlier than the thirteenth century, but where there is support amongst manuscripts which are not cited (notably 8j1, 9d1, 12d1) for any breaks that are not well attested, then the sign + is given after the last Peshitta witness mentioned. The manuscripts cited regularly are 6h3, 6h5, 7a1, 8a1 (1.1–3.24 is in a later hand, but evidently reproducing the original text of the manuscript), 9a1, 10d1 (1.1–3.23 is in a much later hand), 11d1 (1.7–2.7, 7.14–11.15, 27.9–28.21 and 54.6–61.4 are in a later hand), and 12a1.[7] In three of the early manuscripts, 6h3, 6h5 and 8a1,[8] a few lectionary headings are incorporated into the biblical text, and these are indicated by L in Table 1; the lectionary indications added by later hands are not included, since these require separate treatment. The evidence of the important early palimpsest, 5ph1, is not included in Table 1, but is indicated separately below.

In the Hebrew witnesses cited (1QIsa and MT) there is a distinction

---

Reduced Photographic Facsimile: Old Testament, III (London: British Museum, 1936); and J. Cozza-Luzi, *Prophetarum codex graecus vaticanus 2125 qui dicitur Marchalianus* (Rome: Bibliotheca Vaticana, 1890). The evidence of Alexandrinus, in particular, is sometimes ambiguous; I have taken an inclusive approach.

7.   For chs. 40–55 the information can also be found in Korpel and de Moor, *The Structure of Classical Hebrew Poetry*, pp. 649-53, where the verse number *after* which a break occurs is given. It may be noticed that, contrary to their table, there is no Syriac evidence for the break after 45.16. In the few other (small) differences between their table and mine over the Syriac evidence I have checked the microfilms of the manuscripts concerned. My interpretation of the evidence of the Greek manuscripts will be found to differ in a number of cases from theirs; this is usually due to my exclusion of the evidence of breaks introduced by later hands (especially in S and B), and of lighter breaks in Q indicated by a point (as opposed to a small space or the first letter of a new section intruding into the left margin).

8.   On the lectionary system in this manuscript, see K.D. Jenner, 'De perikopentitels van de geïllustreerde syrische kanselbijbel van Parijs (MS Paris, Bibliothèque Nationale, Syriaque 341): Een verglijkend onderzoek naar de oudste syrische perikopenstelsels' (PhD dissertation, Leiden University, 1993). (For the illuminations in this manuscript, see now R. Sörries, *Die syrische Bibel von Paris. Paris BN syr. 341: Eine frühchristliche Bilderhandschrift aus dem 6.* [sic!] *Jahrhundert* [Wiesbaden: Ludwig Reichert, 1991]).

between heavier and lighter breaks: in 1QIsa heavier breaks are denoted by the remainder of a line being left empty (symbolized as ** in the table), while lighter ones are shown by a space left mid-line (symbolized as *). In the MT the heavier breaks are denoted by *petuḥa* (p) and the lighter ones by setuma (s); there is considerable variation in the manuscripts over which of these two is to be found in any one place, and this is denoted in the table by p/s, s/p, where the first denotes the better attested; where s or p is only poorly attested in the manuscripts, then this is indicated by (p) or (s).[9]

In the four Greek manuscripts cited there are different ways of denoting text breaks. In S, the first letter of a new unit extends slightly to the left of the left margin, and the end of the previous line will be left blank (where there is space for this). A second, and later, hand in S has added section numbers; these reach to 441 in Isaiah.

In B, likewise, the first letter of a new unit extends slightly to the left of the left margin, and space is left at the end of the previous line. The original hand supplied chapter numbers in the margin, but these were written over by a later hand, preserving (it seems) the original numbering, which runs from 1 to 74.

In A there are two separate ways of denoting text breaks: after heavier breaks the new unit begins with an enlarged letter which extends to the left of the left margin (as in SB), while lighter breaks are denoted by a short space mid-line. These lighter breaks are denoted in the table below by italicized *A*.

In Q, the first letter of a new unit is extended slightly to the left of the left margin (as in the other manuscripts), though occasionally a small indentation may be used instead. In a few cases, too, larger initial letters (always epsilon, omicron or sigma) are employed, coming in the middle of a line (sometimes preceded by a small space).

Comparison of the incidence of text breaks in Peshitta (P) manuscripts with those in 1QIsa and the MT, shown in Table 1, indicates a high degree of overlap, as can be seen from the following tabulation (where bracketed numbers indicate the number of additional cases where the text break is only attested in a few, or just one, Peshitta manuscript).[10]

9. The evidence is conveniently given in tabular form in Oesch, *Petucha und Setuma*, Tabelle III (= T 4-30, at the end of his book).

10. The figures are based on fuller evidence than those in my 'Text History and Text Revision', p. 67 (the figure given there for P = 1QIsa = MT is a misprint and should read '184', and not '84').

P = 1QIsa = MT	199 times (+ 5)
P = 1QIsa	32 (+ 17); no break in MT
P = MT	7 (+ 7); no break in 1QIsa
1QIsa = MT	22; no break in P
Break in 1QIsa	124; no break in P or MT
Break in MT	5; no break in P or 1QIsa
Break in P	19 (+ 5); no break in 1QIsa or MT

The very large number of cases where P has breaks in common with 1QIsa and/or MT cannot just be a matter of coincidence; rather, it strongly suggests that the extant P manuscripts will reflect the situation already present in the original Syriac translation, and that this in turn simply reflected the situation in the translator's Hebrew *Vorlage*. This of course makes those cases where P goes against 1QIsa and the MT all the more interesting; accordingly, it may be helpful here to draw attention to those places where (a) there is a text break in both 1QIsa and MT, but not in P, and (b) there is a strongly attested text break in P, but none in 1QIsa or the MT:

(a) Text break in 1QIsa and MT, but none in P:
1.18; 3.1; 8.3; 9.13; 14.24; 19.16; 25.6; 26.11, 13; 27.6; 28.7; 36.16; 37.15; 40.17; 44.2; 50.10; 51.11, 22; 53.1; 56.3, 6.

(b) Text break in P, but not in 1QIsa or MT:
1.7; 9.12, 16, 17; 10.15; 25.4; 31.6; 37.5, 18; 38.21, 22; 40.18; 41.4; 50.8b; 55.4; 56.8; 57.19b; 60.8; 63.17.

The earliest witness to the Peshitta text of Isaiah, the palimpsest 5ph1, happens to be the earliest dated Syriac biblical manuscript (459/60 CE). Its evidence has not been included in Table 1, because unfortunately only parts of the undertext can be read, but among these several text breaks (indicated by a circle) can be identified with certainty. These come before the following verses: 17.1, 12; 31.1; 33.20; 34.1; 45.10, 11; 48.12; 49.7, 8, 24; 50.1; 51.1; 57.3; 59.1; 60.1; 61.6, 10; 65.1, 9, 13, 23. For the most part, these represent text breaks that are otherwise well attested; four, however, are of further significance: for 45.10 and 61.6 the only other witness is 9a1, a manuscript that is, on quite other grounds, known to preserve archaic material that has been lost in the rest of the manuscript tradition.[11] For breaks before 65.9 and 23, however, 5ph1 is the unique Syriac witness.

---

11. This was convincingly demonstrated by Michael Weitzman with character-istic acumen and clarity in his 'The Originality of Unique Readings in Peshitta MS

An investigation into the possible significance of the evidence of the Peshitta tradition in these cases must be left for another occasion.

Subsequent Text Divisions in the Syriac Tradition

Two methods of dividing the book of Isaiah into sections (*ṣḥaḥe*) or chapters (*kephalaia*) came into use in the course of the seventh and eighth centuries. The division of biblical books into sections is first found in connection with East Syriac Gospel manuscripts from the early seventh century onwards; this system was then extended to the rest of the New Testament and to most books of the Old Testament. For Isaiah the earliest manuscript with the *ṣḥaḥe* marked in the first hand is 8j1. The system was evidently taken over fairly soon into the West Syriac tradition and so became the standard system in all the Syriac churches.

The book of Isaiah was divided into 30 *ṣḥaḥe*. The correlation of these *ṣḥaḥe* in Peshitta MSS with *kephalaia* in the Syrohexapla and in Septuagint MS B (Vaticanus) is shown in Table 2 in the Appendix. In the manuscript tradition there are two slightly different systems; the main system is to be found in the (later) corrector of 8a1, in 8j1, 9d1, 9d2, 10d1, 11d1, 12a1, 12d1, and 12d2 onwards, while a subordinate variant tradition, where the placing of the *ṣḥaḥe* differs slightly in 12 out of the 30 cases, is to be found in the corrector of 9a1 and in the group of much later manuscripts belonging to that family (16g9, 17a6, 17a7, 17a8, 17a9, 17a11). It is interesting to observe that a number of *ṣḥaḥe* begin at points at which there was not a previous text break recorded in the surviving manuscript tradition (passages for which no text breaks are attested in manuscripts earlier than the ninth century are marked with an asterisk in Table 2). This is also a feature of the later division of the Hebrew text of Isaiah into 25 *sedarim*, the vast majority of which do not correspond to earlier text breaks in the MT.[12]

9a1', in P.B. Dirksen and M.J. Mulder (eds.), *The Peshitta: Its Early Text and History* (Leiden: E.J. Brill, 1988), pp. 225-58; see also his *The Syriac Version of the Old Testament: An Introduction* (Cambridge: Cambridge University Press, 1999), pp. 273-79. In this connection it should be noted that 9a1 is the only Peshitta witness to a text break present in both 1QIsa and MT at 3.13, 7.7, 10.16, 11.1, 45.10 (with 5ph1), 56.10 and 66.12. The break before 61.6 in 5ph1 and 9a1 has no Greek or Hebrew support, but falls at the point where a new *ṣḥaḥe* section occurs in the subordinate *ṣḥaḥe* system (see Table 2).

12. See Oesch, *Petucha und Setuma*, p. 33.

Although the introduction of numbered *shahe* was clearly intended primarily for ease of reference (like chapter *numbers*), it is difficult to see the rationale lying behind the actual choice of places where the text is broken. A certain number happen to coincide with the *kephalaia* introduced by the Syrohexapla (see below), but since this does not apply to any of the cases (asterisked in Table 2, below) where the *shahe* introduce completely new text breaks, influence from this source seems unlikely, and may well be ruled out on chronological grounds, seeing that, for the Peshitta New Testament, *shahe* are already present in a manuscript dated 600 CE. Possibly the placing of the *shahe* was simply aimed at achieving blocks of text of a regular size, since most of them take up approximately the same amount of text space; there are, however, a number of puzzling exceptions, if this were really the criterion. The matter clearly calls for further research.

The division of biblical books into *kephalaia* entered the West Syriac tradition in the early seventh century with Thomas of Harqel's revision of the New Testament and Paul of Tella's translation of the Old Testament (the Syrohexapla, Syh) from the hexaplaric Greek text. No doubt the numbering and placing of *kephalaia* was taken over from Greek manuscripts. Occasionally, *kephalaia* numbering may enter Peshitta manuscripts, and this is the case in 7a1 where a subsequent corrector has added them in the margin (inaccurately in a few places). In Isaiah the text of Syh is divided up into 48 *kephalaia*. Whether any Septuagint manuscripts of Isaiah have the same division is something that requires investigation (the Göttingen edition does not provide information of this nature). In the four Septuagint manuscripts for which there are photographic editions (S, B, A and Q), a later second hand in S (Sinaiticus) and the original hand (re-inked) in B (Vaticanus) have provided chapter divisions (441 in S and 74 in B). As will be seen from Table 2 below, there is not very much overlap in the placing of section/chapter breaks between the various systems; this also applies when this versional evidence is compared with the current chapter division of the Hebrew Bible, taken over from the Vulgate.

Although the evidence of the incipits of liturgical lections is not considered here (beyond the cases covered in Table 1), it might be noted that in several cases these too begin at points where there was no previous break marked in the text, thus further illustrating the great variety of possibilities of dividing up the biblical text into sense units.

Biblical Hebrew, Biblical Texts

The evidence of two other Syriac versions of Isaiah,[13] both fragmentary, is not considered here, though it is worth recording that where
the chapter numbers for the revision by Jacob of Edessa (d. 708) are
available, they agree with those of the Syrohexapla (for *kephalaia* 38
and 39).

Michael Weitzman's *The Syriac Version of the Old Testament*, by
providing a firm methodological basis for the study of the Peshitta in
relationship to its Hebrew *Vorlage*, constitutes a milestone in the
history of scholarship on the Syriac Bible. The aim of the present contribution in honour of his memory is simply to provide some basic
information on one further aspect of the witness of the early Peshitta
manuscripts to the transmission of the biblical text.

Appendix

Sigla and Abbreviations
Peshitta MSS: sigla consist of three elements: first no. = the century of the MS;
letter = the contents of the MS: a = complete or nearly complete Bible; d =
Prophetic books; h = one book only.
Early Septuagint uncials: S = Siniaticus; B = Vaticanus; A = Alexandrinus; Q =
Marchalianus
1QIsa = the Isaiah scroll from Qumran Cave no. 1
Syh = Syrohexapla
D = four points arranged in a diamond shape (or equivalent break)
(D) = ditto, but added in a second hand
K = *Kephalaion* (in Syh; for the numbering, see Table 2).
L = Lection (*qeryana*) incorporated into the biblical text
p = *petuḥa*; s = *setuma*; for s/p, (p), (s), see main text.
**, *, = larger or shorter break in 1QIsa; [*] = shorter break in 1QIsb, absent from
1QIsa.
Note: all biblical references are to the verse *before* which the text break comes.

13. Anonymous and by Jacob of Edessa. The surviving fragments of both these
were edited by A.M. Ceriani, in his *Monumenta Sacra et Profana*, V (Milan:
Bibliotheca Ambrosiana, 1868). For the likelihood that the anonymous version,
made from Greek, represents the version commissioned by Philoxenus, see R.G.
Jenkins, *The Old Testament Quotations of Philoxenus of Mabbug* (CSCO, 514/Sub,
84; Leuven: Peeters, 1989). The character of Jacob's revision of Samuel has
recently been studied by R.J. Saley, *The Samuel Manuscript of Jacob of Edessa: A
Study in its Underlying Textual Traditions* (MPIL, 9; Leiden: E.J. Brill, 1998), and
the text edited by A. Salvesen, *The Books of Samuel in the Syriac Version of Jacob
of Edessa* (MPIL, 10; Leiden: E.J. Brill, 1999).

Table 1

	6h3	6h5	7a1	8a1	9a1	10d1	11d1	12a1	Syh	LXX	1QIsa	MT
1.1		L							K			
.2	D		D			D			D	AQ	*	
.10	D	D				D		D	D	SBA	**	s
.16									L	A		
.21	D	D			D	D				SBA	**	p/s
.22								D	D	A		
.24		D		D					D	A	*	p/s
.27		D		D						A		
.28									D	A		
2.1	D	D	D	D	D			D	K	SBAQ	**	p/s
.5		D	(D)	D	D	D			K	S A	**	s/p
.10			D				D		D	A		
.11								D	D			
.12		D			D					S A	**	p/s
.20						D	D			AQ	**	
.22		D									*	
3.1									D	B AQ	**	p
.36									D	A		
.9b		D							D	A		
.12								D	D	A	*	
.13				D					D	S	**	s/p
.16		(D)			D				K	A Q	**	p/s
.18	D	D	D		D					A	*	p/s
4.1									D	S A	**	
.2			D	D	D	D	D	D	L	S A	*	p/s
5.1	D	L	D	L	D	D	D	D	K	SBA	**	s/p
.8	D		D	D	D	D	D	D	K	SBA	**	s
.11	D	D			D				L	BA	**	p
.18	D	D	D		D	D	D	D	D	S A	**	(s)
.20	D	D	D	D	D	D	D	D	D	S A	*	p/s
.21	D	(D)			D	D	D	D	D	BA	*	s
.22	D	(D)	D	D	D	D	D	D	D	A	*	(s)
.24									D	S A		p/s
.26	D	D	D	D	D				K	S	*	
6.1	D	(D)	D	D	D	D	D	D	K	SBA	**	s/p
.8									D	S A		
.9					D					S A		
.11					D			D	D	A	*	

	6h3	6h5	7a1	8a1	9a1	10d1	11d1	12a1	Syh	LXX	1QIsa	MT
7.1	D	D	D	D	D	D	D	D	K	SBAQ	**	p
.3				(D)	D	D	D	D	L	A	**	s
.5									D	AQ		
.7				D						A	*	s/p
.9						D						
.10	D	L	D	L	D		D		D	S A	**	s/p
.12				D				D	D	S	*	
.13									D	AQ	*	
.14			D						D	A		
.15								D+				
.16b									D			
.18	D	(D)	D		D	D		D	D	S		p/s
.20	D	D+							D	S AQ		(p)
.21		D	D		D			D	D	S A	**	s/p
.23	D	D	D+						D	A	**	(s)
8.1	D	D	D		D	D		D	D	S A	**	p/s
.5	D	D	D		D	D+		D	D	S A	**	s
.9	D	D			D	D		D+	D		**	s/p
.11	D	D	D		D	D				S A	**	s
.16		(D)	D		D	D		D	K	S	*	s/p
.18		(D)								S		
.19		(D)								S A	**	s/p
.23b	D	D						D+	D	A	*	
9.2	D	(D)			D			D			**	
.5		(D)			D					A	*	
.7	D	D		D	D				D	A	**	s/p
.8			D							S		
.12	D	D	D						D	A(11b)		
.16	D				D					A		
.17	D	D						D	D			
10.1	D	D	D	D	D	D		D	D	S	**	s/p
.5		D	D	D	D	D		D	K	A	**	s/p
.10b									D	S AQ		
.12	D	D							D	A	*	s/p
.15	D				D					A		
.16					D					A	**	(s/p)
.20	D	D	D		D	D		D	K	Q	**	p/s
.22						D					*	
.24	D	D		D	D	D		D	D	S A	**	s/p
.27		D	D						D	S AQ	**	(s)

	6h3	6h5	7a1	8a1	9a1	10d1	11d1	12a1	Syh	LXX	1QIsa	MT
.32									L	A		
.33	D	L	D	L	D						**	s/p
11.1				D					K	S AQ	**	s/p
.10		D	D	D	D			D	D	S A	**	p/s
.11	D	D			D			D	D	A	*	p/s
12.1							D		D	S A	**	
13.1		D		D					D	SBAQ	**	p/s
.2									K	BA	*	
.7									D	A		
.9	D	(D)			D	D		D+		Q		(s)
.11					D	D	D+				*	
.17		(D)			D			D	D	S A	**	
.22b		D										
14.3	D	D	D	D	D	D			D	S A	**	s
.4									D	Q		
.7		D								A	*	
.28	D	D	(D)		D			(D)	D	B AQ	**	s/p
.29									K	A		
15.1	D	D	(D)	D		D	D	(D)	K	SBAQ	**	s/p
16.6	D									S AQ	*	
.9									D	A		
17.1	D	D	(D)	D				(D)	K	SBAQ	**	p/s
.3		D									*	
.4			D		D					S A	**	s/p
.7		(D)				D	D	D+		A	*	s
.9	D	D			D			D		S A	**	(s)
.10b									D		*	
.12	D	D				D	D	D	D	A	**	s/p
18.1	D	D		D	D	D	D	D	D	S A	**	s/p
.4		D	D						D	A		s
.7	D	D				D+		(D)		AQ	*	(s)
19.1	D	D	(D)						K	SBAQ	**	s/p
.4b									D	AQ		
.11b									D	A		

	6h3	6h5	7a1	8a1	9a1	10d1	11d1	12a1	Syh	LXX	1QIsa	MT
.16									D	A	*	s
.18	D	D	D		D			D	D	S A	**	s
.19		D	D	D	D			D		A	*	s
.23	D	D	D						D	A	*	s
.24	D	D	D		D		D			S AQ	*	
20.1	D	D	D	D	D	D	D+		K	SBAQ	**	s/p
21.1	D	D	(D)	D		D	D	D	K	SBAQ	**	s/p
.6		D	D		D							p/s
.11	D		(D)	D					K	SBAQ	**	s/p
.13	D	D	D	D					D	A	**	s/p
.17b		D										
22.1	D	D		D					D	SBAQ	**	s/p
.6b					D					A	*	
.14								D				
.15	D	D	D		D	D+			D	AQ	**	(p)
.19b		D										
.20	D									A	**	
.25		D			D					S Q		
23.1		D	(D)	D		D	D	D	K	SBAQ	**	p
.10						D				A		
.14						D				A		
.15	D	D	D		D				D	Q	*	s/p
24.1		D	D		D	D		D	K	SBAQ	**	p
.3							D+				*	
.4	D	D		D						A	*	
.6b		D								A		
.16	D	(D)				D	D	D+		SBA	**	s
.21	D	D		D	D	D					**	s/p
25.1	D	L	D	D	D	D	D	D		AQ	**	p/s
.4b				D		D	D	D+		A		
.9	D	D			D	D	D+			A	**	p/s
26.1	D	(D)			D	D			D	BAQ	**	s
.3b									D	A		
.9b									D	BA		
.12		D								S A		(s)
.13	D									S A	*	(s)

	6h3	6h5	7a1	8a1	9a1	10d1	11d1	12a1	Syh	LXX	1QIsa	MT
.16		D	D	D	D			D	D	S A	**	(p)
.20	D	D	D			D	D	D		B	**	s/p
27.1	D	D	(D)		D	D	D	D	K	AQ	**	s/p
.2	D	(D)	D		D	D	D	D		AQ	**	s/p
.7		D	D		D		D	D		S AQ	*	s/p
.10									D	A	*	
.11b									D	S AQ	*(11a)	
.12	D	D	D		D			D+	D	S AQ	**	s/p
.13		D	D+							AQ	**	s/p
28.1		D		D	D	D		D	D	SBA	**	s/p
.5	D	D	D		D	D		D	D	SBA	**	s/p
.8								D		A		
.9	D	D			D	D+				S A	**	s/p
.14	D			D		D		D+	D	BA	**	p/s
.16		D				D		D+	D	S A	**	s
.23	D	D	(D)		D	D	D	D	K	S A	**	(s)
.29b		D								AQ		
29.1	D				D	D		D	D	SB	**	s/p
.5b						D				A(5a)		
.9	D	D			D	D	D+		D	AQ	**	s
.13	D			(D)	D	D	D	D		BAQ	**	s/p
.15	D	D	D		D	D		D	D	SBA	**	s/p
.18									D	AQ	*	
.22	D		D		D		D	D+	D	SBA	**	s/p
.24b									D	Q		
30.1		D	D	D		D	D	D+		AQ	**	(s)
.6	D	D	(D)	D+					K	SBAQ	**	s
.12	D					D	D+			A	**	s
.15	D	D				D			(D)	A	**	p/s
.20									D	A		
.25	D	D	D		D	D	D	D			*	
.27	D	L	D	D	D	D	D	D	D	A	**	s/p
31.1	D	D			D	D	D	D	D	BAQ	**	s/p
.4			(D)		D	D			K	A	**	s/p
.6	D	D	D		D	D		D		A		
(.7											**	)
.9			D+						D	SB		

	6h3	6h5	7a1	8a1	9a1	10d1	11d1	12a1	Syh	LXX	1QIsa	MT
32.1	D	D				D	D	D+			**	s/p
.9	D	D		D	D		D	D	D	SB	**	p/s
.14			(D)						K			
.20								D	D	S A	**	
33.1	(D)	D		D		D				S A	**	s
.2	(D)	L	D		D				D	B*A*Q	**	s
.5									D	S A		
.7				(D)		D	D	D+			**	s/p
.10	(D)	D	D		D		D	D			**	s/p
.13		D			D	D	D	D		A	*	s/p
.20	D		(D)		D				K	B*A*	*	
.24b		D			D							
34.1	D	D		D					D	SBA	**	s/p
.4									D	A		
.16	D										**	
35.1						D+			D	SBAQ	?	s/p
.2b				D								
.3	L	L		L					D	A	**	s/p
36.1	L	D	D	D	D	D	D	D	K	BA	**	p/s
.11		D		D	D					A		(s)
.12									D	S A		
.13		D	D							S	*	
.21					D					AQ		
.22	(D)	(D)			D+					S AQ	*	
37.1		D	D		D	D	D			*A*		s
.5	D		D		D	D				S AQ		
.8		D			D+					A		
.14	D				D	D		D		BAQ	**	
.18				(D)		D	D	D+		A		
.21		D	D		D	D	D+		D	SBA	**	(s)
.27		D										
.33	D	D	D	D	D	D	D		D	A	**	s/p
.35									D			
.36		D	D		D		D+		D	AQ	**	s
.37		D			D					A		(s)
38.1	·D	L	D	L	D	D	D		D	SBAQ	**	s
.2					D							

	6h3	6h5	7a1	8a1	9a1	10d1	11d1	12a1	Syh	LXX	1QIsa	MT
.4	D	D			D	D		D+		SBAQ	**	s
.9				(D)					D	SBAQ	*	s/p
.21					D+				D	S AQ		
.22	D	D		(D)	D	D	D	D		S A		
39.1		D+							D	B*A*	**	s/p
.3	D				D	D	D	D	D	S AQ	**	(s)
.4b					D					A		
.5					D					S A	**	
.8					D	D	D	D		S AQ	*	
40.1	D	L	D	D	D	D		D	K	SBA	**	p/s
.3	L		D	L	D	D	D	D		SBAQ	*	s
.6		D			D	D		D		BAQ	**	s/p
.9	(D)	D		D	D	D	D	D	D	SBAQ	**	s
.12	D	D	(D)	D	D	D	D	D	K	S A	**	s
(.17											**	s/p)
.18	D	D			D	D+						
.25	D	(D)	D		D	D		D	D	S AQ	**	s
.27		D			D						**	s/p
41.1		D	D	D	D	D	D	D	K	S A	**	s/p
.2						D+				AQ	*	
.4	D				D	D+			D	S	*	
.8				L	D	D	D	D	D	SBAQ	**	s/p
.14	D		D								*	s
.15		D										
.17		L		L	D	D	D+			S A	**	
.21	D	D			D	D	D+			SBAQ	**	p/s
.25	D		D		D					AQ	*	
42.1	D	D	(D)	L	D	D	D		K	B*A*	**	p/s
.5	D	D			D	D	D	D		S*B*A	**	p/s
.10	D	D		D	D+				D	BAQ	**	p/s
.14	D	D	D	D	D	D	D	D		S		s/p
.16b			(D)						K	SB		
.18	D				D	D	D	D+		*A*	**	s/p
.23	D+									S		
43.1	D	D	(D)	D	D	D	D	D	K	SBA	**	p/s
.11	D										**	s/p
.14		D	D	D	D	D			D	A	**	s/p
.16	L	D	D	L	D					S A	**	s/p
.22	D	D	D		D	D	D			SBA	**	s

	6h3	6h5	7a1	8a1	9a1	10d1	11d1	12a1	Syh	LXX	1QIsa	MT
44.1	D	D			D	D	D+			A	**	s/p
.6	L	L	D	L	D	D	D	D	K	AQ	**	p/s
.8b									D	B		
.21	D	D		(D)	D	D	D	D		BA	**	s
.23	D									B	**	
.24	D				D				D	SBA	**	p/s
45.1		D			D	D		D+	D	SBAQ	*	s/p
.8	D	D			D	D	D+		D	SBAQ	**	s/p
.9		D		D	D	D		D+		Q	**	s
.10					D						*	s
.11	D	D			D		D+			S A	*	s/p
.14	D	(D)	D		D	D	D	D	D	SBAQ	**	p/s
.16b									D	BQ		
.18c	(D)	(D)+								SB	**	p/s
.20		D								A	*	
46.1									(D)	S AQ	*	
.3	D	D	D	D	D			D	D	SBAQ	**	s/p
.5	D	(D)			D	D	D	D		S A	*	s/p
.8		D	D		D	D	D+			AQ	*	s
.12	D	D	D	D	D	D	D	D		S A	**	s
47.1	D	D	(D)		D				K	BAQ	**	s/p
.4	D	(D)			D	D	D+				*	s/p
.8	D					D	D+				*	s/p
48.1	D	D			D	D	D	D	D	SBAQ	**	s/p
.3						D+			D	S A	*	s
.12	L	D	D	L	D				D	AQ	**	s/p
.17	D	D			D	D		D+		S A	**	p/s
.20		D			D		(D)	D+	D	S	**	(s)
49.1	L	D	D	D	D	D	D	D	K	AQ	**	s/p
.5	D	D			D	D	D	D		A	**	s
.7		D	D	D	D	D	D	D		S A	**	s/p
.8		D				D+			D	S	**	(s)
.14	D	D	D		D	D	D		D	BAQ	**	s
.22	D	(D)			D	D	D	D		SBA	**	p/s
.24					D	D	D	D	(D)	S A	**	s
.25									D	AQ	*	(s)
50.1	D	D	D		D				D	SBAQ	**	s/p

	6h3	6h5	7a1	8a1	9a1	10d1	11d1	12a1	Syh	LXX	1QIsa	MT
.4	L	L	D	L	D	D		D	K	SBA	**	s/p
.5						D	D+			A	*	
.8b	D	(D)			D	D	D+			S		
.9									D		*	
.11		D								S A		(s)
51.1		D	D	D	D	D			D	SBAQ	**	p/s
.4	D			L	D	D	D	D	D	SBAQ	**	s
.7		(D)			D	D				SBA	**	s/p
.9	L	D		L	D	D	D	D	D	SBAQ	**	s
.12		(D)	D		D	D	D+		(D)	SBA	**	s/p
.15		(D)								AQ	**	
.17	D	D	D		D	D	D	D	D	S AQ	**	s/p
.21	(D)	D	D		D					S A	*	(s)
52.1	D	D	D	L	D				D	S AQ	*	s/p
.4		D							D	SBA		s
.5b									K	SBAQ		
.7	D	L	D	L	D	D	D	D	D	A	**	p/s
.10		D										
.11					D	D	D	D+		AQ	*	s
.13	L	D	D	L	D	D	D	D	D	A	**	s/p
53.4					D					AQ		
54.1	L	L	D	L	D	D	D	D	D	SBAQ	**	s/p
.9					D	D		D+	D			s
.11		D	D		D	D+					**	s/p
55.1	D	D	(D)		D	D		D	K	BA	*	s/p
.4	L	D			D	D		D+		A		
.6		D	D		D	D+			D	AQ	**	s
.12b		(D)				D+					*	
56.1		D			D	D		D+	D	SBA	**	s/p
.4						D+				A	*	s/p
.8	D	D						D+				
.10				D					D		**	s/p
.12				D								
57.3	D	(D)		(D)	D	D		D		BA	**	s
.15			D	L	D	D+				S AQ	*	s/p
.19b						D+				S A		

	6h3	6h5	7a1	8a1	9a1	10d1	11d1	12a1	Syh	LXX	1QIsa	MT
58.1	L	L	D	L	D	D		D	D	SBA	**	s/p
.6	D								D	A		
.13								D+	D	A	**	
59.1	D	D	D		D	D		D	K	S A	**	s/p
.9b		(D)			D			D+		A	*	
.11b		(D)							D	SB*A*		
60.1	L	L	D	L	D	D		D	D	SBA	**	s/p
.8	L	L	D	L	D	D		D		S AQ		
61.1		L	D	L		D		D+	K	SBA	*	s/p
.6					D							
.10	(D)	(D)	D	D	D	D	D	D	D	SB	**	s/p
62.1		D							D	BA		
.6		D			D	D	D+		D		[*]	(p)
.8					D						[*]	(s)
.10	D	D	D	D	D	D	D		D	SBA	**	s/p
63.1	D	L	D	L	D		D	D	K	SBAQ	**	s/p
.7			D	D	D	D	D	D	D	SB	**	s/p
.15		(D)	(D)						K	*A*	*	
.17	D	D			D	D	D	D	D	S A		
64.8b		(D)										
65.1		D		D	(D)	D	D	D	D	SBAQ	**	s/p
.8	L	L	D	L	D	D	D	D	K	SBA	**	s
.11		(D)								S A	**	
.13	D	D		D	D+				D	S *A*	**	p/s
.16b								D	D	S	*(16a)	
.17									D	A	**	
.25									D	BA	*	
66.1	D	(D)	D	D	D	D	D	D	D	BAQ	**	s/p
.5	(D)	D		D	D	D	D	D	D	S AQ	**	s/p
.8	(D)	(D)			D	D	D	D			*	
.10	(D)	D		D	D	D+			D	SBA	**	s/p
.12					D					S AQ	**	s
.15	(D)	(D)							K		**	(s)
.17					D					AQ		
.23		(D)		D	D					AQ	*	

Table 2

Concordance of numbered sections: Syriac and Greek (Vaticanus, B)

* no text break in Peshitta MSS earlier than ninth century
Syr = Syrohexapla Kephalaia
B = Vaticanus Kephalaia

	P shahe		Syr	B		P shahe		Syr	B
	main	sub.				main	sub.		
1.1	1	1	1	1	17.1			17	8
2.1			2	2	18.1	9	9		
.5			3		19.1			18	9
.10*	2				20.1			19	10
.12*		2			21.1	10	10	20	11
3.16*			4		.11			21	12
5.1			5		22.1				13
.8	3	3	6		23.1	11	11	22	14
.26			7		24.1			23	15
6.1			8	3	.16				16
7.1		4	9	4	25.1			(23)	
.3*	4				.3*		12		
8.16			10		.4b*	12			
.23b	5	5			26.1				17
10.5			11		.20				18
.20			12		27.1			24	
.22*	6				.9/10*				19
.24		6			28.1	13	13		20
11.1*			13		.5				21
13.2*			14	5	.14				22
.11*	7	7			.23			25	
14.28				6	29.1				23
.29*			15		.13	14			24
15.1	8	8	16	7					

	P ṣhaḥe		Syr	B		P ṣhaḥe		Syr	B
	main	sub.				main	sub.		
.22		14		25	.22				44
30.6			26	26	44.6			37	
.27	15	15			.8*				45
					.21	22	22		46
31.1				27					
.4*			27		45.1				47
.9*				28	.8				48
					.14				49
32.9				29	.16*				50
.14*			28						
					46.3				51
33.2				30	.12	23			
.5*		16							
.7*	16				47.1		23	38	52
.20			29	31					
					48.1				53
34.1				32	.22*				54
35.1*				33	49.1			39	
					.7	24	24		
36.1	17	17	30	34	.14				55
37.18*	18				50.4			40	56
.21				35					
					51.1				57
38.1				36	.9	25	25		58
.9*		18		37					
.22	19				52.4				59
					.5b*			41	
39.1				38	.7			(41)	
40.1		19	31	39	53.1*				60
.12			32						
					54.1	26			61
41.1			33		.11		26		
.8(*)	20	20		40					
					55.1			42	62
42.1			34	41					
42.16*			35	42	56.3*				63
					.10*				64?
43.1	21	21	36	43					

	P ṣḥaḥe		Syr	B		P ṣḥaḥe		Syr	B
	main	sub.				main	sub.		
57.3	27			65	.6(*)[14]		29		
.7*		27			.10	29			70
58.1				66	63.1			45	71
					.15*			46	
59.1			43						
.9b*	28	28			65.1	30	30		72
.11*				67	.8			47	
60.1				68	66.1				73
					.6*				74
61.1[14]			44	69	.15*			48	

14. See n. 11 above.

SOME SECONDARY EXPANSIONS IN THE MASORETIC
TEXT OF JEREMIAH: RETROVERSION IS PERILOUS
BUT THE RISK MAY BE WORTHWHILE*

Gillian Greenberg

This paper is offered in memory of Dr Michael Weitzman, with whom
this work was first discussed. No student ever had a kinder, more
encouraging, or more stimulating teacher.

An analysis of minuses, that is words or phrases that are present in the
Masoretic Text (= MT[1]) of Jeremiah but are not represented in the
Peshitta (= P), raises a number of interesting questions concerning the
Vorlagen and editorial history of the Septuagint (= LXX) and of the
Peshitta, and relevant to the editorial history of the MT itself.

The hazards of attempting to establish a *Vorlage* from study of a version are well known: see, for example, Driver,[2] and Aejmelaeus,[3] who

* Grateful thanks are due to Dr K. Jenner, the Director of the Peshitta Institute,
and to Dr D. Walter, for their kindness in allowing me to make use of Dr Walter's
work on the variants in the Peshitta MSS to Jeremiah in advance of the publication
of this material; and to Drs A. Gelston, D.J. Lane, A. Rapoport-Albert, A. Salvesen,
and D. Walter for their helpful comments on an earlier draft of this paper.

1.   Since the MT is almost always uniquely defined, despite some MS variation
outlined for instance by Tov (E. Tov, *Textual Criticism of the Hebrew Bible* [Min-
neapolis: Fortress Press; Assen: Van Gorcum, 1992], pp. 25-39) the term will be
used in this discussion without further qualification. For the LXX, Ziegler's edition
(J. Ziegler [ed.], *Septuaginta Vetus Testamentum graecum auctoritate societatis
gottingensis editum. XV. Jeremias, Baruch, Threni, Epistula Ieremias* [Göttingen:
Vandenhoeck & Ruprecht, 1957]) was used. For the Peshitta, the text referred to is
7a1, photolithographice edita, A.M. Ceriani, *Translatio syro pescitto Veteris Testamenti ex codice Ambrosiano sec. fere*, VI (Mediolani, 1876–1883). Where relevant
variants are extant, these are referred to at the appropriate citations.

2.   S.R. Driver, *Notes on the Hebrew Text and the Topography of the Books of
Samuel* (Oxford: Clarendon Press, 1913), xxxviii.

3.   A. Aejmelaeus, 'What Can we Know about the Hebrew *Vorlage* of the
Septuagint', *ZAW* 99 (1987), pp. 58-89 (60).

combine textual criticism of the MT with analyses of translation technique and proceed to an assessment of the probable integrity of the translation, and Goshen-Gottstein[4] who emphasizes the hazards of subjectivity and the difficulty of avoiding this trap. Among modern authors, Lane[5] in the present volume notes that the practice of retroversion is a perilous activity. Many of Weitzman's own papers included discussions of this problem,[6] urging caution even where the agreement of two versions on any individual point seems at first sight to give substantial evidence as to the wording of the *Vorlage*, since such correspondence may also result from influence of one translation on the other, or from the independent reflection of common exegetical tradition, thus manifesting not textual connection but polygenesis. Polygenesis may also, though perhaps rather infrequently, operate to give similar but independent minuses in different versions: faced with a passage of particularly difficult Hebrew, the translators may independently omit the same element, deciding that by doing so they can reach reasonable sense without moving too far away from the intention of the author. Similarly, two translators, dealing with a passage of repetitive Hebrew, might independently opt for an abridged text for the sake of clarity or of literary impact.

In summary, the hazard of attempting to establish a *Vorlage* by retroversion from a translation is that all the elements on which such attempts are based are interdependent: textual criticism of the MT may be supported by study of the versions; use of the versions in textual criticism must be founded on an appreciation of the techniques favoured by their translators; and understanding of these translation techniques must be based on comparison of the versions with the MT. Nonetheless, although proof of the details of the translation process is impossible, well-founded suggestions may be based on such evidence as is available, and an analysis of the minuses in the LXX and the

---

4.   M.H. Goshen-Gottstein, 'Theory and Practice of Textual Criticism—The Text-Critical Use of the Septuagint', *Textus* 3 (1963), pp. 130-58 (133-34).

5.   D.J. Lane, ' "Come Here…, and Let us Sit and Read…": The Use of Psalms in Five Syriac Authors', in the present volume, pp. 412-30.

6.   M.P. Weitzman, 'Peshitta, Septuagint and Targum', in R. Lavenant (ed.), *Symposium Syriacum, VI 1992* (OCA, 247; Rome: Pontificio Istituto Biblico, 1994), pp. 51-84 (52-54), reprinted in A. Rapoport-Albert and G. Greenberg (eds.), *From Judaism to Christianity* (JSS Supplement, 8; Oxford: Oxford University Press, 1999), pp. 181-216 (182-84).

Peshitta in comparison with the MT of Jeremiah has suggested that some of these do indeed yield some information concerning the wording of the *Vorlagen*. The minuses fall into three principal groups:

(a)   a substantial number that do give some insight into the *Vorlagen*: these are characterized by their location at passages where the wording of the MT is such that it is reasonable to ask whether some form of secondary expansion may have occurred during the process of transmission;

(b)   minuses that occur at random, in one version or the other, perhaps resulting from temporary inattention on the part of translator or copyist, and which give no direct insight into the *Vorlage*;[7]

(c)   others that may indicate the translator's deliberate decision not to render a Hebrew term which, if translated, would give awkward or non-idiomatic text in the target language, and which give no insight into the *Vorlage*.

Minuses classified in groups (b) and (c) will be discussed no further here.[8] Clearly, there is some subjective element in this classification, but, on the whole, accidental omissions would be random, with no characteristic unifying the omitted passages, and deliberate omissions would be found at points where the Hebrew grammar or idiom would not translate readily into acceptable Syriac. Neither accidental nor deliberate minuses would in general satisfy the criterion of location at a point where secondary expansion might reasonably be supposed to have occurred; this is the criterion that characterizes group (a), which forms the basis of the following analysis.

The strength of the arguments presented in this paper lies in two

---

7   M.P. Weitzman, *The Syriac Version of the Old Testament: An Introduction* (University of Cambridge Oriental Publications, 56; Cambridge: Cambridge University Press, 1999), pp. 17-18: such minuses may give an *indirect* insight, for instance suggesting a particular layout of the *Vorlage* which led to eye-skip, whether based on a misperception of whole words, on homocteleuton, or on homoiarcton.

8.   These are discussed more fully in G. Greenberg, 'Translation Technique in the Peshitta to Jeremiah' (PhD thesis, University of London, 1999), pp. 169-82. As the thesis emphasizes, the term 'Translation Technique' by no means implies that translation is a mechanical process; see A. Gelston, *The Peshitta of the Twelve Prophets* (Oxford: Clarendon Press, 1987), and D.J. Lane, *The Peshitta of Leviticus* (MPIL, 6; Leiden: E.J. Brill, 1994).

principal factors, first the character of the translation technique of P-Jeremiah as a whole, and second the cumulative nature of the examples. First, the translation technique: this is, essentially, meticulous.[9] the Peshitta is characterized by precision, and is indeed so careful to leave no points unclear that it does occasionally verge on the pedantic. There is also a strong emphasis on accessibility, and to this end, as well as in the course of the drive for precision, a considerable number of additions have entered the translation, making explicit details that are implicit, though nonetheless clear, in the Hebrew: a quantitative analysis has shown that about nine per cent of all sense units in P-Jeremiah include an addition of some kind. Minuses, against a background of such painstaking attention to detail, are particularly striking.

Second, the cumulative weight of the body of evidence to be discussed here: in certain individual cases it would be possible to maintain that some other cause, such as haplography, was responsible for the minus; but it would be implausible to argue that such accidents explain each one of the considerable number of instances that exist.

Examples in this group are themselves divisible into two principal categories.[10]

(1)   those in which the Peshitta and LXX agree with one another against the MT, both versions showing the minus; these examples give insight into the history of the earliest stages of the Peshitta;

(2)   those in which the Peshitta and LXX disagree with one another, the minus affecting the Peshitta, but the LXX agreeing with the MT. These examples give insight into the history of the MT itself.

The Formation of Minuses in Group (a) Category (1)

In these cases, the Peshitta and LXX agree with one another against the MT, both versions showing the minus.

9.   Greenberg, 'Translation Technique', pp. 27, 44, 176-82.

10   There is at least one other group of minuses which would repay study: Gelston (personal communication, 1999) notes that passages in which the Peshitta and LXX agree with one another, and the minus is in the MT itself, would support the suggestion that the MT is a consciously comprehensive text whose editors did not have access to all the amplifications that had been made in other text-forms; this awaits further work.

The Value of the Qumran Evidence

The fragments found at Qumran, in Caves 2 and 4, constitute some of
the rare firm ground on which this discussion may be based: the evidence they provide is indirect rather than direct, but nonetheless
valuable. The importance of these fragments in this context lies in their
demonstration that, at the time when the Qumran documents were
deposited, at least two forms of the book of Jeremiah were extant. The
literature is extensive; see for instance publications by Cross,[11] Tov,[12]
Janzen,[13] Bogaert,[14] and Soderlund[15] in which are discussed the issues
most relevant for present purposes, namely the dating of the manuscripts, their relation to one another in terms of the history of transmission, and the aims of their editors. 4QJer[a] and 4QJer[c], and 2QJer,
correspond to the book of Jeremiah as it appears in P and the MT;
4QJer[b] is closer to the form of the book in the LXX. The two principal
differences between these forms of Jeremiah, that is length and
structure, are both detectable on study of the fragments.[16]

11. F.M. Cross Jr., 'The History of the Biblical Text in the Light of Discoveries
in the Judaean Desert', *HTR* 57 (1964), pp. 281-99; *idem*, 'The Oldest Manuscripts
from Qumran', in F.M. Cross and S. Talmon (eds.), *Qumran and the History of the
Biblical Text* (Cambridge, MA: Harvard University Press, 1975), pp. 147-76.

12. E. Tov, 'Some Aspects of the Textual and Literary History of the Book of
Jeremiah', in Pierre-Maurice Bogaert (ed.), *Le livre de Jérémie, le prophète et son
milieu, les oracles et leur transmission* (BETL, 54; Leuven: Leuven University
Press, 1981), pp. 145-67.

13. J.G. Janzen, 'Double Readings in the Text of Jeremiah', *HTR* 60 (1967),
pp. 433-47; *idem*, *Studies in the Text of Jeremiah* (HSM, 6; Cambridge, MA:
Harvard University Press, 1973).

14. P.-M. Bogaert, 'Le livre de Jérémie en perspective: Les deux redactions
antique selon les travaux en cours', *RB* 101 (1994), pp. 363-406 (403) suggests that
whereas the original form of the book may have been 'La vie et les paroles de
Jérémie selon Baruch', in the development of the longer text the emphasis was
shifted away from the role of Baruch towards the MT presentation of Jeremiah as
the author of the book as a whole rather than of the oracles alone. However, despite
the possibility that this change of emphasis did indeed occur, the reader of the LXX
and MT is in no doubt that these are different forms of the same book; the differences are many, but in essence unimportant and of detail only: the expansion is
literary rather than thematic, largely rhetorical elaboration.

15. S. Soderlund, *The Greek Text of Jeremiah: A Revised Hypothesis* (JSOTSup,
47; Sheffield: JSOT Press, 1985).

16. These differences between LXX-Jeremiah and MT-Jeremiah have of course
long been known. Graf (K.H. Graf, *Der Prophet Jeremia* [Leipzig: T.O. Weigel,

Much of the literature on these two forms of Jeremiah is concerned with their relationship to one another: in brief, one school of thought holds that the longer form represents an expansion of a short *Vorlage* in the process of development of the MT, while the other believes that the short form represents an abbreviation of a longer *Vorlage* in the process of development of the LXX. Decision as to which of these alternatives is the more likely depends to some extent on comparison of the acceptability of deliberate expansion, or deliberate abbreviation, in the course of transmission of a biblical text. A decision to omit any part of a text from a translation would be expected to be more difficult than a decision to add to the text, for there is a psychological gulf between attempting to improve a text, particularly a biblical text, by making restricted additions, and deciding that any word of the original is superfluous and should be excised.

The first school of thought is well represented by Janzen; a major proponent of the other possibility is Soderlund. Their discussions focus on the work of the translator, rather than on the earlier stage shown in the Qumran fragments, but the principles are nonetheless relevant to the present discussion. Janzen argues[17] that texts are more likely to grow than to contract in transmission despite the frequency of haplography: he gives in support of his general argument examples of secondary expansion postulated in textual criticism of, for instance, the Iliad, the Gilgamesh Epic, and Egyptian mortuary texts.[18] Soderlund, on the other hand, gives in support of his belief that the LXX represents a contracted manuscript some instances of suspected condensation in the history of the Gilgamesh Epic, classical texts, and possibly in the Ras Shamra literature.[19] Majority opinion agrees with the first school of thought, that the LXX was translated from a 'short' manuscript, perhaps one of

---

1862], p. xliii) found that LXX-Jeremiah is shorter than MT-Jeremiah by one eighth, approximately 2700 words, this considerable difference being made up mostly of individual words and phrases, though there are some slightly longer passages. The difference in order of the chapters in LXX-Jeremiah and MT-Jeremiah has also been much discussed, and it is generally agreed that the order in the LXX is likely to be the original: see, for example, E. Tov, 'The Literary History of the Book of Jeremiah in the Light of its Textual History', in J.H. Tigay (ed.), *Empirical Models for Biblical Criticism* (Philadelphia: University of Pennsylvania Press, 1985), pp. 211-37 (217 n. 23).

17. Janzen, *Studies*, p. 9.
18. Janzen, *Studies*, pp. 190-91 n. 35.
19. Soderlund, *The Greek Text*, pp. 200-202.

several, and that one or more such manuscripts were expanded to form longer documents in the line of transmission of the MT.

In the light of this transmission history, of which expansion was a substantial component, retroversion at passages where both the Peshitta and LXX have minuses, and where textual criticism suggests some complexity in the Hebrew, may therefore plausibly indicate areas where the gradual expansion of the original short form had not reached the stage represented by the MT at the time when these two versions were translated. Three principal points in manuscript transmission are implied: the LXX represents a stage in the transmission history of a short form of the book; the Peshitta represents a stage a little earlier than the MT in the transmission history of a long form of the book; and the MT has been further expanded from the stage represented by the Peshitta.

The Formation of Minuses in Group (a) Category (2)

In these cases, the Peshitta and LXX disagree with one another, the minus affecting the Peshitta, but the LXX agreeing with the MT.

The explanation suggested here is that editorial work on the MT was still in progress at around the time of translation of the Peshitta, and that in the course of their work the MT editors drew not only on proto-Masoretic MSS, in the line of transmission of the longer text, but perhaps also on the 'short' form of the book which formed the basis of the LXX, or on other 'short' manuscripts that were still extant in Palestine, incorporating any elements they felt constituted valuable expansions of the text before them. Sometimes, such continuing editorial work involved a manuscript that was later than that which formed the *Vorlage* of the Peshitta, or which was for some other reason unavailable to the translator of the Peshitta. This hypothesis fits well with a point made by Gelston[20] who, referring particularly to the Qumran evidence, suggests that several different text-forms may have coexisted for a period before the standardization of the MT, with modifications made inconsistently, and notes that, just as there was probably more than one 'long' text, it may be simplistic to envisage a single 'short' text.

An example will make the suggestion clear: there is, for instance, a

20   A. Gelston, personal communication, 1999.

doublet in 7.27, 28 (discussed on p. 239 below), of which one component appears in the LXX, the other in P, and both in the MT. This picture could result from a sequence of events in which one component was present in the *Vorlage* of the LXX, and thus entered the Greek version(s); the other was present in a proto-MT MS which formed the *Vorlage* of the Peshitta; and at a later stage in the line of transmission of the MT the editors decided that, rather than choose between these two components, they would incorporate both. At other points, other considerations may have influenced the editors' decision to incorporate in the MT words or phrases from a 'short' text: some examples given below show, for instance, the possibility that such decisions were influenced by a tendency towards harmonization with other areas.

The Date and Place of Writing of the Peshitta
These suggestions are compatible with evidence assembled from a number of lines of investigation concerning the date and place of the writing of the Peshitta. On the question of dating, Aphrahat's knowledge of the standard text of the Peshitta[21] gives a probable *terminus ante quem* of the first half of the fourth century CE.[22] Gelston's analysis[23] of the Peshitta of the Twelve Prophets shows that the translator knew the Septuagint, and indeed sometimes showed literary dependence on that version, giving a *terminus post quem* of the middle of the second century BCE. Gelston further refines this period of several centuries during which the Peshitta could have originated, showing the close agreement of the Hebrew *Vorlage* presupposed by the Peshitta with the MT, which suggests a date for the version shortly before the standardization of the MT; although the uncertainty concerning the date of that standardization, and the existence of the proto-Masoretic MSS in the period leading up to that date, make it impossible to infer a precise date for the Peshitta, the balance of probability suggests a date in the middle or later part of the first century CE. Weitzman[24] brings together evidence derived from literary tradition, references to historical events,

21. Aphrahat, *Patrologia Syriaca*, I, II (ed. J. Parisot; Paris, 1894, 1907).
22. D.J. Lane, personal communication, 1999, points out that Aphrahat's own citations may not have been in the exact form in which we have them today: the extant MSS may represent emendations preferred by Aphrahat's scribe; see also Greenberg, 'Translation Technique', pp. 37-39.
23. Gelston, *The Peshitta*, pp. 192-93.
24. Weitzman, *The Syriac Version*, pp. 248-58.

citations of the Peshitta and citations in the Peshitta, vocabulary, and grammar, and on the basis of these additional factors reaches a slightly later date, concluding that a date close to 150 CE is probable for the translation of the canonically earlier books of the Hebrew Bible. By that date, there is general agreement that one or more proto-MT manuscripts would have been in existence (see, for instance, Albrektson,[25] Mulder, [26] Dirksen,[27] and Goshen-Gottstein[28]). The availability of such MSS does not prove that one was offered to the writers of the Peshitta; but it does seem likely that the translators would have sought out a 'model' text, one given high status by those involved in Palestine, as the basis of work of such importance, and that the model they would have wanted to work from would therefore have been in the line of transmission of the MT.

Here, the obvious comparison is with the selection of the MS used by those writing the Septuagint, described by Josephus.[29] This idealized account may well be inaccurate in certain details, but in essence it carries conviction: the best possible MS would have been desired by the translators, and those offering the MS would have felt their own prestige to be reflected in the excellence of that text. It seems probable that those who were planning the preparation of the Syriac translation

25. Albrektson points out that, rather than representing the result of deliberate unification of a text, and including those variants that were judged to be superior, the MT may simply represent one text which, as a result of extraneous events, happened to be the sole survivor of a number of editions: accepting this argument, it is one of those editions which the Peshitta seems to represent (B. Albrektson, *Reflections on the Emergence of a Standard Text of the Hebrew Bible* [VTSup, 29; Leiden: E.J. Brill, 1978], pp. 59-60).

26. M.J. Mulder, 'The Use of the Peshitta in Textual Criticism', in N.F. Marcos (ed.), *La Septuaginta en la investigacion contemporanea: V Congreso de la IOSCS* (Madrid: Instituto Arias Montano, 1985), pp. 37-53 (45), discussing the importance of the Peshitta in establishing, together with the Septuagint, which of a number of text-forms is 'the better' emphasizes that both these versions witness not to '*the* Hebrew text, but to a tradition', that is to one of the several 'pre-Massoretic text-forms'.

27. P.B. Dirksen, 'The Old Testament Peshitta', in M.J. Mulder and H. Sysling (eds.), *Mikra: Text, Translation, Reading and Interpretation of the Hebrew Bible in Ancient Judaism and Early Christianity* (Assen: Van Gorcum; Philadelphia: Fortress Press, 1988), pp. 254-97.

28. M.H. Goshen-Gottstein, 'The Development of the Hebrew Text of the Bible', *VT* 42 (1992), pp. 204-13.

29. Josephus, *Ant.* XII ii, 11(89)-12(107).

would, similarly, have requested the most authoritative possible
Hebrew MS as the basis for their work. It seems unlikely that a MS
from a tradition outside that of the Second Temple, or much older than
the recensions current at that time, would have been acceptable to those
planning the translation into Syriac, or would have been offered by
those whom they approached. By a date as late as 150 CE, the standardization of the MT was complete or almost complete; the MS provided
could therefore have been, virtually, a MT text. Yet the examples
presented in the present paper indicate that there were still some differences between the *Vorlage* and the MT; the geography of the circulation
of proto-MT MSS may be the key factor. It is perfectly plausible that the
Vorlage available in the East, to the Syriac translators, may have been
in a form that had already been superseded in the West at the time when
the Peshitta was being written. Even if those in the East, requesting the
loan of a MS, would have liked to receive the latest possible edition, it
is possible that those in the West in possession of the MSS would have
judged that they should not provide the most up-to-date text, and, given
the difficulties of travel at the time, and the danger that a MS might be
lost or damaged in transit, this would have been an easily defensible
decision: it would have been hardly reasonable to expect the authorities
in the West to offer to their eastern contemporaries a MS which had
perhaps barely reached final form.

Examples of Minuses in Group (a) Category (1)

Some examples follow; because of constraints of space, some selection
was unavoidable, but care has been taken to ensure that passages from
all chapters were given equal consideration.

5.27, 28

על־כן גדלו ויעשירו שמנו עשתו גם עברו דברי רע

ܡܛܠ ܗܢܐ ܥܒܘ ܘܥܬܪܘ ܘܥܒܪܘ ܕ̈ܝܢܐ

διὰ τοῦτο ἐμεγαλύνθησαν καὶ ἐπλούτησαν. καὶ παρέβησαν κρίσιν

שמנו עשתו is rendered in neither version. This is a difficult phrase, but it
seems unlikely that both translators found it too difficult even to
attempt, and it may be a secondary elaboration of ויעשירו גדלו.[30]

---

30. In a small number of the examples discussed in the present paper, there are
Lucianic variants (Ziegler, *Jeremias*) which eliminate the minuses, showing a

8.3

בכל־המקמות הנשארים אשר הדחתים שם
becomes ܒܟܠ ܐܬܪܘܬܐ ܕܐܪܡܐ ܐܢܘܢ ܠܬܡܢ
and ἐν παντὶ τόπῳ, οὗ ἐὰν ἐξώσω αὐτοὺς ἐκεῖ

Neither version gives any equivalent of הנשארים at this point, its second occurrence in the verse. This repetition of הנשארים is probably secondary: it breaks into a word-string which, sometimes with small variations, is well attested within Jeremiah (16.15; 23.3, 8; 24.9; 29.14, 18; 32.37; 40.12; 43.5; 46.28).

8.21

על שבר בת עמי השברתי קדרתי
becomes ܥܠ ܬܒܪܐ ܕܒܪܬ ܥܡܝ ܐܬܟܡܪܬ
and ἐπὶ συντρίμματι θυγατρὸς λαοῦ μου ἐσκοτώθην

There is no equivalent in either version of השברתי, though there is a Lucianic variant in which συντριβην precedes ἐσκοτώθην. The term may be a secondary expansion of קדרתי, or perhaps an imperfect dittography of שבר בת עמי; in either case, it was apparently absent from the *Vorlagen* of the LXX and of the Peshitta.

Greek text in conformity with the MT against P. These are noted against the appropriate verses in the discussion. For instance, such a variant shows ἐλιπανθησαν ἐστεατωθσαν preceding v. 28. Current opinion ascribes an early date to some 'proto-Lucianic' variants, certainly as early as the second half of the first century CE (D. Barthélemy, *Les devanciers d'Aquila* [VTSup, 10; Leiden: E.J. Brill, 1963], pp. 126-27; Cross, 'The History of the Biblical Text', p. 282). E. Tov, 'Lucian and Proto-Lucian', *RB* 79 (1972), pp. 101-13 (107), describing the character of the revisions, notes that many consist of short contextual additions or of additions of subjects, objects and names. Such additions could well have entered the Greek text during the process, discussed by Cross (p. 283), of revision of the Greek to bring it into conformity with a proto-MT MS, for these are points of a kind that might well have entered the Hebrew as a result of secondary expansions. S.P. Brock, *The Recensions of the Septuaginta Version of 1 Samuel* (Turin: Silvio Zamorani, 1996), pp. 204-10 (esp. 204) emphasizes, however, that although the Lucianic text undoubtedly includes recensional elements, it also includes non-recensional variants, which sometimes preserve the original LXX text, lost to the rest of the tradition. Any individual minus discussed in the present paper might, of course, fall into Brock's latter category; but the strength of the argument presented here lies in the cumulative evidence, and it would be unreasonable to reject all the examples on these grounds.

9.16(LXX.17)

התבוננו וקראו למקוננות

becomes ܘܩܪܘ ܠܢܕܒܬܐ

and Καλέσατε τὰς θρηνούσας.

Neither version represents התבוננו, possibly a secondary expansion to harmonize with 2.10 שלחו והתבוננו.

18.8

ושב הגוי ההוא מרעתו אשר דברתי עליו ונחמתי על־הרעה אשר חשבתי
לעשות לו

ܘܢܗܦܘܟ ܥܡܐ ܗܘ ܡܢ ܒܝܫܬܗ ܐܝܟ ܕܡܠܠܬ ܥܠܘܗܝ ܘܐܗܦܟ ܒܝܫܬܐ ܕܐܬܚܫܒܬ
ܠܡܥܒܕ ܠܗ.

καὶ ἐπιστραφῇ τὸ ἔθνος ἐκεῖνο ἀπὸ πάντων τῶν κακῶν αὐτῶν, καὶ
μετανοήσω περὶ τῶν κακῶν, ὧν ἐλογισάμην τοῦ ποιῆσαι αὐτοῖς

Neither version represents אשר דברתי עליו. The MT text is awkward: רעתו in ושב הגוי ההוא מרעתו must mean 'its wrongdoing', but to make sense as the antecedent of אשר in אשר דברתי עליו the meaning 'doom' is required.[31] God has not pronounced that wrongdoing, he has pronounced retribution. If אשר דברתי עליו is seen as a secondary and dubious expansion and considered no further, the verse reads perfectly clearly.

22.11

In translating the apparently straightforward MT שלם בן־יאשיהו מלך יהודה המלך תחת יאשיהו אביו, neither the Syriac nor the Greek render מלך יהודה, although βασιλεως ιουδα appears in a Lucianic recension. There is some uncertainty surrounding the exact details of the succession to Josiah,[32] but no uncertainty in describing Josiah as מלך יהודה, and no evident reason for not translating the phrase, possibly a secondary expansion.

---

31. W. McKane, *A Critical and Exegetical Commentary on Jeremiah*, I (ICC; Edinburgh: T. & T. Clark, 1986), p. 427, comments that 'the shorter text indicated by Sept. and Pesh. is the better one', and refers to the solution adopted by the NEB taking הגוי rather than רעתו as the antecedent of אשר: 'But if the nation which I have threatened turns back from its wicked ways, then I shall think better of the evil I had in mind to bring on it'.

32. See J. Bright, *A History of Israel* (London: SCM Press, 3rd edn, 1981), p. 325 n. 40.

23.20

תתבוננו בה בינה becomes ܬܬܒܝܢܘܢ ܒܗ and νοήσουσιν αὐτά

The form in this verse, with the repetition of the root in the term בינה, is not a standard idiom and is rendered in neither version, though νοησει appears in a Lucianic recension. The passage is duplicated in 30.24, but with no corresponding repetition, supporting the suggestion that 23.20 may include a secondary expansion.

25(LXX 32).18

לחרבה לשמה לשרקה ולקללה כיום הזה
ܠܚܘܪܒܐ ܘܠܬܡܗܐ ܘܠܫܪܘܩܝܬܐ ܐܝܟ ܝܘܡܢܐ
ἐρήμωσιν καὶ εἰς ἄβατον καὶ εἰς συριγμὸν

ולקללה is represented neither in the Peshitta nor in the LXX, and may well be a secondary supplementation on the model of, for instance, 24.9 לחרפה ולמשל לשנינה ולקללה or 44.22 לחרבה ולשמה ולקללה.

29(LXX 36).12, 13, 14

וקראתם אתי	ܘܬܩܪܘܢܢܝ	--------
והלכתם	--------	--------
והתפללתם אלי	ܘܬܨܠܘܢ ܩܕܡܝ	καὶ προσεύξασθε πρός με
ושמעתי אליכם	ܘܐܫܡܥܟܘܢ*	καὶ εἰσακούσομαι ὑμῶν;
ובקשתם אתי	--------	καὶ ἐκζητήσατέ με,
ומצאתם	--------	καὶ εὑρήσετέ με,
כי תדרשני	ܘܟܕ ܬܒܥܘܢܢܝ	ὅτι ζητήσετέ με
בכל לבבכם	ܒܟܠܗ ܠܒܟܘܢ	ἐν ὅλῃ καρδίᾳ ὑμῶν,
ונמצאתי לכם	ܬܫܟܚܘܢܢܝ	καί ἐπιφανοῦμαι ὑμῖν

* This term is present in 9a1 only.[33]

This is a particularly interesting verse, with minuses attributable to more than one cause. Taking the terms in their order in the text:

וקראתם אתי: this is an example of a term present in the *Vorlage* of P

33. Weitzman has shown (M.P. Weitzman, 'The Originality of Unique Readings in Peshitta MS 9a1', in P.B. Dirksen and M.J. Mulder [eds.], *The Peshitta: Its Early Text and History* [Leiden: E.J. Brill, 1988], pp. 225-58 [245], reprinted in Rapoport-Albert and Greenberg [eds.], *From Judaism*, pp. 325-46 [336]) that this MS, with its descendants, often agrees uniquely with the MT, especially in Kings and Jeremiah, and that some of these readings betray the peculiarities and style of the original translators of the Peshitta in the books concerned.

but evidently not in that of the LXX, one of the many such differences between the 'short' and the 'long' text-forms.

והלכתם, which is represented in neither version, seems to obstruct the flow of the sense, and could well be a late gloss presupposing exile and dispersion, and referring to making pilgrimage to Jerusalem.

ובקשתם אתי ומצאתם: this minus could perhaps be deliberate, for the verse is repetitive; but this is by no means a standard approach to the translation of repetitive Hebrew. The sequence of thought is unexpected, too: this phrase would be more logically found following, rather than preceding, כי תדרשני בכל לבבכם. Haplography with ונמצאתי לכם נאם יהוה is just possible, but unlikely, and this minus probably belongs in category (2) that is discussed below, an expansion that was present in the *Vorlage* of the LXX but not in that of the Peshitta, and was copied from that *Vorlage* by the editors of the MT.

34(LXX 41).17

אתם לא־שמעתם אלי לקרא דרור איש לאחיו ואיש לרעהו

becomes ܐܢ̈ܬܘܢ ܠܐ ܫܡܥܬܘܢ ܠܝ ܠܡܩܪܐ ܚܐܪܘܬܐ ܓܒܪ ܠܚܒܪܗ

and οὐκ ἠκούσατέ μου τοῦ καλέσαι ἄφεσιν ἕκαστος πρὸς τὸν πλησίον αὐτοῦ

איש לאחיו is represented neither in P nor in the LXX. Haplography, with a jump from איש (1) to איש (2) in איש לאחיו ואיש לרעהו is just possible but unlikely. It could only explain the omission from both the Syriac and the Greek if there were dependence of the first on the second, and the general picture of the translation technique[34] makes this unlikely at this area of reasonably clear Hebrew. A secondary expansion seems the more likely explanation, and is supported by the resemblance between this verse without לאחיו and v. 15, which reads לקרא דרור איש לרעהו.

36(LXX 43).28

וכתב עליה	ܘܟܬܘܒ ܥܠܝܗ	καὶ γράψον-----
את כל־הדברים	ܟܠܗܘܢ ܦ̈ܬܓܡܐ	πάντας τοὺς λόγους
הראשנים	ܩܕ̈ܡܝܐ	--------
אשר היו על־המגלה	ܕܐܝܬ ܗܘܘ ܥܠ ܡܓܠܬܐ	τοὺς ὄντας ἐπὶ τοῦ χαρτίου
הראשנה	--------	--------

In this verse too, the minuses have evidently developed in more than one way. The final clarifying term, הראשנה, entered the Hebrew too late

---

34. Gelston, *The Peshitta*, pp. 160-77 (176-77); Weitzman, *The Syriac Version*, pp. 68-86 (78-79); Greenberg, 'Translation Technique', pp. 221-51.

for the *Vorlagen* of either the LXX or the Peshitta; in contrast, עליה and הראשנים were absent from the *Vorlage* of the LXX but present in that provided for the Peshitta translators.

43(LXX 50).5

ויקח יוחנן בן־קרח	ܗܘܗ ܡܫܝ ܒܕ ܡܗܢ	καὶ ἔλαβεν Ιωαναν-----[35]
וכל־שרי החילים	ܠܚܠܐܘ ܐܕ, ܣܠܟ	καὶ πάντες οἱ ἡγεμόνες τῆς δυνάμεως
את כל־שארית יהודה	ܘܠܚܠܐܘ ܐܕܐܪ ܐܪܕܟܐܐ	πάντας τοὺς καταλοίπους Ιουδα
	ܟܝ ܗܒܕ ܣܗܘܡ ܐܪ	
אשר־שבו מכל־הגוים	------------	τοὺς ἀποστρέψαντας
אשר נדחו־שם	--------	--------
	--------	--------
לגור בארץ יהודה	--------	κατοικεῖν ἐν τῇ γῇ

The Peshitta renders v. 5a only, with no representation of אשר־שבו..., בארץ יהודה moving straight into the list of social groups given in v. 6. The LXX lacks only מכל־הגוים אשר נדחו־שם, which, as McKane notes,[36] redefines כל־שארית יהודה. This is apparently a further example of a verse with expansions of two distinct origins. One consists of מכל־הגוים אשר נדחו־שם which entered the MT line of transmission too late to be in the *Vorlagen* of either the LXX or the Peshitta; this is enclosed within the other expansion, אשר שבו לגור בארץ יהודה, incorporated by the editors of the MT from a 'short' LXX manuscript.[37]

44(LXX 51).19

עשינו לה כונים להעצבה

becomes ܚܒܪ, ܠܗ ܘܐܕܐܟ

and ἐποιήσαμεν αὐτῇ χαυῶνας.

---

35. υιος καρηε appears in a Lucianic variant.

36. W. McKane, *A Critical and Exegetical Commentary on Jeremiah*, II (ICC; Edinburgh: T. & T. Clark, 1996), p. 1053.

37. לגור בארץ is confirmed in 4QJer[b], but יהודה is not, and McKane notes (*A Critical and Exegetical Commentary*, p. 1053) that 4QJer[b] has a lacuna with a final mem visible, suggesting that מצרים might be a better guess than יהודה here. (There seems to be an error in the Peshitta in the translation of וכל־שרי החילים as ܠܚܠܐܘ ܐܕ, ܣܠܟ: the decision to travel to Egypt seems, judging from the wording of vv. 2 and 4, to have been taken not by Johanan alone, but by his military commanders too. The Peshitta takes וכל־שרי החילים as the object of ויקה, instead of as a supplementary subject.)

Neither version represents להעצבה, a term that may have been a secondary elaboration in the MT. That this term is secondary here is further suggested by its absence from the parallel passage in 7.18, לעשות כונים למלכת השמים, precisely rendered in both the LXX and P: were it a standard component of the description of the cakes referred to here, it would probably have been included at the earlier point. The term is admitedly difficult to translate, and could conceivably have been deliberately omitted from the translation, but this would be an unusual approach in P-Jeremiah.[38]

48(LXX 31).27

אם־בגנבים נמצאה	ܘܒܓܢܒ̈ܐ ܐܫܬ	εἰ ἐν κλοπαῖς σου εὑρέθη
כי־מדי דבריך	------------------	
בו תתנודד	ܗܐ ܒܗ̇ ܗܘܝܬ	ὅτι ἐπολέμεις αὐτόν
	ܡܩܪܒ ܠܗ	

This verse, with its rhetorical question about ישראל, evokes 31.20 where a similar phrase is used with reference to אפרים; possibly כי מדי דברי בו זכר אזכרנו עוד in ch. 31 prompted a secondary addition of כי־מדי דבריך בו to 48.27.[39]

---

38. At most areas of difficult Hebrew the translator restricted any freedom in his approach to the precise area of the problem, rendering the immediate context with his customary care to replicate the sense of the MT, and not taking the difficulty in the *Vorlage* as a justification for veering any further than was necessary from his source document: for books other than Jeremiah, see, for instance, B. Albrektson, *Studies in the Text and Theology of the Book of Lamentations* (Lund: C.W.K. Gleerup, 1963), p. 211; Gelston, *The Peshitta*, p. 158. For Jeremiah, see Greenberg, 'Translation Technique', pp. 221-89 (221-22): study of the translation of the passages of difficult Hebrew shows that this translator took a number of different approaches. Sometimes, he went to the LXX for help; sometimes, he made a guess, often based on his understanding of the etymology of the Hebrew; occasionally, he took a phrase or a word from elsewhere in the Hebrew Bible, paraphrased, or resorted to an atomistic rendering; but to exclude a term from his translation because it was difficult was not an approach he favoured. A similar sense of √עצב is seen at Job 10.8, where P uses √ܥܒܕ: some attempt at translation would be expected in Jeremiah too.

39. The translation implies √נדד rather than √גוד. The LXX is similar in this respect too, reading ὅτι ἐπολέμεις αὐτόν, suggesting that this may indeed have been the root present in the two *Vorlagen*.

51(LXX 28).28

קדשו עליה גוים את מלכי מדי את פחותיה ואת כל סגניה
ואת כל־ארץ ממשלתו

ואת כל־ארץ ממשלתו represented in neither the Syriac nor the Greek; it may be a secondary addition, from 1 Kgs 9.19 where the closely similar phrase, ובכל ארץ ממשלתו, closes an account of some of Solomon's building works.

Examples of Minuses in Group (a) Category (2)

In these cases, the LXX and MT agree with one another against the Peshitta; the minus is evident in the latter only. These minuses have in common their being found at points where both the MT and LXX contain terms that could well be secondary expansions. Some examples follow; as in the examples of minuses in category (1), the constraints of space have made it necessary to include only a selection of passages.

7.16

ואתה אל־תתפלל בעד־העם הזה ואל־תשא בעדם רנה ותפלה ואל־תפגע־בי

becomes ܘܐܢܬ ܠܐ ܬܨܠܐ ܥܠ ܥܡܐ ܗܢܐ ܘܠܐ ܬܒܥܐ ܥܠܝܗܘܢ ܘܠܐ ܬܗܪ ܒܝ

but μὴ προσεύχου...μὴ ἀξίου...μὴ εὔχου...μὴ προσέλθῃς

In the MT and LXX, four terms are used to proscribe three activities: Jeremiah is not to pray for this people, nor to cry to God on their behalf, nor, again, to pray for them, and not to intercede with God for their sake. In the Peshitta, however, there is only one reference to prayer. Not only is this a most striking verse, with its injunction to Jeremiah to refrain from part of his prophetic function, but it is closely similar to 11.14 where there are also two references to prayer: ואתה אל־תתפלל בעד־העם הזה ואל־תשא בעדם רנה ותפלה, and all terms are translated: ܘܐܢܬ ܠܐ ܬܨܠܐ ܥܠ ܥܡܐ ܗܢܐ ܘܠܐ ܬܒܥܐ ܥܠܝܗܘܢ ܒܨܠܘܬܐ, and καὶ σὺ μὴ προσεύχου περὶ τοῦ λαοῦ τούτου καὶ μὴ ἀξίου περὶ αὐτῶν ἐν δεήσει καὶ προσευχῇ. The translation of 11.14 is evidence that the translator of the Peshitta saw no value in avoiding repetition, a conclusion suppported by a good deal of evidence from other areas of this text, so the minus in 7.16 seems unlikely to result from a deliberate omission.

7.27, 28

The whole of 7.28a is absent from P, whereas the LXX has an omission from 7.27b:

Hebrew	Syriac	Greek
וְדִבַּרְתָּ אֲלֵיהֶם	ܘܐܡܪ ܠܗܘܢ	καὶ ἐρεῖς αὐτοῖς
אֶת־כָּל־הַדְּבָרִים הָאֵלֶּה	ܦܬܓܡܐ ܗܠܝܢ ܟܠܗܘܢ	τὸν λόγον τοῦτον
וְלֹא יִשְׁמְעוּ אֵלֶיךָ	ܘܠܐ ܢܫܡܥܘܢܟ	------
וְקָרָאתָ אֲלֵיהֶם	ܘܐܢ ܐܢܬ ܠܗܘܢ	------
וְלֹא יַעֲנוּכָה	ܘܠܐ ܢܥܢܘܢܟ	------
וְאָמַרְתָּ אֲלֵיהֶם	------	------
זֶה הַגּוֹי	------	Τοῦτο τὸ ἔθνος
אֲשֶׁר לוֹא־שָׁמְעוּ	------	ὃ οὐκ ἤκουσεν
בְּקוֹל יְהוָה אֱלֹהָיו	------	τῆς φωνῆς κυρίου
וְלֹא לָקְחוּ מוּסָר	------	οὐδὲ ἐδέξατο παιδείαν
אָבְדָה הָאֱמוּנָה	ܐܒܕܬ ܗܝܡܢܘܬܐ	ἐξέλιπεν ἡ πίστις
וְנִכְרְתָה מִפִּיהֶם	ܘܦܣܩܬ ܡܢ ܦܘܡܗܘܢ	ἐκ στόματος αὐτῶν

Verses 27b and 28a are doublets; one component appears in the LXX, the other in P, and both in the MT. Evidently, one component was present in the *Vorlage* of the LXX, and thus entered the Greek version(s); the other was present in the proto-MT manuscript which formed the *Vorlage* of the Peshitta; and at a later stage, when the MT itself was established, its editors decided that rather than select one of the two components, they would avoid any possibility of making an unwise choice, and would incorporate both.

24.1

אֶת־יְכָנְיָהוּ בֶן־יְהוֹיָקִים מֶלֶךְ־יְהוּדָה וְאֶת־שָׂרֵי יְהוּדָה וְאֶת־הֶחָרָשׁ וְאֶת־הַמַּסְגֵּר מִירוּשָׁלָם

becomes ܠܝܘܟܢܝܐ ܒܪ ܝܘܝܩܝܡ ܡܠܟܐ ܕܝܗܘܕܐ ܘܠܐܘܡܢܐ ܘܠܡܣܓܪܐ ܡܢ ܐܘܪܫܠܡ, with no representation of שָׂרֵי יְהוּדָה; LXX, however, has...καὶ τοὺς ἄρχοντας...

McKane notes[40] that this list is 'to be regarded as a summary of a longer and more informative list'; the statement may have been added in the light of editorial consideration of the 'short' text, in response to a decision that the summary was too limited.

42(LXX 49).2

The epithet in יִרְמְיָהוּ הַנָּבִיא is not represented in the Peshitta ܐܪܡܝܐ, though it is present in the LXX Ιερεμίαν τὸν προφήτην. Deliberate

---

40. McKane, *A Critical and Exegetical Commentary*, I, p. 607.

omission of an epithet would be markedly inconsistent with the translation technique.[41]

42(LXX 49).2

והתפלל בעדנו אל יהוה אלהיך בעד כל־השארית הזאת כי־נשארנו מעט מהרבה

becomes ܟܠ ܥܠܝ ܡܪܢ ܐܠܗܐ ܐܠܗܢ ܘܨܠܐ ܕܐܬܟܪ ܡܠܠ ܡܢ ܣܘܩܠܐ, with no representation of בעד כל השארית הזאת.

LXX, however, has περὶ τῶν καταλοίπων τούτων...

The verse has attracted a good deal of critical interest. Janzen[42] detected a conflate text; his discussion suggests the components בעדנו אל יהוה אלהיך, and בעד כל השארית הזאת. McKane[43] argues that, because the LXX does not represent בעדנו, Janzen's interpretation is unsatisfactory, and that בעדנו should be regarded as an insertion in the MT. Here, editorial awareness of the stereotype to which McKane refers, appearing at 7.16 and 11.14, may have influenced the decision to incorporate the term. Whichever suggestion is accepted, the passage belongs in this category of minuses.

44(LXX 51).27

הנני שקד עליהם לרעה ולא לטובה

becomes ܐܢܐ ܓܝܪ ܡܣܪܗܒ ܐܝܬܝ ܥܠܝܗܘܢ ܒܝܫܬܐ

with no rendering of ולא לטובה.

'Behold, I am watching over them for evil and not for good' thus becomes 'for I bring evil speedily upon them'. The LXX, however, has ὅτι ἰδοὺ ἐγὼ ἐγρήγορα ἐπ' αὐτοὺς τοῦ κακῶσαι αὐτοὺς καὶ οὐκ ἀγαθῶσαι.

48(LXX 31).20

הילילי וזעקי הגידו בארנון כי שדד מואב

becomes ܐܝܠܠܘ ܘܩܥܘ ܐܟܪܙܘ ܒܐܪܢܘܢ ܕܐܬܒܙ ܡܘܐܒ,

with no representation of הגידו.

LXX, however, has ὀλόλυξον καὶ κέκραξον, ἀνάγγειλον ἐν Αρνων...

41. Greenberg, 'Translation Technique', pp. 92-93.
42. Janzen, *Studies*, p. 17.
43. McKane, *A Critical and Exegetical Commentary*, II, p. 1032.

This example is similar to 25.4 discussed above: the omission of a verb would not be in keeping with the translation technique.

48(LXX 31).36

> על כן לבי למואב כחללים יהמה ולבי אל־אנשי קיר־חרש כחלילים יהמה
> becomes ܡܛܠ ܗܢܐ ܠܒܝ ܥܠ ܡܘܐܒ ܐܝܟ ܟܢܪ̈ܐ ܢܝܠܠ, with no equivalent of ולבי אל־אנשי קיר־חרש יהמה.
> LXX, however, has διὰ τοῦτο καρδία μου Μωαβ ὥσπερ αὐλοὶ βουβήσουσιν, καρδία μου ἐπ’ ἀνθρώπους Κιραδας…

Isaiah 16.7, לאשישי קיר חרשת תהגו, may have influenced the editors' decision to incorporate this reference. (Parablepsis, with eye-skip from יהמה[1] to יהמה[2] is possible, either in the Peshitta or in its *Vorlage*.)

50(LXX 27).24

> יקשתי לך וגם נלכדת בבל ואת לא ידעת נמצאת וגם נתפשת כי ביהוה התגרית
> becomes ܐܬܬܩܠܬ ܒܒܠ ܘܐܦ ܐܬܬܨܝܕܬ ܘܠܐ ܝܕܥܬ ܕܠܘܩܒܠ ܡܪܝܐ ܩܡܬ, with no representation of נמצאת וגם נתפשת.
> LXX, however, has εὑρέθης καὶ ἐλήμφθης.

The meaning of the phrase נמצאת וגם נתפשת has been much discussed; McKane[44] points out that it does not seem to add anything to נלכדת, and suggests that its force is to show Babylon's surprise at her sudden change of condition.

51(LXX 28).35

> חמסי ושארי על בבל תאמר ישבת ציון ודמי אל־ישני כשדים תאמר ירושלם
> becomes ܒܙܬܝ ܘܡܚܘܬܝ ܠܒܒܠ ܐܫܬܟܚܘ ܘܕܡܝ ܥܠ ܥܡܘܪ̈ܐ ܕܟܠܕ̈ܝܐ ܬܐܡܪ ܐܘܪܫܠܡ, with no rendering of תאמר ישבת ציון;
> LXX, however, has οἱ μόχθοι μου καὶ αἱ ταλαιπωρίαι μου εἰς Βαβυλῶνα, ἐρεῖ κατοικοῦσα Σιων, καὶ τὸ αἷμά μου ἐπὶ τοὺς καταοικοῦντας Χαλδαίους, ἐρεῖ Ιερουσαλμη.

תאמר ישבת ציון may have been a later insertion, the editors perhaps influenced in their decision to add it by a wish to sharpen the parallelism of 51.35a and 51.35b.

44. McKane, *A Critical and Exegetical Commentary*, II, pp. 1276-77.

51(LXX 28).41

אֵיךְ נִלְכְּדָה שֵׁשַׁךְ וַתִּתָּפֵשׂ

becomes[45] ܪܕ‍ܚܬܝܪ ܐܬܘܕܐܪ ܪܚܒܪ, with no representation of
ותתפש.

LXX, however, has πῶς ἑάλω καὶ ἐθηρεύθη...

ותתפש too may be a later insertion, under the influence of, for instance,
51.31, 32 where the MT has a series of phrases each including a verb of
similar sense, i.e. נלכדה, נתפשו, שרפו באש, and נבהלו.

51(LXX 28).63

תִקְשֹׁר עָלָיו אֶבֶן וְהִשְׁלַכְתּוֹ אֶל תּוֹךְ פְּרָת

becomes ܐܬܒܚ ,ܡܐܚܬܟܐ ܪܐܪܟ ܚܒ ܬܐܠܡ, with no representation of
תוך.

LXX, however, has καὶ ῥίψεις αὐτὸ εἰς μέσον τοῦ Εὐφράτου.

This final example is most striking; omission of any part of this instruction, so short and so full of impact, is surprising.

In conclusion, one further hypothesis remains to be suggested. There
is a marked difference in the prevalence of examples in the different
parts of the book. As noted above, constraints of space make it impossible to give every example in this essay, so it must be admitted that a
bias in selection could, in theory, be responsible for this unequal distribution; great care has been taken, however, to ensure that selection was
fair, and a fuller account will be published in due course in the series of
Monographs of the Peshitta Institute. The book of Jeremiah may be
divided into (a) oracles against the nation and its leaders, approximately
chs. 1–24, and an appendix to these oracles, ch. 25; (b) biographical and
historical chapters, approximately chs. 26–45; and (c) the foreign
oracles and the historical appendix, approximately chs. 46–end 52. The
number of verses in these sections is (a) 626, (b) 473, and (c) 265.
Expressed as percentages of the total book, these figures give (a) 46%,
(b) 35%, and (c) 19%.

In category (1), the examples are distributed evenly, with the largest

45. The Athbash code for Babylon was recognized, as at 25.26, and the biblical
antecedents of Parthia identified with the Babylonians: see M.P. Weitzman, 'The
Interpretative Character of the Syriac Old Testament', in Magne Sæbø (ed.),
Hebrew Bible/Old Testament (Göttingen: Vandenhoeck & Ruprecht, 1996),
pp. 587-611 (607), reprinted in Rapoport-Albert and Greenberg (eds.), *From
Judaism*, pp. 55-89 (80).

number in section (a) and the lowest in section (b). Minuses in category (2), however, present a different picture: here there is an imbalance, with disproportionately more examples in the last part of the book, which suggests that there may have been differences between the transmission histories of the various sections. Possibly, whereas the expansion of the first two sections had progressed to a stage at which editorial review of the 'short' form(s) had been completed by the time the Peshitta was written, editing of the third part was at an earlier stage. This suggestion, made only tentatively here, would be compatible with the theory that the oracles against the nations circulated separately from the rest of the book at some stage.[46]

In summary, the analysis supports the concept of a number of co-existing MT MSS; a linear concept of transmission, starting with a 'short' text and developing this to form a 'long' text, seems to be simplistic. Several factors, including the religio-political power of the groups holding the various texts, were doubtless involved in the preservation or loss of the MSS used, at different times and in different places, by the particular authorities involved in the transmission of the Hebrew Bible.

---

46. See for instance Janzen, *Studies*, p. 115.

TWIN TARGUMS: PSALM 18 AND 2 SAMUEL 22[*]

Marian Smelik and Willem Smelik

1. *Introduction*

Psalm 18 and 2 Sam. 22 are virtually identical copies of a Psalm attributed to David. It comes as no surprise that their variations have received considerable text-critical attention, because they frequently shed light on one another. While some of these variations are apparently due to scribal errors, and others may have resulted from a complicated process in which the texts exercised a mutual influence on each other,[1] there seem to be readings that represent genuine variations, rather than errors and scribal corrections, which have apparently been created by those responsible for the textual transmission, either orally or in written form.[2]

The differences between the later Aramaic versions of these two chapters have received less attention. True, there is a clear consensus among scholars that the Targum of Ps. 18 directly depends on the Targum Jonathan to 2 Sam. 22,[3] but the issue has never been studied in

*   The present article is based on a paper presented at the European Meeting of SBL, Lausanne, 1997, and the 12th World Congress of Jewish Studies, Jerusalem, 1997. We wish to thank the editors, Ada Rapoport-Albert and Gillian Greenberg, for their invaluable remarks in connection with this paper.

1.   F.M. Cross and D.N. Freedman, 'A Royal Song of Thanksgiving: 2 Samuel 22 = Psalm 18', *JBL* 72 (1953), pp. 15-34.

2.   Ps. 18.7 and 32, for example, avoid using אקרא and מבלעדי twice in a bicolon. There is reason to assume that some pluses reflect the flexibility of expansion and contraction in the performance of ancient Near Eastern literature; see J.C. de Moor, 'The Art of Versification in Ugarit and Israel, II: The Formal Structure', *UF* 10 (1978), pp. 187-217 (217) and the literature cited there.

3.   W. Bacher, 'Das Targum zu den Psalmen', *ZDMG* 21 (1872), pp. 408-16, 462-73; P. Churgin, *Targum Jonathan to the Prophets* (New Haven: Yale University Press, 1907 [=1927]), pp. 130-31; *idem*, תרגום כתובים (New York: Horeb, 1945); J. Komlosh, המקרא באור התרגום (Tel-Aviv: Dvir, 1973), pp. 310-11;

great detail. Study of these variant readings yields valuable insight into the textual development and redaction of the Targum to the Prophets. While it is generally agreed that this Targum represents the outcome of a long process of modification and redaction, spanning the Tannaitic and Amoraic periods, the picture of how, when and even by whom editorial changes and modifications have been made remains opaque. There is still little hard evidence for the Tannaitic and Amoraic components, and the suggestions advanced by a number of scholars for dating the Targum are disputed, often remaining inconclusive. For this reason it is important to evaluate the suggestion made by one of the pioneering scholars in Targum studies, Pinkhos Churgin. On the assumption that Targ. Ps. 18 is a copy of Targ. 2 Sam. 22, he claimed that wherever these Targums differ from one another in this chapter, it is the former that preserves the proto-Targum of the latter. Substantiation of this thesis would give invaluable material evidence for the textual history of at least one chapter of Targum Jonathan.[4]

To assess Churgin's claim carefully we have to establish with the utmost precision whether and to what extent Targ. Ps. 18 represents a copy of Targum Jonathan to the Prophets (hereinafter Targ. Neb.). Previous studies have been too heuristic, adducing a few tell-tale examples, with no serious attempt to classify differences between the two Targums. It is necessary not only to distinguish dialectal differences, and variations triggered by the differences in the respective Hebrew parent texts, but also to integrate these results with an assessment of significant similarities between the two Targums, for example, at points where a difference in the Hebrew texts is not reflected in the Targums. When, for example, in a discusssion of the Targum of Psalms published in the nineteenth century, Wilhelm Bacher claimed that Targ. Ps. 18 is a copy of Targ. Neb., he illustrated his opinion with two

---

L. Díez Merino, *Targum de Salmos: Edición principe del Ms. Villa-Amil n.5 de Alfonso de Zamora* (BHBib, 6; Madrid: Consejo superior de investigaciones científicas, 1982), p. 58; E. White, 'A Critical Edition of the Targum of Psalms: A Computer Generated Text of Books I and 2' (Unpublished PhD dissertation, McGill University, Montreal, 1988), pp. 18-19.

4.   For redaction and the proto-Targum (a term not used by Churgin), see, e.g., R.P. Gordon, *Studies in the Targum to the Twelve Prophets: From Nahum to Malachi* (VTSup, 51; Leiden: E.J. Brill, 1994), pp. 108-16; W.F. Smelik, *The Targum of Judges* (OTS, 36; Leiden: E.J. Brill, 1995), pp. 406, 413, 416, 423, 639-42, 644-45, 648.

examples only, and even these two do not withstand careful scrutiny.[5] He added that the translator of Targ. Ps. replaced only relatively unknown words by more common and contemporary equivalents and that he modified the text of his *Vorlage*, Targ. 2 Sam. 22, where the Hebrew text of Ps. 18 differed from that of 2 Sam. 22. He did not point to exceptions, where Targ. 2 Sam. 22 seems to be based on Ps. 18, or where Targ. Ps. 18 follows the different wording of MT 2 Sam. 22. He noted one instance where the Targum of Psalms supplements its *Vorlage*, in v. 29, and pointed to the possibility of a multiple translation in this verse, following Zunz.[6] When Pinkhos Churgin expressed a similar opinion in his study of the Targum to the Prophets, returning to this subject in a study of the Targum to the Writings,[7] he adduced first three and later fifteen examples in support of his opinion that Targ. Ps. 18 preserves an older version of Targum Jonathan. He did not, however, even attempt to categorize these differences, and simply dismissed the possibility that the translator of Targ. Ps. 18, or later copyists, could have contributed to its textual development.[8] Here he simplified matters. Instances where the Hebrew of Ps. 18 differs from 2 Samuel, and the Targum of Ps. 18 keeps pace with the MT, should alert us to the real possibility that the Targum of Ps. 18 is not simply a copy.[9] These instances justify the assumption that the translator was able to make independent contributions to the text.

For these reasons, a reassessment of the evidence is called for, provided that it is based on a critical analysis of all the evidence, rather than a few selected examples, and that it includes a categorization of differences and similarities between the Targums, according to their relationship with the Hebrew parent texts. In the preparation of the

---

5.   Bacher, 'Das Targum zu den Psalmen', p. 472. See below, n. 57 and section 4.3.2.

6.   L. Zunz, *Die gottesdienstlichen Vorträge der Juden historisch entwickelt* (Frankfurt: J. Kaufmann, 2nd edn, 1892), pp. 84-85 n. a; Bacher, 'Das Targum zu den Psalmen', pp. 472-73. For the phenomenon of multiple translation, see D.M. Stec, *The Text of the Targum of Job: An Introduction and Critical Edition* (AGJU, 20; Leiden: E.J. Brill, 1994), pp. 85-94.

7.   Churgin, *Targum Jonathan*, pp. 130-31; *idem*, תרגום כתובים pp. 25-27.

8.   In fact, copyists often would alter their readings, adjusting their text to a variant in their *Vorlage*; see Smelik, *Targum of Judges*, p. 643 n. 15.

9.   He refers just once to a correction after its Hebrew parent text (Churgin, *Targum Jonathan*, p. 57 n. 5).

present article, the authors were able to consult critical editions that were unavailable to these earlier scholars.[10]

Our findings indicate that the author of Targ. Ps. 18 was indeed thoroughly familiar with a copy of Targum Jonathan to 2 Sam. 22. He used this copy, but substituted late Aramaic lexemes for those in Targ. 2 Sam. 22 which had, in his dialect, become obsolete. He also introduced distinct readings at points, but not all points, at which there are differences between the Hebrew parent texts of 2 Sam. 22 and Ps. 18. It is extremely unlikely that all these instances simply escaped his attention; more probably, he intended the text to be read in the light of its parallel text. He preserved almost all supplements to the translation of the Hebrew text as found in the Targum to 2 Sam. 22, together with the substitutions for Hebrew lexemes, that is, words that differ semantically from the Hebrew original. Conversely, he also introduced new translations, on his own initiative, even at points where the Hebrew parent texts do not disagree. The translator thus displays a degree of independence, despite his overall adherence to the model translation of Targ. Neb. His translation strategies sometimes differ from those evident in Targ. Neb., for example in his treatment of metaphors and the preference for theologoumena. Lastly, the Targum of Psalms has been subject to change in the course of textual transmission: some of these changes may reflect alternative translations, which were incorporated into the text during later transmission.

Whether the translator of Targ. Ps. 18 knew Targ. Neb. in written form, or by oral tradition, is not an easy question to answer. Because 2 Sam. 22 and its Targum is part of the lectionary cycle for Pesach, the oral recitation in Aramaic may well have been very familiar to the Targumist. A similar oral link may perhaps also be postulated for some of the variant readings found in the Cairo Genizah fragments of Targ. 2 Sam. 22; here, the reverse process is seen, with occasional influence of either Ps. 18 or Targ. Ps. 18 on Targ. Neb.

10. A. Sperber (ed.), *The Bible in Aramaic* (5 vols.; Leiden: E.J. Brill, 1959–1973); Díez Merino, *Targum de Salmos*; White, *A Critical Edition*. All quotations are from White's edition, but with abbreviations and ligatures filled out, supplemented by Díez Merino's edition for the Targum of Pss. 73–150. In addition we have made use of הקונקורדנציה הממוחשבת לתנ"ך ומפרשיו (Jerusalem: DBS, n.d.). The question of the authorship of Targum Psalms cannot be dealt with within the present study. For the sake of convenience, we refer to 'the targumist': the term is not intended to exclude the possibility of multiple authorship.

Although Wilhelm Bacher, Pinkhos Churgin and Judah Komlosh had already reached some of the conclusions discussed above, they had not identified the relative independence of the translator of Targ. Ps. 18. This observation substantially undermines Churgin's claims concerning the old version of Targum Jonathan as reflected by Targ. Ps. 18. The assumption of a proto-Targum underlying the differences between the Targums is not justified unless additional proof can be adduced in support of it. Admittedly, in a few cases this assumption does provide the most attractive explanation, but the evidence does not permit a clear verdict on the redaction of the chapter as a whole.

In what follows, the observations on which these conclusions are based will be set out.

2. *Types of Relationship*

The relationships between these texts are complicated. Three principal relationships must be defined: that between each Aramaic text and its own Hebrew parent text, that between the two Aramaic texts, and that between each Aramaic text and the other Hebrew parent text. Previous studies have not attempted to explore the third of these relationships. In addition, there is the matter of Hebrew textual criticism, exploring the relationship between the Hebrew *Vorlage* of the Targums and the MT. The complexity of the analysis may be illustrated by a random example of a substantial supplement in v. 49.

Table 1. *2 Samuel 22.49/Psalm 18.49*

תרוממני	----	מן־קמי	אף	מאיבי	מפלטי	MT Ps.
תרוממני	----	ומקמי	----	מאיבי	ומוציאי	MT 2 Sam.
תגברינני	לאבאשא לי	על דקיימין	לחוד[11]	מבעלי דבבי	משיזיב יתי	Targ. Ps.
תגברנני	לאבאשא לי	ועל דקימין	[12]----	מסנאי	ופרקי	Targ. Neb.
תצילני	----	חמס	מאיש	----	----	MT Ps.
תצילני	----	חמסים	מאיש	----	----	MT 2 Sam.
ישיזיבינני[13]	דעימיה	חטופין	עממין	ומשרית	מן גוג	Targ. Ps.
תשיזבנני	דעמיה	חטופין	עממין	ומשרית	מגוג	Targ. Neb.

11. This word is absent in MSS G-I-5 (El Escorial) and Villa-Amil no. 5 (Madrid), whereas MSS Montefiore 7 and Parma 3232 lack the phrase משיזיב יתי מבעלי דבבי לחוד על דקיימין לאבאשא לי.

12. Note, however, that a Cairo Genizah fragment (Sperber) reads ואף על for ועל.

13. But many MSS support the second person singular.

MT: Who rescued me/set me free from my enemies, who raised me clear of my adversaries, saved me from lawless men/man.

Targ. Neb.: And He delivered me from my *haters* [14]/enemies, and/but you made me strong against those who rose up TO DO ME HARM, you saved me from GOG AND (FROM) THE ARMIES OF *the violent nations that came with him.*

Both Targums allude to the eschatological battle against Gog in identical wording, though there is no equivalent in the MT.[15] Further, the Targums translate the first word in Ps. 18, not the more general term used in 2 Sam. 22, but use different roots to do so. Conversely, they reflect the plural of חמס as in 2 Sam. 22, not the singular of Ps. 18: here, they may also have been influenced by the plural מאיש חמסים תנצרני in Ps. 140.2 and 5.[16] The Hebrew lexeme אף is attested only in Ps. 18, and reflected only in Targ. Ps. 18, though a Cairo Genizah fragment of Targ. Neb. adduced by Sperber also supports it.[17] Targ. Neb. reflects ו- as in its *Vorlage*, rather than the particle. The Targums also differ in their translation of מאיבי, identical in the two Hebrew texts.[18]

The data presented above may be summarized as follows: (1) The Targums of Ps. 18 and 2 Sam. 22 may agree with each other where their parent texts do not. (2) The Targums sometimes disagree with each other in the same way as do their parent texts. (3) Both Targums may show the same difference from the Hebrew: substantial supplements may be made, and different lexical equivalents selected (substitutions), suggesting a strong textual link between the Targums.[19] (4) They sometimes disagree at places where the Hebrew texts are similar. (5) Cairo Genizah fragments may display influences from either MT Psalms

---

14. Words printed in italics indicate a semantic difference between the Targum and the Hebrew, words printed in small capitals a supplement in the translation.

15. Komlosh, המקרא באור התרגום, p. 310.

16. The variant reading תנצרני for תצילני, supported by a Qumran text according to BHS, is not supported by the Targums and may, in fact, be based on Ps. 140.

17. See n. 12 above.

18. See below, section 4.3.1.

19. For the coherence between straightforward (or base) translation, substitution, and supplements, see D. Shepherd, 'Translating and Supplementing: A(nother) Look at the Targumic Versions of Genesis 4.3-16', *JAB* 1 (1999), pp. 125-46; W.F. Smelik, 'Translation and Commentary in One: The Interplay of Pluses and Substitutions in the Targum of the Prophets', *JSJ* 29 (1998), pp. 245-60; *idem*, 'Concordance and Consistency: Translation Studies and Targum Jonathan', *JJS* 49 (1998), pp. 286-305.

or Targ. Ps. 18. (6) The picture is complicated by the possibility of Hebrew variant readings in both *Vorlagen*.

The data may be classified into three categories of similarities between the Aramaic versions: (1) those that render similarities between the Hebrew parent texts, (2) those that render differences between the Hebrew parent texts, and (3) those that differ from the Hebrew parent text(s). Differences fall into two groups: (1) those that render differences between the Hebrew parent texts, (2) those between the Aramaic versions only: these may be divided into dialectal differences, substitutions, and pluses. Text-critical observations will be restricted to the points where they are relevant to the present discussion.

3. *Similarities between the Targums*

3.1. *When All Versions Are Similar*
There are many points at which the Hebrew doublets are identical. When their respective Targums follow suit in a straightforward translation, with no significant shift of meaning, dependence of one on the other cannot easily be inferred. Nonetheless, similarities between the Targums, even where the Hebrew parent texts are identical, are important, for such similarities are by no means inevitable. Despite common source texts, many translations differ in vocabulary, syntax and translation strategies, including for instance their approach to metaphors, similes, and descriptions of God. Thus a direct literary relationship may be indicated where translations are identical, but remains unproven in the absence of further evidence.

The discussion that follows is restricted to the particular grammatical and translational differences between Targum Psalms and Targum Jonathan which are relevant to the categories considered below.

3.2. *Similarities Despite Hebrew Dissimilarities*
Similarities between the Targums at points where the Hebrew texts differ are striking.[20] These may be classified as follows.[21]

---

20. Cf. Komlosh, המקרא באור התרגום, p. 311. Interestingly, the Masoretes attest ויהם as the *qere* for ויהמם in 2 Sam. 22, while the *kethib* agrees with Ps. 18. The Targums agree at this point with the *kethib*.

21. Bacher, 'Das Targum zu den Psalmen', p. 464, took אמר דויד בתשבחא in Targ. Ps. 18.4 as proof for the pual of מהלל rather than MT's piel. But the Targums seem to render the text smoothly here, and the result depends on the translation strategies rather than text-critical evidence.

Targums agree, rendering the Hebrew of 2 Sam. 22:[22] in v. 5 the
Targums read עקא for חבלי־מות (Ps. 18) and משברי־מות (2 Sam. 22); in
v. 12, both Targums apparently omit סתרו (Ps. 18; absent in 2 Sam. 22)
(unless שכינתיה is to be understood as its equivalent, in which case they
follow Ps. 18);[23] in v. 14 Ps. 18 reads בשמים whereas 2 Sam. 22 reads
מן־שמים, as the Targums: מן שמיא.[24] In v. 20 Targumic ית reflects את in
2 Sam. 22; in v. 28 ובמימרך does not reflect the suffix עינים (Ps. 18) but
that of עיניך (2 Sam. 22); in v. 36 ובמימרך is the common equivalent for
וענותך, 'your triumph (?)'[25] (Ps. 18) and וענתך, 'your response' (2 Sam.
22); in v. 43 2 Sam. 22 reads אדקם, 'I crushed them', supported by the
Targums with בעטית בהון, 'I trampled them down',[26] whereas Ps. 18
has אריקם, 'I cast them out';[27] in v. 45 יתכדבון corresponds not to the
conjugation יכחשו (Ps. 18) but to יתכחשו (2 Sam. 22); in v. 47 תקוף
reflects צור (2 Sam. 22) which is absent in Ps. 18;[28] in v. 49 עממין חטופין
reflects the plural of חמסים (2 Sam. 22), in contrast to the singular חמס
(Ps. 18).

Targums agree, rendering the Hebrew of Ps. 18: in v. 7 קדמו(ה)י corresponds to לפניו in Ps. 18, lacking in 2 Sam. 22; in v. 11 the translation

---

22. White lists five examples, which he considers to be proof of the dependency
of Targ. Ps. 18 on Targ. Neb. (*A Critical Edition*, p. 19 n. 73); two of them will also
be listed below, but the three others must be rejected. No. 1, the forms where the
difference is related to perfect versus imperfect, and where Targ. Ps. 18 follows MT
2 Sam. 22 may well reflect genuine Hebrew variant readings; such variants are not
at all uncommon. No. 4 (Ps. 18.44) is discussed below. Finally, no. 5 depends on
the equivalent דבר for MT לקח in v. 17, which White contrasts with Targ. Ps. 49.16
(אלף, a co-textual reading as in 68.19). Why White applies this argument to this
verse and not, say, to 51.13 (סלק) or 73.24 (נסב) is unclear; moreover, the Sefardi
MSS *have* דבר in that verse, and a parallel in Ps. 70.17 with David as object and
God as subject is again translated with דבר.

23. See below, n. 144.

24. With the exception of Montefiore 7 (London) and Villa-Amil no. 5 (Madrid),
reading בשמיא.

25. The meaning of this word is uncertain; see *HALAT*, p. 809; M. Dahood,
Psalms I: 1–50 (AB; Garden City, NY: Doubleday, 1965), p. 116.

26. Targ. Ps. 18 reads בעטיתינון, with variants.

27. Cross and Freedman, 'A Royal Song', p. 32 n. 95; J.P. Fokkelman, *Narrative Art and Poetry in the Books of Samuel. III. Throne and City (II Sam. 2–8 and
21–24)* (Assen: Van Gorcum, 1990), pp. 393-94.

28. For this translation equivalent, see also vv. 3 and 32 and Gordon, *Studies in
the Targum*, p. 144.

ודבר, 'drove', reflects וידא (Ps. 18) instead of וירא [29] (2 Sam. 22); in v. 13 שמיא seems to have been triggered by עביו in Ps. 18, again absent in 2 Sam. 22; in v. 15 both versions reflect the suffix of חציו in Ps. 18, in contrast to חצים in 2 Sam. 22; in v. 42 the translation בען סעיד, 'they asked for support', rather reflects ישועו, 'they cried (for help)' (Ps. 18), than ישעו, 'they gazed' (2 Sam. 22); in v. 49, as observed above, ופריק (Targ. Neb.) and משיזיב (Targ. Ps.) reflect מפלטי (Ps. 18) rather than ומוציאי (2 Sam. 22).

A notable exception occurs in v. 44, where Targ. Ps. follows 2 Sam. 22's תשמרני with תיטרינני, except for Sefardi witnesses having יתי מניתא; but Targ. Neb. follows MT Ps. 18's תשימני with its equivalent תמניני.

It is often difficult to determine which of the Hebrew readings triggered the common Targumic rendering. In v. 1 the metaphors ומיד (Ps. 18) and ומכף (2 Sam. 22) have both been substituted with ומחרבא. In v. 7 the translation מתחנן for אשוע (Ps. 18) and אקרא (2 Sam. 22) is appropriate for שוע, but, although it occurs in Targ. Ps. 31.23 for בשועי, is not the standard equivalent. Even in v. 42, the verb has been translated with בעא (followed by supplements), and indeed this verb and צלא are the standard equivalents in Targ. Neb. and Targ. Pss.[30] The verb חנן is the equivalent for Hebrew נשא in Targ. Neb.[31] In v. 12 the metaphors חשרת־מים, 'sieve of waters' (2 Sam.) and חשכת־מים, 'dark waters' (Ps.) have been translated as (ו)מי(י)ן תקיפין, 'heavy rainfall'.[32] In v. 24 the supplement of 'fear' (בדחלתיה) required adjustment of the Hebrew prepositions, עמו in Ps. 18, and לו in 2 Sam. 22. In v. 26 the translation זרעיה does not precisely render גבר (Ps.) or גבור (2 Sam.). Similarly, the translation אלא for זולתי (Ps.) and מבלעדי (2 Sam.) in v. 32 is imprecise.[33] The rare form ויתר [34] in 2 Sam. 22.33, and its

---

29. This seems to be a scribal error in 2 Samuel, as most commentators assume.

30. See further Targ. Neb. Isa. 58.9 תבעי מן קדמוהי; Jon. 2.3 בעיתי; Hab. 1.2 אנא מצלי; Targ. Pss. 22.25 בצלואיהון; 28.2 במצלי (with intentional avoidance of the same root twice, after בעאתי, see n. 127 below); 30.3 צליתי; 31.23 באיתחננותי; 72.12 דבעי; 88.14 צליתי; 119.147 וצליתי.

31. 2 Kgs 19.4; Isa. 37.4; Jer. 7.16; 11.14.

32. The reading חשרת in 2 Sam. 22 is preferable. Cf. S.I. Feigin, 'The Heavenly Siege', *JNES* 9 (1950), pp. 40-43; J.C. de Moor, *The Seasonal Pattern in the Ugaritic Myth of Baʻlu: According to the Version of Ilimilku* (AOAT, 16; Neukirchen–Vluyn: Neukirchner Verlag, 1971), p. 210.

33. As observed in n. 1, Ps. 18 avoids the use of a similar form within a bicolon, as in v. 7.

34. The verb ויתר occurs rarely (cf. *HALAT*, p. 695), but it does not seem to be a

counterpart ויתן in Psalms, have been translated with ומתקן; as this Aramaic form is nowhere the equivalent of נתן in Targ. Neb., there is no evidence to show from which text the Targumists took their cue, though Ps. 18 appears more probable.[35] Finally, in v. 48 the almost synonymous use of וידבר, 'and subjugated' (Ps. 18), and ומוריד, 'and brought down' (2 Sam. 22), has been treated identically in Targ. Neb., ותבר, and Targ. Pss., ומתבר.[36] The particple of Targ. Ps. 18 agrees with its parent text, as does the perfect of Targ. Neb. Here, however, both versions may also reflect the reading in 4QSam[a], ומרדד, 'and subdued'.

One example rewards closer examination. In v. 5 both Targums make the same comparison: distress (עקא) is compared to the condition of a woman in labour, on the verge of dying.

Table 2. 2 *Samuel* 22.5 / *Psalm* 18.5[37]

(חבלי-)	----	----	----	הבלי	אפפוני	---	MT Ps.
(משברי-)	----	----	----	משברי	אפפני	כי	MT 2 Sam.
מתברא	על	דיתבא	כאיתתא	עקא	אקפתני	ארי	Targ. Neb.
מתברא	על	דיתבא	כאיתתא	עקא	אקפתני	----	Targ. Ps.
מות	----	----	----	----	----	----	MT Ps.
מות	----	----	----	----	----	----	MT 2 Sam.
לממת	מסתכנא	והיא	למילד	לה	לית	וחיל	Targ. Neb.
ליממת	מסתכנא	והיא	למילד	לה	לית	וחיל	Targ. Ps.

MT: Ropes of death encompassed me...

Targums: (For) *distress* surrounded me, LIKE A WOMAN WHO IS SITTING ON *a birthstool* AND SHE DOES NOT HAVE THE STRENGTH TO GIVE BIRTH, AND SHE IS IN mortal danger...

The agreement between the translations is marked, but not unique. The same translation (עקא כאתתא דיתבא על מתברא וחיל לית לה למילד) occurs in Targ. Neb. on 2 Kgs 19.3, Isa. 37.3 and Hos. 13.13 as an appropriate explanation of the Hebrew noun משבר, 'mouth of the womb'. This Hebrew word occurs only in those three verses; but in

scribal error for ויתן; cf. P.K. McCarter, *II Samuel* (AB, 9; Garden City, NY: Doubleday, 1984), p. 459; Fokkelman, *Throne and City*, p. 392.

35. The only other qal form of נתר in Job 37.1 has been translated with שפז in Targ. Job.

36. The participle of Targ. Ps. 18 agrees with its parent text, as does the perfect of Targ. Neb.

37. Bracketed words have been repeated in this table to show to which Aramaic words they are equivalent, when they have been translated twice.

2 Sam. 22 a homograph occurs, מַשְׁבֵּר, 'breaker'. The translator sub-stituted one for the other by virtual revocalization, a type of exegesis that is known as paronomasia. The source for this interpretation must have been 2 Sam. 22.5, because Ps. 18.5 reads חֶבְלֵי־מָוֶת, 'the cords of death'. [38] In Ps. 116.3 the same phrase has been translated with מרעי מותא. The wording of Ps. 18 does not lend itself to the technique of paronomasia, so that in this particular instance at least the Targum of Ps. 18 must be dependent on the Targum of 2 Sam. 22.

These examples prove that the Targums are attuned to one another, but also to both parent texts. What are we to make of these relation-ships? It is likely that the Targumist of 2 Sam. 22 had resort to, and was influenced by, the Hebrew doublet of Ps. 18. In at least one case, a Hebrew variant reading may explain the difference between Targ. Neb. and the MT. The Targumist of Ps. 18 followed its Aramaic *Vorlage* at these points, but not invariably: see the exception in v. 44. Whether the agreements are due simply to unthinking copying, or to careful choice, remains to be evaluated.

3.3. *Similarities: When the Hebrew Texts Are Identical*

The Aramaic translations sometimes contain identical, substantial sup-plements to the Hebrew texts (see section 2, Table 1). These supple-ments are usually inextricably interwoven with the translation *sec*.[39] They strongly suggest a direct relationship between the Targums.

1. The Hebrew metaphors in v. 3 spark similar, often identical sub-stitutions and supplements in both Targums, as in the phrase אלהא דאתרעי בי קרבני לדחלתיה, 'My God, who has taken delight in me, who brought me close to his fear', for Hebrew אלי (Ps.) or אלהי (2 Sam.). Yet in subsequent supplements, while there are some similarities, there are also significant differences between the two Targums. These will be discussed in section 4 below, but it is appropriate to emphasize here that strong indications of literary links between the Targums are found together with indications of their independent textual development.

---

38. Most commentators prefer the reading of 2 Sam. 22. Nonetheless, this reading must be maintained for Ps. 18, if only because the phrase אפפוני חבלי־מות occurs in Ps. 116.3 again. It seems to have been a valid alternative. There is no textual evidence that Ps. 18 ever read משברי־מות like 2 Sam. 22. By contrast, a few Hebrew MSS of 2 Sam. 22 read חבלי.

39. See n. 19 above.

2. In v. 9, the smoke rising from God's nostrils (עלה עשן באפו) has effectively been neutralized by a supplement: סליק זדוניה דפרעה כתננא (Targ. Ps), סליק זדוניה דפרעה (רשיעא) היך קיטרא (Targ. Neb.), קדמוהי '(Wicked) Pharaoh's haughtiness went up as smoke before him...'[40]

3. Similarly, in v. 9 the phrase ואש־מפיו תאכל has been neutralized: בכין שלח רגזיה כאישא בערא דמן קדמוהי משיציא, 'therefore he has sent his anger like a burning fire which destroys before him'.[41]

4. The Targums agree in the supplements בגבורתיה and בתקוף, in combination with the substitution קלילין in v. 11. The Hebrew reads וירכב על־כרוב ויעף וידא [42] על־כנפי־רוח and the Targums (here in Targ. Neb.'s dialect) read ואתגלי בגבורתיה על כרובין קלילין ודבר בתקוף על כנפי רוחי, 'He revealed himself in his might on swift Cherubs,[43] and drove powerfully on the wings of the wind'.[44]

5. Both translations substitute גחלי־אש, '(burning) coals of fire' in v. 13 with מזופיתיה כגומרין דנור דלקא ממימריה, God's 'burning anger like coals of fire from his Memra'.[45] This translation both substitutes the metaphor of glowing coals, and retains it, preceded by 'as', in an 'extended simile'.

6. Both translations agree in their supplements and substitutions of v. 17. The Hebrew reads: ישלח ממרום יקחני ימשני ממים רבים, 'He sent down from on high, He took me; He drew me out of the mighty waters'. In the version of Targ. Neb. this has become: שלח נביוהי מלך תקיף דיתיב בתקוף רומא דברני שיזבני מעממין סניאין, 'He sent his prophets, a strong king who dwells in the strength of highness, he took me; he saved me from many nations'.[46]

7. Pluses of precision are common to the Targums. In v. 22 both versions specify דרכי יהוה as (ו)אורחן דתקנן קדם י(ו)י, and explain ולא רשעתי מאלהי as ולא הליכית ברשע קדם אלהי.

---

40. The bracketed word occurs in ten MSS of Targ. Pss. The Sefardi MSS add קדמוי at the end, in agreement with Targ. Neb. For dialectical differences of vocabulary and morphology, see below, pp. 261-66.

41. The text quoted is Targ. Neb.'s; Targ. Ps. differs only in minor details. In our view, משיציא reflects MT's תאכל; contrast the syntax in D.J. Harrington and A.J. Saldarini, *The Targum of the Former Prophets* (The Aramaic Bible, 10; Edinburgh: T. & T. Clark, 1987), p. 201.

42. The variant וידא in 2 Sam. 22 has been discussed above, in §3.2.

43. Apparently, the targumist took ויעף as an adjective, represented by קליל.

44. For dialectical differences in Targ. Ps. 18, see below, §§4.2 and 4.3.2.

45. So Targ. Neb. For a difference, see p. 259.

46. Targ. Pss. only differs in the use of vowel letters.

8. Verse 26 points out how God rewards the pious and the blameless person (עם־חסיד תתחסד עם־גבור תמים תתמם).[47] The Targums identify the pious and the blameless with Abraham and Isaac and offer supplements to the Hebrew in identical wording. But small differences may betray some kind of revision (see below, section 4.3.2, for text and discussion).

9. Similarly, the 'pure' and the 'perverse' in v. 27 have been identified as Jacob and Pharaoh respectively, outlining the result: Jacob's offspring represents the chosen people, whereas the Egyptians are confused. The Targums again use identical wording; there are however important differences to be discussed in 4.3.2.

10. In v. 30 too the Targums substitute the metaphors used with the same nouns and identical supplements; in 2 Sam. 22.30 MT כי בכה ירוץ גדוד באלהי אדלנ־שור, 'With You, I can rush a barrier, With my God, I can scale a wall'; Targ. Neb. ארי במימרך אסגי משרין במימר אלהי אכביש כל כרכין תקיפין, 'For by your Word I will have large armies, by the Word of my God I will conquer all fortified cities'.[48]

11. Literary dependence on the part of Targ. Ps. 18 is further indicated by a stock phrase in v. 32, which has no counterpart in the Hebrew texts, ארום על ניסא ופורקנא דתעביד למשיחך ולשיורי דאישתארון יודון אומיא ועממיא ולישניא,[49] 'therefore, on account of the miracles and the redemption which You will perform for your anointed one and for the remnant of your people who are left over, all nations and peoples and tongues will give thanks...' With ארום for בכין, this is precisely Targ. 2 Sam. 22. The wording and purport of this supplement are typical of the summarizing comments supplemented in Targum Jonathan of the Prophets where it occurs five times; outside this corpus it occurs once only, in this doublet in the Targum of Psalms.[50] It is noteworthy that, when the Targum of Psalms once expresses a similar

47. So 2 Sam. 22; Ps. 18 reads גבר for גבור.

48. Targ. Ps. 18 reads מטול ד- for ארי, ובמימר and אכבוש, and does not have כל. The reading ומבימר in White's edition must be a typographical error; cf. the edition by Díez Merino.

49. In White's edition ופורקנא is not attested by six MSS. The phrase occurs nowhere else, however, with or without פורקנא, and therefore strongly evokes Targ. Neb.

50. Targ. Judg. 5.1, 2; 2 Sam. 22.32, 47; Hab. 3.18. The first part of this plus is repeated in 2 Sam. 22.47, but not in Targ. Ps. 18. Cp. Smelik, *Targum of Judges*, p. 183, p. 380 n. 307, p. 392.

idea without a counterpart in the Hebrew original, independently of Targ. Neb., in the header of Targ. Ps. 18, it uses the expression על נסיא דאתרחישו.[51]

12. According to Levey,[52] the translation of ומי צור מבלעדי אלהינו in the same verse, 'who is a rock except our God?', is reminiscent of the Islamic monotheistic confession: לית אלה אלא יוי ארי לית בר מנך ועמך יימרון לית דתקיף אלא אלהנא, 'there is no God except the LORD, because there is no one apart from you. And your people will say: there is no one as strong as our God.'[53] This notion is, however, firmly rooted in Jewish tradition.[54] Pre-emptive answering of rethorical questions is a well-established characteristic of the Targums, but the verbal agreement between the Targums is nonetheless noteworthy.

13. In v. 47 both Targums translate וברוך צורי, 'blessed be my rock', with (in Targ. Neb.'s version) ובריך תקיפא דמן קדמוהי מתיהיב לנא תקוף ופרקן, 'blessed be the Strong One, because before him we were given strength and redemption!' Apart from orthography, Targ. Ps. differs from this text only in לי for לנא, which reflects the Hebrew more accurately. As in v. 49 discussed above, one MS (London 636) of Targ. Neb. agrees with Targ. Ps. 18 in reading לי.[55]

14. Both Targums supplement (עממיא) דקימין לאבאשא לי, '(the nations) that arose to do me harm', in v. 48, לאבאשא לי, 'to do me harm' and מגוג ומשרית עממין חטופין, 'Magog and the armies of the violent[56] nations', in v. 49.

---

51. In all other instances the noun נסא supplements or explicates the absent or vague object of the sentence. Hence it does not have a similar narrative function. The translation סגיאי נסיא דעבדתא את in Ps. 40.6 is largely based on the Hebrew text: רבות עשית אתה. Cf. 60.6; 75.10; 77.7; 78.42.

52. S.H. Levey, 'The Date of Targum Jonathan on the Prophets', *VT* 21 (1971), pp. 186-96.

53. Targ. Ps. lacks ארי and has the plus בית ישראל after עמך.

54. See A. van der Kooij, *Die alten Textzeugen des Jesajabuches: Ein Beitrag zur Textgeschichte des Alten Testaments* (OBO, 35; Göttingen: Vandenhoeck & Ruprecht, 1981), pp. 189-90; B.D. Chilton, *The Glory of Israel: The Theology and Provenience of the Isaiah Targum* (JSOTSup, 23; Sheffield: JSOT Press, 1983), pp. 6 and 123 n. 32; R. Syrén, *The Blessings in the Targums: A Study on the Targumic Interpretations of Genesis 49 and Deuteronomy 33* (AAAbo.H, 64/1; Åbo: Åbo Akademi, 1986), pp. 154-56; Gordon, *Studies in the Targum*, pp. 142-45.

55. See R. Kasher, תוספות תרגום לנביאים (Jerusalem: World Union of Jewish Studies, 1996), p. 122; the same reading in a Cairo Genizah fragment (Sperber).

56. Harrington and Saldarini, *Former Prophets*, p. 203, mistranslate this word

These common pluses cannot have resulted from similar exegetical techniques or from a common ground of exegetical tradition and theological ideas.[57] There is no question of polygenesis here. They provide solid evidence for a direct literary relationship between both versions, although the exact form of this relationship remains to be discussed. Some supplements point unequivocally to the Targum of 2 Sam. 22 as the original source, and they must have been copied by the translator of Ps. 18. Differences between the Targums will support this conclusion and permit a more detailed analysis; these will now be discussed.

4. *Differences between the Targums*

4.1. *Differences between the Hebrew Parent Texts*
Although the Targums may be identical when the Hebrew texts differ, they may also reflect differences between the parent texts. The translator of Targ. Ps. 18 did not slavishly follow the earlier version of Targ. Neb., but was faithful to his source text, Ps. 18, where it differs from 2 Sam. 22. Small as the number of significant differences between MT Ps. 18 and MT 2 Sam. 22 may be, examples given below show that they exerted considerable influence on the Targumic versions.

1. In v. 1 the Targums clearly reflect their own parent text.[58] The

---

as 'captured'. Targ. Ps. has minor variant readings.

57. The following small supplements shared by both Targums occur: v. 1 בנבואה (in Targ. Neb. this plus often qualifies an inset psalm as prophecy, but it also occurs in the Targum of Psalms at other places, i.e. Targ. Ps. 14.1 לשבחא ברוח נבואה על יד דוד for MT's למנצח לדוד; see also Targ. Ps. 45.1; 46.1; 72.1; 79.1; 98.1; 103.1); in v. 4 both Targums preface the translation by א(ת)ר בתשבחא(ת)ר דו(י)ר אמר (for this incipit formula, see Gordon, *Studies in the Targum*, pp. 74-82), קדם and יתי; v. 5 יתי; v. 6 ן(י)נ(י)נ; v. 19 דמזי; v. 19 מימרא (note also the identical supplement ט(י)לטולי for Hebrew אידי); v. 21 as in v. 4 above אמר דויד, but here only the Sefardi MSS G-I-5 (El Escorial) and Villa-Amil no. 5 (Madrid) of Targ. Ps.; v. 23, the verbs גלא and עבד; v. 24 the verb הוית and the noun נפשי; v. 34 the adjective קלילין; v. 39 the noun פרסת; in v. 40 למעבד, עממיא and לאבאשא; v. 41 מחזרי, where MSS hébreu 110 (Paris) and Villa-Amil no. 5 (Madrid) of Targ. Pss. add קדמי; v. 42 (ו)מצלן and צלותהון; v. 50 קדם.

58. This verse is no proof for the dependency of Targ. Ps. 18 on Targ. Neb., as Bacher, 'Das Targum zu den Psalmen', p. 472, claimed. He wrote: 'Unser Targ., obwohl er dieselben Deutungen im Psalme selbst hat, scheut sich dennoch die Ueberschrift so sehr zu verändern. Daher läßt er aus der Fassung seines Vorgängers Alles weg, was sich auf Israel bezieht, sonst ihm wörtlich folgend'. First, Targ. Ps. reflects the different header of its parent text, and second, it has its own supplement

header of the psalm in the MT is למנצח לעבד יהוה לדוד אשר דבר, but in MT 2 Sam. 22 it is וידבר דוד In Targ. Neb. the words have been translated as follows, ושבח דויד בנבואה, 'And David praised in prophecy', and in Targ. Ps. 18, לשבחא על נישיא דאיתרחישו לעבדא דיי לדוד דשבח בנבואה, 'For praising the miracles which have been performed for the servant of the LORD, David, who praised in prophecy'.

2. In Ps. 18.2 the Hebrew reads ארחמך יהוה חזקי, reflected by אחבבינך יי תוקפי in its Targum. Neither the Hebrew nor the Aramaic versions of 2 Sam. 22 have a parallel phrase here.

3. In v. 7 Ps. 18 has two cola where 2 Sam. 22 has one, apparently summarizing both: ושועתי לפניו תבוא באזניו and ושועתי באזניו respectively. The Targums faithfully reflect this difference: the supplements are recorded in Targ. Ps. 18 only.[59]

4. In 2 Sam. 22.8 the foundations of heaven (השמים) are described as violently trembling and shaking, but in the same verse in Ps. 18 the foundations of the mountains (הרים) tremble. This is reflected in the translations. Targ. Neb. refers to heaven: שכלולי שמיא זעו ואתרכינו, 'The foundations of the heavens trembled and they bent down...', while Targ. Ps. agrees with its own *Vorlage*: אשיית טוריא זעו ואיתרטיטו, 'The foundations of the mountains trembled and shook...'[60] Targ. Ps. alludes to the bending of the heavens in v. 10.

5. The pluses ברד and עביו in MT Ps. 18.13 are combined with a difference, reading עברו where 2 Sam. 22 reads בערו (metathesis). They are reflected in Targ. Ps. with עננו, וברדא and עברו. Targ. Neb. lacks the first two words (although it reads שמי שמיא) and has מבהקין for the latter. These differences stand out amidst identical substitutions for the Hebrew.[61]

6. In v. 14 Ps. 18 has a plus, ברד וגחלי־אש, 'hail and fiery coals', repeating v. 13, and reflected in Targ. Ps. 18, רמא[62] בדרא וגומרין דנור,

---

(miracles); third, it has only the minus ית ישראל in comparison to Targ. Neb. Targ. Ps. 18, however, inserts ישראל in vv. 27 and 32, in contrast to Targ. Neb.

59. The translation of both לפניו and באזניו ה(קדמו)י is a standard, simplifying translational device in the Targums.

60. Because in the Masoretic text of Samuel the heavens tremble, the targumist alludes to an exegetical topic which is connected to God's revelation on Mount Sinai. This resulted in a substitution: heavens bending down instead of shaking. Targ. Pss. does not disagree with this exegetical point; see Smelik, *Targum of Judges*, pp. 402-403.

61. See above, p. 255.

62. This word is lacking in MSS M1106 (formerly in Breslau) and parm. 3095

'he threw hail and fiery coals'. 2 Sam. 22 and its Targum both lack these phrases.

7. In v. 15 Ps. 18 has the plus רב, as reflected in its Targum, absent from both 2 Sam. 22 and Targ. Neb.

8. In v. 16 Ps. 18 reads מים where 2 Sam. 22 has ים; both Targums faithfully reflect their own parent text. This also applies to the difference in preposition, מגערתך in Ps. 18 and בגערתך in 2 Sam. 22, and suffix, אפך in Ps. 18 and אפו in 2 Sam. 22.[63]

9. In v. 25 Ps. 18 has the lexeme יד, absent in 2 Sam. 22.25; the Targums are faithful to their parent texts.

10. Ps. 18.28 opens with כי, reflected by מטול in its Targum. 2 Sam. 22 has the particle את,[64] reflected in Targ. Neb. as ית, while Ps. 18 reads אתה, reflected in its Targum with דאנת.

11. Ps. 18.33 המאזרני, 'who girded me', and 2 Sam. 22.33 מעוזי, 'my stronghold', seem to be faithfully reflected in their respective Targums with דמזרז לי קמור,[65] 'who girded me with a belt', and דסעיד לי, 'who supports me', respectively.[66] However, Targ. Pss. retains the metaphor, which Targ. Neb. is unlikely to do,[67] as is evident in v. 40, where Targ. Neb. renders ותזרני, 'and you girded me', with וסעדתני, 'and you supported me'. Targ. Ps. renders this literally with וזרזת, 'and you girded me', adding היך קמור, 'as a belt'.

12. The plus וימינך תסעדני, 'your right hand has sustained me', in Ps. 18.36 is reflected in Targ. Ps. 18 only, וימינך תסייעינני.

13. The difference between ואשיגם, 'and I overtook them' (Ps. 18.38) and ואשמידם, 'and I destroyed them' (2 Sam. 22.38) is faithfully reflected in their Targums with ואדבקינון and ושצתנון respectively.[68]

14. Similarly, the plus ואכלם, 'and I will devour them', in 2 Sam. 22.39 is reflected only in Targ. Neb. (ושיציתנון).

(Cod. De–Rossi 732); MS E.e5.9 (Kennicott 92) has רמיא.

63. Targ. Ps. רוגזך except for White's basic MS.

64. This particle may, however, be a shortened form; see Cross and Freedman, 'A Royal Song', p. 28 n. 62; Fokkelman, *Throne and City*, p. 348 n. 36.

65. The supplement of קמור, 'belt', follows from the verb; some MSS erroneously have קמות (El Escorial G-I-5 and Villa-Amil no. 5).

66. Note, however, that 4QSam[a] supports the reading of Ps. 18.

67. See also below, section 4.3.1 under 2.

68. In Targ. Ps. 18 Codex Solger 7 (Nürnberg) follows Targ. Neb. by substituting ושיציתינון.

15. In v. 43, the phrase על־פני־רוח in Ps. 18 corresponds to ארץ in 2 Sam. 22; the Targums render this faithfully with על אפי זעפא and דארעא respectively. In the same verse 2 Sam. 22 reads אדקם ארקעם, 'I crushed and stamped them down', where Ps. 18 has אריקם, 'I cast them out'; the Targums resemble one another in part, and support אדקם rather than אריקם,[69] but Targ. Neb. retains the plus in its parent text with רפסתנון, 'I crushed them', absent from Targ. Ps. 18.

16. The order of the two cola in v. 45 differs between 2 Sam. 22 (בני לשמע אזן ישמעו לי (נכר יתכחשו־לי לשמוע אזן ישמעו לי) and Ps. 18 (בני־נכר יכחשו־לי), and their respective Targums follow suit (Targ. Neb. לשמע אוזן;[70] Targ. Pss. בני עממיא יתכדבון לי לשמיע אודן ישתמעון לי (ישתמעון לי בני עממיא יתכדבון קדמי).

Though one version is dependent on the other, it is not a slavish copy, and we should perhaps say that Targ. Neb. served as a blueprint for the translator of Targ. Ps. 18. Even where substitutions abound, in which case the relationship between the Hebrew and the Aramaic may be difficult to determine, the translator of Targ. Ps. 18 duly observed what his own parent text required, and did not gloss over differences as he did in the instances discussed above (section 3.2). In these latter instances, the Targumist's deviation from Ps. 18 may be due to inattention, or to a deliberate decision;[71] his careful handling of differences suggests the latter, with a conscious retention of the reading of Targ. Neb. as an adequate rewording of MT Ps. 18.

4.2. *Dialectal substitutions*
Elijah Levita must have been one of the first authors to draw attention to dialectal markers in the Targum of the Writings,[72] shared by the Targum of Psalms. The linguistic provenance of Targ. Ps. 18 has often been adduced as one of the main reasons for the differences between this Targum and Targum Jonathan.[73] Common as this assumption is, it

69. See n. 27 above.
70. MS w (Sperber; a Yemenite MS) reads אוזן.
71. Admittedly, it is possible that he had a copy of MT Ps. 18 that was closer to 2 Sam. 22 at these points (section 3.2). The cases where Targ. Neb. follows MT Ps. 18 and those that are too ambiguous to determine the Hebrew *Vorlage* have to be left out of the present discussion.
72. Quoted by White, *A Critical Edition*, pp. 17-18.
73. Bacher, 'Das Targum zu den Psalmen', p. 472; Díez Merino, *Targum de Salmos*, p. 58; White, *A Critical Edition*, p. 19, but we disagree with his first

is not self-evident. It is noteworthy that ch. 18 in this Targum betrays no influence of the dialect of Targum Jonathan greater than that in the other Psalms, though this would be probable in a copy of Targ. Neb. lacking independent contributions.[74] The examples adduced below mark its dialect as Late Jewish Literary Aramaic,[75] consistent with Targ. Pss. as a whole, the dialect shared by the distinctive parts of Targ. Ps.-J. and Targ. Job. [76]

1. The Hebrew word בליעל is almost invariably translated by רשיעא or רשעא, '(sons of) wickedness' in the Targum of the Prophets.[77] The use of טלומייא in Targ. Ps. 18.5 for חייבין in Targ. Neb. is typical of the later dialect of the former, where it occurs frequently;[78] the word occurs neither in Targ. Onq. nor in Targ. Neb. Dialect is not, however, a satisfactory explanation for the substitution of חייבין by טלומיא in Targ. Ps. 18, for the translator was content to use חייבין in v. 6 and many other instances outside this psalm.[79] In fact, both Targums opted for unusual

observation, since orthographical observations have no bearing on dialectology (E.M. Cook, 'Rewriting the Bible: The Text and Language of the Pseudo-Jonathan Targum' [unpublished PhD dissertation, University of California, 1986], p. 19).

74. The expressions עלמא דעתיד למיתי (see below, 4.3.2 point 6) and the one discussed in section 3.3, point 11, are exceptions.

75. The term has been coined by S. Kaufman, 'Dating the Language of the Palestinian Targums and their Use in the Study of First Century CE Texts', in D.R.G. Beattie and M.J. McNamara (eds.), *The Aramaic Bible: Targums in their Historical Context* (JSOTSup, 166; Sheffield: JSOT Press, 1994), pp. 118-41 (125).

76. The use of קוטרא in Targ. Ps. 18 for תננא (Targ. Neb.) in 18.9 is ambiguous; the first noun occurs in Targ. Pss. 119.83 and 148.8 but it is balanced by five instances of the latter noun, three times in Ps. 68.3, 9 (2×), where it may depend on Targ. Judg. 5 (Churgin, *Targum Jonathan*, p. 50; Smelik, *Targum of Judges*, p. 413) and in 102.4 and 144.5. The morphology of the verbs shows no difference in, for example, the perfect of the third person masculine plural (ו-, not ין -); cf. Cook, *Rewriting the Bible*, p. 178; D.M. Golomb, *A Grammar of Targum Neofiti* (HSM, 34; Chico, CA: Scholars Press, 1985), p. 125.

77. Targ. Judg. 19.22; 20.13; 1 Sam. 1.16; 2.12; 10.27; 25.17, 25; 30.22; 2 Sam. 16.7; 20.1; 23.6; 1 Kgs 21.10, 13 (2×); Nah. 1.11; 2.1. Exceptions: חיבא in 2 Sam. 22.5; שט in 1 Sam. 25.25 and שקרין in 2 Sam. 22.5, both as a variant reading. Cp. Targ. Onq. Deut. 13.14; 15.9; Targ. Ps.-J. זידנין and זדנותא in these verses.

78. 12 times: Targ. Ps. 7.4; 10.3; 18.5; 37.1; 41.9; 43.1; 72.4; 103.6; 105.14; 119.121, 134; 146.7. It also occurs in Targ. Prov. (6.12; 16.27; 29.25) and Targ. Job (35.9), as well as Targ. 1 Chron. 16.21. The verb occurs three times in Targ. Ps.-J. and twice in Targ. Job.

79. In this verse, Targ. Neb. uses רשיעין.

equivalents.[80] Apparently the translator preferred the political connotation of 'oppressors' to the moral translation he found in Targ. Neb.

2. Palestinian Aramaic tends to sever the pronominal suffix from
verbal forms and present it separately with יַת, even where the Hebrew
does not have אֵת. See Targ. Ps. 18.6 אקדימו יתי where 2 Sam. 22 reads
קדמוני; Targ. Ps. 18.49 משיזיב יתי for ופרקי in Targ. Neb.[81]

3. The suffix ending on וֹי- in Targ. Ps. 18 for וֹהי is Palestinian;[82] see
18.7 באודנוי where Targ. Neb. lacks the word; see further 18.3, 10, 23,
27. Although the Standard Literary Aramaic ending on והי- occurs 17
times in Targum Psalms (including 18.17, ניביוהי), the former ending is
by far the more common, occurring over 300 times.[83] Because it occurs
elsewhere in the corpus, its occurrence in Targ. Ps. 18 may be due to
influences other than Targ. 2 Sam. 22, for instance that of Onqelos on
later copyists.[84]

4. The use of מטול (18.8, 20, 22, 23, 29, 30) or ארום (18.18; 2×)
rather than ארי,[85] or אמול היכנא rather than על כין (18.50), comes as no
surprise. מטול occurs over 130 times in Targ. Pss., and היכנא מטול 17
times, whereas ארי occurs only in Targ. Ps. 71.3. The use of ארום in
Targ. Pss. for בכין in 18.32 also forms a dialectal substitution; בכין is
Western Aramaic,[86] but appears neither in Targ. Pss., nor in Targ.
Prov., nor in Targ. Job.

5. The different words for 'foundation', שכלולא (Targ. Neb.) in v. 8
and 16 in comparison with אשיתא and שתסא in Targ. Ps. 18.8 and 16
may well reflect a dialectal difference between the Aramaic versions.

---

80. See n. 77 above. The equivalent טלומא occurs again in Targ. Ps. 41.9 but in
101.3 רשיעא is used. The latter form, or the variant רשעא, is the equivalent usually
chosen.

81. Cf. Golomb, *Grammar of Targum Neofiti*, p. 209.

82. So also White, *A Critical Edition*, p. 19.

83. The unusual form is not restricted to words expressing 'inalienable possession'; cf. Golomb, *Grammar of Targum Neofiti*, p. 52. Both forms occur with one
type of noun, e.g., קדמוהי (22.25) and קדמוי (28.7).

84. The variant קדמוהי for קדמוי occurs in 18.3, 9, 10; באודנוהי for באודנוי in
18.7; בנוהי for בבנוי in 18.27. Most of these are found in Sefardi MSS, which also
replace במני in 18.6 with בזיני.

85 So also Bacher, 'Das Targum zu den Psalmen', p. 472; White, *A Critical
Edition*, p. 19.

86. Cf. A. Tal, *The Language of the Targum of the Former Prophets and its
Position within the Aramaic Dialects* (Tel-Aviv: Tel-Aviv University Press, 1975),
p. 58 (Hebrew).

שתסא occurs six times, evenly distributed over Targ. Pss. and Targ. Prov.[87] אשיתא occurs four times, twice in Targ. Pss. (11.3; 18.8), once in Frag. Targ. (Deut. 27.15) and once in Targ. Neb. (Jer. 50.15) where it represents the *hapax legomenon* in the Bible. שכלולא does not occur in the Targum of the Writings.[88]

6. In many instances Targ. Ps. 18 reads היך rather than -כ as in 18.5.[89] היך does not appear in Targ. Onq. or Targ. Neb., but occurs frequently in the Palestinian Targums. The use of היך כ-, 'as, like, in the manner of', occurs in v. 15 according to two MSS only,[90] but is found elsewhere in Targ. Pss.,[91] and appears to be typical of Late Jewish Literary Aramaic.[92]

7. In v. 11 Targ. Neb. reads כנפי, where Targ. Ps has גדפי (for MT כנפי).[93] כנפא occurs twice in Targ. Ps, in 55.7 and 104.3, while גדפא occurs here and in 148.10. In Targ. Neb., כנפא appears to be the more usual choice, but גדפא is also found, although mostly in variant readings, possibly suggesting a change of preference.[94]

8. In v. 11 Targ. Neb. has רוחא, Targ. Ps זעפא (for MT רוח). זעפא belongs to Late Jewish Literary Aramaic, occurs for רוח in v. 43 again, and at ten other points in Targ. Pss. but never occurs in Targ. Neb.[95]

9. The use of ואיתחזר for סחור סחור in v. 12 is a clear example of Palestinian Aramaic in Targ. Pss.,[96] which never uses סחור סחור, but

87. Targ. Pss. 18.16; 24.2; 137.7; Targ. Prov. 3.19; 8.29; 10.25.

88. It occurs in Targ. Ps.-J. Gen. 22.13; Lev. 22.27; Num. 22.28; Targ. Neb. 2 Sam. 22.8, 16; Frag. Targ. Exod. 12.42; Lev. 22.27.

89. Targ. Ps. 18.9, 15, 21, 25, 34, 35, 43; in vv. 21 and 25 most MSS have -כ, however.

90. MSS G-I-5 (El Escorial) and Villa-Amil no. 5 (Madrid).

91. But not in all MSS. See 22.14, 17; 48.11; 59.7, 15; 69.17; 72.16; 78.27; 104.3; 106.9; 124.7; 133.3; Targ. Prov. 26.11, 23; Targ. Job. 14.6; 31.18; 40.17 (only in the Rabbinic Bible of Venice, 1517, probably following Cod. Solger [Nürnberg]); Targ. Lam. 1.15; 3.52.

92. The only other instances in the Targums are in Fragmentary Targum (Gen. 42.23, Exod. 14.13); in Neofiti and Pseudo-Jonathan it does not occur at all.

93. According to Bacher, 'Das Targum zu den Psalmen', p. 470, the use of גדפי is a real Aramaic word instead of Targ. Neb.'s hebraizing כנפי.

94. Targ. Neb. 2 Sam. 22.11 variant; 1 Kgs 8.7; Isa. 40.31; Ezek. 1.9 variant; Mic. 1.16 variant.

95. Targ. Pss. 11.6; 18.11, 43; 35.5; 55.9; 83.14, 16 (2×); 103.16; 107.25; 135.7; 139.7. It also occurs in Targ. Ps.-J. Lev. 15.19; Targ. Prov. 19.12; Targ. Job 1.19; 4.9; 8.2; 15.2, 30; 21.18; 30.15.

96. So also White, *A Critical Edition*, p. 19; cf. R. Weiss, התרגום הארמי לספר

instead has חזור חזור (3.7; 12.9; 27.6; 31.14 etc.), or a form of חזר.

10. The use of חמא (18.16, 29) in Targ. Pss. rather than חזא (Targ. Neb.) forms a litmus test of dialect.[97] The latter form does not occur in Targ. Pss.

11. 18.18 reads עשן for תקף; the root עשן occurs only in the Targum of the Writings, with one exception at Targ. Ps.-J. on Num. 25.8.[98]

12. The vocabulary of Targ. Ps. 18.29 belongs to Late Jewish Literary Aramaic; examples are שרגא,[99] 'light', חברייא,[100] 'dark' (for Targ. Neb. חשוכא), and some lexemes noted above.[101]

13. Targ. Ps. 18.35 reads כרכומיא, 'bronze', instead of Targ. Neb.'s synonym נחשא which occurs once in Targ. Pss.[102]

14. The use of סגע, instead of סני, in Targ. Ps. 18.37 belongs to the Late Jewish Literary Aramaic dialect; the verb occurs in Targum Pseudo-Jonathan and the Targums to Psalms, Proverbs, Job and Chronicles only.[103]

15. The resolution of gemination with nun in אנפי in Targ. Ps. 18.43, instead of פני, is a phenomenon that disappeared by the end of the first century CE; it may, however, reflect the influence of Biblical Aramaic.[104]

איוב (Tel-Aviv: Tel-Aviv University, 1979), p. 313.

97. So also White, *A Critical Edition*, p. 19, following Bacher, 'Das Targum zu den Psalmen', p. 472.

98. Targ. Pss. 9.20; 18.18; 21.2; 24.8; 29.1; 30.8; 31.3; 52.9; 59.4; 68.29; 71.3; 75.9; 78.4; 89.14; Targ. Prov. 7.26; 8.28; 9.3, 14; 10.29; 11.16; 14.26; 18.19, 23; 21.14; 24.5; 29.25; 30.25; Targ. Job 26.2; Targ. 1 Chron. 4.32; 6.44.

99. Only in Targ. Pss. 18.29; 78.36; 119.105; 132.17; Prov. 6.23; 20.20, 27; 24.20; 31.18; Job 18.6; 21.17; 29.3; 1 Chron. 8.33; 2 Chron. 3.15.

100. Targ. Pss. 18.29; 35.6, 14; 38.7; 43.2; Prov. 4.19.

101. מטול אנת, and חמא.

102. Targ. Ps. 107.16. כרכומא occurs in Targ. Ps. 18.35, Targ. Job. 20.24, 28.2 and 41.19 only.

103. Verb and noun occur about 100 times. Cf. J. Levy, *Chaldäisches Wörterbuch über die Targumim und einen grossen Theil des rabbinischen Schriftums* (Leipzig: Baumgärtners Buchhandlung, 1867–68), II, p. 144. MS hébreu 114 of the Bibliothèque Nationale, Paris, agrees with Targ. Neb. (אסגיתא); Cod. Solger 7 (Nürnberg) offers an alternative reading: אפתיתא, 'you have widened'.

104. So Cook, *Rewriting the Bible*, pp. 126-29. In 18.28, 29 את is the form of Targ. Neb. for the current form אנת in Targ. Pss. (45 instances overall). This latter form does not occur in the Palestinian Targums (Neof., Genizah, Ps.-J.) but it is, of course, an archaic form. Note that את occurs 53 times in Targ. Pss., but not in ch. 18.

16. The use of אשקקי, 'lane, street', in Targ. Ps. 18.43 belongs to Palestinian Aramaic,[105] whereas שוקא, 'street', occurs in all Targums including Targ. Pss.

4.3. *Non-dialectal Differences Originating in the Aramaic Versions*

Despite the obvious similarity of the Targumic versions, there are numerous differences between them which are inexplicable either by variation within the Hebrew source-texts (4.1) or by dialectal differences (4.2). The assumption of a proto-Targum of the Prophets, which may have been preserved in Targ. Ps., may solve this problem; the remaining differences could perhaps be explained as revisions of Targum Jonathan. Synonyms, substitutions and supplements will be discussed separately where possible.

4.3.1. *Synonyms and Substitutions*[106]

1. In v. 1 השירה has been rendered with תשבחתא in Targ. Neb. but with the rather more literal שירתא in Targ. Ps. 18. Targ. Neb. is consistent in its translation of שירה and the related noun שיר is also invariably translated by תשבחתא,[107] apart from negative contexts such as wailing, punishment or disobedience, where זמרא is used.[108] Targ. Pss. is less consistent: it uses תשבחתא for שיר 10 times,[109] 5 times when the verb

105. M. Sokoloff, *A Dictionary of Jewish Palestinian Aramaic of the Byzantine Period* (Ramat Gan: Bar Ilan University Press, 1990), p. 78, cf. Levy, *Chaldäisches Wörterbuch*, I, p. 73.

106. The following small differences are to be noted: in v. 6 חייבין (Targ. Ps.) versus רשיעין (Targ. Neb.); in v. 25 Targ. Neb. is slightly more literal in rendering וישב with ואתיב, while Targ. Pss. has the more idiomatic translation ופרע; in v. 27 קלקילתינון (Targ. Ps.) versus בלבילתנון (Targ. Neb.; but most MSS of Targ. Pss. agree with Targ. Neb.); in v. 32 אומיא ועממיא (Targ. Ps.) versus עממיא אומיא (Targ. Neb.; the order in Targ. Neb. mirrors Dan. 3.4, 7, 29, 31; 5.19; 6.26; 7.14); in v. 48 דילי (the Sefardi MSS of Targ. Ps., El Escorial G-I-5, Villa-Amil no. 5 [Madrid], Montefiore 7 [London] and hébreu 110 [Paris], also inverting word order) versus לי (Targ. Neb.); in v. 49 משיזיב (Targ. Ps.) versus ופרקי (Targ. Neb.; two Sefardi MSS of the former agree with the latter).

107. שירה: Targ. 2 Sam. 22.1; Isa. 5.1; 23.15; שיר: Targ. Judg. 5.12; 1 Kgs 5.12; Isa. 26.1; 30.29; 42.10: Amos 8.10.

108. שירה: Targ. Neb. Amos 8.3; שיר: Targ. Neb. Isa. 23.16; 24.9; Ezek. 26.13; 33.32 (Amos 5.23); Amos 6.5.

109. In some MSS שבחא is used; Targ. Pss. 28.7; 30.1; 40.4; 42.9; 45.1.

שיר has also been used in the MT,[110] and שירתא 31 times,[111] including 12 cases where תשבחתא renders Hebrew מזמור in the same verse.[112] These findings do not support Churgin's view that Targ. Ps. 18 preserves the unrevised version of Targum Jonathan.

2. In v. 3 מגני, 'my Shield', is rendered with תקפי, 'my Strength' in Targ. Neb. and תריסי, 'my Shield' in Targ. Ps. respectively. Preservation of the metaphor is not characteristic of Targ. Neb., though it is of Targ. Ps. 18, where the same metaphor is also found in v. 31, תריס (Targ. Neb. has תקוף again). Targum Jonathan has a strong and consistent tendency to substitute real or abstract terms for metaphors,[113] but Targ. Ps. 18 is no less consistent in its adoption of a different translation strategy at this point, as in v. 33 (above, section 4.1). Targ. Pss. is far less inclined to substitute metaphors, although it often does.[114] These findings do not support the assumption that Targ. Ps. 18 here reflects the proto-Targum of the Prophets.

3. In v. 13 Hebrew מגנה has been translated by מזיו in Targ. Neb. Although this word occurs 12 times in Targ. Pss, this Targum has מזיהור here, a word that occurs nowhere else in Targ. Pss., and is found only infrequently in the Targum of the Writings as a whole.[115] This suggests that Targ. Ps. here depends on the proto-Targum of the Prophets, as זיוהרא is the standard translation of נגה in Targ. Neb.;[116] Churgin, however, does not give this example.

---

110. Targ. Pss. 96.1; 98.1; 137.4; 144.9; 149.1; the only exceptions to this combination are 33.3 and 137.3.

111. Targ. Pss. 33.3; 46.1; 69.31; 120.1; 121.1; 122.1; 123.1; 124.1; 125.1; 126.1; 127.1; 128.1; 129.1; 130.1; 131.1; 132.1; 133.1; 134.1; 137.3.

112. Targ. Pss. 48.1; 65.1; 66.1; 67.1; 68.1; 75.1; 76.1; 83.1; 87.1; 88.1; 92.1; 108.1. Cf. 98.1.

113. For this device, see L. Díez Merino, 'Procedimientos targúmicos', in V. Collado-Bertomeu and V. Vilar-Hueso (eds.), *II. Simposio bíblico español (Córdoba 1985)* (Valencia: Monte de Piedad; Córdoba: Caja de Ahorros de Córdoba, 1987), pp. 461-86; F. Böhl, 'Die Metaphorisierung (Metila) in den Targumim zum Pentateuch', *FJB* 15 (1987), pp. 111-149; Smelik, 'Concordance and Consistency', pp. 301-302.

114. Cf. White, *A Critical Edition*, pp. 106-11.

115. Targ. Prov. 4.23 and Targ. Lam. 4.7.

116. Targ. Neb. 2 Sam. 23.4; Isa. 50.10; 60.3, 19; Ezek. 1.4, 13, 27, 28; 10.4; Joel 2.10; 4.15; Amos 5.20; Hab. 3.4; in Hab. 3.11 it is dissolved, in Isa. 4.5 אמיטתא; in Isa. 62.1 ניהור.

4. In v. 15, Targ. Ps. and Targ. Neb. differ markedly in their choice of verb and object in their translations of וישלה חציו/חצים, 'He sent (his) arrows'; Targ. Neb. ושלה מחתיה כגרין, 'He sent his plague as arrows' versus Targ. Ps. 18 ושדר מימריה היך גיררין, 'And he sent his Memra as arrows'.[117] Both take 'arrows' for a metaphor, substitute it, but retain the literal meaning in a comparison (extended simile). The choice of using either שדר or שלח, both denoting 'send', does not depend on semantic function.[118] In Targ. Ps. Memra serves as sparks of God's activity in the form of lightning from heaven. Vestiges of similar representations are present in Targ. Neb. and perhaps מימריה once formed the original translation, as Churgin suggested;[119] without additional support this, however, remains speculative.

5. In v. 21 יגמלני has been translated by ישלמיני in Targ. Neb. and by יגמליני in Targ. Ps. 18, with the exception of two Sefardi MSS which agree with Targ. Neb.[120] Both Targums vary in their translation of this verb, but if we confine ourselves to the connotation of retribution, the choices are גמל,[121] גרם,[122] פרע,[123] שלם,[124] and שלם גומלא.[125] From these observations we can infer only that both translations were viable options for the translators, and there is no reason to assume that the reading in Targ. Neb. is secondary.

---

117. The translation 'and his Memra sent [?] as arrows' is implausible, because the comparison needs a referent.

118. Cf. E. van Staalduine-Sulman, *Samuel* (A Bilingual Concordance to the Targum of the Prophets, 3; Leiden: E.J. Brill, 1996), pp. 224 and 241-44; for Targ. Pss., see 20.3, 43.3, 57.4, 105.17 etc. and 78.25, 105.26 and 111.9. For Imperial Aramaic, see M.L. Folmer, *The Aramaic Language in the Achaemenid Period: A Study in Linguistic Variation* (Leuven: Peeters, 1995), pp. 652-57. For a distinct semantic function in Syriac, see J. Joosten, 'Materials for a Linguistic Approach to the Old Testament Peshitta', *JAB* 1 (1999), pp. 203-18 (207-208).

119. Churgin, תרגום כתובים, p. 26.

120. G-I-5 (El Escorial) and Villa-Amil no. 5 (Madrid).

121. Targ. 1 Sam. 24.18 (twice); 22.21 variant; Isa. 63.7; Joel 4.4; Targ. Pss. 18.21; 116.7; 137.8. As White's edition of Targ. Pss. does not go beyond Ps. 72, while most occurences in the Psalms do, we could only consult a Sefardi edition.

122. Targ. Neb. Isa. 3.9.

123. Targ. Pss. 7.5.

124. Targ. 2 Sam. 19.37; 22.21; Targ. Pss. 13.6; 18.21 variant (see previous note); 103.10; 119.17.

125. Targ. Ps. 142.8.

6. In v. 37 תחת(נ)י has been represented with קדמי in Targ. Neb., but its Ashkenazi MSS have תחותי, while Targ. Ps. has באתרא. In v. 10 both versions render תחת רגליו with קדמו(ה)י, and in v. 39 both Targums give תחות פרסת ר(י)גלי for the same phrase. With Churgin, we may assume that the translation באתרא is original in Targ. Neb., as this equivalent for תחת occurs frequently,[126] whereas the equivalent קדם is unique in Targ. Neb. But the evidence for the proto-Targum of the Prophets here is circumstantial, so this assumption depends on the degree of conservation of the Aramaic *Vorlage* in Targ. Ps. 18.

7. A peculiar phenomenon occurs in v. 41, where the Hebrew uses the synonyms איבי and סנאי, faithfully reflected by Targ. Ps. with בעלי דבבי and סנאי respectively. Targ. Neb. inverts their order with סנאי and בעלי דבבי, for no apparent reason. The same inversion occurs in Targ. Onq. Num. 10.35. The translation of אויב with the more poignant סנאה occurs a few times in Targ. Neb.,[127] whereas the more neutral term בעיל דבבא is used for שנה only once, in Ezek. 16.27.[128] These instances exemplify semantic shift, and are thus more easily explained than the inversion in 2 Sam. 22. In v. 18, the same inversion occurs in Targ. Neb. and Targ. Ps. 18, with the exception of the Sefardi MSS.[129] Presumably the translator of Targ. Pss. overlooked the inversion in v. 18, where the components may have appeared to be near-synonyms, while in v. 41 he may have been alerted by a difference between the Hebrew texts. Still, Targ. Ps. goes its own way in v. 18 as well, using עשינין אינון instead of תקפוני as in Targ. Neb. We have shown above that this latter difference does not constitute proof of a revision of Targ. Neb., *pace* Churgin, as it reflects Late Jewish Literary Aramaic.

8. In v. 43 Targ. Ps. has היך גרגישתא, 'as a clod of earth', which occurs once in Targ. Neb., four times in Targ. Ps.-J. and Targ. Job, and

---

126. Josh. 5.7, 8; Judg. 7.21; 1 Sam. 14.9; 2 Sam. 2.23; 3.12; 7.10; 2 Kgs 3.27 variant; Jer. 38.9.

127. Judg. 5.31; 2 Sam. 22.38, 49 (not in Targ. Ps. 18.38); 2 Kgs. 21.14 variant; Ezek. 36.2. See also Targ. Onq.

128. The occurence in Targ. Onq. Deut. 32.41 follows a stylistic device, avoiding two identical equivalents for different Hebrew lexemes (here the standard translation בעיל דבבא for Hebrew צר immediately precedes the word). For this device, see Smelik, 'Concordance and Consistency', p. 248.

129. El Escorial G-I-5, Villa-Amil no. 5 (Madrid), Montefiore 7 (London) and hébreu 110 (Paris). These MSS corrected the text after מה.

once in Targ. Chron.,[130] for Targ. Neb.'s כעפרא, 'as dust'; the latter noun is used in Targ. Pss.[131]

9. In v. 44 David is saved מפלוגת עמא, 'from the contest of the people', in Targ. Neb.; Targ. Ps. 18 makes the danger a non-Israelite one by its translation מפלוגתא דעממיא,[132] reinforced by the supplement במזלי מזיין, '(you appointed me) when I walked along armed (at the head of the nations)'.[133] This difference reflects deliberate exegesis.

10. A case of metathesis occurs in v. 46 where 2 Sam. 22 reads ויחגרו, 'they were limping (?)',[134] but Ps. 18 ויחרגו, 'they trembled'; remarkably, Targ. Neb. reflects the latter with ויזועון, 'they trembled', and Targ. Ps. 18 displays a semantic shift from 'trembling' to ויטלטלון, 'they were shaken'.

4.3.2. *Supplements*[135]

So far we have been able to produce no unarguable evidence in support of Churgin's claims. The pluses in Targ. Ps. 18 argue against his view, showing as they do that scribes and copyists in fact *did* alter the text of Targ. Ps. 18.[136] This section will shed more light on the matter.

---

130. Targ. Neb. 1 Kgs 7.46; Targ. Ps.-J. Gen. 1.24; 4.10; 6.21; 15.19; Targ. Job 7.5; 11.17; 21.33; 38.38; Targ. 2 Chron. 4.17. Cf. Tal, *Language*, pp. 138 and 206.

131. 7.6; 30.10; 44.26; 72.9; 78.27; 88.11; 89.48; 90.10; 103.14; 113.7; 119.25.

132. This shift is shared by Western variant readings of Targ. Neb. and a Cairo Genizah fragment (Sperber); cf. Kimḥi's interpretation.

133. A shift occurs at the end of the verse where Hebrew ידע is translated with ידע in Targ. Neb. but with חכם in Targ. Ps. 18.

134. I suggest this translation on the basis of its occurrence in Qumran Hebrew (see D.J.A. Clines, *The Dictionary of Classical Hebrew*, III [Sheffield: Sheffield Academic Press, 1996], p. 161, although they list this occurrence under 'gird', p. 160) and Rabbinic Hebrew and Aramaic; cf. Fokkelman, *Throne and City*, p. 394.

135. Minuses rarely occur, except in some cases of 'free translation' where the equivalence between source and target text is beyond reconstruction. In Targ. Ps. 18.1 the text does not reflect MT's כל. In Targ. Ps. 18.8 the text does not reflect חרה in the phrase כי חרה לו, and merely states מטול דתקיף ליה where Targ. Neb. reads ארי תקיף רגזיה. See also below, on vv. 26-27.

136. Many single supplements are found in Targ. Ps. 18. In 18.9 the Targum characterizes Pharaoh as רשיעא, which is a fairly standard supplement for this noun; see Targ. Ps.-J. Exod. 15.1, 9, 21; Targ. Ps. 89.11; Frag. Targ. and Targ. Cairo Genizah Exod. 15.9. but not in Targ. Neb. However, in the manuscripts of Ashkenazi provenance it does occur, as well as in one Yemenite manuscript. All this may not prove much more than that the combination was a common one, and that

1. Despite obvious correspondences, Targum Jonathan deviates from Targ. Pss. in vv. 2-3, and not only where its Hebrew parent text differs:

Table 3. *Targum 2 Samuel 22.2-3 and Targum Psalm 18.2-3*

ומצודתי	סלעי	יהוה	חזקי:	יהוה	ארחמך	ויאמר	MT Ps.
ומצדתי	סלעי	יהוה	----	-----	-----	ויאמר	MT 2 Sam.
ורוחצני	תוקפי	יי	תוקפי:	יי	אחבבינך	ואמר	Targ. Ps.
ורחצני	תקפי	יוי	----	----	----	ואמר	Targ. Neb.
בו	אחסה־	----	צורי	אלי	----	ומפלטי	MT Ps.
בו	אחסה־	----	צורי	אלהי	לי	ומפלטי	MT 2 Sam.
לדחלתיה	קרבני	בי	דאתרעי	אלהא	יתי	ומשיזיב	Targ. Ps.
לדחלתיה	קרבני	בי	דאתרעי	אלהי	יתי:	ומשיזיב	Targ. Neb.
ישעי	וקרן	----	----	----	----	מגני	MT Ps.
ישעי	וקרן	----	----	----	----	מגני	MT 2 Sam.
ופורקן	תקוף	לי	מתייהב	קדמוי	דמן	תריסי	Targ. Ps.
ופרקן	תקוף	לי	מתיהיב	קדמוהי	דמן	תקפי	Targ. Neb.
----	----	משגבי	----	-----	----	----	MT Ps.
----	----	משגבי	----	----	----	----	MT 2 Sam.
----	----	רוחצני	דבבי	בעלי	על	----	Targ. Ps.
מימריה	דעל	רחצני	דבבי	בעלי	על	לאתגברא	Targ. Neb.
----	----	----	----	----	----	----	MT Ps.
----	----	מגני	----	בו	[אחסה	----	MT 2 Sam.
----	----	----	----	----	----	----	Targ. Ps.
מבעלי	עלי	מגין	עקא	בעדן	רחיץ	אנא	Targ. Neb.
----	----	----	----	-----	----	----	MT Ps.
----	[משגבי]	ישעי	וקרן	----	-----	----	MT 2 Sam.
----	----	----	----	-----	----	----	Targ. Ps.
דהוה	סמכני	בפרקניה	קרני	לארמא[137]	ואמר	דבבי	Targ. Neb.

scribes may have supplemented any reference to Pharaoh with this qualification.

For additional supplements to Targ. Ps. 18, see הא in 18.9; the identification of 'your people' as ישראל in v. 27; in v. 45 the Sefardi MSS El Escorial G-I-5, Villa-Amil no. 5 (Madrid), Montefiore 7 (London) and hébreu 110 (Paris) have the supplement נוכראין which agrees with the substitution נכר in a Cairo Genizah fragment of Targ. Neb. (Sperber); the same plus in MS Villa-Amil no. 5 in v. 46.

In Targ. Neb. 2 Sam. 22.1 the supplement ואף לדויד is related to the substitution ית ישראל for MT's אתו (reflected in Targ. Ps 18.1: יתיה). The Targum of the Prophets indicates that this song of praise is not just about David, but about Israel and *also* about David. See also n. 57 above.

137. For this correction of Sperber, based on the MSS, see Van Staalduine-Sulman, *Samuel*, III, p. 193; Churgin, *Targum Jonathan*, pp. 130-31.

Biblical Hebrew, Biblical Texts

----	----	----	----	-----	----	----	MT Ps.
----	----	----	----	-----	ומנוסי	----	MT 2 Sam.
----	----	----	----	-----	----	----	Targ. Ps.
מן	עריק	הויתי	כד	לי	סמך	מימריה	Targ. Neb.
----	----	----	----	----	----	----	MT Ps.
----	----	----	----	משעי	----	----	MT 2 Sam.
----	----	----	----	----	----	----	Targ. Ps.
מיד	ואף	דבבי	מבעלי	פרקני	רדפי	קדם	Targ. Neb.
			----	-----	----	----	MT Ps.
			----	תשעני:	מחמס	----	MT 2 Sam.
			----	----	----	----	Targ. Ps.
			יתי	פריק	חטופין	כל	Targ. Neb.

Targ. Ps.: [2]And he said: '**I adore you, LORD, my strength**. [3] The Lord is my strength and my safety and he saves me;[a] God, who has taken delight in me, has led me to the fear of him. My *shield*—from Him strength and redemption are given to me over my enemies—my safety.

Targ. Neb.: [2] And he said: 'The Lord is my strength and my safety and he saves me. [3] My God who has taken delight in me, he has led me to the fear of him. My *strength*—from Him strength and redemption are given to me TO OVERPOWER my enemies. My safety—IN TIMES OF DISTRESS I RELY ON HIS WORD. HE SHIELDS ME FROM MY ENEMIES AND HE PROMISED TO RAISE MY HORN IN HIS REDEMPTION. **My support**—HIS WORD SUPPORTED ME WHEN I WAS FLEEING FROM MY PURSUERS; **my redemption—He saved me from** MY ENEMIES AND ALSO FROM THE HAND OF ALL **robbers**.

a. Words printed in italics represent substitutions (Aramaic–Aramaic); in small capitals, pluses (Aramaic–Aramaic); in boldface, a Hebrew plus faithfully reflected in the Targums.

Those differences which relate to the Hebrew parent texts are printed in boldface in the translation. The Hebrew plus in Ps. 18.2 is faithfully reflected in its Targum, while that in 2 Sam. 22 is reflected in Targum Jonathan.[138] The latter, characteristically, gives explanatory supplements to these pluses.

Not all differences can be accounted for in this way. Part of Targ. Neb.'s supplement, דעל מימריה אנא רחיץ בעדן עקא מגין עלי מבעלי דבבי ואמר לארמא קרני בפרקניה, is a double translation of the Hebrew אחסה-בו מגני וקרן ישעי, 'I take refuge in him, my shield and the horn of

---

138. For the Hebrew variation, see G. Schmuttermayr, *Psalm 18 und 2 Samuel 22: Studien zu einem Doppeltext* (SANT, 25; Munich: Kösel, 1971).

my salvation'.[139] Interestingly, this second translation is of the associative kind, referring to 1 Sam. 2.10: וירם קרן משיחו, 'he will raise the
horn of his anointed one'. There, however, Targum Jonathan interprets
the metaphor as follows: וירבי מלכות משיחיה, 'he will magnify the
kingdom of his Messiah'. Here the metaphors have been retained,
which, as we have seen, is not Targ. Neb.'s usual translation strategy.
Churgin rightly suggests that this supplement represents a late textual
development. Notably, Targ. Ps. 18 does not elaborate on its final key-
word, רוחצני. It is not clear, however, whether the second translation of
Targ. Neb. was absent from the Targum of the Prophets from which the
translator worked, or whether he himself omitted it.

The first translation, then, of צורי אחסה־בו מגני וקרן ישעי is less
literal: דאתרעי בי קרבני לדחלתיה, 'who took delight in me, has led me
to the fear of him'. Here אחסה must have been related to the verb חוס
rather than חסה. The fact that Targ. Ps. 18 continues this translation
with תריסי, seamlessly reflecting MT מגני, justifies this deduction.

It is tempting to connect the translation in Targ. Neb. to a period of
political distress, as the supplement implies, when the self-confident
tone of the reference to 'the kingdom' (of God's anointed one) seemed
misplaced. An earlier reference to periods of distress in Targum
Jonathan has been related to the aftermath of the Second Revolt against
Rome.[140] The proto-Targum of the Prophets underwent some sort of
revision, specifically expansion, in the aftermath of the Bar Kokhba
revolt. This plus effectively reminds the reader or listener that God will
not forsake his people, in agreement with a plus in the next verse, 22.4,
which claims that God's saving acts may occur in any period.[141] Thus
the Targum of 2 Sam. 22 may have been revised in order to console an
audience that had suffered, but it is impossible to date this revision
precisely.

2. In Targ. Neb. 22.7 the verse opens with אמר דויד, a device often
used to identify the speaker; this device is itself known elsewhere in the
Targum of Psalms,[142] and both versions share this supplement at the

139. So Churgin, *Targum Jonathan*, pp. 130-31.

140. L. Smolar and M. Aberbach, *Studies in Targum Jonathan to the Prophets*
(Baltimore: Ktav, 1983), p. 85.

141. The supplement דבכל עדן in Targ. Neb. 22.4.

142. 14.1; 32.1; 49.16; 57.1; 58.1; 59.1; 60.3; 75.1; 84.9; 91.2; 118.28. See
M. Bernstein, 'Translation Technique in the Targum to Psalms. Two Test Cases:
Psalms 2 and 137', in E.W. Lovering (ed.), *SBL 1994 Seminar Papers* (Atlanta:

beginning of vv. 4 and 21; Targ. Pss. lacks it here.

3. In the Sefardi textual tradition of Targ. Ps. 18.7 a plus occurs that is absent in the Ashkenazi manuscripts, ומקביל צלותי מהיכל קודשיה דבשמיא, 'And [He] received my prayer from his *holy* temple *which is in heaven*' (Targ. Neb. agrees with the Ashkenazi text, ומקביל מהיכליה צלותי). The plus refers to the heavenly temple, possibly as a consolation to the generations living after the destruction of the Second Temple: God still hears one's prayers. Apparently later scribes changed the text according to their own exegetical notions.[143] Such pluses point to scribal activity in the textual history of Targ. Pss.

4. In 22.10 the subject has been supplemented: it is God's Glory, יקריה, which has been revealed. The Targum of Psalms does not attest to this plus. In general, it is far less consistent in using metonyms for God, an inconsistency that may well reflect carelessness toward this particular use of language on the part of the copyist/Targumist responsible for Targ. Pss.[144] A related supplement is מן קדם preceding יוי in 22.16, lacking in Targ. Ps. 18.

5. The plus in Targ. Ps. 18.12, introducing God's glory, is interesting.

Table 4. *Targum 2 Samuel 22.12 and Targum Psalm 18.12*

סביבתיו	----	חשך	----	וישת	MT 2 Sam.
סביבתיו	סתרו[145]	חשך	----	וישת	MT Ps.
←	----	בערפילא	שכינתיה	אשרי	Targ. Neb.
ואיתחזר	----	בערפילת	שכינתיה	אשרי	Targ. Ps.
----	----	----	----	סכות	MT 2 Sam.
----	----	----	----	סכות	MT Ps.
----	----	----	----	ענן יקר	Targ. Neb.
דרעוא	מיטרין	דאחיד	היך מטללתא	בענני יקריה	Targ. Ps.

Scholars Press, 1994), pp. 326-45 (341); M. Bernstein, 'Specification of Speakers as an Interpretive Device in the Targum of Psalms' (paper given at the Twelfth World Congress of Jewish Studies, Jerusalem, 1997). For Targum Jonathan, see Gordon, *Studies in the Targum*, pp. 74-82.

143. Unusually, for the translator(s), the variant reading does not reflect the Hebrew word order faithfully.

144. J. Shunary, 'Avoidance of Anthropomorphism in the Targum of Psalms', *Textus* 5 (1966), pp. 133-44.

145. This word appears not to be reflected in the Targums, unless we are to assume that שכינתיה has been understood as its equivalent. That is not impossible, as this equivalent occurs in Targ. Ps. 61.5 and 91.1; cf. 81.8 where it is associated with it, linked to סתר's meaning of 'hiding'; cf. Targ. Isa. 28.17; 32.2.

עבי שחקים	חשרת־מים	----	----	→	MT 2 Sam.
עבי שחקים	חשכת־מים	----	----	→	MT Ps.
מרכפת עננין	מין תקיפין[146]	מחית	ליה	סחור סחור	Targ. Neb.
מריכפת עננין	ומיין תקיפין	----	על עמיה	→	Targ. Ps.
----	----	----	----	----	MT 2 Sam.
------	----	----	----	----	MT Ps.
עלמא:	ברום	מחית	------	קלילין	Targ. Neb.
דעלמא:	מן רומיה	על רשיעיא	דקיבלא		Targ. Ps.

Targ. Neb.: He made his Shekinah dwell in a dark cloud, a cloud of Glory all around him, *pouring down* heavy showers from the mass of swift clouds on the height of the world.

Targ. Ps.: He made his Shekinah dwell in the dark cloud, *and he surrounded himself with the* clouds *of his* Glory AS A SHELTER, *containing* rains OF DELIGHT FOR THE SAKE OF HIS OWN PEOPLE, BUT showering waters from the mass of the clouds of *darkness* ON THE WICKED ONES from the height of the world.

In Targ. Ps. 18, God's Glory is compared to a protective covering of clouds in the traditional interpretation of Lev. 23.43 in Targum Onqelos and parallels.[147] Based on the lexeme סוכה in Isa. 4.6 and Exod. 12.37, the *Mekhilta*, *Sifra* and *Tanhuma* attribute this interpretation to R. Akiva;[148] *b. Suk.* 11b attributes it to R. Eliezer on the basis of Lev. 23.43.[149] The same motif occurs in Targum Jonathan on Isa. 4.6 and Ezek. 16.12. The interpretation hangs on the differentiation of clouds and the comparison of the clouds to booths, סכות. The same idea is, however, expressed in Targ. Neb. with the words ענן יקר. Interestingly, the interpretation of סכות as מטללתא in Targ. Ps. 18 occurs in Targ. Neb. 2 Sam. 11.11. Both Targums relate the Hebrew word סכות (or

146. We differ slightly from the equation in Van Staalduine-Sulman (ed.), *Samuel*, where Targ. Neb. מחית is equated to חשרת.

147. Targum Pseudo-Jonathan, *Neofiti*, the *Fragmentary Targum*, Cairo Genizah fragments.

148. *Mekhilta dRY* פסחא 14 (edn Lauterbach, I, pp. 108); בשלח 1 (edn Lauterbach, II, pp. 182-83); *Sifra* אמור 17.11; *Tanh.* 21.9.

149. As Grossfeld observes, the positions of Eliezer and Akiva seem to be reversed in these sources; B. Grossfeld, *The Targum Onqelos to Leviticus* (The Aramaic Bible, 3; Edinburgh: T. & T. Clark, 1988), p. 53 n. 12. However, he overlooked the fact that the prooftexts of Eliezer and Akiva differ. It is possible that Eliezer and Akiva agreed on both the existence of real booths and the cloud of Glory in the wilderness, but disagreed with one another about the texts that buttress these opinions.

סכתו in Ps. 18) to the first colon, in agreement with the Masoretic division by accents.[150]

The Targum differentiates the two dark clouds mentioned in the text: here are the clouds full of rain for the righteous, and there are the clouds full of destructive power for the wicked. The reference here is to the exodus, more specifically the crossing of the Sea of Reeds, when the Israelites were protected but the Egyptians were drowned. The distinction is based on the principle that the Hebrew Bible contains no redundancy, so that the repetition of clouds requires interpretation. This exegetical technique was especially favoured by R. Akiva, to whom the present explanation has been attributed in some rabbinic sources.[151] The parallels are of an early origin and suggest that this explanation circulated at an early date.

The priority of one version or the other here remains uncertain, but the examples given above do suggest that the translator of Targ. Ps. 18 felt free to incorporate a well-known motif into his translation. Note the change of word order, when סהור סחור becomes a verbal form, אתחזר. There is no evidence here to support Churgin's belief that the proto-Targum of the Prophets contained this version.

6. In vv. 26-29, although the Targums have much in common, there are also many points at which they differ. It is worthwhile to consider these verses in their entirety here (even though some of the differences belong rather to section 4.3.1). In 2 Sam. 22.26 Targum Jonathan reads בכין twice whereas Targ. Ps. 18 has עם, as do the Hebrew texts.[152]

Table 5. *Targum Psalm 18.26 and Targum 2 Samuel 22.26*

----	----	----	→	----	חסיד	עם־	MT 2 Sam.
-----	----	----	→	----	חסיד	עם־	MT Ps.
אסניתא	בכין	קדמך	חסיד	דאשתכח	אברהם	----	Targ. Neb.
אסניתא	-----	קדמך	חסיד	דאישתכח	אברהם	עם	Targ. Ps.
תמים	-----	→	גבור	עם	תתחסד	----	MT 2 Sam.
תמים	-----	→	גבר	עם	תתחסד	----	MT Ps.
שלים	דהוה	יצחק	זרעיה	עם	חסדא	למעבד	Targ. Neb.
שלים	דהוה	יצהק	זרעיה	עם	חיסדא	למעבד	Targ. Ps.

150. A similar example of targumic interpretation agreeing with these accents is to be found in Judg. 5.13 and 20.

151. See n. 147 above.

152. See also section 4.2 above.

----	-----	----	תתמם	----	----	MT 2 Sam.
----	----	----	תתמם	----	----	MT Ps.
עמיה	רעותך	מימר	אשלימתא	בכין בדחלתך		Targ. Neb.
עימיה	רעותך	מימר	אשלמתא	---- בדחלתא		Targ. Ps.

Targ. Neb.: (Because of) Abraham who was found to be pious before you, *therefore* you did much kindness with his offspring. (Because of) Isaac who was blameless in (his) fear for you, *therefore* you fulfilled the word of your will with him.

Targ. Pss.: *With* Abraham who was found to be pious before you, you did much kindness. With his offspring, Isaac, who was blameless in (his) fear for you, with him you fulfilled the word of your will.

In *b. Ned.* 32a this verse has been applied to Abraham, in *Lev. R.* 11.5 and *Midr. Teh.* 18.22 to Abraham or Moses, but not to Isaac. The inclusion of Isaac is apparently based on the Aqedah,[153] linked to גב(ו)ר תמים in the Hebrew.

There is reason to believe that Targ. Neb. has been revised (although Churgin does not suggest this), while Targ. Ps. 18 preserved the older reading. Because Targ. Neb. does not retain עם at the beginning of the verse, but reads בכין at a different position, the syntax of Targ. Ps. 18 is smoother than that of Targ. Neb.[154] As a result, the phrase עם זרעיה now belongs to the first half of the verse about Abraham, v. 26a, in Targ. Neb. The parallel Hebrew text, however, belongs to v. 26b. Indeed, it seems obvious that the 'hero' of 26b has been identified with Abraham's offspring Isaac, as in Targ. Ps. 18.

There are, however, three objections to the view that Targ. Neb. is the result of a revision. The smooth syntax of Targ. Ps. and its reflection of the MT's עם twice could result from the work of the translator of Targ. Pss. The use of בכין in Targ. Neb. highlights any cause or result, especially the reward of the faithful as in the present verse,[155] or the

153. White refers to *Gen. R.* 64.3 where Isaac is called a עולה תמימה (*A Critical Edition*, p. 99).

154. One Yemenite MS and two Ashkenazi MSS restore the preposition עם (Sperber's ybc) in the first case, as does a gloss in Codex Reuchlin, but this appears to be a correction; 'y', often together with 'w', frequently contains small revisions towards the MT, in contrast to Sperber's basic text. The MSS ybd also restore עם once in v. 27.

155. Targ. Judg. 5.2 and 2 Sam. 23.5. It does not mark the resumption of the standard translation here, as it seems to do in Targ. Judg. 5.2, 1 Sam. 2.1 and the Pal. Targ. of 1 Kgs 16.34/17.1. Cf. A. Samely, *The Interpretation of Speech in the Pentateuch Targums: A Study of Method and Presentation in Targumic Exegesis*

punishment for the wicked.[156] Significantly, Targ. Neb. also omits עם twice in v. 27, in contrast to Targ. Ps. 18; here it does not insert בכין:

[157]יעקב דהליך בברירותא קדמך בחרתא בנוהי מכל עממיא אפרישתא זרעיה מכל פסולא פרעה ומצראי דחשיבו מחשבן על עמך בלבילתנון כמחשבתהון	עם יעקב דהוה בריר קדמך בחרתא בבנוי מכל עממיא ואפרישתא זרעיה מכל פסילן [158]ועם פרעה ומצראי דחשיבו מחשב בישׁן על עמך[159] קלקילתינון במחשבתהון
Targ. Neb.: Jacob who was *walking in purity* before you, you have chosen his sons from all the nations, you have separated his offspring from every *blemish*; Pharaoh and the Egyptians, who plotted plans against your people, you have *scattered* [160] them *according to their plans.*	Targ. Pss.: *With* Jacob who was *pure* before you, you have chosen his sons from all the nations *and* you have separated his offspring from all *the idols*; *but with* Pharaoh and the Egyptians, who plotted *evil* plans against your people, you have *destroyed* them *with their plans.*

There is therefore a possibility, which cannot be discounted, that the absence of עם is original in Targ. Neb., and that Targ. Ps. 18 supplied it on the basis of the Hebrew text in vv. 26-27. A strong case can be made for the claim that the translator of Targ. Ps. 18 was more independent than previous authors have believed. It is in any case important to emphasize that both Targums are internally consistent. This is well shown in the following verses.

Targ. Neb. emphasizes the eschatological motif of *this* world and the world *to come* in vv. 28-29, whereas Targ. Ps. 18 refers to the exile.[161]

(TSAJ, 27; Tübingen: J.C.B. Mohr, 1992), p. 77 n. 18; Smelik, *Targum of Judges*, p. 393. Cf. Targ. Ezek. 28.13 (where it introduces a comment on the orifices and organs, similar to *b. B. Bat.* 75a/b and the traditional morning blessings).

156. As in 2 Sam. 23.7; Jer. 4.12; 17.4; 48.27; 51.7 and Ezek. 28.13. See also Judg. 11.1 (variant); 2 Sam. 2.2; 22.32, 47, etc.

157. Note that עם has been restored in Sperber's witnesses 'ybd'; see n. 153 below. It is not original, for Targ. Neb. reads the preposition ב, see text.

158. In White's basic MS על עמך has been omitted; in another MS it has been replaced by על ישראל.

159. So Targ. Pss, but also the Western MSS of Targ. Neb. and a Cairo Genizah fragment.

160. Most MSS of Targ. Pss. follow this reading.

161. MT 2 Sam. 22.28-29: כי־אתה עם עני תושיע ועיניך על־רמים תשפיל: ואת נירי יהוה ויהוה יגיה חשכי.

(28) וית עמא בית ישראל דמתקרן בעלמא
הדין עם חשיך את עתיד למפרק ובמימרך
תקיפיא דמתגברין עליהון תמאיך:

(28) מטול דאנת ית עמא בית ישראל
דחשיכין[162] ביני עממיא בגלותא אנת
עתיד למפרוק ובמימרך אומיא תקיפיא
דמתגברין עליהון[163]
תמאיך:

(29) ארי את הוא מריה נהוריה דישראל
יוי וייי יפקנני מחשוכא לנחורא ויחזינני
בעלמא דעתיד למיתי לצדיקיא

(29) מטול דאנת תנהר שרגא דישראל
דמיטפיא בגלותא דאנת הוא מרי דאנהורא
דישראל ייי אלהי יפקינני מחברייא[164]
לנהור (וינהר קבלי) ויחמינני בנחמותא
לעלמא דעתיד למיתי לצדיקיא

Targ. Neb.: The people, the House of Israel, who are called a poor *people in this world*, you will save, and by your Memra you will humble the strong ones who are overpowering them (now).

Targ. Pss: For you, you will save them, the people of Israel who are poor among the *nations in exile*, and by your Memra you will humble the strong PEOPLES who are overpowering them (now).

For You are its master, the LORD is Israel's light. And the LORD will bring me forth from darkness into light and show me the world that is to come for the righteous.

For YOU WILL MAKE SHINE ISRAEL'S LIGHT, WHICH WAS EXTINGUISHED IN THE EXILE, for you, LORD, are the master of Israel's light. My God will bring me forth from the dark to light (and he will brighten my darkness)[165] and he will show me the CONSOLATION of the world that is to come for the righteous.

The contrast between this world and the world to come is one of the hallmarks of rabbinic eschatology, and Targum Jonathan shares this theologoumenon.[166] It is consistent with the messianic interpretation of 2 Sam. 23.1-8.[167] The reference to the world to come occurs in v. 29, thus making Targ. Neb. consistent in these verses. Targ. Ps. 18 is no

162. Five manuscripts have the variant reading דחשבין, 'considered' (White's edition, p. 72); but in the light of the Hebrew equivalent עני this must be an inner-Aramaic corruption.

163. This word is missing in White's basic MS.

164. The bracketed words only appear in the Sefardi MSS and seem to represent a gloss, an alternativetranslation of the Hebrew, יגיה חשכי.

165. מחכיריא in Díez Merino's edition must be a scribal error (ב/כ) in MS Villa-Amil no. 5, or a typo.

166. Smolar and Aberbach, *Studies*, pp. 179-83.

167. See E. van Staalduine-Sulman, 'Reward and Punishment in the Messianic Age (Targum 2 Sam. 23.1-8)', *JAB* 1 (1999), pp. 273-96.

less consistent in its reference to Israel's exile, to which it refers in both verses, but in v. 29 it shares the reference to the world to come with Targ. Neb., possibly suggesting that Targ. Ps. 18 combined two distinct traditions. The vocabulary of Targ. Ps. 18 is Palestinian Aramaic,[168] but the reference to the 'world to come' in v. 29 is clearly borrowed from Targ. Neb., לעלמא דעתיד למיתי, for Targ. Pss. always refers to it as עלמא דאתי.[169]

The distinct motifs are not characteristic of one or the other. The contrast between this world and the world to come (עלמא דאתי) occurs frequently in Targ. Pss.,[170] even more often than in Targ. Neb. where it occurs only here, in 1 Kgs 5.13, Isa. 5.20 and in Mal. 3.6. On the other hand, the motif of the exile occurs frequently in Targ. Neb. too,[171] and is not more characteristic of the Targum of Psalms.

As Zunz suggested, followed by Bacher and Churgin,[172] the supplement 'You will make shine Israel's light...' in Targ. Ps. 18 represents an alternative translation of the MT כי־אתה תאיר נרי, juxtaposed to the one found in Targum Jonathan. This alternative translation, however, is probably not an example of the secondary phenomenon of multiple translations, seen in the Targum of Job, for it accords with the translator's tendency to reflect his own Hebrew parent text which has the plus תאיר,[173] in contrast to 2 Sam. 22, כי־אתה נירי. The translation as found in Targ. Neb. could not easily be adjusted without changing its purport, something the translator was apparently unwilling to do; he therefore adjusted Targ. Neb.'s reading only to the extent that its dialect was made to conform to that of Targ. Pss. (so that even this phrase does not appear to be secondary in Targ. Ps. 18).

168. For example: חמא, מטול, אנת, חבירא, שרגא.

169. Targ. Pss. 41.14; 50.21; 61.7; 63.4, 5; 73.12; 89.53; 90.2, 10; 92.9; 103.17; 106.48; 119.165; 128.2; 139.18; 143.3.

170. See the previous note.

171. Smolar and Aberbach, *Studies*, pp. 201-204; Chilton, *Glory of Israel*, pp. 28-33.

172. Zunz, *Die gottesdienstlichen Vorträge*, pp. 84-85 n. a; Bacher, 'Das Targum zu den Psalmen', pp. 472-73; Churgin, תרגום כתובים, p. 26.

173. The same strategy accounts for a difference in v. 29b, where ויהוה in 2 Sam. 22 is reflected with ויוי in Targ. Neb., and אלהי in Ps. 18 by אלהי in its Targum. In v. 41 תתה (2 Sam. 22) and נתתה (Ps. 18) are both translated with תברתא. Targ. Ps. 18, however, has the supplement יהבתנון, a second translation of the Hebrew verb.

While familiar with the version of Targ. Neb., the translator of Targ. Ps. 18 deviated from his model in v. 28 and retained it in v. 29, only to insert another translation with a quite different emphasis. This may have been his own composition, but the possibility remains that he was influenced by a translation of Targ. Pss. extant at his period but lost to present-day students.[174] The Sefardi witnesses of Targ. Ps. 18 add a further double translation in v. 29b, indicating that the Targum of Psalms underwent textual development beyond the text of Targum Jonathan.

All in all, analysis of vv. 26-29 confirms the relative independence of the translator of Targ. Ps. 18.

7. In v. 40 Targ. Pss. has the supplement חמטתנון, 'I subdued them'; a Cairo Genizah fragment of Targ. Neb. has a similar supplement with תברת (Sperber).

8. In Targ. 2 Sam. 22.47 the stock phrase on miracles is repeated before the actual translation: בכין על נסא ופרקנא דעבדתא לעמך אודיו ואמרו, 'Therefore, on account of the miracle and redemption which You performed on behalf of your people, they gave thanks and said...' This plus presumably entered the Targum after the Targum of Ps. 18 was composed.[175] The translator of Targ. Ps. 18 did not omit a similar phrase in vv. 1 and 32. That such pluses were sometimes added is evident from variant readings in the Targums. In the Targum of Judges the very phrase is sometimes found as a variant reading, and in Targ. 2 Sam. 22 one codex has an even more expanded reading.[176]

174. That such translations existed, is evident from a Frag. Targ. to 2 Sam. 22.28. See Kasher, תוספות תרגום לנביאים, p. 122, also quoted by Sperber, *Bible in Aramaic*, II, p. 204; cf. M.H. Goshen-Gottstein and R. Kasher (eds.), שקיעים מתרגומי המקרא הארמיים, I (Ramat Gan: Bar Ilan University Press, 1983), p. 142.

175. See Churgin, *Targum Jonathan*, p. 130.

176. Kasher, תוספות תרגו לנביא, p. 122.

MAKING SENSE OF JOB 37.13: TRANSLATION STRATEGIES
IN 11Q10, PESHITTA AND THE RABBINIC TARGUM

Sally L. Gold

Introduction

Synoptic comparison of the Aramaic versions of the book of Job found
in 11Q10 (the Qumran Job scroll, QJ), the Peshitta (PJ) and in the
rabbinic Targum (TJ) forms the basis of a study[1] which aims to explore
the translators' understanding of this complex text and the strategies
they employed in order to produce their translations.[2] The aim is, in
effect, to see 'how—and how well—the text was understood', as
Michael Weitzman expressed it in his paper on the Hebrew and Syriac
texts of Job.[3]

In his study of cases of serious semantic discrepancy between the
Hebrew text and the Syriac translation of Job, Weitzman articulates a
set of translation techniques which together form a rational and coherent approach to the task of transmitting the Hebrew text. Seven translational devices are defined: (1) working within the constraints of the

1. This paper is part of a doctoral research project under the supervision of Dr
Piet van Boxel (Leo Baeck College) and Professor Philip Alexander (Manchester).
With characteristic generosity, Michael Weitzman gave me a pre-publication copy
of his paper on the Hebrew and Syriac texts of the book of Job, modestly commenting that I might find in it something of interest.
2. The following editions are used: F. García Martínez, E. Tigchelaar and
A. van der Woude (eds.), *11Q10* (DJD, 23; Oxford: Clarendon Press, 1998), pp.
79-180. J.P.M. van der Ploeg, O.P van der Woude, A.S van der Woude and
B. Jongeling (eds.), *Le Targum de Job de la grotte XI de Qumran* (Leiden: E.J. Brill
1971). D.M. Stec (ed.), *The Text of the Targum of Job: An Introduction and Critical
Edition* (Leiden: E.J. Brill, 1994). L.G. Rignell (ed.), 'Job', in The Peshitta Institute, *The Old Testament in Syriac according to the Peshitta Version* (Leiden: E.J.
Brill, 1982).
3. 'The Hebrew and Syriac Texts of the Book of Job', in *From Judaism to
Christianity* (JSS Supplement, 8; Oxford: Oxford University Press, 1999), pp. 130-48.

consonantal Hebrew text, while selecting a particular meaning, or changing the grammar; (2) manipulating, or, in other words, deliberately misreading the consonantal Hebrew text; (3) manipulating the Syriac equivalent translation, that is starting with a provisional translation and reworking it until sense is achieved; (4) guesswork to achieve a sense to fit the context; (5) using influences from outside the text, such as a neighbouring or more distant passage in Job, or other biblical books, non-biblical literature, theological doctrine or other versions; (6) abdication of the translation role, either by leaving an obscure translation or by omitting a translation; (7) the drive for continuous sense, which often determined the translator's choice of translation device.[4] He notes two further explanations for semantic discrepancy: corruption of the Syriac translation during transmission, and a *Vorlage* different from the Masoretic text (MT); it is the explanation of semantic discrepancy through translation technique that he both prefers and pursues.

Weitzman's method is simple—nine categories suffice to cover all cases of semantic divergence from HT—and decisive—the categories are clear and straightforward to apply.

Furthermore, it avoids the complexity involved in a more atomistic classification of the PJ translation technique.[5] While the criticism may be levelled that it risks being subjective in reasoning—Weitzman admits to trying to read the mind of the translator—his method offers accessible, comprehensive and innately satisfying solutions to the cases of semantic discrepancy that are described. His observations form an inspirational background to the current synoptic study of the three Aramaic versions of Job. Some of the translation techniques that he identified in PJ may be identified also in the Qumran translation, though it is not at this stage clear whether they may need adjustment when applied more thoroughly to QJ. It also remains to be seen how they hold up

4. I wonder whether this is more accurately a motive that underpins the translation devices rather than a device itself. The question will be addressed in the wider study rather than in this paper.

5. An example of an atomistic approach to translation technique in PJ is H.M. Szpek, *Translation Technique in the Peshitta to Job* (SBLDS, 137; Atlanta: Scholars Press, 1992). In brief, her four-part model classifies each divergence from the MT four times, i.e. according to the linguistic area into which it falls (grammar, syntax, semantics, style), the type of adjustment it represents (e.g. addition, transposition, interpretation), the motivation for the change (e.g. ideology, textual difficulty, language difference), and its effect on the translation (e.g. clarity, confusion, innovation).

when applied to passages in Job that Weitzman did not include in his selective survey. As regards analysis of the rabbinic version of Job, the fertile field of Targum studies provides additional theories and tools with which to do this. Here, too, there is some overlap with Weitzman's theories: his category 'manipulation of the Hebrew consonantal text' recalls the rabbinic אל תקרי; the role of influences outside the immediate text, scriptural or otherwise, and the selection of meaning from the consonantal Hebrew are well known from Targum.

Although these three versions of Job have previously been studied individually,[6] a synoptic study offers a fresh approach to their complexities, both singular and collective.[7] It may be that translators of the same text are likely to see in it the same problems,[8] particularly when

---

6. The literature is fairly extensive and scattered. The following list is useful but by no means comprehensive. On the rabbinic Targum to Job see Stec, *Targum of Job*; also R. Weiss, *The Aramaic Targum of the Book of Job* [Hebrew] (Tel Aviv: Tel Aviv University Press, 1979); C. Mangan, *The Targum of Job: Translated with Critical Introduction, Apparatus and Notes* (The Aramaic Bible, 15; Edinburgh: T. & T. Clark, 1991). For literature on Peshitta Job, see Weitzman, *The Hebrew and Syriac Texts*; also Szpek, *Translation Technique*; H.M. Szpek, 'On the Influence of the Targum on the Peshitta to Job', in P.V.M. Flesher (ed.), *Targum Studies. II. Targum and Peshitta* (Atlanta: Scholars Press, 1998), pp. 141-58. On Qumran Job, see the critical editions, and M. Sokoloff, *The Targum to Job from Qumran Cave XI* (Ramat Gan: Bar Ilan University, 1974). Also Weiss, *The Aramaic Targum*, Appendix 1 to ch. 1; J.C. Lübbe, 'Describing the Translation Process of 11QtgJob: A Question of Method', *RevQ* 13 (1988), pp. 543-93; S. Kaufman, 'The Job Targum from Qumran', *JAOS* 93 (1973), pp. 317-27; J. Gray, 'The Massoretic Text of the Book of Job, the Targum and the LXX in the Light of the Qumran Targum', *ZAW* 86 (1974), pp. 331-50; J. Fitzmyer, 'The First-Century Targum of Job from Qumran Cave XI', in *idem, A Wandering Aramean* (Missoula, MT: Scholars Press, 1979), pp. 161-82; P. Grelot, 'Le Targum de Job de la grotte XI de Qumran', *RevQ* 8 (1972–75), pp. 105-14.

7. David Shepherd's article, 'Will the Real Targum Please Stand Up? Translation and Coordination in the Ancient Aramaic Versions of Job', *JJS* L1/1 (2000), pp. 88-116, was published just as the current paper was submitted. While we share the broad methodology of a synoptic approach to the same material, the detailed application and the foci of attention are different. His observations deserve the fullest consideration which cannot be undertaken here.

8. Robert Gordon has commented to this effect in regard to the ancient Versions: 'Methodological Criteria for Distinguishing between Variant Vorlage and Exegesis in the Peshitta Pentateuch', in P. Dirksen and A. van der Kooij (eds.), *The Peshitta as a Translation* (MPIL, 8; Leiden: E.J. Brill, 1995), pp. 121-22.

the original is difficult; in the case of Job it is notoriously so, both linguistically and semantically. Yet their solutions to particular difficulties, be they similar or different, can tell us what it is that the translators found problematic and what their strategies were for dealing with
the problems. This in turn, through the comparison and contrast facilitated by synopsis, may help to clarify in a wider sense the natures of
their translations both individually and vis-à-vis each other and to suggest the nature of any influences upon them, common or particular.

The present study makes two assumptions: (1) that all three translators worked with a Hebrew *Vorlage* that differed little from the MT,
and (2) that the three translations are independent of each other.[9] The
primary focus of the analysis is on the semantic content of the translations where this differs from the Hebrew text, rather than on differences from the Hebrew text that can be accounted for as simply
linguistic, stylistic or idiomatic concerns.[10] Job 37.13 is a semantic
challenge, and the three Aramaic translations provide a clear example
of the different approaches of the translators to their task, and of some
of their strategies. For the purposes of analysis the verse is broken into
four parts, with each translation of each part examined in terms of its
linguistic and semantic content, and with suggestions, where possible,
of a reasoned route from Hebrew text to translation.[11] The main characteristics of the three translations to emerge from this analysis are then

9. Both assumptions are in line with the current consensus. See, for example,
on 11Q10: Sokoloff, 'Targum to Job from Qumran', pp. 6-7, and Fitzmyer, 'The
First-Century Targum', p. 168; on TJ: Mangan, *Targum of Job Translated*, p. 14,
and Weiss, *The Aramaic Targum*, pp. xi, 35-36; on PJ: Weitzman, 'The Hebrew
and Syriac Texts', pp. 140, 146-47, and Szpek, 'On the Influence', pp. 157-58.

10. See the examination of such cases in PJ by Szpek, *Translation Technique*,
and to some extent in TJ by Weiss, *The Aramaic Targum*.

11. Weitzman, regarding the P translation, and Le Déaut before him, regarding
QJ, both noted the desirability of tracing a logical pathway from Hebrew text to
translation before seeking an explanation through different Vorlage or translator or
copyist error. See Weitzman, 'The Hebrew and Syriac Texts', p. 131; R. Le Déaut,
'Usage implicite de l'al tiqre dans le Targum de Job de Qumrân?', in D. Muñoz
Leon (ed.), *Salvacion en la Palabra: Homenaje al Prof. A. Diez Macho* (Madrid:
Ediciones Cristiandad, 1986), pp. 419-31. In previous studies of PJ and of QJ both
different Vorlage and error have been presented as explanations for semantic
discrepancy; the current study considers them only as last resorts where no other
reasoned method can be suggested.

summarized. A discussion of some features of the translations that arise out of this analysis concludes the paper.[12]

Analysis of Job 37.13

The wider preceding context for Job 37.13 describes how natural events come to pass through God's will: thunder and lightning, snow, frost, rain, wind and clouds are all divinely directed (vv. 3-11). In v. 12, however, although it is apparently a continuation of what precedes, the language and sense become more obscure:

והוא מסבות מתהפך בתחבולתו לפעלם כל אשר יצום על פני תבל ארצה

The variety evident in modern translations is testimony to its difficulties. The Authorized Version (AV) rendering, for example, is confused: 'And it [the bright cloud] is turned round about by his counsels: that they may do whatsoever he commandeth them upon the face of the world in the earth'. The New English Bible (NEB) admits to paraphrase: 'they [the clouds] travel round in their courses, steered by his guiding hand to do his bidding over all the habitable world'; the Jewish Publication Society (JPSV) translation notes that the meaning of the Hebrew is uncertain: 'He keeps turning events by His stratagems, that they might accomplish all that He commands them throughout the inhabited earth'.[13]

In that it appears to present a series of alternatives which are in some sense mediated by the divine will, v. 13 too seems to make sense as a continuation of the preceding verses, although its precise relationship with v. 12 is debatable. The Hebrew text (HT)[14] of Job 37.13 reads as follows:

אם לשבט אם לארצו אם לחסד ימצאהו

While word-for-word the Hebrew is linguistically relatively straightforward, the sense overall and relative to v. 12 is not. The structure looks as if it ought to be antithetical, contrasting שבט and חסד but לארצו

---

12. A systematic analysis of PJ and QJ in the light of the translation techniques identified by Weitzman in 'The Hebrew and Syriac Texts' does not form part of the current paper.

13. The translations of QJ, PJ and TJ for 37.12 are given below in the Summary.

14. Whilst it is possible that the translators had recourse to a tradition of pronunciation, we do not know that it was that of the MT. The abbreviation HT is therefore preferred.

אם constitutes the chief difficulty in that it sits in the first hemistich
where one might expect a verb to balance ימצאהו in the second. Several
translators in the modern era have regarded the phrase as corrupt.
Dhorme in 1926 described the phrase as 'embarrassing',[15] and favoured
radical emendation to ימלא רצונו 'he accomplishes his will'; Tur-Sinai[16]
and Gordis[17] read אם לא רצו 'if they do not obey', taking אנשי in v. 7b
as the antecedent. Grabbe sought a solution through comparative philological evidence for cognates of רצה with prosthetic א, and suggested
that ארצו be translated as 'his pleasure' or 'his grace'.[18] ימצאהו is
another difficulty. Though it is vocalized as hiphil 'he causes it to find'
in the MT, most modern translators adjust the sense to be consistent
with what precedes. Tur-Sinai, Gordis and Dhorme, for example,
favour the qal sense of 'to attain, reach' (as in Job 11.7; 31.29) and the
nuance of fate this allows, that is, through natural forces God lets man
reach his appropriate fate. Job 34.11 contains the same idea.[19] Modern
biblical translations offer various solutions for these uncertainties. For
example, 'He causeth it to come, whether for correction, or for his land,
or for mercy' (AV); 'Causing each of them to happen to His land,
whether as a scourge or as a blessing' (JPSV); 'Whether he makes him
attain the rod, or his earth, or constant love' (NEB). As we shall now
see, the ancient translators of the verse sought yet other solutions to its
semantic puzzles. They render as follows.[20]

PJ: ܐܝ ܠܫܒܛܐ ܐܘ ܠܐܪܥܐ ܐܘ ܠܛܝܒܘܬܐ ܕܡܫܬܟܚܐ ܒܗ
Whether for the rulers, or whether for the earth, or whether for the kindness which is found in it.

QJ: הן למכתש הן לארעא הן לכפן וחסרנה והן פתגם //ב להוא עליה
Whether for affliction, or for an unexpected event, or for hunger and
want, or whether [for] a shameful matter, it comes to pass on it.

15. P. Dhorme, *A Commentary on the Book of Job* (trans. H. Knight; London:
Nelson, 1967).
16. N.H. Tur-Sinai, *The Book of Job: A New Commentary* (Jerusalem: Kiryath
Sefer, 1957).
17. R. Gordis, *The Book of Job* (New York: Jewish Theological Seminary of
America, 1978). See Gordis and Dhorme (*Commentary*) for a survey of commentaries on this verse, including Hitzig's suggested reading אם לא רצו in F. Hitzig,
Das Buch Hiob uebersetzt und ausgelegt (Leipzig, 1874).
18. L.L. Grabbe, *Comparative Philology and the Text of Job: A Study in Methodology* (SBLDS, 34; Missoula, MT: Scholars Press, 1977).
19. Job 34.11 uses the same form of the verb, though with energic-nun suffix.
20. The English translations throughout are mine.

TJ: אין מטרא דפורענותא בימי ובמדברא אין מטרא רזיא לאילני טווריא
וגלימתא אין נחיא דחסדא לחקלי וכרמי ופירי יספקניה

Whether the rain of punishment in the seas and in the desert, or the
heavy rain for the trees of the mountains and hills,[21] or the gentle [rain]
of kindness for the fields and vineyards and crops, he supplies it.

שבט אם לשבט. שבט 'rod, staff' is found in Biblical Hebrew (BHeb) both as a
symbol of authority (e.g. Isa. 14.5; Zech. 10.11; Ps. 45.7) and as an
instrument of chastisement (e.g. Exod. 21.20), and frequently in this
latter sense as a metaphor for divine punishment (e.g. Job 9.34; 21.9;
Lam. 3.1).[22]

שבט occurs three times in Job, at 9.34, 21.9 and 37.13. At the first
two occurrences, the HT is unambiguous, with שבט clearly a symbol of
affliction; in these two verses, the Peshitta translator uses the cognate
ܫܒܛܐ, possibly because the range of meanings of the root in Hebrew
and in Syriac is similar. At 37.13, however, he has identified a different
shade of meaning, that of leadership; שבט is then treated as a metonym,
that is, the rod or sceptre as symbolic of power and authority, person-
ified and rendered as the plural ܫܠܝܛܢܐ 'rulers, leaders'. ܫܠܝܛܢܐ is
something of a standard or favoured expression in PJ, being used to
translate several different lexemes in HT,[23] all of them unambiguously
types of leaders. Its use here is presumably intended to clarify a potential ambiguity.

Whence the Qumran translator's למכתש? The noun[24] derives from the
Aramaic root כתש 'to crush; to touch, strike, afflict'. At the simplest
level the use of מכתש avoids the possible confusion inherent in שבטא,
which, like the Hebrew, can mean both 'staff' and 'tribe'. Furthermore,

21. גלימא may mean 'valley'; 249a; M. Jastrow, *A Dictionary of the Targumim:
The Talmud Babli and Yerushalmi and the Midrashic Literature* (London: Shapiro
Valentine & Co., 1926), p. 249a.

22. In addition, it regularly means 'tribe'. The meanings may be connected in
that a staff is symbolic of tribal leadership, e.g. Gen. 49.16 which could be translated: 'Dan will judge his people as one of the staffs (i.e. leaders) of Israel'; cf.
Judg. 18.1 where again שבט may perhaps be understood as 'leader'. Interestingly,
the alternative מטה 'staff, rod' can also mean 'tribe'. See the editors' note in BDB,
p. 641b. Note also Ps. 23.4 where שבט is a symbol of comfort.

23. It is used to render HT's שרים (3.15), נדיבים (12.21; 34.18), יעצים (3.14)
and נוגש (39.7).

24. Following Sokoloff, *Targum to Job from Qumran*, ad loc., who argues
against taking this as an infinitive on the grounds that the root is not found in the
Peal.

however, the translator has used the Aramaic equivalent of BHeb נגע 'wound; plague; mark of affliction'; נגע is used frequently to describe disease, which itself is often understood as divine punishment. So by using מכתש, the translator not only avoids ambiguity but also clarifies the sense of HT's שבט as divinely administered chastisement or affliction. There are some suggestive scriptural occurrences of שבט and נגע which may have informed QJ's treatment of the two nouns as synonyms. For example, 2 Sam. 7.14 where בשבט אנשים and בנגעי בני אדם are in parallel; likewise בשבט and בנגעים in Ps. 89.33. In addition, Ps. 38 is redolent throughout of Job in its depiction of a man in the throes of great physical and spiritual stress; he is beset by those who vex him with specious argument, while his family and friends withdraw from his plight, which he describes as 'my affliction נגעי' (Ps. 38.12). There are, then, scriptural links between שבט and נגע which would allow their interpretation as synonyms; moreover, the language and imagery of Ps. 38 suggest a special relevance in the context of Job. QJ's choice of translation with מכתש suggests that such contiguities did not escape the notice of its translator.

If scripture informs the Qumran translation of Job 37.13, it is rabbinic tradition, itself, of course, based on scripture, that informs the rabbinic translation. The entire verse is elaborated into a description of different kinds of rain which reflects a highly developed tradition in which rainfall and lack of rain are seen as symbolic of relations between Israel and God: provision of rain in due season is a blessing, failure of the rains is punishment or warning. The scriptural background to this tradition is Deut. 11.8-17: brought out of Egypt, the Israelites stand to possess 'a land which the Lord your God cares for; the eyes of the Lord your God are always upon it' (v. 12). If they are obedient, then God will send rain (v. 14), but if they transgress, then 'the Lords's anger will erupt…and he will shut up the heavens so that there will be no rain and the land will not yield its produce' (v. 17). In rabbinic discussion it is material from Job that frequently provides the proof-texts. Commenting on Deut. 11.12—'a land which the Lord your God cares for…'—*Sifre* 40 describes how, at Rosh HaShanah, if Israel is first thought to deserve reward, that is, rain, but then is found to have sinned, then God will cause the rain to fall at the wrong time and in the wrong places: 'causing it to descend on [parts of] the land that do not need it, on seas and on wildernesses, as it is said: "Drought and heat consume the snow waters, and Sheol those who have sinned" '—the proof-text is Job

24.19. Here we see TJ's first category, מטרא דפורענותא, reflecting the rabbinic understanding of שבט: affliction in the sense of rain which falls as a punishment.

There are many rabbinic references to different kinds of rain. The mishnaic prescriptions (*m. Ta'an.* 3.2) for fasting at times of drought include a description of three: לצמחים 'for the crops', לאילן 'for the trees', לזה ולזה 'for both' (but insufficient for storage in cisterns and other containers). Honi prays for three kinds: גשם רצון 'rain of benevolence', גשם ברכה 'rain of blessing' and גשם נדבה 'rain of generosity' (*m. Ta'an.* 3.8). There are distinct echoes of both passages in TJ's interpretation of Job 37.13. The links are even stronger in talmudic comment: 'Rava said: Snow [is good] for mountains תלגא לטורי, heavy rain [is good] for trees מטרא רזיא לאילני, light rain [is good] for produce מטרא ניחא לפירי, and drizzle עורפילא [for germination]' (*b. Ta'an.* 3b)—Job 37.6 is cited as the proof-text. Here we see the second and third of TJ's categories: heavy rain, which provides the quantities required by trees without risk of damage, and gentle rain, which is better for crops.[25]

אם לארצו. In the context of v. 13 it is difficult to be sure of the sense of ארץ and of what appears to be a 3 m. sg. possessive suffix, as the variety of modern translations of this phrase would indicate. None of our translations directly renders the suffix. PJ reproduces the sense of 'land' or 'earth' but adds the conjunction, perhaps to achieve a better flow, and omits the suffix in what is apparently a deliberate and simple solution to the difficulty in the sense of HT.[26]

While the TJ translation does not represent לארצו overtly, the sense of 'the land' is subsumed in, yet also underpins, the interpretation of the whole verse. A particularistic understanding, grounded in the 3 m. sg. suffix, is almost certain. Compare, for example, Job 5.10: 'He gives rain upon [the] earth and sends water upon [the] fields'. In the rabbinic translation of 5.10 'the land' is identified as 'the land of Israel'. In *Sifre* 42, where Deut. 11.14 is understood to imply God's own personal concern for Israel's welfare,[27] Job 5.10 is brought as confirmation; and

---

25. Cf. *b. Ta'an.* 8b where Job 37.13 is interpreted as referring only to blessings.

26. Szpek, *Translation Technique*, p. 98, attributes the omission of the suffix here to 'language difference and redundancy' and judges that synonymy is unaffected.

27. *Sifre* 42 reads, ' "I will give"—I Myself, not by the hands of an angel nor by

elsewhere Job 5.10 is illuminated further: 'the earth' is Israel and 'the fields' means other lands[28].

The QJ translation הן לארעא would appear to be almost literal, and indeed is so described by Sokoloff[29] and by Garcia Martinez *et al.*[30] The latter see no merit in deriving it either from רעע 'to shatter, break' (as van der Ploeg *et al.*[31]) or from ערע 'to join, come in contact' with scribal change of ע to א, giving ארעא 'accident'. Yet the suffix of HT is not translated. Did the translator abdicate his role here, or is there something more to this omission? Looking again at the possibilities, it may be that QJ's לארעא is not a translation in the sense of 'land'. The root רעע has an aphel ארע 'to do harm' with the infinitive ארעא—precisely the form found in QJ. Alternatively, derivation from ארע 'to join, meet; attack' (rather than from ערע and contrary to Garcia Martinez *et al.*) would obviate the requirement of scribal emendation and would yield the derived noun ארעא 'occurrence, accident'.[32] By itself the change of consonant from צ to ע (ארע > ארץ) is unexceptional and suggests a straightforward translation. However, when coupled with the omission of a translation of the suffix, and with the potential sense achieved by reading it as a derivation from ארע, it is just possible that the translator intended a sense that would be less incongruous than a literal translation meaning 'his land' and more consistent with his understanding of the verse (thus, either 'occurrence' or 'harming').[33]

אם לחסד. The Peshitta adds the conjunction but is otherwise straightforward. In the TJ translation the sense of חסד is both retained and interpreted: it becomes נחיא דחסדא, the 'gentle [rain] of kindness' which is the type most beneficial to crops; cf. the earlier reference to *b. Ta'an.* 3b: מטרא נחיא לפירי 'light rain for the crops'.

It is generally agreed that QJ's לכפן וחסרנה 'hunger and want' has

the hands of a messenger—"the rain of your land"—not the rain of all lands.'

28. See *b. Ta'an.* 10a; also *b. Ta'an.* 8b.

29. See Sokoloff, *Targum to Job from Qumran*, ad loc.

30. That is, García Martínez, Tigchelaar and van der Woude, *11Q10*, ad loc.

31. That is, van der Ploeg, O.P. and A.S. van der Woude and Jongeling, *Le targum de Job*, ad loc.

32. The form ארע is listed in Jastrow, *Dictionary of the Targumim*, p. 124b as that found in *Pseudo-Jonathan*, with the form ערע found in *Onqelos*.

33. The question does remain, however, as to why the translator would be content with such an ambiguous result; ארעא would appear to be more obviously 'land' than 'accident'.

resulted from reading לחסר (i.e. reading ר instead of ד).[34] The reasons
for this misreading, and for the double translation, are uncertain; both
may have been deliberate. The misreading has been explained by
Weiss[35] who postulates that the translator was influenced by Job 30.3
בְּחֶסֶר וּבְכָפָן 'in want and famine'.

The double rendering of the single Hebrew noun may be accounted
for by supposing that the QJ translator, influenced by knowledge of the
alternative and rare BHeb noun חֶסֶר 'want, lack', deliberately read ר
rather than ד and has supplied both חסרנה and כפן in order to represent
both possible vocalizations of חסר.[36] Why the translator might have
read ר (and thus חסר) here at all, let alone the unusual noun חֶסֶר, is a
question that will be taken up below in the Discussion section. Second,
in addition to accounting for the double translation which has resulted
from reading חסר (with ר), it is possible to argue that the QJ translator
may also have read and translated the noun as חסד (with ד). Any understanding of the QJ rendering at this point is hampered by the condition
of the manuscript. Of the third word only the bottom parts of the letters
survive; the final letter of the third word is generally agreed to be ב.
After פתגם van der Ploeg *et al.*[37] suggest reading either ריב 'conflict', or
טב, this latter reflecting the sense of חסד in HT.[38] Garcia Martinez *et al.*
reject both these suggestions: ריב because the traces of letters are too
close together to allow this reading, and טב for reasons expounded
below. They suggest instead פתגם חוב , citing in support the expression
פתגם דחוב in *Onqelos* (O) to Exod. 22.8 which translates HT דבר
פשע.[39]

Were the reading טב correct, this would support the theory proposed

34. Sokoloff, 'Targum to Job from Qumran', ad loc., understands חסרנה as noun
+ possessive suffix—'for hunger and its want'—which is without correspondence
in HT.

35. Weiss, *The Aramaic Targum*, p. 26.

36. Double translation of a single Hebrew word is a common feature in the
Palestinian Pentateuchal Targumim, though not always because the consonantal
text offers an alternative reading. The motivation seems to be to bring out the fullest
possible sense of HT. Klein has labelled such cases as 'Targumic doublets'.
M. Klein, *Genizah Manuscripts of the Palestinian Targum to the Pentateuch* (Cincinnati: Hebrew Union College Press, 1986), I, p. xxxi; II, p. 4.

37. *Le targum de Job*, ad loc.

38. This is the reading accepted by Sokoloff, 'Targum to Job from Qumran',
ad loc.

39. García Martínez *et al.* (eds.), *11Q10*, ad loc.

herein that QJ has intentionally read both חסד and חסר. But such a
reading must be rejected on the grounds that there are no remains which
could be those of a ס. However, in support of reading חוב in the lacuna,
it is here proposed that the translator understood the noun in HT as חֶסֶד
meaning 'shame, reproach' rather than 'kindness'. The BHeb noun חסד
in this sense may well be an Aramaism,[40] the Aramaic root חסד 'to be
put to shame' yielding the noun חסדא 'shame, revilement'. It is rare in
BHeb, occurring twice: in Lev. 20.17, 'He who sees the nakedness of
his sister and she his nakedness, it is a shameful thing חֶסֶד הוּא'; and in
Prov. 14.34 where it is equated with חטאת, 'sin is a reproach to
peoples'. If the translator of QJ sought scriptural support for understanding חסד in Job 37.13 as 'shame', or by extension 'sin', such support is available. While Garcia Martinez *et al.* translate פתגם חוב as 'a
case of law-breaking', it might be better translated as 'shameful/sinful
thing'.[41] The addition of a conjunction suggests that the phrase והן פתגם
[חו]ב is to be taken as directly joined to the preceding phrase, and that
the entire phrase הן לכפן וחסרנה והן פתגם [חו]ב is a translation of HT
אם לחסד, intended to extract the maximum meaning from it.[42]

ימצאהו. The Peshitta translates with a passive verb[43] and so treats the
object suffix separately, transposing it into the preposition + suffix
(presumably referring to the earth in v. 12), while the imperfect of HT
becomes participial; the added relative particle allows us to understand

40. See P.W. Skehan and A. Di Lella, *The Wisdom of Ben Sira: A New
Translation and Notes, Introduction and Commentary* (AB; Garden City, NY:
Doubleday, 1987), regarding חסד in Ben Sira 41.22c (Masada text). It is a marginal
variant to חרפה in the B text (which is believed to represent the original Hebrew
version), but is the preferred reading since חרף is the parallel in v. 22d. See Y.
Yadin, *The Ben Sira Scroll from Masada* (Jerusalem: The Israel Exploration
Society and The Shrine of the Book, 1965), ad loc., pp. 7, 10.

41. פתגם חוב would be a passable translation of חסד הוא as found in Lev.
20.17, though none of the Targumim render it thus; *Pseudo-Jonathan* has both גני
'disgrace' and חסדא; *Onqelos* has קלנא הוא; *Neofiti* has חסד הוה.

42. J.T. Sanders examines the concept of shame as a significant theme in wisdom literature, tracing its development from an Egypto-Israelite wisdom tradition
from before the beginning of the second century BCE and on into the Hellenistic
period. He observes that 'shame is the key ethical sanction in Ben Sira'. J.T.
Sanders, 'Ben Sira's Ethics of Caution', *HUCA* 50 (1979), pp. 73-106.

43. The form ימצאהו could be understood as *qal*, *hiphil* (defective), or, theoretically, as *niphal* with the suffix understood as the subject: ימצא הוא 'it will be
found'.

that the subject is ܐܝܢܐ: 'the kindness which is found in it'. The over-all effect of these adjustments is that the difficulties and uncertainties of HT are avoided.

Of the two words that conclude the verse in QJ, עליה would appear to translate the 3 m. sg. object suffix of HT; as in PJ, it is treated separately and transposed into preposition + suffix: 'upon it' (again, as in PJ, presumably referring back to תבל in v. 12). Assuming that the QJ rendering includes a representation of the verb of HT, then it must be the form להוא. The form appears to be an imperfect of √ הו\א 'to be, occur, come to pass' with preformative -ל; the QJ translator has, then, preserved the imperfect of HT, but apparently without any causative sense.[44] As a hiphil the Hebrew is written defectively, giving the QJ translator scope to treat it as qal. But the qal of מצא has the sense of 'to find', not the sense of 'to be'.[45] The qal is, however, found with the sense 'to befall, happen to'. Given this sense here, the HT could be understood as ימצא הו(א) 'it happens/will happen', becoming in QJ 'it will be/come to pass'.[46]

מצא in this particular sense of 'to befall, happen to' is found almost exclusively with reference to unwelcome events, for example Job 31.29: 'Did I rejoice at the destruction of my enemy, did I stir myself because evil befell him? כי מצאו רע'; Ps. 119.143: 'Although trouble and anguish have come upon me צר ומצוק מצאוני, your commandments are my delight'; also Gen. 44.34; Deut. 4.30; 31.17, 21; 2 Kgs 7.9. In all

---

44. According to Sokoloff, *Targum to Job from Qumran*, ad loc., להוא is the only verbal form in the biblical and Qumran dialects with prefix -ל in the imperfect. He renders להוא עליה as 'he will be over it', understanding God as the subject; but this is interpretative, for the subject could equally well be impersonal and the sense thus simply 'it will be upon it'. Alternatively, the preformative -ל may express a jussive (see W.M. Stevenson, *Grammar of Palestinian Jewish Aramaic* [Oxford: Clarendon Press, 1924], §18.6), in which case the sense is 'may he/it be upon it'.

45. The niphal often can mean 'to be', e.g. Deut. 17.2; 18.10; Isa. 51.3; 65.8; and several times in Job: 19.28; 28.12, 13; 42.15.

46. Cf. the emphatic or sometimes pleonastic use of the (usually preverbal) personal pronoun. See C.H.J. van der Merwe, J.A. Naudé and J.H. Kroeze, *A Biblical Hebrew Reference Grammar* (Sheffield: Sheffield Academic Press, 1999), pp. 251-54, 344-50; also P. Joüon, *A Grammar of Biblical Hebrew* (trans. and rev. T. Muraoka; Rome: Pontificio Istituto Biblico, 1993), §146b (3). What such an explanation of the QJ translation may suggest about the translator's skill is discussed further below.

these cases it is used with רשׁעה ,עוון or צרה.[47] Perhaps it was his awareness of this association of qal מצא with negative events that informed the QJ translator's understanding of ימצאהו here in Job 37.13, this in turn allowing him to give each of the three Hebrew nouns a negative connotation. This would reinforce the suggestion that it is indeed the noun חוב which has been lost in the lacuna, and strengthen the claim herein that ארעא is to be understood in the sense of 'unexpected (bad) event'.

In TJ the causative sense of ימצאהו is achieved by transposing into the active peal √ ספק with object suffix: 'he supplies it', with God as the unequivocal subject.[48] This understanding is consistent with the rest of TJ's elaboration on this verse.

Summary

As an overall assessment it seems fair to say that in their strategies for producing a translation of Job 37.13 our three translations exhibit marked preferences. The PJ translation works within the confines of the Hebrew consonantal text, achieving its translation by employing exclusively linguistic means: it omits the awkward possessive suffix on אצו, adds conjunctions, and reworks the grammar (active verb becomes passive, verbal suffix becomes preposition + suffix). These strategies serve to clarify individual Hebrew lexemes, but not the overall sense of the verse. Thus, although the result may well be idiomatic Syriac, the additional impression is that the translator has sought simply to transmit a translation, albeit modified, of the Hebrew words, rather than also to find a good sense in them.[49] A lack of cohesion, which many find in HT

47. מצא also has the niphal sense 'be found' used with רעה ,עולה; e.g. 1 Sam. 25.28; 2 Kgs 1.52; Ezek. 28.15; Mal. 2.6. It seems that in these combinations the root is strongly associated with negative events.

48. TJ contains several orthographic variants on יספקניה.

49. Regarding the Peshitta translation as a whole, it is commonly accepted that, in most books, it remains close in sense to the Hebrew of the MT, translating phrase by phrase rather than word by word. The acknowledged exceptions are Qohelet, Song of Songs and Chronicles. Where the sense was difficult to recover, however, the translator could resort to word by word translation or to free translation. See M.P. Weitzman, *The Syriac Version of the Old Testament: An Introduction* (University of Cambridge Oriental Publications, 56; Cambridge: Cambridge University Press, 1999), pp. 15, 22-23, 61-62, 111-21. PJ to 37.13 may be an example of this. Furthermore, bearing in mind Weitzman's observation that the problems of

itself, remains; the personification of שבט as 'rulers' may clarify the individual Hebrew lexeme but does not help to elucidate the wider sense as it runs on from the previous verse.[50]

The QJ translator too works largely within the confines of the Hebrew consonantal text and seeks clarification of it. In addition, however, the translation gives the distinct impression, through its creative manipulation of both the content and sense of HT, that the intention is not simply to translate the words, but also to represent their sense. It was argued above that the translator has turned to Scripture, both to the wider Job text and beyond, in order to do this. Thus ימצאהו provides the key to interpreting HT as a series of negatives, so that שבט becomes מכתש, ארצו becomes ארעא 'unforeseen event', and the richness of interpretation available in חסד, including a deliberate reading of ר, is exploited. The sense fits well with the preceding verse,[51] and achieves a coherence that is difficult to find in the apparent incongruities of the HT, where 'chastisement', 'his earth' and 'kindness' make an uneasy sense. By contrast, QJ's 'plague', 'accident', 'famine and want' and 'sinful/shameful thing' produce a consistent theme of negative events which can all come about on earth.

The rabbinic version also achieves a cohesion, seeing in HT the combination of three key nouns which are linked by their association with rain and reflect traditions found in other rabbinic works of interpretation. It is shot through with references to and echoes of such themes and uses HT as a hook on which to hang a translation that itself is entirely interpretative. Thus שבט is understood as 'curse' and becomes the rain of punishment: precious water which is wasted upon the sea and desert; חסד is the opposite: rain of appropriate quality, quantity and location which is counted as a blessing; and ארץ, the land of Israel, over which God takes especial and personal care, remains the

semantic correspondence between the MT and the Syriac are 'particularly acute' in the book of Job (see Weitzman, 'The Hebrew and Syriac Texts', p. 130), it may be that a full assessment of such problems and of their significance for the character of the PJ translation remains to be made.

50. Such judgments are bound in some degree to be subjective. Nevertheless, although the semantic route to the translation seems clear, I cannot see that 'rulers' makes transparent sense in the larger context. PJ to 37.12 reads, 'And it [the cloud] circles round and is turned in order to carry out counsels; everything that he has commanded them upon the face of the world, his earth.'

51. QJ to 37.12 reads, 'And he speaks [and] they obey him and go to their tasks; he has command over everything which he created on the face of the world.'

essential flavour of the entire interpretation even though the lexeme is dissolved and no longer explicitly represented.[52] This elaboration on the theme of rain fits the wider context of Job 37, and that of 37.12 as understood in TJ.[53]

Discussion

Analysis of a single verse can be suggestive at best; only the weight of further illustrative analyses can show whether such observations amount not merely to impressions but to the demonstration of characteristic tendencies, or whether there is sufficient evidence to support more concrete conclusions. It is with this caveat that some particular points of interest that arise from this analysis are now considered.

As noted earlier, while the translation techniques identified by Weitzman in PJ have informed the current analysis, it is not the intention here to undertake a systematic evaluation of the translations in these terms. However, one example may serve to illustrate their utility beyond the PJ translation. Omission, or failure to translate, may be the result of error (either original to the translator or subsequently in the transmission of the text) or it may be deliberate (again, on the part of the translator or copyist).[54] Omission as a deliberate device is described by

52. The rabbinic translation of Job 37.13 recalls Alexander's Type B Targum which 'dissolves' the translation in paraphrase. This style does not characterize the whole translation, for many other verses in Job are rendered in a straightforward manner. See P.S. Alexander, 'Jewish Aramaic Translations of Hebrew Scriptures', in M.J. Mulder and H. Sysling (eds.), *Mikra: Text, Translation, Reading and Interpretation of the Hebrew Bible in Ancient Judaism and Early Christianity* (Assen: Van Gorcum; Philadelphia: Fortress Press, 1988), pp. 217-53.

53. There are two versions of 37.12 in TJ; the second makes a particularly fitting precursor to TJ 37.13: 'And in his mercy he restores the hidden waters in his store-houses to the labours of humankind; he reveals them and sends them to the earth for all whom he commands upon the face of the world.' The issue of alternative translations in TJ is important but cannot be elaborated here. See Stec, *Targum of Job*, Introduction.

54. The possibility of deliberate copyist 'corrections' has been noted by, e.g., Flesher in relation to the Palestinian Pentateuchal Targumim. See P.V.M. Flesher, 'Exploring the Sources of the Synoptic Targums to the Pentateuch', in *idem* (ed.), *Targum Studies. I. Textual and Contextual Studies in the Pentateuchal Targums* (Atlanta: Scholars Press, 1992), pp. 101-34. The current study is concerned with the texts in their present forms rather than with a history of their transmission; copyist error, deliberate or otherwise, would only be considered in the absence of any other explanation.

Biblical Hebrew, Biblical Texts

Weitzman as 'abdication of translation role'.[55] Though, as Weitzman claims, instances of this may be rare, PJ's handling of HT אצרו in Job 37.13 is such a case; the translator simply omits a translation of the suffix in order to avoid its awkwardness. While the dropping of the suffix in QJ is also intentional, the motive is more substantial. The translator has not simply translated the Hebrew minus the suffix, but rather he has brought out of the text a different understanding (i.e. ארעא = 'accident'). It is this which justifies the omission.[56] In effect, what he has done is to translate with the straight Aramaic equivalent of HT (minus suffix) but to understand its alternative Aramaic sense. This is akin to Weitzman's identification in PJ of cases where the translator has exploited the ambiguity of the Syriac equivalent. There is an interesting contrast here between the use of omission by PJ and QJ and the eschewing of omission by rabbinic translation conventions.[57] It is not yet clear how the legitimacy accorded to intentional omission by PJ and QJ can be of use in an assessment of the development of the tools and conventions of scriptural translation and interpretation in Judaism and in early eastern Christianity.[58] In this context, Heinemann's observation

55. Weitzman, 'The Hebrew and Syriac Texts', p. 140. He acknowledges that in some cases the omission may suggest physical damage to the Vorlage. In her model for evaluating PJ, Szpek includes omission as a manner of adjustment in the translation. Szpek, *Translation Technique*.

56. Le Déaut ('Usage implicite', p. 430) has remarked on the need to consider whether omissions in QJ are intentional. Where Weiss noted omissions in the QJ translation he characterized them as carelessness or misunderstanding (*The Aramaic Targum*, p. 22).

57. In his dissection of the literary characteristics of the Pentateuchal Tar- gumim, Samely rules omission as 'flouting the conventions of Targumic literature' since it is not Targum's task to correct or 'purge' the scriptural text of problematic elements. See A. Samely, *The Interpretation of Speech in the Pentateuch Targums: A Study of Method and Presentation in Targumic Exegesis* (TSAJ, 27; Tübingen: J.C.B. Mohr [Paul Siebeck], 1992), pp. 97, 105. Earlier, in discussing the character- istics of a Type B Targum, Alexander had cautioned that the apparent lack of representation of elements of the original HT may in fact be a failing on the part of the (modern) reader and 'our ignorance of the underlying exegetical processes' (Alexander, 'Jewish Aramaic Translations', p. 237).

58. This touches on the question of the background(s) and milieu(x) of the Peshitta translator(s). The issues are too complex to be dealt with here. For a presentation of the issues and proposed solutions, see P.B. Dirksen, 'The Old Testament Peshitta', in M.J. Mulder and H. Sysling (eds.), *Mikra: Text, Trans- lation, Reading and Interpretation of the Hebrew Bible in Ancient Judaism and*

that the occasional cases of omission of the negative particle in the Pentateuchal Targums are examples of an early and undeveloped mode of translation, takes on new significance.[59] What does seem clear is that a synoptic study presents another way of contributing to the investigation of such issues.

The analysis of the QJ translation of ימצאהו hinted that it may reveal something of the translator's linguistic skills. Although the QJ translation itself has been recognized for its reworking of the poetry of the original into more readily understandable, coherent and consistent paraphrase,[60] the prerequisites of an easy, if not bilingual, familiarity with and a poet's appreciation both of his source language and of the nature of his text are not things with which the QJ translator has been expressly credited. Yet it would require either a shaky appreciation of the conventions of the biblical language, or alternatively a creative, if perhaps somewhat unorthodox, approach to the same in order to read ימצאהו as ימצא הו(א). Neither an assumption of bilingualism nor one of poetic appreciation of the linguistic and formal features of scriptural text would be remotely notable were this a rabbinic work. The origins of the QJ translation are unknown and probably unknowable, but features that suggest the translator's skills in these areas may help to clarify quite where it sits in the development of Jewish scriptural translation and interpretation.[61]

Finally, the role of Scripture in the translation process must be considered. That a rabbinic Targum should manifest associations with Scripture and with rabbinic material found elsewhere is not unexpected.[62] What the present synoptic analysis adds to the picture, however, is the suggestion that Scripture had an influential role in the

---

Early Christianity (Assen: Van Gorcum; Philadelphia: Fortress Press, 1988), pp. 255-97; Weitzman, *The Syriac Version*, pp. 206-62).

59. Heinemann's observations are cited by Michael Klein in 'Converse Translation: A Targumic Technique', *Bib* 57 (1976), pp. 515-37.

60. For example, Sokoloff, *Targum to Job from Qumran*, p. 8.

61. Although commonly referred to as the 'Targum' of Job from Qumran (perhaps under the influence of the title given to it by the editors of the first edition), and although clearly a 'Targum' in the most basic sense of an Aramaic translation of scripture, its status vis-à-vis the genre is debated. See Samely's discussion of the issues, where he categorizes QJ alongside the Peshitta among the ancient versions (*Interpretation of Speech*, pp. 158-84).

62. Weiss discusses the interpolations in this verse (*The Aramaic Targum*, pp. 278-79).

translation process of the Qumran Job text too. In this context QJ's reading of ר for ד and thus of חסר is of particular interest. The double translation לכפן ולחסרנה may be accounted for by assuming that it exploits an opportunity to represent both possible vocalizations (חֶסֶר and חֹסֶר). Yet this begs the question why, firstly, the translator might have read ר for ד, and secondly, why, given its rarity, the translator might have read חֹסֶר here at all. As further explanation, then, is it not possible that QJ's translation of חסד is offered precisely here not simply because the language of HT presented an ambiguity, but also because of something the translator understood to be implicit in the content? Regarding the TJ translation, while there is no question that it is influenced by rabbinic traditions, one must wonder why it is that the interpretation focuses on rain at this point, when the overt content of Job 37.13 does not concern rain at all. Perhaps it is, as suggested above, the juxtaposition in HT of three key nouns which are linked by their association with rain and reflect rabbinic traditions found elsewhere. Or perhaps the surrounding context which speaks of thunder, lightning and rain-clouds is sufficient explanation. Alternatively, or indeed additionally, it may be that the translator was sensitive to something else implicit in the particular content of this verse which made the elaboration appropriate.[63]

The rabbinic traditions regarding rain which underpin the TJ version are themselves founded on Scripture, on passages such as those cited earlier, and others such as Amos 4.[64] The Amos passage (4.5-13) describes the Lord's attempts to bring Israel back to obedience, including, explicitly, withholding of rain, blighted crops, destroyed vineyards and olive groves, pestilence and 'want of bread חֹסֶר לחם'. There are strong similarities of theme and content between it and Deut. 28, a passage that details the blessings the Lord will bestow on Israel for

63. Ambiguity in the biblical text and its exploitation by the Targumist as a means to fuller understanding of its message has been explored by Golomb. In his opinion, the question that is not asked often enough of Targumic exegesis is precisely that which is asked here, i.e. why does it appear where it does? See D.M. Golomb, ' "A liar, a blasphemer, a reviler": The Role of Biblical Ambiguity in the Palestinian Pentateuchal Targumim', in P.V.M. Flesher (ed.), *Targum Studies*. I. *Textual and Contextual Studies in the Pentateuchal Targums* (Atlanta: Scholars Press, 1992), pp. 135-46.

64. Amos 4 provides the proof-text in *m. Ta'an.* 3.3 in connexion with fasting when rain fails to fall on a city.

obedience, such as rain in due season (v. 12); and conversely the curses that will accrue for disobedience, such as drought (vv. 23-24), hunger, thirst, nakedness and servitude 'in want of all things וּבְחֹסֶר' כֹּל (v. 48). The parallels between the two passages are striking: the Amos verses read like a realization of the threats detailed in the Deuteronomy verses. Together they read like a background to the rabbinic interpretation of Job 37.13, which, in almost a synthesis, describes the rains that fall for both retribution and for kindness. Most notable of all for our purposes is the fact that it is in these two passages only that the rare noun חֹסֶר occurs. Could it not be that חֹסֶר is pivotal to the rabbinic elaboration of Job 37.13, since it is so rare and occurs in two such closely linked contexts, both of which speak of rain/drought, fulfilment/want?[65] Perhaps the term was traditionally associated with these passages. One might expect a Targumic interpretation which draws on ideas in Deut. 28 and Amos 4 to hinge on a third occurrence of חֹסֶר to pull the threads of such an interpretation together. Yet it is not, of course, חֹסֶר that appears in Job 37.13, but rather חֶסֶד. If this suggestion is correct and חֹסֶר is indeed the key to understanding why the rabbinic version is elaborated at 37.13, then the implication is that the translator of TJ read and translated the explicit content (חסד > דחסדא נחיא) but also recognized and exploited an ambiguity and read חֹסֶר, thereby alluding to an implicit connexion with ideas in the Deuteronomy and Amos passages and allowing the rain-centred interpretation to be incorporated at this point.[66]

The questions raised by the QJ translation are resolved if it is accepted that this translator too recognized the opportunity for exegesis inherent in חסד, involving re-reading with ר and the scriptural associations of חסר with 'want of rain'. With the guide provided by the earlier text of HT, which concerns divine providence in nature, including the provision of the great and small rains (v. 6), and with his understanding that v. 13 concerns negative events, he was able to incorporate both חסד and חסר in a remarkable, interpretative translation.[67]

---

65. The noun חֹסֶר is found but three times: Deut. 28.48 (as detailed), 57 (where the context is ravening hunger during a siege) and Amos 4.6.

66. The reading of ר for ד or vice versa is common in rabbinic interpretative re-reading. See Le Déaut, 'Usage implicite', p. 423. TJ being a Targumic text, there is no formulaic אל תקרי here to herald the process.

67. While it is not my intention to enter here into the intricacies of the essential debate about the definition and nature of Targum—a key element of which is the

The suggestion, then, is that both the QJ translator and the rabbinic Targumist saw an ambiguity in HT's חסד, and that both their translations allude to the scriptural association of חֶסֶר with lack of rain. Though speculative, this reasoning does offer an explanation for otherwise unexplained features of the Qumran and the rabbinic versions. It also suggests that an evaluation of the depths of the Qumran version is justified and may be fruitful.[68] It does not imply that the rabbinic Targumists knew of QJ's translation; rather, the coincidence should be seen as suggestive of a similarity in their strategies when producing a translation and of the importance of Scripture in those strategies.

question of the status of QJ—I wonder whether at this point QJ could be said to combine both an exegetical interest in its source text and a conscious reflection of the wording of HT. This definition of Targum (so nicely summarized by Smelik) forms the bedrock for Samely's objection to the conventional tagging of QJ as a Targum. See Samely, *Interpretation of Speech*, p. 159, and W.F. Smelik, *The Targum of Judges* (OTS, 36; Leiden: E.J. Brill 1995), p. 647.

68. The original editors of QJ observed that it had recourse, along with LXX, to 'une tradition exégétique commune', examples of which they note in situ but with little elaboration, and added that 'le Targum de Job de 11Q est du type simple et ne connaît pas des longue paraphrases et amplifications des Targums postérieurs' (van der Ploeg *et al.*, *Le targum de Job*, p. 7). It is perhaps as a result of this that QJ has often been considered transparent (its fragmentary nature notwithstanding) and without depth. This recalls the historic and still pervasive description of *Onqelos* as literal and, in comparison with the Palestinian Targumim, uninteresting. Yet, as Samely reminds us (*Interpretation of Speech*, p. 178), as long ago as 1963 Vermes had suggested otherwise when he identified in O the use of abbreviated allusional references to traditions found in more detail in other Targumim (G. Vermes, 'Haggadah in the Onkelos Targum', *JSS* 8 [1963], pp. 159-69). Leaving aside the wider questions regarding the place of O within the genre of Targum and of the definition of QJ, Vermes's observations regarding the nature of aggadah in *Onqelos* seem pertinent to the current suggestion regarding the QJ translation, viz. that there may be unexplored depths to it. Furthermore, in the light of his opinions regarding the status of QJ, Samely's own comments regarding O are interesting. He concludes that though O is different, it is still 'within the range of Targums' because the concerns of its author are exegetical. A translator, by contrast, is a 'reluctant exegete', since his product is intended to take the place of the original rather than to supplement it. This provokes a fascinating question: Given that the purpose of the QJ version is as yet unestablished, and if there are as yet unexplored exegetical depths to the QJ version, how well does this sobriquet fit its author? Was QJ's author a reluctant exegete, or a subtle one? It is hoped that the research to which this paper is a preliminary will go some way towards illuminating these issues.

Part III
INTERTESTAMENTAL TEXTS

THE QUMRAN PESHARIM AND THE TEXT OF ISAIAH IN THE CAVE 4 MANUSCRIPTS

George J. Brooke

1. *Introduction*

This study addresses once again the issue of the value for text-critical purposes of quotations of authoritative texts in other compositions. I have addressed this issue before[1] and am still inclined to believe that if used cautiously quotations of texts can be of some value for the text critic, most often if there is other textual evidence for assessing any variant which such quotations may contain. Put another way, some variants within quotations may represent features of the textual transmission of the cited material and not just the adjustment of the quotation for the purposes of the context within which the quotation is housed: not all variants in quotations are exegetical alterations, though some may well be.

This short study has been provoked in particular by the 1997 publication of the principal edition of the fragmentary Isaiah scrolls from Cave 4 at Qumran.[2] These Isaiah manuscripts have been edited by the late Patrick W. Skehan and Eugene Ulrich. When reviewing the volume for the *Journal of Theological Studies*,[3] I was struck by the editorial policy on the presentation of variants. The policy is worth citing in full:

---

1.   See especially my study, 'The Biblical Texts in the Qumran Commentaries: Scribal Errors or Exegetical Variants?', in C.A. Evans and W.F. Stinespring (eds.), *Early Jewish and Christian Exegesis: Studies in Memory of William Hugh Brownlee* (SBL Homage Series, 10; Atlanta: Scholars Press, 1987), pp. 85-100.

2.   E. Ulrich, F.M. Cross, R.E. Fuller, J.E. Sanderson, P.W. Skehan and E. Tov (eds.), *Qumran Cave 4.X: The Prophets* (DJD, 15; Oxford: Clarendon Press, 1997).

3.   *JTS* 50 (1999), pp. 651-55.

> The catalogue of VARIANTS lists only those readings where the manu-
> script is extant (certain or highly probable on the scroll) and differs from
> one of the major Hebrew texts—other Qumran scrolls, 𝔐, or 𝔐 q, mss.
> Ideally, 𝔊 should also be included as one of the criteria, and some editors
> systematically have, while others have not, made variation from 𝔊 a
> criterion for inclusion in the catalogue of VARIANTS. In the latter case,
> however, the NOTES often mention some of the more significant
> divergences from 𝔊. Variants that have been reconstructed are normally
> described only in the NOTES and are not included in the VARIANTS
> section.[4]

Not only has this policy resulted in some unevenness in the presentation
of the evidence by the various editors involved in the volume, but it has
also meant that the principal edition is self-avowedly only a first step on
the road in understanding the significance of these biblical scrolls for
the history of the texts of the biblical books which they represent.

From one perspective this editorial policy has resulted in a product
that takes one step forwards in providing us with all the fragments but
two steps backwards in their limited assessment. In his 1973 dissertation on the text of Isaiah at Qumran, which was completed under
the direction of Patrick Skehan himself at the Catholic University of
America, Francis J. Morrow had already offered a preliminary listing
and analysis of the variants in the Qumran Cave 4 Isaiah manuscripts.[5]
Morrow's work included consideration of much of the evidence from
the scriptural citations in the Isaiah pesharim and some other non-
biblical compositions which contained either explicit or implicit citations of Isaiah. The 1997 principal edition of the Cave 4 Isaiah manuscripts contains no references to any of the non-biblical compositions to
which Morrow referred.

This lack of reference to Hebrew manuscripts more or less contemporary with the Qumran Isaiah manuscripts themselves is puzzling.
It is undoubtedly good text-critical practice to treat the text-critical
information of quotations in non-biblical manuscripts with caution.
Long before the Qumran discoveries text critics were aware that
explicit scriptural quotations can undergo various transformations at the
hands of those who use them and that implicit quotations are of even

---

4.   *Qumran Cave 4.X: The Prophets*, p. 5.

5.   F.J. Morrow, 'The Text of Isaiah at Qumran' (PhD dissertation, Catholic
University of America, Washington, DC, 1973). This was never published other
than by University Microfilms International (No. 74-5079).

more limited text-critical worth for not dissimilar reasons. Nevertheless, despite the exercise of due caution, it is relatively easy to argue that explicit quotations do indeed have some text-critical value and that such evidence as they may provide should be included in a principal edition such as that of the Qumran Cave 4 Isaiah manuscripts.

The particular problems of the biblical quotations in the Qumran pesharim have been noted often. In 1987 I myself wrote that

> scholars interested in the history of the biblical text should be very cautious in their use of the variants in the biblical quotations in the commentaries in any reconstruction of the overall history of traditions. Many variants may be local and unique to the particular commentary; only indirectly can they be used for the understanding of textual recensions.[6]

This statement applied especially to the handling of unique variants found in the scriptural quotations in the pesharim. However, I continued by citing approvingly the programmatic statement of Shemaryahu Talmon:

> What is especially required…is a careful collation of the MT and the Vss with the text preserved in Qumran biblical mss and fragments, in the Pesher literature, and in quotations from the Bible which abound in the covenanters' non-biblical writings.

Such a collation, Talmon went on to suggest, would be conducive 'to a better understanding of scribal techniques, and of human failings and weaknesses which affected the text of the Bible in the long history of its transmission'.[7]

Most recently the matter has been studied again in detail by T.H. Lim.[8] Lim has argued that the first task must be to establish precisely what is meant by the label 'variant', since the Masoretic tradition itself is far from textually uniform, and so it is far from clear in every case from what a variant may be varying. The problem is made all the more acute for consideration of biblical texts from the first century BCE since in many cases what might be taken as representative

---

6.   'The Biblical Texts in the Qumran Commentaries', p. 99.

7.   S. Talmon, 'The Ancient Hebrew Alphabet and Biblical Text Criticism', in A. Caquot, S. Légasse and M. Tardieu (eds.), *Mélanges bibliques et orientaux en l'honneur de M. Mathias Delcor* (AOAT, 215; Neukirchen–Vluyn: Neukirchener Verlag, 1985), pp. 387-402 (401).

8.   T.H. Lim, *Holy Scripture in the Qumran Commentaries and Pauline Letters* (Oxford: Clarendon Press, 1997), esp. chs. 5 and 6.

of the (proto-)Masoretic tradition can only be postulated. Lim's second step is to acknowledge the existence of exegetical variants: 'the ancient exegete modified his biblical text'.[9] However, Lim is careful to delineate precisely how such an exegetical variant might be recognized. His concern is to pay attention predominantly to the context in which the biblical passage is quoted for signals that the author might provide, which can reveal that the text interpreted is indeed different from the text as the author received it.

As for the text of Isaiah at Qumran in general, Patrick Skehan offered a preliminary characterization a long while ago:

> Though the manuscripts of Qumran are not held, for the text they offer, to the rigidly controlled transmission of a definitively fixed consonantal text such as we later find in the Masora, those cases are extremely rare in which any combination of them, published or unpublished, gives exclusive or predominant witness to a non-masoretic reading.[10]

1QIsa[a] has been extensively studied with regard to its variants[11] and Morrow's work on the Cave 4 Isaiah manuscripts has been widely consulted.[12]

2. *The Cave 4 Isaiah Manuscripts and the Pesharim*

What follows in this study is a complete collation of all the textual variants in the biblical quotations in the six Isaiah pesharim[13] with the Cave 4 Isaiah manuscripts as published in the 1997 principal edition. References to Morrow's earlier work will be found in several cases, though there is more to be said than is laid out in his listing of variants.

---

9. *Holy Scripture*, p. 95.

10. P.W. Skehan, 'The Text of Isaias at Qumrân', *CBQ* 12 (1955), p. 162.

11. See, especially on linguistic matters, E.Y. Kutscher, *The Language and Linguistic Background of the Isaiah Scroll (1QIsa[a])* (STDJ, 6; Leiden: E.J. Brill, 1974); and, on some key exegetical issues arising from variants, W.H. Brownlee, *The Meaning of the Qumrân Scrolls for the Bible with Special Attention to the Book of Isaiah* (New York: Oxford University Press, 1964).

12. Though it is interesting to note that in its place it is common to encounter reference to the more general but very important survey by P.W. Skehan, 'Littérature de Qumrân: A) Textes bibliques', *DBSup*, IX (1978), pp. 805-22.

13. The most convenient presentation of the Isaiah pesharim is to be found in M.P. Horgan, *Pesharim: Qumran Interpretations of Biblical Books* (CBQMS, 8; Washington, DC: Catholic Biblical Association of America, 1979), pp. 70-138, 260-61.

The study ends with a list of all the places where the variants occur so that the principal edition of the Cave 4 Isaiah manuscripts may be readily updated.

All the manuscripts we are considering here are very fragmentary. The places where there are overlaps between at least one Isaiah manuscript and one commentary are relatively few. In some places, however, there is some small amount of textual overlap but no variant reading between the witnesses.

a. *The Less Weighty Evidence*
1. *Minor orthographic variants.* Scholars are inclined to categorize orthographic variants separately from other kinds of variant reading. Morrow omits what he considers to be orthographic variants from his study altogether. Building on the work of Skehan, and as has become common practice in the editions of biblical manuscripts from Qumran, Ulrich places the orthographic variants for each Cave 4 Isaiah manuscript in a separate section in the introduction to each manuscript.

One clear example of an orthographic variant occurs in Isa. 19.11. 4QIsa[b] reads פרעה while 4QpIsa[c] includes a waw as vowel letter: פרעוה. Ulrich has noted that the orthography of 4QIsa[b] 'is often less full, but occasionally more full, than that of 𝔐, since neither is consistent'.[14] Given that 4QpIsa[c] is a community composition, it is not surprising to find that its orthography is more full, since a majority of community compositions tend towards a fuller orthography. A further example of the same phenomenon can be seen in Isa. 9.18, in which 4QIsa[e] reads לא with the MT, whereas 4QpIsa[c] reads the plene form with waw as also in this instance does 1QIsa[a]. Overall this phenomenon of more and less full orthographies, together with some other factors, has led E. Tov to describe the fuller system as reflecting the practices of a Qumran scribal school.[15]

---

14. *Qumran Cave 4.X: The Prophets*, p. 20.

15. See his essay 'The Significance of the Texts from the Judean Desert for the History of the Text of the Hebrew Bible: A New Synthesis', in F.H. Cryer and T.L. Thompson (eds.), *Qumran between the Old and New Testaments* (JSOTSup, 290; Sheffield: Sheffield Academic Press, 1998), pp. 294-96 and the other studies cited there; now revised and updated in 'Die biblischen Handschriften aus der Wüste Juda—Eine neue Synthese', in U. Dahmen, A. Lange and H. Lichtenberger (eds.), *Die Textfunde vom Toten Meer und der Text der Hebraïschen Bibel* (Neukirchen–Vluyn: Neukirchener Verlag, 2000), pp. 15-17.

Another minor orthographic variant is visible for Isa. 5.25 in 4QpIsa[b] where כסהה is represented in defective spelling whereas in 4QIsa[b] the scribe first wrote כסומ which was then corrected with a supralinear letter to כסומה which agrees with the MT.

2. Another orthographic issue can be seen in Isa. 8.7. 4QIsa[e] and the MT agree in reading אפיקיו, the regularly formed third person singular suffix for nouns in the plural.[16] In 4QpIsa[c] the shorter form אפיקו occurs (this phrase is not preserved in 1QIsa[a]). Writing in 1986 E. Qimron commented that

> there are about 30 cases where we find ו- instead of יו-… Such instances
> of non-standard spelling for the 3rd person singular suffixes—with both
> singular and plural nouns—indicate that these suffixes were pronounced
> alike ($\bar{o}$ or $\bar{u}$). The scribes, however, almost always succeeded in
> preserving the orthographic distinction. The pronunciation $\bar{o}$ in the plural
> (יו-) suffix resulted from the contraction of the 'long' diphthong *aw* in
> this suffix.[17]

Qimron has also noted that the manuscript in which the scribe was least successful in maintaining the difference is 1QIsa[a] rather than in any of the non-biblical scrolls. The association of 1QIsa[a] with the Qumran scribal school in this way may assist in explaining why it is in the community's biblical commentaries that this phenomenon also surfaces. Perhaps the commentaries were based on some such text of Isaiah as is found in 1QIsa[a].

Another example of this same phenomenon confirms the phrasing of the previous statement, that perhaps the commentaries were based on *some such text* of Isaiah as is found in 1QIsa[a], not on 1QIsa[a] itself. For Isa. 8.8 4QIsa[e] reads the regularly formed third person singular suffix for a plural noun, as does 1QIsa[a] (כנפיו), whereas 4QpIsa[c] reads a waw alone as the suffix which might be construed as above for Isa. 8.7 or as the suffix for a singular noun (כנפו). The two Qumran biblical manuscripts thus agree with one another and the MT (and Peshitta) against the quotation in the commentary. Before concluding that this variant is of little significance, it should be recalled that the LXX for Isa. 8.8 represents something of an alternative text and that כנפיו is only

16. The Greek witnesses represent a second person plural suffix; the Peshitta agrees with the MT.

17. E. Qimron, *The Hebrew of the Dead Sea Scrolls* (HSS, 29; Atlanta: Scholars Press, 1986), p. 59.

represented in the Greek tradition in Symmachus and Theodotion, and there in the singular (του πτερυγιου) as in 4QpIsaᶜ.

These variations from the MT (or proto-MT) in the presentation of the suffix would seem to be secondary, but may be of assistance in the assessment of the overall placing of certain manuscripts on the text-critical stemma. When that is done, it should be constantly recalled, however, that even manuscripts containing relatively recent secondary features may nevertheless contain some earlier or more original readings.

3. Slightly more significant than the orthographic variants mentioned so far are those in which the longer form of the suffix is used. Two examples of this are visible in this collated material. In Isa. 21.10 4QIsaᵃ agrees with the MT and 1QIsaᵃ in reading לכם, whereas 4QpIsaᵉ 5.2 has the longer form: לכמ[ה. It may be tempting to suggest that these long suffixes represent something particular, but there seems to be nothing particularly sectarian about them, even though for the second person plural a large number of the instances of the longer form are to be found in the Temple Scroll.[18] A second example can be seen in Isa. 30.16. Whereas 4QIsaᶜ reads the shorter form (רודפ[כם) with 1QIsaᵃ and the MT, 4QpIsaᶜ has the longer form (רודפיכמה).

4. A more complicated matter, which may still be classified as an orthographic variant, can be seen in Isa. 8.7. The MT reads גדותיו, a reading which is probably also to be found in 4QpIsaᶜ (גדו]תו\יו) and with the reduplication of the medial waw in 1QIsaᵃ (גדוותיו) which Kutscher characterized as an Aramaism even though the root גדה is unattested in Aramaic.[19] 4QIsaᵉ probably reads a yod as third letter. Ulrich lists this variant in two places: in his list of orthographic differences between 4QIsaᵉ, other Qumran Isaiah manuscripts and the MT, and also in his list of textual variants.[20] Morrow comments that the reading in 4QIsaᵉ should be compared with the *kethib* of 1 Chron. 12.16

18. *The Hebrew of the Dead Sea Scrolls*, p. 62. Though the Temple Scroll may not be viewed as strictly sectarian in composition, the principal copy from Cave 11 (11Q19) may well have been copied by a member of the Qumran community or the wider movement of which it was a part, and in the act of copying some orthographic adjustments could have been made.

19. *Language and Linguistic Background*, p. 207.

20. *Qumran Cave 4.X: The Prophets*, pp. 90, 93.

and he notes that 'it is possible that the word has come under the influence of גְּדִי, גְּדִיָּה, "kid" '.[21] Whatever the variant represents in terms of textual transmission, the reading in 4QIsaᵉ appears secondary, while that in 4QpIsaᶜ reflects the original text. Here is a variant that is suggesting that the text in the biblical commentary may be used as a source of supportive evidence for what is more likely to be the earlier and more original reading.

5. Verbs sometimes prove problematic. In Isa. 5.25 4QpIsaᵇ presents the standard apocopated form of היה with the conjunction, in agreement with the MT. 4QIsaᶠ presents an unapocopated form in agreement with 1QIsaᵃ (ו[]תהיה). This feature would seem to be secondary and of text-critical significance only in signalling that some late Second Temple biblical manuscripts carry features of the language of their scribes; this example is illustrative of the collapse in the later half of the Second Temple period of the previously highly nuanced role of the conjunction.[22] Nevertheless, this item also suggests that the text of Isaiah as represented in 4QpIsaᵇ is not necessarily based on a local form of the text.

In Isa. 9.17, 4QIsaᵉ, 1QIsaᵃ and the MT agree in reading ותצת, a qal imperfect, 'it [wickedness] set on fire the thickets of the forest'. In 4QpIsaᶜ there is a hiphil form, ותצית, which can be translated identically as 'it [wickedness] set on fire the thickets of the forest'. The problem here is a classic example of a text-critical conundrum. 4QIsaᵉ, 1QIsaᵃ and the MT represent the *lectio difficilior*, since it would be idiomatically more normal for the qal to be followed by באש סבכי היער. For the Hebrew represented in Isaiah, the hiphil would be more appropriate as it is followed by an object phrase introduced by beth, as commonly seen in Amos, Jeremiah, Lamentations and Ezekiel. The Greek provides a future passive (καυθησεται ἐν) 'will be burnt among the bushes of the forest' perhaps more readily representing the hiphil than the qal, but requiring the reader to understand that it is the wickedness that is destroyed as the first half of the verse states. Faced with the choice between qal and hiphil, most text critics would probably opt for the

21. 'The Text of Isaiah at Qumran', p. 31. Morrow fails to mention the reading in 4QpIsaᶜ when discussing this verse.

22. See especially the study by M.S. Smith, *The Origins and Development of the Waw-Consecutive: Northwest Semitic Evidence from Ugarit to Qumran* (Atlanta: Scholars Press, 1991).

lectio difficilior, and see the 'improved' reading in the Qumran commentary as an example of the common scribal activity of improving the idiom of earlier authors.

6. Conjunctions may also provide ambiguous evidence for the text critic. One possible variant can be noticed in Isa. 30.23. All the witnesses agree that להם should be preceded by the conjunction, but in 4QpIsa[c] the phrase occurs after an introductory formula without it. One may readily suppose that the Qumran commentator saw fit to omit the conjunction as he cited the phrase and the difference should not be deemed to be a textual variant at all.

However, the conjunction is altogether more difficult to assess in the opening verse of the book of Isaiah when all the evidence is put together. What is more original in Isa. 1.1 and how have the variations come about? The MT and 1QIsa[a] (and one suspects, because of its orthography, also 4QIsa[j]) have no conjunction between the proper names. The text of Isa. 1.1 in 3QpIsa presents two conjoined pairs of kings, with some neat sense of poetic asyndeton, while the Greek (and the Peshitta) provides three conjunctions, a straight list. What should be made of all this text-critically? If it is commonly the case that as texts are transmitted from one generation to the next they are expanded in small ways, then the evidence that represents the shortest form of the text is likely to be the more original. Of note is the possibility that 3QpIsa may represent a form of the verse which in this respect is earlier than the Greek translation of Isaiah, though obviously a general theory on the age of the text of Isaiah in 3QpIsa cannot be constructed on the basis of the absence of a single waw.

So far this study has considered very minor issues which many commentators would not think worthy of a sentence of comment. Indeed both Morrow and Ulrich barely comment on any of the items that we have considered briefly so far. The collation of readings between the Cave 4 Isaiah manuscripts and the text of Isaiah in the pesharim throws up a few more intricate and intriguing pieces of evidence which will command our attention for the rest of this essay.

b. *The More Weighty Evidence.*
1. First, there is the matter of the suffix in Isa. 14.8 which is rendered in the NRSV as follows:

The cypresses exult over you,
   the cedars of Lebanon, saying,
'Since you were laid low,
   no one comes to cut us down.'

1QIsaᵃ and the MT read the last two words of the verse as הכרת עלינו, 'the one who cuts us down'; the trees are speaking of themselves. This reading is supported by the Greek and other versions. In 4QpIsaᶜ the text is quoted with its final suffixed preposition as עלימו. Whereas the MT and its allies take the two types of tree in the first half of the verse as being in apposition (as in the NRSV rendering above), 4QpIsaᶜ seems to understand the 'cedars of Lebanon' to be the sole object of the lumberjack's concern, an object cited first in anticipation of the third person suffix to come: 'Indeed, the cypresses rejoice over you, "(as for) The cedars of Lebanon, since you lay down, a hewer has not arisen against them" '. E. Qimron acknowledges the existence of this form of the third person suffix without comment.[23] The reading in 4QpIsaᶜ is now confirmed by 4QIsaᵉ where the more regular form עליהם is found. Morrow did not notice this variant in his dissertation where the relevant fragment is assigned to 4QIsaˡ.[24] Ulrich lists it but without any mention of the supporting evidence of 4QpIsaᶜ, despite his citing the Greek, the Targums, the Peshitta and the Vulgate in support of the MT's reading.[25]

How is one to assess this variant? There are two possibilities. The commentary in 4QpIsaᶜ is too fragmented for us to be able to see any clear reason for the change in understanding, though elsewhere Lebanon is identified either as the Kittim (4QpIsaᵃ fragments 8-10, lines 2-3) or with the council of the community (1QpHab 12.3-4 on Hab. 2.17)[26] and so here the commentator might have thought he needed to distinguish the cedars of Lebanon from the cypresses. In light of 4QIsaᵉ, it seems as if there were two understandings of the syntax of the verse and the author of 4QpIsaᶜ exploited one of these for his own purposes. Though we might be inclined to think that the MT represents the more original form of the text in light of the Greek evidence in particular, nevertheless the point can be made that the author of 4QpIsaᶜ

23. *The Hebrew of the Dead Sea Scrolls*, p. 58.
24. 'The Text of Isaiah at Qumran', p. 56.
25. *Qumran Cave 4.X: The Prophets*, p. 96.
26. On this identification, see the analysis by G. Vermes, *Scripture and Tradition in Judaism: Haggadic Studies* (SPB, 4; Leiden: E.J. Brill, 2nd edn, 1983), pp. 26-39, esp. pp. 32-33.

probably did not introduce a variant into his text for exegetical reasons but used an alternative understanding of the structure of the verse which was available to him.

On the other hand, however, it is also possible to argue that, since 4QIsa^e is written in a Herodian hand with a slightly fuller orthography than is found in the MT, perhaps 4QIsa^e was itself corrupted by a scribe who knew the exegetical reading offered in 4QpIsa^c. In this case the text-critical value of 4QIsa^e is marginally reduced. Whatever the case, I would argue that it is irresponsible of Ulrich not to have mentioned in his description of the variant in 4QIsa^e that it was also to be found in 4QpIsa^c.

2. A second weightier matter concerns the divine name and associated phraseology. Here there are some intriguing observations to be made since it is well known that the divine name in Isaiah is the subject of continuous 'improvement' and embellishment. A good example of the problem can be seen in the representation of Isa. 5.24 in 4QpIsa^b 2.7. In 4QpIsa^b the tetragrammaton is not qualified by צבאות as it is in the MT and 1QIsa^a, as well as the Greek and other versions. Commentators note the lack of צבאות in 4QpIsa^b but usually make no detailed comment.[27] Considered in isolation it might be seen as an omission,[28] perhaps even a deliberate omission by the Qumran commentator. However, it might also represent the more original form of the text.

In the next verse, Isa. 5.25, 4QpIsa^b agrees with the MT (and Peshitta and Vulgate) and 1QIsa^a, as well as the majority of the Targumic evidence, in simply presenting the tetragrammaton without qualification, and yet 4QIsa^b shows the same verse in which the tetragrammaton is provided with a supralinear correction to read יהוה צבאות. This is supported by the Greek and a few manuscripts of the Targum. Ulrich has also noted that 4QIsa^b also reads יהוה צבאות at Isa. 19.19 against most of the evidence which reads the tetragrammaton alone.[29]

27. E.g., Horgan (*Pesharim*, p. 93) notes baldly: '*yhwh* (MT and 1QIsa^a: *yhwh sb'wt*)'. J.M. Allegro, apparently without any text-critical intention, says that the MT 'adds' צבאות: J.M. Allegro with A.A. Anderson, *Qumrân Cave 4.I (4Q158–4Q186)* (DJD, 5; Oxford: Clarendon Press, 1968), p. 16.

28. Morrow, 'The Text of Isaiah at Qumran', p. 24: 'inadvertently omitted'.

29. *Qumran Cave 4.X: The Prophets*, pp. 26, 31. Several Peshitta manuscripts agree in this respect with 4QIsa^b at Isa. 19.19.

The overall evidence for Isa. 5.24-25 is thus that 4QpIsa[b] offers a consistent presentation of the tetragrammaton without any qualification, a state of affairs that may now be supported by the uncorrected form of 4QIsa[b]. 4QIsa[b] corrector offers יהוה צבאות for Isa. 5.25 (5.24 not being extant) with the Greek and some targumic support, and the MT (and Peshitta) offers יהוה צבאות for 5.24 but not for 5.25. The Greek has σαβαωθ consistently in both verses, which may represent the text that the correcting hand of 4QIsa[b] may be working towards. What can be made of this? Perhaps not much, without studying the way the divine sobriquets are given elsewhere in the manuscript evidence for the whole of the book of Isaiah. However, if the text-critical maxim 'the shorter the earlier, the longer the later' applies, then the text of 4QpIsa[b] may represent the oldest form of the text, the Greek the most recent or most developed, with the other witnesses somewhere in between or containing scribal errors. Whatever the case, it is clear to me that the text of Isa. 5.24-25 as it is represented in 4QpIsa[b] needs to be included in this discussion of textual variants.

3. The last set of variants to be considered comes from the most extensive section of overlap between a Cave 4 biblical manuscript and a Qumran Isaiah commentary. Here we shall briefly consider five variants in Isa. 10.27-32 which are variously found in 4QpIsa[a] and 4QIsa[c] (as listed by Ulrich). In textual order we can begin with the minor matter of the verb tense in Isa. 10.27. As can be seen from Ulrich's apparatus, there is some reason to suppose that this is not simply a matter of a scribal error which Ulrich claims the scribe himself later corrected.[30] It might be that an intertextual resonance of Isa. 7.17 is at stake. Whatever is made of 4QIsa[c] text-critically, the point that must be urged is that the evidence of 4QpIsa[a] should be set alongside that of 1QIsa[a], the MT, the Greek witnesses, the Targums, the Peshitta and the Vulgate with all of which it clearly agrees.

The second variant should also be annotated with evidence from 4QpIsa[a]. The Greek (and so the Peshitta and the Vulgate) represents the reading of אל with 4QIsa[c]. 4QpIsa[a] also reads אל against על of 1QIsa[a], the MT and the manuscripts of the Targum. Whereas the previous example may be merely a matter of scribal error, this second example poses the question concerning which is the preferable reading. The

---

30. *Qumran Cave 4.X: The Prophets*, p. 51: 'the original scribe inserted a supralinear *yod*'.

interchange of אל and על is sufficiently common in Qumran textual witnesses that it is virtually impossible to suggest which is more likely to be the original here without recourse to an analysis of the idiomatic usage of בא in first Isaiah. Such analysis produces the intriguing result that the verb occurs in only one other verse of first Isaiah with על, namely in Isa. 7.17, the very verse that may provide the intertextual source for the perfect tense of the verb in Isa. 10.27. Isa. 7.17 may explain the use of the preposition in the MT of Isa. 10.28 as later harmonization and so suggest that אל of 4QIsa^c and 4QpIsa^a is more original.

The third variant concerns the immediately following place name in Isa. 10.28. Here there is a rich range of possibilities with 4QIsa^c representing a plene spelling. Ulrich's apparatus conveniently summarizes all the versional evidence.[31] The text of the previous half verse with its place names is somewhat corrupt and various emendations have been suggested. It is not surprising to discover further variety in the representation of Aiath or Aioth. Whatever is made of the variety of evidence, it is important to note that 4QpIsa^a agrees with the correcting hand of 1QIsa^a by providing an old accusative ending: עיתה. Qimron has noted that 'a number of locative expressions (compounded with prepositions) terminate with *ā* (*he*)',[32] commonly in the idiom of the Temple Scroll. He went on to say that

> the *he* in these expressions does not designate the direction, since the *he* of direction lost its syntactical function in DSS Hebrew. It was rather perceived as a locative termination without any syntactical function. It is known that *ā* is an ancient locative termination. It occurs in BH, in MH and in Aramaic.

If Qimron is right, then there is a problem which is only solved by reckoning that the oldest form of the proper name in this context is represented by 4QpIsa^a which contains both the preposition אל, supported by 4QIsa^c, and the final he (אל עיתה). The preposition clearly provides the directional force to allow the final he to be understood as what used to be described as a directional accusative. The other possibility is that Qimron is wrong and that the directional he survived into late Second Temple times as the reading of 4QpIsa^a might suggest.

---

31. *Qumran Cave 4.X: The Prophets*, p. 51.
32. *The Hebrew of the Dead Sea Scrolls*, p. 69.

With regard to the unique reading in 4QIsa^c (עיות), it should be noted that the introduction of a waw may provide an example of the vowel shift which is widely apparent in the Hebrew of the Dead Sea Scrolls in which an *o* sound can represent not only qameṣ but also pataḥ and segol. Although Qimron has commented that this is largely restricted to vowel sounds carried by liquid and labial consonants,[33] the phenomenon could have been more widespread. However, caution needs to be exercised with this suggestion since a proper name is involved and the possibilities for variation are clearly plentiful.

The fourth variant in Ulrich's list, this time in Isa. 10.31, is also in need of some further comment. To the evidence cited by Ulrich should be added that provided by 4QpIsa^a whose reading (מדמנה) agrees with that found in the MT and its related witnesses against 1QIsa^a (מרמנה) and the Peshitta. Since in many ways 4QpIsa^a agrees with 4QIsa^c, it is possible to argue that the second letter of the word, which it is impossible to read in Isa. 10.31 in 4QIsa^c, should be restored in accordance with 4QpIsa^a and the MT and the majority of the versions.

The last variant in this intriguing section supports further associating the text forms 4QIsa^c and 4QpIsa^a. Both manuscripts agree with 1QIsa^a, the versions, and the *qere* of the MT in their reading of בת in Isa. 10.32. Again, it seems that 4QpIsa^a provides text-critical evidence which should be cited.

What should the overall assessment of these five variants be? Does the evidence of 4QpIsa^a make a difference as to how the character of 4QIsa^c should be described? If we are inclined to associate the readings of 4QpIsa^a and 4QIsa^c, then is the way forward to suggest that the biblical text represented in 4QpIsa^a must be factored in to any consideration of text-critical matters? This is surely the case. E. Tov has pointed out that 4QIsa^c is one of the 25 per cent of biblical manuscripts from the Qumran caves that are written according to the so-called Qumran scribal practice.[34] Although there is insufficient evidence to say that this group of manuscripts represents a fully fledged text type of its own, like that represented in the proto-MT, the *Vorlage* of the LXX, or the Samaritan Pentateuch, it is indeed evident that the type of text found in 4QIsa^c shares certain features with the biblical text as represented in 4QpIsa^a, which overall is indeed a sectarian composition. 4QIsa^c has a striking characteristic that confirms its sectarian association, though

33. *The Hebrew of the Dead Sea Scrolls*, pp. 39-40.
34. 'The Significance of the Texts', p. 295 n. 59.

such a characteristic does not make its text into a distinctive type. 4QIsa^c represents a wide range of divine epithets in palaeo-Hebrew, just as the tetragrammaton is so represented in 11QPs^a and some other biblical manuscripts found at Qumran. Such a feature might incline some modern analysts to think that 4QIsa^c is a sectarian version of Isaiah with characteristics they would also associate with the (in their view) non-scriptural 11QPs^a. 4QIsa^c then becomes yet another brick in the construction of an argument against the authoritative status of 11QPs^a. However, there is no such thing as a truly sectarian version of a biblical text in the Qumran caves, sectarian in the sense that the Samaritan Pentateuch is sectarian,[35] so 4QIsa^c should be classified more appropriately as a type of non-aligned text.

4. *Conclusion*

What is to be done with the evidence of the biblical quotations in the Qumran pesharim? More particularly, what is to be done with the evidence of the Isaiah quotations in the Isaiah pesharim in relation to the manuscripts of Isaiah from Qumran's Cave 4? It is quite possible that many of the unique variants in the scriptural citations in the pesharim are to be understood as reflecting the exegetical concerns of the Qumran commentators. However, where there is no obvious explanation for the variants on the basis of a close reading of the commentary and where there is corroborating textual evidence for the variants from what may be classified as biblical manuscripts, even if they are written in the so-called Qumran scribal practice, then it must be supposed that the quotations in the pesharim contain representations of earlier variant readings. As such, the biblical quotations in the pesharim must be included in any critical apparatus of a biblical manuscript. *Qumran Cave 4.X: The Prophets* edited by Eugene Ulrich and others needs to be adjusted to include the information discussed in this study.

35. As I have argued in '*E pluribus unum*: Textual Variety and Definitive Interpretation in the Qumran Scrolls', in T.H. Lim, L. Hurtado, A.G. Auld and A. Jack (eds.), *The Dead Sea Scrolls in Their Historical Context* (Edinburgh: T. & T. Clark, 2000), pp. 107-19. The argument is against the proposals of Tov to insist that some of the biblical manuscripts found at Qumran are of a sectarian character, even if only in terms of their scribal practices; see his essay 'The Significance of the Texts'.

Appendix

List of overlaps between Cave 4 Isaiah MSS and Qumran Isaiah Pesharim.

Isaiah	Information on the text in the overlap[36]

a. Overlap without variants

5.11-14	No variants in the overlap between 4QpIsa^b and 4QIsa^f
5.29-30	No variants in the overlap between 4QpIsa^c and 4QIsa^p
10.24	No variants in the overlap between 4QpIsa^c and 4QIsa^c
14.28-30	No variants in the overlap between 4QpIsa^c and 4QIsa^o
21.13	No variants in the overlap between 4QpIsa^e and 4QIsa^b

b. Orthographic differences

5.24-25	5.25a ותהיה [M 4QpIsa^b ותהי 1QIsa^a 4QIsa^f 5.25b כסוחה 4QpIsa^b [כסוהה 1QIsa^a 4QIsa^b M (כסוח{ה})
8.7-8	8.7 אפיקיו [4QpIsa^c אפיקו 4QIsa^e M; G υμων
9.17-18	9.18 לוא 1QIsa^a 4QpIsa^c [לא 4QIsa^e M
19.9-12	19.11 פרעוה 4QpIsa^c [פרעה 1QIsa^a 4QIsa^b M
21.10	21.10 לכמ[ה 4QpIsa^e [לכם 1QIsa^a 4QIsa^a M
30.15-16	30.15 Divine name in paleo-Hebrew 4QIsa^c [יהוה 1QIsa^a 4QpIsa^c M 30.16 רודפיכמה 4QpIsa^c [רודפיכם 1QIsa^a 4QIsa^c (רודפי[כם) M

c. Variants

1.1-2	1.1 [ויותם אחז וי] 3QpIsa [יותם אחז יחזקיהו 1QIsa^a M] G (και Ιωαθαμ και Αχαζ και Εζεκιου) S] V (Iothan, Achaz, et Ezechiae); not enough text survives of this verse in 4QIsa^{a,b,j} to use them for this phrase
5.24-25	5.24 יהוה 4QpIsa^b V] יהוה צבאות 1QIsa^a M T G S 5.25a {צבאות} יהוה 4QIsa^b G T^mss] יהוה 1QIsa^a M T S V 4QpIsa^b
8.7-8	8.7 גדותיו 4QpIsa^c (גדו]תיו) M 1QIsa^a (גדוותיו) G S V] גדיותיו 4QIsa^e 8.8 וה[יו מטות כנפיו 4QpIsa^c σ´ θ´] והיה מטות כנפיו 1QIsa^a 4QIsa^e M S V
9.17-18	9.17 ותצית 4QpIsa^c G?] ותצת 1QIsa^a 4QIsa^e M S
10.22-34	10.27 יסור 1QIsa^a 4QpIsa^a M G T S V] סור {י} 4QIsa^c 10.28 אל 4QIsa^c 4QpIsa^a G S V] על 1QIsa^a M T

---

36. { } = supra-linear correction.

10.28 עיות 4QIsa^c] עיה 1QIsa^{a}*; עיתה 1QIsa$^{a\ corr}$ 4QpIsa^a; עית M T
S V (Aiath); G (την πολιν Αγγαι)

10.31 מדמנה 4QpIsa^a M G T V; probably 4QIsa^c] מרמנה 1QIsa^a S

10.32 בת 1QIsa^a 4QIsa^c 4QpIsa^a M^q G S V] בית M^k T(vid)

14.8   14.8 עלימו 4QpIsa^c 4QIsa^e (עליהם)] עלינו 1QIsa^a M T G S V

19.9-12   19.11 אנו בני 4QpIsa^c G S] אני בן 1QIsa^a 4QIsa^b M V

30.23   30.23 לחם 4QpIsa^c] ולחם 1QIsa^a 4QIsa^r M G S V

3 MACCABEES, HANUKKAH AND PURIM*

Philip S. Alexander

A Neglected Apocryphon

3 Maccabees is one of the most neglected of the Jewish texts to have survived from Second Temple times. Preserved only by the Greek, Syriac and Armenian Churches, it seems to have been unknown in the West before the time of the Reformation. It is oddly named, given that it does not once mention the Maccabees and, in fact, purports to record events in the time of Ptolemy Philopator (Ptolemy IV, 221–203 BCE), over forty years before the Maccabaean revolt. It may have acquired its title simply because it was placed in a stichometry or in a Greek Bible codex immediately after the first two books of Maccabees. The name, however, is not entirely inappropriate, since there are numerous similarities between its story and the history of the Maccabaean rebellion, and, as we shall see, its strong intertextuality with 2 Maccabees is significant for its interpretation. Interest in *3 Maccabees* is beginning to grow. The New Revised Standard Version (NRSV) has included it for the first time in an English Bible. As a result it will feature in both the new one-volume Bible commentaries, the 'Peake' replacements, which are in an advanced state of preparation—the *Eerdmans Bible Commentary* and the *Oxford Bible Commentary*,[1] both of which take the NRSV as their base. *3 Maccabees* seems set to be more in the public eye in the next few decades. It has been neglected too long. The most thorough commentary on it remains C.L.W. Grimm's in the *Kurzgefasstes exegetische Handbuch zu den Apokryphen des Alten Testament* which

* The present essay develops some ideas set out in my analysis of *3 Maccabees* in J.W. Rogerson and J.D.G. Dunn (eds.), *Eerdmans Bible Commentary* (Grand Rapids: Eerdmans, forthcoming). It benefited from criticism by members of the Ehrhardt Seminar, Manchester, to whom I presented a version of it.

1. J. Barton, M. Goodman and J. Muddiman (eds.), *The Oxford Bible Commentary* (Oxford: Clarendon Press, forthcoming).

appeared in 1857. Most subsequent commentaries to greater or lesser degree 'crib' from this. There are useful studies by C.W. Emmet (in Charles, *Apocrypha and Pseudepigrapha of the Old Testament*, 1913), by Moses Hadas (in the Jewish Apocryphal Literature Series, 1953), and, in Hebrew, by Theodore Gaster (in Abraham Kahana's pioneering *Ha-Sefarim ha-Ḥitzonim*, 2nd edn, 1956). However, Hugh Anderson's contribution on *3 Maccabees* to Charlesworth's *Old Testament Pseudepigrapha* (1985) is disappointing: it seems to be heavily dependent on Hadas and represents a missed opportunity to advance our knowledge of the work.[2] Some of the basic problems of *3 Maccabees* have barely been tackled. Its text is problematic: the Syriac[3] and Armenian versions of it have hardly been investigated. There are numerous cruces in the Greek. A glance at the NRSV version will show an unusual number of footnotes suggesting alternative renderings, and the attentive reader of the NRSV will, I think, come away from it with a feeling that it does not always provide a totally convincing translation.

3 Maccabees 1.2 presents a typically niggling crux, and, incidentally, illustrates the author's style:

> Θεόδοτος δὲ τις ἐκπληρῶσαι τὴν ἐπιβουλὴν διανοηθεὶς παραλαβὼν τῶν προϋποτεταγμένων αὐτῷ ὅπλων Πτολεμαϊκῶν τὰ κράτιστα διεκομίσθη νύκτωρ ἐπὶ τὴν τοῦ Πτολεμαίου σκηνὴν ὡς μόνος κτεῖναι αὐτὸν καὶ ἐν τούτῳ διαλῦσαι τὸν πόλεμον.

---

2. For a preliminary bibliography of *3 Maccabees* see C.W. Emmett, 'The Third Book of Maccabees', in R.H. Charles (ed.), *Apocrypha and Pseudepigrapha of the Old Testament*, I (Oxford: Clarendon Press, 1913), pp. 155-73; T.H. Gaster, '3 Maccabees', in A. Kahana (ed.), *Ha-Sefarim ha-Hitzonim* (repr.; Jerusalem: Makor, 2nd edn, 1978 [1956]), II, pp. 231-57 (Hebrew); C.L.W. Grimm, *Das zeite, dritte und vierte Buch der Maccabäer* (Kurzgefasstes Exegetische Handbuch zu den Apokryphen des Alten Testament (Liepzig: S. Hirzel, 1857); R. Hanhart, *Maccabaeorum liber III* (Septuaginta: Vetus Testamentum Graecum auctoritate Societatis Litterarum Gottingensis editum, IX, 3; Göttingen: Vandenhoeck & Ruprecht, 2nd edn, 1980); M. Hadas, *The Third and Fourth Book of Maccabees* (Jewish Apocryphal Literature; New York: Harper, 1953), pp. 1-85; V.A. Tcherikover, 'The Third Book of Maccabees as a Historical Source of Augustus Time', *Scripta Hierosolimitana* 7 (1961), pp. 1-25 translated from *Zion* 10 (1944–45), pp. 1-20 (Hebrew); H. Willrich, 'Der historische Kern des III Makkabäerbuches', *Hermes* 39 (1904), pp. 244-58.

3. Syriac MS 3, fols. 63a-74a of the John Rylands University Library Manchester (15th–17th century) contains a version of the work. See J.F. Coakley, 'A Catalogue of the Syriac Manuscripts in the John Rylands Library', *BJRL* 75 (1993), pp. 106-207.

The context here is the battle of Raphia in 217 BCE between Ptolemy Philopator and Antiochus III. Theodotus had been a high-ranking officer in the Ptolemaic forces who some time previously had deserted to Antiochus's side. Just before the battle he stole across the lines under cover of darkness and attempted to assassinate his old master. The NRSV gives the standard rendering in its footnote:

> But a certain Theodotus, determined to carry out the plot he had devised, took with him the best of the Ptolemaic soldiers previously put under his command, and crossed over by night to the tent of Ptolemy, intending single-handed to kill him and thereby end the war.

There are obvious difficulties here: ὅπλα can certainly mean soldiers,[4] but this hardly fits the context which stresses that Theodotus planned to do the deed alone. The NRSV text gives a more literal rendering of the crucial words: 'took with him the best of the Ptolemaic arms that had previously been issued to him', but this does not convey any clear sense. The meaning must surely be that Theodotus dressed up in his old Ptolemaic regimentals, in order to insinuate himself unchallenged into the Ptolemaic camp as a high-ranking Ptolemaic officer (which, of course, he once had been), so that he could get close to the king. A more enlightening translation might be: 'he took the best Ptolemaic armour that had previously been issued to him', or more freely, 'he donned the best', or, drawing out a possible nuance of κράτιστα, 'the highest-ranking Ptolemaic uniform that had previously been issued to him...' It must be admitted, however, that the Greek of *3 Maccabees*, though in its way educated, is not entirely felicitous—a point to which I shall return presently.

The Argument of 3 Maccabees

3 Maccabees is almost certainly from the pen of a single author. It does contain a number of puzzling inconsistencies, but they are not such as to call into question the overall integrity of the book.[5] Its structure holds

---

4.   See LSJ, s.v. (p. 1240), II 4, 'ὅπλα = ὁπλῖται, *men-at-arms*', noting that it is frequent in prose and quoting Thucydides and inscriptions.

5.   The most obvious inconsistency is at 2.25, where reference is made to the 'previously mentioned drinking companions and comrades of the king'. In fact they have not been previously mentioned. The sudden blackening of the king's character at this point in the narrative is also rather disconcerting. Some commentators have felt that the book opens very abruptly with the sudden introduction of Theodotus, as

the key to its interpretation. It falls into two carefully balanced parts, which tell the tale of two cities and their respective Jewish communities—Jerusalem and Alexandria. The first part, which runs from 1.1 to 2.24, focuses on Jerusalem. It begins with an account of the battle of Raphia in spring 217 in which Ptolemy Philopator defeated Antiochus III. After his victory Ptolemy decides to visit the neighbouring regions, doubtless to try and secure their loyalty. A Jewish delegation meets him and invites him to Jerusalem. When he arrives in the city he naturally visits the Temple. Impressed by the magnificence of the building he decides that he wants to enter the Holy of Holies. The priests are horrified by his proposal and explain to him that it is against the Jewish law. Stubbornly he insists. As the news of the king's intention spreads, a hubbub breaks out: Jews rush to the Temple to protest and make such a noise that it sounds as if the very Temple buildings themselves are crying out against the sacrilege (1.29). Suddenly the commotion is stilled and attention focuses on the lone figure of the High Priest Simon on his knees, with hands outstretched in supplication. He utters a noble and moving prayer calling upon God to protect his sanctuary against the arrogant king. God obliges and, when the king tries to enter the Holy Place, he strikes him down with a fit, and the king has to be dragged unceremoniously away by his courtiers.

The king returns to Alexandria in high dudgeon, determined to avenge his humiliation at the hands of the Jerusalem Jews on their Egyptian co-religionists (2.25). First he spreads evil reports about the Jews among the non-Jewish population; then he moves to judicial measures, decreeing that the Jews should first lose whatever rights and privileges they had as citizens; second that they should be subject to poll tax; and third that they should be forbidden to worship their own God if they did not participate in the official state cult of Dionysus. The Jews do their best by passive resistance to avoid the evil decrees; they try to maintain communal solidarity by putting Jewish collaborators under the ban, withdrawing from all religious, social and commercial intercourse with them, and thus denying them the possibility of having the best of both worlds, namely participating in the state cult and at the same time retaining their links with their own ethnic and religious community. When the king hears of this he is furious and, just as his anger

if we already know who he is. It is possible something has been lost from the beginning of the work, but it is just as easy to suppose that our author is combining different sources but not reconciling them thoroughly.

against the Jews of Jerusalem spilled over against the Jews of Alexandria, so now it spills over against the Jews of the countryside, the *chora*. The king decides on a policy of genocide: the Jews as a whole cannot be trusted and so must all be put to death. He issues a decree in the form of a letter 'to his generals and soldiers in Egypt and all its districts' (3.12), instructing them to round up all the Jews of the country and send them in chains to Alexandria. This is duly done. The prisoners arrive at Schedia, the dock area of Alexandria at the end of the great canal, and from there they are marched to the hippodrome outside the eastern or Canopic gate, where their sorry plight could serve as a stern warning to those going in and out of the city (the author's knowledge of the topography of Alexandria and, indeed of Egypt, is very good). Up to this point the prisoners comprise only Jews from the *chora*, but the Jews of the *polis* now show sympathy with the plight of their country brethren. This enrages the king still further and results in the action being extended to them (4.13).

He devises for the Jews a cruel fate: they are to be trampled to death in a great public spectacle by elephants maddened by draughts of wine and frankincense. Two attempts to implement this cruel decree are thwarted by divine providence, but finally it is set in train. The third attempt is vividly imagined from the standpoint of the Jews themselves, incarcerated and helpless in the hippodrome (5.48-51). A cloud of dust coming from the direction of the city gate gives them early warning of the approach of the elephants, soldiers and spectators. Pandemonium breaks out among the prisoners. The parallelism with the early scene in the Jerusalem Temple is obvious, and here, as there, the general cries of supplication are silenced and a single voice of a priest, in this case Eleazar, leads the intercessions. Eleazar's prayer, like Simon's, is noble and well constructed, and it calls on God to deliver his people. God again duly obliges by manifesting a dreadful epiphany of two angels (6.18-21). Frightened by the apparition, the elephants turn back and trample the crowd of Egyptians that is following them. The king, chastened by the mayhem, has a dramatic change of heart and realizes the folly of his ways. Like many tyrants caught doing wrong he blames his advisers. Acknowledging publicly the loyalty of the Jews and the role they have played in the past in the defence of the country, he orders them to be released, and invites them to hold a feast at royal expense celebrating their deliverance in the very hippodrome where they were supposed to die. The feasting runs for seven days from the 7th to the

13th of the Egyptian month Epeiph (1–7 July), a period ordained to be an annual festival. The king also issues a letter countermanding his earlier decree, and, recognizing the Jews' loyalty, he gives orders that no-one is to harm them (7.1-9). The Jews petition the king to allow them to deal with the renegades in their community, arguing that the loyalty to the state of those who violate God's law must be suspect. The king gives them leave to act as they see fit and they put 300 renegades to death.

The country Jews now return to the *chora* and celebrate their deliverance for another seven days at Ptolemais Hormos (7.17), the well-known commercial entrepôt at the entrance of the Fayum in the Arsinoite nome. They dedicate there an inscription and a synagogue to commemorate the events. The book ends with a benediction: 'So the supreme God perfectly performed great deeds for the deliverance of the Jews. Blessed be the Deliverer of Israel through all times! Amen' (7.23).

3 Maccabees' Use of Sources

It is hard in this brief summary to do justice to the author's narrative skill or to the vigour with which he tells his tale. His literary textures are rich, with a pleasing variation between direct speech and third person narrative. In particular, the fine liturgical simplicity of the prayers of Simon and Eleazer contrasts starkly with the Asianic exuberance of the main narrative, which in turn contrasts with the dry chancery style of the two imperial letters. This is an author who can skilfully manage different styles. He is also an author with a vivid, visual imagination. His constantly shifting perspectives are cinemato-graphic. If Cecil B. De Mille had made a Holywood 'blockbuster' of this tale he would not have had to work much on his storyboard. Two sequences of 'camera angles' are, I think, particularly effective: the first is the zooming in from the crowd scene and the general pandemonium to the lone figure of Simon in the Temple wrapt in prayer (1.28–2.1). The author liked this so much that he repeated it in the Eleazar scene at the end of the book (5.50–6.2). The second sequence is the final dramatic climax in the hippodrome (5.48–6.21). As I noted earlier, the denouement is visualized first from the standpoint of the wretched prisoners, who first become aware of their impending doom when they see a cloud of dust emerging from the Canopic gate. Our attention is focused on this phenomenon, which we see through their eyes. The 'camera' then swings round to their reaction: realization dawns on them as to what the dust-cloud signifies; pandemonium breaks out. It then zooms in on the figure of Eleazar engaged in prayer. It swings round again to the approaching elephants, soldiers, courtiers and spectators. Finally, we are shown the mysterious apparition, followed by the stampede. It is masterly. I can think of few works from antiquity that visualize their story as effectively.

The author's generally good command of his material is important for our purposes, for, despite his narrative skill and force of imagination, there are a number of 'glitches' in the story which he has been unable to smooth over. First, I do not find that his claim that the king attacked the Egyptian Jews because of what happened in Jerusalem totally convincing. It is not clear at first reading why so much time is spent in Jerusalem when the main theatre of action is Egypt. Second, the involvement of the country Jews and their relationship to the city Jews is rather puzzling. The king's anger is first directed towards the Jews of Alexandria, but then somehow spreads to the country Jews (3.1 is hardly an adequate explanation). However, puzzlingly, it is initially only the country Jews who are put in irons. The city Jews do not get involved until they show solidarity with the Jews from the *chora* (4.13). Finally, there is the question of why there is a double celebration of the festival—once for seven days in Alexandria (6.30-40) and then again for seven days at Ptolemais Hormos (7.17-20). At first sight it looks as if the book has two alternative endings.

None of this suggests to me that *3 Maccabees* is composite. Rather, these problems are most satisfactorily explained by supposing that our author is adapting, and, according to his lights, remaining faithful to, separate sources of information. It is tempting to dismiss the whole tale as a fabrication, to see it effectively as a novella, but this would be a misjudgment. There may be a great deal more history behind *3 Maccabees* than at first might be supposed.[6] The author was trying to explain a real historical phenomenon—the origins of a festival in which he himself may have participated every year. He has done research and uncovered a number of bits of information, which he does his best, not

6.   It is interesting to note that the historians who have looked seriously into the matter have been rather impressed by the *historicity* of *3 Maccabees*; see, e.g., H. Willrich, 'Der historische Kern des III Makkabäerbuches', *Hermes* (1904), pp. 244-58.

always successfully, to link together and interpret. It is worth recalling the more obvious evidence for his use of sources.

First, for his account of the battle of Raphia and of Philopator's visit to Jerusalem (1.1-28), and possibly for other information about the Ptolemaic court and the king's Friends (a class of court official), he may have drawn on Ptolemy of Megalopolis's lost history of the reign of Ptolemy Philopator, a source Polybius also employed in Book 5 of his *Histories*. Careful comparison with Polybius gives us access to Ptolemy's work and suggests that our author, while remaining generally faithful to his source, decorated it a little. He gives the king's sister Arsinoe a more dramatic role. According to Polybius, who is here almost certainly following Ptolemy of Megalopolis faithfully, Ptolemy Philopator and Arsinoe addressed their troops *before* the battle. Our author has her alone intervene when the engagement is at its height and the issue hangs in the balance. It is hard to see why he does this. Perhaps it is yet another example of his penchant for the dramatic. However, there may also be literary reasons: Arsinoe provides the kind of feminine interest that Esther provides in the book of Esther, and her disregard of social norms (she appears with 'her locks all dishevelled', 1.4), points up the extreme peril of the situation. Our author also puts Theodotus's treachery in a more dramatic light by making him act alone, whereas Polybius, again following his source, says he took two companions with him. The reason for this is probably because our author wants to make Theodotus a more effective foil to the Jew Dositheus son of Drimylus, who by a clever stratagem saves the king. Our author has introduced Dositheus (Polybius knows nothing of him), but he is not an invention. By chance we happen to know that he actually existed, for he is mentioned in Papyrus Hibeh 90.[7] The loyalty of Dositheus contrasts sharply with the disloyalty of Theodotus. He plays the same role in *3 Maccabees* as Mordechai plays in Esther.

Second, our author's account of the measures against the Jews in 2.25-30 is probably derived, as the text claims, from a real Ptolemaic decree recorded in the form of a public inscription. Some of the phrasing used there may plausibly be taken as preserving the precise wording of that decree. Our author has, however, probably got a bit muddled.

---

7. *CPJ*, I, pp. 235-36 (nos. 127*d* and 127*e*). The fact that our author scrupulously mentions the fact that Dositheus was an apostate (1.3) rather supports the historicity and vouches for his honesty. He had little sympathy for renegades (2.31-33; 7.10-14).

The decree to which he alludes may well have been issued by Philopator after the battle of Raphia. Its primary purpose was to extend citizenship to non-Greeks, perhaps in recognition of the services they had rendered in his army. However, citizenship was granted only to anyone who participated in the cult of Dionysus, whose symbol was the ivy leaf. The Ptolemies claimed descent from Dionysus, and Philopator was particularly famous for his devotion to the god.[8] Anyone who did not participate in the cult of Dionysus was not permitted to worship his own gods. Such a religious and ideological unification of the kingdom would make good political sense in the aftermath of Raphia. Though possibly not directed at them specifically, it would have created problems particularly for Jews, and may well have provoked resistance on their part, which resulted in persecution. The situation is analogous to Antiochus IV's Hellenization programme which sparked off the Maccabaean revolt. However, it makes little sense to say, as our author does, that it was the Jews who *refused* to take part in the cult who were branded with the ivy leaf. The branding with the ivy leaf is better understood as the sign of a *devotee* of Dionysus, and would have been a crude but highly effective way of keeping track of those who *conformed*.[9] Our author, coming across a reference in his sources to branding with the ivy leaf, and possibly abhorring branding as a mutilation or possibly because of its association with thieves and slaves, assumed that it was meant as a *punishment* of the Jews. But if this is the correct understanding of the confusion here, then it strongly suggests that our author is doing his best to make sense of real sources.

8.   See P.M. Fraser, *Ptolemaic Alexandria* (Oxford: Clarendon Press, 1972), I, pp. 202-204; J. Tondriaux, 'Les Thiases dionysiaques royaux de la Cour ptolémaïque', *Chronique d'Egypte* 41 (1946), pp. 149-71.

9.   It is clear from *3 Macc.* 2.29 that branding with a hot iron is meant: τούς τε ἀπογραφομένους χαράσσεσθαι καὶ διὰ πυρὸς εἰς τὸ σῶμα. Philopator himself, the supreme devotee of Dionysus, is said to have been branded with the ivy leaf, though in the form of a tattoo. See Fraser, *Ptolemaic Alexandria*, I, p. 204, quoting the *Etymologicum Magnum*: ΓΑΛΛΟΣ: ὁ Φιλοπάτωρ Πτολεμαῖος· διὰ τὸ φύλλοις κισσοῦ κατεστίχθαι ὡς οἱ Γάλλοι. ἀεί γάρ ταῖς Διουσιακαῖς τελεταῖς [κισσῷ ἐστεφανοῦντο]. See further, T.H. Gaster, '3 Maccabees', in A. Kahana (ed.), *Hasefarim ha-ḥitzonim* (repr.; Jerusalem: Makor, 2nd edn, 1978 [1956]), II, pp. 231-57 (244); C.W. Emmet, 'The Third Book of Maccabees', in R.H. Charles (ed.), *Apocrypha and Pseudepigrapha of the Old Testament*, I (Oxford: Clarendon Press, 1913), pp. 155-73 [165]; A. Kasher, *The Jews in Hellenistic and Roman Egypt* (Tübingen: Mohr Siebeck, 1985), pp. 216-17.

Third, Philopator's plan to kill the Jews by having them crushed by drunken elephants (5.1–6.21) is almost certainly based on an incident recorded also by Josephus in *Apion* 2.53-55. If Josephus is to be believed (and in this case he probably is) the incident occurred in the reign not of Philopator but of Ptolemy Physcon (Ptolemy IX, 146–117 BCE). Physcon, angry at the Alexandrian Jews because they had backed Cleopatra rather than him after the death of Philometer, arrested them and threatened to have them trampled by elephants. However, the combination of an apparition and the entreaties of his favourite concubine dissuaded him from carrying out his threat, and 'that' concludes Josephus, 'is the origin of the well-known festival which the Jews of Alexandria keep, with good reason, on this day, because of the deliverance so manifestly vouchsafed to them by God'. The dating of this incident to Physcon's reign may have been less clear in our author's than in Josephus's source.

Finally, our author doubtless consulted the inscription in the synagogue at Ptolemais mentioned at 7.20, which may well have contained a brief account of the festival it commemorated. There is surely no reason to doubt the historicity either of this synagogue or of its inscription.[10] *3 Maccabees* was written for the Jews of Egypt and would have been intended to be read especially by the Jews of Fayum, who play such a prominent and honourable role in it. Our author would have been taking a risk with his credibility if no such synagogue or inscription existed. The festival that *3 Maccabees* describes was a real festival, in which, as I suggested, our author probably participated. It was held over seven days from the 7th to the 13th of the Egyptian month of Epeiph. It involved feasting, choral singing (6.32, 35; 7.16), floral tributes (7.16) and the cry 'Hallelujah' (7.13), and the final day seems to have been reserved especially to commemorate the destruction of the Jewish renegades (7.15).[11] This festival, as festivals do, would have attracted folk-traditions over the years, which our author knew. Our author, then, did not make everything up. He had sources that he collected and carefully pondered, drawing inferences from them (some of which were probably

10. For Jewish synagogues in the region see W. Horbury and D. Noy (eds.), *Jewish Inscriptions of Graeco-Roman Egypt* (Cambridge: Cambridge University Press, 1992), no. 117 (pp. 201-203).

11. I assume here that 6.30-40, 7.15-16 and 7.17-20 all describe aspects of the same festival.

false) and weaving them together with embellishments supplied by his own fertile imagination to create the present tale.

The Genesis of 3 Maccabees and its Historical Setting

How are we to unravel this tangled skein? I would like to make a proposal which I think reasonably accommodates all the facts. I would suggest that the origins of *3 Maccabees* lie in a festival that was celebrated by the Jews of the Arsinoite nome in Ptolemais Hormos. This was where the inscription and the synagogue commemorating the festival were to be found. The festival commemorated some deliverance of the Jews in the past from official persecution. The inscription would surely have dated this persecution and it would have been from it that our author derived the link with the reign of Ptolemy Philopator. The persecution may have been a rather local affair. This would explain why the Jews of the *chora* (which would refer most naturally to the Jews of the Fayum) are the real heroes of the story, and why the Jews of Alexandria get drawn in only secondarily. It is possible that our author was an Arsinoite Jew (though he knows the topography of Alexandria rather well). It has often been noticed that his religious ideas are very unsophisticated, and show little evidence of the advanced thinking of Alexandrian Judaism. I have already commented on his Greek, which, though vigorous and educated, is not stylistically assured. It would fit rather well with the style and level one would expect of a country schoolmaster. All this might point to the author being a 'country cousin', and not one of the Alexandrian sophisticates.

Our author probably lived long after the events commemorated in the festival. He may have celebrated the festival himself, and if he did he doubtless read the inscription in the Ptolemais synagogue and knew the folk-stories linked to the festival. But these did not satisfy him. He wanted to know more. He set out to research the origins of the festival. His researches took him to Alexandria, where he found another local festival of deliverance, probably commemorating events in the reign of Ptolemy Physcon. He identified the two. He also found in Alexandria a Ptolemaic inscription dating to the reign of Philopator which he deduced—whether rightly or wrongly is unclear—had something to do with the festival. So far so good. But there are certain features about *3 Maccabees* that still remain unexplained. *3 Maccabees* is promoting the festival as worthy of being celebrated by *all* Jews in Egypt. If the festival was originally local, why would he want to do that? And why does he bring in, possibly gratuitously since it may never actually have happened, the incident in the Jerusalem Temple?[12]

Let us consider the second of these questions first. *3 Maccabees* clearly intends to show that the Jews of Egypt are as pious and as loyal to the Torah of Moses and the ancestral traditions as are the Jews of Jerusalem. This is the whole point of the work's structure, in which the heroic actions of the Jews in Jerusalem are closely matched by the heroic actions of the Jews in Egypt. There is surely an element of local pride here. But what could have provoked our author into such an outburst? I would suggest that it may have been the promotion in Egypt of the festival of Hanukkah. It has long been recognized that there are numerous echoes in *3 Maccabees* of 2 Maccabees.[13] 2 Maccabees is a rather curious work. Its author tells us that it is an epitome of a much longer account of the Maccabaean struggle written in five books by Jason of Cyrene. Jason probably composed his original work around 130 BCE and the epitome dates probably from some thirty years later. The work of Jason of Cyrene seems to have been a rather straight-

12. The historicity of the Temple incident is much disputed. It should not be dismissed as outright fiction. Emmet, 'Third Maccabees', p. 160, makes a good case for its basic historicity: 'In his triumphal progress after Raphia the king would not be likely to leave out the Jewish capital. With his love of architecture and interest in religion he would certainly wish to enter the Temple. The Jews would no less certainly have tried to prevent him, and his superstitious fears may well have been worked on in some such manner as to give rise to the highly coloured narrative of our book. It is even possible that the story may have been taken in substance from the memoirs of Ptolemy Megalopolitanus.' He points out (p. 159) that the characteristics that Polybius attributes to Ptolemy of Magalopolis, 'love of "miraculous occurrences and embellishments", and the fondness for tracing out causes, are exactly those of *3 Maccabees*, and would make him a congenial pattern for the author of the latter book'. The parallels with the Heliodorus episode in 2 Macc. 3.22-31 are obvious, and *3 Maccabees* may indeed have had this in mind (see below), but there is also one major difference: Heliodorus was prevented from entering the Temple *treasury*; Philopator was prevented from entering the Holy of Holies. In this respect the parallel with the story of Ptolemy's penetration of the sanctuary in 63 BCE, as told by Josephus, *War* 1.152, is more exact, but it is unlikely that *3 Maccabees* is echoing that incident. It is just as possible that Pompey shows how any conqueror would have been tempted to behave in Jerusalem, if backed by his legions.

13. One is the Heliodorus incident in 2 Maccabees: see n. 12. Emmet, 'Third Maccabees', pp. 156-57, gives a useful list of the major parallels.

forward, perhaps somewhat dry history of the revolt. Where and why it was written is hard to say. The epitome, however, tells a much more dramatic tale,[14] which was clearly composed to promote the observance of Hanukkah. Its intended audience was the Egyptian Diaspora, as the prefaced letters indicate (1.1, 10). The genuineness of these letters has been much debated. The first (1.1-10), which is dated to 124 BCE and refers to an earlier communication dated to 143, is almost certainly genuine. The second (1.10–2.18), the implied date of which is 165 BCE, is much more questionable. There were evidently earlier efforts to get the Egyptian Jews to embrace Hanukkah, but these having come to nothing, another attempt was made around 100 BCE. Our epitomist reworked the history of Jason of Cyrene into a festal scroll and sent it to Egypt prefaced by copies of the two earlier letters from the Jerusalem authorities to give authority to his advocacy of the festival. It is hard not to detect Hasmonaean political ambition behind this tireless promotion of Hanukkah. Hanukkah and the Hasmonaeans cannot be divorced: the rededication of the Temple was their finest hour. Hanukkah was a potent vehicle of Hasmonaean propaganda.[15] It may have been the appearance of 2 Maccabees in Egypt that provoked our author, either in a spirit of emulation or (as I shall argue presently) of opposition, to compose *3 Maccabees* to glorify the fidelity to Torah of local Jewish heroes.

There is another piece of even more intriguing intertextuality which points in a similar direction. *3 Maccabees* does not actually mention the Hasmonaeans, but it is not difficult to detect hints about them in it. In the late second century BCE any story about the Jerusalem Jews' doughty defence of the sanctity of the Temple and their zealous adherence to the ancestral laws would have raised in most reader's minds the analogy of the Hasmonaeans. But in addition to Hanukkah, there is a second festival whose ghostly presence can be felt in our work—the festival of Purim. The similarities in plot between the scroll of Esther and *3 Maccabees* are obvious, but there are also numerous details that suggest our author was acquainted with the Esther story. His description of the carousing of Philopator with his royal Friends is reminiscent of Ahasuerus's feast in Esther, though both possibly owe something to

---

14. 2 Maccabees' stress on the theme of martyrdom is noteworthy.

15. I find the claim that there are anti-Hasmonaean elements in 2 Maccabees implausible. It is surely difficult if not impossible to promote Hanukkah without glorifying the Hasmonaeans.

stock descriptions of the dissipations of oriental tyrants. I have already suggested that Dositheus the son of Drimylus plays a Mordechai-like role in saving the king's life, and that Arsinoe may have been fore-grounded to provide a focus of feminine interest somewhat comparable to Esther in the book of Esther. In both Esther and *3 Maccabees* the Jews, in the end triumphant, avenge themselves on their enemies, though in Esther they engage in wholesale slaughter of the gentiles (Est. 8.11-12; 9.16), whereas in *3 Maccabees* only 300 renegade *Jews* are killed (*3 Macc.* 7.15).[16] *3 Maccabees* knew the Greek Esther. Why, then, did its author not explicitly mention Esther? A reference would have been more than appropriate in the prayer of Eleazar, when he is citing examples of divine deliverance.

This deserves a closer look. The section in question is found in 5.48–6.15. Eleazar's prayer is simple, affecting and in good liturgical style. Like Simon's in 2.1-20, its language contrasts with the bombast of the surrounding narrative. Eleazar, like Simon, quotes biblical exempla, in this case to illustrate how God has delivered his people in dire circum-stances in the past. The first, appropriately, is the deliverance of Israel from Pharaoh, 'the former ruler of this Egypt' (6.4). The second is the deliverance of Jerusalem from the Assyrian Sennacherib (cf. 2 Kgs 19.35). The third is the deliverance of the three Hebrews from the fiery furnace: the verbal echoes here of the story as told in the book of Daniel are particularly strong.[17] The fourth example is Daniel's deliverance from the lions' den (Dan. 6.24). *3 Maccabees*' retelling of examples two to four curiously makes no mention of the angelic agents who, according the biblical story, were involved in each of these saving acts. In 2 Kgs 19.35 it is the 'angel of the Lord' who destroys the Assyrians. In Dan. 3.25 Nebuchadnezzar sees a fourth figure in the fiery furnace whose appearance is 'like a son of the gods'. And in Dan. 6.22 Daniel tells King Darius, 'My God sent his angel and shut the lions' mouths'. The author of *3 Maccabees* has nothing against the idea of angelic intervention: he himself is just about to introduce angels to deliver the Jews of Alexandria (5.16-21). He may have avoided bringing them in

---

16. Note, however, that the number of those killed in Shushan was three hund-red (Est. 9.15). Another interesting parallel that might be mentioned is the fact that the contrast between Shushan ha-Birah and the 'villages' in Esther (see ch. 7) is mirrored by the contrast between Alexandria and the *chora* in *3 Maccabees*.

17. Cf. 6.6 with Dan. 3.27, and for 'turning the flame against all their enemies' see The Prayer of Azariah 24-25, itself probably suggested by Dan. 3.22.

here, so as not to blunt the dramatic impact of the climax. Eleazar's final example from Jonah (cf. Jon. 1.17–2.9) is at first sight surprising. However, it is possible that he takes Jonah as a symbol of Israel. Jonah tried to flee from the presence of the Lord, but found that wherever he went, even to the depths of sea, God was still there to hear his prayer and to save him. This would chime well with the ending of Eleazar's prayer with its quotation of Lev. 26.44, 'When they are in the land of their enemies, I will not spurn them, neither will I abhor them so as to destroy them utterly and break my covenant'. The one exemplum conspicuous by its absence is the story of Esther. This surely cannot be because *3 Maccabees* predates or did not know the book of Esther. It is much more probable that the omission is deliberate: the silence about the Esther story is thunderous. It could have so easily been introduced, and there would have been no problem of anachronism, as there would have been with more explicit allusions to the Maccabees.

The relationship of *3 Maccabees* to the book of Esther is complex. *3 Maccabees*, I have suggested, presupposes a knowledge of the Esther story. However, confusingly, some of the additions found in the Greek Esther (notably Additions B and E) seem to show a knowledge of *3 Maccabees*.[18] How can this be explained? I would suggest that a Greek version of Esther close in content to our current Hebrew text was introduced to Egypt in 114 BCE. The date can be deduced from the colophon to the Greek Esther (Addition F 11), which probably belongs to the original Greek form. This colophon, which is almost certainly genuine, tells us that the Greek translation, which was done by Lysimachus, son of Ptolemy, in Jerusalem, was brought to Egypt from Palestine by one Dositheus, a priest and levite, and his son Ptolemy. The purpose of introducing the work to Egypt can only have been to encourage Egyptian Jews to celebrate Purim. The book of Esther enjoins the observance of the festival on Jews throughout the Persian empire, which, as it is careful to point out, extended all the way to Egypt (Est. 1.1; 9.20).

18. See C.A. Moore, 'On the Origins of the LXX Additions to the Book of Esther', *JBL* 92 (1973), pp. 382-93 (384-85). Note the fact that the Additions rather exonerate the king and blame the 'Macedonian' Haman (Addition E 7-14). This is parallel to the rather lame attempt in *3 Maccabees* to excuse Ptolemy and pin the blame on his advisors (7.2-4), and even more particularly to the pointed exoneration of the ordinary, decent 'Greeks' in 3.8-10, implying, perhaps, that it was the 'Macedonians' who caused the problem.

Who would have wanted to promote this festival in Egypt? The origins of Purim are highly obscure. C.A. Moore and others are convinced that the book of Esther does commemorate, albeit in a highly exaggerated way, a genuine 'deliverance' experienced by the Jews of Persia (possibly in the fourth century BCE).[19] The Esther story originated in Persia but was brought to Palestine, perhaps by immigrating Persian Jews, and attracted interest there. That interest would unquestionably have been stimulated by the Hasmonaean revolution. The similarities between the story of Esther and the story of Hanukkah are obvious: both involve a deliverance from tyranny that is commemorated by an annual festival. Some Palestinian Jews began to celebrate Purim. Certainly the festival was recognized by the rabbinic movement after 70 CE: a whole tractate of the Mishnah is devoted to it.[20] It was from Palestine, or more specifically Jerusalem, as the colophon of the Greek Esther shows, that the book of Esther was carried into Egypt. The promotion of Purim in Egypt seems to have had the backing of the Jerusalem authorites. Is it possible that, as with the festival of Hanukkah, Hasmonaean political ambition lies behind the promotion of Purim in Egypt?[21] They may have been playing on a well-established link

19. C.A. Moore, *Esther* (AB, 7B; Garden City, NY: Doubleday, 1971), p. lix.

20. Rabbinic recognition of Purim is rather surprising, given the religiously dubious character of the book of Esther and the fact that Purim is not a Torah festival. This might suggest that by the second century CE the festival was so popular among Palestinian Jews that the Rabbis simply could not ignore it. Their support for Purim contrasts with their lack of support for Hanukkah. The Mishnah and the earlier layers of Talmudic literature show no interest in Hanukkah. This is all of a piece with their lack of interest in, or even denigration of, the Hasmonaeans. It is only in the late Amoraic period that Hanukkah gains recognition by the Rabbinic establishment, perhaps, again, under pressure of popular support. Hanukkah and Purim, as we have noted, are similar in many ways: Jewish liturgy and folk-tradition constantly make cross-reference from one to the other. So why did the Rabbis accept one and not the other? I have suggested elsewhere that they perceived an important difference: Hanukkah celebrates a deliverance *in Eretz Israel*; it is, therefore, inextricably bound up with Jewish nationalism and messianism. Purim celebrates a deliverance *in the Diaspora*. Purim was politically much less dangerous. It was at least in part because they were worried, in the aftermath of the Bar Kokhba revolt, about an upsurge of Jewish nationalism and messianism that the Rabbis were so cool towards Hanukkah. See my essay, 'From Poetry to Historiography: The Image of the Hasmonaeans in Targum Canticles and the Question of the Targum's Provenance and Date', *JSP* 19 (1999), pp. 103-28, esp. 115-19.

21. The absence of Esther from Qumran might be linked to the fact that Purim

between the two festivals in the popular imagination. Was Purim to be yet another instrument for asserting the political and spiritual hegemony of Jerusalem? The Hasmonaeans had much to gain by encouraging loyalty to Judaism among Diaspora Jews, especially if *they* monopolized the definition of Judaism.

Our traditional, pious author of *3 Maccabees*, living probably in the Arsinoite nome, might well have reacted negatively to the publication of the original Greek Esther. He could have found it objectionable on two counts. First, the tone of the book of Esther is remarkably unreligious. There is no mention of Torah, or of the commandments, or even of God. Second, he might well have asked himself why the proud Jewish community of Egypt should celebrate the achievements of the Jews in far-away Persia? Were there not closer to home similarly stirring examples of loyalty to Torah and divine deliverance to be remembered? And so, I would suggest, in face of propaganda in favour of two alien festivals (Hanukkah and Purim), both linked (in differing degrees) to Hasmonaean political ambitions, our author decided to promote a local Egyptian festival of deliverance and to remind the Jews of Jerusalem that Egyptian Jews were just as loyal to the Torah, and just as willing to embrace martyrdom, as they were. The scroll of Esther was designed to be read on the festival of Purim: it was part of the celebration. 2 Maccabees was also, I suggested, intended as a festal scroll.[22] Our author in *3 Maccabees* provided a festal scroll for the unnamed festival of 7–13 Epeiph. Note in this connection its concluding benediction. The publication of *3 Maccabees*, however, in its turn had an impact on the Greek Esther. A new version of this was produced incorporating additions (some modelled on parts of *3 Maccabees*), which were intended to give the work a much more religious colouring. The additions found only in the Greek text are all secondary (they show little sign of having had a Hebrew *Vorlage*) and may be largely from the same hand.[23]

---

was being promoted by the Jerusalem authorities. However, the situation at Qumran is complicated; Esther-like fragments have now been identified at Qumran (4Q550). These may, however, like the Daniel stories and the book of Esther, simply be evidence of a penchant for oriental tales in Palestine in late Second Temple times.

22. Hanukkah was, of course, furnished sometime later with another festal scroll, the Scroll of Antiochus—but that is another story.

23. I am not sure how the A text or so-called 'Lucianic' recension of Esther fits into the picture. I do not think that it is early or throws light on the origins of either

I am tempted to push my analysis a little further. If my reading of *3 Maccabees* against 2 Maccabees and Esther is correct, then it suggests that *3 Maccabees* contains an anti-Hasmonaean sub-text. But why such anti-Hasmonaean bias? The answer may lie in the communal politics of Egyptian Jewry. Egypt had given refuge to the Oniads. It was there at Leontopolis that they built a temple to rival the Temple in Jerusalem. The Oniads were not driven out of Jerusalem in the first instance by the Hasmonaeans but by the Hellenists (Menelaus or Alcimus). However, it was the Hasmonaeans who *kept* them out of Jerusalem, for when they recaptured the city they did not recall them but firmly installed themselves in power and finally usurped the High Priesthood. There was surely no love lost between the Hasmonaeans and the Oniads. The Oniads prospered in Egypt and wielded considerable political influence there. The Hasmonaeans could hardly have viewed with complacency the powerful position enjoyed by their rivals in the most populous and prosperous community in the Diaspora. It makes good sense to suppose that they would have done all they could to extend their influence in Egypt.

At first sight *3 Maccabees'* very positive view of the Jerusalem Temple sits uneasily with this position. However, there is no real problem here. Even Jews disillusioned with the Hasmonaeans would have retained a pride in their ancient homeland and in its magnificent Temple. Besides, the events in Jerusalem which *3 Maccabees* describes took place long before the wicked Hasmonaeans usurped the priestly mitre. They happened back in the days of the godly high priest Simeon the Just—a man respected by all Jewry and an Oniad! His name had been immortalized by the great panegyric in ch. 50 of Ben Sira, a Greek version of which became available in Egypt in the late second century CE, at roughly the same time as *3 Maccabees* was being composed.[24]

---

the Hebrew or the Greek Esther. It is more likely to be a late revision of the B text in the light of the Hebrew. The fact that the differences between the A and B texts are largely confined to the sections that overlap with the MT makes perfectly good sense on this surmise. These were the only sections that could be revised in such a way, since they alone had a Hebrew *Vorlage*. Thus it is not at all clear that the Additions in the A text are secondary and borrowed from the B text. For a discussion, see D.J.A. Clines, *The Esther Scrolls: The Story of a Story* (Sheffield: JSOT Press, 1984), pp. 69-92.

24. The Simeon the Just of rabbinic fame (e.g. *m. Ab.* 1.2) is more likely to be Simeon II (219–196) and therefore the same as the high priest praised by Ben Sira.

But Egypt too, *3 Maccabees* implies, had nurtured a priest to rival the great Simeon in piety—the priest Eleazar. Our author pointedly tells us that Eleazar was 'famous among the priests *of that country* [i.e. Egypt]' (7.13). The land of Israel has no monopoly on priestly piety. There is surely an oblique reference here to Leontopolis, though Leontopolis could not of course be named since it was only founded in the 140s BCE by Onias IV, the grandson of Simeon the Just—well after the events that *3 Maccabees* purports to describe.

3 Maccabees cannot be understood in isolation. It must be read in the context of the subtle inter-textual relations that it bears with 2 Maccabees, the Greek Esther and the Greek Ben Sira. It cannot be accidental that all these works appeared in Egypt at roughly the same time as *3 Maccabees*, around 100 BCE. When we read these texts together a pattern emerges of local Egyptian religious pride (perhaps allied to support for the Oniads) resisting attempts by the Hasmonaeans and the Jerusalem authorities to impose their authority upon them. The reading is speculative but it tells a coherent and, I trust, a convincing story which accounts reasonably well for all the data.

THE TRANSLATION OF *1 ENOCH* 70.1:
SOME METHODOLOGICAL ISSUES*

Michael A. Knibb

I

Chapters 70–71 of the Ethiopic book of Enoch form a separate section
at the end of the Parables of Enoch (chs. 37–71) in which Enoch's
ascent to heaven and identification as the son of man, apparently the
individual whom Enoch had previously seen enthroned in heaven, are
described. There are grounds for thinking that the passage was intended
as an account of Enoch's final translation to heaven at the end of his
life, in contrast to the accounts of Enoch's earlier, temporary, translations to heaven (14.8; 39.3), whose purpose was to carry up to God
the petition of the watchers and to receive a revelation of the secrets of
the cosmos and of heaven.[1] It seems quite likely that chs. 70–71 are
secondary in comparison with the main body of the Parables, but as the
Ethiopic text stands, they serve as a conclusion to the Parables, and
there are allusions back both to the Parables[2] and to the Book of

* This brief study is dedicated to the memory of Michael Weitzman whose
death has deprived us of a remarkable friend and colleague.
    1.   Cf. A. Caquot, 'Remarques sur les chapitres 70 et 71 du livre éthiopien
d'Hénoch', in L. Monloubou (ed.), *Apocalypses et théologie de l'espérance* (Association catholique française pour l'étude de la Bible: LD, 95; Paris: Cerf, 1977), pp.
111-22 (112-13); J.C. VanderKam, 'Righteous One, Messiah, Chosen One, and Son
of Man in 1 Enoch 37–71', in J.H. Charlesworth (ed.), *The Messiah: Developments
in Earliest Judaism and Christianity* (Minneapolis: Fortress Press, 1992), pp. 169-
91 (178-79). According to the fiction reflected in 81.5-6, Enoch was to teach his
children for one year all that he had learnt in these heavenly journeys before finally
being taken from them.
    2.   Cf. 70.2 with 39.3; 70.3 with 61.1; 71.7 with 61.10; 71.8 with 40.9; 71.10
with 46.1; 71.14 with 46.3; 71.16 with 48.7; 62.14. See Caquot, 'Remarques',
p. 114; M.A. Knibb, 'Messianism in the Pseudepigrapha in the Light of the Scrolls',
DSD 2 (1995), pp. 165-84 (179-80).

Watchers (chs. 1–36).[3] The text divides on formal grounds into two parts, a third person narrative, which gives a summary account of Enoch's ascent (70.1-2), and an autobiographical report in which Enoch describes his ascent and identification as son of man (70.3–71.17).

According to the autobiographical report, the ascent occurred in three stages[4] (70.3-4; 71.1-4; 71.5-11), and in broad terms the description may be compared with the account of the ascent in 14.8-25, which also occurred in three stages (14.8-9, 10-14a, 14b-25). The language used in 70.3–71.11 is reminiscent of that used in 14.8-25, and in particular the house built of crystal and tongues of fire (71.5), from which the Head of Days emerges (71.10), recalls the description of the houses in 14.10-13, 15-17.

The climax of the autobiographical report comes in 71.14 in which Enoch is addressed—according to what seems to me the most natural understanding of the Ethiopic text—as follows:

> And he [or 'that one'; var. 'that angel'][5] came to me, and greeted me with his voice, and said to me. 'You are the son of man who was born to righteousness,[6] and righteousness remains (*hadara*) over you, and the righteousness of the Head of Days will not leave you.'

There seems little doubt that a deliberate link back is intended in this verse with the description of the son of man in 46.3: 'This is the son of man who has righteousness, and with whom righteousness dwells (*hadara*)', and thus that Enoch himself is here identified with the figure whom he had seen enthroned next to God during his visionary journeys through the heavenly regions, the one who would act as the judge at the end of the age, who is called 'righteous one',[7] 'chosen one',[8] and 'messiah'[9] as well as 'son of man'.[10] But the identification comes as

---

3. Cf. 70.3–71.11 with 14.8-25.

4. Cf. Caquot, 'Remarques', p. 114 ('par palliers').

5. There are no other significant variants in this passage apart from this.

6. This sentence could also be translated 'You are a son of man [or 'a man'] who was born to righteousness'. See further Caquot, 'Remarques', pp. 115-18; S. Mowinckel, *He that Cometh* (Oxford: Basil Blackwell, 1959), pp. 441-44.

7. See 38.2 (although the reading 'righteousness' is perhaps to be preferred); 53.6.

8. See, e.g., 40.5; 45.3-4.

9. See 48.10; 52.4.

10. See, e.g., 46.1-6; 48.1-10.

something of a surprise, both because throughout the main body of the Parables (chs. 38–69) Enoch seems clearly to be distinguished from the heavenly figure he saw, the chosen one/the son of man, and because, even within chs. 70–71, a clear distinction seems to be drawn in 70.1 between Enoch and the son of man. A number of different strategies have been adopted to deal with the apparent difficulty,[11] but it is not my intention, nor is it really possible, to pursue these here. Rather, my intention is to focus on the translation of 70.1 in view of the role this passage has played in the question of the identification of Enoch as son of man.

The summary account of Enoch's ascent in 70.1-2 is cast, as we have noted, as a third person narrative. It serves both to link chs. 70–71 to chs. 37–69 and as an introduction to the autobiograpical report that follows. The Ethiopic text of the majority of the manuscripts, both those belonging to the older type of text and those belonging to the younger type of text, may be translated, fairly literally, as follows:

> And it came to pass after this (that), while he was living, his name was lifted to the presence of the [or 'that'] son of man and to the presence of the Lord of Spirits [*tala'ala semu ḥeyaw baḥabehu lawe'etu walda 'eguala 'emmaḥeyaw wabaḥaba 'egzi'a manafest*[12]] from among those who dwell upon the dry ground. And he was lifted on the chariots of the wind [or 'of the spirit'], and his name vanished among them.

This translation is an adapted version of the one I gave in my translation of Enoch,[13] but in all essentials it is also the translation given by Flemming, Charles, and Uhlig;[14] it likewise corresponds in all essentials

---

11. See, e.g., M. Casey, 'The Use of the Term "Son of Man" in the Similitudes of Enoch', *JSJ* 7 (1976), pp. 11-29 (18-19, 22-29); VanderKam, 'Righteous One', pp. 182-85; J.J. Collins, 'The Son of Man in First-Century Judaism', *NTS* 38 (1992), pp. 448-66 (453-57); Knibb, 'Messianism', pp. 177-80.

12. For the purposes of this article I have thought it unnecessary to use anything more than a simple system of transliteration.

13. M.A. Knibb in consultation with E. Ullendorff, *The Ethiopic Book of Enoch: A New Edition in the Light of the Aramaic Dead Sea Fragments.* I. *Text and Apparatus*; II. *Introduction, Translation and Commentary* (Oxford: Clarendon Press, 1978) (II, p. 165).

14. See J. Flemming and L. Radermacher, *Das Buch Henoch* (GCS; Leipzig: J.C. Hinrichs, 1901), p. 90; R.H. Charles, *The Book of Enoch* (Oxford: Clarendon Press, 2nd edn, 1912), p. 141; S. Uhlig, *Das äthiopische Henochbuch* (JSHRZ, 5/6; Gütersloh: Gütersloher Verlagshaus Gerd Mohn, 1984), p. 631.

to the translation given by Dillmann,[15] who, however, had at his disposal only manuscripts belonging to the younger type of text. In this passage, as in 48.3, the 'name' stands for the person, and the statement that Enoch's name was lifted to the presence of the son of man and the Lord of Spirits refers to the taking up of Enoch into heaven. This is made clear by the parallel statement in v. 2 ('he was lifted on the chariots of the wind') which alludes to the narrative of the taking up of Elijah into heaven (2 Kgs 2.11-12).

The manuscripts I used for my edition of the Ethiopic text of Enoch,[16] which, with some exceptions, had been known for some time and had been used by Charles and Flemming in the early part of the last century, reveal a number of textual variants in 70.1-2, but only two are of significance in relation to the above translation. First, for *baḥabehu lawe'etu* ('to the presence of the/that'), the variants *baḥaba we'etu* and *baḥaba lawe'etu* occur, but with no real difference in meaning. However, Tana 9 has a double reading (*baqedma baḥaba lawe'etu*), and Abbadianus 55 has only *lawe'etu*. The significance of the reading in Abbadianus 55 is discussed below, but it should be noted here that the support for this reading is now known to be stronger than was earlier thought. Second, the conjunction 'and' (*wa*) before 'to the presence of the Lord of Spirits' is only attested by four manuscripts belonging to the older type of text.[17] But whether the conjunction is original or not, it is clear on the basis of the majority text reflected in the above translation that Enoch was taken up into the presence of both the son of man and the Lord of Spirits and is thus distinguished from the son of man.

However, in a valuable article published in 1977, Caquot argued that the text contained in the majority of the manuscripts and reflected in the above translation preserved the *lectio facilior* and was intended to accommodate ch. 70 to the main part of the Parables, and in particular to the vision of the Head of Days and the son of man in ch. 46. Caquot maintained instead that the original text was preserved by Abbadianus 55 in which *baḥabehu* (or *baḥaba*,[18] 'to the presence of') does not

15. See A. Dillmann, *Das Buch Henoch* (Leipzig: F.C.W. Vogel, 1853), p. 40.

16. See above, n. 13.

17. British Library Orient. 485 (early 16th cent.), Berlin Peterm. II Nachtr. 29 (16th cent.), Abbadianus 35 (end of the 17th cent.), Tana 9 (first half of the 15th cent.).

18. The two forms differ only in the presence or absence of the anticipatory suffix.

occur.[19] I reproduce his translation as he subsequently gave it in *La Bible: Ecrits intertestamentaires*:

> Ensuite, il arriva que le nom de ce fils d'homme fut élevé vivant auprès du Seigneur des Esprits [Abbadianus 55 *tala'ala semu ḥeyaw lawe'etu walda 'eguala 'emmaḥeyaw baḥaba 'egzi'a manfasat]* (et retiré) d'entre les habitants de l'aride. Il fut élevé sur le char du vent, et son nom fut retiré d'entre eux.[20]

This translation presupposes that in *semu...lawe'etu* we have an instance of the use of an anticipatory pronominal suffix followed by the preposition *la*; the absence of the conjunction before 'to presence of the Lord of Spirits' then gives the translation 'the name of the [or 'that'] son of man was raised, while he was living, to the presence of the Lord of Spirits'.[21] Thus according to the text preserved by Abbadianus 55— and, as we now know, by other older manuscripts—Enoch was here identified as the son of man.

The decision as to which of these two texts represents, if not the original Ethiopic text, at least the oldest Ethiopic text accessible to us, is finely balanced. On the one hand, Abbadianus 55—to focus, for the time being, just on this manuscript—dates from about 1500 and is one of the comparatively small number of manuscripts of Enoch that are old by Ethiopic standards.[22] It is a representative of the older type of text, and its evidence in a case such as this certainly deserves consideration. Furthermore, acceptance of the text represented by Abbadianus 55 as the best Ethiopic text available would mean that there was no inconsistency within chs. 70–71 between 70.1 and 71.14 over the identification of Enoch as the son of man. On the other hand, even if this text were accepted, there would still remain the problem posed by the fact that within chs. 38–69 Enoch seems clearly to be distinguished from the chosen one/the son of man. Furthermore, while it is true that

19. See Caquot, 'Remarques', p. 113.

20. See Caquot, 'Hénoch', in A. Dupont-Sommer and M. Philonenko (eds.), *La Bible: Ecrits intertestamentaires* (Bibliothèque de la Pléiade; Paris: Gallimard, 1987), pp. 463-625 (549); cf. Casey, 'The Use of the Term "Son of Man" ', pp. 25-27.

21. The text of Abbadianus 55 could in fact also be translated 'while he was living, his name was raised to the [or 'that'] son of man' (cf. VanderKam, 'Righteous One', p. 184), but this seems less likely.

22. For the date of this manuscript, see O. Löfgren, *Die äthiopische Übersetzung des Propheten Daniel* (Paris: Paul Geuthner, 1927), p. xxvii.

Abbadianus 55 deserves consideration as a representative of the older type of text, three other important manuscripts containing this type of text—British Library Orient. 485 (early 16th cent.), Berlin Peterm. II Nachtr. 29 (16th cent.), and Abbadianus 35 (end of the 17th cent.)—all attest the majority text, and Tana 9 (first half of the 15th cent.), with its double reading (*baqedma bahaba lawe'etu*) should also be included here; these four manuscripts are representative of at least two different strands within the older tradition. In addition, Abbadianus 55 cannot be regarded as a particularly reliable representative of the older text of Enoch both because in Enoch, apart from other defects, there are very significant omissions in its text from ch. 83 onwards, and thus the significance of any omission in this manuscript is diminished; and because in other books there is evidence that it contains a revised type of text. Thus Löfgren, in his exemplary edition of Daniel, did not assign Abbadianus 55 to the 'Old Ethiopic' and noted that it shared a number of readings with the later type of text,[23] while in my own work on Ezekiel I have observed that Abbadianus 55 frequently attests the revised type of text. Finally, it could as easily be argued that the non-occurrence of *bahabehu* or *bahaba* in Abbadianus 55 is simply a mistake, or was intended to accommodate 70.1 to 71.14,[24] as that the text of the majority of the manuscripts was intended to accommodate 70.1 to the Parables that precede it.

A case can thus be made, it seems to me, for the originality of either the text of the majority of the manuscripts or for that represented by Abbadianus 55, and in the end a decision between the two readings is likely to depend on a consideration of wider issues relating to the interpretation of this section of *1 Enoch*. But in a recent article, Daniel Olson has argued very strongly for the originality of the text represented by Abbadianus 55 and has claimed that other scholars have mistranslated and misinterpreted the passage. To quote his own words:

> It is a simple fact that all the discussions to date [of *1 En*. 70.1] have been hobbled by serious deficiencies. First, debates about *1 En*. 70–71 over the past few decades have overlooked the important new manuscript evidence available. Second, at least in the Anglo-Saxon world, questionable English translations have been consistently and uncritically relied upon to the detriment of accurate exegesis. Third, in considering the

23. Löfgren, *Die äthiopische Übersetzung*, pp. xli-xlii.
24. Cf. VanderKam, 'Righteous One', p. 184; Collins, 'The Son of Man', pp. 453-54.

textual problems involved practically no attention has been paid to the environment in which *1 Enoch* has come down to us. Correcting these oversights clarifies the disputed passages in these chapters, and a much firmer foundation is then laid for interpreting them.[25]

It is to issues arising from these claims that I now turn.

II

It has long been known that the non-occurrence of *baḥabehu* or *baḥaba* in Abbadianus 55 was supported by two late manuscripts, Abbadianus 99 and 197[26] (both 19th cent.[27]), but the number of manuscripts with this type of text has now been increased as a result of the Ethiopian Manuscript Microfilm Library (EMML) project. The manuscripts photographed as part of this project include at least 30 copies of Enoch, of which four (EMML 1768, 2080, 6281 and 7584) have been identified as representative of the older type of text.[28] Olson notes that three of these (EMML 1768, 2080, 7584) as well as two manuscripts with the later type of text (EMML 2436 [17th cent.] and 6974 [18th cent. ?]) have virtually the same text as Abbadianus 55 in *1 En.* 70.1. He repeats the claim made when EMML 2080 was first identified that it 'may be the oldest Ethiopic MS of *1 Enoch* extant, possibly dating to the twelfth century', and he argues that the support from the EMML manuscripts shows that the text represented by Abbadianus 55 should be regarded as a genuine alternate reading. He concludes that because only Tana 9 (which, as we have seen, has a double reading) can claim equal antiquity with Abbadianus 55, EMML 1768, 2080 and 7584, 'from a purely text-critical point of view, it can be persuasively argued that the balance of evidence now tilts slightly in favour of the minority reading',[29] that is the text represented by the latter manuscripts. This is a strong claim to make, and for a number of reasons it must be doubted whether it can be

25. D.C. Olson, 'Enoch and the Son of Man in the Epilogue of the Parables', *JSP* 18 (1998), pp. 27-38 (30).

26. J. Flemming, *Das Buch Henoch* (TU, NS 7.1; Leipzig: J.C. Hinrichs, 1902), p. 86.

27. See C. Conti Rossini, 'Notice sur les manuscrits éthiopiens de la collection d'Abbadie', (suite) *JA* 10.20 (1912), pp. 5-72 (7-8, 34).

28. Cf. P.A. Tiller, *A Commentary on the Animal Apocalypse of 1 Enoch* (SBL Early Judaism and its Literature, 4; Atlanta: Scholars Press, 1993), p. 129 n. 8, p. 143.

29. Olson, 'Enoch and the Son of Man', pp. 30-32.

justified. The comments that follow are based on knowledge of Abbadianus 55, EMML 1768 and 2080, but not of EMML 7584, which is said to date to the late fifteenth century.

First, the claim that EMML 2080 may be the oldest Ethiopic manuscript of Enoch extant and possibly dates to the twelfth century is certainly wrong. I note that Olson does not discuss the palaeography of the manuscript, nor even refer to what is now the standard treatment of Ethiopic palaeography, Uhlig's *Äthiopische Paläographie*. But even a superficial examination of the manuscript shows that from a palaeograpical point of view it belongs clearly with manuscripts from Uhlig's Period III, that is, in the period from the middle of the fifteenth to the middle of the sixteenth century. Uhlig himself, in the light of his discussion of the characterisics of the script, concludes that there is much to be said for the view that EMML 2080 dates from the latter part of his Period III.[30] But the manuscript has been subjected to extensive revision and correction at different times, and the reading that corresponds with that of Abbadianus 55 is a correction; the original reading, as Olson himself notes, was very probably *baḥaba we'etu*.[31]

Second, there is some reason to doubt whether the testimony of EMML 1768 is all that significant in support of that of Abbadianus 55. EMML 1768 is, like Abbadianus 55 and EMML 2080, a large manuscript containing the prophetic and wisdom books of the Old Testament and dates from the same general period as the other two manuscripts, that is, the end of the fifteenth or the early sixteenth century. I have collated the text of Ezekiel in this manuscript, and its readings agree so often with those of Abbadianus 55 that it is clear that, at least in the case of Ezekiel, there is some connection between the two manuscripts; such limited soundings as I have undertaken suggests the likeliehood of this in *Enoch* also. In any case, the evidence in relation to Ezekiel calls into question the value of EMML 1768 as independent additonal testimony alongside Abbadianus 55.

---

30. S. Uhlig, *Äthiopische Paläographie* (Äthiopistische Forschungen, 22; Stuttgart: Franz Steiner Verlag, 1988), pp. 419-20. See on Uhlig's book the reviews by E. Ullendorff in *JSS* 36 (1991), pp. 128-34 and by Knibb in *ZDMG* 141 (1991), pp. 405-408.

31. Olson, 'Enoch and the Son of Man', pp. 37-38. Olson argues that the original copyist simply made a mistake and corrected it himself from his master copy, but in the light of the other manuscript evidence it is very hard to believe that the reading *baḥaba we'etu* was a spontaneous mistake made by the copyist.

Third, Olson is inclined to dismiss the value of the evidence of Tana 9 on the grounds that it contains a double reading (*baqedma baḥaba lawe'etu*), but this seems to me mistaken. Here it would appear that the copyist inadvertently wrote *baqedma* ('before') and then immediately corrected himself, but without deleting the word written in error; this kind of phenomenon can be observed not infrequently in older Ethiopic manuscripts. But be that as it may, the crucial point is that Tana 9 provides evidence that the reading *baḥaba lawe'etu* was known in the first half of the fifteenth century and is thus attested at an earlier date than the reading without *baḥaba* or *baḥabehu*.

In summary, the evidence of EMML 1768, 2080 and 7584 has strengthened the claim for the reading of Abbadianus 55 in *1 En.* 70.1 to be taken seriously as representing the oldest accessible Ethiopic text of this passage, and has made it less likely that the non-occurrence of *baḥabehu* or *baḥaba* is simply a mistake. However, the original reading in EMML 2080 has been corrected at the key point in *1 En.* 70.1, and it is not clear at what stage the correction was inserted, while in general it may be wondered how far EMML 1768 provides genuinely independent additional evidence by the side of Abbadianus 55. More importantly, these manuscripts all date from the same general period, the end of the fifteenth century and the early part of the sixteenth, and it is in this same general period that two of the oldest representatives of the majority reading, British Library Orient. 485 (early 16th cent.) and Berlin Peterm. II Nachtr. 29 (16th cent.), belong, while Tana 9 carries the evidence for the majority reading back to the first half of the fifteenth century. The dates of the different manuscripts do not provide sufficient grounds for asserting the priority of either the majority or the minority reading, and certainly not for the claim that on purely text-critical grounds the balance of evidence has now tilted slightly in favour of the latter.

III

Olson has not only argued in favour of the originality of the minority text in *1 En.* 70.1-2, but has also offered what he suggests might be a better translation of this text:

> And it happened afterwards that the immortal name of that Son of Man was exalted in the presence of the Lord of Sprits beyond all those who live on the earth. He was raised aloft on a chariot of wind, and his name was spoken among them.

This translation should be compared with that of Caquot, reproduced above. It will be apparent that Olson has given an interpretative paraphrase rather than a translation in one or two places. But this aside, his translation is based on taking three phrases in the Ethiopic text in a different way from virtually all his predecessors,[32] and in each case his decision must be regarded as problematic in the context.

First, Olson has argued that the translation of *semu ḥeyaw* as 'his name during his lifetime' is forced and implausible, and that the phrase means 'his living name'. In itself such a translation is perfectly possible, but it has to be asked whether this translation is plausible in the context. Olson in fact argues that the intended meaning is likely to be 'his ever-living name', and he ultimately renders the phrase as 'his immortal name'; but if this were the intended meaning it has to be wondered why the word 'immortal' was not used. It would be interesting to know what Greek, not to mention Semitic, phrase Olson believes lay before the Ethiopic translator. To my knowledge, neither the phrase 'living name',[33] nor the phrase 'immortal name', occurs in the Hebrew Bible or in the Septuagint, but the phrase 'everlasting name' (ὄνομα αἰώνιον) does occur in a few places (e.g. Isa. 56.5; 63.12) and is routinely rendered in Ethiopic by *sem zala'alam*. On the other hand, it is not the case that the rendering of *semu ḥeyaw* by 'his name during his lifetime' or 'his name while he was living' is forced or implausible. Also, while it is true that no exact parallel occurs in *1 Enoch* for the use of Enoch's 'name' to represent Enoch himself, a very close parallel does occur in 48.3.

Secondly, Olson has argued that *tala'ala semu* does not mean 'his name was lifted' or 'his name was raised aloft', but 'his name was exalted'. Again, Olson's translation is in itself perfectly possible. Ethiopic *tala'ala* occurs with the meaning 'laudibus extolli' in Ps. 98.5, 9 (LXX ὑψοῦν; MT 99.5, 9), and the causative form of the verb (*'al'ala*) is used with the word 'name' in *1 En.* 39.9, 61.12 and Ps. 33.4 (MT 34.4).[34] But in *1 En.* 70.1-2 *tala'ala* is clearly used in v. 2 to refer to the

32. Olson, 'Enoch and the Son of Man', pp. 32-33.

33. In Sirach we three times find the statement 'and his name will live forever' or similar: see 37.26 (καὶ τὸ ὄνομα αὐτου ζήσεται εἰς τὸν αἰῶνα); 39.9; 44.14. It is of interest that the Ethiopic does not use the verb 'to live' for ζῆν but instead *nabara* ('to sit', 37.26) or *qoma* ('to stand', 39.9; 44.14), both here with the meaning 'to endure'.

34. Cf. A. Dillmann, *Lexicon linguae aethiopicae* (repr.; New York: Ungar,

'raising aloft', the taking up, of Enoch into heaven, and it seems much more natural to assume that the verb is being used in the same way in v. 1, and that both verses are describing the same event. Further, while it is certainly possible to give a comparative meaning to the preposition *'em* ('from'), the statement that the name of the son of man was exalted 'beyond all those who live on the earth' would hardly seem appropriate to the context.

Finally, Olson has argued that in v. 2 the phrase *waḍ'a semu* refers to the spreading of Enoch's fame. Here Olson follows the suggestion of Black: 'Eth. waḍ'a = יצא promulgari and sem = שם in the sense of "fame" '.[35] This is of course perfectly possible, but in a context referring to the taking up of Enoch into heaven, it might seem easier to assume that the phrase refers to the disappearance of Enoch. The statement in 70.2 may then be understood as a counterpart to 12.1, where, in the context of Enoch's earlier translation to heaven, it is said that Enoch was 'hidden', and that no one knew where he was. Comparison might also be drawn with 2 Kgs 2.16-18 where the sons of the prophets cannot believe that Elijah has disappeared.

I conclude that it is still more plausible to assume that vv. 1 and 2 of *1 En.* 70 refer to the same event, the taking up of Enoch—whether or not identified as the son of man—into heaven, and his disappearance from among men, than that v. 1 refers to the exaltation of the name of the son of man, and v. 2 to the taking of him up into heaven. Thus, if the minority text (Abbadianus 55, EMML 1768, 2080, 7584) does represent the oldest acessible form of the Ethiopic text, the translation of Caquot is still to be preferred as a more accurate indication of the meaning of the passage.

IV

In the final section of his article Olson argues that attention to the fact 'that *1 Enoch* as we now have it is, among other things, a document of the Ethiopian Orthodox Church and part of its canon of scripture' can help us to understand particular readings in the Ethiopic text of Enoch, and notably in *1 En.* 70.1 and 71.14. He is quite right to highlight the fact that *1 Enoch* has been transmitted in the context of the Ethiopian

1955 [1865]), col. 55; Caquot, 'Remarques', p. 113.

35. M. Black, *The Book of Enoch or 1 Enoch: A New English Edition* (SVTP, 7; Leiden: E.J. Brill, 1985), p. 250.

Church,[36] and that within that context the Parables naturally lent themselves to christological interpretation, as is well illustrated by the fifteenth-century homiletical work Maṣḥafa Milad ('the Book of Nativity'), to which Olson (and others) have drawn attention. Maṣḥafa Milad,[37] whose composition is attributed to King Zar'a Ya'qob (1434–68), contains extensive extracts from the Parables and from other sections of *1 Enoch*, which are interspersed with christological comment. Thus the quotation of *1 En*. 46.1–51.5 is introduced by the following statement: 'Hear, O Christian, Enoch the prophet was not content with the numbers of the weeks of years, but reported further how he had seen the son of God and the son of the virgin Mary.'[38] Similar comments are interspersed at various points in the quotation of *1 En*. 46.1–51.5 that follows.

In view of the fact that *1 Enoch* was transmitted in a Christian context, it would not be surprising to find that the text has in places been Christianized, and indeed this can be shown to be the case in some passages and/or manuscripts. Thus, for example, it is perhaps hardly surprising that in 62.5 the Ethiopic expression used here for 'the son of man', *walda be'esi* (*filius viri*), should have been changed in manuscripts with the later type of text to 'the son of the woman' (*walda be'esit*), that is Mary,[39] although it is also possible, as VanderKam notes, that the change was made under the influence of the reference in

36. Transmitted, but not of course translated, in this context. Thus, while it is very likely that the text of *1 Enoch* was influenced during its transmission by the context in which it was transmitted, at the time of the original translation the theology of the Ethiopian Orthodox Church hardly existed and was certainly insufficiently developed to have had any influence on specific details of the text.

37. For an edition and translation, see K. Wendt, *Das Maṣḥafa Milad (Liber Nativitatis) und Maṣḥafa Sellase (Liber Trinitatis) des Kaisers Zar'a Ya'qob* (4 vols.; CSCO, 221-22, 235-36, Scriptores Aethiopici, 41-44; Louvain: Secrétariat du Corpus SCO, 1962, 1963).

38. For the text, see Wendt, *Das Maṣḥafa Milad*, I, p. 54.

39. Olson ('Enoch and the Son of Man', pp. 35-36) gives some other examples of changes of this kind in *1 Enoch*. He suggests that many Ethiopian copyists would have found *walda be'esi* unacceptable as a term for 'son of man' because it would have implied that Jesus is the biological son of Joseph, and thus they deliberately made changes. But it is not clear that the changes were in all cases deliberately made for theological reasons, and the possibility that the changes were made spontaneously must also be kept in mind. See also, in relation to 62.5, the suggestion of VanderKam (n. 40). The text of Tana 9 in 62.5 means 'when those sons of men see him', not, as Olson states, 'when the sons of men have seen that one'.

the previous verse to a woman in the pangs of childbirth.[40] Outside the Parables Christian influence can be seen in 105.2.

Olson is thus certainly right to draw attention to the context in which the text of *Enoch* has been transmitted. But his explanation of the texts of *1 En.* 70.1 and 71.14 in the light of supposed concerns generated within this Christian environment seems misconceived. Olson draws attention to the three expressions used for 'son of man' in the Parables: *walda 'eguala 'emmaheyaw* ('son of the offspring of the mother of the living', i.e. Eve), *walda sabe'* (*filius hominis*), and *walda be'esi* (*filius viri*),[41] and argues that the three expressions 'are *not* all neutrally applicable to Jesus Christ in Ethiopia'. He maintains that *1 En.* 70.1, where *walda 'eguala 'emmaheyaw*—the normal Ethiopic equivalent for 'son of man' in both the Old and the New Testament—is used, invited a christological application, but that this created a problem in that on a straightforward reading of the minority text Enoch was identified with the son of man. The minority text could be interpreted to mean 'his name was raised to that son of man',[42] but eventually, in order to make clear the distinction between Enoch and the son of man, the preposition *bahabehu* (or *bahaba*) was inserted to produce the majority text. In contrast, Olson argues that there was no temptation to find a christological interpretation in *1 En.* 71.14. In this verse the Ethiopic phrase for 'son of man' is *walda be'esi*, which Olson states is 'never used of Jesus Christ in Ethiopic literature'. Whereas Ethiopian copyists were anxious to dissociate Enoch and the *walda 'eguala 'emmaheyaw*, they were only too happy to attach the 'troublesome'[43] *walda be'esi* to Enoch. Thus the text, understood in an 'Ezekielic' way as 'You are a son of man who was born...' or 'You are a man who was born...', survived unscathed.[44]

This argument seems to me to be based on an artificial distinction, but in any case ignores the fact that *1 En.* 71.14 was given a christological interpretation in Ethiopian Christianity. Olson has overlooked the fact that the quotation of *1 En.* 71.12-17 in Mashafa Milad is introduced by the statement 'Hear, O Jew, from the prophet Enoch what he prophesied concerning Jesus Christ, the son of Mary and the son of

40. VanderKam, 'Righteous One', p. 174 n. 15.
41. For these three expressions, see, e.g., Black, *The Book of Enoch*, p. 206.
42. See above, n. 21.
43. For Olson's view that *walda be'esi* was 'troublesome', see n. 39.
44. Olson, 'Enoch and the Son of Man', pp. 33-36.

God'.[45] In reality no distinction is drawn between the three expressions used for 'son of man' within the Parables of Enoch, and the use of different terms has to be understood within the context of the wider problem of consistency and diversity in the use of translation equivalents in the Ethiopic Bible.[46] The use of different expressions for 'son of man' does not, in my view, shed any light on the problem of the relationship between *1 En.* 70.1 and 71.14, and the text-critical problem of 70.1 has to be resolved, if at all, on the basis of the normal criteria. In fact, as I have already argued, it is possible to make a plausible case in 70.1 for both the majority and the minority reading, and a decision between the two is likely to depend on a consideraton of wider issues relating to the interpretation of this section of *1 Enoch*.

In his edition of the Aramaic fragments of *Enoch*, Milik commented that it was strange that no edition of the *Ethiopic Enoch* had taken account of the numerous quotations of the book to be found in Ge'ez literature, and he gave a provisional list of such quotations.[47] One of the most important sources for these quotations was Maṣḥafa Milad, which includes extensive extracts from *1 Enoch*, as we have seen, as well as from other biblical books. Subsequently, both Berger and Piovanelli have drawn attention to Maṣḥafa Milad as an important textual witness for *1 Enoch*, and Berger worked through the list of quotations given by Milik and noted that the text of the extracts from *Enoch* in Maṣḥafa Milad agreed with that of the older group of manuscripts.[48]

I have examined the text of *1 En.* 46.1–51.5 and 62.1-16 in Maṣḥafa Milad as a test. There is no question but that its text belongs with that of the older group of manuscripts, and there is some evidence, as Berger noted, of a connection with Tana 9. There are some 26 readings in these

45. For the text, see Wendt, *Das Maṣḥafa Milad*, p. 62.

46. Cf. M.A. Knibb, *Translating the Bible: The Ethiopic Version of the Old Testament* (The Schweich Lectures of the British Academy 1995; Oxford: Oxford University Press for the British Academy, 1999), pp. 87-112. It is to be observed that *sabe'*, *be'esi*, and *'eguala 'emmaḥeyaw* are all routinely used as translation-equivalents for ἄνθρωπος; cf. Ps. 48.13, 21 (MT 49.13, 21) where *sabe'* is used for ἄνθρωπος in the first occurrence of the refrain, but *'eguala 'emmaḥeyaw* in the second.

47. J.T. Milik, *The Books of Enoch: Aramaic Fragments of Qumrân Cave 4* (Oxford: Clarendon Press, 1976), pp. 85-88.

48. K. Berger, review of M.A. Knibb, *The Ethiopic Book of Enoch*, in *JSJ* 11 (1980), pp. 100-109 (108); P. Piovanelli, 'Sulla *Vorlage* aramaica dell'Enoch etiopico', *Studi Classici e Orientali* 37 (1987), pp. 545-94 (563-64).

chapters that I have not—at least as yet—found in other manuscripts. But none of these unique readings appears to represent the original Ethiopic text; rather they represent the kind of changes that regularly occur when manuscripts are copied (omissions, occasionally additions, of odd words, substitution of one word by a synonym, use of different tenses or constructions, minor mistakes). And unfortunately in key passages Maṣḥafa Milad does not help us, at least so far as I have seen. For example, in 70.1 it gives essentially the same text as Berlin Peterm. II Nachtr. 29, *tala'ala semu ḥeyaw baḥaba* (Berl + *we'etu*) *walda 'eguala 'emmaḥeyaw wabaḥaba* (Berl *waḥaba*) *'egzi'a manafest*,[49] that is the majority text. And in 62.2, where scholars have long thought that the reading of all the manuscripts 'And the Lord of Spirits sat (*nabara*) on the throne of his glory' ought to be emended to 'And the Lord of Spirits set him (*'anbaro*; sc. the Chosen One) on the throne of his glory', Maṣḥafa Milad reads, 'And that (or 'the') Chosen One, the Lord of Spirits sat (*nabara*) on the throne of his glory (*wanabara zeku ḥeruy 'egzi'a manafest diba manbara sebḥatihu*)'.[50] Here it seems to me that 'that Chosen One' is a gloss, and that the passage is not somehow to be understood as meaning 'The Lord of Spirits set that Chosen One on his glorious throne'.[51] Rather the text in Maṣḥafa Milad is to be understood in the light of the later comment that follows the quotation of 63.11-12: 'Son of man Enoch calls him, and Lord of Spirits Enoch calls this Christ, the son of Mary and the son of God'.[52]

The quotations of Enoch in Maṣḥafa Milad are important, probably not for any individual reading they attest, but because they reinforce our knowledge of the Ethiopic text of Enoch that was in circulation in the fifteenth century. This is, of course, also the date of the oldest manuscripts of Enoch that we possess. Unless and until a manuscript of Enoch that genuinely dates from before the fifteenth century comes to light, the fifteenth century, or perhaps shortly before, will remain the earliest period to which we can carry back knowledge of the Ethiopic text.[53]

---

49. For the text, see Wendt, *Das Maṣḥafa Milad*, I, p. 61.
50. For the text, see Wendt, *Das Maṣḥafa Milad*, I, p. 59.
51. Cf. Uhlig, *Das äthiopische Henochbuch*, p. 613.
52. For the text, see Wendt, *Das Maṣḥafa Milad*, I, p. 61.
53. See further, Knibb, *Translating the Bible*, p. 41.

JEWISH AND CHRISTIAN COLLABORATION IN ANCIENT SYRIA

Michael M. Winter

Although the book of Ben Sira is not now in the Hebrew canon, it seems to have been present when the Septuagint and Syriac translations were made, since it is in all the manuscripts of both those versions of the Bible. In short it is a book about which Jews and Christians have disagreed, but upon which they have also collaborated, as I will show in the course of this chapter.

The relationship between Ben Sira's Hebrew text and its most ancient translations has long been recognized as one of the thorniest problems of textual research. Not only do the versions differ from the text at many points, but the original Hebrew has undergone a complicated evolution, displaying reduplications and even triplications of many verses. Various theories have been advanced to account for these differences. Nearly a century ago, I. Levi suggested that some 25 of them were translations from the Syriac.[1] More recently, the re-translation theory was studied again by A. Di Lella, who defended its occurrence in a detailed study of half a dozen instances, three of which had been noted only briefly by Levi.[2] More recently, H.P. Ruger published an indispensable study of the Hebrew text of Ben Sira[3] in which he accounts for the complex state of the Hebrew text on the assumption that it is the amalgamation of two basic text forms. In his explanation of the reduplications, as well as the differences between Hebrew manuscripts, he has offered an alternative explanation for all Di Lella's retranslations and most of Levi's. Although I accept the accuracy of nearly all that

---

1. I. Levi, *L'Ecclesiastique* (Paris: Bibliotheque de l'Ecole des hautes études, 1901).
2. A. Di Lella, *The Hebrew Text of Sirach* (The Hague: Mouton & Co., 1966), à propos of 5.4-6, 10.31, 15.14, 15.15, and 16.3.
3. H.P. Ruger, *Text und Textform im hebräischen Sirach* (Berlin: W. de Gruyter, 1970), p. 115.

Ruger has demonstrated, I maintain that the retranslation phenomenon is still the correct explanation of a small number of verses, whose peculiarities cannot otherwise be accounted for satisfactorily. I offer here a couple of instances that other authors have not investigated.

It may be helpful to the reader if I describe the process taken to underlie my hypothesis. Originally a problem arose because the scholar who first translated Ben Sira from Hebrew into Syriac did not understand every word in the Hebrew text, and rendered some of them by paraphrases. This fact is undeniable and will have been noted by all those who have studied the Syriac version. At a later stage I envisage that a Jew who knew both languages well, read both texts and was surprised to see that the Syriac contained phrases that were not clearly in the Hebrew text. Accordingly, as if to make good the omissions, he translated those phrases accurately from Syriac back into Hebrew, and added them in the margins of the Hebrew manuscripts he possessed. He may have been emboldened to do this innovative work because Ben Sira was no longer in the Hebrew canon, although it was still valued in Jewish communities, as can be deduced from the large number of quotations from it in rabbinic writings even after the eighth century CE.[4] At a later date copyists drew them from the margins into the main body of the text.

The first example I will discuss is 32(35).11c, d, since the puzzling addition is still in the margin of manuscript B, as can be seen clearly in the excellent modern edition of the Hebrew text edited by P.C. Beentjes.[5]

The Hebrew that has survived in manuscript B has a number of lacunae in this passage, together with some marginal additions. But the Septuagint is complete, and bears the symmetry of a text that seems not to have been altered. It can be translated as follows:

11   Add a smiling face to all your gifts,
       and be cheerful as you dedicate your tithes.
12   Give to the Most High as he has given to you,
       generously as your means can afford;

---

4.   Seventy-nine quotations of Ben Sira in rabbinic literature were published by A.E. Cowley and A. Neubauer, in *The Original Hebrew of a Portion of Ecclesiasticus* (Oxford: Clarendon Press, 1897), pp. xix-xxx. Nine of these are from the writings of Saadia, gaon of the academy at Sura.

5.   P.C. Beentjes, *The Book of Ben Sira in Hebrew* (Leiden: E.J. Brill, 1997), p. 61.

13   for the Lord is a good rewarder,
  and he will reward you seven times over.[6]

It is reasonable to suppose that this is a faithful rendering of the Hebrew, which makes the divergences in the present state of the surviving Hebrew and the Syriac translation difficult to account for.

A valuable clue is provided by the omission of the word 'tithe' from the Syriac in 11b. It is perfectly clear in the Hebrew מעשרך מעשר מעשיך as can be seen in the text and the marginal variants. All the Greek manuscripts use the technical term δεκατην, but the Syriac has re-written it thus:

and in joy lend to him who does not repay thee.

ܘܠ ܦܪܥ ܠܐ ܠܡܢ ܐܘܙܦ ܒܚܕܘܬܐ

The inspiration for these words may well have been Lk. 6.35 'Lend without hope of return'. The thoughts embodied there (11b) are sufficiently close to the content of 13 to account for the inclusion of 13 immediately after 11b in the Syriac, though in a slightly different wording from the Hebrew and Greek, thus:

ܡܛܠ ܕܐܠܗܐ ܦܪܘܥܐ ܗܘ
ܘܚܕ ܒܚܕ ܗܘ ܦܪܥ ܠܟ

Written thus, it supplied the perfect parallelism to the first Syriac alteration to 11b. One is naturally led to ask what motive could have inspired the Syriac translator to alter v. 11 in this manner. The answer is close at hand. Elsewhere I have shown that this part of ch. 32 (35) has undergone large-scale modifications at the hands of the Ebionites, a Judaeo-Christian sect who were strongly opposed to sacrifices, the Temple, priesthood, and greatly favoured the Mosaic Law and the poor.[7] In fact in the first 11 verses of this chapter there are 13 alterations in the Syriac translation, all of which are consistent with Ebionite theology. The elimination of a reference to tithes would be totally consistent with this outlook.

---

6. English version as in the Jerusalem Bible, following the verse numbers as in the Göttingen Septuagint edited by J. Ziegler.

7. M.M. Winter, 'The Origins of Ben Sira in Syriac (Part I)', *VT* 26 (1977), pp. 237-41. My conclusions have been accepted by the standard authors, cf. P.W. Skehan and A. Di Lella, *The Wisdom of Ben Sira* (AB; Garden City, NY: Doubleday, 1987), p. 57 n. E. Schürer, *The History of the Jewish People in the Time of Jesus Christ* (rev. and ed. G. Vermes, F. Miller and M. Goodman; Edinburgh: T. & T. Clark, 1986), III.1, p. 205 n.

Verse 12 is substantially the same in the three languages, despite some lacunae and marginal additions in the Hebrew. After that the Syriac version has two more lines, whose addition would seem to indicate that the translator was carried away by his enthusiasm for supporting the poor. They are as follows:

For he who gives to the poor lends to God,
for who is a rewarder if not He.

ܡ̇ܢ ܕ̇ܝܗܒ ܠܡܣܟ̈ܢܐ ܠܐܠܗܐ ܗܘ ܡܘܙܦ
ܘܡ̣ܢ ܗ̣ܘ ܦ̇ܪܘܥܐ ܐܠܐ ܐܢ ܗܘ

Presumably the Syriac writer was influenced by Prov. 19.17 ('The man who is kind to the poor lends to God'), but clearly he was not following it slavishly. Perhaps he quoted from memory? The words that occur in the margin of Hebrew manuscript B, written at right angles to the main text, are a literal translation of the Syriac:

מלוה ייי נותן לאביון
ומי בעל גמולות כי אם הוא

This explanation, I maintain, accounts for the divergences of the three languages at this point.

The next example I will discuss is 35(32).11, 12, whose theme is the homely subject of etiquette at dinner parties. Of the three languages it is the Greek that seems to have preserved the original, since it is both coherent and symmetrical. It can be translated thus:

11 On the hour rise up and do not delay,
   Return home and do not be sluggish.
12 There relax and do what you want,
   And do not sin by extravagant speech.

The Hebrew text as preserved in manuscript B bears a strong resemblance to the Greek, but it has been complicated by another line which initially bears some similarity to v. 11, but then diverges from it considerably. There are a couple of lacunae in v. 12, but the sense is clear, except for one phrase.

11 בעת מפקד אל תתאחר   פטר לביתך ושלם רצון
בעת שלחן אל תרבה דברים   ואם עלה על לבך דבר
12 [ ] ל[ ]ך ושלם רצון ביראת אל ולא בחסר כל

In attempting to unravel the complications, it seems advisable to start with the puzzling phrase 'in the time of the table' בעת שלחן. Not only is it meaningless, but such a phrase is found nowhere else in the Hebrew

Bible. The Syriac version contains the same meaningless phrase in exactly the same words: ܟܪܣܝܐ ܕܦܬܘܪܐ. Clearly one was translated from the other, but the question is, in which direction did the translation occur? There is a possible explanation. I suggest that the original, and intelligible, Hebrew בעת מפקד may have been written carelessly, and the Syrian translator, with perhaps a limited knowledge of Hebrew could perhaps have read it as בעת מסבו which is a rare word, but in Song 1.12 it means a round table.[8] Being aware of his limited knowledge of Hebrew, he felt obliged to translate it literally, although it did not quite make sense. Other examples of this kind of translator's humility are to be found in the Vulgate, where Mount Sion was described as 'mons pinguis, mons coagulatus'.

The next phrase in Syriac, is enigmatic 'Do not prolong the talking', ܠܐ ܬܘܓܪ ܠܡܡܠܠܘ. It could be the translation of a Hebrew form different from manuscript B, and which has not survived. But in the interests of restricting the number of hypothetical unknowns, I think it would be safer to regard it as a rather free rendering of the Hebrew, as in manuscript B and that which must have lain behind the Greek. This kind of paraphrase is not uncommon in the Syriac version of Ben Sira. Having translated the words in this way, the writer supplies a virtual comment on the activity that would delay the departure of the guests saying 'even if you remember something', ܘܐܢ ܐܝܬ ܒܟ ܣܘܟܠܐ. On reflection it seems obvious that an amplification of this kind is more likely to have been done by a translator who was prone to paraphrases, rather than by the custodians of the original language. Putting together his slavish translation of the table phrase, interpretative renderings, and accurate translation, the Syriac writer produced a version of these verses as follows:

> At the time of the table do not prolong the talking,
> even if you remember something. Return to your house,
> and do what you want
> in the fear of God and not through vacuousness.

> ܒܙܒܢܐ ܕܦܬܘܪܐ ܠܐ ܬܘܓܪ ܠܡܡܠܠܘ
> ܘܐܢ ܐܝܬ ܒܟ ܣܘܟܠܐ ܦܢܝ ܠܒܝܬܟ
> ܘܥܒܕ ܨܒܝܢܟ ܒܕܚܠܬܗ ܕܐܠܗܐ ܘܠܐ ܒܣܪܝܩܘܬܐ

At a later date a Jewish scholar possessed of a competent knowledge of Syriac, read Ben Sira in that language, and perceived the divergence

8. BDB, p. 687.

from the Hebrew text that he knew. Accordingly, he translated from Syriac into Hebrew so that, in his estimate, the parent text should have no lacunae. This, I suggest, is the most reasonable account for the confused state of the Hebrew text at this point.

An equally fascinating problem, and whose solution is of much wider amplitude, is to ask where and when this exchange between the languages took place. In attempting to solve that problem it seems reasonable to link the retranslations with that other cultural borrowing, namely the system of vowel points.

In the most general terms one can state with reasonable assurance that both communities took vowel points into their biblical (and other) manuscripts after the Arab conquest of the Persian empire, and a large part of the Byzantine empire too. Arabic eventually became the universal language of everyday life and the Jews and Christians kept Hebrew and Syriac for religious purposes. Clearly there was a danger that the correct pronunciation of both languages was threatened as their common use receded from everyday life. For the Jews this was not a new danger. Hebrew had been under threat since the return from the Babylonian exile, when it had to compete with the widespread use of Aramaic in all parts of the Persian empire. Although the Targums were developed from that time onwards, it seems that the correct pronunciation of Hebrew was preserved in the oral tradition of the scribes and later by the Rabbis and their schools.

The Syrians displayed no similar confidence, as Arabic was supplanting their ancestral language. In 640 CE the Arabs annexed the Iranian plateau, and a decade later the last Sassanian emperor, Iazgard III, was assassinated. The Arabs advanced as far as the Oxus river, thus securing the whole of the ancient Persian empire. In the eighth century CE Arabic became the spoken language of all the conquered regions.[9] It is difficult to estimate how long the process took, and how widely Arabic was adopted by minorities who possessed ancient languages reinforced by religious literature and liturgy. Alfred von Kremer has drawn attention to the significance of a regulation issued by Harun Rashyd I who commanded that the Jews and Christians must wear clothes that were

9.   T.W. Arnold, 'Muslim Civilization during the Abbasid Period', in J.A. Tanner, C.W. Brevite-Orton and Z.N. Brooke (eds.), *Cambridge Mediaeval History*, IV (Cambridge: Cambridge University Press, 1927), p. 286. A. Lewis, 'Egypt and Syria', in A.K.S. Lambton and B. Lewis (eds.), *The Cambridge History of Islam*, I/2 (Cambridge: Cambridge University Press, 1970), p. 176.

different from those of the Arabs. He maintains that this was because both groups were speaking Arabic, and would otherwise be indistinguishable from the Arabs. He considered that Arabic took about 200 years to become used universally.[10]

In that overall context it is possible to seek for precise information about the invention of vowel points. The earliest direct evidence is a Syriac manuscript dated 411 CE in the British Library (Add. 12150) which has diacritical points. This was a primitive system of dots written above or below the line to remove any ambiguity about the pronunciation (and by implication, the vowels) of words whose consonants were identical. In the same library, another manuscript (Add. 12136) has a colophon written in 899 CE by Mar Babai of Harran. He stated that the system of nine accentual points was devised by Joseph Huzaya, who was the fourth director of the Christian school at Nisibis. J.B. Segal has suggested that the reality was probably more complicated than Mar Babai envisaged. Some of the accents may have been in use before the time of Joseph Huzaya, and his own specific contribution may have been to separate the pausal from the other accents.[11] Joseph Huzaya directed the school towards the middle of the sixth century CE. By the end of that century the tragic division in the Syriac Church was virtually complete. The frontier between the Persian and Byzantine empires separated the Nestorians from the Jacobites, and indeed the persecuted Nestorians fled into Persia for safety. In the Western part of the Syriac cultural milieu Jacob of Edessa devised another system of vowel pointing about the year 700, which developed eventually into the use of Greek letters above and below the line, to supply the vowels.

It is generally agreed by the standard authors that the Jews borrowed the system of vowel points from the Syrian Christians.[12] Paul Kahle had accepted this unhesitatingly, on account of the similarity between the

10. A. von Kremer, *Culturgeschichte des Orients under den Chalifen*, II (Vienna, 1877), p. 168.

11. J.B. Segal, *The Diacritical Point and the Accents in Syriac* (Oxford: Oxford University Press, 1953), p. 67.

12. T. Nöldeke, *Compendious Syriac Grammar* (London: Williams & Norgate, 2nd edn, 1904), pp. 8, 9. S. Morag, *The Vocalisation Systems of Arabic, Hebrew and Aramaic* (The Hague: Mouton & Co., 1962), pp. 47, 48. D. Barthélemy, *Etudes d'histoire du texte de l'Ancien Testament* (Fribourg: Universitaire Fribourg, 1978), p. 358.

Syriac signs and the most primitive Hebrew pointings.[13] This direction of the cultural flow is also consonant with the fact that Hebrew had survived for many centuries without vowel pointing, although the purity of language was under threat from Aramaic as the vernacular. The swift adoption of vowel pointing by the Syrians, when their language came under threat, must have impressed the Hebrew scholars, if only on account of the foolproof character of the remedy.

Assuming that the Jews and Christians were in sufficiently close and sympathetic contact for the vowel system to have been adopted from one to another, then it is reasonable, I think, to suggest that the retranslations took place in the same milieu.

In trying to decide where these important cultural interchanges might have taken place we are reduced to conjecture, in the absence of specific information. The most obvious region to examine is the northern part of Mesopotamia, since the Christians were very numerous there, and on reasonably good terms with the Jews. In fact, it has been suggested that on the eve of the conquest the majority of the people there were Christians.[14] A likely place for serious dialogue would be a town that had Jewish and Christian communities, and, moreover, schools of both persuasions. The city of Nisibis must be considered as the most likely candidate fulfilling these conditions.

Our knowledge of the Christian school there is due to the chronicle written by Barhadbessabba at the end of the sixth century.[15] The school was founded by Narsai, who had been expelled from Edessa, with the help of Barsauma the bishop of Nisibis. The exact date of the foundation is disputed among the experts. It was some time between 457 (the death of Hiba) and 489 when the school of Edessa (on the Byzantine side of the frontier), was closed by order of the Emperor Zeno.[16] The

---

13. P. Kahle, *Masoreten des Westens*, I (Stuttgart: Kohlhammer Verlag, 1927), p. 52.

14. J.B. Segal, 'The Jews of Northern Mesopotamia before the Rise of Islam', in J.M. Grintz and J. Liver (eds.), *Studies in the Bible Presented to Professor M.H. Segal* (Jerusalem: Israel Society for Biblical Research by Kiryat Sepher, 1964), pp. 32-63.

15. F. Nau (ed.), *La Second Partie de l'Histoire Ecclesiastique de Barhadbessabba* (PO, 9; Paris: Firmin et Didot, 1913). It is the source of a number of later studies such as J. Chabot, *L'école de Nisibe* (Paris: Gabalda, 1909), and A. Vööbus, *A History of the School of Nisibis* (CSCO, 226, Subs 26; Leuven: Peeters, 1965).

16. A. Vööbus, *The Statutes of the School of Nisibis* (Stockholm, 1961), p. 16.

chronicle of Barhadbessabba records that the third director of the school, Mar Abraham, was respected by the Jews of Nisibis, but the same source mentions trouble between the two communities later.[17] The fourth director of the school was Joseph Huzaya, whose work on the pointing system has been discussed above. There seems little doubt that it was this school that produced the system of vowel pointing which was finally adopted by all the East Syrian Christians,[18] particularly in view of the information in the colophon of manuscript Add. 12136.

Granted that the Christians had a school at Nisibis, what of the Jews? Did they have a similar establishment which could adopt and disseminate a vowel system that could be adapted easily to the Hebrew script? At various times in the Persian empire the Jews had schools at Huzal, Nehardea, Mahoza, Pumbeditha, Sura, and indeed at Nisibis. The information about this school is fragmentary. No chronicle has survived from the pen of a grateful alumnus like that of Barhadbessaba concerning the Christian school. Working from notices in the Babylonian Talmud, J. Neusner had deduced that it was founded by R. Judah ben Bathyra (II) at the time of Bar Kochba's rebellion about 135 CE. He left Palestine for Nisibis before the outbreak of hostilities and there received the former students of Rabbi Akiba, who sought refuge in Babylonia. After the cessation of hostilities in Palestine there is no further information about the academy for some centuries, but Neusner considered that it continued working.[19] This opinion is confirmed by the evidence of Cassiodorus. In connection with his desire to found a school of theology in Rome, Cassiodorus wrote the 'Institutiones Divinarum Litterarum' in the middle of the sixth century, as a sort of programme and rationale for theological education. In the preface he mentions other theological schools including Nisibis: 'sicut apud Alexandriam multo tempore fuisse traditur institutum, nunc etiam in Nisibi civitate Syrorum Hebraeis sedulo fertur exponi'[20] ('Just as it is related that instruction [on the Bible] was given for a long time at Alexandria, now also it is reported that in Nisibis of Syria it is taught carefully by the Hebrews'). The sentence is not free from ambiguities, and Baumstark originally considered that he referred to the well-known

17. *Patrologia Orientalis*, vol. 9, pp. 621 and 626.

18. Vööbus, *A History of the School of Nisibis*, pp. 196-203.

19. *b. Yeb.* 108b, and *b. Sanh.* 96a, discussed in J. Neusner, *A History of the Jews in Babylonia* (Leiden: E.J. Brill, 1969), I, pp. 156, 159.

20. Cassiodorus, *Institutiones*; Migne, *PL*, LXX, col. 1105.

Christian school.[21] P. Kahle stated firmly that it was to be understood of the Jewish academy, which was then ('nunc') working at the time when Cassiodorus wrote, that is the middle of the sixth century.[22]

There can be no reasonable doubt about the invention of the system of vowel points by the Christians in Nisibis, and it is highly probable that the Jews adopted it in that same city. We are left with one unanswered question: When did this momentous cultural transaction take place?

In general terms one can surmise that the motive for adopting the vowel pointing would have been when Arabic was being diffused in the erstwhile Persian empire in the seventh and eighth centuries. A more precise indication has been suggested by a modern writer. The colophon of a Cairo manuscript of the prophets, dated 895 CE speaks of Moses ben Asher as then being alive. He is cited in evidence of a particular Tiberiad reading of a disputed word, and this implies a system of vowel pointing. He is the fifth generation in a list of rabbis, and allowing an average of about 25 years for each generation of teachers, one can deduce that the system of vowel pointing was in place by 770 CE at the latest.[23] Joseph Huzaya, referred to above, was the director of the Christian school in the middle of the sixth century. Although the parameters are imprecise, one can conjecture that the adoption of vowel pointing took place between the middle of the sixth century and the middle of the eighth century, at Nisibis. Since one linguistic transaction was taking place in that city, it is not unreasonable to suggest that the textual retranslations between Syriac and Hebrew also took place in the same place and within the same period.

The theory I have outlined is no more than a hypothesis, but it is consistent with all the known facts, and supplies a coherent explanation of the origin of the retranslations in Ben Sira, together with the much wider phenomenon of the diffusion of vowel pointing.

---

21. A. Baumstark, *Geschichte der syrischen Literatur mit Ausschluß der christlich-palästinenischen Texte* (Berlin: W. de Gruyter, 1968 [1922]), p. 114.

22. P. Kahle, *Masoreten des Westens*, p. 53. Baumstark later accepted this view.

23. B. Chiesa, *The Emergence of Hebrew Biblical Pointing* (Frankfurt, 1979), pp. 37-40.

A KARSHUNI (CHRISTIAN ARABIC) ACCOUNT OF THE DESCENT OF THE WATCHERS[*]

Siam Bhayro

In this paper I propose to examine a short section of the British Library manuscript BMOr 4402, a Karshuni[1] version of the *Chronicle* of Michael the Syrian. The section of interest is an extract from the book of *Enoch*. I shall first consider the relationship between the Karshuni account and the other versions of the book of *Enoch*, and then look at some aspects of the extract itself.[2]

The oldest account of the descent of the Watchers is that described in the book of *Enoch*, specifically *1 En.* 6–11. These six chapters are fully attested only in the Ge'ez, or Classical Ethiopic, version which has been preserved by the Ethiopian Church. In addition to the Ethiopic version, there is a Greek version attested in one manuscript, P. Cairo 10759, known as Codex Panopolitanus (hereafter CP). The Ethiopic version appears to have been translated from a Greek *Vorlage* very much akin to CP. The Greek version was itself a translation, probably based upon an Aramaic original. Fragments of an Aramaic version of the book of *Enoch* were discovered among the finds of Qumran Cave 4 (see Fig. 1 below).[3]

*   An earlier version of this paper was presented at the British Association of Jewish Studies annual conference held at the University of Leeds, 4–6 July 2000. Sincere thanks are due to M. Said of the School of Oriental and African Studies, London, for assistance with the Arabic translation. Thanks are also due to Dr S.P. Brock for reading an earlier draft and making a number of valuable comments, especially in relation to the Aleppo manuscript.

1.   Karshuni is Arabic written with a Syriac script.

2.   The summary of the relationship between the different versions which is presented in this paper was given a more in-depth treatment in my PhD thesis, 'A Text-Critical and Literary Analysis of 1 Enoch 6–11' (PhD thesis, University College London, 2000).

3.   The latest critical edition of the Ethiopic version of the book of *Enoch* is

Alongside this sequence, however, runs what we call the *Chronicle Tradition*, that is the use of sections from *1 En.* 6–11 in the wider context of a chronicle of the history of the world. A good example of this is the *Chronicle* of Michael I, or Michael the Syrian, the twelfth-century Jacobite Patriarch of Antioch.

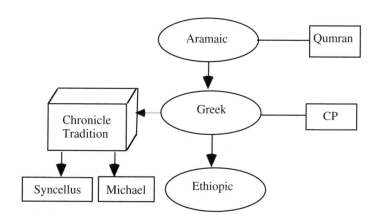

Figure 1. *The relationship between the different versions of 1 Enoch 6–11*[4]

Comprising 21 books, Michael's *Chronicle* runs up until the year 1195 CE. While describing the antediluvian period, in ch. 4 of book 1 Michael relates the origins of kingship upon the earth. According to Michael, kingship did not exist upon the earth before the descent of the 'sons of God'. Adam governed as the father of humanity, and was succeeded by his son Seth. During the reign of Seth, however, humankind

that of M.A. Knibb, *The Ethiopic Book of Enoch* (Oxford: Clarendon Press, 1978). In this paper, the Ethiopic text is based upon my readings of EMML 6686, a seventeenth-century manuscript from the monastery Debra Libanos in the Shewa region of Ethiopia. Print-outs of this manuscript were kindly supplied by Dr Getatchew Haile of the Hill Monastic Manuscript Library, Collegeville, MN. The most recent edition of CP is that of M. Black (ed.), *Apocalypsis henochi graece* (Leiden: E.J. Brill, 1970). For the *editio princeps* of the Qumran Aramaic fragments, cf. J.T. Milik, *The Books of Enoch: Aramaic Fragments of Qumran Cave 4* (Oxford: Clarendon Press, 1976).

4.   In this diagram, the oval boxes represent the languages in which the Enoch traditions are extant whilst the rectangular boxes represent actual versions. The three-dimensional box represents the original chronicle upon which the later chronicles of Michael and Syncellus were based.

divided between those who chose to live in celibacy on Mount Hermon, and those who married and lived on a less exalted plain. Those who dwelt in Mount Hermon were called the 'sons of God' and 'angels'. The descent of these 'angels' in the fortieth year of Jared and the installation of their leader, Shemyazos, as king shattered the peace that previously had reigned upon the earth. Eventually the flood destroyed the empire of Shemyazos.[5]

This account is supported in the margins by excerpts from a number of sources including the book of *Josephus* (ܣܘܦܘܣ ܟܬܒܐ) and the book of *Enoch* (ܚܢܘܟ ܟܬܒܐ).

Michael's excerpt from the book of *Enoch* is rather short, covering approximately *1 En.* 6.1-7, plus some extra material. It was published by Chabot in 1899 and analysed by Brock in 1968.[6]

Regarding the source of Michael's *Enoch* passage, Gelzer demonstrated how later Byzantine scholarship on the Apocrypha and Pseudepigrapha was based upon the accounts of two early fifth-century Alexandrian chronographers, Annianos and Panodoros.[7] Furthermore, it is suggested that Michael the Syrian did not know of these two sources directly, but through a Syriac intermediary—possibly either of the two seventh/eighth-century chroniclers Jacob of Edessa and John of Litarba (see fig. 2 below).[8]

---

5.   Cf. W. Adler, *Time Immemorial: Archaic History and its Sources in Christian Chronography from Julius Africanus to George Syncellus* (Washington, DC: Dumbarton Oaks, 1989), pp. 118-22. Adler discusses the literary context in which the 'sons of God' of Gen. 6.2 are interpreted as being humans rather than angels as in the Book of Watchers.

6.   Cf. J.B. Chabot (ed. and transl.), *Chronique de Michel le Syrien: Patriarche jacobite d'Antioche 1166–1199* (Paris: Ernest Leroux, 1899), pp. 3-4 (text), pp. 7-8 (translation); S.P. Brock, 'A Fragment of Enoch in Syriac', *JTS* NS 19 (1968), pp. 626-31.

7.   Gelzer suggested that it was from Panodoros through Annianos that Old Testament Apocryphal sources reached later Byzantine scholarship. This was demonstrated with reference to *Jubilees* and argued that it was the same for *Enoch*; cf. H. Gelzer, *Sextus Julius Africanus und die byzantinische Chronographie* (2 vols., Leipzig; 1880–98), II, pp. 262-64. Cf. also the discussion in Brock, 'Fragment of Enoch', p. 628.

8.   Brock, 'Fragment of Enoch', pp. 626, 629.

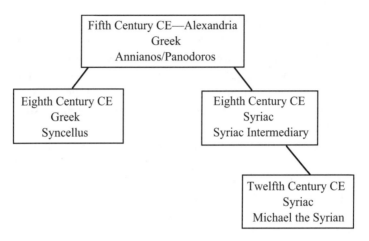

Figure 2. *The Sources of the* Chronicle tradition

The other important chronography is that of Georgius Syncellus. Writing at the end of the eighth century, Syncellus quotes twice from *1 En.* 6–11. It is interesting that our knowledge of Panodoros is almost exclusively derived from Syncellus. As we can see from Figure 2 above, it is possible that both Michael's Syriac source and Syncellus were translated from the same Alexandrian source in the same period.

In view of this, Brock notes that 'it is not surprising…that Michael's Syriac quotation agrees most closely with the Greek of Synkellos'.[9]

We see two examples of this agreement between the chroniclers Michael and Syncellus, on the one hand, and the Ethiopic and CP on the other, right at the start of our passage. The first example relates to the description of the birth of human females in *1 En.* 6.1. Both the Ethiopic and CP use two adjectives for the daughters, while the chronicle sources only use one:

1 Enoch 6.1

Ethiopic   ተወልዳ ፡ ሎሙ ፡ አዋልድ ፡ ሠናያት ፡ ወሳሁያት ::
           …beautiful and pretty daughters were born to them.

Michael   ܐܬܝܠܕ̈ܝ ܠܒܢ̈ܝ ܐܢܫܐ ܒܢ̈ܬܐ ܫܦܝܪ̈ܬܐ
           …fair daughters were born to the sons of man.

Greek   CP: ἐγεννήθησαν θυγατέρες ὡραῖαι καὶ καλαί.
                …fitting and beautiful daughters were born.

9.   Brock, 'Fragment of Enoch', p. 629.

Syn: ἐγεννήθησαν αὐτοῖς θυγατέρες ὡραῖαι.
...fitting daughters were born to them.

In the next verse, the angels conspire to take human wives for themselves. Both the Ethiopic and CP use the imperative 'Come!' whilst the Chronicle sources omit this:

1 Enoch 6.2

Ethiopic ንዑ ፡ ንኅረይ ፡ ለነ ፡ አንስተ ፡ እምውሉደ ፡ ሰብእ
Come! Let us choose for ourselves wives from the sons of men.

Michael ܟܣܬܟܐ ܟܙܝܟ (*sic*)[10] ܟܕܝܢ ܡܢ ܟܢܫ ܠ ܟܠܝ
Let us choose for ourselves wives from the daughters of the men of the earth.

Greek   CP: Δεῦτε ἐκλεξώμεθα ἑαυτοῖς ψυναῖκας ἀπὸ τῶν ἀνθρώπων
Come! Let us choose for ourselves wives from the men.

Syn: ἐκλεξώμεθα ἑαυτοῖς γυναῖκας ἀπὸ τῶν θυγατέρων τῶν ἀνθρώπων τῆς γῆς
Let us choose for ourselves wives from the daughters of the men of the earth.

In the above example, both the Ethiopic and CP share readings that are identical save for a slight difference between 'sons of men' (ውሉደ ፡ ሰብእ) and 'men' (ἀνθρώπων). Both the chronicler sources differ considerably, however, using the longer phrase 'the daughters of the men of the earth' (ܟܣܬܟܐ ܟܙܝܟ ܟܕܝܢ; τῶν θυγατέρων τῶν ἀνθρώπων τῆς γῆς) rather than sons.

This use of *daughters* rather than *sons* represents the triumph of sense over a literal word-for-word rendering in the priority of the original chronicler—it is far more sensible for the angels to choose their partners from the female inhabitants of the earth. It also demonstrates the extent to which the interpretation of the 'sons of God' as being particularly pious humans (discussed above) influenced the chronographer. Thus the issue is no longer angels choosing humans but the 'sons of Seth' choosing wives from the 'daughters of Cain'. It is this mingling of the pious Sethites with the impious Cainites which brings ruin to the earth.

---

10. The Aleppo manuscript appears to have ܟܙܝ ܕܝܢ which differs from Chabot's copy.

Thus we have a number of readings that may be assigned specifically to the chronicle tradition, of which we have seen three examples: the use of only one adjective for the daughters in *1 En.* 6.1 and, in *1 En.* 6.2, the omission of the imperative 'Come!' and the use of the longer phrase 'daughters of the men of the earth'.

In addition to the differences between the Chronicle tradition and the main Enoch tradition, there are also variations within the chronicle tradition itself. Thus in *1 En.* 6.1, Michael's Chronicle has a longer text, with Syncellus not representing Michael's 'upon the earth in those days' (ܟܕ ܐܝܬ ܒܝܘܡܬܐ ܗܢܝܢ):

1 Enoch 6.1

Michael   ܘܗܘܐ ܗܕܐ ܕܟܕ ܣܓܝ ܒܢܝ̈ܐ ܐܢܫܐ ܥܠ ܐܪܥܐ ܒܝܘܡܬܐ ܗܢܝܢ
            And it was that when the sons of man increased upon the earth in
            those days...

Syncellus καὶ ἐγένετο ὅτε ἐπληθύνθησαν οἱ υἱοὶ τῶν ἀνθρώπων
            And it happened when the sons of men multiplied...

The Chronicle tradition, therefore, is not a uniform one—there are differences between its two attestations. This has implications for the textual analysis of *1 En.* 6–11, where an often complex series of relationships between the different versions must be taken into consideration. It was in the process of gathering the data for such an analysis that I came across the British Library manuscript BMOr 4402, which is a Karshuni translation of Michael the Syrian's *Chronicle*.

Dated to 1846, this Karshuni version was translated directly from the Syriac *Vorlage* of the copy made for Chabot. This Syriac *Vorlage* is housed in the Church of the Edessenes (St George) in Aleppo.[11] For the purpose of the present discussion, the relevant section appears in lines 8-26 on the left-hand column of page 3 recto (see photograph below), beginning with the opening 'From the Book of Enoch' (ܡܢ ܟܬܒܐ ܕܚܢܘܟ) and ending at the start of the next quote 'From the Book of Josephus' (ܡܢ ܟܬܒܐ ܕܝܘܣܝܦܘܣ).[12]

---

11. I am grateful to Dr S. Brock for this information.
12. A transcription and translation of the extract is given at the end of the paper. Nestorian script is used for transcribing BMOr 4402 because it is closer than the Estrangela to the Serta script of the manuscript.

We note firstly that the Karshuni version corresponds to Chabot's facsimile of the Syriac version with respect to the readings that are peculiar to the Chronicle tradition. Thus the Chronicle tradition reading of *1 En*. 6.1 is reflected in the Karshuni version which also has only the one adjective: ܘܘܠܕ ܠܠܒܫܪ ܒܢܐܬ ܚܣܢܐܬ 'and fair daughters were born to the men.'

We note further that the Karshuni version also agrees with Chabot's Syriac text in *1 En*. 6.2, omitting the imperative 'Come!' and reading the 'daughters of the men of the earth': ܦܠܢܟܬܐܪ ܠܢܐ ܢܣܐ ܡܢ ܒܢܐܬ ܒܢܝ ܐܠܐܪܕܝܝܢ 'Let us choose for ourselves wives from the daughters of the men of the earth'.

As one would expect, where there are differences between Syncellus and Michael, the Karshuni version agrees with the text of Michael rather than with Syncellus's. We noted above that the Syriac version of *1 En*. 6.1 includes the phrase ܥܠ ܐܪܥܐ ܒܗܢܘܢ ܝܘܡܬܐ 'upon the earth in those days', which is omitted in Syncellus's version. The Karshuni version's ܥܠܝ ܐܠܐܪܨ ܦܝ ܬܠܟ ܐܠܐܝܐܡ corresponds to the ܥܠ ܐܪܥܐ ܒܗܢܘܢ ܝܘܡܬܐ of Michael's text.

In view of all this, it is surprising that the Karshuni version diverges from the 'expected reading' when introducing the central characters of the narrative in *1 En*. 6.2. In the Ethiopic and CP, those who descend from heaven to earth are called 'the angels—the sons of heaven' (መላእክት ፡ ውሉደ ፡ ሰማያት; οἱ ἄγγελοι υἱοὶ οὐρανοῦ), while in Michael and Syncellus they are called simply 'the Watchers' (ܥܝܪ̈ܐ; οἱ ἐγρήγοροι).

Both terms represent a distinct treatment of the Hebrew expression בני־האלהים as found in Gen. 6.2. The Ethiopic and CP clarify who these are, while the chroniclers make use of a specific technical term and assume that the reader would understand to whom it refers. Surprisingly, the Karshuni extract rejects both of these methods, reverting back to the form found in Gen. 6.2 (which is not attested in any of the Enoch versions), transliterating the Hebrew expression as ܒܢܘ ܐܠܠܘܗܝܡ.[13] This

13. We have two possible explanations for the use of ܒܢܘ ܐܠܠܘܗܝܡ rather than the expected ܥܝܪ̈ܐ. It is possibly derived from the Peshitta's use of ܒܢܝ ܐܠܠܘܗܝܡ in Gen. 6.2. It could also be derived from the two earlier occurrences of this phrase in the Karshuni version, both of which are found on p. 2 verso of BMOr 4402: line 2—ܒܢܘ ܐܠܠܘܗܝܡ, line 24—ܒܢܝ ܐܠܠܘܗܝܡ.

suggests that the Karshuni version is capable of furnishing the Enoch tradition with original, independent readings.

We note, finally, that when Brock published the Syriac excerpt in 1968, he identified two rather problematic phrases which occur towards the end of the extract. The Karshuni version sheds an interesting light upon these problems.

Phrase 1

ܘܗܠܝܢ ܐܬܝܗܘܢ ܗܘܘ ܐܟ̈ܝܐ ܕܣܡܝܢ ܪ̈ܝܫܝ ܥܣܪ̈ܐ ܕܝܠܗܘܢ

And these, their chiefs of ten, were ?ܕܣܡܝܢ ܐܟ̈ܝܐ?

In particular, ܐܟ̈ܝܐ ܕܣܡܝܢ is problematic. Brock suggested that it must be corrupt.[14] The Karshuni version reads ܩܕ ܥܡܝܬ ܥܩܘܠ ܪ̈ܘܣ ܥܫܪ ܥܘܪܗܡ 'the senses of their chiefs of tens had been blinded', offering ܥܡܝܬ ܥܩܘܠ '(whose) minds were blinded' for the problematic ܐܟ̈ܝܐ ܕܣܡܝܢ. The Karshuni version's ܥܡܝܬ implies that the ܕܣܡܝܢ should be read as ܕܣܡܝܐ.[15]

Phrase 2

ܘܟܘܟܒܐܝܠ ܪܝܫܐ ܗܘ̇ ܕܪ̈ ܐܠܦ ܠܒܢܝܢܫܐ ܐܣܛܪܘܢܘܡܝܐ
ܗ ܚܘܕܪ̈ܝܬܐ ܕܫܡܫܐ ܫܤ ܐܘܕ̈ܝܐ ܡܬܡܢܝܢ

Kokab'il, who was head of the two hundred, taught the sons of man astronomy, that is the orbit of the sun, 360 ?ܐܘܕܝܐ? being numbered.

For ܐܘܕܝܐ, Brock gives the Greek ζώδια 'zodiacs',[16] which assumes that the scribe has confused ܐ with ܙ (a confusion which is certainly possible in the Serta script). This appears to be confirmed by the Karshuni version's ܒܪ̈ܘܓ 'horoscopes'.

It is worth noting at this point the use of ܘ to represent two different Hebrew vowels. Its use in ܥܘܪܗܡ makes sense, but we would have expected ܥܡܝ rather than ܥܡܘ. A close examination of the manuscript appears to suggest that ܥܡܝ was originally written but later changed to ܥܡܘ.

14. Brock, 'Fragment of Enoch', p. 631 n. 1.

15. Chabot's copy can certainly be read this way. Brock has further confirmed that this is the case for the Aleppo manuscript. This still leaves the ܐܟ̈ܝܐ / ܥܩܘܠ unexplained. It is possible that the Syriac version's ܐܟ̈ܝܐ was originally a reference to the 'Watchers' (ܥܝܪ̈ܐ)—'the Watchers who were blinded'——and that a problem with the *Vorlage* has produced both ܐܟ̈ܝܐ and ܥܩܘܠ.

16. Brock, 'Fragment of Enoch', p. 631.

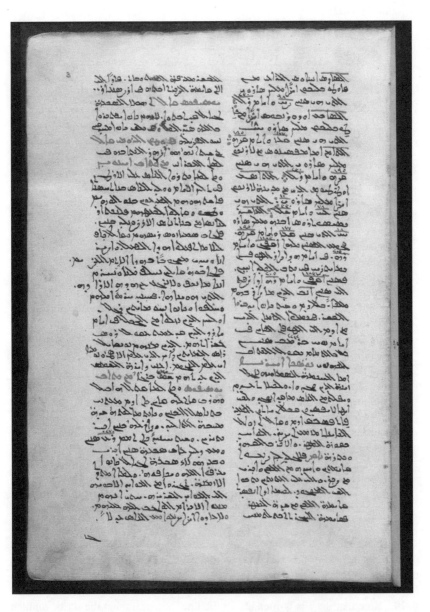

BMOr 4402, p. 3 recto. Reproduced by permission of the British Library.

BMOr 4402

Transcription:

ܡܢ ܟܬܒܐ ܕܚܢܘܟ

ܘܗܘܐ ܟܕ ܣܓܝܘ ܒܢܝ ܐܢܫܐ ܥܠ ܐܪܥܐ ܒܗܢܘܢ ܝܘܡܬܐ ܘܐܬܝܠܕ ܠܗܘܢ ܒܢܬܐ ܫܦܝܪܬܐ [17]ܕܐܬܩܪܝܘ ܒܢܝ ܐܠܗܐ ܘܐܬܪܓܪܓܘ {erasure} ܘܐܡܪܘ ܚܕ ܠܚܕ ܢܓܒܐ ܠܢ ܢܫܐ ܡܢ ܒܢܬ ܒܢܝ ܐܢܫܐ ܕܐܪܥܐ ܘܢܘܠܕ ܒܢܝܐ. ܘܥܢܐ ܣܡܝܐܙܘܣ ܪܫܗܘܢ ܘܐܡܪ ܕܚܠ ܐܢܐ ܕܠܡܐ ܠܐ ܬܥܒܕܘܢ ܗܢܐ ܣܘܥܪܢܐ ܘܐܢܐ ܒܠܚܘܕܝ ܐܬܚܝܒ ܒܗܢܐ ܚܛܗܐ ܪܒܐ. ܘܥܢܘ ܐܡܪܝܢ ܠܗ ܡܘܡܝܢܢ ܟܠܢ ܘܢܕܪܝܢܢ ܢܕܪܐ ܕܠܐ ܢܫܠܐ. [18]ܘܥܢܘ[19] ܬܡܢ ܟܠܗܘܢ ܢܣܟ ܚܠܦܐ ܘܣܥܪ ܪܢܗ ܡܢ ܢܚܬ ܘܐܪܢܕܟܝܠ ܡܢ ܗܘܐ ܪܝܫ ܕܬܪܝܢܡܐ ܘܗܘ ܐܠܦ. ܟܘܢܣ ܣܦܪܘܬܐ ܚܠܦܐ ܘܣܟܠܐ ܘܚܕܢܐ ܒܝܬ ܡܢܬܢܡ ܗܘ ܐܘܠܦܢ ܕܝܠܗ ܗܘ ܐܘܠܦ ܬܠܬܡܐܐ. ܕܐܪܝܥ ܡܢ ܐܝܠܝܢܐ ܟܕ ܐܝܠܐ ܪܒ ܠܢܝܗ ܣܥܪ ܪܫܐ ܗܘ ܚܣܡܬ ܟܒܐ. ܬܠܬܡܐܐ[20]ܕܐܪܡܓܙܘܣ ܚܕ ܡܢܗܘܢ ܟܘܟܒܐܝܠ. ܝܝܢܐ ܕܬܪܝܢܡܐ ܬܠܬܡܐ[21] ܪܣܐܡ ܒܓܝܗ.

Translation:

From the book of Enoch

And it was when the men increased upon the earth in those days, and fair daughters were born to the men, that those who are named the *sons of God* lusted after them. And they said to each other, 'Let us choose for ourselves wives from the daughters of the men of the earth and beget sons.'

And Semi'azos, their head, answered and said, 'I fear lest you will not do this action, and I alone will become condemned in this great sin.'

And they answered him saying, 'We swear, all of us, and we make a vow that we shall not stop nor turn from this purpose which we desired.'

And there all of them were excommunicated and they swore. And they were about two hundred persons, those who descended from the mountain in the days of Jared, those that the senses of their chiefs of tens had been blinded.

One of whom, *Kokabil*—the head of the two hundred, that one taught astronomy, that is the science of the stars, I mean the cycle of the sun whose number is 360 horoscopes.

17. Note that the ܐ is written above the line. It is possible that the scribe ran out of space as the end of the rest of the word already exceeds the end of the previous nine lines on the page.

18. Part of the ܡ is missing in the manuscript, but the reading is not in doubt.

19. Note that the ܘ is written above the line. It appears that the scribe omitted this originally.

20. Note that the ܒܝܬ is written above the line. As the word ܕܐܪܡܓܙܘܣ is rather long, the scribe appears to have attempted not to exceed the established column width. Furthermore, note the way in which the ܒ is written above the ܬ.

21. Above the ܫܒ—360, the same number is written in Arabic numerals. This appears to have been added by a later scribe.

Part IV
THE EASTERN CHURCH TRADITION

THE RELATION BETWEEN BIBLICAL TEXT AND LECTIONARY SYSTEMS IN THE EASTERN CHURCH[*]

Konrad D. Jenner

This contribution is dedicated to the memory of the late Michael Weitzman. When Michael and I first met, I found that his approach complemented that of our Institute in Leiden: where we were concentrating primarily on textual criticism and history, and the relations between MSS, Michael's principal interests were the Syriac language itself, its linguistic features, to the study of which he applied statistical techniques, the development of textual traditions, and related cultural and historical issues. It was a privilege to discuss with him our studies of the relationship between the Hebrew Bible or Christian Old Testament and the ancient versions, especially with respect to the Syriac Bible, known as the Peshitta. Our discussions concentrated on the use of the Peshitta in general, rather than on its use in liturgy: the present essay is intended to fill this gap. The analysis builds on my early research, under the supervision of Dr W. Baars, which led to my dissertation and to other subsequent work.[1] It is based on manuscripts up to and including the tenth century,[2] that is the ancient representatives of the Syriac Old

*   Acknowledgement: I owe much gratitude to Gillian Greenberg for her kind assistance in upgrading the quality of the English and in preparing this contribution for publication.

1.   K.D. Jenner, *De perikopentitels van de geïllustreerde Syrische kanselbijbel van Parijs (MS Paris, Bibliothèque Nationale, Syriaque 341): Een vergelijkend onderzoek naar de oudste syrische perikopenstelsels* (Dissertation, Leiden University, 1993); K.D. Jenner, 'The Development of Syriac Lectionary Systems: A Discussion of the Opinion of P. Kannookadan', *The Harp* 10.1 (1997), pp. 9-24.

2.   Manuscripts later than the tenth century are excluded from this study. The ninth- and tenth-century lectionary manuscripts or pericope books are also excluded, since their systems of lessons are based on a more extensive liturgical calendar and reflect a different selection criterion. The meticulous description of the

Testament, and it offers a comparison of the lectionary systems as represented in:

1. the ancient biblical manuscripts of the Peshitta;
2. manuscripts of Jacob of Edessa's revised Bible;
3. Syrohexaplaric manuscripts;
4. a lectionary system listed in a seventh century survey and edited in translation by F.C. Burkitt.[3]

The overall aim of this comparison is to determine whether these lectionary systems are related to one another. The specific issue is to identify the basis of the system developed by Jacob of Edessa, showing how, and to what extent, he depended on any of the other systems. Did he know these systems, did he copy or modify one of them, or did he conflate specific elements from more than one? There are further important questions, outside the scope of the present paper: what were the theological and other (hidden) motives and criteria that determined the selections of pericopes, and why were many pericopes excluded from the selections? The answer to these questions must wait for another study.

The findings presented here may serve as guidelines for further investigation into the reception history of the Syriac Bible, particularly the way in which the ancient text of the Old Testament was actualized by the Syrian Christians in the course of centuries, in the pluriformity of cultural areas, and in the different rites. This actualization may be seen as an indicator of the interaction between culture, society and religion, between church and secular institutions. Viewed thus, the actualization of the Bible in liturgy is not only a matter of church history, but also forms an integral part of cultural, social and sometimes political history.

Of Jacob's edition, only Genesis, Exodus, Samuel, Isaiah, Ezekiel and Daniel are known to have survived.[4] The Syrohexapla is not extant for every biblical book. Ancient manuscripts containing some or all of a system of lessons or pericopes survive for the following books: Genesis,

---

lectionary MSS by W. Baars is to be found in the keeping of the Peshitta Institute, Leiden.

3.   F.C. Burkitt, 'The Early Syriac Lectionary System', *Proceedings of the British Academy* 10 (1923), pp. 301-38.

4.   See W. Baars, 'Ein neugefundenes Bruchstück aus der syrischen Bibelrevision des Jakob von Edessa', *VT* 18 (1968), pp. 548-49.

Exodus, Job, Joshua, Judges, Samuel, Kings, Proverbs, Ecclesiastes, Wisdom, Isaiah, Ezekiel, Daniel and Ben Sira.[5] The seventh-century survey of lessons does not refer to pericopes in the books of Ecclesiastes, Wisdom of Solomon, Song of Songs, Nahum, Zephaniah, Bel and the Dragon, or Maccabees. The comparisons on which the present analysis is based are therefore derived from study of 44 MSS, of which 26 are Peshitta MSS, 12 are Syrohexaplaric, 5 are MSS of Jacob of Edessa's revision, and 1 is that of Burkitt's edition of the lectionary system referred to above. Details of these MSS, and of the libraries where they are held, are given in Appendix 2.

The ancient Old Testament Peshitta manuscripts contain elements of a number of different lectionary systems; this was discussed in my dissertation.[6] The differences concern the selection and length of pericopes, the ecclesiastical or liturgical calendar, the connection between pericopes, festival and commemoration days, as well as the terminology, layout, and orthography of the titles. The liturgical titles in Jacob of Edessa's biblical manuscripts (JE) vary, as do those in the Peshitta manuscripts (P). However, all copies of Jacob's Bible have similar layout: all liturgical titles are placed in the margins,[7] never appearing in a column of text.

In the JE manuscript *MS Paris, Bibliothèque Nationale, Syr 26* the following seven titles are added to the text of Genesis and Exodus:[8]

1. Gen. 41.41   p. 84   Commemoration of ////
Tuesday in the [week] of Rest = 7h5

ܡ̇ܘ, ܒܪܗܕܝܐ ܪ /// ܥܛܪܝܬܐ ܟܝܟ̈ ܪ /// ܪ ܝܒܘܝܢܬܐ   1

2. Gen. 41.53   p. 84   Sunday after Epiphany

ܡ̇ܘ, ܫܘܒܚܪܐ ܪܕܢܚܐ ܪܚܕ   2

3. Gen. 48.22   p. 85   Ascension of our Lord
Hosanna (Palm Sunday)

ܡ̇ܘ, ܣܘܠܩܐ ܪܕܡܪܢ ܥܘܫܥܢܐ   3

---

5. See W. Baars, *New Syro-Hexaplaric Texts, Edited, Commented upon and Compared with the Septuagint* (Leiden: E.J. Brill, 1968), pp. 1-40.

6. See Jenner, *De perikopentitels*, ch. 2 and supplements B and C. See also Burkitt, 'Lectionary System', pp. 301-18.

7. Most of these titles, outside the textual columns, have apparently been added by a later, though pre-tenth century, hand.

8. The manuscript contains Gen. 1.1-16, 3.21–32.12, 33.11–43.32, 44.29–50.26 and Exod. 1.1–15.20, 17.7–25.17, 26.12–33.19, 34.30–35.22, 36.13–40.38. No lessons have been taken from the portions of Leviticus, Numbers or Deuteronomy.

4. Exod. 2.23   p. 111   the Departed

ܩ 4 ܕܥ̈ܢ̈ܝܕܐ

5. Exod. 3.1   p. 111   the Departed = L 7h13 8b1mg SH2 [DT DEC]
                              Sunday after Christmas

ܩ 5 ܕܥ̈ܢ̈ܝܕܐ ܘܒܚܕܒܫܒܐ ܕܒܬܪ ܝܠܕܐ

6. Exod. 4.18   p. 116   Sunday /////

ܩ 6 ܕܒܚܕܒܫ/////

7. Exod. 12.29   p. 135   the Departed = 7h13 8b1mg SH2 [DEC] 7

ܗܘ ܕܝܠ̈ܝܕ̈ܐ 7

Comparison of the lessons listed above with those in the P manuscripts (5b1, 7a1, 7h5, 7h13, 7k4, 7k12, 8a1 and 8b1), the Syrohexaplaric manuscripts (SHM, SH1 and SH2, details see Appendix 3), and
in Burkitt's lectionary edition (L) shows:

1. JE and 7h5 share the lesson of Gen. 41.41 for Tuesday of the
    week of rest. The titles differ hardly at all in terminology (i.e.
    the word 'week'), but do differ with respect to the eccles-
    iastical calendar in that JE reads, in addition, the lesson for the
    commemoration of an unknown person.

2. Exod. 3.1 is related to the commemoration of the departed in
    JE as well as in 8b1mg and SH2. However, the terminology of
    the three titles differs: two, 8b1mg and SH2, explicitly add the
    liturgical marker 'for the commemoration of'; JE does not.

3. JE, L, 7h13, 8b1mg and SH2 twice share an incipit, but do not
    relate the pericopes in question to the same day of the eccles-
    iastical calendar: Exod. 3.1 (Christmas = 7h13, 8b1mg and
    SH2; Saturday of the first (?) week of the Fast = L; Sunday 6 =
    8b1mg), and Exod. 12.29 (Good Friday = L and 7h13; Holy
    Saturday = 8b1mg; Eve of Easter or the Night of the Gospel =
    SH2; Sunday 20 = 8b1mg SH2).

Thus, Gen. 41.41 and Exod. 3.1 are the only two lessons shared by
JE-Genesis and JE-Exodus with the Genesis and Exodus lessons
attested in the other manuscripts, that is: 37 lessons in L, 137 in the P
manuscripts,[9] and 68 in both SH1[10] and SH2.[11] The JE manuscripts

9.   Only 35 titles of the lessons in the P-MSS are written in the textual column.
10. The incipits of this MS refer to liturgical titles.
11. 65 of the incipits of this MS refer to liturgical titles.

have no incipit in common with the three pericopes[12] as attested for these two books in the Syrohexaplaric Pentateuch manuscript SHM.

The titles of L, P and JE employ remarkably varied terminology: four different marks identify the incipits of lessons and pericopes. The evidence in Genesis and Exodus thus suggests a discrepancy, or even a complete lack of any relationship or correspondence, between the lectionary system in JE-Genesis and JE-Exodus on the one hand and those of L, the P and SH manuscripts on the other. There is no apparent reason to assume a source common to JE-Genesis, JE-Exodus, and any of the other systems, and it therefore seems reasonable to conclude that, with respect to Genesis and Exodus, Jacob of Edessa did not use an existing lectionary system but made his own selection of lessons.

This conclusion is strongly supported by the discussion below. For SHM, the picture is as follows for the three pericopes Exod. 15.22, 19.17 and 34.27. The first incipit is testified once as a lesson in the text column of 7h13 (Epiphany), and twice in the margins of 8b1 ([Thursday] in the second week of baptism, and the consecration of the cross).[13] The second incipit is not testified,[14] whereas the third one is attested for the sixth Sunday after Epiphany in the margin of 8b1.[15] These three instances are insufficient to establish a relationship between the lectionary systems attached to SHM and 8b1. The findings in Leviticus, Numbers and Deuteronomy are similar. For Leviticus, the six incipits in the margins of 8b1[16] do not correspond with the four in the margins of SHM,[17] of which details are given in Appendix 2. In Numbers, four incipits and corresponding titles are found in the margins of 5b1; seven in L, one in the margin of 7a1, 16 in the margins of 8b1, and

---

12. The term pericope is used, since in this Syrohexaplaric manuscript the incipits of the lessons are not related to a title referring to a day of the ecclesiastical or liturgical calendar. This manuscript must be considered here, although its date is uncertain; A. Vööbus suggests the twelfth century.

13. Jenner, *De perikopentitels*, p. 376.

14. The nearest incipit is Exod. 19.20 (lesson 27), see Jenner, *De periko-pentitels*, p. 376.

15. See Jenner, *De perikopentitels*, p. 376.

16. Lev. 8.1 (twice), 12.1, 16.1, 23.1, and 26.3 (Jenner, *De perikopentitels*, p. 377).

17. There is no lectionary system for Leviticus in L and the ancient P-MSS; SHM is the only witness for a lectionary system in the Syro-hexaplaric tradition for Leviticus.

six in the text columns of 8a1.[18] In SHM, however, there are seven instances, one of which (Num. 20.1) corresponds with the lesson for Tuesday in the Great Week;[19] the remainder (for details see Appendix 3) have a different incipit. In Deuteronomy in 26 cases a lesson is attested in the margins of 8b1, whereas four are preserved in L, two in 6h6, and four in 8a1.[20] Deuteronomy 16.1 (fol. 171b) is the only one of the six pericopes in SHM to correspond with one of the instances listed; there is no correspondence with the remaining five (see Appendix 3).

There is no evidence for a liturgical relationship between SH1 and the P manuscripts.[21] It seems, however, that there is a close relationship between SH2 and the marginal readings in 8b1; details are given in Appendix 3. Nearly all incipits of SH2 are shared with 8b1mg, and in many cases the titles of both manuscripts are related to the same ecclesiastical festival days.[22] SH3 contains eight incipits (see Appendix 3) of which six are shared with 8b1mg; there is no reason to assume a liturgical relationship between these manuscripts. Four of the eight pericopes in SH3 lack a liturgical title; the titles of the remaining four do not refer to the same festival day as that specified in 8b1mg.[23] In Deuteronomy, only the P manuscripts present a lectionary system.[24]

Since the books of Job, Joshua, Judges and Ruth are not extant in the copies of Jacob of Edessa's Bible, we have no evidence of the lectionary systems attached thereto. The Syrohexaplaric manuscripts SH4, SH5,[25] SH6 and SH7 (for details see Appendix 3) each contain a lectionary system,[26] none of which corresponds with that of the P manuscripts.[27]

---

18. See Jenner, *De perikopentitels*, p. 377.

19. L, 8a1 and 8b1mg.

20. See Jenner, *De perikopentitels*, pp. 377-78.

21. See Jenner, *De perikopentitels*, p. 374. This similarity in the system of lessons and ecclesiastical calendar between a SH-MS and a P-MS may indicate the milieu of 8b1, which has a different type of P-text (see M.D. Koster, *The Peshitta of Exodus: The Development of its Text in the Course of Fifteen Centuries* (Studia Semitica Neerlandica, 19; Assen: Van Gorcum, 1977), pp. 14, 136, 168-70).

22. See Jenner, *De perikopentitels*, pp. 419-20.

23. See Jenner, *De perikopentitels*, p. 377.

24. See Jenner, *De perikopentitels*, pp. 377-78. There is no JE- and SH-evidence.

25. The ancient P-MSS give no lectionary system for this book.

26. With the exception of Judg. 5.1-11, these MSS lack liturgical titles, and give in the margin only the markers of the incipits and explicits of the lessons.

27. See Jenner, *De perikopentitels*, pp. 378-81. Cf. Burkitt, 'Lectionary System'.

The JE manuscript *MS London, British Library, Additional 14429* contains the following 29 titles attached to the text of Samuel.[28]

1. 1 Sam. 1.1-13 fol. 5a New Sunday = 6h4mg 7h12 7k3
   1 ܩܪ̈ܝ، ܕܚܕܒܫܒܐ ܒܫܒܐ ܚܕܬܐ
2. 1 Sam. 1.19-28 fol. 7a the Birth of our Lord (Christmas) = 6h1mg 6h4mg(?!) 7k3mg 8a1 [DT]
   2 ܩܪ̈ܝ، ܕܝܠܕܗ ܕܡܪܢ
3. 1 Sam. 2.1-10 fol. 8a the Mother of God (the Virgin Mary)
   3 ܩܪ̈ܝ، ܕܝܠܕܬ ܐܠܗܐ
4. 1 Sam. 2.11-27 fol. 9b Sunday of the fifth (week) of fasting
   4 ܩܪ̈ܝ، ܕܚܕܒܫܒܐ ܕܚܡܫܐ ܕܨܘܡܐ
5. 1 Sam. 3.1-14 fol. 12b Tonsure
   5 ܩܪ̈ܝ، ܕܣܘܦܪܐ
6. 1 Sam. 4.18-22 fol. 16b Monday in the Great (Holy) week = 7h12mg
   6 ܩܪ̈ܝ، ܕܬܪ̈ܝܢ ܒܫܒܐ ܕܫܒܬܐ ܪܒܬܐ
7. 1 Sam. 7.2-17 fol. 21b the beginning of the Fast (Lent) = L
   Tuesday in the Great (Holy) week = L
   7 ܩܪ̈ܝ، ܕܡܫܪܝ ܨܘܡܐ ܘܕܬܠܬܐ ܒܫܒܐ ܕܫܒܬܐ ܪܒܬܐ
8. 1 Sam. 8.4-18 fol. 23b Sunday in the second week of the Fast (Lent)
   8 ܕܚܕܒܫܒܐ ܕܬܪ̈ܬܝܢ ܕܨܘܡܐ
9. 1 Sam. 9.1-14 fol. 25b Wednesday in the Great (Holy) week = L <8a1>
   9 ܩܪ̈ܝ، ܕܐܪܒܥܐ ܒܫܒܐ ܕܫܒܬܐ ܪܒܬܐ
10. 1 Sam. 10.17 fol. 30b Thursday of the Mystery (Maundy Thursday) = L 6h4mg 7h12mg {8a1} [DT]
    10 ܩܪ̈ܝ، ܕܚܡܫܐ ܕܪܐܙܐ
11. 1 Sam. 11.13–12.5 fol. 33a Commemoration of the Bishops and Departed = L 7h12mg [DT DEC DI]
    11 ܩܪ̈ܝ، ܕܥܘܗܕܢ ܐܦܝܣܩܘܦܐ ܘܕܥܢܝ̈ܕܐ
12. 1 Sam. 12.6-12 fol. 34a Wednesday in the week of Rest Rogations
    12 ܩܪ̈ܝ، ܕܐܪܒܥܐ ܒܫܒܐ ܕܫܒܬܐ ܕܢܝܚܬܐ ܘܕܒܥܘ̈ܬܐ
13. 1 Sam. 14.24-29 fol. 41a the Consecration of the Cross (Enkainia)
    13 ܩܪ̈ܝ، ܐܢܘܢܝܐ ܕܨܠܝܒܐ

28. In addition to my own investigation into the Samuel Manuscript of Jacob of Edessa, I have been able to compare my data with those of A. Salvesen.

14.	1 Sam. 14.30-45	fol. 42a	Sunday in the third (week) of the Fast 14 ܩܪ̈, ܕܚܕܒܫܒܐ ܕܬܠ̱ ܕܨܘܡܐ
15.	1 Sam. 16.1-13	fol. 48a	Epiphany = L 6h1mg 6h19 7h12mg 8a1 Pentecost = L 6h19 Thursday of the Mystery (Maundy Thursday) [DEC] 15 ܩܪ̈, ܕܚܡܫ ܕܦܨܚܐ ܘܕܦܢܛܩܘܣܛܐ ܘܕܕܢܚܐ ܕܪ̈ܐܙܐ
16.	1 Sam. 17.37-51	fol. 54a	Easter = 6h1mg[29] Commemoration of the Martyrs 16 ܩܪ̈, ܕܚܕܒܫܒܐ ܪ̈ܒܐ ܘܕܘܟܪ̈ܢܐ ܕܣܗ̈ܕܐ
17.	1 Sam. 21.1-19	fol. 66a	John the Baptist Monday in the week of Rest Sunday in the sixth (week) of the Fast 17 ܩܪ̈, ܕܝܘܚܢܢ ܡܥܡܕܢܐ ܘܕܬܪ̈ܝܢ ܒܫܒܐ ܕܫܒܬܐ ܕܢܝܚܬܐ ܘܕܚܕܒܫܒܐ ܕܫܬܐ ܕܨܘܡܐ
18.	1 Sam. 24.2-20	fol. 73b	Commemoration of the Apostles 18 ܩܪ̈, ܒܕܘܟܪ̈ܢܐ ܕܫܠܝ̈ܚܐ
19.	1 Sam. 26.1-13	fol. 78b	Tuesday in the Great (Holy) week = L <8a1> 19 ܩܪ̈, ܕܬܠܬܐ ܒܫܒܐ ܕܫܒܬܐ ܪ̈ܒܬܐ
20.	1 Sam. 26.14-25	fol. 80a	Good Friday 20 ܩܪ̈, ܕܥܪ̈ܘܒܬܐ ܕܚܫܐ
21.	2 Sam. 1.1-16	fol. 91b	Commemoration of the Just 21 ܩܪ̈, ܒܕܘܟܪ̈ܢܐ ܕܟܐܢ̈ܐ
22.	2 Sam. 5.23b-39	fol. 99b	Commemoration of the Bishops 22 ܩ ܒܕܘܟܪ̈ܢܝ ܐܦܣܩܘ̈ܦܐ
23.	2 Sam. 6.1-23	fol. 104b	Hosanna (Palm Sunday) Ascension = L 6h19 7h12 8a1 [DT DEC] 23 ܩ ܕܐܘܫܥܢ̈ܐ ܘܕܣܘܠܩܐ
24.	2 Sam. 7.1-17	fol. 107a	Consecration of the Church 24 ܩ ܕܚܘܕܬܐ ܕܗܝܟܠܐ
25.	2 Sam. 7.18-29	fol. 108b	Friday of the week of Rest 25 ܩܪ̈, ܕܥܪ̈ܘܒܬܐ ܕܫܒܬܐ ܕܢܝܚܬܐ
26.	2 Sam. 20.4-13a	fol. 148a	Commemoration of the Prophets Commemoration of one of the Priests 26 ܩܪ̈, ܒܕܘܟܪ̈ܢܐ ܕܢܒܝ̈ܐ ܘܕܟܗ̈ܢܐ

29. The incipit is known, but the title is illegible.

27. 2 Sam. 23.13-17   fol. 157a Sunday of the fourth (week) of the Fast (Lent)

ܒ̈ܗܕ ܐ̇ܪܒܝܥܝܬܐ ܕܨܘܡܐ ܕܚܕ 27

28. 2 Sam. 23.13-17   fol. 157a Epiphany in the night = 6h4mg [DT]

ܒ̈ܗܕ ܕܫܗܪܐ ܕܕ̈ܢܚܐ 28

29. 2 Sam. 24.1-25   fol. 159b Saturday of the Evangile in the evening
                                  = L 6h4mg
                                  Rogations
                                  in case of pestilence

ܒ̈ܗܕ ܕܫܒܬܐ ܕܣܒܪܬܐ ܒ̈ܪܡܫܐ ܘܒܒ̈ܥܘܬܐ ܘܒܡܘܬܢܐ 29

Comparison of the titles attached to the text of Jacob's Samuel with those in L, 6h4, 6h19, 7h12, 7k3 and 8a1, shows that in 9 of the 29 instances above, the JE titles show a connection between the lesson and the ecclesiastical calendar which is similar to that in at least one of the ancient P manuscripts. In numbers 2, 10, 11, 15, 23 and 28 above, the terminology in the relevant JE titles differs from that in the other manuscripts studied here. In three, numbers 11, 15 and 23, the same lesson is related to an extra day of commemoration or to a festival day, and in one case, number 11, the lesson according to JE begins one verse earlier than the lessons in the other manuscripts. Though the incipits of the JE lessons as given in numbers 3, 19, 21, 23, 24, 26 and 27 are shared with the lessons in the other manuscripts, the titles of these latter lessons refer to a different ecclesiastical calendar. Further, in numbers 6, 16 and 28, only one of the other manuscripts supports the JE title; the title of the supporting manuscript is, however, unlikely to be original, and should probably be given a considerably later date. To sum up, in the absence of the Syrohexaplaric text of the book of Samuel, it seems probable that although JE-Samuel does give evidence of a selection from and a reworking of the ancient lectionary system(s), its lectionary system is far too individual to support an assumption that Jacob deliberately accepted or adapted an existing lectionary system.

The findings presented above for Samuel yield no clear evidence for the criteria used by Jacob in the selection of lessons; we may only guess at the arguments that determined his choice in relation to the ecclesiastical calendar.

Only 18 verses of the first chapter of the books of Kings have survived. No marker of the incipit of a lesson, nor any liturgical title, is connected with these verses. There is a good deal of evidence in L and the P manuscripts 6h18, 7a1, 7h10, 8a1 and 8h4 to suggest that a variety of lectionary systems may have been in use. The Syrohexaplaric manuscript SH8 contains only three lessons (see Appendix 3), which share no data with the lessons in the P manuscripts. Though there are two lessons in common between the six (details in Appendix 3) in the Syrohexaplaric manuscript SH9 and the P manuscripts, this is insufficient evidence on which to base an assumption of any liturgical relationship or dependence between these texts. The lesson for the night of Epiphany in SH9 is identical with that in the margin of 6h18, while the terminology of the title in the margin of the corresponding lesson in 7h10 is different. According to SH9 the pericope of 2 Kgs 13.14 is read in the services on Maundy Thursday; however, in 8a1 this lesson is related to the commemoration of the Departed.[30]

Proverbs, Wisdom and Ecclesiastes are not extant in the copies of Jacob's edition. For Proverbs, there is evidence in L, four P manuscripts (6h16, 7a1, 7h6 and 8a1) and one Syrohexaplaric manuscript, SH7 (for details, see Appendix 3), that this biblical book did form a part of some ancient lectionary system(s). There is no evidence that the selections of lessons as testified in the manuscripts in question belong to one and the same system. It seems clear that SH7 has no liturgical relationship with the P manuscripts, since the former shares only four of the 15 pericopes with the latter. In two of these four instances the explicit in SH7 differs from that in the P manuscripts; in one instance the difference is in the incipit (see n. 30 above).

In contrast with the two lessons in 8a1 for Wisdom, the only liturgical representative of biblical manuscripts according to the Peshitta, SH7 (for details see Appendix 3) presents the markers of the incipits and explicits of 15 lessons. In only one instance does the lesson in 8a1 correspond with a pericope in SH7: there is thus no evidence of a liturgical relationship between the two manuscripts.

That Ecclesiastes formed a part of an ancient lectionary system is testified by 7g2mg 8a1[31] and SH7.[32] There is no evidence whatever to support the assumption that there was a liturgical relationship between SH7 and the P manuscripts.

The JE manuscript *MS London, British Library, Additional 14441* contains 21 titles in the book of Isaiah, listed below.[33] These titles and

---

30. See Jenner, *De perikopentitels*, p. 385.

31. See Jenner, *De perikopentitels*, p. 388.

32. The MS contains one marker of the incipit of a lesson, viz. Eccl. 5.4-11 (fol. 67a).

33. This MS contains: Isa. 2.22–3.11, 7.3-14, 8.2-11, 12.3–13.7, 13.21–19.2,

lessons have been compared with those in SH7, SH10, SH11 (the details are set out in Appendix 2), L and in the P manuscripts 6h3, 6h5 and 8a1.

In some cases the text presents an explicit while the corresponding incipit is lacking because of the loss of folios: Isa. 40.11 (fol. 41b); 46.4 (fol. 43a). In one case, Isa. 59.11a-21, the marker of the incipit is placed without any reference to the lectionary system; in another, a lesson seems to be related to two explicits: Isa. 58.9 and 59.2.

1. Isa. 7.14 fol. 4b Rogations

1 ܩܪ ܕܒܥܘ̈ܬܐ

2. Isa. 25.1-12 fol. 21a Commemoration of the Exiles = SH10 [DEC]

2 ܩܪ، ܒܕܘܟܪܢܐ ܕܐܟܣܢ̈ܝܐ

3. Isa. 25.6–26.15 fol. 21b the Departed

3 ܩܪ، ܒܕܘܟܪܢܐ ܕܥܢܝ̈ܕܐ

4. Isa. 26.16–27.6 fol. 23a Friday of the week of Rest = {8a1} [DT]

4 ܩܪ، ܕܥܪܘܒܬܐ ܕܫܒܬܐ ܕܢܝܚܬܐ

5. Isa. 28.9-23 fol. 25b Monday in the Great (Holy) week = 6h5mg SH10 [DT]

5 ܩܪ، ܕܬܪܝܢ ܒܫܒܐ ܕܫܒܬܐ ܪܒܬܐ

6. Isa. 29.9-24 fol. 29a Rogations = 6h5mg SH10

6 ܩܪ ܕܒܥܘ̈ܬܐ

7. Isa. 32.9-15 fol. 36a Rogations = SH10
Rogation in case of drought = 6h5mg SH10 [DT]

7 ܩܪ، ܕܒܥܘ̈ܬܐ ܘܕܡܛܪܘܬܐ ܡܛܠܪܐ

8. Isa. 33.2-12 fol. 37a Rogations = 6h5*
Earthquake = 6h5mg [DT]

8 ܩܪ، ܕܒܥܘ̈ܬܐ ܘܕܙܘܥܐ

9. Isa. 33.13-22 fol. 38a Second Sunday of the Fast = SH10 [DEC]

9 ܩܪ، ܕܚܕܒܫܒܐ ܕܬܪܝܢ ܕܨܘܡܐ

10. Isa. 48.12-22 fol. 46a Pentecost = L 6h3 6h5mg {8a1} SH10 [DT]

10 ܩܪ ܠܐ ܕܦܢܛܩܘܣܛܐ

11. Isa. 49.1-14 fol. 47a Birth of our Lord (Christmas) = SH10 [DEC]

11 ܩ ܕܝܠܕܗ ܕܡܪܢ

20.1–35.1, 40.4-15, 45.7-16, 46.2–51.2, 57.2–63.8, 65.25, 66.4. Cf. W. Wright, *Catalogue of Syriac Manuscripts in the British Museum, Acquired since the Year 1838*, I (London: The Trustees of the British Museum, 1870), p. 39.

12. Isa. 50.4-11 fol. 50a Commemoration of the Bishops = L 6h3 6h5mg SH10 SH11 [DI DEC]

12 ܩܪ̈, ܕܘܟܪܢܐ ܕܐܦܝܣܩܘ̈ܦܐ

13. Isa. 58.1-9a /59.2 fol. 53a Beginning of the Fast (Lent) = L 6h3 6h5 <8a1> SH7 SH10 SH11 [DE]

13 ܩܪ̈, ܕܫܘܪܝ ܨܘܡܐ

14. Isa. 59.2-8 fol. 54b Fourth Sunday of the Fast (Lent) = 6h5mg SH10 [DI DT]

14 ܩܪ̈, ܕܚܕܒܫܒܐ ܕܐܪܒܥܐ ܕܨܘܡܐ

15. Isa. 60.1-7 fol. 56a the Dawn of Easter (Great Sunday) = L 6h3 6h5 6h5mg <8a1> SH7 SH10 [DT DE DEC?]

15 ܩܪ̈, ܕܢܓܗ ܕܚܕܒܫܒܐ ܪܒܐ

16. Isa. 60.8-22 fol. 57a the Innocents = 6h5mg SH10 [Palm Sunday] Wednesday in the week of ////// = SH10??

16 ܩ ܕܛܠܝ̈ܐ ܘܕ[ܐܘܫܥܢܐ] ܘܕܐܪܒܥܒܫܐ ܒܫܒܐ ܕܫܒܬܐ////

17. Isa. 61.1–62.2 fol. 58b Maundy Thursday, in the morning (Thursday of the Mystery in the morning) = L 6h5mg SH10 [DT] the Priests = L 6h5 [DT] Baptism

17 ܕܚܡܫܒܫܐ ܕܐܪܙܐ ܒܨܦܪܐ ܘܕܟܗ̈ܢܐ ܘܕܡܥܡܘܕܝܬܐ

18. Isa. 61.10–62.12 fol. 59b Easter (Resurrection) = L 6h5mg SH7 SH10 SH11 [DT DI DE]

18 ܩ ܕܩܝܡܬܐ

19. Isa. 62.3-12 fol. 60a Thursday in the week of Rest

19 ܕܚܡܫܐ ܒܫܒܐ ܕܫܒܬܐ ܕܢܝܚܬܐ

20. Isa. 63.1-6 fol. 61a Friday of the Crucifixion (Good Friday) = 6h5mg SH10 [DT]

20 ܩܪ̈, ܕܥ[ܪܘܒܬܐ] ܕܙܩ[ܝܦܘܬܐ]

21. Isa. 63.7 fol. 61b On the day of the Commemoration of the Martyrs = SH7 SH10 SH11 [DEC]

21 ܩ ܒܝܘܡ ܕܘܟܪܢܐ ܕ[ܣܗ̈ܕ]ܐ

The lessons witnessed for the book of Isaiah present a picture completely different from those attested for the other biblical books. The discussion that follows shows the complexity of the findings. In three instances only, numbers 1, 3 and 19, the incipit of the lesson as prescribed by Jacob of Edessa is peculiar to his lectionary system. In the remaining 18 cases the lesson from Jacob's lectionary system is shared with a pericope in at least one of the following: L, 6h3, 6h5, 8a1, SH7, SH10 and SH11. In three of the 18 cases, that is numbers 10, 13 and 17, L and the biblical manuscripts of the Peshitta, the Syro-hexapla and Jacob of Edessa, provide the same lesson. Thus, in these instances, all four source categories indicate the same lesson, that is the connection of the same pericope with the same festival or commemoration day. Nonetheless, despite this similarity in ecclesiastical or liturgical calendar and lectionary system, there is diversity in the terminology of the titles, shown in numbers 10 and 17, as well as in the length of the pericope, evident in number 13. There are two cases, numbers 12 and 15, in which the same pericope is witnessed for all four source categories, but not related to the same festival or commemoration day; in other words, each lectionary has its own lesson. In one case, number 18, the same lesson is found in L, P and JE, though the titles of the witnesses differ in terminology and the pericopes differ in length. In six instances, viz. numbers 5, 6, 7, 14, 16 and 20, the same lesson is shared by P, SH and JE, despite differences in terminology of the titles in numbers 5, 7, 14 and 20, and in the length of the pericope in number 14. JE and SH share one lesson, number 8, but four pericopes in numbers 2, 9, 11 and 21, though these are related to different festival and commemoration days. JE and P share only one lesson, number 4, and the terminology of the titles differs. These data indicate a remarkable variety in the lectionary systems. Furthermore, although on the one hand the great majority of JE-Isaiah lessons is in some way related to the other lectionary systems, the JE lessons on the other hand apparently form part of an independent lectionary system.

The Syrohexaplaric manuscript SH7, which is lacking in titles, contains 31 pericopes, of which 8 are shared with no other manuscripts. SH10, presenting 98 lessons, provides the greatest number of lessons, of which 21 are peculiar to this manuscript. Of the 26 lessons in SH11,[34] 6 are singular lessons. The same incipit is shared in 10 instances by SH7, SH10 and SH11, in 22 instances by SH7 and SH10, in 10 instances by SH7 and SH11, and in 18 instances by SH10 and SH11. The Syrohexaplaric manuscripts SH7, SH10 and SH11 thus share a remarkable number of pericopes and liturgical titles. The relationship is strongest for SH7 and SH10, and for SH10 and SH11.

---

34. This MS contains only part of the text of Isaiah.

Nevertheless, the differences between the three manuscripts are sufficient to amount to evidence against any form of mutual dependency: each apparently presents its own lectionary system. There is, however, good reason to believe that the lectionary system of 6h5mg is dependent on that of SH10.

All in all, the variety in the choice of pericopes and the liturgical titles attached to them described above strongly suggests that each individual witness of the ancient biblical manuscripts, L, the Syrohexaplaric manuscripts and the JE-Isaiah manuscript provides its own lectionary system. There is no strong support for the assumption that Jacob of Edessa made use of the same ecclesiastical calendar as that attested by the other manuscripts. He seems to have developed his own calendar.

The text of Jeremiah is wanting in Jacob of Edessa's revision, and his lectionary system for that book is therefore unknown. SH7 (for details see Appendix 3) contains 13 pericopes; on four occasions, the incipit of these pericopes is shared with that of an ancient P manuscript.[35]

The greatest number of lessons, a total of 74, is presented in JE manuscript *MS Rome, Vatican Library, Siriaco 5.*[36] The greater part of these belong to an elaborate system of extra Sundays added to the ancient ecclesiastical and liturgical calendar(s). The manuscript contains an illegible index to its lectionary system. The 74 lessons[37] are as follows:

1. Ezek. 2.1-6   fol. 4b   Sunday of Pentecost

   ܪ‍ܠ‍ܥܐ‍ܦܝ.ܪ ܪܒܪܐ .ܫ.ܪ ,ܡ   1

2. Ezek. 2.6–3.3   fol. 5a   When someone becomes a Priest (Ordination)

   ܪܝܡܐ ܪܐܡ.ܪ ܪܣ ,ܡ   2

3. Ezek. 3.4-13   fol. 6a   Monday in the Great (Holy) week = 6h15

   ܪܐܣܬ ܪܐܒܪܝ.ܪ ܪܒܪܐ ܝܬܐ.ܪ ܐ   3

35. See Jenner, *De perikopentitels*, pp. 392-93. There are three further instances in which there is a difference of four verses or less between the incipit of SH7 and that of the P manuscripts. The corresponding liturgical titles are usually added in the margin.

36. The MS contains: Ezek. 1.15–16.47, 17.10–19.11, 20.13-39, 20.48–21.23, 21.30–27.20, 27.30–29.13, 29.20–36.8, 36.16-19, 36.35–37.19, 37.27–38.23, 39.16–46.13.

37. Some passages of the translations of the liturgical titles are put between square brackets. These brackets refer to the abbreviations in the Syriac titles.

4. Ezek. 3.14-15 fol. 7a Sunday of the fourth (week) of the Fast (Lent)
4 ܦܪ, ܕܚܕ ܒܫܒܐ ܕܐܪ̈ܒܥܐ ܕܨܘܡܐ

5. Ezek. 3.16-21 fol. 7a Sunday of the beginning of the Fast (Lent) = 7h2 8a1
5 ܦܪ, ܕܚܕ ܒܫܒܐ ܕ[ܡܥܠܝ] ܨܘܡܐ

6. Ezek. 3.22 fol. 8a Commemoration of the Prophets
Commemoration of the Martyrs = L 7h2 8a1
Sunday of the third (week) after Easter (Resurrection)
6 ܦܪ, ܒܕܘܟܪܢܐ ܕܢܒܝ̈ܐ ܘܕܣܗ̈ܕܐ ܘܚܕ ܒܫܒܐ ܕܬܠܬܐ ܕܒܬܪ ܩܝܡܬܐ

7. Ezek. 4.9-15 fol. 9b Wednesday [in the first week] of the Fast (Lent) = SH7 [DE]
7 ܕ ܒܫ ܕܒܫ ܕܨܘ

8. Ezek. 4.16 fol. 10b Ascension = L 6h15 <8a1> [DEC][38]
8 ܦܪ, ܕܣܘܠܩܐ

9. Ezek. 4.17 fol. 10b Tuesday ////// = L 6h15 <8a1> [DI][39]
9 [ܦܪ,] ܕܬܠܬܐ ܒܫܒܐ///

10. Ezek. 5.11-17 fol. 11b [Saturday of the first week of the Fast] (Lent)
10 ܕܫܒ ܕܫ ܩܕ ܕܨܘ

11. Ezek. 6.1-14? fol. 12b Thursday///////
11 /// ܚܡܫܐ /// ܬܐ

12. Ezek. 7.1 fol. 14b Sunday of the sixteenth [week] after Easter (Resurrection)
12 ܦܪ, ܕܚܕܒܫܒܐ ܕܫܬܬ [ܥܣܪ̈ܐ] ܕܒܬܪ ܩܝܡܬܐ

13. Ezek. 7.5 fol. 15a Sixth [Sunday] after [Easter (Resurrection)]
13 ܕܚܕܒܫ ܘ ܕܒܬܪ ܩܝ

14. Ezek. 7.10 fol. 15b Wednesday in the Great (Holy) week = L 6h15 <8a1>
14 ܦܪ, ܕܐܪ̈ܒܥܐ ܒܫܒܐ ܕܫܒܬܐ ܪܒܬܐ

15. Ezek. 8.1 fol. 17b Second Sunday of the Fast (Lent)
15 ܦܪ, ܕܚܕܒܫܒܐ ܕܬܪܝܢ ܕܨܘܡܐ

16. Ezek. 10.1 fol. 21a Seventh [17?] Sunday after Easter (Resurrection)
16 ܦܪ, ܕܚܕܒܫܒܐ ܕܙ [ܥܣܪܝ?] ܕܒܬܪ ܩܝܡܬܐ

17. Ezek. 10.18-22 fol. 24a Ninth Sunday after Easter (Resurrection)
17 ܦܪ, ܕܚܕܒܫܒܐ ܕܛ ܕܒܬܪ ܩܝܡܬܐ

38. But cf. no. 9.
39. But cf. no. 8.

18. Ezek. 11.1 fol. 24b Great (Holy) Saturday = L <8a1>
ܩܪ̈، ܕܥܪܘܒܬܐ ܪܒܬܐ 18

19. Ezek. 11.14 fol. 26a Tenth Sunday [after] Easter (Resurrection)
ܩܪ̈، ܕܚܕܒܫܒܐ ܕܝ، ܩܝܡܬܐ 19

20. Ezek. 11.22 fol. 27a the Bishops = L 7h2
the Departed
ܩܪ̈، ܕܐܦܝ̈ܣܩܘܦܐ ܘܕܥܢܝ̈ܕܐ 20

21. Ezek. 12.3-24 fol. 27b Eleventh Sunday after Easter (Resurrection)
ܩܪ̈، ܕܚܕܒܫܒܐ ܕܝܐ ܕܒܬܪ ܩܝܡܬܐ 21

22. Ezek. 13.1-23 fol. 30a Thirteenth Sunday after Easter (Resurrection)
ܩܪ̈، ܕܚܕܒܫܒܐ ܕܝܓ ܕܒܬܪ ܩܝܡܬܐ 22

23. Ezek. 14.1 fol. 33a Fourteenth Sunday after Easter (Resurrection)
ܩܪ̈، ܕܚܕܒܫܒܐ ܕܝܕ ܕܒܬܪ ܩܝܡܬܐ 23

24. Ezek. 14.13 fol. 35a Third Sunday of the Fast (Lent)=L [DEC]
Commemoration of the Just and the Blessed Doctors
And the rogation against the paucity of rain
ܩܪ̈، ܕܚܕܒܫܒܐ ܕܓ ܕܨܘܡܐ ܘܕܘܟܪܢܐ ܕܟܐ̈ܢܐ ܘܕܡܠ̈ܦܢܐ ܘܥܠ 24
ܒܨܝܪܘܬ ܡܛܪܐ

25. Ezek. 15.1 fol. 36b Fifteenth Sunday after Easter (Resurrection)
ܩܪ̈، ܕܚܕܒܫܒܐ ܕܝܗ ܕܒܬܪ ܩܝܡܬܐ 25

26. Ezek. 16.36 fol. 41a Sixteenth Sunday after Easter (Resurrection)
ܩܪ̈، ܕܚܕܒܫܒܐ ܕܝܘ ܕܒܬܪ ܩܝܡܬܐ 26

27. Ezek. 17.11 fol. 43a Seventeenth Sunday after Easter (Resurrection)
ܩܪ̈، ܕܚܕܒܫܒܐ ܕܝܙ ܕܒܬܪ ܩܝܡܬܐ 27

28. Ezek. 17.22 fol. 44a Twenty-fourth [Sunday] after Easter (Resurrection)
ܕܚܕܒܫ ܟܕ ܕܒܬܪ ܩ، 28

29. Ezek. 18.1 fol. 44b Friday in the week of Rest = L 6h15 {8a1}
Commemoration of the Bishops = L 8a1
And the Departed
ܘ ܕܥܪܘܒܬܐ ܕܫܒܬܐ ܕܢܝܚܬܐ ܘܕܘܟܪܢܐ ܕܐܦܝ̈ܣܩܘܦܐ ܘܕܥܢܝ̈ܕܐ 29

30. Ezek. 18.5 fol. 45a Monday [in the middle week of the Fast] (Lent)
ܒ ܒܫܒ ܕܫ ܡܨܥ ܕܨܘ 30

31. Ezek. 18.20 fol. 46a Eighteenth Sunday after Easter (Resurrection)
ܕܚܕܒܫܒܐ ܕܝܚ ܕܒܬܪ ܩܝܡܬܐ 31

32. Ezek. 18.21 fol. 46a Tuesday [in the middle week of the Fast] (Lent)
ܓ ܒܫܒ ܕܫ ܡܨܥܐ ܕܨܘ 32

33. Ezek. 19.1 fol. 47b Saturday of (the week of) Rest = L 6h15 [DT]

33 ܩܪ̈، ܕܫܒܬܐ ܕܫܠܝܐ

34. Ezek. 20.13 fol. 49a /////// Ninth week after Easter (Resurrection)

34 ܫܒܘܥܐ ܕܛ ܕܒܬܪ ܩܝܡܬܐ

35. Ezek. 20.13 fol. 49a Friday [in the middle week of the Fast] (Lent)

35 ܕܥܪ̈ܘܒܬܐ ܕܫܒ ܡܨ̈ܥ ܕܨܘ

36. Ezek. 20.27 fol. 50b Twentieth Sunday after Easter (Resurrection)

36 ܘ ܕܚܕܒܫܒܐ ܕܟ ܕܒܬܪ ܩܝܡܬܐ

37. Ezek. 20.30 fol. 51a Thursday of the Mystery (Maundy Thursday) = L 6h15 [DT]
Thursday in the week of Rest

37 ܩܪ̈، ܕܚܡܫܐ ܫܒܐ ܕܐܪܙܐ ܘܕܚܡܫܐ ܫܒܐ ܕܫܒܬܐ ܕܫܠܝܐ

38. Ezek. 20.39 fol. 52b Thursday [in the middle week of the Fast] (Lent)

38 ܗ ܫܒܐ ܕܫ ܡܨ̈ ܕܨܘ

39. Ezek. 20.39 fol. 52b Twenty-first Sunday after Easter (Resurrection)

39 ܩܪ̈، ܕܚܕܒܫܒܐ ܕܟܐ ܕܒܬܪ ܩܝܡܬܐ

40. Ezek. 21.14 fol. 54a Thursday in the Great (Holy) week
Friday in the Great week (Good Friday) = 6h15 [DI]

40 ܩܪ ܕܚܡܫܐ ܫܒܐ ܕܫܒܬܐ ܪܒܬܐ ܘܕܥܪܘܒܬܐ ܕܫܒܬܐ ܪܒܬܐ

41. Ezek. 21.29 fol. 55b Twenty-fifth [Sunday] after [Easter (Resurrection)]

41 ܕܚܕܒܫ ܟܗ ܕܒܬܪ ܩܝ

42. Ezek. 22.1 fol. 56a Twenty-second Sunday after Easter (Resurrection)

42 ܘ ܕܚܕܒܫܒܐ ܕܥܣܪܝܢ ܘܬܪܝܢ ܕܒܬܪ ܩܝܡܬܐ

43. Ezek. 22.17 fol. 58a Third Sunday after Easter (Resurrection)

43 ܕܚܕܒܫܒܐ ܕܓ ܕܒܬܪ ܩܝܡܬܐ

44. Ezek. 24.1 fol. 65b Twenty-sixth [Sunday] after [Easter (Resurrection)]

44 ܕܚܕܒܫ ܟܘ ܕܒܬܪ ܩܝ

45. Ezek. 25.1 fol. 69a Twenty-seventh [Sunday] after [Easter (Resurrection)]

45 ܕܚܕܒܫ ܟܙ ܕܒܬܪ ܩܝ

46. Ezek. 26.1 fol. 71b Twelfth [Sunday] after [Easter (Resurrection)]

46 ܕܚܕܒܫ ܝܒ ܕܒܬܪ ܩܝ

47. Ezek. 27.1 fol. 73b Twenty-seventh [Sunday] after [Easter (Resurrection)]

47 ܕܚܕܒܫ ܟܙ ܕܒܬܪ ܩܝ

48. Ezek. 28.20 fol. 80a Twenty-ninth [Sunday] after [Easter (Resurrection)]

48 ܕܚܕܒܫ ܟܛ ܕܒܬܪ ܩܝ

49. Ezek. 30.1 fol. 83a ////

49 ܩ //////

50. Ezek. 30.13 fol. 84b Second [Sunday] after [Easter (Resurrection)]

50 ܕܚܕܒܫ ܒ ܕܒܬܪ ܩ݂

51. Ezek. 31.15 fol. 88b Third [Sunday] after [Easter (Resurrection)]

51 ܕܚܕܒܫ ܓ ܕܒܬܪ ܩ݂

52. Ezek. 32.1 fol. 89b Thirty-first [Sunday] after [Easter (Resurrection)]

52 ܕܚܕܒܫ ܠܐ ܕܒܬܪ ܩ݂

53. Ezek. 33.1 fol. 93b the Priests = 8h2
Baptism and John the Baptist = <8a1>
Monday in the week of Rest
Sunday of the fourth week of the Fast (Lent)

53 ܩܪ، ܕܟܗ̈ܢܐ ܘܕܡܥܡܘܕܝܘܬܐ ܘܕܝܘܚܢܢ ܡܥܡܕܢܐ ܘܬܪ̈ܝܢ ܒܫܒܐ
ܕܫܒܬܐ ܕܢܝܚܬܐ ܘܕܚܕܒܫܒܐ ܕܐܪ̈ܒܥܐ ܕܨܘܡܐ

54. Ezek. 33.7 fol. 94b Monday [in the week] of Rest = 6h15 7h2 [DT]

54 ܒ ܒܫܒ ܕܢܝܚܬܐ

55. Ezek. 33.21 fol. 96b Thirty-second [Sunday] after
[Easter (Resurrection)]

55 ܕܚܕܒܫܒ ܠܒ ܕܒܬܪ ܩ݂

56. Ezek. 34.1 fol. 98b Tuesday [in the week of Rest]

56 ܓ ܒܫܒ ܕܢܝܚܬܐ

57. Ezek. 34.9 fol. 99b ///////// and the Departed ?

57 ܕܫ[///]ܐ [ܕܥܢܝ̈ܕܐ]

58. Ezek. 34.11 fol. 100a Thursday in the week of Rest =
L 6h15 8a1 7h2 [DI]

58 ܩܪ، ܕܚܡܫܐ ܒܫܒܐ ܕܫܒܬܐ ܕܢܝܚܬܐ

59. Ezek. 34.20 fol. 101a Commemoration of the Innocents

59 ܩܪ، ܒܕܘܟܪܢܐ ܕܛܠܝ̈ܐ

60. Ezek. 35.6 fol. 103b Thirty-third [Sunday] after [Easter (Resurrection)]

60 ܕܚܕܒܫ ܠܓ ܕܒܬܪ ܩ݂

61. Ezek. 36.1 fol. 104a Second Sunday after Epiphany

61 ܩܪ، ܕܚܕܒܫܒܐ ܕܒ ܕܒܬܪ ܕܢܚܐ

62. Ezek. 36.13 fol. 106a Sunday before Christmas (the Birth) =
7ph9mg [DEC]

62 ܕܚܕܒܫ ܕܩܕܡ ܒܝܬ ܝܠܕܐ

63. Ezek. 37.15 fol. 109a Saturday of the Evangile (Holy Saturday) =
L SH7 [DI]

63 ܩܪ، ܕܫܒܬܐ ܣܒܪܬܐ

64. Ezek. 38.1 fol. 110a Fifth [Sunday] after Epiphany

64 ܕܚܕܒܫܒܐ ܗ ܕܒܬܪ ܕܢܚܐ

65. Ezek. 38.18 fol. 113a Sixth [Sunday] after Epiphany = 7ph9mg [DI]

65 ܕܚܕܒܫܒܐ ܘ ܕܒܬܪ ܕܢܚܐ

66. Ezek. 39.17 fol. 114a Seventh [Sunday] after Epiphany

66 ܕܚܕܒܫܒܐ ܙ ܕܒܬܪ ܕܢܚܐ

67. Ezek. 43.1 fol. 131b Hosanna (Palm Sunday) = 7h2mg SH7

67 ܕܐܘܫܥܢܐ

68. Ezek. 43.10 fol. 133a Sixth [Sunday] of the Fast (Lent) = 7ph9mg [DI]

68 ܕܚܕܒܫܒܐ ܘ ܕܨܘܡܐ

69. Ezek. 44.1 fol. 136b Commemoration of the Mother of God = 8a1 [DEC]

69 ܩܪ، ܒܕܘܟܪܢܐ ܕܝܠܕܬ ܐܠܗܐ

70. Ezek. 44.17 fol. 140b Commemoration of one of the Bishops and the Priests = 7ph9mg SH7 [DI]

70 ܩܪ، ܒܕܘܟܪܢܐ ܕܚܕ ܡܢ ܐܦܝܣܩܘܦܐ ܘܕܟܗ̈ܢܐ

71. Ezek. 45.1 fol. 141b Eighth [Sunday] after Epiphany

71 ܕܚܕܒܫܒܐ ܚ ܕܒܬܪ ܕܢܚܐ

72. Ezek. 45.10 fol. 143a Thursday [in the week before the Fast (Lent)]

72 ܗ ܒܫܒܐ ܕܩܕܡ ܕܨܘܡܐ

73. Ezek. 45.18 fol. 144b Great [Sunday] (Easter) = 7h2 [DEC]

73 ܕܚܕܒܫܒܐ ܪܒܐ

74. Ezek. 46.8 fol. 146b [Sunday] after Christmas

74 ܕܚܕܒܫܒܐ ܕܒܬܪ ܝܠܕܐ

Comparison of these 74 lessons with L, 6h15, 7h2, 7ph9, 8a1, 8h2 and SH7 shows the relationships described below.

There are no instances in which L,[40] P manuscripts,[41] SH7 (see Appendix 3), and JE have the same incipit. In one instance (number 63) JE, L and SH7 seem to share the same pericope; however, the incipit in SH7 differs slightly from those for the lessons of the other two witnesses. In one other instance (number 67) JE, 7h2 and SH7 share the same pericope. Thus, there are only two cases in which the same

40. See Jenner, *De perikopentitels*, pp. 393-95, and Bijlage C, Tafel 6. Cf. Burkitt, 'Lectionary System', pp. 301-38.

41. See Jenner, *De perikopentitels*, pp. 393-95, and Bijlage C, Tafel 6. Cf. Burkitt, 'Lectionary System', pp. 301-38.

pericope is attested in all three categories of ancient lectionary systems, and only one other in which JE and SH7 share a pericope. This amounts to trivial evidence only of agreement between the JE lectionary system and that in the Syrohexaplaric cases. L, or one of the biblical manuscripts of the Peshitta tradition, support the JE lectionary system in 18 cases.[42] In four of these (numbers 24, 62, 69 and 73) the JE lectionary system is based on a different ecclesiastical calendar. Twice (numbers 33 and 37) the lessons are the same, but the terminology in the liturgical titles is different; in three cases (numbers 40, 65 and 70) the incipit is different.[43] These findings support an overall conclusion that no relationship can be established in Ezekiel between the lectionary systems of JE and the Syrohexapla. There is insufficient evidence of a relationship between the lectionary systems of JE and those of the Peshitta tradition. There is no basis for an assumption that the JE lectionary system for Ezekiel is dependent on the lectionary system(s) as reflected in L or the P manuscripts. If Jacob of Edessa used the lectionary system(s) of these categories of manuscripts, his sources are, for the most part, lost.

The book of the Twelve Prophets is wanting in Jacob of Edessa's revision. The limited number of lessons in L and the P manuscripts,[44] and the very few pericopes attested in SH7 (for details see Appendix 3) suggest that there were only a small number of lessons marked in the lectionary system of this book. The lectionary systems of these three categories of MSS share a pericope only as a result of accident.

The lectionary system(s) related to Daniel in the JE manuscript MS *Paris, Bibliothèque Nationale, Syriaque 27* consists of 22 lessons.[45] These are shown below, in a list based on the current text as presented in the Leiden Peshitta edition; the order in this JE manuscript is slightly different, as the listed folio numbers show. In several cases the explicit of the corresponding lesson in the Peshitta manuscripts is in a different

42. 6h15 and <8a1> presumably support the lesson of no. 9, though the incipit would be different in that case.

43. Whether the incipits in the palimpsest manuscript 7ph9 are correct, may be a matter of dispute.

44. See Jenner, *De perikopentitels*, pp. 395-97 and Bijlage C, Tafel 6.

45. The MS contains: the complete text of Daniel, Bel and the Dragon, Susannah. Cf. H. Zotenberg, *Manuscrits orientaux: Catalogues des manuscrits syriaques et sabéens (mandaïtes) de la Bibliothèque nationale* (Paris: Imprimerie nationale, 1874), p. 10.

place, that is: the lessons in the JE and P manuscripts differ in length. The explicits under discussion are given after the oblique stroke of the sigla of the corresponding P-manuscripts.

1. Dan. 1.1-21 fol. 94b Sunday of the beginning of the Fast[46]
= 6h10mg [DE /v. 17] 8a1
Commemoration of the blessed[47] =
6h10mg [DE /v. 9]
New Sunday = 6h10mg [DE /v. 9]
Pentecost = L 6h10 8a1

1 ܗܘ̇ ܕܪܝܫ ܨܘܡܐ ܘܕܘܟܪܢܐ ܕܛܘܒܢܐ ܘܕܚܕܒܫܒܐ ܚܕܬܐ
ܘܕܦܢܛܩܘܣܛܐ

2. Dan. 2.1-12 fol. 96b Sunday in [week] two of the Fast (Lent) =
6h10mg [DT DE /v.16 DT]
Tuesday [of the week] of Rest
[Sunday] of Hosannah (Palm Sunday) =
6h10 8a1 [DT]
Tuesday(?) in the Great (Holy) week =
6h10mg [DT]

2 ܗܘ̇ ܕܚܕܒܫܒܐ ܒܫ ܒ ܕܨܘܡ ܓ ܒܫܒ ܕܢܝܚ ܘܕܚܕ ܕܐܘܫܥܢ [ܘ?ܓ] ܒܫܒ
ܕܫܒ ܪܒܬܐ

3. Dan. 2.31 fol. 99a Birth (Christmas) = 6h10 8a1
Sunday of the week of the Fast = 6h10 8a1

3 ܗܘ̇ ܕܒܝܬ ܝܠܕܐ ܘܕܚܕܒܫܒܐ ܕܫܒܬܐ ܕܨܘܡܐ

4. Dan. 3.16 fol. 102b Commemoration of the Innocents
Commemoration of the Martyrs

4 ܗܘ̇ ܕܘܟܪܢܐ ܕܛܠܝܐ ܘܕܣܗܕܐ

5. Dan. 3.26-37 fol. 104a Commemoration of the Just = 6h10mg [DI]
Saturday of the Great Week (Holy Saturday) =
L [DE /Dan. 4.3]

5 ܗܘ̇ ܠܗ ܕܘܟܪܢܐ ܕܟܐ̈ܢܐ ܘܕܫܒܬܐ ܕܫܒܬܐ ܪܒܬܐ

6. Dan. 3.37-45 fol. 105a Saturday of the week of Rest = 6h10mg [DEC]

6 ܗܘ̇ ܠܗ ܕܫܒܬܐ ܕܫܒܬܐ ܕܢܝܚܬܐ

7. Dan. 3.51-86 fol. 106a the Attendants of the Oblation = 6h10mg [DEC]

7 ܗܘ̇ ܕܬܫ̈ܡܫܝܐ ܩܘܪܒܢܐ

8. Dan. 4.1 fol. 110a Monday in the week of Rest =
L 6h10* 6h10mg [DEC]

8 ܗܘ̇ ܕܬܪܝܢ ܒܫܒܐ ܕܫܒܬܐ ܕܢܝܚܬܐ

46. Sunday before Lent.
47. Theodore of Mopsuestia.

9. Dan. 5.1 fol. 120a Thursday in the week of Rest = L 6h10* <8a1>

9 ܗܘ̇ ܕܚܡܫܐ ܒܫܒܐ ܕܫܒܬܐ ܕܢܝܚܬܐ

10. Dan. 6.1-11 fol. 123a Commemoration of John the Baptist = 6h10mg [DE /v. 13]
[Wednesday] of the Great (Holy) [week] = 6h10mg [DE /v. 13]
Commemoration of the Martyrs = 6h10

10 ܗܘ̇ ܒܕܘܟܪܢܗ ܕܝܘܚܢܢ ܡܥܡܕܢ[ܐ] ܘܕܐܪܒܥ[ܒ]ܫܒܐ ܕܫܒ ܪܒܬܐ
ܘܒܕܘܟܪܢܗ ܣܗ̈ܕܐ

11. Dan. 6.12-15 fol. 124b Friday of the Crucifixion = 6h10mg [DEC]

11 ܗܘ̇ ܕܥܪܘܒܬܐ ܕܙܩܝܦܘܬܐ

12. Dan. 6.20-25 fol. 124b Great Sunday (Easter) = 6h10mg [DT DI DE /vv. 19-29]

12 ܗܘ̇ ܕܚܕܒܫܒܐ ܪܒܐ

13. Dan. 7.1 fol. 114a Thursday in the week of the Mystery (Maundy Thursday) = 6h10 8a1

13 ܗܘ̇ ܕܚܡܫܐ ܒܫܒܐ ܕܐܪܙܐ

14. Dan. 7.6-14 fol. 114b Ascension Day = 6h10mg [DT]

14 ܗܘ̇ ܕܣܘܠܩܐ

15. Dan. 7.21-28 fol. 116b Commemoration of the Bishop(s) = L 6h10mg 8a1 [DT DE]

15 ܗܘ̇ ܒܕܘܟܪܢܐ ܕܐܦܝܣܩܘܦܐ

16. Dan. 8.1-15 fol. 117a Friday of the week of Rest = L 6h10mg <8a1> SH7 [DE]

16 ܗܘ̇ ܕܥܪܘܒܬܐ ܕܫܒܬܐ ܕܢܝܚܬܐ

17. Dan. 9.4-10a fol. 138b Rogations = 6h10mg [DE /v.14]

17 ܗܘ̇ ܕܒܥܘ̈ܬܐ

18. Dan. 9.15-19 fol. 140a Wednesday, the halfway point of the Fast = 6h10mg [DE]

18 ܗܘ̇ ܕܐܪܒܥܐ ܒܫܒܐ ܕܦܠܓܗ ܕܨܘܡܐ

19. Dan. 9.20-27 fol. 140b Tuesday in the Great (Holy) week = 6h10mg [DEC]
Dedication of the Cross = 6h10mg [DT]

19 ܗܘ̇ ܕܬܠܬܐ ܒܫܒܐ ܕܫܒܬܐ ܪܒܬܐ ܘܕܐܢܩܢܝܐ ܕܨܠܝܒܐ

20. Dan. 10.1 fol. 126b Sunday of the fifth week of the Fast = 6h10mg
The Commemoration of the Apostles = L 6h10mg
Wednesday of the week of Rest = 6h10 8a1

20 ܗܘ̇ ܕܚܕܒܫܒܐ ܕܚܡܫܐ ܕܨܘܡܐ ܘܒܕܘܟܪܢܐ ܕܫܠܝ̈ܚܐ
ܘܕܐܪܒܥܐ ܒܫܒܐ ܕܫܒܬܐ ܕܢܝܚܬܐ

21. Dan. 10.4   fol. 127b   when someone becomes a priest (Ordination)
                             = 6h10mg

21 ܡܬ, ܕܗܘܐ ܟܗܢܐ

22. Bel Dr 23-31 fol. 136b   Commemoration of the Prophets = 6h10mg [DEC]
                             Commemoration of one of the Bishops =
                             6h10mg [DEC]

22 ܡܬ, ܕܘܟܪܢܐ ܕܢܒܝܐ ܘܚܕ ܡܢ ܐܦܣܩܘܦܐ

Comparison of the lessons in L,[48] the ancient Peshitta manuscripts (6h10, 6h21 and 8a1),[49] JE-Daniel and of the pericopes of SH7 (for details see Appendix 3) shows that a considerable number of pericopes are shared by the lectionary system of JE and that preserved in the margins of 6h10. This observation does not, however, constitute evidence that the later system is dependent on the former or vice versa. There are three principal arguments against such an assumption. First, there is a discrepancy in the terminology of the liturgical titles (numbers 2, 12, 14, 15 and 19); second, the two systems either make a different use of the same ecclesiastical calendar, or they use different calendars (numbers 6, 7, 8, 11, 19 and 22); third, in a number of cases the explicits differ. In only one case (number 16) does the pericope of SH7 apparently support a lesson which L, P manuscripts and the JE manuscript share.

Fol. 92 of the JE manuscript of Daniel contains an index to its lectionaries, in which the terminology sometimes differs from that in the titles in the manuscript itself. There is a further difference that is more significant: the index includes a selection of 21 lessons, instead of the 22 marked in its manuscript. Further, the reader searches in vain in the manuscript for lesson number 17 as listed in the index, while lessons numbers 3 and 16 are absent from the index (see below). The scribe of the titles in the margins of the JE manuscript and its index made use of abbreviations; the style of these titles is telegraphic. The terminological differences concern not only the formulae of the titles, but also the markers of the incipits.

48. See Jenner, *De perikopentitels*, pp. 397-400 and Bijlage C, Tafel 6. Cf. Burkitt, 'Lectionary System', pp. 301-38.
49. See Jenner, *De perikopentitels*, pp. 397-400 and Bijlage C, Tafel 6. Cf. Burkitt, 'Lectionary System', pp. 310-38.

fol. 92a

1 ܩܪܝܢܐ ܕܥܡܠ ܨܘܡܐ ܘܒܥܘܗܕܢܝ̈ ܠܦܘ̈ܫܩܐ ܘܕܚܫ ܒܫܒܐ ܫܒܬܐ
ܘܕܦܢܛܩܘܣܛܐ ܬܪ ܠܚܡܐ

2 ܩܪܝܢܐ ܒܥܘܗܕܢܐ ܕܟܗ̈ܢܐ ܘܕܫܡܫܬܐ ܕܫܡܫܬܐ ܛܒܬܐ. ܒܨܦܪܐ ܕܬܪܝܢ ܒܫܒܐ
ܕܐܪܒܥܐ:·

3 ܩܪܝܢܐ ܬܪܝܢ ܒܫܒܐ ܕܫܒܬܐ ܕܚܫܐ ܒܨܦܪܐ ܕܬܪܝܢ ܒܫ ܕ,

4 ܩܪܝܢܐ ܒܥܘܗܕܢܝ̈ ܐܦܝܣܩܘܦܐ ܒܨܦܪܐ ܕܬܠܬܐ ܒܫܒܐ ܕܚܡܫܐ

5 ܩܪܝܢܐ ܕܚܕܒܫܒܐ ܕܬܪܝܢ ܕܨܘܡܐ ܘܕܠ ܒܫܒܐ ܕܫܒ ܕܚܫ ܘܕܐܘܫܥܢܐ
ܘܕܠ ܒܫܒܐ ܕܫܒ ܬܠܬܐ ܒܨܦܪܐ ܘܕܡܫܡܫܢܐ ܒܫܒ ܕܫܒܥܐ

6 ܩܪܝܢܐ ܕܫܒܬܐ ܕܫܒܬܐ ܕܚܫܐ ܒܨܦܪܐ ܕܬܪ̈ܝܢ ܒܫܒܐ ܕܫܒܥܐ

7 ܩܪ, ܕܫܒܥܐ ܫܒܬܐ ܕܬܐܪܐ ܒܨܦܪܐ ܕܬܠܬܐ ܒܫܒܐ ܕܐܪܒܥܐ

8 ܩܪܝܢܐ ܒܥܘܗܕܢܐ ܕܡܠ̈ܦܢܐ ܘܕܣ̈ܗܕܐ ܒܨܦܪܐ ܕܬܪܝܢ ܒܫܒܐ ܕܬܪܝܢ

9 ܩܪܝܢܐ ܕܥܕܬܐ ܕܢܚ ܒܥܕܢܐ ܕܩܘܪܒܢܐ ܒܨܦܪܐ ܕܬܪܝܢ ܒܫܒܐ ܕܫܬܐ

10 ܩܪܝܢܐ ܕܫܘܠܡܗ ܕܡܪܝ, ܒܨܦܪܐ ܕܬܠܬܐ ܒܫܒܐ ܕܐܪܒܥܐ

11 ܩܪ, ܕܫܒܥܐ ܫܒܬܐ ܕܫܒܬܐ ܕܚܫܐ ܒܨܦܪܐ ܕܬܠܬܐ ܒܫܒܐ ܕܥܣܪܐ

fol. 92b

12 ܩܪ, ܒܥܘܗܕܢܝ, ܡܫܝܚ ܡܥܡܕ[ܢܘ]ܬܐ ܫܒܬܐ ܕܫܒܬܐ ܪܒ ܘܕܣܗܕܐ ܒܨܦܪ[ܐ]
ܕܐܪܒܥܐ ܦ ܕܬܠܬܐ

13 ܩ ܕܒܥܘܕܬܐ ܕܐܘܦܩ ܒܨܦܪܐ ܕܐܪܒܥܐ ܦ ܕܐܪܒܥܐ

14 ܩ ܕܚܕܒܫܒܐ ܬܠܬ ܐܝܟ ܒܨܦܪܐ ܕܐܪܒܥܐ ܦ ܕܗ

15 ܩܪ, ܕܚܕܒܫܒܐ ܕܗ ܕܨܘܡܐ. ܘܒܥܘܗܕܢܝ, ܫܠܝܚܐ ܘܕܚܫ ܒܫܒܐ ܕܫܒ ܕܚܫ.
ܒܨܦܪ ܕܕ ܒܫܒ ܕܘ

16 ܩܪ, ܗܘ ܕܗܘܐ ܒܗܝܠܐ. ܒܨܦܪܐ ܕܐܪܒܥܐ ܒܫܒܐ ܕܫܒܥܐ

17 ܩܪ, ܒܥܘܗܕܢܝ, ܒܬܘ̈ܠܐ. ܘܕܐܦܝܣܩܘ ܘܕܟܗ̈ܢܐ. ܘܕܝܠܕܬ ܐܠܗܐ ܘܕܚܫ ܒܫܒܐ
ܕܘ ܕܨܘܡ ܘܕܒ ܒܫܒܐ ܕܫܒ ܕܚܫ ܘܕܚܕܒܫܒܐ ܕܫܒܬܐ ܕܚܫܬܐ. ܒܨܦܪܐ
ܕܫܒܥܐ ܒܫܒܐ ܕܠ

18 ܩܪܝܢܐ ܒܥܘܗܕܢܐ ܕܒܬܘܠܐ ܘܕܚܫ ܗܝ ܐܦܝܣܩܘܦܐ. ܒܨܦܪܐ ܕܫܒܥܐ ܒܫܒܐ
ܕܫܒܥܐ:·

19 ܩܪܝܢܐ ܕܒܥܘܬܐ. ܒܨܦܪܐ ܕܫܒܥܐ ܒܫܒܐ ܕܬܫܥܐ

20 ܩܪܝܢܐ ܕܐܪܒܥܐ ܫܒܬܐ ܕܦܠܓܗ ܕܨܘܡܐ. ܒܨܦܪܐ ܕܫܒܥܐ ܒܫܒܐ
ܕܥܣܪܐ

21 ܩܪܝܢܐ ܕܬܪܝܢ ܒܫܒܐ ܕܫܒܬܐ ܬܠܬܐ ܘܕܐܢܦܠܝܢܐ [????], ܕܨܠܝܒܐ.
ܒܨܦܪܐ ܕܫܒܥܐ ܒܫܒܐ ܕܥܣܪܐ

Ben Sira is wanting in Jacob of Edessa's revision; no lectionary system for this book is preserved in L or the ancient biblical P-MSS. SH7 (for details see Appendix 3) is the only ancient biblical manuscript that contains a number of pericopes that are marked as belonging to some lectionary system.

To sum up, in evaluating the evidence of the ancient lectionary system or systems, one must take into account both the absence of sufficient MSS, and also the lacunae in the systems of which we do have remnants. These two areas of incomplete data warn the comparative scholar against jumping to hasty conclusions. Thus, although the data often show the same combination of pericope and ecclesiastical festivity or day of commemoration to be present in the lectionary system of Jacob of Edessa and in those systems preserved in the ancient biblical manuscripts, a detailed study also shows a substantial number of cases where there are considerable differences in terminology and in length of pericopes, as well as combinations peculiar to the system of Jacob of Edessa. The differences can be classified as follows:

a.   The lessons have the same incipits but differ in explicits.
b.   The lessons are based on the same pericope or part of it, but are read on different festival days and on different ecclesiastical occasions.
c.   The lessons are the same, but the terminology in their liturgical titles[50] differs.

There is thus some evidence to suggest that Jacob of Edessa selected a number of pericopes that were in common use in the whole ancient Syrian church; however, he seems to have developed in addition his own lectionary system.

The following reconstruction gives a fair picture of the elements of Jacob's lectionary system:

Holy Days (Celebrations)

Christmas	1 Sam. 1.19-28; Isa. 49.1-14; Dan. 2.31
Epiphany (night)	2 Sam. 23.13-17
Palm Sunday	Gen. 48.22; 2 Sam. 6.1-23; Isa. 60.8-22; Ezek. 43.1; Dan. 2.1-12

Holy week

Monday	1 Sam. 4.18-22; Isa. 28.9-23; Ezek. 3.4-13
Tuesday	1 Sam. 7.2-17; 1 Sam. 26.1-13; Dan. 9.20-27
Wednesday	1 Sam. 9.1-14; Ezek. 7.10; Dan. 6.1-11
Thursday	1 Sam. 10.17; 1 Sam. 16.1-13; Isa. 61.1-62.2; Ezek. 20.30; 21.14; Dan. 7.1-8
Good Friday	1 Sam. 26.14-25; Isa. 63.1-6; Ezek. 21.14; Dan. 6.12-15
Saturday	2 Sam. 24.1-25; Ezek. 11.1; 37.15; Dan. 3.26-37
Easter	1 Sam. 17.37-51; Isa. 60.1-7; 61.10–62.12; Ezek. 45.18; Dan. 6.20-25

50. I.e. the phrase in the manuscript which relates the pericope in question with a festival day or occasion.

Week of Rest

	Monday	1 Sam. 21.1-19; Ezek. 33.1; 33.7; Dan. 4.1
	Tuesday	Gen. 41.41; Ezek. 34.1; Dan. 2.1-12
	Wednesday	1 Sam. 12.6-12; Dan. 10.1
	Thursday	Isa. 62.3-12; Ezek. 20.30; 34.11; Dan. 8.1-15
	Friday	2 Sam. 7.18-29; Isa. 26.16–27.6; Ezek. 18.1; Dan. 8.1-15
	Saturday	Ezek. 19.1; Dan. 3.37-45
New Sunday		1 Sam. 1.1-13; Dan. 1.1-21
Ascension		Gen. 48.22; 2 Sam. 6.1-23; Ezek. 4.16; Dan. 7.6-14
Pentecost		1 Sam. 16.1-13; Isa. 48.12-22; Ezek. 2.1-6; Dan. 1.1-21

Normal Sundays

before *Christmas*   Ezek. 36.13
after *Christmas*   Exod. 3.1; Ezek. 46.8
after *Epiphany*

	First	Gen. 41.53; 1 Sam. 16.1-13
	Second	Ezek. 36.1
	Fifth	Ezek. 38.1
	Sixth	Ezek. 38.18
	Seventh	Ezek. 39.17
	Eighth	Ezek. 45.1

the weeks of the *Fast (period of Lent)*

	Beginning	1 Sam. 7.2-17; Isa. 58.1-9a + 59.2; Ezek. 3.16-21; Dan. 1.1-21; 2.31
	Second	1 Sam. 8.4-18; Isa. 33.13-22; Ezek. 8.1; Dan. 2.1-12
	Third	1 Sam. 14.24-29; Ezek. 14.13
	Fourth	2 Sam. 23.13-17; Isa. 59.2-8; Ezek. 3.14-15; 33.1
	Fifth	1 Sam. 2.11-27; Dan. 10.1
	Sixth	1 Sam. 21.1-19; Ezek. 43.10

the weeks after *Easter*

	Second	Ezek. 30.13
	Third	Ezek. 3.22; 22.17; 31.15
	Sixth	Ezek. 7.5
	Ninth	Ezek. 10.18-22; 20.13
	Tenth	Ezek. 11.14
	Eleventh	Ezek. 12.3-24
	Twelfth	Ezek. 22.1; 26.1
	Thirteenth	Ezek. 13.1-23
	Fourteenth	Ezek. 14.1
	Fifteenth	Ezek. 15.1
	Sixteenth	Ezek. 7.1; 16.36
	Seventeenth (?)	Ezek. 10.1; 17.11

Eighteenth	Ezek. 18.20
Twentieth	Ezek. 20.27
Twenty first	Ezek. 20.39
Twenty fourth	Ezek. 17.22
Twenty fifth	Ezek. 21.29
Twenty sixth	Ezek. 24.1
Twenty seventh	Ezek. 25.1; 27.1
Twenty ninth	Ezek. 28.20
Thirty first	Ezek. 32.1
Thirty second	Ezek. 33.21
Thirty third	Ezek. 35.6

On Week Days
in the week before *the Fast*

Thursday	Ezek. 45.10

in the weeks of *the Fast (period of Lent)*
First week

Wednesday	Ezek. 4.9-15
Saturday	Ezek. 5.11-17

Middle week

Monday	Ezek. 18.5
Tuesday	Ezek. 18.21
Wednesday	Dan. 9.15-19
Thursday	Ezek. 20.39
Friday	Ezek. 20.13

Commemorations

(Illegible)	Gen. 41.41
Apostles	1 Sam. 24.2-20; Dan. 10.1
John the Baptist	1 Sam. 21.1-19; Ezek. 33.1; Dan. 6.1-11
Bishop(s)	1 Sam. 11.13–12.5; 2 Sam. 5.23b-39; Isa. 50.4-11; Ezek. 11.22; 18.1; 44.17; Dan. 7.21-28; Bel Dr 23-31
Blessed doctors	Ezek. 14.13
Blessed (Theodore of Mopsuestia)	Dan. 1.1-21
Departed	Exod. 2.23; 3.1; 12.29; 1 Sam. 11.13–12.5; Isa. 25.6–26.15; Ezek. 11.22; 18.1; 34.9
Exiles	Isa. 25.1-12
Innocents	Isa. 60.8-22; Ezek. 34.20; Dan. 3.16
Martyrs	1 Sam. 17.37-51; Isa. 63.7; Ezek. 3.22; 34.9; Dan. 3.16; 6.1-11
Mother of God	1 Sam. 2.1-10; Ezek. 44.1
Priests	2 Sam. 20.4-13; Isa. 61.1–62.2; Ezek. 33.1; 44.17

| Prophets | 2 Sam. 20.4-13; Ezek. 3.22; Bel Dr 23-31 |
| The Just | 2 Sam. 1.1-16; Ezek. 14.13; Dan. 3.26-37 |

Rituals and Ceremonies

Attendants of the offering	Dan. 3.51-86
Baptism	Isa. 61.10–62.1; Ezek. 33.1
Dedication of the church	2 Sam. 7.1-17
Consecration of the Cross	1 Sam. 14.30-45; Dan. 9.20-27
Ordination (Priest)	Ezek. 2.6–3.3; Dan. 10.4
Tonsure	1 Sam. 3.1-14

Prayers/Rogations

Earthquake	Isa. 33.2-12
For rain/against drought	Isa. 32.9-15; Ezek. 14.13
Pestilence	2 Sam. 24.1-25
Rogations	1 Sam. 12.6-12; 2 Sam. 24.1-25; Isa. 7.14; 29.9-24; 32.9-15; 33.2-12; Dan. 9.4-10a

In short, the lectionary system(s) as reflected in the JE biblical manuscripts present the basic structure of the ancient ecclesiastical calendar of the whole Syrian Church as found in L and the ancient Peshitta manuscripts, that is: the celebration of the high feasts and fragments of the period of the great Fast. The data in the JE biblical manuscripts indicate an expansion similar to but not identical with that found in the ancient Peshitta manuscripts, particularly with reference to the lessons as marked in the margins.[51] These lessons in the margins of the Peshitta manuscripts correspond largely, though not in all respects, with those in the Syrohexaplaric manuscripts.

Comparison of the lectionary systems under investigation thus shows some overlap of the systems in the JE and P manuscripts. However, this overlap does not amount to evidence of a special relationship between these systems. The striking areas of overlap relate to the lessons of the relevant JE manuscripts, those in the margins of 6h5, 6h10 and to a lesser extent 7ph9. Elucidation of the nature, if any, of the relationship between the lessons in these manuscripts is beyond the scope of the present paper. The areas of overlap in the remaining biblical manuscripts of JE, P and SH relate to the ancient lectionary system(s) and reflect the ecclesiastical and liturgical calendar of that period.

51. Cf. Jenner, *De perikopentitels*, pp. 65-155.

Appendix 1

Abbreviations and symbols:

DE	Difference(s) in explicit(s)
DEC	Difference(s) in ecclesiastical calendar(s)
DI	Differences in incipit(s)
DT	Differences in terminology
*	Reading before it had been corrected in the MS
{ }	Reconstruction of a completely illegible portion of a liturgical title in 8a1
< >	Liturgical title in 8a1 part of which is not completely damaged, erased or faded, so that the traces of ink are legible.

Appendix 2
The MSS on which this Paper is Based

(N.B. MS München, Bayerische Staatsbibliothek, Syr. 1 (= JE) includes no reference to a lectionary system.)

Peshitta MSS

London, British Library
5b1: add. 14425
6h3: add. 12175, fols. 81-254
6h4: add. 14431
6h5: add. 14432, fols. 1-120/122
6h10: add. 14445
6h15: add. 17107
6h16: add. 17108
7g2: add. 14443, fols. 72-98
7h2: add. 12136
7h5: add. 14426
7h6: add. 14443, fols. 35-71
7h13: add. 12133, fols. 1-108
7k3: add. 14442, fols. 47-65
7k4: add. 14444, fols. 1-24
7ph9: add. 17191
8b1: Oriental 4400
8h2: add. 12135, fols. 1-43
8h4: add. 14430

Leningrad, M.E. Saltykov-Shedrin State Public Library
6h1: New Series 2

Dair as-Suryan
6h19: Syr. 22, fols. 41-104
6h21: Syr. 28, fols. 64-132

Milan, Ambrosian Library
7a1: B. 21 Inf.
7h10: A. 296 Inf., frags. 26-25

Monastery of St Catherine
7h10: Syriac 28
7h12: Syriac 35

Paris, Bibliothèque Nationale
8a1: Syriaque 341

Syrohexaplaric MSS

London, British Library
SH1: add. 14442, fols. 1-46
SH2: add. 12134, fols. 8-132
SH3: add. 14437, fols. 1-46
SH4: add. 17103, fols. 1-62
SH5: add. 17103, fols. 62-70
SH6: add. 12133, fols. 109-169
SH8: add. 14437, fols. 47-124
SH10: Oriental 8732, fols. 57-126

Milan, Ambrosian Library
SH7: C. 313 Inf.

Paris, Bibliothèque Nationale
SH9: Syriaque 27, fols. 1-91

Jerusalem, Monastery of St Marcus
SH11: no. 1

Midyat
SHM: s.n. (According to A. Vööbus (*The Pentateuch*, p. 29) now in the possession of Hans Lill.)

MSS of Jacob of Edessa's Revision

London, British Library
add. 14429
add. 14441

Rome, Vatican Library
Siriaco 5, fols. 91-141

Paris, Bibliothèque Nationale
Syriaque 26
Syriaque 27, fols. 91-141

Burkitt's Lectionary Edition

London, British Library
add. 14528, fols. 152-191

Appendix 3
SH MSS

SH1 Genesis: Gen. 37.17b-28 (fol. 26a) and 50.22-26 (fol. 46a); but note that 7h5mg and 8b1mg begin a lesson at Gen. 37.23 for Maundy Thursday.

SH2 Exodus: In this MS the liturgical titles and markers of the incipit are written in the text column. Exod. 1.1 (Third Sunday, fol. 8b), 1.8 (Sunday before Christmas, fol. 8b), 1.15 (Innocents | Fourth Sunday, fol. 9b), 2.11 (Fifth Sunday, fol. 11b), 3.1 (Christmas | the Departed, fol. 13a), 3.18 (Sixth Sunday, fol. 14b), 4.1 (mg, only incipit, fol. 15b), 4.18 (Sunday after Christmas, fol. 17b), 4.28 (Seventh Sunday, fol. 18b), 5.15 (Ninth Sunday, fol. 20b), 6.28 (Tenth Sunday, fol. 24a), 7.14 (Eleventh Sunday, fol. 25a), 7.19 (Palm Sunday, fol. 27a), 8.20 (Twelfth Sunday, fol. 29a), 9.1 (Thirteenth Sunday, fol. 30b), 9.13 (Fourteenth Sunday, fol. 32a), 9.27 (Fifteenth Sunday, fol. 34a), 10.3 (Sixteenth Sunday, fol. 35a), 10.12 (Seventeenth Sunday, fol. 36a), 10.21 (Eighteenth Sunday, fol 37a), 11.1 (Nineteenth Sunday, fol. 38a), 12.1 (Maundy Thursday, hora 9, fol. 39b), 12.29 (Twentieth Sunday | Easter Eve, fol. 42b), 12.41 (Easter Day, fol. 44a), 13.11 (Twenty-first Sunday, fol. 46a), 13.19 (Ascension, fol. 47a), 14.5 (Twenty-second Sunday, fol. 47b), 14.15 (Martyrs, fol. 49a), 14.21 (Twenty-third Sunday, fol. 49b), 15.1 (Enkainia = finding of the Cross, fol. 52b), 16.4 (Third Sunday of the Fast, fol. 53b), 16.22 (Fourth Sunday of the Fast, fol. 55b), 16.33 (Mother of God, fol. 56b), 17.1 (Tuesday in the Holy week, fol. 57a), 17.8 (Twenty-fourth Sunday, fol. 58a), 18.1 (Twenty-fifth Sunday, fol. 59a), 18.13 (Twenty-sixth Sunday, fol. 60a), 19.1 (Pentecost, fol. 62a), 19.9 Second Sunday of the Fast, fol. 62b), 19.17 (mg, only marker of the incipit, fol. 63b), 19.20 (Twenty-seventh Sunday, fol. 64a), 20.22 (Sunday 28, fol. 66b), 21.15 (Twenty-ninth Sunday, fol. 68b), 21.22 (Thirtieth Sunday, fol. 69b), 22.14 (Thirty-first Sunday, fol. 72a), 23.20 (Thirty-second Sunday, fol. 75a), 24.1 (Sunday of the beginning of the Fast, fol. 76b), 24.9 (Saturday of the week of Rest, fol. 77a), 25.1 (Thirty-third Sunday, fol. 78a), 28.1 (Thirty-fourth Sunday, fol. 87a), 30.12 (Thirty-fifth Sunday, fol. 97a), 30.34 (Thirty-sixth Sunday | Maundy Thursday, fol. 98a), 31.12 (Thirty-seventh Sunday, fol. 100a), 32.7 (Thirty-eighth Sunday, fol. 101b), 32.17 (Thirty-ninth Sunday, fol. 103a), 32.30 (Sunday after Epiphany, fol. 104a), 33.7 (Second Sunday after Epiphany, fol. 105a), 33.17 (Third Sunday after Epiphany, fol. 107a), 34.4b (Fourth Sunday after Epiphany, fol. 108a),

34.12 (Fifth Sunday after Epiphany, fol. 109a), 34.27 (Sixth Sunday after Epiphany, 110b), 35.30 (Seventh Sunday after Epiphany, fol. 114a), 40.17 (mg, Eighth Sunday after Epiphany, fol. 130b).

SH3 Numbers: Num. 11.16 (fol. 11a), 12.1 (fol. 13a), 17.1 (Christmas, fol. 24b), 20.1 (Epiphany, fol. 30a), 20.22 (fol. 32a), 21.4 (Good Friday, fol. 33a), 21.10 (fol. 33b), 22.22 (Palm Sunday, fol. 37a).

SH4 Judges: Judg. 2.4-9 (fol. 6b), 5.1-11 (Palm Sunday, fol. 14a), 13.12-18 (fol. 39a), 15.9-13 (fol. 42b), 20.26-28 (fol. 57a).

SH5 Ruth: Ruth 4.18-end (fol. 69b).

SH6 Joshua: Josh 5.9-10 (fol. 117b), 20.1-6 (fol. 154a), 24.29-end (fol. 168a).

SH7 Isaiah: The MS presents only the incipit and explicit of the lessons and is lacking in the titles: Isa. 1.16-27 (fol. 173b-174a), 4.2-6 (fol. 174b), 5.11-23 (= SH10, fol. 175a), 7.3–8.4 (= SH 10, fol. 175b), 8.9-20 (= SH10, fol. 175b-176a), 9.1-7 (fol. 176a), 10.32–11.10 (= SH10, DI, fol. 177a), 12.1-6 (= SH10, fol. 177a), 27.1-9a (= SH10, fol. 180a-180b), 31.4–32.4 (fol. 182b), 32.1-8 (= 6h5mg SH10, fol. 182b), 40.1-11 (= 6h5 SH7 SH10, fol. 185a), 42.1-13 (= SH10, fol. 186a), 43.1-10 (fol. 186a-186b), 43.1-15 (= SH10, fol. 186a-186b), 48.20–50.11 (= SH7 SH10, fol. 188a-188b), 51.1-3/11 (= 6h5mg SH10, fol. 188b/188b-189a), 52.6-12 (= SH10, DI, fol. 189a), 52.13 (= 6h3 SH10, fol. 189a-189b), 55.3–56.1 (= SH7 SH10, fol. 190a), 56.10–57.4 (= SH10, fol. 190a), 58.1-8a (= 6h3 6h5 <8a1> JE SH7 SH10, fol. 190b), 58.6-12 (fol. 190b), 60.1 (= L 6h5mg SH7 SH10, DT, fol. 191a), 60.18–61.9 (= SH7 SH10, DI, fol. 191b), 61.10–62.5 (= L 6h5mg SH7 SH10, DE, fol. 191b), 62.10-12 (= SH7 SH10, fol. 191b), 63.7-14 (= SH7 SH10, fol. 192a), 65.8-16 (= SH7 SH10, fol. 192b), 65.16-24 (fol. 192b), 66.18-24 (= SH10, fol. 193a).

SH7 Jeremiah: The MS does not provide the title to which the markers of the incipits in the margin refer: Jer. 3.14-22 (fol. 117a-117b), 11.15-19 (fol. 121a), 18.18-23a (fol. 123b), 23.2-8 (fol. 125a), 30(H)/ 37(GR).8-10 (fol. 128a), 30(H)/ 37(GR).18-31(H)/ 38(GR).3 (fol. 128a-128b), 30(H)/ 37(GR).18-23 (fol. 128a-128b), 31(H)/ 38(GR).1-9 (fol. 128b), 31(H)/ 38(GR).10-14 (fol. 128b), 31(H)/ 38(GR).15-25 (fol. 128b), 31(H)/ 38(GR).23-34 (fol. 128b-129a), 34(H)/ 41(GR).8-16 (fol. 130b), 36(H)/ 43(GR).4-10 (fol. 131a), 38(H)/ 45(GR).1-6 (fol. 132a), 50(H)/ 27(GR).33–51(H)/ 28(GR).6 (fol. 136b-137a).

SH7 Ezekiel: The MS does not provide the title to which the markers of the incipits in the margin refer: Ezek. 4.9-11 (fol. 153b), 16.1-9 (fol. 157a), 17.9-24 (fol. 138a-138b), 36.22-28 (fol. 167a), 36.33-38 (*idem*), 37.1-15 (fol. 167a-167b), 37.16-26 (fol. 167b), 39.1-10 (fol. 168a), 43.1-9 (fol. 170a), 43.18a–44.4 (fol. 170b), 44.15-19 (fol. 171a), 47.1-12 (fol. 172a), 47.2-12 (*idem*).

SH7 The Twelve Prophets: The MS does not provide the title to which the markers of the incipits in the margin refer: Hos. 6.5-7.1 (fol. 98a), Amos 8.5-13 (fol. 101a-

101b), Mic. 4.1-8 (fol. 102b), 5.2-10 (fol. 103a), Joel 2.12-20 (fol. 104a), 3.1-21 (fol. 104b), Jon. 1.11-17 (105b), Zech. 6.10-15 (fol. 110b), 7.1-11 (fol. 111a), 8.3-8 (fol. 111a), 9.9-16 (fol. 111b), 11.10-14 (fol. 112a), 12.8-13 (fol. 112a), 13.7–14.10 (fol. 112b), Mal. 2.5-7 (fol. 113a).

SH7 Proverbs: The MS does not provide the title to which the markers of the incipits in the margin refer: Prov. 1.10-19 (DE, fol. 53a-53b), 1.19-21 (fol. 53b), 1.22-33 (fol. 53b), 2.20b–3.8 (fol. 54a), 3.11-18 (fol. 54a), 3.27–4.9 (= 8a1, fol. 54a-54b), 4.10-22 (fol. 54b), 5.7-16 (fol. 55a), 8.5-21a (fol. 56a), 8.22-31 (DE, fol. 56a-56b), 8.32 (fol. 56b), 10.20-25 (fol. 57a), 10.27–11.7 (fol. 57a), 13.9-21 (fol. 58a), 24.10b-18 (DI, fol. 62b). Compared with the evidence in P-MSS, the MS in some pericopes shows up a different incipit or explicit.

SH7 Job: The MS does not provide the title to which the markers of the incipits in the margin refer: Job 11.12-19 (fol. 42a-42b), 19.20-29 (fol. 44b), 30.6-13 (fol. 47b), 31.3-22 (fol. 47b-48a), 31.23-35a (fol. 48a), 37.1-5 (fol. 50a), 38.1-17 (fol. 50a-50b).

SH7 Wisdom: The MS does not provide the title to which the markers of the incipits in the margin refer: Wis. 1.1-15 (1, fol. 72a-72b), 1.16 (2, fol. 72b), 2.12-21 (3, fol. 72b), 3.1 (4, fol. 72b), 4.1-9 (5, fol. 73a), 4.17–5.5 (6, fol. 73b), 6.10-19 (7, fol. 74a), 7.7-17a (= 8a1, 8, fol. 74a-74b), 7.15-27 (9, fol. 74b), 10.9-14 (10, fol. 75b), 10.10-14 (11, fol. 75b), 10.15-21 (12, fol. 75b), 11.23–12.2 (13, fol. 76a), 14.1-6 (14, fol. 77a), 19.5 (15, fol. 79b). The incipit of each pericope is related to a number, so the composer of the lectionary system took 15 pericopes from Wisdom.

SH7 Daniel: The MS does not provide the title to which the markers of the incipits in the margin refer: Dan. 1.3-5 (fol. 143b), 5.13-29 (fol. 147a), 6.11-17 (fol. 147b), 7.13-22 (fol. 148a), 8.1-17a (fol. 148a-148b).

SH7 Ecclesiastes: The MS does not provide the title to which the markers of the incipits in the margin refer: Eccl. 5.4-11 (fol. 67a).

SH7 Ben Sira: The MS does not provide the title to which the markers of the incipits in the margin refer: Sir. 1.16-27 (fol. 81a), 17.1-26 (fol. 85b), 18.25–19.6 (fol. 86a), 19.22-28 (fol. 86a), 22.27–23.6 (fol. 87a-87b), 24.19–31.9 (fol. 88a), 29.1-12 (fol. 89b), 32/35.17–33/36.11 (fol. 89b-90a), 37.16-26 (fol. 92a-92b), 38.1-14 (fol. 92b), 39.1-10 (fol. 93a), 39.12-32 (fol. 93a), 48.1-5 (fol. 96a).

SH8 Kings: The MS does not provide us with titles; the incipits 1 Kgs 13.20 (fol. 90b), 19.2 (fol. 107b) and 21.28 (116b) are marked in the margin, only the first is shared with all the P-MSS under investigation.

SH9 Kings: The MS contains six lessons, each of which is connected with a liturgical title: 2 Kgs 2.13-22 (Easter Day, fol. 13a), 2.19-22 (mg, the night of Epiphany, fol. 13b), 4.1-17 (commemoration of *kamptria*, fol. 17b), 4.30-37 (Easter Day, fol. 20a), 13.14 (Maundy Thursday, fol. 49b), 23.21-24 (Easter Day, 81b).

SH10 Isaiah: The manuscript contains the following lessons: Isa. 5.1 (= 6h5, Wednesday in the Great Week, fol. 57a), 5.8 (= 6h5mg, DEC, Wednesday in the week of the beginning of the Fast, Twelfth Sunday, fol. 57b), 5.11 (= SH7, Thirteenth Sunday, fol. 58b), 6.1-8 (Ascension, fol. 59a), 7.3 (= SH7, Good Friday, fol. 60b), 7.10 (= 6h5 8a1, Christmas, fol. 60b), 8.1-5 (= 6h5mg, DE, the Mother of God, fol. 62a), 8.9 (= SH7, Mar Zakkay, the Saints, fol. 62b), 9.7 (= 6h5mg, Fourteenth Sunday, fol. 64a), 10.1 (= 6h5mg, Seventh Sunday after Epiphany, fol. 65a), 10.12 (Sunday of the forty [Martyrs], fol. 65b), 10.33 (= L 6h5mg SH7, DT DI, Epiphany, fol. 66b), 11.11 (Twentieth Sunday, fol. 67a), 12.1-6 (= SH7, Epiphany, fol. 67b), 13.1 (= 6h5mg, Fifteenth Sunday, fol. 68a), 13.9 (= 6h5mg, DI, Rogations, fol. 68b), 13.17 (= 6h5mg, Sixteenth Sunday, fol. 69a), 17.7 (= 6h5mg, DI, Seventeenth Sunday, fol. 73a), 19.1 (= 6h5mg, Sunday after Christmas, fol. 74b), 22.15 (Third Sunday before Christmas, fol. 78a), 24.1 (= 6h5mg, Rogation against drought, fol. 79b), 24.16 (the Cross, fol. 80b), 25.1-10 (= 6h5mg, the Departed, fol. 81a), 26.1 (= 6h5mg, Second Sunday after Epiphany, fol. 81b), 26.12 (= 6h5mg, in time of wrath and death, fol. 82a), 27.1-9a, (= SH10, Sunday before the first week of the Fast, fol. 82b), 28.9 (= 6h5mg, Monday in the Great Week, fol. 84a), 29.9 (= 6h5mg, Nineteenth/Twenty-ninth? Sunday, Rogations, fol. 86a), 30.6 (= 6h5mg, Twentieth Sunday, fol. 87a-b), 30.20 (= 6h5mg, DI, Twenty-first Sunday, fol. 88b), 31.1 (= 6h5mg, Twenty-second Sunday, fol. 89b), 32.1 (= 6h5mg SH7, Twenty-third Sunday, fol. 90a), 32.9 (= 6h5mg, Rogations, especially against drought, fol. 90b), 32.14 (St Drusius, Eighth Sunday after Epiphany, fol. 91a), 33.1 (Second Sunday of the Fast, fol. 91b), 33.13-22 (= 6h5mg, Twenty-fourth Sunday, fol. 92a), 34.1 (= 6h5mg, Twenty-fifth Sunday, fol. 93a), 35.1-10 (= SH11, Second Sunday of the Fast, Monday in the week of white/ Easterweek, Tonsure, Sixth week of the Fast, Baptism, fol. 94a), 36.1 (= L 6h3 6h5mg, Thursday of the week of Rest, fol. 94b), 37.21 (= 6h5mg, Twenty-sixth Sunday, fol. 97b), 38.1 (= 6h5mg, the Prophets, fol. 98b), 38.9/10 (= 6h5mg SH11, Sunday of the middle of the Fast, the Departed, fol. 99a), 38.29 (= 6h5mg, DI, Twenty-seventh Sunday, fol. 99b), 40.1 (= 6h5 SH7 SH11, John the Baptist, fol. 100a), 40.12 (= 6h5mg, Twenty-eighth Sunday, fol. 101a), 40.25 (prime of Nocturn, the monks, fol. 101b), 41.1 (= 6h5mg, Twenty-ninth Sunday, fol. 102a), 41.8 (= SH11, DEC, the oblation of the nun, fol. 102b), 41.17b/18 (Thirtieth Sunday, fol. 103a), 42.1 (= 8a1 SH7, St Stephen, first of the Martyrs, fol. 104a), 42.10 (Anthony, fol. 104b), 42.16b (Thirty-first Sunday, fol. 104b), 43.1 (= SH7, the Innocents, the forty Martyrs, fol. 105b), 43.15 (= 6h5mg, DI, Fifth Sunday of the Fast, Baptism, fol. 106a), 43.25 (= SH11, Friday of the week of white, fol. 106b), 44.6 (= L 6h3 6h5mg 8a1, Saturday of the week of Rest, the Martyrs, fol. 107a), 44.21 (= 6h5mg, Thirty-second Sunday, fol. 108a), 45.1 (Fifth Sunday after Easter, fol. 108b), 45.9 (Thirty-third Sunday, fol. 109a-b), 45.17 (= SH 11, New Sunday, Thirty-fourth Sunday, fol. 110a), 46.3 (Thirty-fifth Sunday, fol. 110b), 47.1 (Thirty-sixth Sunday, fol. 111b), 48.1 (= SH11, DEC, Thirty-seventh Sunday, fol. 112b), 48.12 (= L 6h3 6h5mg {8a1}, Pentecost, fol. 113a), 48.20 (= SH7 SH11, Sunday before Epiphany, fol. 113b), 49.1 (DEC, Ascension, fol. 114a), 49.8 (= 6h5mg , Fifth Sunday after Epiphany, fol. 114b), 49.21b (Thirty-eighth Sunday, fol. 115b), 50.4 (= L 6h3 6h5mg SH11, DI DEC, Good Friday, fol.

116a), 51.1 (= 6h5mg SH7, Fourth Sunday after Easter, the saints, St John bar Eph-tonia and St Severus, fol. 116b), 51.4 (= SH11, Wednesday in the week of white/ Easterweek, fol. 117a), 51.17 (= SH11, DEC, Tuesday in the week of Rest, fol. 117b), 52.1 (= 6h5 SH11, DI, Second Sunday before Christmas, the Apostles, patriarch Peter, John bar Qursis, fol. 118b), 52.7 (= 6h5mg, Palm Sunday, fol. 119a), 52.13 (= 6h3 SH7 SH11, Maundy Thursday, fol. 119b), 54.1 (= 6h5mg 8a1 SH11, DEC, Sixth Sunday after Easter, Restoration of the Temple, fol. 120b), 54.9 (= 6h5mg SH11, DI DEC, Third Sunday after Easter, fol. 121a), 54.14 (= SH11, DT, tonsure of the monks, fol. 121a), 55.1 (= 6h5mg, Tuesday in the Great Week, fol. 121b), 55.3 (= SH7 SH11, Third Sunday of the Fast, fol. 121b), 56.1 (Thirty-seventh Sunday, fol. 122b), 56.9/10–57.4 (= SH7, Easter Eve, fol. 123a), 58.1 (= 6h3 6h5 <8a1> SH7 SH11 JE, Sunday of the beginning of the Fast, fol. 124b), 59.1 (= 6h5mg JE, DI, Fourth Sunday of the Fast, fol. 126a), 59.11b (Sunday of the forty, fol. 126b), 60.1 (= L 6h5mg SH7, DT, baptism, fol. 127b), 60.8 (= 6h5mg JE, the Apostles, the Innocents, Wednesday in the week of Rest, fol. 127b), 60.17 (the first in Kanun II, St Ignatius, Basilius, Gregorius, fol. 128b), 61.1-6 (= L, DT, Thursday of the Chrisma, fol. 129a), 61.10–62.5 (= L 6h5mg SH7 SH11, DT DI, Easter, St Drusius, fol. 129b), 62.10 (= SH7 SH11, Palm Sunday, fol. 130a), 63.1 (= 6h5mg, Good Friday, fol. 130b), 63.7 (= JE SH7 SH11, DEC, Easter, Pentecost, fol. 131a), 63.15 (= 6h5mg, Rogations in case of Earthquake, fol. 131b), 65.8 (= SH7 SH11, DEC, the Apostle Paul, fol. 133a), 65.13 (= 6h5mg, 22 Nisan, patriarch Peter, the Martyrs, the unleavened bread, the Just, fol. 133b), 66.8 (= 6h5mg, Saturday in the week of white/Easterweek, the Departed, fol. 135a), 66.18 (= SH7, the first in the month Ayr, St Athanasius, Simeon Saba, the Apostle Thomas, fol. 136a).

SH11 Isaiah: The MS contains the following lessons (the folio numbering is made from the film): Isa. 35.1 (= SH10, Sunday of the second week of the Fast, Monday in the week of white, fol. 11a), 38.9/10 (= 6h5mg SH10, Sunday of the beginning of the Fast, fol. 17a), 40.1 (= 6h5 SH7 SH10, John the Baptist, fol. 19a), 40.18 (the Martyrs, fol. 20a), 41.8 (= SH10, DEC, the Apostles, fol. 21b), 43.25 (= SH10, Friday in the week of white, fol. 27a), 45.17 (= SH10, New Sunday, fol. 31a), 48.1 (= SH10, DEC, Pentecost, fol. 34b), 48.20 (= SH7 SH10, Sunday before Epiphany, fol. 35b), 49.13-23 (Tuesday in the week of white, fol. 36b), 50.4-11(= SH10 6h3 6h5mg, DI DEC, Good Friday, fol. 38a), 51.4-12 (= SH10, Wednesday in the week of white, fol. 39a), 51.17 (= SH10, DEC, Easter eve, fol. 40b), 52.1-12 (= SH10, Second Sunday before Christmas, the Apostles, fol. 41a), 52.13 (= SH7 SH10 6h3, Maundy Thursday, fol. 42a), 54.1 (= SH10, DEC, Tuesday of the week of Rest, fol. 43b), 54.9 (= SH10, DEC, Wednesday of the week of Rest, fol. 44a), 54.14 (= SH10, DT, Tonsure, fol. 44b), 55.3 (= SH7 SH10, Sunday of the third week of the Fast, fol. 45a), 58.1 (= SH7 SH10 JE 6h3 6h5 <8a1>, Sunday of the beginning of the Fast, fol. 48a), 58.6-12 (= SH7, Sunday of the fifth week of the Fast, fol. 49a), 60.1 (= SH7 SH10, DEC, Tuesday of the week of Rest, fol. 51b), 60.19 (the Bishops, fol. 52b), 61.10 (= SH7 SH10, DEC, Easter Eve, fol. 53b), 62.10-12 (= SH7 SH10, Palm Sunday, fol. 54b), 63.7-14 (= SH7 SH10 JE, DEC, Easter Sunday, Pentecost, fol. 55a), 65.8 (= SH7 SH10, DEC, Easter, fol. 59b).

SHM Leviticus: Lev. 7.19b (fol. 72b), 22.31 (fol. 93b), 23.26 (fol. 94b), and 26.42 (fol. 100b).

SHM Numbers: Num. 5.10b (fol. 110b), 9.4-14 (fol. 116b and 117a), 15.1 (fol. 125a), 20.1 (fol. 130a), 21.10 (fol. 130a), 21.10 (fol. 132a), 22.21 (fol. 133b), and 24.3 (fol. 136a).

SHM Deuteronomy: Deut. 15.1 (fol. 170b), 16.1 (fol. 171b), 21.21 (fol. 177a), 24.8 (fol. 179b), 26.17 (fol. 181b), and 28.66 (fol. 185b).

'COME HERE...AND LET US SIT AND READ...':
THE USE OF PSALMS IN FIVE SYRIAC AUTHORS

David J. Lane

Preface

These words of Jacob of Serugh[1] introduce an article that considers
ways in which five Syriac authors quoted Scripture. It provides warnings about the use of patristic material for critical editions of biblical
books, and shows this to be as perilous an activity as the use of back
translations of versions to suppose *Vorlage*. It also expresses my gratitude for discussions and correspondence with Michael Weitzman,
whose death has deprived Syriac studies of a fine scholar in mid-career.
He has joined others whose premature death robbed Syriac studies of
great light:[2] William Cureton, cataloguer and editor of Syriac manuscripts, who died as the result of a railway accident in 1863; Mgr Addai
Scher, another cataloguer and editor, killed in the massacres of 1915;
and two notable contributors to Peshitta studies: John Pinkerton killed
in action in 1916, and C. Peters who perished in the Nazi period. From
these we have gained much, but could have gained so much more.

Introduction

In recent years much valuable work has been done on the Syriac Bible,
Old and New Testaments alike. The Leiden Peshitta project,[3] and the

---

1. *Against the Jews* 4.177. The references are taken from Micheline Albert,
Jacques de Saroug: Homélies contre les juives (PO, 38; Turnhout: Brepols, 1976).
2. P.B. Dirksen, *An Annotated Bibliography of the Peshiṭta of the Old Testa-
ment* (MPIL, 5; Leiden: E.J. Brill, 1989). C.B. Moss, *Catalogue of Syriac Printed
Books and Related Literature in the British Museum* (London: Trustees of the
British Museum, 1962).
3. Various editors, *The Old Testament in Syriac According to the Peshiṭta
Version* (Leiden: E.J. Brill, 1962–). Psalms was published in 1980.

Munster New Testament project[4] provide necessary basic tools; the related works of concordances[5] and monographs[6] make them applicable. Consequently Syriac Bible studies are emerging from an isolation that was inevitable when they were a matter chiefly for textual critics[7] or, more recently, of translation technique.[8] This article looks at a related topic, also being currently addressed: the use of Scripture by Syriac authors.[9] The term 'use of Scripture' is deliberately chosen, rather than 'quotation of Scripture', which oversimplifies a complex matter.

The matter is complex for four reasons. First, successive scribes may have consciously or unconsciously modified an author's biblical phrases so that they accord with what was to them a familiar or standard text pattern: hence an accurate edition of the author's work is a prerequisite for study of the author's use of Scripture. Secondly, a judgment as to whether an author is citing from a text *sous les yeux*, from memory, or from personal composition requires knowledge of what text traditions were available to that author. This could be a local text, or one recognizable as more or less standard within the Peshitta text tradition, or one having fresh points of contact with Greek or Hebrew patterns. To use such terms as 'Peshitta', 'MT' or 'LXX' confuses: they refer to general patterns of text, within which there are variations, the consequence of

---

4. Barbara Aland and Andreas Juckel (eds.), *Das Neue Testament in syrischer Überlieferung* (Arbeiten zur Neutestamentliche Textforschung; Berlin: W. de Gruyter, 1986–).

5. The Peshiṭta Institute, *The Old Testament in Syriac According to the Peshiṭta Version*. V. *Concordance* (Leiden: E.J. Brill, 1997). W. Strothmann, *Konkordanz zur syrischen Bibel* (14 vols.; Wiesbaden: Otto Harrassowitz, 1984–1995). George Anton Kiraz, *A Computer Generated Concordance to the Syriac New Testament* (6 vols.; Leiden: E.J. Brill, 1993).

6. Monographs of the Peshiṭta Institute, Leiden, 9 volumes so far, from 1972 onwards.

7. E.g. P.B. Dirksen and M.J. Mulder (eds.), *The Peshiṭta: Its Early Text and History* (MPIL, 4; Leiden: E.J. Brill, 1988).

8. E.g. P.B. Dirksen and A. van der Kooij (eds.), *The Peshiṭta as a Translation* (MPIL, 8; Leiden: E.J. Brill, 1995).

9. R.G. Jenkins, *The Old Testament Quotations of Philoxenus of Mabbug* (CSCO, 514, Subs, 84; Leuven: Peeters, 1989). D.J. Lane, 'The Well of Life: Šubḥalmaran's Use of Scripture', *OCA* 256 (1998), pp. 49-59. R.J. Owens, *The Genesis and Exodus Citations of Aphrahat the Persian Sage* (MPIL, 3; Leiden: E.J. Brill, 1983). M.J. Suggs, 'The Use of Patristic Evidence in the Search for a Primitive New Testament Text', *NTS* 4 (1957–58), pp. 139-47 provides a valuable introduction to the matter.

different attempts at translation, of difference in time or place of manuscript copying, or even fashion. The western part of the Syriac church came to regard the Greek Bible as normative, letting that influence text or promote revision. Philoxenus's use of Scripture is a case in point: he uses a text for Psalms that has different characteristics from that which he used for Genesis, Exodus and Isaiah.[10] Hence there is need for critical editions of biblical texts, with provision for variant readings.

However, quotation is a matter of mind as well as text. Philoxenus varied his method as well as his exemplars, on occasion manipulating quotation in the service of argument.[11] This is the third element of complexity. Like scribes of liturgical manuscript, authors modify the syntax or vocabulary of quoted passages to suit their nature as excerpts rather than as a running text. Introductory phrases appear; there are insertions of *dalath* or *lam* to mark quotation; and there are alterations of syntax appropriate to a change from direct to indirect speech, for example the change of grammatical number or case, or the replacement of pronoun by proper name. The fourth element of complexity is the chief concern of this article. An author may completely reshape a biblical passage or phrase to make it more effectively persuasive. The quotation may be made straightforwardly as a ground for argument, incidentally as illustration, or obliquely as allusion. Quotation is a literary genre, a category of rhetoric. It is a means of persuasion, of inviting consent on the part of the reader or listener. It may achieve this by eliciting pleasurable recognition, by laying a ground for consent on the basis of mutually accepted authority, or by making a case sound eminently reasonable. Rules, or at any rate customs, may be identified. What follows examines the intention and context of Psalm quotations made by five Syriac authors who have different aims and methods, and provides illustration of these rules or customs.

Five Authors and their Purposes

The five authors selected are Narsai[12] from the fifth century, Jacob of Serugh[13] from the fifth and sixth, John of Dalyatha[14] and Joseph

---

10. Jenkins, *Philoxenus*, p. 177.

11. Jenkins, *Philoxenus*, p. 169.

12. Philippe Gignoux, *Homélies de Narsaï sur la création: Edition critique du texte syriaque, introduction et traduction française* (PO, 34; Turnhout: Brepols, 1968).

Ḥazzaya[15] from the eighth, and Ishodad of Merv[16] from the ninth. They are chosen to represent a spread of literary activity in time, genre and method. Psalm quotations have been selected in order to limit the scope of the study while still showing representative material. Further, Psalms play a large part in Syriac ascetical and liturgical life: Ishodad of Merv states that the church requires candidates for all ecclesiastical degrees to be able to recite the Psalms without carelessness or hurry,[17] Joseph Ḥazzaya that solitaries in their cell must recite the whole of David between night and day.[18]

The range of these authors' genre and method is suggested by their lives. Narsai was born at the end of the fourth century; in his early years he was a refugee from Sasanian persecution of Christians, and in his later from the results of Sasanian–Roman hostilities. Theological and military conflicts led him to flee from the school at Edessa to develop that at Nisibis. His writings reflect scientific as well as biblical bases, and the pragmatic approach of the school of Antioch and Theodore of Mospuestia. Half a century later, Jacob of Serugh was educated at the school of Edessa, but took up a position contrary to its Christology. He shows the metaphoric slant of that school, but friendship with Severus, Philoxenus of Mabbug and John of Tella suggests that he was of a more conceptual cast of mind. This is even more markedly so in the case of John of Dalyatha, born in the north of present Iraq in the early part of the eighth century, and who entered the religious life on Mount Qardu, now in eastern Turkey, where Syriac, following Jewish, tradition placed the resting of Noah's ark. Later he moved further east to the monastery of Dalyatha, 'Vineshoots'. Following Evagrius he brings a philosophical and psychological dimension to asceticism. His near contemporary

---

13. Albert, *Contre les juives*; Frédéric Rilliet, *Jacques de Saroug: Six homélies festales en prose: Edition critique du texte syriaque, introduction et traduction française* (PO, 43; Turnhout: Brepols, 1986).

14. Robert Beulay, *La collection des lettres de Jean de Dalyatha: Edition critique du texte syriaque inédit, traduction française, introduction et notes* (PO, 39; Turnhout: Brepols, 1978).

15. Paul Harb, François Graffin and Micheline Albert, *Lettre sur les trois étapes de la la vie monastique: Edition critique du texte syriaque, traduction et introduction* (PO, 45; Turnhout: Brepols, 1992).

16. Ceslas van den Eynde, *Commentaire d'Išoʻdad de Merv sur l'Ancien Testament. VI. Psaumes* (CSCO, 185 [texte], 186 [translation]; Leuven: Peeters, 1981).

17. Van den Eynde, *Psaumes*, Introduction §5.

18. Harb *et al.*, *Trois Etapes*, §73.

Joseph Ḥazzaya is in a similar mould. His own life as monk, solitary and Superior are reflected in his approach to the spiritual life. The development of the soul is modelled on changes in practical life, from monastic to partly and then completely solitary. Ishodad of Merv, Bishop of Ḥdatta and (happily for him) unsuccessful candidate for the Catholicate in 852, brings us back to the approach of Narsai. Like him, his approach is pragmatic and exegetical, and, most usefully for us, draws on the work of his predecessor commentators.

The five authors between them exemplify two different approaches, expository and exegetical. The distinction between these is important in any assessment of authors' use of Scripture. Expository authors, like Jacob of Serugh, but more obviously John of Dalyatha and Joseph Ḥazzaya, make conceptual points for which quotations provide example, allusion or illustration. Exegetical authors, like Narsai and Ishodad of Merv, take a theme or, more usually, a biblical text, and explain points that readers or listeners may find difficult or interesting, and provide explanation or illustration from other biblical passages or from science, philosophy or history. They usually provide extensive extracts: commenting on Acts, Ishodad of Merv cites short or long blocks of text, and then answers the questions that a practical person might want to have answered, providing additional useful information. Ephrem, commenting on the Diatessaron, starts with almost a running text, and provides such information as an imaginative person might wish to know. The distinction, though important, is not necessarily absolute. Ephrem the exegete also writes hymns that are so allusive that it has been said that to reconstruct his biblical text from them is like attempting to put together the King James version from the hymns of John Wesley.[19] Jacob of Serugh the expositor illustrates the human need for divine nourishment by associating Jesus in the manger with a physical metaphor in Ps. 49.20, 'mankind, of its own free-will, is become like a beast'. So an author may not be exclusively one or the other, but a particular piece of work will tend to one rather than the other. The effect of this is that if comment is based on a running text or significant phrases, a plain meaning of text may be supposed, and a known, identifiable text form will most likely be used. If, on the other hand, there is a running argument, quotations may be closely referenced to the text, but are

19. Jeffrey Paul Lyon, *Syriac Gospel Translations: A Comparison of the Language and Translation Method in the Old Syriac, the Diatesseron, and the Peshitto* (CSCO, 548, Subs, 88; Leuven: Peeters, 1994), p. 6.

more likely to be brief or in a free style or in allusion. The appeal here
is not to an objective text, but to the memory of a text in the reader's
mind. The selectivity of material is more marked. For example, the
seventh-century expository author Shubḥalmaran, writing on the ascetic
life,[20] uses much Scripture, but not the Psalter. He demonstrates the
pattern set by Jesus in the mould of Old and New Testament fellow-
ascetics, and so uses only material that plainly describes relevant
action: the conceptual approach of Psalms is not relevant. All these
considerations affect 'reliability' in the matter of quotation. A rule may
be formulated:

> Ignorance of an author's aim and method invalidates use of that author's
> quotations as evidence for a particular reading or type of text.

We now turn to our examples.

Ishodad of Merv

Ishodad is taken first, because he is the most straightforward of the
authors. He is a pragmatic commentator who quotes only the few words
he thinks merit a comment with reference to their plain meaning. He
provides a useful yardstick by which to assess the others, earlier though
they be. The plain meaning is elicited by associating Psalms with events
in the time of David, dated on internal grounds. Their present order, he
explains,[21] is set by Ezra, who collected the surviving fragments after
the exile. Hence Ps. 39 'Deliver me O Lord from the...man' should
precede Ps. 6 'Do not...in your anger...' because (chronologically)
David's persecution by Saul took place earlier than his sin with Bath-
sheba; in the same way Ps. 22 'My God my God why have you
abandoned me', appropriate to his persecution by Absalom, is earlier
than Ps. 18 which relates to the end of his life. This method of 'dating'
is found, of course, in Psalm headings which are the work of editors
and collectors, not the original author.

Ishodad's brevity in quotation enables his treatment of Ps. 28 to be
given in entirety:

---

20. *The Book of Gifts*, British Library Oriental MS 6714 fols. 1-73. See Lane,
'The Well of Life'.

21. Van den Eynde, *Psaumes*, Introduction §X.

3. 'They are saying "Peace".' That is, they are praying with their mouth that I am restored to health. 'And wickedness in their heart'. That is, inwardly they are seeking that I die, so that they might escape fearing me, and effect all they desire.

4. 'Reward them': like you did the Assyrians.

5. 'Because they do not understand what you did to them' chase them, like them, from your land. 'Save your people': as you saved them from the Egyptians, etc.

The interpretation follows the method given in his Introduction §XIII: David composed his Psalms in a historical rather than allegorical sense. So Ps. 28 is related to Ps. 27, which David as a prophet uttered in the person of Ezekiel the prophet, the link being that both were treated alike by their parents. He denies the validity of allegory, admitting only that some phrases are to be understood as metaphor: 'He speaks of God as if he has a body...for corporal beings can understand only what is adapted to their way of thinking'. Hence Ps. 1 'blessed is the man who has not gone in the way of the unrighteous...I have not sat down with the ungodly' has the meaning 'I have not sinned'. That 'there' refers not to physical place but manner of acting is shown by Ps. 50.23: 'There I will show the salvation of...' which means 'to those who offer a sacrifice, that is praise and thanksgiving, I will show the way of salvation'. Similarly Ps. 85.10 'Mercy and truth have come before us' is taken to show the permanence of God's pity, and Ps. 82.6 'As for me, I have said you are gods and sons...' that where there is a resemblance of action it is expressed as identity of being. The metaphoric use of language is shown also in his comment on Ps. 1.1: the normal actions of walking, stopping and sitting are metaphors for movements of the soul. First comes pressure of thought to imitate the actions of others; then comes association with the actions of others; next comes pleasure in voluntarily joining in the actions of others. But, as Ishodad points out, this is the order of a Greek rather than Syriac text.

Ishodad's quotations in Introduction and Commentary allow three observations to be made. First, the longer quotations in the commentary are more easily compared with the text and apparatus of the Leiden Peshitta. For the most part, the text used is a familiar Peshitta type of text, although corrections are sometimes made, and in many instances Ishodad himself assists by giving other Syriac or Greek or Hebrew readings.[22] For example, the reading of Ps. 45 'I will speak of my words

22. The provenance of the quotations is discussed in J.-M. Vosté, 'Les citations

to the king' understands the Syriac to be *w-'īmar 'nā 'bāday l-malkā*, as the Leiden text, but he notes that it can be found in MSS with the last two words *'bādēy malkā*, that is 'I will speak the deeds of the king'. Second, there is no general tendency to manipulate the quotations, for in Commentary and Introduction alike a simple meaning is aimed at: the objective is the explanation of Scripture and its handling, in the manner of Theodore of Mopsuestia. But, thirdly, what may seem to be an Old Testament quotation may not be so. Introduction §XII presents a compound quotation where Old Testament and New Testament and LXX play a part. Ps. 31.4 and Lk. 23.46 combined result in 'Father into thy hands I commend my Spirit'; again a quotation from Ps. 14.1-3 is in fact mediated through its rearrangement in Rom. 3.10-12.

Narsai

Narsai has been referred to above as a pragmatic or exegetical author, although poetic. Not surprisingly, therefore, when he writes *On Creation*, there are few Psalm quotations, for mostly he quotes from Genesis. The few Psalm quotations accord with his habitual method: they provide physical metaphors for discussion of non-physical beings. For example, in 1.121 he writes, 'He made the heavenly multitudes fire and spirit', alluding to Ps. 104.4, and again,

> He made his messengers wind, and his servants burning fire. Without, therefore, revealing the mystery of his being, he revealed the nature of those who are with him...

The same theme and reference recur in 5.287, 'They are servants, just as if it were said "They are spirit" ', and also in 5.301, 'He named them fire and wind by the mouth of the son of Jesse'. The same text has a different point at 5.479, namely that the order of non-physical beings lies within the divine power:

> For he said, 'he will make his messengers spirit'; 'his messengers' he named them, not 'messengers'.

At 3.204 use is made of Ps. 148.5: 'He showed his creative power in his deeds, "for he said, and they were" '. This is as the Leiden text, with the omission of the pronoun and particle *d-hū*. The next verse is also quoted, in a modified way, referring now to the sun and the heavenly bodies: 'He established a law that it would not transgress the course of the day and the night'—an allusion also to the sun and moon as lightbearers to mark out the day and the night (Gen. 1.16).

On Creation confirms points made earlier. First, pragmatic authors make little use of such conceptual material as Psalms. Second, that where they do, they provide metaphor rather than allegory. Third, if quotations are not for comment but exposition, they will be brief, and by way of illustration and allusion. They will seldom be long enough for textual comparison.

Jacob of Serugh: Against the Jews

Jacob may also be described as a pragmatic rather than a conceptual author. In the verse homilies *Against the Jews* he does not comment on a text, but on the institutions of the Old Testament: sabbath, sacrifice, circumcision and so on.

But he provides more quotation from Psalms than does Narsai, and moves in a wider range of metaphors and poetic imagery: homily 6 is a most attractive verse dialogue between Church and Synagogue, making much use of Song of Songs. In this collection of five early and two later homilies his argument is simple and attractive: Scripture and reason show that God could have a son, to be identified with Jesus. Both points Israel misguidedly failed to recognize. So his purpose is not to explain what is difficult to understand in Scripture, but to win assent by reference to texts and phrases mutually accepted as authoritative, whose plain meaning is deeply reasonable. The quotations may be expected to be shaped to serve the thesis.

There are 24 quotations from the Psalms; those from Ps. 2.7 plunge us straight into the difficulties. He quotes from this verse four times, 3.307, 311, 313 and 351:

> 1. *If God said to him* 'You are my son'
> 2. *Why did he say*, 'I today begot you m*y son…*'
> 3. *First of all behold* I begot you *a child*
> 4. *It is written 'He, the Lord, said to me* "you are *my* son" '.

Divergences from the text[23] of the Leiden Peshitta are italicized. The quotations are shaped to fit Jacob's argument. The first fits the context

---

23. 'Text' here means the printed text of the Leiden edition. Notice is given where the first or second apparatus records variant reading(s).

'If God said...why do you deny...?'; the second fits the context 'Why did he say...he acknowledges...'; the third expands the quotation with allusion to Prov. 8.20; and the fourth overtly claims scriptural authority. The first shows a further difference from the familiar 'the Lord said to me' because for Jacob 'Lord' might refer to Jesus, or the Holy Spirit, but is required by his argument to be taken as 'God'.

The next points are those of text: first that of Jacob's homilies, and second of the Syriac Bible. The editor of the homilies notes the following variants. In the first quotation, 'you' is omitted—but as the quotation is used the word occurs twice 'you are my son...why do you...', and the variant is probably an error, that is the omission of one of the two adjacent Syriac pronouns 'you'. In the second there are orthographic variants: *yawmānā* for the Syriac 'today' *yawmān*; an initial *alaph* is omitted from *'īladtāk*. There are additions: *lam* which signals a quotation, and the addition of 'you' with the noun 'child'.

As against the text printed in the Leiden Peshitta there are differences in addition to those noted above. The first differs from the familiar: it reads 'and I this day begot you', with the orthography *'īladtāk*, and the form *yawmānā*. The apparatus, however, notes manuscripts that omit the conjunction. The same pattern is seen in the remainder of the Psalm quotations in these homilies.

There are only two straight quotations:

24.1 'The earth is the Lord's', 7.390.
To confirm the belief that all, not just the heavens, belongs to God.

118.22 'He was *indeed* the stone that the builders rejected', 6.152.
The same as Leiden text except for the *tūb*, required for emphasis.

Eight adapt direct speech by changes of pronoun, tense or mood, or omission/addition of conjunction where the phrases are re-applied

22.17, 19 'He showed them in advance that his hands and his feet would be pierced, and his garment obtained by lot', 1.259, 262-63.

45.11 *'Forget* your people and your father's household', 6.109.
The only difference here is that the text of Jacob omits *wau* before 'forget'; the context of the quotation demands its absence, 'the prophet cried to me...', but the omission or addition of conjunctions and particles is in any case a feature of scribal activity.

47.1 *'And because of this* all the nations clap the hand', 2.169.
The quotation is prefaced by these words, for it is a Davidic comment on what has gone before.

50.13 '*(He teaches him) that* he does not eat the flesh of *calves, and young bullocks,* nor yet drink the blood of goats', 8.23, 24.
Differences from the Leiden text are: flesh is a construct form, rather than absolute with *dalath*; there is a doublet, 'calves'.

50.1 'That it was necessary for him to *offer a sacrifice of all kinds of* thanksgiving', 7.25.
As against the Leiden text, *d-kull* is inserted as examples follow.

69.22 '*And would be giving him* to drink *poison at the time of his thirst*', 1.260. There is also conflation: in the Psalm text 'give' belongs to the first part of the verse, to drink is *d-nešteh* rather than *ašqyōny*, and 'at the time of his thirst' rather than 'for his thirst'. This has the feel of mental reference rather than exact citation.

89.27 '*In prophecy he is mentioned as being* Father', 3.317.
Indirect speech, referring to the phrase 'He will call me "You are my Father...my God and mighty saviour." '

107.20 '*It is written in the prophet that* he sent out his word and healed them', 1.157.
This supporting the relation of Word and Son.

Five adapt for the sake of the argument

2.9 '*That he* might rule them, *all the nations*, with a rod of iron', 3.304.
He argues that as Israel has rejected their Lord, he will rule over the Gentiles instead, and so asks the question 'Why is it said in David, King and Prophet...?' *All the nations* picks up 'the nations as your inheritance' in v. 8.

19.11 '*Your words* are sweeter than honey *of* the comb', 6.336.
This redirects the phrase 'the judgments of the Lord...are sweeter than honey and the honeycomb'. Neither Leiden nor Hexapla apparatus shows the phrase 'of the comb' for 'and the comb.' The phrase is part of a dialogue between the Church and the Synagogue, which leans heavily on Song of Songs, with elements of Ezekiel, as each party claims to be the acknowledged true bride: here, for example, our phrase is prefaced by 'How lovely you are, how lovely you are, daughter of the Amorites...', cf. Song 1.15; Ezek. 16.3. This is a good example of a pastiche where scriptural phrases come as a natural way of expressing perceptions formed on other grounds.

33.6 'By the word of the Lord were the heavens made, David is witness, and by the breath of his mouth the *hidden forces which are above*', 1.91-92.
The context here is the creative activity of the word, and so embraces the unseen as well as the seen. Peshitta text has 'by the breath of his mouth

all his forces', Jacob's text presents a construct *brūḥ* instead of absolute. Syrohexapla suggests the reason for the change: for *ḥaylwāteh* it reads *ḥalwātā dīlhōn*, referring back to the plural *šmayyā* rather than the singular *maryā*. There are no relevant variants in the editions of Peshitta, Syrohexapla, or Jacob.

106.37 'Your sons and your daughters you sacrificed to demons *and luminaries*', 5.180.
The addition, not attested in text or apparatus of Leiden or Syrohexapla, reflects a background of Persian concern with heavenly bodies.

137.3, 4 'Among the Babylonians the sons of the people were required *to sing some of the Lord's songs* there; *they said, "How can there be a way to sing some* of the praise of the Lord in a land *which is not his*" ', 7.408.
The first part is a paraphrase, using the verb *tb* rather than *š'l*, but expanding the phrase 'words of songs' with the next phrases 'songs of Sion' and replacing 'Sion' with 'Lord', as suggested a little further on. The second part likewise expands, with periphrasis for 'how can we sing...' and 'strange land' interpreted as 'Land not his'. Some MSS of Peshitta Psalms supply *men*, 'some of'. This is a good example of quotation by free association of words in the same passage.

Five are allusions

8.3 'In the mouth of children a single praise', 1.307.
This is an allusion to Ps. 8.3 'Out of the mouth of young men and children you have brought your praise to perfection' and to its quotation in Mt. 21.16. Children is *šabrē* as in Syrohexapla[24] where Peshitta text has *'laymē*; the praise is single, or unique, because only Jesus fulfilled the prophecy of riding on a colt, the foal of an ass, Zech. 9.9, and embodied the single shoot from Jesse's tree.

19.4 *'The word raises itself, and without the ears of faith, cannot be heard'*, 3.23, 24.
This is allusion, to Ps. 19.4: 'There is neither speech nor words, so that it is not heard with their sound'. Hence 'heard' is a participle rather than an imperfect and infinite.

51.9 'The bridegroom has scoured me and *I am much whiter than* snow *and light*', 6.320.
This alludes to Ps. 51.9 and Isa. 1.18. The tense is perfect, rather than imperfect; the noun *light* is added, the comparison is strengthened by the addition of *ṭab* before *men*. The bride, changed by the groom, is no

24. Syrohexapla has been examined in the diplomatic critical edition of Robert J.V. Hebert, *The 'Syrohexaplaric' Psalter* (SBLSCS, 27; Atlanta: Scholars Press, 1989).

longer 'black but comely', Song 1.5. Ps. 19.6 provides further allusion: the sun's rising is compared to a bridegroom emerging from the wedding banquet. *Light* alludes to Mt. 17.2: the garments of the transfigured Jesus were as white as light.

80.9 *'The Father brought a choice vine out of Egypt'*, 5.80; *'I am the bride that Moses brought out of Egypt'*, 6.15.
In the first, Peshitta and Syrohexapla editions present *gbettā* not *sattā*, and lack *choice*. In the second the allusions are to Zipporah whom Moses married (Exod. 2.21) in Midian.

114.4 *'I am the one before whom* the mountains danced, *for I was beloved, and the* heights *danced to accompany us when I passed across'*, 6.23-24.
This cites just three words, *ṭūrē*, *rqedu* and *rmātā*, but weaves them into the song dialogue between Church and Synagogue.

Jacob of Serugh: Six Prose Homilies

The seven homilies just discussed are in verse, so it is worthwhile to consider if there is a different method of quotation in prose style. These prose homilies on church festivals form a systematic approach to the mystery of salvation.

Five seem to be exact.

45.7 'Thy throne O God is for ever and ever', 4.13.
The Leiden text has 'The throne of God is for ever and ever', but important MSS (the corrector of 8a1 and 12a1 etc.) in the apparatus give the reading found in Jacob. However, Jacob quotes, and the MSS are assimilated to, Heb. 1.8. Linked with this is a reference to Ps. 102.28.

77.17 'The waters saw you O God, the waters saw you and feared; the depths also trembled , and the clouds rained down their water', 2.33.
Exactly as the Leiden text, and is used in association with Christ's baptism. His descent into the river caused it to tremble, and the heavens rain so that their waters may share in the baptising.

116.11 'Every man is a liar', 4.3.
This is as the Leiden text, except for the replacement of a *dalath* by *wau*. The quotation is in fact from Rom. 3.4 'Let God be true and every man a liar', all of which is quoted to support the argument that things earthly and things divine must be approached appropriately to their nature.

118.24 'This is the day that the Lord has made; let us rejoice and be glad in it', 6.1.

This is a direct quotation, introducing the homily on the Resurrection. It corresponds with the Leiden text, except for the particle *dalath* to introduce the quotation as the word of the prophet.

118.26 'Blessed is he who comes in the name of the Lord', 4.17, 40, 46. This quotation is as the Leiden text, but here is in fact from Mt. 21.9.

One is an adaptation, a good example of how phrases from different Psalms are amalgamated to form a single unit within the argument.

63.4 is added between words from 116.12 '(How shall I repay the Lord for all his forgivenesses extended towards me?) For *his* mercy is better than *my* life, (for to him be praise and blessings for ever and ever. Amen.)', 3.44.
The personal pronoun suffixes are changed to suit the indirect rather than direct quotation. As against the Leiden text, Jacob's adds an enclitic pronoun, *'nōn* to the noun 'mercy'. This kind of addition or omission is common in scribal activity. The words are ascribed to Adam, restored by Christ's conquest of nature by his grace and the power of his fasting, who must surely express himself in these words.

Three are allusions

8.3 *'The praise that vanished from the mouth of old men is restored in the mouth of young men and children, as it is written'*, 4.20.
This is a loose quotation, to fit the context. The fact that 'The praise' instead of 'Thy praise' is found in MSS in the Leiden apparatus is not therefore significant.

18.11 *'If the Lord of the cherubim rode on an ass without a saddle...'*, 4.8.
This is an allusion to 'He rode upon the cherubim and flew...' and provides a useful example of how a very brief phrase can sometimes be detected in its context. It is also a reminder that the word 'Lord' is frequently redeployed with reference to Jesus. Also used in the teaching on humility is Ps. 131.1, see below.

49.20 *'who by their own will are become* like beasts', 1.14, linking Christ in the manger and mankind's free conformity to the beasts, has been mentioned earlier.

If anything, the prose works are more poetic in their use of quotation, and both prose and verse writings confirm the conclusions reached earlier. There is a further reminder to be wary of Old Testament phrases presented in a New Testament guise, and of compound quotations.

John of Dalyatha: Letters

An allusive and associative use of quotations is much more in evidence in the letters of John of Dalyatha, unsurprisingly, as he is writing of modes of being effected by prayer. His letters are about the ascetic life, which is an anticipation of the resurrection, and the end of which is the vision of the glory (not the nature) of God. Prayer may be knocking at the door, but true prayer is a given knowledge of the glory that surrounds God.

Eight Psalm quotations are straightforward, though context has necessitated minor adaptations.

24.3 'Who *then* shall ascend your *holy* mountain?', 51.7.
The conjunction and change of pronoun suffix result from the context of continuous writing. The quotation combines both halves of the verse 'Who shall ascend the mountain of the Lord', and 'who shall stand on his holy mountain'. The phrase 'holy mountain' is also familiar from such passages as Isa. 27.13, 56.7.

34.9 *'O taste, my brother, and see the sweetness of our good father'*, 7.2.
The context alters plural verbs to singular: experience (*theoria*) of the hidden father is the end of ascetic life. The Leiden text is (plural) 'O taste and see that the Lord is good'.

34.19 *'He hears* the broken in heart', 30.3.
The context is 'there is not a day which is empty of his God...' The text alluded to is 'The Lord is near the broken in heart', cf. also Isa. 61.1 and Lk. 4.18, 'I was sent to heal the broken in heart'. The letter gives encouragement in the face of suffering, whether physical or spiritual, active or passive.

35.19 *'our enemies* hate *us* without a cause', 17.4.
This is almost a set phrase, cf. Ps. 69.5. The context changes the person and number.

35.21 'Aha, aha, our eye has seen him', 17.1.
There is a deliverance from enemies who have rejoiced in the downfall and darkness of the would-be ascetic: 'him' therefore rather than 'it'.

38.17 *'Pray for me, I beseech you, that I am not a cause of joy* to those who hate me', 17.4.
The reference is 'I said, let them not rejoice...', context causing the changes.

39.8 'What, therefore, is my hope other than you, O Lord?', 4.4.
Against the Leiden text, *dalath*, a sign of quotation, stands first. This letter is one of encouragement to a solitary.

55.23 *'Let us lay our* care on the Lord', 32.2.
The context alters the pronouns: Leiden text gives 'Cast your (sing.) care upon the Lord'.

The remaining seven quotations show a blending of passages and an inbuilt interpretation.

15.1 *'I, too, with David, proclaim* blessed *whoever, at every moment, thinks of his departure (from this world),* and without spot ponders on the way of the Lord', 47.3.
This is a blend of quotation and interpretation. The underlying quotations are Ps. 119.2 'Blessed are those who are without spot on the way, and walk in the law of the Lord'; v. 15 'I meditate on your commands and have knowledge of your ways'; Ps. 15.2 refers to one who walks, or conducts himself, without spot. Lk. 9.31 uses the word *mappqānā* of Jesus' journey to be accomplished at Jerusalem. The context, of renunciation of the world, sets the pattern for the quotations and allusions and their deployment.

45.8 *'He has anointed you with choice oil,* the oil of gladness', 11.2.
The phrase fits with the anointing of a sick person, but carries with it the overtones of Mary's *mešḥā d-besmā* of Mt. 26.7 of which this is the contrasting oil of life.

63.2 'My soul is athirst for you, my flesh seeks you', 51.6.
The quotation is adapted for the sake of the argument, an account of Paradise desired and the hoped for vision of God. The words of the Leiden text are: 'My soul is athirst for you, and my flesh waits for you'. John presents *ba'e* instead of *mesakkē*.

89.16 *'He reveals and shows you the uncreated* light *so that you might* walk by it', 15.9/10.
An allusion, to suit the argument that discussion of lofty affairs proves pleasing where that of lowly and dark does not. The Leiden text is 'O Lord let us walk in the light of your countenance'.

124.7 *'When our soul is stripped of these things, it no longer falls into the traps of the enemy, but is able to fly swiftly towards God, and is saved by him',* 4.2.
This is closer to allusion, where it is the image rather than the phrasing that suggests dependency. The text of the Psalm is 'our soul, like a bird, is delivered from the snare of the hunter. The snare is broken and we are delivered.' It is rash to conclude from such a case that John had a text different from the Peshitta pattern.

136.23 'Who raises up our lowly state and brings down our enemies who without cause have raised themselves against us', 17.1.

This is a conflation of phrases. From Ps. 136.2 comes 'Who raises up our lowly state', Ps. 35.19 provides 'who hate me without a cause' and Ps. 35.26 'those who have raised themselves against me'. This is only in part a quotation, but rather an example of how Psalm vocabulary expresses underlying thought, itself informed by Scripture.

142.8 'Deliver *our* soul from the house of bondage *which we ourselves have shut up*'.
This is a quotation and comment: the first part is a quotation, with the plural for the singular possessive pronoun, and the second a comment to the effect that we are our own prison house.

From John's letters a further conclusion may be added to the ones already reached: illustrative and allusive usage makes literal comparison of quotation and origin a difficult matter.

Joseph Ḥazzaya

In Joseph's *Letter on the Three Stages* the tendencies noted in John of Dalyatha are carried further. The genre of writing is indicated by this author, who asks God to give his correspondent the key of understanding the songs of blessed David,[25] and has prayed[26] that the holy divine light might shine in his heart so that his understanding might enter the created body of ink and he might see with an enlightened eye of the soul the holy mysteries concealed within God's gospel.

Ten quotations are simple quotations, with minimal change to suit context.

6.7 '*Namely* I have watered my couch *all* night, and dissolved my bed with my tears', §84.
As the Leiden text, except that quotation requires *dalath* (Leiden *wau*) on the first verb; *all night* replaces *every night*, as does Leiden MS 12t1.

7.7 'May the wickedness of one who hates return on his own head', §126.
As Leiden text.

18.35 'And the Lord teaches my hands for war *and blessed is the Lord who teaches my hands for war*', §126.
The passage, as an apostrophe, repeats the phrase.

25. Harb *et al.*, *Trois étapes*, §75.
26. Harb *et al.*, *Trois étapes*, §73.

51.14; 44.8 'And surround me with your salvation, and I will put to shame those who hate me, with your help', §126.
Phrases from both verses are combined.

70.2, 3, 4. Cf. 40.15; 71.13 'And O God deliver me, Lord remain as my helper; let those who seek *the destruction of* my soul be ashamed and made to blush', §126.
This is as the Leiden text, except for the addition of 'the destruction of'.

71.4 'and deliver me O *God* from the hand of the wicked', §126.
As Leiden text, except for 'God' rather than 'Lord', by assimilation to the preceding phrase quoted.

86.1 'Incline your ear O Lord and answer me', §126.
As Leiden text.

91.6 This is a reference to the mid-day demon: however his activity extends from 9 am until 4 pm. §88.

117.1, 2 'O praise the Lord all peoples; *and praise* for ever', §85.
As a prophylactic for accidie, Ps. 117 is summarized. Only the first four words are quoted, then the verb is repeated and the very last word added.

140.9 'And do not grant O Lord the desire of the wicked, and do not bring his evil belief on my head'.
This is as the Leiden text. A variant in Joseph's text gives 'his' for 'my'.

141.2 'May the offering of my hands be *accepted before you* as an evening sacrifice'.
As Leiden text, but for the addition of two Syriac words.

The significance of the quotations lies not in their content, but in their application to a spiritual or mental state of being, not physical: *rūḥānā* or *mad'ānā* not *pagrānā*.

One quotation is more complex: there is a reshaping of the material for the sake of the argument.

68.2, 3, introduced by 'strike upon the lyre of the Son of Jesse':
'Let God arise and all his enemies be scattered, and those who hate *you* flee from before *you*; and as wax *is melted* in front *of the heat* of the fire *let your enemies be dispersed before you*', §126.
There are differences from the Leiden text. The pronouns are second person rather than third: the correspondent's enemies are being considered. 'And as a cloud is dispersed let them be dispersed' does not appear, though 'let them be dispersed' is retained for later use. 'In front of the heat' appears before 'of the fire'. 'Wax' and 'is melted' are transposed. 'Let the wicked perish from before God' is replaced by 'let your enemies be dispersed from before you'.

The patterns previously observed are found here too, with one modification. In a conceptual, expository, writer phrases may be unmodified in quotation: their application is a shift in key, not content.

Conclusion

The use of Syriac patristic writings is not a simple matter. The examples provided in this article alert us to elements that take the argument away from a straightforward choice, quotation from text or quotation from memory. First, critical texts (and apparatus) of the Syriac Bible, Peshitta and Syrohexapla, need to be consulted to give evidence of the kinds of text an author may have had *sous les yeux*. Second, critical editions of the authors' work are needed, to assess the extent to which copyists made the text conform to one familiar or normative to them. Third, quotations are excerpts from a larger text, and as such are likely to have been modified to suit a different context and status. Fourth, the mind of the author determines the purpose and the content and shape of the quotation. The exegete quotes with closer reference to an exemplar, the expositor with closer reference to the argument. The exegete's quotations provide material more useful for comparison of texts, the expositor's quotations material more useful for studying the history of thought. Fifth, caution is needed in detecting quotations that are not quotations: either where the quotation is at second hand, Old Testament mediated through New Testament, or where it is evidence of a mind that is not a treasury of biblical texts, but one so saturated in biblical material that this becomes its natural vocabulary of discourse. Quotation is an art, not a science, and allusion not reproductive but creative writing.

THE HEBREW AND THE GREEK AS ALTERNATIVES TO THE SYRIAC VERSION IN IŠOʻDAD'S COMMENTARY ON THE PSALMS*

R. Bas ter Haar Romeny

When I first met Michael Weitzman, I had just started my doctoral research on Eusebius of Emesa and his use of alternatives to the Septuagint in his *Commentary on Genesis*. We had a lengthy discussion on Eusebius's use of the term ὁ Σύρος, 'the Syrian', a label he uses in order to refer to his own renderings of the Peshitta into Greek. Weitzman's keen interest in the subject, his vast knowledge, and his patience in listening to the ideas and questions of a newcomer in the field made a lasting impression on me. I am glad to have had the opportunity to discuss Peshitta and related issues with him on that occasion and several others. My contribution to this volume, dedicated to him, again deals with alternative readings: I consider the use of the *'Ebrāyā*, 'the Hebrew', and the *Yawnāyā*, 'the Greek', as alternatives to the Peshitta in the ninth-century commentary on the Psalms by Išoʻdad of Merv.[1]

Weitzman himself discussed the *'Ebrāyā*. In his book *The Syriac Version of the Old Testament*,[2] he explains that the term has a number of uses. First, the *'Ebrāyā* may indicate an alternative rendering of the Hebrew text, closer to the MT than is the Peshitta. Second, there are instances where the *'Ebrāyā* and the Peshitta are comparably close to the MT but differ from one another. Third, the *'Ebrāyā* sometimes

* My research is funded by the Royal Netherlands Academy of Arts and Sciences. I am grateful to Dr C. Molenberg for supplying me with the text of Išoʻ bar Nun's Selected Questions on the Psalms, and to Dr C. Leonhard for sending me copies of two of his unpublished works.

1. C. van den Eynde, *Commentaire d'Išoʻdad de Merv sur l'Ancien Testament. VI. Psaumes*, ed., transl. (CSCO, 433-34; Syr 185-86; Leuven: Peeters, 1981).

2. M.P. Weitzman, *The Syriac Version of the Old Testament: An Introduction* (University of Cambridge Oriental Publications, 56; Cambridge: Cambridge University Press, 1999), pp. 139-42.

offers an interpretation known through *Targum Onqelos* and different
from the Peshitta. Yet other cases suggest confusion consequent on a
number of different factors. Lastly, the word is also used in commentaries to refer directly to the Hebrew language or a Hebrew word in
transliteration. Weitzman concludes that this variety of uses suggests
that the word *'Ebrāyā* functioned as a generic term for information
drawn piecemeal from Jewish tradition, either through direct contacts
with Jews—converted or not—or as an inheritance from the Jewish
antecedents of the Syriac church. The term *Yawnāyā* likewise combines
different traditions. As *Yawnāyā* readings are often found in conjunction with *'Ebrāyā* readings, I deal with both categories here.

Weitzman drew a distinction between the material he found in writings attributed to Ephrem, and material from later authors. He realized
the importance of studying the alternative readings author by author.
Only in this way is it possible to discern the distinct traditions that
come together under the names *'Ebrāyā* and *Yawnāyā*. Moreover, an
author-by-author approach enables us to address two other issues: the
reasons for quoting alternatives to the Peshitta, and the position of these
alternatives within an author's exegetical method. The present essay is
based on a study of the work of Išo'dad of Merv, which constitutes one
of the most important sources of *'Ebrāyā* and *Yawnāyā* readings. This
author, Bishop of Ḥdatta in the middle of the ninth century, wrote one
of the most extensive commentaries on the Old and New Testaments.
He used material from his own East Syrian tradition, but also from other
sources. For a study of the use of *'Ebrāyā* and *Yawnāyā* references in
the Church of the East, Išo'dad's commentaries form the obvious starting point. Even before this work had been fully edited, its biblical quotations attracted the attention of scholars. I refer here to a chapter on the
Yawnāyā in Diettrich's 1902 study of Išo'dad's position in the history
of exegesis,[3] Baumstark's review of this work as well as his own
1911 study of Išo'dad's Greek and Hebrew Pentateuch quotations,[4]

---

3. G. Diettrich, *Išôdâdh's Stellung in der Auslegungsgeschichte des Alten
Testamentes an seinen Commentaren zu Hosea, Joel, Jona, Sacharja 9–14 und
einigen angehängten Psalmen veranschaulicht* (BZAW, 6; Giessen: Ricker, 1902),
pp. xlii-lvi.

4. A. Baumstark, review of Diettrich, *Išôdâdh's Stellung*, in *OrChr* 2 (1902),
pp. 451-58, and *idem*, 'Griechische und hebräische Bibelzitate in der Pentateucherklärung Išô'dâôs von Merw', *OrChr* NS 1 (1911), pp. 1-19.

and Vosté's 1945 study of the quotations from the Psalms.[5]

Baumstark deals extensively with the identity of the *Yawnāyā*, 'the Greek', which in his opinion reflected two different sources: one was the Syrohexapla, a Syriac version made at the beginning of the seventh century by the West Syrian bishop Paul of Tella on the basis of Origen's edition of the Greek Septuagint; the second was a putative East Syrian version made on the basis of the Lucianic recension. Following a suggestion by Diettrich, Baumstark attributes this Syro-Lucianic version to Mar Aba,[6] the sixth-century Catholicos mentioned as a translator of the Bible in 'Abdišo' bar Brika's catalogue, dating from the early fourteenth century, of the writings of the Fathers. Baumstark stresses that Išo'dad had worked only with pre-existing material and had not himself added readings. On the *'Ebrāyā*, Baumstark is brief: in his view, it reflects either a Targum related to the three Targums on the Pentateuch,[7] or a Jewish school tradition that had not otherwise been recorded in writing. He also explains that some *'Ebrāyā* readings came into existence as a result of confusion: the Syriac letter ܥ, with the numerical value of 70, may have been intended in some cases as a rendering of the Greek οἱ ο´, which is used as an indication of the Septuagint, whereas it can also be taken as an abbreviation of ܥܒܪܝܐ, *'Ebrāyā*.

Baumstark is severely criticized by Vosté, who explains that the hypothesis of a version attributable to Mar Aba in fact rests on two assumptions: first, that a number of quotations in Išo'dad may be ascribed to a version of which no trace is left but the name of the author; second, that Mar Aba did indeed use the Lucianic recension of the Septuagint. The total lack of other vestiges of Mar Aba's version makes it impossible to test either of these assumptions. Vosté therefore concludes that Baumstark took his readers into the 'région nébuleuse des pures hypothèses'. Vosté's own solution is to ascribe some differences between Išo'dad's quotations and the Syrohexapla to a literary revision of the latter, and others to errors stemming from the fact that Išo'dad was not quoting this translation at first hand. With regard to the *'Ebrāyā*, he does not deny that Jewish scholars might be the ultimate

5. J.-M. Vosté, 'Les citations syro-hexaplaires d'Išo'dad de Merw dans le Commentaire sur les Psaumes', *Bib* 26 (1945), pp. 12-36.
6. The readings differ from the known fragments of the Syro-Lucianus usually attributed to Polycarp, who worked by order of Philoxenus.
7. *Onqelos, Pseudo-Jonathan*, and the *Fragmentary Targum; Neofiti* had not yet been discovered in Baumstark's time.

source of the material. He does assume, however, that the immediate source of Išo'dad's readings was the marginal apparatus of the Syrohexapla.

The problem with Vosté's solutions is exactly that for which he rebukes Baumstark: they are based on new, unprovable assumptions. First, the *Yawnāyā*: there is no evidence of the existence of a reworked literary version of the Syrohexapla that could explain Išo'dad's Greek readings. Second, the *'Ebrāyā*: the margins of the Syrohexaplaric manuscripts known to us do not give readings of the Hebrew in translation. In the following pages, I shall address the problem of the *Yawnāyā* first. Here, the evidence is clearer than that relating to the *'Ebrāyā*, and has already been presented in a number of publications.

The Yawnāyā

The scholarship of past decades has drawn attention anew to another suggestion by Diettrich, which was rejected out of hand by Baumstark in favour of the Mar Aba hypothesis. Diettrich conjectured that some readings of the Septuagint may have been translated into Syriac 'in and together with' Theodore of Mopsuestia's commentary, as an aid for Syriac readers.[8] This hypothesis was proved to be true when additional fragments of the Syriac translation of Theodore's Old Testament commentaries were published. The fifth-century translators of Theodore appear to have used the Peshitta reading when they had to render the Greek biblical text that formed the subject of his comments. In some cases, however, they kept to Theodore's Greek reading, especially when they found a difference in the choice of words, or in the construction or extent of a phrase. Often they did so tacitly, adapting all or only part of the Peshitta reading to the Greek. Sometimes, however, they must have thought that this procedure would cause insurmountable difficulties for the Syriac reader who was used to the Peshitta. In such cases, the translators gave the quotation first in the form of the Peshitta and then in the form of the Septuagint, which they explicitly introduced as *Yawnāyā*, 'the Greek'.[9]

---

8.   Diettrich, *Išôdâdh's Stellung*, pp. liv-lv.

9.   This procedure was first described by T. Jansma, 'Théodore de Mopsueste, Interprétation du livre de la Genèse. Fragments de la version syriaque (B.M. Add. 17,189, fol. 17–21)', *Mus* 75 (1962), pp. 63-92 (82-83). All references and a nuanced discussion of the practice can be found in L. Van Rompay, *Le*

The study of Išoʻdad's use of sources in his commentary on Genesis showed clearly that he had taken some quotations from his principal immediate sources, Išoʻ bar Nun and the Diyarbakır commentary. These works, probably dating from the end of the eighth century, do not quote the Syrohexapla; they adopted the 'Greek' readings from the commentaries which they copied or summarized: of these, the works of Theodore of Mopsuestia, the Blessed Interpreter of the East Syrian Church, took pride of place. Salvesen, who has studied all readings of the Greek in Išoʻdad's commentary on Genesis, concludes that more than half the readings were taken from the Syrohexapla—sometimes with minor changes—and the remainder from other commentaries. The Diyarbakır commentary supplied the bulk of these non-Syrohexaplaric readings, but it is clear that in a number of cases Išoʻdad consulted the sources of this commentary or parallels to it.[10] Thus it is possible that Išoʻdad had direct access to the Syriac version of Theodore of Mopsuestia's *Commentary on Genesis*, and it is certain that he copied, from a Syriac intermediary, a number of comments made by Eusebius of Emesa.[11]

It is understandable that most research has concentrated on the book of Genesis, because here the difficult matter of Išoʻdad's sources has been substantially clarified—in fact, the biblical quotations were instrumental in solving this issue. The problem with the book of Genesis, however, is first that we have only small fragments of Theodore's commentary. It is therefore difficult to confirm that the *Yawnāyā* readings taken from the Diyarbakır commentary do ultimately go back to Theodore, though this is indubitably the most likely hypothesis.[12] A second problem is the fact that the Syrohexapla is not extant for the whole book of Genesis, so that there are several points at which it is impossible to be absolutely certain that a reading was indeed taken from this version. In the book of Psalms the situation is different. For

commentaire sur Genèse–Exode 9,32 du manuscrit (olim) Diyarbakır 22, transl. (CSCO, 483, Syr, 205; Leuven: Peeters, 1986), p. xxxviii.

10. A. Salvesen, 'Hexaplaric Readings in Išoʻdad of Merv's Commentary on Genesis', in J. Frishman and L. Van Rompay (eds.), *The Book of Genesis in Jewish and Oriental Christian Interpretation: A Collection of Essays* (TEG, 5; Leuven: Peeters, 1997), pp. 229-52 (234-36).

11. Van Rompay, *Le commentaire*, transl., pp. xlix-l with nn. 47 and 48.

12. Van Rompay, *Le commentaire*, transl., p. xxxvii.

Pss. 119 (LXX[13] 118) and 139 (138)–148 a Syriac version of Theodore's commentary has been handed down to us, and for Pss. 1–81 (80) there are extensive Greek and Latin fragments.[14] The Syrohexapla of the Psalter has been preserved in a number of manuscripts, among which is the well-known Codex Ambrosianus C. 313. Inferiore, available in a facsimile edition since 1874.[15]

A discussion of the relationship between the Syriac fragments of Theodore's Commentary on the Psalms and Išoʿdad's work is already available in the recent study by Leonhard,[16] who devoted a chapter to the question of the biblical quotations. With regard to the provenance of the *Yawnāyā* readings, Leonhard's findings corroborate Salvesen's conclusions. Leonhard stresses a point also observed by Salvesen: the

---

13. In this article, references to the Psalms are given first according to the numbering in the *BHS*, and then, between brackets, according to the Septuagint (when there is a difference). Note, however, that the numbering of the Psalms in Peshitta manuscripts and older editions differs from the *BHS* from Ps. 115 (Peshitta 114.9-26) to 147 (Peshitta 146 and 147), and that there are differences in verse numbering between the older Peshitta editions (and thus Van den Eynde's edition of Išoʿdad) and the editions of other witnesses. In both respects, the Leiden Peshitta edition adopts the numbering of the Hebrew Bible. For the sake of clarity, I follow this practice here. Readings can easily be traced in Van den Eynde's edition with the help of the index.

14. On the different traditions of Theodore's *Expositio in Psalmos*, see L. Van Rompay, *Théodore de Mopsueste: Fragments syriaques du Commentaire des Psaumes (Psaume 118 et Psaumes 138–148)*, transl. (CSCO, 436, Syr, 190; Leuven: Peeters, 1982), pp. v-ix, and *idem*, 'The Christian Syriac Tradition of Interpretation', in M. Sæbø *et al.* (eds.), *Hebrew Bible/Old Testament. The History of its Interpretation*. I. *From the Beginnings to the Middle Ages (until 1300)*, 1, *Antiquity* (Göttingen: Vandenhoeck & Ruprecht, 1996), pp. 612-41 (633-34). For the Greek text I follow R. Devreesse, *Le commentaire de Théodore de Mopsueste sur les Psaumes (I–LXXX)* (Studi e testi, 93; Vatican City: Biblioteca Apostolica Vaticana, 1939). The Latin texts are available in L. De Coninck and M.J. D'Hont, *Theodori Mopsuesteni Expositionis in Psalmos Iuliano Aeclanensi interprete in latinum versae quae supersunt* (CCSL, 88A; Turnhout: Brepols, 1977).

15. A.M. Ceriani, *Monumenta sacra et profana*. VII. *Codex Syro-Hexaplaris Ambrosianus photolithographice editus* (Milan: Bibliotheca Ambrosiana, 1874). The variants of the other manuscripts and a study of the text can be found in R.J.V. Hiebert, *The 'Syrohexaplaric' Psalter* (SBLSCS, 27; Atlanta: Scholars Press, 1989).

16. C. Leonhard, 'Ishodad of Merv's Exegesis of the Psalms 119 and 139–147: A Study of his Interpretation in the Light of the Syriac Translation of Theodore of Mopsuestia's Commentary' (unpublished doctoral thesis, Katholisch-theologische Fakultät der Universität Wien, 1999), pp. 39-60.

correlation between the position of the quotation in Išo'dad's text, and its provenance. In his discussion of Išo'dad's parallels to Theodore's commentary, Leonhard says that when a *Yawnāyā* reading is appended without explanation at the end of a paragraph of commentary, it is likely to have been taken from the Syrohexapla;[17] when a reading is given at the beginning of a comment and is subsequently interpreted, it is likely to have been quoted from the source of its interpretation.[18] Sometimes, however, the biblical quotations in the Syriac version of Theodore are not exactly identical to the readings that probably derive from that text. There are a number of explanations of these differences: Leonhard notes the history of transmission, the fact that the reading may have reached Išo'dad through an intermediary such as the Diyarbakır commentary for Genesis, and Išo'dad's own interventions. In some cases, it seems that, rather than simply copying versions, Išo'dad apparently tried to reconstruct readings. He must have been led to do this especially in cases where he was confronted with differences between the Syrohexapla and the Greek reading of a commentary he wanted to use. Thus there are some points at which Išo'dad replaced the reading of the source on which his discussion was based by the Syrohexaplaric reading, and at others, as Salvesen also noted, combinations and doublets are found.

It is worth examining whether these conclusions can be applied more widely. To this end I propose to check those Psalms for which we have the Greek version of Theodore. In the present essay, the discussion is restricted to Pss. 33–61 (32–60), for which the Greek text is largely complete.[19] There are two discrete questions: first, can the *Yawnāyā*

17. Salvesen needed to determine the criteria for attributing a reading to the Syrohexapla in her work on Genesis, as the Syrohexapla is not extant for the whole book. She formulates these as follows: it is likely that Išo'dad quoted the Syrohexapla when his *Yawnāyā* is a legitimate rendering of the Septuagint and when there is no sign that he is relying on an earlier commentary. This is even more probable where Išo'dad has placed the reading without explanation at the beginning or end of a paragraph, and especially when more alternatives to the Peshitta are given ('Hexaplaric Readings', p. 232).

18. See also his 'Īšō'dāḏ's Commentary on Psalm 141,2. A Quotation of Theodore of Mopsuestia's Lost Commentary', in E.J. Yarnold (ed.), *Studia Patristica: Papers Presented to the Thirteenth International Conference on Patristic Studies Held in Oxford 1999* (Leuven: Peeters, forthcoming).

19. A full listing of all biblical quotations in Išo'dad's commentary on the Psalms is being undertaken as part of the *Text and Context* programme of the

readings that differ from the Syrohexapla be explained as translations from Theodore's Greek? Second, what is the significance of the position of these readings in Išoʻdad's commentary; that is, is there a correlation between position and provenance?

The results of this analysis are as follows. There are 40 *Yawnāyā* readings in these chapters, two of which give a different version of a *Yawnāyā* reading quoted earlier. Of these 40 readings, 15 are identical to the Syrohexapla,[20] eight additional readings differ only in that they add directly to the noun a possessive suffix which was constructed with -ܠܗ in the Syrohexapla,[21] and three show other minor variations,[22] which may also result from an effort to make the text more readable (Paul of Tella's version was very literal) or to make the reading fit better into the context. These minor changes do not amount to evidence that would warrant the assumption of a full stylistic revision of the entire Syrohexapla.

Of these 26 readings that are close, or even identical, to the Syrohexapla, 19 are quoted without explanation, and are placed either at the end of a paragraph of interpretation (15 times), or as the only comment on a verse or an expression (4 times). Of the remaining seven cases, four are given a short, and three a long explanation. Similarly, of the four readings with a short explanation, two appear at the end of a paragraph, and two constitute the only remark made; the other three, however, appear at the beginning of a full paragraph, at the end of a paragraph which clearly explains the Greek reading, and in the middle of the paragraph respectively. In some cases it is possible to assume

---

Peshitta Institute. Note that the lemmata in the catena fragments have not always been written in full. The readings given by Devreesse do not always represent Theodore's Septuagint text, which can often be reconstructed from his explanations. The most complete study on this matter is still E. Große-Brauckmann, 'Der Psaltertext bei Theodoret' [the author in fact deals with Theodoret, Theodore, and Chrysostom], *NGG* Ph.-h. Klasse (1911), pp. 336-65 (also printed in MSU 1), especially pp. 348ff.

20. Pss. 33(32).15; 35(34).15; 38(37).21; 40(39).7A (Van den Eynde, *Psaumes*, ed., p. 62,16), 40(39).16, 18; 41(40).4, 14; 44(43).20B (Van den Eynde, *Psaumes*, ed., p. 66 n. 3); 48(47).15; 49(48).3, 19; 60(59).8c (the peʻal also occurs as a variant in the tradition of the Syrohexapla, cf. Hiebert, *The 'Syrohexaplaric' Psalter*, p. 82 [ad 59.6]); 60(59).9b; and 61(60).8.

21. Pss. 39(38).11, 12; 41(40).10 (provided that *syāmē* are added on the word ܠܒܘܫܐ in Išoʻdad's text); 42(41).9; 44(43).26; 49(48).8-9, 12; and 59(58).12.

22. Pss. 34(33).22; 35(34).17b-c; and 45(44).9-10.

that the readings accompanied by an explanation go back to the commentary from which the explanation was taken, that is, from Theodore of Mopsuestia[23] and in one case perhaps from Išoʻ bar Nun,[24] but this is never the only admissible assumption. The cases that are not accompanied by an explanation include a number where Theodore—even when his explanation is cited for the Peshitta reading of the same verse—cannot be the source of the reading, since his Septuagint reading differs from that reflected in Išoʻdad and the Syrohexapla.[25]

The remaining 14 readings differ from the Syrohexapla in whole or in part. Nevertheless, Vosté maintains that 8 of these 14 readings must go back to the version of Paul of Tella.[26] They employ synonyms, or show stylistic corrections, that would confirm the hypothesis of a literary revision which Vosté had postulated to explain these readings. Two others would belong to a set of special cases showing a number of errors and conflations,[27] and the remaining four are not listed in his article.[28] Let us now see whether the study of Theodore's commentary can change this picture.

First of all, in the case of Ps. 60(59).6, it is not difficult to agree with Vosté that it goes back to the Syrohexapla. The Milan manuscript reads

23. One could instance Ps. 41(40).10; compare Theodore, ed. Devreesse, *Le commentaire*, p. 258,12-19. See especially, however, the three cases of Pss. 35(34).15, 17bc, and 49(48).12, where Van den Eynde refers to Theodore's explanation. Pss. 40(39).16 and 49(48).3, where the reading of the Greek also follows Theodore's explanation, may be comparable with the example last mentioned. In these two cases, however, it is not evident that the explanation refers to the Greek biblical text; for this reason, they are here counted with cases not accompanied by an explanation.

24. Ps. 59(58).12; the text is found in MS Cambridge Add. 2017, fol. 54r 1. Cf. also Theodore, ed. Devreesse, *Le commentaire*, p. 386,15.

25. Pss. 40(39).7A; 41(40).4; 42(41).9 (division of sentences); and 45(44).9-10 (division of sentences). The same holds true for Išoʻ bar Nun. This exegete explains 39(38).11 and appears to be followed by Išoʻdad, but he gives no reading of the Greek. He does give a reading for Ps. 45(44).9-10, but that of Išoʻdad is different (MS Cambridge Add. 2017, fol. 51r 6-7; quoted and discussed in C. Molenberg, *The Interpreter Interpreted: Išoʻ bar Nun's Selected Questions on the Old Testament* [doctoral thesis, Groningen: Rijksuniversiteit, 1990], pp. 253-58).

26. Pss. 35(34).17a; 37(36).1; 38(37).8, 9; 45(44).2a; 55(54).22; 58(57).4; and 60(59).6. For this paragraph, see Vosté, 'Les citations syro-hexaplaires', pp. 24-30.

27. Pss. 49(48).14 and 55(54).10.

28. Pss. 34(33).6; 40(39).7B (Van den Eynde, *Psaumes*, ed., p. 69,21); 44(43).20A (Van den Eynde, *Psaumes*, ed., p. 66,6-7); and 45(44).2b.

ܠܕܡ ܟܐܘ̈ܓܐ ܩܕܡ ܡܢ ܠܡܥܪܩ,[29] 'to flee from before the face of the bow', for LXX τοῦ φυγεῖν ἀπὸ προσώπου τόξου. It is conceivable that Išoʻdad or an earlier collector wanted to simplify this into the reading ܠܕܡܘ ܩܕܡ ܡܢ ܠܡܥܪܩ 'to flee from before the bow'. Moreover, there is no reason to suggest that this represents an independent translation taken from the Syriac Theodore, since Išoʻdad does not quote Theodore at this point. The situation is different, however, in Pss. 34(33).6, 37(36).1, 38(37).8,[30] 38(37).9 and 45(44).2b. Išoʻdad's explanations of these verses either actually use Theodore's wording, or at least correspond very closely to his interpretation. The *Yawnāyā* readings use different words or constructions giving approximately the same meaning as the Syrohexapla. In none of these cases, however, can the choice of these synonyms easily be explained on the basis of literary concerns such as the wish to write better Syriac or to produce a more readable text. It therefore seems more logical to assume that Išoʻdad adopted an independent rendering given by the translators of Theodore.

Three additional cases can, without doubt, be associated with Theodore. For Ps. 49(48).14, we find a Peshitta reading that has been adapted to fit Theodore's comment, which is in fact based on Symmachus. The Peshitta and Symmachus also play a role in the reading of Ps. 55(54).10, where Išoʻdad's Greek appears to follow Theodore's quotation from Symmachus,[31] while preserving the structure of the Peshitta reading. These two instances are especially important, as they constitute the clearest demonstration of the connection between the wording of Išoʻdad's explanation and *Yawnāyā* reading, and Theodore's commentary. In the third case, Ps. 55(54).22, no such connection can be discerned. There is, however, another relevant observation: Išoʻdad quotes the *Yawnāyā* as ܡܢ ܪܘܓܙܐ ܕܐܦ̈ܝܗܘܢ, 'from the anger of their face [Aramaic word]'. The Syrohexapla reads ܡܢ ܪܘܓܙܐ ܕܦܪܨܘܦܗ, 'from the anger of his face [Greek loanword]'. In the choice of the word for 'face' one might see the hand of an editor, but the difference in the number of the possessive suffixes is the result of there having been two different Greek models: the common reading αὐτοῦ

---

29. Vosté corrects this into ܠܕܡ ܟܐܘ̈ܓܐ ܡܢ ܠܡܥܪܩ. This has no bearing on the argument.

30. Note, however, that Išoʻdad's reading here also occurs without attribution in the margin of three Syrohexapla manuscripts (see Hiebert, *The 'Syrohexaplaric' Psalter*, p. 59 ad 37.7).

31. Cf. Van den Eynde, *Psaumes*, transl., p. 94 n. 5.

was translated in the Syrohexapla, and the rare αὐτῶν was the basis of Išoʻdad's rendering. The latter reading was also found in Theodore's Septuagint.[32]

There are three further instances where Theodore's commentary (or that of another author) may well have been the source of a non-Syrohexaplaric reading. In Ps. 35(34).17a the reading is associated with a very short explanation which, while it does not contradict Theodore's comment, is too short to confirm that there has been contact. In the case of Ps. 45(44).2a, Theodore is clearly quoted, but the reading given is not a correct translation of his biblical text. A more interesting case is that of Ps. 44(43).20. The first two words of the *Yawnāyā* reading (A) differ from the Syrohexapla. The Syrohexaplaric reading is also given, however (B). Two manuscripts quote it in the margin, and another gives it in the main text but explicitly marks it as coming from another text (ܪ܏ ܏ܘܪ ܏ܘܘܝ). These differing positions of the note could indicate that it was not added by Išoʻdad himself. However, there are comparable notes in Išoʻdad's commentaries on other books, some of which are more firmly integrated into the text. Whoever added the note referring to the Syrohexapla, it was clear to him that the two versions could not easily be identified.

The two remaining readings can be explained otherwise. For Ps. 58(57).4 we find a combination of the Syrohexapla and the Peshitta,[33] in a reading that is also attributed to the *'Ebrāyā*. We shall see below that the information pertaining to the Hebrew text probably relates to the first word only.[34] It is possible that this prompted Išoʻdad to combine data. Finally, Ps. 40(39).7 (B) is taken from the Peshitta of Heb. 10.5. Only in the verb is there any difference from the Syrohexaplaric quotation given earlier in the commentary.

To sum up, we have seen that 8 of 14 readings that differ substantially from the Syrohexapla can best be explained as independent

---

32. The lemma in Devreesse's edition does not reflect Theodore's actual text (cf. the explanation which follows). See Große-Brauckmann, 'Der Psaltertext', p. 360 ad loc. Van den Eynde notes that Išoʻdad quotes an interpretation of Theodore. This text, which does not quote Theodore literally, is attributed by Išoʻdad himself to Išoʻyahb and Ḥenana, and has been adapted to the singular.

33. There is a misprint here in Van den Eynde's edition: read ܏ ܏ܬܝܕܪ instead of ܏ ܏ܬܝܕܪ (p. 89,7). Išoʻ bar Nun also deals with this verse (and is probably quoted by Išoʻdad), but does not quote the Greek.

34. See n. 67 below.

renderings taken directly or indirectly from the Syriac version of Theodore's commentary. This explanation may also apply in three further cases; in the remaining instances, other explanations are more probable. In only a very small number of instances does the connection to Theodore seem to be the only possible explanation; with one exception, however, none of the 14 cases can easily be explained by Vosté's assumption of a full literary revision of the Syrohexapla. This one exception may be explained as the result of an emendation by Išoʻdad or by an earlier exegete from whom he adopted the reading, as were the readings with -ܠ.ܕ and a possessive suffix.

The position of the readings does indeed prove to be relevant. A *Yawnāyā* reading placed without explanation at the end of a comment, or as the only remark on a verse, has nearly always been taken from the Syrohexapla. A clear exception is Ps. 58(57).4, a reading attributed to both the *Yawnāyā* and the *'Ebrāyā*. There is room for doubt in a small number of instances where a reading of the Greek is placed without further remarks at the end of a paragraph taken from Theodore, but the data are equivocal. On the one hand, the explanation of Ps. 49(48).12 does relate to the *Yawnāyā* reading that follows, though this text is, perhaps coincidentally, identical to the Syrohexapla.[35] On the other hand, Išoʻdad does not present Theodore's explanation of Ps. 37(36).1 as building on the text of the Greek Bible, but the *Yawnāyā* reading that follows, differs from the Syrohexapla, and must have been taken from the Syriac Theodore. Neither of the two further readings[36] that are quoted, without their own explanations, at the beginning of a longer paragraph, appear to have been taken from the Syrohexapla.

Leonhard also states that when a reading is given at the beginning of a comment and is subsequently interpreted, it is likely to have been quoted from the source of its interpretation. This is usually true, but as he and Salvesen have already observed, we must allow for some influence of the Syrohexapla. After all, Išoʻdad was able to use this tool, and we may conjecture that when he was confronted with mixed readings without a *Yawnāyā* label in the Syriac Theodore, he sometimes used it in an attempt to clarify the text.[37]

---

35. Compare also the cases of Pss. 40(39).16 and 49(48).3, see n. 23 above.

36. Pss. 45(44).2a (unexplained); 55(54).22 (Theodore).

37. The readings of the Three were investigated but cannot be dealt with in detail here. The results are comparable with those of the *Yawnāyā* readings.

The ʿEbrāyā

The trouble with Vosté's hypothesis regarding the origin of the *ʿEbrāyā* material is that the margins of the extant Syrohexaplaric manuscripts of Psalms do not give Išoʿdad's readings of the Hebrew. Vosté himself was aware of this problem,[38] but refers to the way the *ʿEbrāyā* is cited in Išoʿdad: that is, in the same way as, and sometimes even together with, the *Yawnāyā*, Symmachus and Aquila. The fact that Išoʿdad or his source quoted different readings of one verse that are not always found in the Milan manuscript should show that the Syrohexapla originally contained many more marginal readings than does this copy. In this putative larger stock of marginal readings, there must have been references to the Hebrew. Vosté admits that these were probably not very numerous, since the patriarch Timothy I does not mention them in his description of the process of copying Syrohexaplaric manuscripts.[39] However, the presence of one single transliteration of Hebrew into Syriac characters, at Ps. 110(109).1, is for him proof that there were at least some such references: where else could this transliteration have originated?

The presence of transliterations is, indeed, undeniable. In fact, the Milan manuscript itself does not lack such material. Thus at Ps. 40(39).6 we find the note 'All translators said *ears*, and with regard to the Hebrew: *'sn'ym*, ωσναϊμ'.[40] Such notes are natural, since Origen's Hexapla included a Hebrew column in Greek transliteration. The Hexapla did not, however, include a translation from the Hebrew explicitly marked as τὸ Ἑβραϊκόν or ὁ Ἑβραῖος. These terms are used to identify ad hoc translations of a single expression or verse in the works of Greek exegetes, who based themselves on informants. It is possible that some of these readings had been added in the margins of the Syrohexapla or its Greek models,[41] as were a number of other scholia. Thus the Milan

38. 'Les citations syro-hexaplaires', pp. 33-35.

39. Vosté, 'Les citations syro-hexaplaires', p. 34 n. 3. The text of Timothy's letter has been edited by O. Braun, 'Ein Brief des Katholikos Timotheos I über biblische Studien des 9. Jahrhunderts', *OrChr* 1 (1901), pp. 299-313. For an English translation, see S.P. Brock, *A Brief Outline of Syriac Literature* (Mōrān 'Eth'ō, 9; Kottayam: SEERI, 1997), pp. 245-50.

40. .ωσναϊμ ܒܝܬ ܐܘܕܢܐ ܐܡܪܘ ܟܠܗܘܢ ܡܦܫܩܢܐ ܘܠܒܪ

41. It would appear from the colophons that we have to reckon with different models. The most probable hypothesis is that these models already contained most

manuscript gives scholia from Cyril, as a result of which this Alexandrian author makes an unexpected appearance in Išoʻdad.[42] This might be the origin of marginal readings such as the one found at Exod. 6.12, where we do find a Syriac translation of the last words of the verse labelled as *'Ebrāyā* (abbreviated as ܥܒ).[43]

It is thus true that there are some *'Ebrāyā* readings that actually give a translation, not a transliteration, in Syrohexaplaric manuscripts. It is also true that copyists did sometimes make their work easier by copying only some of the marginal notes: there are indeed examples of this practice to be found on studying Syrohexaplaric Psalter manuscripts. There is, however, not a single indication that there were many of these *'Ebrāyā* translations in the margins of Syrohexaplaric manuscripts. In the Psalter Vosté found none. Hiebert has shown that the number of readings differs substantially in the ten manuscripts that contain Syriac versions of the Greek Psalms, but that the choice of readings is

of the marginal material in that form, though the possibility remains that Paul of Tella used a full Hexapla for some books. The most complete discussion of the colophons is still that of G. Mercati, 'Di varie antichissime sottoscrizioni a codici esaplari', in *idem, Nuove note di letteratura biblica e christiana antica* (Studi e testi, 95; Vatican City: Biblioteca Apostolica Vaticana, 1941), pp. 1-48. An interesting hypothesis (Paul's model was a Tetrapla, and a Tetrapla was a Septuagint column with a marginal apparatus culled from the Three) is defended by R.G. Jenkins, 'Colophons of the Syrohexapla and the *Textgeschichte* of the Recensions of Origen', in C.E. Cox (ed.), *VII Congress of the International Organization for Septuagint and Cognate Studies, Leuven 1989* (SBLSCS, 31; Atlanta: Scholars Press, 1991), pp. 261-77.

42. See C. Van den Eynde, *Commentaire d'Išoʻdad de Merv sur l'Ancien Testament. IV. Isaïe et les Douze*, transl. (CSCO, 304, Syr, 129; Leuven: Secrétariat du CorpusSCO, 1969), pp. xix-xxi.

43. That is, unless this is a mistake. Theodotion's reading ἀπερίτμητος τοῖς χείλεσιν could very well also be translated as ܪܟܝܟ ܐ ܠܝ ܐ ܕܝ ܐܪܟ ܐܘܬ ܐ. However, the attribution ܥܒ is found in both the London Exodus and the Midyat Pentateuch manuscripts, and the agreement may well be accidental. For the London manuscript (BL Add. 12,134), see P. de Lagarde, *Bibliothecae syriacae quae ad philologiam sacram pertinent* (Göttingen: Dieterich, 1892), ad loc.; for the Midyat manuscript, see A. Vööbus, *The Pentateuch in the Version of the Syro-Hexapla: A Fac-simile Edition of a Midyat MS. Discovered 1964* (CSCO, 369, Subs, 45; Leuven: Peeters, 1975), fol. 24r. Cf. the retroversion in F. Field, *Origenis Hexaplorum quae supersunt; sive Veterum interpretum graecorum in totum Vetus Testamentum fragmenta*, I (Oxford: Clarendon Press, 1875), p. 90 ad loc. For the *'Ebrāyā* in the margins of the Syrohexapla of 3 and 4 Kingdoms, cf. n. 55 below.

remarkably consistent in those manuscripts in which larger numbers of readings are to be found.[44] Since the Psalter manuscripts known today have no translations labelled *'Ebrāyā*, we have no reason to expect that, even if one containing a few such examples were found, it would include a number comparable to the 40 or so found in Išo'dad's commentary on Psalms. Such a finding is possible, but not probable. In short, neither the textual history of the Syrohexapla nor the present state of the text support Vosté's conclusion.

I do not have a solution for all the pieces of the puzzle, but I believe that a fresh look at Išo'dad's sources will enable us to put some pieces into place. For Genesis, Van Rompay noted that a small number of the *'Ebrāyā* readings were actually translated from Greek Ἑβραῖος readings stemming from Eusebius of Emesa, and that a number of others stemmed from the Diyarbakır commentary. As the latter commentary draws heavily on Theodore of Mopsuestia, it is possible that some readings ultimately go back to his work. For the Psalms, we are once again in a far better position to check this, as much more of Theodore's commentary on this book is extant. Moreover, Theodore's *Commentary on the Psalms* must date to an early period in his career. What remains of this shows that Theodore still refers quite often to alternative readings, although the beginnings of a more critical attitude can be seen.[45] If a link between Theodore's Ἑβραῖος and Išo'dad's *'Ebrāyā* exists anywhere, then we should expect to see it here.

In the light of all this, the findings are far from spectacular. In those parts of Išo'dad's commentary that are parallelled in the Syriac Theodore, Leonhard found four *'Ebrāyā* readings, but none of these seems to have been taken from Theodore. In the Greek and Latin remains for Pss. 1–81 (80), the situation is only a little better. Išo'dad has 21 *'Ebrāyā* readings,[46] three of which appear to go back to Theodore: Pss.

44. Hiebert, *The 'Syrohexaplaric' Psalter*, p. 261.

45. On this issue, see R.B. ter Haar Romeny, *A Syrian in Greek Dress: The Use of Greek, Hebrew, and Syriac Biblical Texts in Eusebius of Emesa's Commentary on Genesis* (TEG, 6; Leuven: Peeters, 1997), pp. 135-39, with further references.

46. Vosté's list ('Les citations syro-hexaplaires', p. 32) is not complete. Add Pss. 29.6, 40.7 and 55.15, and read 74.5 for 78.5. On the reading of Ps. 72(71).5, which he attributes to Symmachus, see below. The reading of Ps. 69(68).13, where he wants to read *'Ebrāyā* instead of *Yawnāyā*, is taken from the Syrohexapla with a small adaptation to the Peshitta. On the other hand, Van den Eynde's attribution of the reading of the Greek of Ps. 81(80).7 to the Hebrew must be correct (it is included in the figure of 21 mentioned above).

29(28).6,[47] 8[48] and 40(39).7.[49] The last instance, however, can be included only if one assumes that Theodore's long sentence has been completely misunderstood: he is in fact explaining that the Hebrew does not read the way Išoʻdad maintains. In addition to these three readings, an explanation of Hebrew idiom given with regard to Ps. 36(35).7 is based on Theodore's commentary,[50] as is the remark that Pss. 9 and 10 are taken together in the Greek but not in the Hebrew text.[51]

It is of course possible that the limited number of Hebrew readings found to have been taken from Theodore is a consequence of the process of transmission. It is striking, after all, that these three readings are all located in that section of Theodore's commentary that has been handed down to us in its most complete Latin and Greek form, that is, the section on Pss. 1–61 (60). Indeed, if one compares the two Latin versions of Theodore's work, it becomes clear that the alternative readings did not survive the process of abbreviation—as if the editor was aware of Theodore's change in attitude and wanted to represent the later Theodore. Even in the original Latin version one can understand that a Hebrew reading would not survive in a case such as the commentary on Ps. 16(15).2, where the translator had to compare his Latin lemma first with the Greek and then with the Syrian.[52] Thus we can assume that the vicissitudes of transmission explain a number of lost parallels; it is, however, clear that not all the 18 remaining cases can be explained in this way, if only because several of them concern the same Pss. 1–61 (60). Although Theodore's text is apparently largely complete here, and deals with all the verses concerned, we find no more Ἑβραῖος readings that could have been Išoʻdad's source.[53]

47. Latin text: De Coninck, *Expositio in Psalmos*, p. 130,49-50. On the connection with Theodore, see Molenberg, 'The Interpreter Interpreted', pp. 213-15.

48. Latin text: De Coninck, *Expositio in Psalmos*, p. 131,71. The connection with Theodore had already been indicated by Vosté, 'Les citations syrohexaplaires', p. 32.

49. Greek text: Devreesse, *Le commentaire*, p. 249,23-24.

50. Greek text of Theodore: Devreesse, *Le commentaire*, p. 199,3-11; Išoʻdad: Van den Eynde, *Psaumes*, ed., p. 56,22-24; transl., p. 66,5-7.

51. Latin text of Theodore: De Coninck, *Expositio in Psalmos,* p. 43,16-17; Išoʻdad: Van den Eynde, *Psaumes*, ed., p. 28,10-11; transl., p. 33,14-15.

52. Latin text: De Coninck, *Expositio in Psalmos*, p. 75,16-22.

53. For Pss. 16(15).2, 50(49).2, 68(67).23, 74(73).5 and 78(77).8 he even gives alternative readings—but not the Hebrew.

In a small number of cases a mistake may have been made. Baumstark mentioned the possible interchange of ܐ for οἰ οʹ and ܐ for ܥܒܪܝܐ, *'Ebrāyā*.[54] The usual indications for the Septuagint are ܫܒܥܝܢ, 'seventy', and ܝܘܢܝܐ, 'Greek', sometimes abbreviated as ܝܘ. Theoretically, however, the mistake is possible, if the ܐ was indeed used to indicate the Septuagint in one of Išoʿdad's direct or indirect sources. A mistake more likely to occur is that a ܠ (*l*, for λ), indicating Lucian's recension, was not understood, and was read incorrectly as an ܐ.[55] An interchange of ܐ for *'Ebrāyā* and ܓ (*g*) for οἰ γʹ, the Three, may also be postulated.[56] It appears that οἰ γʹ is usually rendered as ܓ ܗܠܝܢ or ܓ ܗܢܘܢ (that is, with a demonstrative to indicate the Greek article), but there are indeed cases where we find only ܓ. There is the further possibility that Išoʿdad, his source, or a copyist simply mixed up attributions: a small number of such cases are discussed by Van den Eynde in the introductions to his translations. For the list of 18 remaining cases, Vosté's suggestion that the *'Ebrāyā* reading of Ps. 72(71).5 should be attributed to Symmachus is the most important, though it should be recognized that the agreement may well be accidental: both Symmachus and the *'Ebrāyā* are, after all, renderings of the Hebrew text.[57]

All in all, there is certainly some scope for confusion, but human fallibility can explain all our 18 cases no better than can the transmission history of Theodore's commentary or the theory that some

54. Baumstark, 'Griechische und hebräische Bibelzitate', p. 17.

55. The ܠ is still found in some instances in the Paris manuscript of 4 Kingdoms (BN Syr. 27, fol. 1-90; first example at 4 Kgdms 9.9, see the edition of Lagarde, *Bibliothecae Syriacae*, ad loc., and cf. Field, *Origenis Hexaplorum quae supersunt*, I, pp. lxxxiv–lxxxv). In 3–4 Kingdoms several examples of a loose ܐ are found. This situation is exceptional. It is not impossible that in many cases the original reading was a ܠ.

56. See, for example, the way ܓ is written in the margin of fol. 52r of the Midyat manuscript (ed. Vööbus), where only the ܗܠܝܢ before it makes clear the copyist's intention, and the large ܐ or ܓ in the top margin of fol. 19v of the same manuscript (ad Exod. 8.1; Lagarde's edition of the London Exodus reads ܓ here).

57. In fact, the issue is even more complicated here, as the Syriac reading also occurs in the margin of the Milan manuscript, but without attribution. If Išoʿdad's Syrohexapla had the same reading without attribution, it is possible that he or somebody else conjectured that it must represent the Hebrew. Note, however, that one of the codices collated by Hiebert has the same reading with a small variant and an attribution to Symmachus; see Hiebert, *The 'Syrohexaplaric' Psalter*, p. 267.

'Ebrāyā readings had found a place in the Syrohexaplaric manuscript used by Išo'dad. It therefore seems possible that Išo'dad obtained his readings from more than one source.

Other Sources for Išo'dad's 'Ebrāyā?

When it comes to Greek exegetes who could be the ultimate source of some readings, one thinks in the first instance of Eusebius of Emesa, Išo'dad's source for some *'Ebrāyā* readings in Genesis. There is, however, no commentary on the Psalms known under his name. Modern scholarship does attribute an Antiochene commentary to his follower Diodore, but this work gives few Ἑβραῖος readings. This dearth of alternative biblical quotations is readily understandable, since Diodore obtained such material for his commentary on Genesis from Eusebius. For the book of Psalms, this rich source was apparently not available to him. In Pss. 1–50, the only part of Diodore's commentary that has been edited,[58] there are no readings that could have been Išo'dad's source. Theodoret of Cyrrhus and, on the Palestinian-Alexandrian side, Eusebius of Caesarea, yield no more than does Diodore in this respect.[59]

We must, therefore, turn to the Syriac writers who may have been among Išo'dad's sources. This is problematic, in the absence to date of a full picture of the relation to other East Syrian exegetical works; in this respect, the student of the book of Genesis has a clear advantage over the student of the Psalter. Most of these works have not even been edited. Van den Eynde surveyed all Nestorian works on the Psalms and their possible relations with Išo'dad.[60] In terms of possible sources for Išo'dad—or works using the same sources—the most promising avenue would seem to be study of the *Scholion* or *Book of Scholia* of Theodore bar Koni (791/792), the *Selected Questions* of Išo'dad's contemporary Išo' bar Nun, and the commentaries of MS Sachau 215 and of Denḥa-Gregory, both of which are of uncertain date. The Nestorian 'masoretic' manuscript 9m1 (British Library Add. 12,138), which dates from 899, might also repay study.

---

58. J.-M. Olivier, *Diodori Tarsensis Commentarii in Psalmos*, I (CCSG, 6; Turnhout: Brepols; Leuven: Leuven University Press, 1980).

59. Theodoret has a number of Ἑβραῖος and Σύρος readings, which are recorded already in Field's *Origenis Hexaplorum quae supersunt*. Eusebius of Caesarea is quoted there especially for his readings of the Three.

60. *Psaumes*, transl., pp. xxi-xxiii and xxxii-xli.

The latter manuscript does indeed contain some marginal notes referring to alternative readings, as Wright has already noted.[61] However, none of the *'Ebrāyā* readings of Pss. 1–81 (80) are found here, nor did I find any other alternative readings in the Psalms under discussion. The cases mentioned by Wright are apparently exceptional. Theodore bar Koni, who probably had a source in common with Išo'dad, devotes four questions to the Psalter.[62] These do not contain alternative readings either. In discussions of the *Yawnāyā* above, I have referred to Išo' bar Nun's *Selected Questions*, and identified him as the possible source of the *Yawnāyā* reading of Ps. 59(58).12. He does not quote any of the *'Ebrāyā* readings of Pss. 1–81 (80), however. Molenberg has shown that although Išo'dad indeed appears to have used Išo' bar Nun's work for his commentary on the Psalms, he did not content himself with simply copying this source. He often composed a new text, in the process of which he added information from other sources and checked the biblical quotations.[63]

Molenberg also notes the importance of the commentary which, to judge by its heading, is attributed by some to Denḥa, possibly a student of Išo' bar Nun and by others to a monk by the name of Gregory. This work, preserved in the Paris manuscript BN Syr. 367 dating from 1252, incorporates the commentary of MS Sachau 215, a work deriving largely from Theodore of Mopsuestia, but commenting on the Peshitta instead of on the Greek text. In its turn, the Denḥa-Gregory commentary is included in a larger collection which includes several discourses on the Psalms, preserved in a number of nineteenth-century manuscripts.[64] In this version, some fragments are added from a work by

61. W. Wright, *Catalogue of Syriac Manuscripts in the British Museum Acquired since the Year 1838*, I (London: The Trustees of the British Museum, 1870), p. 104.

62. Edition: A. Scher, *Theodorus bar Kōnī: Liber Scholiorum 1* (CSCO, 55, Syr, 19; Paris: Imprimerie Nationale, 1910), pp. 353,6–359,8. Translation: R. Hespel and R. Draguet, *Théodore bar Koni, Livre des Scolies (recension de Séert)*. I. *Mimrè I–V* (CSCO, 431, Syr, 187; Leuven: Peeters, 1981), pp. 294-98.

63. She examines three examples relating to the Psalter (Molenberg, *The Interpreter Interpreted*, pp. 208-36; see also pp. 253-58). In two of these Išo'dad happens to give quotations of the Hebrew, which are not shared by Išo' bar Nun.

64. On this tradition, see also Van Rompay, *Théodore de Mopsueste: Fragments syriaques*, transl., pp. ix-xiv. I take the manuscript Mingana Syr. 58 (Selly Oak Colleges Library, Birmingham) as a sample of this tradition, as did Van den Eynde. Some sections were published from a manuscript in his possession by

Aḥob of Qaṭar, partly in the margins and partly in the text itself. There are points of agreement between Išoʿdad on the one hand and Denḥa-Gregory and Aḥob on the other. Van den Eynde suggested the possibilities of interdependence and a common source as possible origins of this agreement, but did not choose between them.[65] Molenberg argues that the only conclusion to be drawn from the agreement is that Išoʿdad had at his disposal the same material as that which has been preserved in the nineteenth-century manuscripts.[66] This could imply that neither Denḥa-Gregory nor Aḥob borrowed from Išoʿdad, but because of the uncertainty attaching to the dating of these authors this possibility is hard to exclude from the outset.

The commentary of Denḥa-Gregory itself is interesting because it contains a number of very close parallels with Išoʿdad, sometimes closer to Išoʿdad than are the parallels in Išoʿ bar Nun. It does not yield any of our *ʿEbrāyā* readings, however. More important for our purpose are the additions attributed to Aḥob. Six of Išoʿdad's 21 *ʿEbrāyā* readings in Pss. 1–81(80) appear among these, four of which are explicitly under Aḥob's name.[67] It is conceivable that the attributions were dropped in the remaining two cases, if only because they begin with the word *ʿEbrāyā*, next to which the attribution to Aḥob may have seemed redundant. Several *ʿEbrāyā* readings in the remaining Psalms are also found in this source. Thus one of the four readings studied by Leonhard, Ps. 119(118).83, has a parallel here.[68] There are also a number of *ʿEbrāyā* readings that are not paralleled in Išoʿdad. The question is, of course, whether Aḥob was Išoʿdad's source or the other way round. This brings us to the important issue of the dating of Aḥob.

B. Vandenhoff, *Exegesis Psalmorum, imprimis messianicorum, apud Syros Nestorianos e codice adhuc inedito illustrata* (Rheine: Altmeppen, 1899).

65. Van den Eynde, *Psaumes*, transl., p. xxiii.

66. Molenberg, *The Interpreter Interpreted*, p. 219.

67. With attribution: Pss. 45(44).9 (MS Mingana 58, fol. 64r margin; Vandenhoff, *Exegesis Psalmorum*, text p. 37 n. 7 [on p. 38]; transl. p. 41); 58(57).4 (fol. 77r boxed; Aḥob quotes only the first word, but there is no reason to assume that Išoʿdad knew more); 68(67).14, 16-17 (fol. 86r margin). For the latter two readings Van den Eynde already mentioned the parallel in Aḥob (*Psaumes*, transl., pp. 112 n. 15 and 114 n. 23). Without attribution: Pss. 66(65).11 (fol. 84v margin) and 68(67).23 (fol. 87r margin). The latter case was noted by Van den Eynde, *Psaumes*, transl., p. 115 n. 28, who does attribute it to Aḥob.

68. Text in the margin of MS Mingana 58, fol. 148v, without attribution to Aḥob.

Assemani says in a footnote to his edition of 'Abdišoʿ bar Brika's catalogue, where Aḥob is presented as the author of biblical commentaries, that he lived around the year 990.[69] Baumstark already voiced some doubts, noting that Aḥob's quotations of Persian words might point to pre-Islamic times.[70] The fact that he may also have given one quotation in the language of the *Ṭayyāyē*,[71] that is, Arabic, does not invalidate this suggestion: Arabic is known to have been a spoken language long before the rise of Islam. Cowley argued that our Aḥob should be identified with Ayyub, 'the interpreter of Seleucia', who lived at the end of the sixth century.[72] An additional argument is that in all likelihood Christianity had already disappeared from the Bet Qaṭraye region by the beginning of the tenth century.[73] In any case, it would seem wise not to date him much later than other important scholars from Bet Qaṭraye such as Isaac of Nineveh, Dadišoʿ and Gabriel of Qaṭar.

Another clue can be found within the texts attributed to Aḥob themselves. This is a point that requires further study, but my first soundings show that some of the notes clearly present the exegesis of Theodore of Mopsuestia. Where Išoʿdad has a parallel comment, it can be seen that both authors give the same reworked version of Theodore's exegesis,[74] and that this version is sometimes developed further by Išoʿdad. For instance, at Ps. 5.4 Theodore offers three explanations of the word

69. J.S. Assemani, 'Carmen Ebedjesu metropolitae Sobae et Armeniae continens catalogum librorum omnium ecclesiasticorum', in *idem* (ed.), *Bibliotheca Orientalis Clementino-Vaticana*, III.1 (Rome: Sancta Congregatio de Propaganda Fide, 1725), pp. 3-362 (175 n. 4).

70. Baumstark, *Geschichte der syrischen Literatur mit Ausschluß der christlich-palästinensischen Texte* (Berlin: W. de Gruyter, 1968 [1922]), p. 132 n. 1.

71. Text in the margin of MS Mingana 58, fol. 100r, without attribution to Aḥob.

72. R.W. Cowley, 'Scholia of Aḥob of Qaṭar on St John's Gospel and the Pauline Epistles', *Mus* 93 (1980), pp. 329-43 (338-39). Cowley supposes that he was born in Qaṭar and migrated to Seleucia. For the person of Ayyub, cf. the Chronicle of Seert: A. Scher and R. Griveau (eds.), *Histoire nestorienne (Chronique de Séert)*, II/2 (PO, 13.4; Paris: Firmin-Didot, 1918), p. 438,6.

73. See J.-M. Fiey, 'Diocèses syriens orientaux du Golfe Persique', in F. Graffin (ed.), *Mémorial Mgr Gabriel Khouri-Sarkis (1898–1968)* (Leuven: Imprimerie Orientaliste, 1969), pp. 177-219 (211-12).

74. Compare, for example, the Greek text of Theodore, Devreesse, *Le commentaire*, p. 261,5-12, with Aḥob, MS Mingana 58, fol. 60v boxed, and Išoʿdad, Van den Eynde, *Psaumes*, ed., p. 64,3-9; transl., p. 74,39.

'morning'. Aḥob quotes only these three, whereas Išo'dad adds a fourth.[75] These parallels between Aḥob and Išo'dad can be explained by assuming that Išo'dad used Aḥob, but not the other way round. Thus even if one decides on other grounds to ascribe a very late date to Aḥob, the material attributed to him must go back to an earlier source also used by Išo'dad. Theoretically one might exclude the alternative readings from this conclusion, since in individual cases it is not possible to show that Aḥob's reading represents an earlier stage than an identical one given by Išo'dad. Aḥob's collection of quotations as a whole, however, can hardly be explained as having been taken from Išo'dad. It contains mainly readings of the Hebrew and a small number of non-Syrohexaplaric *Yawnāyā* readings: even if all of these were found in Išo'dad's commentary, it would be difficult to explain how Aḥob had made this selection, leaving out the large number of Syrohexaplaric readings.

An interesting detail which may also suggest that the Aḥob material was added to Išo'dad's commentary, possibly even at a later stage, is the fact that some of Aḥob's notes and readings appear at different places in the three manuscripts of Išo'dad: they appear to have been added as marginal notes by Išo'dad himself or by a later author.[76] This brings us to the last issue: what was the place of the alternative readings in Išo'dad's comments?

The Use of Alternative Readings

Salvesen has shown that Išo'dad's use of alternatives to the Peshitta is neither systematic nor polemical in purpose.[77] She mentions the desire to clarify the biblical text, the wish to seem erudite, and a belief in the plurality of the biblical text as the main motives. In the few cases where Išo'dad makes his choice explicit, the meaning is decisive: he adopts

75. Latin text of Theodore: De Coninck, *Expositio in Psalmos*, p. 26,44-47. Aḥob: MS Mingana 58, fol. 20v margin. Išo'dad: Van den Eynde, *Psaumes*, ed., p. 24,15-18; transl., pp. 28,25-29,2. Cf. also a case relating to the introduction to Ps. 45(44): Greek text of Theodore, Devreesse, *Le commentaire*, p. 277,19-21. Aḥob: MS Mingana 58, fol. 63v margin. Išo'dad: Van den Eynde, *Psaumes*, ed., p. 66,15-16; transl., p. 76,22-23.

76. See, for example, Van den Eynde, *Psaumes*, transl., pp. 69 n. 3, 113 n. 16, and 115 n. 28 (ed., p. 104 n. 54). This issue was already mentioned by Leonhard, 'Ishodad of Merv's Exegesis', p. 59 n. 206.

77. Salvesen, 'Hexaplaric Readings', p. 238.

the reading most useful to his explanatory and theological purposes.[78] This holds true in a sense also for the cases where Išo'dad is apparently making an implicit choice, explaining the alternative reading only. In such cases we must assume that he adopted an explanation from a commentary relating to the Greek or Hebrew[79] text, and needed the alternative reading to make the whole understandable.

However, a large majority of Išo'dad's alternative readings appear without any comment. In some cases the presentation can be deceptive. For instance, the reading of the Greek and the Hebrew of Ps. 81(80).5 seems to be a gloss without further purpose:[80]

ܗ̇ܘ, ܕܟܕ ܢܦܩ ܠܐܪܥܐ ܕܡܨܪܝܢ. ܥܒܪ̈ܝܐ ܘܝ̈ܘܢܝܐ ܡܢ ܐܪܥܐ ܐܡܪܝܢ.

> The (expression) *when he went out to the land of Egypt*: the Hebrew and the Greek say: 'out of the land (of Egypt)'.

In the paragraph in question, Išo'dad quotes Išo' bar Nun extensively. When we compare Išo'dad's text with its source, it appears that Išo'dad gives the alternative reading as an answer to a problem that Išo' bar Nun had solved in a speculative way. The latter reads:[81]

ܗ̇ܘ, ܕܝܢ. ܕܠܐܪܥܐ ܕܡܨܪܝܢ: ܗܢܘ ܟܕ ܢܦܩܘ ܟܕ ܒܗ ܒܐܪܥܐ ܕܡܨܪܝܢ ܡܬܗܦܟ ܗܘܐ: ܐܘ ܕܢܓܠܝܬ ܝܬܝܪ. ܟܕ ܢܦܩ ܡܢ ܐܪܥܐ ܕܡܨܪܝܢ.

> Now the (expression) *to the land of Egypt*: that is, *when they*[82] *went out*—in the sense of: '(when) he passed through the land of Egypt'; or to put it more clearly: 'when he went out of the land of Egypt'.

This example, however, cannot dispel the general impression that those readings that are given without explanation at the end of a paragraph

---

78. For this point, see also K.D. Jenner, 'Syrohexaplarische und proto-syro-hexaplarische Zitate in syrischen Quellen außer den individuellen Exemplaren des syrohexaplarischen Psalters', in A. Aejmelaeus and U. Quast (eds.), *Der Septuaginta-Psalter und seine Tochterübersetzungen. Symposium in Göttingen 1997* (MSU, 24; Göttingen: Vandenhoeck & Ruprecht, 2000), pp. 147-73.

79. Diettrich, *Išôdâdh's Stellung*, pp. xlvi-xlvii, says that only the Greek is explained on the same level as, or instead of, the Peshitta. This cannot be maintained for the commentary on the Psalms (cf. for instance the presentation of the *'Ebrāyā* readings of Pss. 29[28].8, 66[65].11 and 68[67].14).

80. Van den Eynde, *Psaumes*, ed., p. 125,11-12.

81. Text quoted from MS Cambridge Add. 2017, fol. 62r 4-7.

82. Išo' bar Nun also expresses the idea here that Joseph, who is taken as the subject of the phrase 'he went out', represents the people as a whole. Išo'dad had expressed this explicitly at the beginning of his paragraph.

serve no more than a documentary purpose. What could be the motive for this collecting of data?

Among Antiochene exegetes, the importance of the Hebrew text had been recognized since Eusebius of Emesa. East Syrian exegetes had not failed to notice that Theodore of Mopsuestia, at least in his later works, had come to prefer the Septuagint as the most reliable means of access to the Hebrew original. He despised the Peshitta, which was quoted so often by Eusebius because of the affinity of the Hebrew and the Syriac languages. As far as we can see, Theodore's East Syrian followers did not adopt his harsh judgment, but held the view of their countryman Eusebius. They were, however, more inclined to take into consideration the possibility of a corrupted Hebrew text than he was.

The result was a mixed approach, as can be seen in Išo'dad's works: the Peshitta remained the basis of his commentaries, but in addition to some references to the Hebrew, he incorporated many quotations from the Greek. These served the practical purpose of making Theodore's comments intelligible, and may also be seen as a token of reverence for Theodore and his Greek Bible. There is, however, a third factor. Biblical studies had taken on an apologetic dimension in Išo'dad's day, as is evident in the example of Catholicos Timothy I. This prelate had introduced the Syrohexapla to the Church of the East shortly before Išo'dad started writing his commentaries.[83] Timothy believed that the original Hebrew text by then existed in three recensions: the text as translated by the Seventy, the text used by the Three—with whom he associated the Peshitta—and the Hebrew text as preserved among the Jews.

Rather than assuming that Išo'dad held the belief in the plurality of scriptures found in Origen's exegesis, I would suggest that the background to Išo'dad's documentary approach is the judgment that the

83. For this point, see R.B. ter Haar Romeny, 'Biblical Studies in the Church of the East: The Case of Catholicos Timothy I', in E.J. Yarnold (ed.), *Studia Patristica 34: Papers Presented to the Thirteenth International Conference on Patristic Studies Held in Oxford 1999* (Leuven: Peeters, forthcoming). For the link between biblical studies and apologetics in this period, see K.D. Jenner, 'Some Introductory Remarks Concerning the Study of 8a1', in P.B. Dirksen and M.J. Mulder (eds.), *The Peshiṭta: Its Early Text and History. Papers Read at the Peshiṭta Symposium Held at Leiden 30–31 August 1985* (MPIL, 4; Leiden: E.J. Brill, 1988), pp. 200-24 (209-15). For the connection between Timothy and Išo'dad, see Leonhard, 'Ishodad of Merv's Exegesis', pp. 39-43.

different versions together ensure the reliability of the biblical text. The results can be closely similar, however: in a number of cases the presentation of different versions suggests that their meanings complement each other, as in Origen. Early Antiochenes such as Eusebius and Theodore would not have approved of that outcome.

Conclusion

An author-by-author approach is not only the best way to study how and why alternative readings were used: where different traditions may have come together under a single label such as 'the Hebrew' or 'the Greek', it is also the only approach that can help us discern what is behind these names. Išoʿdad's commentary on the Psalms forms a good illustration. A large proportion of his *Yawnāyā* readings was taken from the Syrohexapla. Some others can best be explained as deriving directly or indirectly from the Syriac translation of Theodore of Mopsuestia's *Expositio in Psalmos*; one reading reflects a mixed text, and another has apparently been influenced by the way the text was quoted in the Peshitta of the New Testament. Mistakes may account for a small group of *ʿEbrāyā* readings. A number of other readings must derive from the Interpreter, but the majority of the readings which could be traced appeared to come from Aḥob of Qaṭar. If this author wrote more than the additions to the Denḥa-Gregory commentary, we may suppose that he supplied some of the unexplained readings which still make up more than half of the total number. If this is so, the situation is comparable to that in Genesis, where Išoʿdad also adopted the majority of the *ʿEbrāyā* readings from an earlier Syriac work, the Diyarbakır commentary.

Let us return finally to Weitzman's categorization of the *ʿEbrāyā* readings with respect to the Hebrew text. The readings going back to the Interpreter—Greek ad hoc renderings of the Hebrew that have been translated into Syriac—all belong to Weitzman's fourth category, cases that suggest confusion of various sorts, whereas Aḥob's readings, together with most of the unexplained ones, belong to the first and second categories. They give other interpretations of the MT (in two cases of hapax legomena), which are either just as close to it as is the Peshitta, or even closer, for instance because they are more literal or because they represent the Masoretic vocalization rather than any other. This division between the Theodore and the Aḥob readings is striking, but the data presented here constitute too small a basis to allow firm conclusions to be drawn (apart from the obvious observations that Aḥob must have had excellent means of access to the Hebrew text, and that Išoʻdad did not distinguish between his sources). This analysis does, however, strongly suggest that the approach is valuable, and that study of the readings that were not included in selections studied here, and exploration of the Denḥa-Gregory commentary with its additions, are well worthwhile.

DID JACOB OF EDESSA KNOW HEBREW?

Alison Salvesen

The Syrian Orthodox scholar Jacob of Edessa is a major figure in the history of Syriac scholarship. Born around 630 CE, he was a learned exponent of the Syriac language, but also a strong advocate of Greek learning. He took an uncompromising line on canon law, and was a biblical scholar of the first order. His linguistic ability and his interest in biblical interpretation have often led to comparisons with Jerome, and some modern writers have stated that, like Jerome, he was trilingual: the Victorian scholar William Wright said that Jacob of Edessa was 'an ἀνὴρ τρίγλωττος, who was equally conversant with Syriac, Greek and Hebrew',[1] and more recently Graffin has spoken of Jacob's 'maîtrise de la langue hébraïque'.[2] Others have been more sceptical: even in 1878 Nöldeke described Jacob's ability in Hebrew as 'sehr, sehr fadenscheinig', and contrasted it with Jerome's true working knowledge of the language.[3]

It is worth reviewing the evidence for and against Jacob of Edessa's supposed knowledge of Hebrew. There are a number of places where it might be found:

    a.   Jacob's own version of the Old Testament, of which some manuscripts remain;

    b.   his letters on biblical interpretation;

---

1. W. Wright, 'Two Epistles of Mar Jacob, Bishop of Edessa', *Journal of Sacred Literature and Biblical Record* NS 10 (1867), pp. 430-60 (430).

2. F. Graffin, 'Jacques d'Edesse réviseur des Homélies de Sévère d'Antioche d'après le ms. syriaque B.M. Add 12.159', in F. Graffin and A. Guillaumont (eds.) *Symposium Syriacum 1976, Chantilly, France* = OCA 205 (Rome: Istituto Pontificio Biblico, 1978), pp. 234-55 (250).

3. E. Nestle, 'Jakob von Edessa über den Schem hammephorasch und andere Gottesnamen. Ein Beitrag zur Geschichte des Tetragrammaton', *ZDMG* 32 (1878), pp. 465-508 (473-74 n. 3).

    c.   his scholia on the Old Testament;

    d.   marginal notes Jacob made to his revision of the Greek translation of the *Homiliae Cathedrales* of Severus of Antioch.

a. Jacob's version of the Old Testament is still largely unpublished.[4] Richard Saley and I have separately spent some years working on his version of Samuel,[5] but it is clear that for this book at least Jacob relied solely on the Greek Bible (the Septuagint), the Syriac Peshitta, and to a lesser extent the Syrohexapla, the Syriac translation of Origen's Septuagint text. The influence of the Greek reviser of the Septuagint, Symmachus, is apparent in 1 Sam. 13.1, but Jacob's accompanying note demonstrates that Severus of Antioch was the intermediary. At no time does Jacob appear to have consulted a Hebrew text, even for the many difficult names in 1–2 Samuel. So there is no sign that he knew Hebrew in his revision of the books of Samuel. The situation in other books requires investigation, but this will have to await the production of suitable editions.

b. Jacob's letters to John the Stylite are more promising.[6] John has asked some difficult questions about various passages in the Bible, especially in the Old Testament, and on the whole Jacob answers convincingly and with great authority. Occasionally he makes explicit reference to Jewish legends or traditions, such as the Ten Trials of Abraham,[7] but we will leave these aside, since one could be familiar with Jewish traditions without actually knowing Hebrew, as is clear in the case of Ephrem. Some of the ideas Jacob mentions seem to come from early Jewish writings such as the books of *Jubilees* and *Enoch*, and even Josephus. However, Jacob does demonstrate a high regard for the Hebrew language, saying that it was the original, 'Adamic'

---

    4.   W. Baars, 'Ein neugefundenes Bruchstück aus der syrischen Bibelrevision des Jakob von Edessa', *VT* 18 (1968) pp. 548-54, gives details of the MSS of Jacob's version on pp. 548-49, and lists published excerpts on p. 551 n. 4.

    5.   R.J. Saley, *The Samuel Manuscript of Jacob of Edessa: A Study in its Underlying Textual Traditions* (MPIL, 9; Leiden: E.J. Brill, 1998), and Salvesen, *The Books of Samuel in the Version of Jacob of Edessa* (MPIL, 10; Leiden: E.J. Brill, 1999).

    6.   Wright 'Two Epistles', pp. 430-33 and ܪ-ܪܒ, and F. Nau, 'Traduction des lettres XII et XIII de Jacques d'Édesse', *Revue de l'orient chrétien* 10 (1905), pp. 197-208, 258-82.

    7.   Wright, 'Two Epistles', p. ܐ, and Nau, 'Traduction', pp. 204-205.

language,[8] that the Hebrew script and writings in Hebrew existed even before Moses.[9] The most interesting passages are where Jacob actually cites a Hebrew word in the course of his explanation.

1. John asks three questions concerning creatures in the book of Job, asking specifically for literal, not allegorical, identifications.[10] The three are Behemoth (Peshitta Job 40.15), the bird called *knpy šbḥyn* (Peshitta Job 39.13) and Leviathan (Peshitta Job 3.8, also the Hebrew of 40.25). Jacob promises not only to do this but to interpret their Hebrew names. He states, correctly, that the word Behemoth is a plural form in Hebrew, means 'animals', and is translated thus (i.e. as θηρία) in the LXX. Modern scholars believe that the animal in Job is a hippopotamus, but Jacob holds that it refers to locusts, who are many but act as one, hence the singular verbs used of the Behemoth in Job 40. The *knpy šbḥyn* is a splendid bird (*prḥt' šbyḥt'*). It is very strong and is called the 'elephant bird' because it carries off young elephants. Leviathan is a great serpent of the waters (*tnyn' rb'*), greater than any other creature on land or in the water, and is called κῆτος ('whale', 'sea monster') in Greek. No one knows its exact size.

Apart from the fanciful zoology, what were the sources of Jacob's information about these Hebrew names? He is correct that Behemoth is a plural form,[11] but is his statement based on a knowledge of Hebrew grammar? In fact we find that not only does the LXX have a plural, 'animals', but Aquila and Theodotion have κτήνη, 'beasts'. The Peshitta of Job 40.25 does not have Leviathan but *tnyn'*, though 'Leviathan' does appear in 3.8. Could Jacob have known that the Hebrew text of 40.25 had 'Leviathan'? He could certainly have deduced that it did, since Aquila and Symmachus read 'Leviathan' there instead of LXX δράκων. Either δράκων or *tnyn'* would have supplied the meaning of Leviathan, and LXX Job 3.8 renders the word as μέγα κῆτος. As for the 'splendid bird', Symmachus's reading for Job 39.13 is πτέρον ἀγλαισμοῦ, 'bird of splendour'.

2. John is puzzled by the plants mentioned in 2 Kgs 4.39.[12] Jacob gives the Greek and Syriac versions for them, and says that corresponding to Syriac *rw'n'*, 'wild herbs', the Greek has *'rywt* (αριωθ). This is a

---

8. Wright, 'Two Epistles', p. ܪܐ, and Nau, 'Traduction', pp. 273-74.
9. Wright, 'Two Epistles', p. ܠܒ, and Nau, 'Traduction', pp. 207-208.
10. Wright, 'Two Epistles', pp. ܣܚ-ܣܒ, and Nau, 'Traduction', pp. 262-67.
11. BDB, p. 97, suggest that it is an intensive plural of the singular בהמה, 'beast'.
12. Wright, 'Two Epistles', p. ܚܝ, and Nau, 'Traduction', p. 270.

Hebrew expression, he says, but he confesses that neither he nor Greek readers know what it means. He then makes the important admission 'I cannot readily explain to you Hebrew words such as these with precision'. The MT has the form ארה, which is a hapax legomenon in this sense. The example here shows that Jacob did not know the actual Hebrew text, only its transliteration, and was unable to find an informant to supply a definition.[13]

3. Jacob supports his assertion that Hebrew was the first language of humanity by demonstrating that the wordplay in Gen. 2.23, that woman was so named because she was taken from man, does not work at all in Syriac, but that it does in Hebrew. He even gives the Hebrew words transliterated into Syriac, '*š*' ('woman') and '*yš* ('man'), which do correspond closely to the Hebrew spelling.[14] But it is likely that he owes this explanation and the Hebrew words to Eusebius of Emesa, whom he has just cited as having written a discourse (*m'mr'*) on the priority of Hebrew. This work is no longer extant. However, a similar argument based on transliteration of the Hebrew words for man and woman appears in an anonymous catena fragment and Diodore.[15] Ter Haar Romeny suggests that both are based on a lost comment by Eusebius of Emesa, which was in turn derived from Eusebius of Caesarea, who wrote in *Praeparatio Evangelica* 11.6.18, 'as for the woman, since it was said that she was taken from the man, she also shares a name with man. For woman is called *essa* among them [i.e. the Jews], as man is called *heis*.'[16]

---

13. This contrasts with the practice of Jerome: instead of following the LXX interpretation κολοκύνθη 'gourd', he retranslated the word קיקיון in Jon. 4.6 as *hedera* 'ivy' on the basis of his acquaintance with Palestinian botany, the reading of Symmachus (κισσός), and a first-hand knowledge of the Hebrew, Syrian and Phoenician words for 'gourd'. However, Augustine says that the local North African Jews disagreed with Jerome's definition. See J.N.D. Kelly, *Jerome: His Life, Writings and Controversies* (London: Duckworth, 1975), pp. 221, 266.

14. Wright, 'Two Epistles', p. ܪܒ, Nau, 'Traduction', p. 274.

15. The catena fragment is §314 in F. Petit, *La chaîne sur la Genèse: Edition intégrale*, I (TEG, 1; Peeters: Leuven, 1992), that of Diodore is §100 in *idem, Catenae graecae in Genesim et in Exodum 2: Collectio coisliniana in Genesim* (CCSG, 15; Leuven: Peeters, 1986).

16. See R.B. ter Haar Romeny, *A Syrian in Greek Dress: The Use of Greek, Hebrew, and Syriac Biblical Texts in Eusebius of Emesa's Commentary on Genesis* (TEG, 6; Leuven: Peeters, 1997), pp. 203-206, which includes a discussion of the ways in which Greek and Latin authors tried to represent shin.

c. In Jacob's scholia on the Bible, he occasionally refers to Hebrew words.[17]

1. On Gen. 22.13, Jacob says that the vegetation in which the ram was caught was called *sbq* in Hebrew.[18] This is incorrect: the Hebrew word is in fact spelt סבך with a kaph, not a qoph. The information was probably taken directly from the LXX, which has the reading ἐν φυτῷ σαβέκ: Jacob's use of the term *nṣbt'* in his explanation looks suspiciously like φυτόν, and he must have guessed that σαβέκ was a transliteration of the Hebrew, though he was wrong in his Semitic retroversion. Since similar comments on Gen. 22.13 appear in several Greek scholia, most of them ultimately dependent on Eusebius of Emesa, it is possible that Jacob was influenced by one of these as well.[19] But if so, it is remarkable that he never mentions any of their fanciful etymologies of Sabek or speculated like them on the typology of the ram. In fact his interpretation concerning the ram is extremely prosaic.

2. In his 36th scholion, addressing the question of why Esau was called Edom, Jacob recounts the episode of Gen. 25.30, where Esau asks his brother to feed him the red lentils he has cooked. Jacob connects the name Edom with the Hebrew word *'dm*, which he says means 'red' and is derived from the noun *'dmt'*, 'red earth' (the Hebrew form is actually אדמה).[20] There are similarities with two catena fragments on Gen. 2.16: τὸ ἀδάμ ἐστι γῆ ἐρυθρά, 'adam is "red earth" ',[21] and Ἐδὼμ γὰρ τὸ πυρρόν, ὥς που καὶ ὁ Ἠσαῦ, πυρρᾶς φακῆς πεπρακὼς αὐτοῦ τὰ πρωτοτόκια, τὴν προσηγορίαν εἴληφεν, 'Edom is "red", as in the case of Esau, who received the name after he had sold his rights as first-born for red lentil pottage'.[22] Whatever the true source of Jacob's comments, it is clear that they required no real knowledge of the Hebrew language.

17. G. Phillips, *Scholia on Passages of the Old Testament, by Mar Jacob, Bishop of Edessa* (London: Williams & Norgate, 1864), p. 12.

18. In his 33rd scholion, Phillips, *Scholia*, p. 13 and p. ܞ.

19. §1277 in F. Petit, *La chaîne sur la Genèse: Edition intégrale*, II (TEG, 2; Leuven: Peeters, 1994). It is repeated in similar forms by Procopius, Diodore, Gennadius, and eventually Isho'dad of Merv.

20. Phillips, *Scholia*, pp. 13-14. and pp. ܞ.

21. §274 in Petit, *La chaîne sur la Genèse*, I. One manuscript attributes it to Eusebius of Emesa, though Romeny considers this insufficient to establish authorship (*Syrian in Greek Dress*, p. 196). Compare also Origen, *Hom. Gen.* 12.4: 'Esau vero—ut aiunt qui Hebraea nomina interpretantur—vel a rubore vel a terra, id est rubeus vel terrenus vel, ut aliis visum est, factura dictus esse videatur'.

22. §86 in Petit, *Collectio Coisliniana*. It is attributed to Diodore.

3. Jacob's 23rd scholion concerns the identity of Eliezer the Damascene (Gen. 15.2).[23] Towards the end, in rather a convoluted manner, he says,

> The name of the mother of Eliezer is known and published in divine Scripture in this place, as may be seen in copies of the Scriptures of the translation of the Greeks (that is, what was translated from the Hebrew language into Greek by the seventy two, the translations, the books of the Hebrews [*mpšqn' spr' d'bry'*] in what was written instead of those words: 'behold Eliezer the son of Maseq, the Damascene woman (*dmsqyt'*), the son of my house, inherits from me'.

This text does not correspond to either LXX or Syrohexapla. However, there is a slight resemblance to a catena fragment attributed to Eusebius of Emesa and found also in Diodore: ἡ Ἐβραία Δαμασκήνος λέγει, ὅθεν ἦν αὐτῷ ἡ μήτηρ, 'the Hebrew says "Damascene", from where his mother was'.[24] Did Jacob have a muddled recollection of this reading of the 'Hebrew'?

d. Judging from the manuscript evidence of Jacob's revision of Severus's *Homiliae Cathedrales*, he often felt the need to amplify or even correct tactfully what the great Master had said.[25] Some of his remarks, recorded in the margins of certain manuscripts, concern Hebrew words.

1. Severus explains the word *iōbēl*, 'Jubilee' , as a combination of two words for God, *iaō* and *ēlaa* (the Greek forms are given in the margin of the manuscript). This is suspect even to the non-Hebraist, for in that case, where does the *b* in *iōbēl* come from? Jacob glosses over Severus's explanation by observing that 'the Master (i.e. Severus) supposes that the word Jobel is a composite word'.[26] However, Jacob does not add any etymology of his own.

---

23. Phillips, *Scholia*, pp. 7-10 and pp. ٦-١.

24. §945 in F. Petit, *La chaîne sur la Genèse*, III (TEG, 3; Leuven: Peeters, 1995). Diodore's version is §185 in Petit, *Collectio Coisliniana*. However, Romeny (*Syrian in Greek Dress*, p. 298) thinks the original form of Eusebius's comment did not have the second part of the phrase.

25. Especially in British Museum Additional MS 12,159 (L), a ninth-century copy of Jacob's revision of the earlier Syriac translation of the Homilies of Severus of Antioch carried out by Paul of Callinicum. Jacob's revision was finished in 701, according to the colophon to Vat. Sir. 141, another MS of the revision. See Brière's introduction to the edition of the Homilies, in PO 29 (1960), pp. 33-50.

26. In Severus, Hom. 84, PO 23 (1932), ed. Brière, p. 19.

2. In Hom. 119, Severus is addressing a certain Romanos, whose ideas he is trying to refute. Severus says that according to this Romanos, the name Beelzebub (*b'lzbwb*) means 'swallower of flies' (*bālaʿ debābā*).[27] In another marginal note, Jacob emphasizes this was not Severus's own opinion on the matter, but compared with rebutting Romanos's heretical opinions it was too trivial for the great man to bother correcting. After some rude remarks about Cilicia, Romanos's place of origin, as a place that breeds flies, Jacob himself gives the real meaning of Beelzebub as 'God-Fly', *'alāhā' debābā*, since *b'l* is equivalent to Syriac *ba'lā* and means 'god' in Canaanite. 'As for *zbwb*, this is [Syriac] *debābā*, "fly", reading *z* for *d*. This is the god of Ekron to whom Ahaziah sent after his accident' (2 Kgs 1.2).

Jacob's explanation comes close to a correct rendering of the Hebrew, but how did he come about it? He may have obtained a hint from the Septuagint, which renders Beelzebub in 2 Kgs 1.2, 3, 6, 16 as βάαλ μυῖα, 'Baal the Fly', while the versions have transliterations of the Hebrew form: Aquila βααλ ζεβουβ, Symmachus βεελ ζεβουλ, and, perhaps most importantly, the reading of the 'Hebrew' version: εβρ.´ , βαβαλ ζεβουβ ελων εκρων. This reading of the 'Hebrew' appears also in the Syrohexapla as *b'lzbwb*, at 2 Kgs 1.3, 6. Jacob did not need to have first-hand knowledge of Hebrew to arrive at the definition, only access to the versions through witnesses to the Hexapla or through the Syrohexapla.

3. On the slightly odd syntax of Severus's text of Ezek. 13.10, 'if it will fall',[28] Jacob comments in the margin that it is customary in Hebrew to say 'if this should befall us' rather than 'it shall not be', that is the expression is a statement, not part of a conditional clause.[29] However, though this is true of oath formulae in Hebrew, it has nothing to do with this particular verse in Ezekiel: the Hebrew has no conditional (i.e. no אִם), and some Greek manuscripts lack εἰ. Jacob had probably worked out from the context the real meaning of Hebrew oaths rendered literally into Greek or Syriac from the Hebrew, and then misapplied his observation in this case.

---

27. In Severus, Hom. 119, PO 26 (1950) ed. Brière, p. 407.

28. 'Fall' is the LXX and Peshitta interpretation of the Hebrew consonants תפל (as if from נפל) in Ezek. 13.10, but the root is actually תפל 'to be insipid', and this meaning is reflected in the revisions of Aquila, Symmachus and Theodotion.

29. Severus, Hom. 76, PO 12 (1919) ed. Brière, p. 145.

4. In the course of Severus's discussion of Mk 7.11 and Mt. 15.5, Jacob explains to the Syriac reader that the Greek text of Mark has the word *qwrbn'*, 'offering', in the Hebrew form *qwrbn*, whereas the parallel passage in Matthew has the Greek word δῶρον, 'gift'.[30] But the words are so similar in Syriac and Hebrew that this instance does not prove much about Jacob's knowledge of Hebrew.

5. In Hom. 29 Severus is discussing the episode of Josh. 7, where an Israelite appropriates devoted goods for himself.[31] The text gives the man's name as 'Achar, and Jacob adds a marginal note to applaud the Syriac version of Josh. 7.25: 'since you have troubled us, may the Lord trouble you', against the LXX 'you have destroyed us, the Lord will destroy you'.[32] He says that the name 'Achar in the Hebrew language means 'troubler', *dlḥ*, or rather 'dregs', *ṭṭr'*.[33] Achar's father was called *krm'*, 'vine' (Josh. 7.1), and he called his son 'dregs' or 'troubler'.

Jacob is correct in giving the meaning of the Hebrew root *'kr* as 'trouble' and in saying that the Syriac of Josh. 7.25 reproduces an original Hebrew wordplay. What he is unaware of (and it proves that he was not using a Hebrew text) is the fact that the man's name in Hebrew is 'Achan not 'Achar: the event takes place in the valley of 'Achor, and the wordplay is related to the place name, not the personal name. However, in both the Syriac and LXX versions of Josh. 7, the man's name has been assimilated to that of the place, and these are the texts on which Jacob is relying.[34] The wordplay on Hebrew *'kr* is reproduced in the later Greek versions, such as Symmachus (v. 25 τί ἐτάραξας ἡμᾶς), and Aquila (κοιλάς ταραχοῦ), and in the Syrohexapla the reading of the 'Rest of the Interpreters', *lmn' dlḥt ln*. Knowing that these versions were closer to the Hebrew, Jacob may have adopted their understanding of the passage, and he would have appreciated their support of the rendering of the Peshitta.

---

30. Severus, Hom. 79, PO 20 (1929) ed. Brière, pp. 309-10. The Peshitta text has the word *qwrbny* in both places, hence the Syriac reader's need for an explanation.

31. PO 36 (1974), ed. Brière and Graffin, 'Jacques d'Edesse', pp. 594-95.

32. However, the 'Syriac' version that Jacob cites here is not identical to the Peshitta of Josh. 7.25, though the main point, the use of the verb *dlḥ*, is the same. Was Jacob quoting from memory?

33. The connection between the two words is not apparent in English, but both Syriac words can refer to clouded or turbid water.

34. The form Achan does appear in some Hexaplaric manuscripts.

6. More intriguing are the two long notes Jacob has on the meaning of Hosanna.[35] In the first he is diplomatically correcting Severus's belief that Greek Ὡς αννα means 'like praise' (αννα being taken to mean 'praise'), and 'Jesus' in Greek relates to ἴασις, 'healing'. Jacob explains that Greeks cannot say Shin or *'Ay*, hence the error, since Hosanna in Hebrew and Syriac contains both. He himself correctly says that Hosanna is connected with salvation rather than healing, citing Zech. 9.9 in support, that the name Isaiah means 'the salvation of Yahweh', and that the Hebrew word for salvation is *yšw't*, and this is true, though the form he gives is the construct form and strictly speaking means 'salvation of—'.

Jacob is certainly on the right lines, but it is evident that he knows only the Syriac form of Hosanna and not the Hebrew. He explains *'wš'n'* as meaning 'O salvation', as if the word was a composite of *'w* and *š'n'*, and is unaware that the Hebrew form has an initial he. In the second note he also mistakenly analyses the end of the word (*-n'*) as a first person objective suffix, 'me' (i.e. 'save me!'). It is actually a second, separate particle in Hebrew, נא, with the sense of entreaty.

Jacob cites with surprising accuracy the 'Hebrew' of Ps. 118.25 (LXX 117.25): *'nn' 'dwny 'wšy'n' 'nn' 'dwny 'šlyḥ 'n'*. There is also a Greek version in the margin supplied with Syriac consonants where necessary: ΑΝΝΑ ΑΔΟΝΑΙ ΩΣΙ'ΑΝΑ ΑΝΝΑ ΑΔΟΝΑΙ Α ṣΛΙ ḥΑΝΑ. This looks quite impressive (apart from the lack of 'Hé's for the hiphil verbs) until we remember that a very similar Greek transliteration appears in Origen's *Commentary on Matthew* 16.19: οὕτω δὲ καὶ ἡ ἑβραικὴ δέξις, 'Thus the Hebrew tradition had ΑΝΝΑ ΑΔΩΝΑΙ ΩΣΙΑΝΝΑ, ΑΝΝΑ ΑΔΩΝΑΙ ΑΣΛΙΑΝΝΑ, ΒΑΡΟΥΧ ΑΒΒΑ ΒΣΑΙΜ ΑΔΩΝΑΙ.' The Greek transliteration also appears in Jerome's *Letter XX to Damasus*. All in all, there is nothing in Jacob's notes on Hosanna that demonstrates direct knowledge of Hebrew, only some facts obtained indirectly.

7. There is one very extensive scholion of Jacob's, found between Severus's *Homilies* 123 and 124 and relating especially to comments made by Severus on the names of God.[36] In the course of Hom. 123

35. In Severus, Hom. 20, PO 37 (1975), eds. Brière and Graffin, pp. 52-55. See also Graffin, 'Jacques d'Edesse', p. 250.

36. In PO 29 (1960), ed. Brière, pp. 190-99. It was published earlier with a German translation and comments by Nestle, in 'Jakob von Edessa'. Also Graffin, 'Jacques d'Edesse', p. 250.

Jacob explains the meaning of Adonai Sabaoth and informs the reader that 'the Master' was unaware that the Hebrew of Ps. 110.1 used two different names, *yhyh* (*sic*) and *'dwny*, and says that he has written a lengthy scholion on the Divine Name among the Hebrews which he is going to place at the end of this homily.[37]

This scholion on the Most Sacred Name of God concerns the confusion that has arisen in the Syriac church over the 'true' name of God, which appears to be written in Greek manuscripts as PIPI (ΠΙΠΙ) and has been so represented in copies of the Syrohexapla (*pypy*). Jacob's argument is a carefully structured piece of rhetoric in the first half: he seems aware that he will have his work cut out persuading others that this name PIPI is a Satanic deception and not the true name of God at all. But the error has crept in, and he believes that the scholars of the past who mistakenly introduced it will be thankful to him if he can eradicate it now.

Jacob explains that centuries ago the pious Jewish translators of the Septuagint feared to render into Greek the Most Sacred Name of God (YHWH) which they themselves avoided pronouncing, substituting the name Adonai instead when reading. So they left the Divine Name in Hebrew characters in the Greek text, and placed the word κύριος in the margins as a reminder to substitute it for the Tetragrammaton. Ignorant readers then mistook these Hebrew letters as Greek, and read them from left to right as 'PIPI'. The true name of God is represented *Yod-He-Yod-He* (*sic*), and is known as the 'name set apart', *šm' prwš'*. At the end of the scholion Jacob has composed a table setting out the true and false names of God in Syriac, Greek and Hebrew. Underneath he supplies Syriac and Greek versions of Ps. 110.1, with a Greek transliteration of the 'Hebrew' text.

Jacob presents his case persuasively, with full explanations and examples. He declares his intention of eradicating every single example of the deceptive name PIPI from the scriptures. This appears to have taken place in the Syrohexapla version of Isaiah found in the eighth century Codex Ambrosianus, where *mry'* is the name used throughout the main text, and *yhyh* in the marginal notes.[38] As pointed out over a

---

37. These notes are on pp. 142-43 of the edition.

38. A.M. Ceriani (ed.), *Monumenta Sacra et Profana. VII. Codex Syro-Hexaplaris Ambrosianus* (Turin: Hermann Loescher; London: Williams & Norgate, 1874).

century ago, this must be due to Jacob's influence.[39] Clearly he knew that PIPI was a blasphemous absurdity, and was prepared to face hostility in declaring this. But what he says is the true name, *yhyh*, does not correspond to the actual Hebrew Tetragrammaton, though it is a distinct improvement on PIPI. The information that he deploys so effectively against possible opponents is likely to have come from earlier Greek sources, and the Greek transliteration of Ps. 110.1 could ultimately have originated from the Hexapla. Anyway, whatever Jacob's sources in this learned scholion, they do not point to a first-hand knowledge of the Hebrew language.

Nothing in all the examples examined above indicates certain and independent knowledge of Hebrew language or the Hebrew biblical text on Jacob's part. Where there is a close correspondence with the meaning of the Hebrew, there is almost always evidence to suggest that Jacob's information came from versions in Greek that closely resembled the Hebrew, like the 'Hebraios' or Aquila, Symmachus and Theodotion, or alternatively from commentators who themselves used these versions, such as Origen or Eusebius of Emesa. And to be fair, Jacob himself never claims to know Hebrew, only interpretations of it. It is some of his modern admirers who have wanted to see him as a Syrian Origen or Jerome.

In his recent monograph on Jacob's version of Samuel, Richard Saley remarks in passing that 'Jacob had, at minimum, some knowledge of Hebrew and Jewish biblical tradition'.[40] I suggest that this was in fact the absolute limit of his abilities in Hebrew, a minimal knowledge of Hebrew biblical tradition. This is not to diminish him, for the fact that he uses such sources at all shows his open-mindedness and great learning. And considering the strong criticism he received in his own day from his fellow churchmen for advocating even Greek learning in the Syriac church, it would have been difficult to take Hebrew more seriously than he did.

39. Discussed by Nestle, 'Jakob von Edessa', pp. 507-508, also Field, *Origenis Hexaplorum quae supersunt*, II (Oxford: Oxford University Press, 1875), p. 429, and A.M. Ceriani, *Monumenta Sacra et Profana*, II (Milan: Bibliotheca Ambrosiana, 1863), pp. 106-12.

40. Saley, *Samuel Manuscript*, p. 15.

Part V
'SIMPLE HEBREW: A STRANGE GIBBERISH KIND OF STUTTERING'

GOETHE ON HEBREW

Edward Ullendorff

The dismayingly premature death of Michael Weitzman, in the prime
of his life and work, has not only brought consternation to his family,
friends and admirers, but it has also robbed Hebrew scholarship of
one of the ever diminishing number of practitioners of this crucial
discipline.

Our last meeting occurred, not long before that cruel event, at a fine
lecture Michael delivered at Oxford on the *Qaddish* prayer, a subject
close to his heart and upon which I had heard him discourse before. We
then talked about the relationship between the *Qaddish* and the *pater-
noster* on which I had been meaning to write something for the past
sixty years—ever since I had studied my teacher Ismar Elbogen's
Der jüdische Gottesdienst. A memorial contribution to a volume in
Michael's honour would have been the appropriate occasion for such a
subject. Alas, two bouts of illness made it impossible to follow so complex a trail within the time prescribed; thus I had to turn to a topic with
an equally distant background in my academic peregrinations—but of a
much lesser intricacy. It so happens that Michael and I conversed on
my present subject when discussing the well-nigh catastrophic diminu-
tion of Hebrew language studies in Great Britain and elsewhere. He
then opined that Hebrew (and no doubt other classical languages) was
perhaps perceived as too difficult a discipline. I countered with the
substance of the following desultory observations.

When settling down to penning these notes and opening my volume
of Goethe's *Aus meinem Leben: Wahrheit und Dichtung*,[1] I found at the

---

1. Vol. 22 of the Cotta edition of 1871, pp. 79-97—to which Goethe had prefaced the motto ὁ μὴ δαρεὶς ἄνθρωπος οὐ παιδεύεται 'the unchastised man is not
being educated' or 'spare the rod and spoil the child'—incidentally the maxim of
my school and of one of the universities in which I had taught (without the rod!).

appropriate place a note penned by the late Enoch Powell (whom I had taught some Hebrew and Aramaic) asking for the references to 'Goethe's Hebrew hints'. Nearly twenty years later I performed the same service for my friend Michael Weitzman. Goethe in his auto-biographical sketches gives hardly any dates or indications of his age at any particular point of time. It is, however, possible in most instances to posit an approximate dating from the external circumstances of the narrative. Thus the time-frame of his Hebrew studies can be roughly assessed by the period of the French occupation of Frankfurt (1756–1763) and the billeting of a French officer in his paternal home. This corresponds to Goethe's age seven to about thirteen. Taking the latter age, twelve to thirteen, as a basis, Goethe revealed remarkable polyglot talents. We know from p. 79 of *Aus meinem Leben* that about that time an English 'Sprachmeister' was at Frankfurt and offered his services to teach English to anyone who was not entirely obtuse—at any rate up to the point from which the pupil could proceed on his own with a measure of diligence. The exercise turned out to be successful, and Goethe, accompanied by his father and sister, worked hard during those four weeks. Indeed, they continued on their own beyond that period, and the teacher occasionally looked in to check on their progress, which gave satisfaction to all concerned.

Goethe now produced an ingenious literary device in order to keep all his languages acquired so far in reasonable repair. He had found it tedious to work on the grammatical paradigms to maintain his know-ledge; instead he invented a method, in the form of a novel, which should achieve a much better result: this novel involved six or seven siblings who were dispersed over several countries and who wrote to each other in the languages of the area in which they lived. The eldest brother composed his letters in excellent German and reported the events of his journeys. Another brother studied theology and wrote in 'formal Latin' to which he frequently added a postscript in Greek. Goethe had, of course, learnt Latin at an early age, and the study of Greek had been essential for him to read the New Testament in the original language. The latter he read 'quite comfortably' (p. 80) because the Gospels and Epistles were recited, translated and submitted to exe-gesis after Sunday church services. Another brother lived in Hamburg as a trade representative and 'naturally' wrote in English, while a younger brother was domiciled at Marseilles and corresponded in French. Italian was represented by a musician sibling on his first visit abroad—which naturally meant the quasi-obligatory journey to Italy. The youngest of all, cut off from other languages, had specialized in 'Judendeutsch' (= Yiddish) and 'by this terrible code' led the others to despair, while the parents were amused by this strange idea.

Those were the seven languages which Goethe could handle, actively as well as passively, as a young adolescent. But he adds that the mere language form was not enough for him, for he endeavoured to enliven this fictional correspondence with the geography of those areas and with the people and their customs who inhabited the regions which Goethe at that time knew from the perusal of their literatures only.

He now continues (p. 80):

> These pursuits are apt to become ever more fascinating and extensive. When I sought to acquire the 'barocke Judendeutsch' and to write it as well as I could read it, I soon found that I lacked a knowledge of Hebrew from which alone the modern corrupt and distorted form had to be derived.

Quandoque bonus dormitat Goethe!—with apologies to Horace; for Goethe could no doubt see himself that the structure of Yiddish was almost entirely Teutonic and only the vocabulary manifested a good many relics from Hebrew—possibly more than is the case in contemporary Yiddish. In any event, his acquaintance with this quaint *Misch-sprache* led inexorably to approaching his father with the request, indeed the necessity, to enable him to learn Hebrew: 'I pursued his consent very vigorously'. 'I had indeed an even more elevated purpose. Everywhere I heard it being said that for an understanding of the Old Testament (as indeed for that of the New) a knowledge of the original languages was essential.' We have already seen that he was familiar with Greek, and he now proposed to apply the same linguistic rigour to the Hebrew Bible, for the latter had 'always appealed to me very specially on account of its peculiarities'.

Goethe's dictum about the need for a knowledge of Greek and Hebrew as the languages of the Bible (Latin was, of course, taken for granted) remained an absolute requirement in the training of the clergy until twenty or thirty years ago. During the nineteen-fifties and sixties I taught Hebrew to generations of theological students in Scotland and England. And when occasionally some of them complained about the difficulty of learning Hebrew, I invariably referred them to the following passage in Goethe's autobiography:

> My father, who did not like to do things by halves, decided to request the Rector of our *Gymnasium*, Doctor Albrecht, to give me private tuition on a weekly basis until I had grasped the rudiments of so simple ('einfach') a language. His hope was that Hebrew might be disposed of, if not as quickly as English, then certainly in double the time needed for the latter.

Goethe tells us that Rector Albrecht was one of the strangest characters in the world:

> small, not fat but broad, ungainly, yet not crippled. His face, over seventy years old, was screwed up by a sarcastic smile. He lived in the old monastery of the discalced monks, the seat of the school. His inclination was to pay the closest attention to his pupils' mistakes or shortcomings and to treat them with allusions and innuendoes taken from classical or biblical sources.

Goethe went to see him every evening at 6 pm; they would be seated in the Rector's library, with a well-thumbed copy of the second-century satirist Lucian always by his side. The teacher was unable to suppress mocking remarks about the pupil's wish to study Hebrew. Goethe never mentioned his interest in the *Judendeutsch* of his native city and its relevance to Hebrew; instead, he referred to a better understanding of the Old Testament *Urtext*. Albrecht just smiled and suggested that his pupil should be content with learning to read Hebrew. This irked Goethe, and he paid the closest attention to the alphabet, which was not unlike its Greek counterpart, its shapes readily comprehensible and the names of the letters not alien to him. Having understood and retained all this and having been long aware that the direction of Hebrew writing was from right to left, young Goethe thought he was now ready to start reading a text:

> But now a new army of little characters and signs appeared, points and lines which are intended to be vowels. I was astonished about this, for the main alphabet contained vowel-like symbols (he was no doubt referring to *w* and *y*). It was known that the Jewish nation in its heyday was content with the main characters of its script and had no knowledge then of any other mode facilitating reading and writing. I would have preferred to adhere to this more ancient and more convenient procedure, but my old teacher declared with some severity that one had to comply with grammatical rules as they had evolved. Reading without those dots and squiggles was a difficult task and could only be accomplished by the learned and the most experienced (p. 81).

> Thus I had to submit to his guidance that these small symbols required to
> be learnt, but the matter seemed to me increasingly confused. At times
> some of the original characters (p. 82) appeared to count for little by
> themselves and served merely as carriers for their tiny successors
> (*matres lectionis* no doubt). At other times they were to indicate a
> smooth or soft breathing or a harsh guttural sound (i.e. '*aleph* or '*ayin* or
> merely act as support). Finally, when one had come to terms with all
> these details, it emerged that some of the main characters as well as the
> small ones might be relegated into retirement, so that the eyes had to
> work a lot, while the lips did very little.

Goethe was now encouraged to read Hebrew which appeared to him 'a
strange gibberish kind of stuttering', while any more authentic pronunciation, accompanied by some nasal and gurgling sounds, was
represented to him as being 'unattainable'. In the event the entire mode
of learning repelled him and, instead, he found some 'childish amuse-
ment' with the odd names of those many marks of pronunciation aids
(Masoretic pointing). Yet in the course of reading, translating, repeating, and reciting from memory he developed a fresh relationship to the
contents of the Old Testament texts, for it was that aspect after all for
which he had requested elucidation from his teacher. Even earlier on he
had come across contradictions in the transmission (*sic*) of the biblical
narrative and had caused some embarrassment to his domestic tutors
when he drew their attention to such incongruities as the Sun standing
still upon Gibeon and the Moon in the valley of Ayalon (Josh. 10.12).
'All this came back to me when I endeavoured to master the Hebrew
language by concentrating exclusively on the Old Testament, eschewing Luther's translation and turning to the original version.' Goethe's
interest in the substance of the biblical narrative led inevitably and
'unfortunately' to a certain curtailing of the grammatical exercises. The
youngster's doubts and constant questionings produced only smiles and
guffawing from the Rector and an occasional exclamation in the then
customary third person pronoun: 'Er närrischer Kerl! Er närrischer
Junge!' (you dotty fellow! you dotty lad!).

Goethe's Hebrew studies are followed in his autobiography by a
detailed and somewhat idiosyncratic summary of Old Testament history
and theology, a subject to which he devoted much time and thought. He
tells us that 'ein so grosses Werk als jenes biblische prosaisch–epische
Gedicht hatte ich noch nicht unternommen' (p. 92). When the work was
finished (for it was completed—to his own astonishment), he thought of
combining these biblical studies with some unpublished poems which

in retrospect seemed to him not altogether negligible. The collection might get the title 'Gemischte Gedichte' (miscellaneous poems) which 'appealed to me, because in this way I confessed to myself I might imitate some famous authors'.

His next venture was connected with the Frankfurt *Judenstadt*, in fact called 'Judengasse', because it consisted essentially of one single street. The dirt, the multitude of people and their accent did not make an agreeable impression. It took a long time for young Goethe to summon up the courage to enter into the ghetto, for somewhere he had heard malicious rumours of what Jews might do to Christian children. However, in recent times, he realized, the situation had improved, and such stories no longer circulated.

> In the meantime they still remained God's chosen people and represented a kind of surviving memory of ancient times. After all, they were human beings, active, obliging, and even the stubbornness with which they adhered to their age-old customs deserved respect. Moreover, the girls were pretty and were pleased when a Christian youth met them on the Sabbath on their walks and showed himself friendly and attentive to them. I was, therefore, extremely curious to get acquainted with their ceremonies and did not rest until I was able to visit their school (in this context almost certainly 'shul' = synagogue) quite often and be present at a circumcision, a wedding, or their *Lauberhüttenfest* (*sic*; i.e. *Sukkoth*). Everywhere I was well received, provided with hospitality, and invited to return.

Frankfurt's Jewish quarter was, of course, as well known as its future cosmopolitan Jewish community became in the following century and a half. And Goethe, too, as a native of this city—despite the fact that most of his life was spent at Weimar—was markedly cosmopolitan and worldly in his mode of life, his languages, and his tastes. His youthful interest in Hebrew and the Hebrew Bible is just one facet of his remarkable personality—widely celebrated again in this 250th anniversary year of his birth (1999).

BIBLIOGRAPHY

Abrahams, I (ed. and trans.), *Hebrew Ethical Wills* (Philadelphia: Jewish Publication Society of America, 1926), I, p. 63.

Abramsky, S., 'סיגים ובדילים בישעיהו פרק א', *Eretz-Israel* 5 (1958), pp. 105-107.

Adler, W., *Time Immemorial: Archaic History and its Sources in Christian Chronography from Julius Africanus to George Syncellus* (Washington, DC: Dumbarton Oaks, 1989).

Aejmelaeus, A., 'What Can we Know about the Hebrew Vorlage of the Septuagint', *ZAW* 99 (1987), pp. 58-89.

Aland, Barbara, and Andreas Juckel (eds.), *Das Neue Testament in syrischer Überlieferung* (Arbeiten zur Neutestamentliche Textforschung; Berlin: W. de Gruyter, 1986–).

Albert, Micheline, *Jacques de Saroug: Homélies contre les juives* (PO, 38; Turnhout: Brepols, 1976).

Albertz, R., 'Das Deuterojesaja-Buch als Fortschreibung der Jesaja-Prophetie', in E. Blum *et al.* (eds.), *Die hebräische Bibel und ihre zweifache Nachgeschichte: Festschrift für Rolf Rendtorff zum 65. Geburtstag* (Neukirchen–Vluyn: Neukirchener Verlag, 1990), pp. 241-56.

Albrekston, B., *Studies in the Text and Theology of the Book of Lamentations* (Studia Theologica Laudensia, 21; Lund: C.W.K. Gleerup, 1963).

—*Reflections on the Emergence of a Standard Text of the Hebrew Bible* (VTSup, 29; Leiden: E.J. Brill, 1978).

Alexander, P.S., 'Jewish Aramaic Translations of Hebrew Scriptures', in M.J. Mulder and H. Sysling (eds.), *Mikra: Text, Translation, Reading and Interpretation of the Hebrew Bible in Ancient Judaism and Early Christianity* (Assen: Van Gorcum; Philadephia: Fortress Press, 1988), pp. 217-53.

—'From Poetry to Historiography: The Image of the Hasmoneans in Targum Canticles and the Question of the Targum's Provenance and Date', *JSP* 19 (1999), pp. 103-28.

Allegro, J.M., with A.A. Anderson, *Qumrân Cave 4.1 (4Q158–4Q186)* (DJD, 5; Oxford: Clarendon Press, 1968).

Alter, R., *The Art of Biblical Poetry* (Edinburgh: T. & T. Clark, 1990).

Anderson, A.A., *The Book of Psalms* (NCB; London: Oliphants, 1972)

Anderson, H., '3 Maccabees', in J.H. Charlesworth (ed.), *The Old Testament Pseudepigrapha*, II (Garden City, NY: Doubleday, 1985), pp. 509-29.

Aphrahat, *Patrologia Syriaca* (2 vols.; ed. J. Parisot; Paris, 1894, 1907).

Arnold, T.W., 'Muslim Civilization during the Abbasid Period', in *Cambridge Mediaeval History*, IV (Cambridge: Cambridge University Press, 1927), p. 286.

Arragel, Moses, *La Biblia de Alba: An Illustrated Manuscript Bible in Castilian* (Madrid: Fundación de Amigos de Sefarad; London: Facsimile Editions, 1992).

Assemani, J.S., 'Carmen Ebedjesu metropolitae Sobae et Armeniae continens catalogum librorum omnium ecclesiasticorum', in *idem* (ed.), *Bibliotheca Orientalis Clementino-Vaticana*, III.1 (Rome: Sancta Congregatio de Propaganda Fide, 1725), pp. 3-362.

Avigad, N., *Beth She'arim. Report on the Excavations, 3, Catacombs 12-23* (Jerusalem: Masada Press, 1976).

Avigad, N., and Y. Yadin, *Genesis Apocryphon*, X.2 (Jerusalem: Magnes Press, 1956).

Baars, W., 'Eine neue griechische Handschrift des 3 Makkabäerbuches', *VT* 13 (1963), pp. 82-87.

—'Ein neugefundenes Bruchstück aus der syrischen Bibelrevision des Jakob von Edessa', *VT* 18 (1968), pp. 548-54.

—*New Syro-Hexaplaric Texts, Edited, Commented upon and Compared with the Septuagint* (Leiden: E.J. Brill, 1968).

Bacher, W. 'Das Targum zu den Psalmen', *ZDMG* 21 (1872), pp. 408-16, 462-73.

Baer, Isaac, עבודת ישראל (Rödelheim, 1868).

Barr, J. 'St Jerome's Appreciation of Hebrew', *BJRL* 49 (1966–67), pp. 281-302.

—*Comparative Philology and the Text of the Old Testament* (Oxford: Clarendon Press, 1968).

Barth, H., *Die Jesaja-Worte in der Josiazeit: Israel und Assur als Thema einer produktiven Neuinterpretation der Jesajaüberlieferung* (WMANT, 48; Neukirchen–Vluyn: Neukirchener Verlag, 1977).

Barthélemy, D., *Les devanciers d'Aquila* (VTSup, 10; Leiden: E.J. Brill, 1963).

—*Etudes d'histoire du texte de l'Ancien Testament* (Fribourg: Universitaire Fribourg, 1978).

—*Critique Textuelle de l'Ancien Testament*. II. *Isaïe, Jérémie, Lamentations* (OBO, 50/2; Fribourg: Editions universitaires; Göttingen: Vandenhoeck & Ruprecht, 1986).

Baumstark, A., review of Diettrich, *Isôdâdh's Stellung*, in *OrChr* 2 (1902), pp. 451-58.

—*Festbrevier und Kirchenjahr der syrischen Jakobiten* (Paderborn: F. Schoening, 1910).

—'Griechische und hebräische Bibelzitate in der Pentateucherklärung Isô'dâds von Merw', *OrChr* NS 1 (1911), pp. 1-19.

—'Neuerschlossene Urkunden altchristlicher Perikopenordnung des ostaramäischen Sprachgebietes', *OrChr* 3.Serie I (1927), pp. 1-22.

—*Comparative Liturgy* (London: A.R. Mowbray, rev. edn, 1958).

—*Geschichte der syrischen Literatur mit Ausschluß der christlich-palästinensischen Texte* (Berlin: W. de Gruyter, 1968).

—*Nichtevangelische syrische Perikopenordnungen des ersten Jahrtausends im Sinne vergleichender Liturgiegeschichte* (Münster: Aschendorff, 2nd edn, 1972).

Baxter, J.H. *et al.* (eds.), *Medieval Latin Word List from British and Irish Sources* (Oxford: Oxford University Press, 1934).

Beentjes, P.C., *The Book of Ben Sira in Hebrew* (VTSup, 68; Leiden: E.J. Brill, 1997).

Beeston, A.F.L., *et al.*, *Sabaic Dictionary* (Louvain-la-Neuve: Peeters; Beirut: Librairie du Liban, 1982).

Bellinger, A.R., C.H. Kraeling *et al.*, *The Excavations at Dura-Europos, Final Report*, 8 (New Haven: Yale University Press, 1956).

Belot, J.B., *Vocabulaire Arabe–Français* (Beirut, 1899).

Ben Yehuda, E., *Thesaurus totius hebraitatis* (Berlin: Schoeneberg, n.d.; repr. New York: Thomas Yoseloff, 1959).

Bergmeier, R., 'Das Streben nach Gewinn—des Volkes עוֹן', *ZAW* 81 (1969), pp. 93-97.

Berlin, A., *The Dynamics of Biblical Parallelism* (Bloomington: Indiana University Press, 1985).

Berliner, A. (ed.), *Targum Onkelos* (2 parts; Berlin, 1884).

Bernstein, M. 'Translation Technique in the Targum to Psalms. Two Test Cases: Psalms 2 and 137', in E.W. Lovering (ed.), *SBL 1994 Seminar Papers* (Atlanta: Scholars Press, 1994), pp. 326-45.

—'Specification of Speakers as an Interpretive Device in the Targum of Psalms' (paper given at the Twelfth World Congress of Jewish Studies, Jerusalem, 1997).

Bettenzoli, G., *Geist der Heiligkeit: Traditionsgeschichtliche Untersuchung des QDŠ-Begriffes im Buch Ezechiel* (Quaderni di Semitistica, 8; Florence: Università di Firenze, 1979).

Beulay, Robert, *La collection des lettres de Jean de Dalyatha: Edition critique du texte syriaque inédit, traduction française, introduction et notes* (PO, 39; Turnhout: Brepols, 1978).

Bhayro, S., 'A Text-Critical and Literary Analysis of 1 Enoch 6–11' (PhD thesis, University College London, 2000).

Birt, T., *Die Buchrolle in der Kunst* (Leipzig: Teubner, 1907).

Black, M., *Apocalypsis henochi graece* (Leiden: E.J. Brill, 1970).

—*The Book of Enoch or 1 Enoch: A New English Edition* (SVTP, 7; Leiden: E.J. Brill, 1985).

Blau, J., 'Etymologische Untersuchungen auf Grund des Palestinischen Arabisch', *VT* 5 (1955), pp. 339-44.

Blenkinsopp, J., *Wisdom and Law in the Old Testament: The Ordering of Life in Israel and Early Judaism* (Oxford: Oxford University Press, 1983).

—*A History of Prophecy in Israel: From the Settlement in the Land to the Hellenistic Period* (London: SPCK, 1984).

Bloedhorn, Hanswulf, and Gil Hüttenmeister, 'The Synagogue', in W. Horbury *et al.* (eds.), *The Cambridge History of Judaism*, III (Cambridge: Cambridge University Press, 1999), pp. 267-97.

Bogaert, P.-M., 'Le Livre de Jérémie en perspective: Les deux redactions antique selon les travaux en cours', *RB* 101 (1994), pp. 363-406.

Böhl, F. 'Die Metaphorisierung (Metila) in den Targumim zum Pentateuch', *FJB* 15 (1987), pp. 111-49.

Bonnard, P.-E., *Le second Isaïe, son disciple et leurs éditeurs: Isaïe 40–66* (Paris: J. Gabalda, 1972).

Borbone, P.G., *Il libro del profeta Osea: Edizione critica del testo ebraico* (Turin: Silvio Zamorani, 1987).

Borbone, P.G., J. Cook, K.D. Jenner and D.M. Walter, *The Old Testament in Syriac According to the Peshitta Version*, Part V, *Concordance*, Volume 1, *The Pentateuch* (Leiden: E.J. Brill, 1997).

Bosshard-Nepustil, E., *Rezeptionen von Jesaia 1–39 im Zwölfprophetenbuch: Untersuchungen zur literarischen Verbindung von Prophetenbüchern in babylonischer und persischer Zeit* (OBO, 154; Freiburg: Universitätsverlag; Göttingen: Vandenhoeck & Ruprecht, 1997).

Brand, Y., *Klei haheres besifrut hatalmud (Ceramics in Talmudic Literature)* (Jerusalem: Mosad Harav Kook, 1953).

Braun, O., 'Ein Brief des Katholikos Timotheos I über biblische Studien des 9. Jahrhunderts', *OrChr* 1 (1901), pp. 299-313.

Bredenkamp, C.J., *Der Prophet Jesaia* (Erlangen: Andreas Deichert, 1886).

Brière, M. (ed.), *Les Homiliae Cathedrales de Sévère d'Antioche; Homilies 70–76*. PO 12 (1919), pp. 1-163.

—*Les Homiliae Cathedrales de Sévère d'Antioche; Homilies 78–83*. PO 20 (1929), pp. 273-434.

—*Les Homiliae Cathedrales de Sévère d'Antioche; Homilies 84–90*. PO 23 (1932), pp. 1-176.

—*Les Homiliae Cathedrales de Sévère d'Antioche; Homilies 113–119*. PO 26 (1950), pp. 257-450.

—*Les Homiliae Cathedrales de Sévère d'Antioche; Homilies 120–125*. PO 29 (1960), pp. 1-262.

Brière, M., and F. Graffin, *Les Homiliae Cathedrales de Sévère d'Antioche; Hom. 40–45*. PO 36 (1974), pp. 1-137.

—*Les Homiliae Cathedrales de Sévère d'Antioche; Hom. 18–25*. PO 37 (1975), pp. 1-180.

Bright, J., *A History of Israel* (London: SCM Press, 3rd edn, 1981).

Brock, S.P., 'A Fragment of Enoch in Syriac', *JTS* NS 19 (1968), pp. 626-31.

—'Some Aspects of Greek Words in Syriac', in A. Dietrich (ed.), *Synkretismus im syrisch-persischen Kulturgebiet* (AAWG, 96; Göttingen: Vandenhoeck & Ruprecht, 1975), pp. 80-108.

—*The Old Testament in Syriac According to the Peshitta Version. III.1. Isaiah* (Leiden: E.J. Brill, 1987).

—'Text History and Text Division in Peshitta Isaiah', in P.B. Dirksen and M.J. Mulder (eds.), *The Peshitta: Its Early Text and History* (Leiden: E.J. Brill, 1988), pp. 49-80.

—'The Use of the Syriac Fathers for New Testament Textual Criticism', in B.D. Ehrman and M.W. Holmes (eds.), *The Text of the New Testament in Contemporary Research* (Studies and Documents, 46; Grand Rapids: Eerdmans, 1995), pp. 224-36.

—*The Recensions of the Septuagint Version of 1 Samuel* (Quaderni di Henoch, 9; Turin: Silvio Zamorani, 1996).

—*A Brief Outline of Syriac Literature* (Mōrān 'Eth'ō, 9; Kottayam: SEERI, 1997).

Brockelmann, K., *Lexicon syriacum* (Halle: M. Niemeyer, 2nd edn, 1928).

Brooke, G.J., 'The Biblical Texts in the Qumran Commentaries: Scribal Errors or Exegetical Variants?', in C.A. Evans and W.F. Stinespring (eds.), *Early Jewish and Christian Exegesis: Studies in Memory of William Hugh Brownlee* (SBL Homage Series, 10; Atlanta: Scholars Press, 1987), pp. 85-100.

—Review of E. Ulrich *et al.* (eds.), *Qumran Cave 4.X: The Prophets* in *JTS* 50 (1999), pp. 651-55.

—'*E pluribus unum*: Textual Variety and Definitive Interpretation in the Qumran Scrolls', in T.H. Lim *et al.* (eds.), *The Dead Sea Scrolls in their Historical Context* (Edinburgh: T. & T. Clark, 2000), pp. 107-19.

Brown, J.P., *Israel and Hellas* (BZAW, 231; Berlin: W. de Gruyter, 1995).

Brownlee, W.H., *The Meaning of the Qumrân Scrolls for the Bible with Special Attention to the Book of Isaiah* (New York: Oxford University Press, 1964).

Brüll, A., *Das samaritanische Targum zum Pentateuch* (Frankfurt am Main, 1874–75).

Bultmann, C., *Die biblische Urgeschichte in der Aufklärung* (BHT, 110; Tübingen: Mohr Siebeck, 1999).

Burkitt, F.C., 'The Early Syriac Lectionary System', *Proceedings of the British Academy* 10 (1923), pp. 301-38.

—'The Old Lectionary of Jerusalem', *JTS* 24 (1923), pp. 415-24.

Caquot, A., 'Remarques sur les chapitres 70 et 71 du livre éthiopien d'Hénoch', in
L. Monloubou (ed.), *Apocalypses et théologie de l'espérance* (Association catholique
française pour l'étude de la Bible: LD, 95; Paris: Cerf, 1977), pp. 111-22.

—'Hénoch', in A. Dupont-Sommer and M. Philonenko (eds.), *La Bible: Ecrits
intertestamentaires* (Bibliothèque de la Pléiade; Paris: Gallimard, 1987), pp. 463-625.

Casey, M., 'The Use of the Term "Son of Man" in the Similitudes of Enoch', *JSJ* 7 (1976),
pp. 11-29.

Ceriani, A.M., *Monumenta sacra et profana*, II (Milan: Bibliotheca Ambrosiana, 1863).

—*Monumenta sacra et profana*, V (Milan: Bibliotheca Ambrosiana, 1868).

—*Monumenta sacra et profana*. VII. *Codex syro-hexaplaris Ambrosianus photolithographice editus* (Milan: Bibliotheca Ambrosiana, 1874).

Chabot, J.B., *Chronique de Michel le Syrien: Patriarche jacobite d'Antioche 1166–1199*
(Paris: Ernest Leroux, 1899).

—*L'Ecole de Nisibe* (Paris: Gabalda, 1909).

Charles, R.H., *The Book of Enoch* (Oxford: Clarendon Press, 2nd edn, 1912).

Chiesa, B., *The Emergence of Hebrew Biblical Pointing* (Frankfurt, 1979).

Childs, B.S., *Isaiah and the Assyrian Crisis* (SBT, 2nd series, 3; London: SCM Press,
1967).

Chilton, B.D., *The Glory of Israel: The Theology and Provenience of the Isaiah Targum*
(JSOTSup, 23; Sheffield: JSOT Press, 1983).

Churgin, P., *Targum Jonathan to the Prophets* (New Haven: Yale University Press, 1907
[=1927]).

—תרגום כתובים (New York: Horeb, 1945).

Clements, R.E., *Isaiah 1–39* (NCB; Grand Rapids: Eerdmans; London: Marshall, Morgan
& Scott, 1980).

—' "Arise, Shine; for your Light has Come"; A Basic Theme of the Isaianic Tradition', in
C.C. Broyles and C.A. Evans (eds.), *Writing and Reading the Scroll of Isaiah:
Studies of an Interpretive Tradition*, I (VTSup, 50, 1; Leiden: E.J. Brill, 1997),
pp. 441-54.

Clines, D.J.A., *The Esther Scrolls: The Story of a Story* (JSOTSup, 30; Sheffield: JSOT
Press, 1984).

Clines, D.J.A. (ed.), *The Dictionary of Classical Hebrew*, I (Sheffield: Sheffield Academic
Press, 1993).

—*The Dictionary of Classical Hebrew*, III (Sheffield: Sheffield Academic Press, 1996).

Coakley, J.F., 'A Catalogue of the Syriac Manuscripts in the John Rylands Library', *BJRL*
75 (1993), pp. 106-207.

Cohen, J., *Judaica et Aegyptica: De Maccabaeorum Libro III, Quaestiones Historicae*
(1941).

Collins, J.J., 'The Son of Man in First-Century Judaism', *NTS* 38 (1992), pp. 448-66.

Conti Rossini, C., 'Notice sur les manuscrits éthiopiens de la collection d'Abbadie', (suite)
JA 10.20 (1912), pp. 5-72.

Cook, A.K., *About Winchester College* (London: Macmillan, 1917).

Cook, E.M., 'Rewriting the Bible: The Text and Language of the Pseudo-Jonathan Targum' (unpublished PhD dissertation, University of California, 1986).

Cooke, G.A., *A Critical and Exegetical Commentary on the Book of Ezekiel* (Edinburgh:
T. & T. Clark, 1936).

Cowley, A.E., and A. Neubauer, *The Original Hebrew of a Portion of Ecclesiasticus*
(Oxford: Clarendon Press, 1897).

Cowley, R.W., 'Scholia of Aḥob of Qaṭar on St John's Gospel and the Pauline Epistles', *Mus* 93 (1980), pp. 329-43.

Cozza-Luzi, J., *Prophetarum codex graecus vaticanus 2125 qui dicitur Marchalianus* (Rome: Bibliotheca Vaticana, 1890).

Cross, F.M., Jr, 'The History of the Biblical Text in the Light of Discoveries in the Judaean Desert', *HTR* 57 (1964), pp. 281-99.

—'The Evolution of a Theory of Local Texts', in F.M. Cross and S. Talmon (eds.), *Qumran and the History of the Biblical Text* (Cambridge, MA: Harvard University Press, 1975), pp. 306-20.

—'The Oldest Manuscripts from Qumran', in F.M. Cross and S. Talmon (eds.), *Qumran and the History of the Biblical Text* (Cambridge, MA: Harvard University Press, 1975), pp. 147-76.

Cross, F.M., and D.N. Freedman, 'A Royal Song of Thanksgiving: 2 Samuel 22 = Psalm 18', *JBL* 72 (1953), pp. 15-34.

Dahood, M., *Psalms I:1–50* (AB; Garden City, NY: Doubleday, 1965).

Davies, G. Henton, 'Ark of the Covenant', *IDB* 1 (1962), pp. 222-26.

Day, J., 'Pre-Deuteronomic Allusions to the Covenant in Hosea and Psalm lxxviii', *VT* 36 (1986), pp. 1-12.

De Coninck, L., and M.J. d'Hont, *Theodori Mopsuesteni Expositionis in Psalmos Iuliano Aeclanensi interprete in latinum versae quae supersunt* (CCSL, 88A; Turnhout: Brepols, 1977).

Derenbourg, J. (= Naphtali), *Version arabe de Pentateuque de R. Saadia* (Paris, 1893).

Derenbourg, J., *Oeuvres complètes de R. Saadia ben Iosef Al-Fayyoûmî. III. Version arabe d'Isaïe* (Paris: Ernest Leroux, 1896).

Devreesse, R., *Le commentaire de Théodore de Mopsueste sur les Psaumes (I–LXXX)* (Studi e testi, 93; Vatican City: Biblioteca Apostolica Vaticana, 1939).

Dhorme, P., *A Commentary on the Book of Job* (trans. H. Knight; London: Nelson, 1967).

Di Lella, A., *The Hebrew Text of Sirach* (The Hague: Mouton & Co., 1966).

Dietrich, W., *Jesaja und die Politik* (BEvT, 74; Munich: Chr. Kaiser Verlag, 1976).

Diettrich, G., *Isôdâdh's Stellung in der Auslegungsgeschichte des Alten Testamentes an seinen Commentaren zu Hosea, Joel, Jona, Sacharja 9–14 und einigen angehängten Psalmen veranschaulicht* (BZAW, 6; Giessen: Ricker, 1902).

Díez Merino, L., *Targum de Salmos: Edición príncipe del Ms. Villa-Amil n.5 de Alfonso de Zamora* (BHBib, 6; Madrid: Consejo superior de investigaciones científicas, 1982).

—'Procedimientos targúmicos', in V. Collado-Bertomeu and V. Vilar-Hueso (eds.), *II Simposio bíblico español (Córdoba 1985)* (Valencia: Monte de Piedad; Córdoba: Caja de Ahorros de Córdoba, 1987), pp. 461-86.

Dillmann, A., *Das Buch Henoch* (Leipzig: F.C.W. Vogel, 1853).

—*Lexicon linguae aethiopicae* (repr. New York: Ungar, 1955 [1865]).

Dillmann, A., and R. Kittel, *Der Prophet Jesaja* (Leipzig: S. Hirzel, 6th edn, 1898).

Dirksen, P.B., 'The Old Testament Peshitta', in M.J. Mulder and H. Sysling (eds.), *Mikra: Text, Translation, Reading and Interpretation of the Hebrew Bible in Ancient Judaism and Early Christianity* (Assen: Van Gorcum; Philadelphia: Fortress Press, 1988), pp. 254-97.

—*An Annotated Bibliography of the Peshiṭta of the Old Testament* (MPIL, 5; Leiden: E.J. Brill, 1989).

Dirksen, P.B., and M.J. Mulder (eds.), *The Peshiṭta: Its Early Text and History* (MPIL, 4; Leiden: E.J. Brill, 1988).

Dirksen, P.B., and A. Van der Kooij (eds.), *The Peshiṭta as a Translation* (MPIL, 8, Leiden: E.J. Brill, 1995).

Dittenberger, W., *Orientis Graeci Inscriptiones Selectae* (2 vols.; Leipzig, 1903).

Doniach, N.S., *Oxford English–Arabic Dictionary of Current Usage* (Oxford: Oxford University Press, 1972).

Doniach, N.S., and A. Kahane, *The Oxford English Hebrew Dictionary* (Oxford: Oxford University Press, 1996).

Donner, H., *Israel unter den Völkern* (VTSup, 11; Leiden: E.J. Brill, 1964).

Douglas, M., *Leviticus as Literature* (Oxford: Oxford University Press, 1999).

Driver, G.R., 'Hebrew Notes', *ZAW* 52 (1934), pp. 51-56.

—'Notes on the Psalms', *JTS* 36 (1935), pp. 147-56.

—'Hebrew *'al* ("high one") as a Divine Title', *ExpTim* 50 (1938), pp. 92-93.

—*Semitic Writing from Pictograph to Alphabet* (The Schweich Lectures, 1944; London: Oxford University Press, 1948; 3rd edn, 1976).

—'Hebrew Notes on "Song of Songs" and "Lamentations" ', in W. Baumgartner *et al.* (eds.), *Festschrift Alfred Bertholet zum 80. Geburtstag* (Tübingen: J.C.B. Mohr [Paul Siebeck], 1950), pp. 134-46.

—'Babylonian and Hebrew Notes', *WO* 2 (1954–1959), pp. 21-24.

—'Notes on Isaiah', in J. Hempel and L. Rost (eds.), *Von Ugarit nach Qumran* (Festschrift O. Eissfeldt; BZAW, 77; Berlin: Alfred Töpelmann, 1958), pp. 42-48.

—*The Judaean Scrolls* (Oxford: Basil Blackwell, 1965).

—' "Another Little Drink'—Isaiah 28:1-22', in P.R. Ackroyd and B. Lindars (eds.), *Words and Meanings* (Festschift D.W. Thomas; Cambridge: Cambridge University Press, 1968), pp. 47-67.

Driver, S.R., *Notes on the Hebrew Text and the Topography of the Books of Samuel* (Oxford: Clarendon Press, 2nd edn, 1913).

du Cange, D., *Glossarium mediae et infimae Latinitatis* (Paris, 1766).

Dübner, F. (ed.), *Epigrammatum anthologia palatina* (Paris: Didot, 1864–90).

Duhm, B., *Das Buch Jesaia* (Göttinger Handkommentar zum Alten Testament; Göttingen: Vandenhoeck & Ruprecht, 3rd edn, 1914).

Dürrbach, F. *et al.* (eds.), *Inscriptions de Délos* (2 vols.; Académie des Inscriptions et Belles Lettres; Paris: Champion, 1926, 1929).

Eaton, J.H., 'The Origin of the Book of Isaiah', *VT* 9 (1959), pp. 138-57.

Efros, I., *English-Hebrew Dictionary* (ed. J. Kaufman; Tel Aviv: Dvir, 1929).

Ehrlich, A.B., *Randglossen zur hebräischen Bibel*. IV. *Jesaia, Jeremia* (Leipzig: J.C. Hinrichs, 1912).

Elbogen, I., *Der jüdische Gottesdienst* (Frankfurt: Kauffmann, 2nd edn, 1924).

Elias, E.A., *Elias' Modern Dictionary English–Arabic* (Cairo: Elias' Modern Press, 3rd edn, 1929).

Elliger, K., *Deuterojesaja*. I. *Jesaja 40,1–45,7* (BKAT, 11/1; Neukirchen–Vluyn: Neukirchener Verlag, 1978).

Emerton, J.A., 'Comparative Semitic Philology and Hebrew Lexicography', in J.A. Emerton (ed.), *Congress Volume Cambridge 1995* (VTSup, 66; Leiden: E.J. Brill, 1997), pp. 1-24.

Emmerson, G.I., *Isaiah 56–66* (OTG; Sheffield: Sheffield Academic Press, 1992).

Emmet, C.W., 'The Third Book of Maccabees', in R.H. Charles (ed.), *Apocrypha and Pseudepigrapha of the Old Testament*, I (Oxford: Clarendon Press, 1913), pp. 155-73.

Eynde, C. van den, *Commentaire d'Išoʻdad de Merv sur l'Ancien Testament*. IV. *Isaïe et les Douze* (trans.; CSCO, 304, Syr, 129; Leuven: Secrétariat du CorpusSCO, 1969).

—*Commentaire d'Išoʻdad de Merv sur l'Ancien Testament*. VI. *Psaumes* (CSCO, 433-34, Syr 185-86; Leuven: Peeters, 1981).

Fassberg, S.E., 'The Orthography of the Relative Pronoun -שׁה in the Second Temple and Mishnaic Periods', *Scripta classica israelica* 15 (1996), pp. 240-50.

Fehérvári, G., 'Miḥrab', in *Encyclopaedia of Islam*, VII (Leiden: E.J. Brill, 1993), pp. 7-14.

—'Masdjid, 2, c', in *Shorter Encyclopedia of Islam* (Leiden: E.J. Brill, 1961), p. 343.

Feigin, S.I., 'The Heavenly Siege', *JNES* 9 (1950), pp. 40-43.

Fey, R., *Amos und Jesaja: Abhängigkeit und Eigenständigkeit des Jesaja* (WMANT, 12; Neukirchen–Vluyn: Neukirchener Verlag, 1963).

Field, F., *Origenis Hexaplorum quae supersunt* (2 vols.; Oxford: Clarendon Press, 1875).

Fiey, J.-M., 'Diocèses syriens orientaux du Golfe persique', in F. Graffin (ed.), *Mémorial Mgr Gabriel Khouri-Sarkis (1898–1968)* (Leuven: Imprimerie Orientaliste, 1969), pp. 177-219.

Fischer, J., *In welcher Schrift lag das Buch Isaias den LXX vor? Eine textkritische Studie* (BZAW, 56; Giessen: Alfred Töpelmann, 1930).

Fishbane, M., *Biblical Interpretation in Ancient Israel* (Oxford: Clarendon Press, 1985).

Fitzmyer, J., 'The First-Century Targum of Job from Qumran Cave XI', in *idem*, *A Wandering Aramean: Collected Aramaic Essays* (Missoula, MT: Scholars Press, 1979), pp. 161-82.

—'The Phases of the Aramaic Language', in *idem*, *A Wandering Aramean: Collected Aramaic Essays* (Missoula, MT: Scholars Press, 1979), pp. 57-84.

Flemming, J., *Das Buch Henoch* (TU, NS 7.1; Leipzig: J.C. Hinrichs, 1902).

Flemming, J., and L. Radermacher, *Das Buch Henoch* (GCS; Leipzig: J.C. Hinrichs, 1901).

Flesher, P.V.M., 'Exploring the Sources of the Synoptic Targums to the Pentateuch', in *idem* (ed.), *Targum Studies*. I. *Textual and Contextual Studies in the Pentateuchal Targums* (Atlanta: Scholars Press, 1992), pp. 101-34.

Flusser, David, 'The Text of Isa. xlix, 17 in the DSS', in C. Rabin (ed.), *Textus: Annual of the Hebrew University Bible Project*, II (Jerusalem: Magnes Press, The Hebrew University, 1962), pp. 140-42.

Fokkelman, J.P., *Narrative Art and Poetry in the Books of Samuel*. III. *Throne and City (II Sam. 2–8 and 21–24)* (Assen: Van Gorcum, 1990).

Folmer, M.L., *The Aramaic Language in the Achaemenid Period: A Study in Linguistic Variation* (Leuven: Peeters, 1995).

Fraser, P.M., *Ptolemaic Alexandria* (Oxford: Clarendon Press, 1972).

Frazer, J.G. (ed.), *Letters of William Cowper*, I (London: Macmillan, 1912).

Gammie, J.G., *Holiness in Israel* (OBT; Minneapolis: Fortress Press, 1989).

Gaon, S. (ed.), *Book of Prayer of the Spanish and Portuguese Jews' Congregation*, II New Year (London, 1971).

García Cordero, M., 'El Santo de Israel', in *Mélanges bibliques rédigés en l'honneur de André Robert* (Paris: Bloud & Gay, 1957), pp. 165-73.

García Martínez, F., E. Tigchelaar and A.S. van der Woude (eds.), *11Q10* (DJD, Oxford: Clarendon Press, 1998).

Gaster, T.H., '3 Maccabees', in A. Kahana (ed.), *Ha-sefarim ha-hitzonim* (repr.; Jerusalem: Makor, 2nd edn, 1978 [1956]), II, pp. 231-57.

Geiger, A., *Urschrift und Uebersetzungen der Bibel* (Breslau: Julius Hainauer, 1857).

Gelston, A., *The Peshitta of the Twelve Prophets* (Oxford: Clarendon Press, 1987).

Gelston, A. (ed.), *Vetus Testamentum Syriace* III, 4 (Leiden: E.J. Brill, 1980).

Gelzer, H., *Sextus Julius Africanus und die byzantinische Chronographie* (2 vols.; Leipzig, 1880–98).

Gignoux, Philippe, *Homélies de Narsaï sur la création: Edition critique du texte syriaque, introduction et traduction française* (PO, 34; Turnhout: Brepols, 1968).

Ginsburger, M., *Das Fragmententhargum (Thargum jeruschalmi zum Pentateuch)* (Berlin: Calvary, 1899).

—*Pseudo-Jonathan* (Berlin: Calvary, 1903).

Goitein, S.D., *A Mediterranean Society, The Jewish Communities of the Arab World as Portrayed in the Documents of the Cairo Genizah*. IV. *Daily Life* (Berkeley: University of California Press, 1983).

Golomb, D.M. *A Grammar of Targum Neofiti* (HSM, 34; Chico, CA: Scholars Press, 1985).

—' "A Liar, a Blasphemer, a Reviler": The Role of Biblical Ambiguity in the Palestinian Pentateuchal Targumim', in P.V.M. Flesher (ed.), *Targum Studies 1: Textual and Contextual Studies in the Pentateuchal Targums* (Atlanta: Scholars Press, 1992), pp. 135-46.

Gonçalves, F.J., *L'expédition de Sennachérib en Palestine dans la littérature hébraïque ancienne* (EBib NS, 7; Paris: J. Gabalda, 1986).

Goodenough, E.R., *Jewish Symbols in the Greco-Roman Period* (13 vols.; New York: Pantheon, 1953–68).

Gordis, R., *Koheleth: The Man and his World* (Texts and Studies of the Jewish Theological Seminary of America, 19; New York: Bloch Publishing Co., 2nd augmented edn, 1955).

—*The Book of Job* (New York: Jewish Theological Seminary of America, 1978).

Gordon, R.P., ' "Isaiah's Wild Measure": R.M. McCheyne', *ExpTim* 103 (1992), pp. 235-37.

—*Studies in the Targum to the Twelve Prophets: From Nahum to Malachi* (VTSup, 51; Leiden: E.J. Brill, 1994).

—'Methodological Criteria for Distinguishing between Variant Vorlage and Exegesis in the Peshitta Pentateuch', in P. Dirksen and A. van der Kooij (eds.), *The Peshitta as a Translation* (MPIL, 8; Leiden: E.J. Brill, 1995), pp. 121-22.

Görg, M., 'Jesaja als "Kinderlehrer"? Beobachtungen zur Sprache und Semantik in Jes 28,10 (13)', *BN* 29 (1985), pp. 12-16.

Goshen-Gottstein, M.H., 'Theory and Practice of Textual Criticism—The Text-Critical Use of the Septuagint', *Textus* 3 (1963), pp. 130-58.

—'The Development of the Hebrew Text of the Bible', *VT* 42 (1992), pp. 204-13.

Goshen-Gottstein, M.H. (ed.), *The Book of Isaiah* (The Hebrew University Bible Project; Jerusalem: Magnes Press, The Hebrew University, 1995).

Goshen-Gottstein, M.H., and R. Kasher (eds.), שקיעים מתרגומי המקרא הארמיים, I (Ramat Gan: Bar Ilan University Press, 1983).

Grabbe, L.L., *Comparative Philology and the Text of Job: A Study in Methodology* (SBLDS, 34; Missoula, MT: Scholars Press, 1977).

Graf, K.H., *Der Prophet Jeremia* (Leipzig: T.O. Weigel, 1862).

Graffin, F., 'Jacques d'Edesse réviseur des Homélies de Sévère d'Antioche d'après le ms. syriaque B.M. Add 12.159', in A. Guillaumont and F. Graffin (eds.), *Symposium Syriacum 1976, Chantilly, France* (OCA, 205; Rome: Istituto Pontificio Biblico, 1978), pp. 243-55.

Grätz, H., *Emendationes in plerosque sacrae scripturae VT libros* (Breslau, 1893).

Gray, G.B., *The Book of Isaiah I–XXXIX (XXVII)* (ICC; Edinburgh: T. & T. Clark, 1912).

Gray, J., 'The Massoretic Text of the Book of Job, the Targum and the LXX in the Light of the Qumran Targum', *ZAW* 86 (1974), pp. 331-50.

Greenberg, G., 'Translation Technique in the Peshitta to Jeremiah' (PhD thesis, University of London, 1999).

Grelot, P., 'Le targum de Job de la grotte XI de Qumran', *RevQ* 8 (1972–75), pp. 105-14.

Grimm, C.L.W., *Das zweite, dritte und vierte Buch der Maccabäer* (Kurzgefasstes exegetische Handbuch zu den Apokryphen des Alten Testament; Leipzig: S. Hirzel, 1857).

Grintz, Y.M., 'Ark of the Covenant', *EncJud* 3 (1971), pp. 459-66.

Große-Brauckmann, E., 'Der Psaltertext bei Theodoret', *NGG* Ph.-h. Klasse (1911), pp. 336-65.

Grossfeld, B., *The Targum Onqelos to Leviticus* (The Aramaic Bible, 3; Edinburgh: T. & T. Clark, 1988).

Guidi, I., 'Note Miscellanee', *Giornale della Società Asiatica Italiana* 3 (1889), pp. 164-81.

Gutridge, C.A., 'Wisdom, Anti-wisdom and the Ethical Function of Uncertainty: The Book of Qoheleth / Ecclesiastes in the Context of Biblical and Greek Wisdom Theory' (PhD thesis, University College London, 1998).

Haar Romeny, R.B. ter, 'Techniques of Translation and Transmission of the Earliest Text Forms of the Syriac Version of Genesis', in P.B. Dirksen and A. Van der Kooij (eds.), *The Peshitta as a Translation* (MPIL, 8; Leiden: E.J. Brill, 1995), pp. 177-85.

—*A Syrian in Greek Dress: The Use of Greek, Hebrew, and Syriac Biblical Texts in Eusebius of Emesa's Commentary on Genesis* (TEG, 6; Leuven: Peeters, 1997).

—'Biblical Studies in the Church of the East: the Case of Catholicos Timothy I', in E.J. Yarnold (ed.), *Studia Patristica 34: Papers Presented to the Thirteenth International Conference on Patristic Studies Held in Oxford 1999* (Leuven: Peeters, forthcoming).

Hachlili, R. (ed.), *Ancient Synagogues in Israel, Third–Seventh Century C.E.* (BAR, 499; Oxford: British Archaeological Reports, 1989).

Hadas, M., 'III Maccabees and Greek Romance', *Review of Religion* 13 (1949), pp. 155-62.

—*The Third and Fourth Book of Maccabees* (Jewish Apocryphal Literature; Harper: New York, 1953).

Hallo, W.W., 'Isaiah 28 9-13 and the Ugaritic Abecedaries', *JBL* 77 (1958), pp. 324-38.

Hallo, W.W. (ed.), *The Context of Scripture. I. Canonical Compositions from the Biblical World* (Leiden: E.J. Brill, 1997).

Halpern, B., ' "The Excremental Vision": The Doomed Priests of Doom in Isaiah 28', *HAR* 10 (1986), pp. 109-21.

Hanhart, R., *Zum Text des 2. und 3. Makkabäerbuches: Problem der Überlieferung, der Auslegung und der Ausgabe* (Göttingen: Vandenhoeck & Ruprecht, 1961).

—*Maccabaeorum liber III* (Septuaginta: Vetus Testamentum Graecum auctoritate Societatis Litterarum Gottingensis editum, IX, 3; Göttingen: Vandenhoeck & Ruprecht, 2nd edn, 1980).

Harb, Paul, François Graffin and Micheline Albert, *Lettre sur les trois étapes de la vie monastique: Edition critique du texte syriaque, traduction et introduction* (PO, 45; Turnhout: Brepols, 1992).

Harl, M., 'Le nom de "l'arche" de Noe dans la septante. Les choix lexicaux des traducteurs alexandrins, indices des d'interpretations théologiques?', *ΑΛΕΞΑΝΔΡΙΝΑ: Mélanges Claude Mondésert, S.J.* (Paris: Cerf, 1987), pp. 15-43.

Harland, P.J., 'בצע: Bribe, Extortion or Profit?', *VT* 50 (2000), pp. 310-22.

Harper, W.R., *Amos and Hosea* (ICC; Edinburgh: T. & T. Clark, 1905).

Harrington, D.J., and A.J. Saldarini, *The Targum of the Former Prophets* (The Aramaic Bible, 10; Edinburgh: T. & T. Clark, 1987).

Harris, J.R., 'Metrical Fragments in III Maccabees', *BJRL* 5 (1919), pp. 195-207.

Harrison, R.K., *Introduction to the Old Testament* (London: The Tyndale Press, 1970).

Head, B.V., *Catalogue of the Greek Coins of Phrygia* (London: British Museum, 1906).

—*Historia Numorum: A Manual of Greek Numismatics* (Oxford: Clarendon Press, 2nd edn, 1911 [1887]).

Healey, J.F., 'Lexical Loans in Early Syriac: A Comparison with Nabataean Aramaic', *SEL* 12 (1995), pp. 75-84.

Henten, J.W. van, *The Maccabean Martyrs as Saviours of the Jewish People: A Study of 2 and 4 Maccabees* (JSJ Supplement, 57; Leiden: E.J. Brill, 1997).

Hepworth, B., *Robert Lowth* (Boston: Twayne Publishers, 1978).

Hespel, R., and R. Draguet, *Théodore bar Koni, Livre des Scolies (recension de Séert)*. I. *Mimrè I–V* (CSCO, 431, Syr, 187; Leuven: Peeters, 1981).

Hiebert, R.J.V., *The 'Syrohexaplaric' Psalter* (SBLSCS, 27; Atlanta: Scholars Press, 1989).

Hintze, J.L., *NCSS 2000: User's Guide* (3 vols.; Kaysville, UT: NCSS, 1998).

Hitzig, F., *Das Buch Hiob uebersetzt und ausgelegt* (Leipzig, 1874).

Hoftijzer, J., and K. Jongeling, *Dictionary of the North-West Semitic Inscriptions*, Parts 1 and 2 (Handbuch der Orientalistik; Leiden: E.J. Brill, 1995).

Høgenhaven, J., *Gott und Volk bei Jesaja: Eine Untersuchung zur biblischen Theologie* (ATDan, 24; Leiden: E.J. Brill, 1988).

Holl, K., (ed.), *Epiphanius (Ancoratus und Panarion)*, I (Die griechischen christlichen Schriftsteller der ersten drei Jahrhunderte; Leipzig: J.C. Hinrichs, 1915).

Holladay, W.L., *Isaiah: Scroll of a Prophetic Heritage* (Grand Rapids: Eerdmans, 1978).

—*Jeremiah*, I (Philadelphia: Fortress Press, 1986).

—*Jeremiah*, II (Philadelphia: Fortress Press, 1989).

Horbury, W., 'Early Christians on Synagogue Prayer and Imprecation', in G.N. Stanton and G. Stroumsa (eds.), *Tolerance and Intolerance in Ancient Judaism and Christianity* (Cambridge: Cambridge University Press, 1998).

—*Jews and Christians in Contact and Controversy* (Edinburgh: T. & T. Clark, 1998).

Horbury, W., and D. Noy (eds.), *Jewish Inscriptions of Graeco-Roman Egypt* (Cambridge: Cambridge University Press, 1992).

Horgan, M.P., *Pesharim: Qumran Interpretations of Biblical Books* (CBQMS, 8; Washington: Catholic Biblical Association of America, 1979).

Houbigant, K.F., *Biblia Hebraica cum Notis criticis et versione Latina ad notas criticas facta*, IV (Paris: C. Briasson & L. Durand, 1753).

Huber, F., *Jahwe, Juda und die anderen Völker beim Propheten Jesaja* (BZAW, 137; Berlin: W. de Gruyter, 1976).

Ibn Barun, see under Wechter, P.

James, M.R., 'Books and Writing', in L. Whibley (ed.), *A Companion to Greek Studies* (Cambridge: Cambridge University Press, 1931), pp. 606-10.

—'Books and Writing', in J.E. Sandys (ed.), *A Companion to Latin Studies* (Cambridge: Cambridge University Press, 1935), pp. 237-42.

Jansma, T., 'Théodore de Mopsueste, Interprétation du livre de la Genèse. Fragments de la version syriaque (B.M. Add. 17,189, fol. 17–21)', *Mus* 75 (1962), pp. 63-92.

Janzen, J.G., 'Double Readings in the Text of Jeremiah', *HTR* 60 (1967), pp. 433-47.

—*Studies in the Text of Jeremiah* (HSM, 6; Cambridge, MA: Harvard University Press, 1973).

Jastrow, M., *A Dictionary of the Targumim: The Talmud Babli and Yerushalmi and the Midrashic Literature* (London: Shapiro Valentine & Co., 1926).

Jellicoe, S., *The Septuagint and Modern Study* (Oxford: Clarendon Press, 1968).

—'Colophons of the Syrohexapla and the *Textgeschichte* of the Recensions of Origen', in C.E. Cox (ed.), *VII Congress of the International Organization for Septuagint and Cognate Studies, Leuven 1989* (SBLSCS, 31; Atlanta: Scholars Press, 1991), pp. 261-77.

Jenner, K.D., 'Some Introductory Remarks Concerning the Study of 8a1', in P.B. Dirksen and M.J. Mulder (eds.), *The Peshitta: Its Early Text and History. Papers Read at the Peshitta Symposium Held at Leiden 30–31 August 1985* (MPIL, 4; Leiden: E.J. Brill, 1988), pp. 200-24.

—*De perikopentitels van de geïllustreerde syrische kanselbijbel van Parijs (MS Paris, Bibliothèque Nationale, Syriaque 341): Een vergelijkend onderzoek naar de oudste syrische perikopenstelsels* (Dissertation, Leiden University, 1993).

—'The Development of Syriac Lectionary Systems: A Discussion of the Opinion of P. Kannookadan', *The Harp* 10/1 (1997), pp. 9-24.

—'Syrohexaplarische und proto-syrohexaplarische Zitate in syrischen Quellen außer den individuellen Exemplaren des syrohexaplarischen Psalters', in A. Aejmelaus and U. Quast (eds.), *Der Septuaginta-Psalter und seine Tochterübersetzungen. Symposium in Göttingen 1997* (MSU, 24; Göttingen, Vandenhoeck & Ruprecht, 2000), pp. 147-73.

Jensen, J., *The Use of* tôrâ *by Isaiah: His Debate with the Wisdom Tradition* (CBQMS, 3; Washington: The Catholic Biblical Association of America, 1973).

Jesi, F., 'Notes sur l'édit dionysiaque de Ptolémée IV Philopator', *JNES* 15 (1956), pp. 236-40.

Jones, B.A., *The Formation of the Book of the Twelve* (SBLDS, 149; Atlanta: Scholars Press, 1995).

Jones, D.R., 'The Traditio of the Oracles of Isaiah of Jerusalem', *ZAW* 67 (1955), pp. 226-46.

—'Exposition of Isaiah Chapter One Verses One to Nine', *SJT* 17 (1964), pp. 463-77.

Joosten, J., 'Greek and Latin Words in the Peshitta Pentateuch. First Soundings', in R. Lavenant (ed.), *Symposium Syriacum VII 1993* (OCA, 256; Rome: Pontificio Istituto Biblico, 1998), pp. 37-47.

—'Materials for a Linguistic Approach to the Old Testament Peshitta', *JAB 1* (1999), pp. 203-18.

—'χαλκηδών', *RHPR* 79 (1999), pp. 135-43.

Joüon, P., *A Grammar of Biblical Hebrew* (trans. and rev. T. Muraoka; Rome: Pontificio Istituto Biblico, 1993).

Kahle, P., *Masoreten des Westens*, I (Stuttgart: Kohlhammer Verlag, 1927).

Kaiser, O., *Das Buch des Propheten Jesaja: Kapitel 1–12* (ATD, 17; Göttingen: Vandenhoeck & Ruprecht, 5th edn, 1981) (ET, *Isaiah 1–12: A Commentary* [OTL; London: SCM Press, 1983]).

Kannookadan, P., *The East Syrian Lectionary. An Historico-Liturgical Study* (Rome: Har Thoma Yogan, 1991).

Kasher, A., 'Anti-Jewish Persecutions in Alexandria in the Reign of Ptolemy Philopator

According to III Maccabees', in U. Rappaport (ed.), *Studies in the History of the Jewish People in the Land of Israel*, IV (Haifa, 1978), pp. 59-76 [Hebrew].

—*The Jews in Hellenistic and Roman Egypt* (Tübingen: Mohr Siebeck, 1985).

Kasher, R., מקורות לחקר תרבות ישראל) תוספות תרגום לנביאין, II (Jerusalem: World Union of Jewish Studies, 1996).

Kaufman, S., 'The Job Targum from Qumran', *JAOS* 93 (1973), pp. 317-27.

—'Dating the Language of the Palestinian Targums and their Use in the Study of the First Century CE Texts', in D.R.G. Beattie and M.J. McNamara (eds.), *The Aramaic Bible: Targums in their Historical Context* (JSOTSup, 166; Sheffield: JSOT Press, 1994), pp. 118-41.

Kelly, J.N.D., *Jerome: His Life, Writings and Controversies* (London: Gerald Duckworth, 1975).

Kennedy, J., *A Popular Argument for the Unity of Isaiah* (London: James Clarke, 1891).

Kennett, R.H., *Ancient Hebrew Social Life and Custom as Indicated in Law, Narrative and Metaphor* (The Schweich Lectures, 1931; London: Oxford University Press, 1933).

Kennicott, B., *Vetus Testamentum hebraicum cum variis lectionibus* (2 vols.; Oxford: Clarendon Press, 1776).

Kenyon, F.G., *The Codex Alexandrinus in Reduced Photographic Facsimile: Old Testament*, III (London: British Museum, 1936).

Kiraz, George Anton, *A Computer Generated Concordance to the Syriac New Testament* (6 vols.; Leiden, E.J. Brill, 1993).

Kitchen, K., 'The Aramaic of Daniel', in D.J. Wiseman (ed.), *Notes on Some Problems in the Book of Daniel* (London: Tyndale Press, 1965), pp. 31-79.

Klein, M., 'Converse Translation: A Targumic Technique', *Bib* 57 (1976), pp. 515-37.

—*Genizah Manuscripts of the Palestinian Targum to the Pentateuch I, II* (Cincinatti: Hebrew Union College Press, 1986).

—*Targumic Manuscripts in the Cambridge Genizah Collections* (Cambridge University Library Genizah Series, 8; Cambridge: Cambridge University Press, 1992).

Klostermann, A., 'Schulwesen im alten Israel', in N. Bonwetsch *et al.* (eds.), *Theologische Studien* (Festschrift T. Zahn; Leipzig: A. Deichert, 1908), pp. 193-232.

Knibb, M.A., in consultation with E. Ullendorff, *The Ethiopic Book of Enoch: A New Edition in the Light of the Aramaic Dead Sea Fragments*. I. *Text and Apparatus*; II. *Introduction, Translation and Commentary* (Oxford: Clarendon Press, 1978).

—'Messianism in the Pseudepigrapha in the Light of the Scrolls', *DSD* 2 (1995), pp. 165-84.

—*Translating the Bible: The Ethiopic Version of the Old Testament* (The Schweich Lectures of the British Academy, 1995; Oxford: Oxford University Press for the British Academy, 1999).

Koenen, K., *Ethik und Eschatologie: Eine literarkritische und redaktionsgeschichtliche Studie* (WMANT, 62; Neukirchen–Vluyn; Neukirchener Verlag, 1990).

Kohut, A., *Aruch Completum*, I–VIII (New York: Pardes, 1955).

Komlosh, J., המקרא באור התרגום (Tel-Aviv: Dvir, 1973).

Kooij, A. van der, *Die alten Textzeugen des Jesajabuches: Ein Beitrag zur Textgeschichte des Alten Testaments* (OBO, 35; Göttingen: Vandenhoeck & Ruprecht, 1981).

Kornfeld, W., 'QDŠ und Gottesrecht im Alten Testament', in J.A. Emerton (ed.), *Congress Volume: Vienna 1980* (VTSup, 32; Leiden: E.J. Brill, 1981), pp. 1-9.

Korpel, M.C.A., and J.C. de Moor, *The Structure of Classical Hebrew Poetry: Isaiah 40–55* (OTS, 41; Leiden: E.J. Brill, 1998).

Koster, M.D., *The Peshitta of Exodus: The Development of its Text in the Course of Fifteen Centuries* (Studia Semitica Neerlandica, 19; Assen: Van Gorcum, 1977).

Krauss, S., *Griechische und lateinische Lehnwörter im Talmud, Midrasch und Targum*, Parts 1 and 2 (Berlin: Calvary, 1898; repr. Hildesheim: G. Olms, 1987).

—*Synagogale Altertümer* (Berlin: Harz, 1922).

Krauss, S., and W. Horbury, *The Jewish–Christian Controversy*. I. *History* (Tübingen: J.C.B. Mohr [Paul Siebeck], 1995).

Kremer, A. von, *Culturgeschichte des Orients unter den Chalifen*, I (Vienna, 1877).

Kugel, J.L., *The Idea of Biblical Poetry: Parallelism and its History* (New Haven: Yale University Press, 1981).

Kutscher, E.Y., *The Language and Linguistic Background of the Isaiah Scroll (1QIsaᵃ)* (STDJ, 6; Leiden: E.J. Brill, 1974; Hebrew Edition, Jerusalem: Magnes Press, 1959).

Lagarde, P. de, *Bibliothecae syriacae quae ad Philologiam Sacram Pertinent* (Göttingen: Dieterich, 1892).

Lagarde, P. de (ed.), *Prophetae Chaldaice* (Leipzig, 1872).

Lake, H., and K. Lake, *Codex sinaiticus petropolitanus et Friderico-Augustanus Lipsiensis: The Old Testament...now Reproduced in Facsimile from Photographs* (Oxford: Clarendon Press, 1922).

Lambert, Elie, 'La synagogue de Douro-Europos et les origines de la mosquée', *Semitica* 3 (1950), p. 67.

Lampe, G.W.H. (ed.), *Patristic Greek Lexicon* (Oxford: Clarendon Press, 1961).

Landsberger, Franz, 'The Sacred Direction in Synagogue and Church', *HUCA* 28 (1957), pp. 181-203.

—*History of Jewish Art* (Cincinnati: Hebrew Union College).

Lane, D.J., *The Peshitta of Leviticus* (MPIL, 6; Leiden: E.J. Brill, 1994).

—'The Well of Life: Šubḥalmaran's Use of Scripture', *OCA* 256 (1998), pp. 49-59.

Lane, D.J., *et al.*, *The Old Testament in Syriac According to the Peshitta Version*, Part I, fascicle 2; Part II, fascicle 1b (Leiden: E.J. Brill, 1991).

Lane, E.W., *An Arabic-English Lexicon* (London: Williams & Norgate, 1863–93). For supplements, see vol. VIII.

Larsen, M.T., *Old Assyrian Caravan Procedures* (Istanbul: Nederlands-historisch-archaeologisch instituut in het Nabije Oosten, 1967).

Lau, W., *Schriftgelehrte Prophetie in Jes 56–66: Eine Untersuchung zu den literarischen Bezügen in den letzten elf Kapiteln des Jesajabuches* (BZAW, 225; Berlin: W. de Gruyter, 1994).

Le Déaut, R., 'Usage implicite de l'al tiqre dans le targum de Job de Qumran?', in D. Muñoz Leon (ed.), *Salvacion en la palabra Homenaje al Prof. A. Díez Macho* (Madrid: Ediciones Cristiandad, 1986), pp. 419-31.

Le Déaut, R., and J. Robert, *Targum des Chroniques* (Cod. Vat. Urb. Ebr. 1) (2 vols.; Analecta Biblica, 51; Rome: Pontificio Istituto Biblico, 1971).

Leonhard, C., 'Ishodad of Merv's Exegesis of the Psalms 119 and 139–147: A Study of his Interpretation in the Light of the Syriac Translation of Theodore of Mopsuestia's Commentary' (unpublished doctoral thesis, Katholisch-theologische Fakultät der Universität Wien, 1999).

—'Išō'dād's Commentary on Psalm 141,2. A Quotation of Theodore of Mopsuestia's Lost Commentary', in E.J. Yarnold (ed.), *Studia Patristica: Papers Presented to the Thirteenth International Conference on Patristic Studies Held in Oxford 1999* (Leuven: Peeters, forthcoming).

Levene, D., and B. Rothenberg, 'בא ברזל—A Fundamental Aspect of the Nature of Metal', *JAB* 2.1 (2000), pp. 75-87.

Levey, S.H., 'The Date of the Targum Jonathan on the Prophets', *VT* 21 (1971), pp. 186-96.

Lévi, I., *L'Ecclésiastique* (Paris: Bibliotheque de l'Ecole des hautes études, 1901).

Levine, Lee I. (ed.), *The Synagogue in Late Antiquity* (Philadelphia: American Schools of Oriental Research, 1987).

Levy, J., *Chaldäisches Wörterbuch über die Targumim und einen grossen Theil des rab-binischen Schrifttums* (2 vols.; Leipzig: Baumgärtner's Buchhandlung, 1867–68).

—*Neuhebräisches und chaldäisches Wörterbuch* (4 vols.; Leipzig: Brockhaus, 1876–89).

Lewis, A., 'Egypt and Syria', in *The Cambridge History of Islam*, I/2 (Cambridge: Cambridge University Press, 1970), p. 176.

Lewis, J.P., *A Study of the Interpretation of Noah and the Flood in Jewish and Christian Literature* (Leiden: E.J. Brill, 1968).

Lewy, H., *Die semitischen Fremdwörter im Griechischen* (Berlin, 1895).

Lias, J.J., 'The Unity of Isaiah', *BibSac* 72 (1915), pp. 560-91.

Liddell, H.E., R. Scott and H. Jones, *Greek-English Lexicon* (Oxford: Oxford University Press, 1940).

Lieberman, S., *Tosefeth Rishonim: A Commentary Based on the Manuscripts of the Tosefta and Works of the Rishonim and Midrashim in Manuscripts and Rare Editions* (Jerusalem: Bamberger & Wahrmann, 1939).

Lim, T.H., *Holy Scripture in the Qumran Commentaries and Pauline Letters* (Oxford: Clarendon Press, 1997).

Loewe, R., 'Potentialities and Limitations of Universalism in the *Halakhah*', in *idem* (ed.), *Studies...in Memory of Leon Roth* (London: Routledge and Kegan Paul, 1966), pp. 115-50.

—'Gentiles as seen by Jews after 70 CE', in W. Horbury *et al.* (eds.), *The Cambridge History of Judaism*, III (Cambridge: Cambridge University Press, 1999), pp. 250-66.

Löfgren, O., *Die äthiopische Übersetzung des Propheten Daniel* (Paris: Paul Geuthner, 1927).

Loretz, O., *Der Prolog des Jesaja Buches (1,1–2,5): Ugaritologische und kolometrische Studien zum Jesaja-Buch*, I (UBL, 1; Altenberge: CIS-Verlag, 1984).

Löw, I., *Flora der Juden* (4 vols.; repr.; Hildesheim: Olms, 1967 [1928]).

Lowth, R., *De sacra poesi Hebraeorum: Praelectiones academicae oxonii habitae* (Oxford: Clarendon Press, 1753).

—*Isaiah: A New Translation: With a Preliminary Dissertation, and Notes Critical, Philological, and Explanatory* (London: J. Dodsley & T. Cadell, 1778).

—*Sermons and Other Remains of Robert Lowth* (repr.; London: Routledge/Thoemmes Press, 1995).

Lübbe, J.C., 'Describing the Translation Process of 11QtgJob: A Question of Method', *RevQ* 13 (1988), pp. 543-93.

Lukyn Williams, A., *Adversus Judaeos* (Cambridge: Cambridge University Press, 1935).

Lundbom, J., *Jeremiah: A Study in Ancient Hebrew Rhetoric* (SBLDS, 18; Missoula, MT: Scholars Press, 1975; 2nd edn; Winona Lake: Eisenbrauns, 1997).

Lyon, Jeffrey Paul, *Syriac Gospel Translations: A Comparison of the Language and Trans-lation Method in the Old Syriac, the Diatessaron, and the Peshitto* (CSCO, 548, Subs, 88; Leuven: Peeters, 1994).

Macintosh, A.A., *Hosea* (ICC; Edinburgh: T. & T. Clark, 1997).

Macomber, W.F., 'The Chaldean Lectionary System of the Cathedral of Kokhe', *OCP* 33 (1967), pp. 483-516.

Maigne d'Arnis, W.-H., *Lexicon manuale ad Scriptores mediae et infimae latinitatis* (Paris: Migne, 1866).

Mangan, C., *The Targum of Job: Translated with Critical Introduction, Apparatus and Notes* (The Aramaic Bible, 15; Edinburgh: T. & T. Clark, 1991).

Maori, Y., 'The Tradition of Pisqa'ot in Ancient Hebrew Manuscripts: The Isaiah Texts and Commentaries from Qumran' [in Hebrew], *Textus* 10 (1982), pp. 1*-50*.

—*The Peshitta Version of the Pentateuch and Early Jewish Exegesis* [Hebrew] (Jerusalem: Magnes Press, 1995).

Margalioth, M., *Sepher Ha-Razim: A Newly Recovered Book of Magic from the Talmudic Period* (Jerusalem: The Louis M. and Minnie Epstein Fund of the American Academy for Jewish Research, 1966).

Margalioth, R., *The Indivisible Isaiah: Evidence for the Single Authorship of the Prophetic Book* (New York: Yeshiva University, 1964).

Margoliouth, J.P., *Supplement to the Thesaurus Syriacus of R. Payne Smith* (Oxford: Clarendon Press, 1927).

Marti, K., *Das Buch Jesaja* (HKAT, 10; Tübingen: J.C.B. Mohr [Paul Siebeck], 1900).

—*Dodekapropheton* (KHAT, 13; Tübingen: J.C.B. Mohr [Paul Siebeck], 1904).

Mazar, B. (Maisler), *Beth She'arim, Report on the Excavations, 1, Catacombs 1-4* (Jerusalem, 1957; repr.; New Brunswick: Rutgers University Press, 1972).

McCarter, P.K., *II Samuel* (AB, 9; Garden City, NY: Doubleday, 1984).

McKane, W.A., *Critical and Exegetical Commentary on Jeremiah*, II (ICC; Edinburgh: T. & T. Clark Ltd, 1996).

Meade, D.G., *Pseudonymity and Canon: An Investigation into the Relationship of Authorship and Authority in Jewish and Earliest Christian Tradition* (Grand Rapids: Eerdmans, 1987).

Menasseh b. Israel, *Humas o cinco libros de la Ley Divina...juntas las Aphtarot* (Amsterdam [1655]).

Mercati, G., 'Di varie antichissime sottoscrizioni a codici esaplari', in *idem*, *Nuove note di letteratura biblica e christiana antica* (Studi e testi, 95; Vatican City: Biblioteca Apostolica Vaticana, 1941), pp. 1-48.

Merwe, C.H.J. van der, Naude J.A. and J.H. Kroeze, *A Biblical Hebrew Reference Grammar* (Sheffield: Sheffield Academic Press, 1999).

Meyer, R., and H. Donner (eds.), *Wilhelm Gesenius: Hebräisches und aramäisches Handwörterbuch über das Alte Testament*, I (Berlin: Springer-Verlag, 18th edn, 1987).

Meyers, Eric M., James F. Strange and Carol L. Meyers, 'The Ark of Nabratein—A First Glance', *BA* 44 (1981), pp. 237-43.

Michaelis, J.D., 'Vorzügliche Varianten in Propheten Jesaia', *Orientalische und Exegetische Bibliothek + Anhang* 14 (1779), pp. 99-224.

—*Supplementa ad lexica hebraica* (Göttingen: J.G. Rosenbusch, 1792).

—*Die Weissagungen Jesaia* (Deutsche Uebersetzung des Alten Testaments, 8; Göttingen: Vandenhoeck, 1779).

Mikra'ot Gedolot 'Haketer': Isaiah (ed. M. Cohen; Ramat-Gan: Bar Ilan University, 1996).

Milbank, J., *The Word Made Strange: Theology, Language, Culture* (Oxford: Basil Blackwell, 1997).

Milik, J.T., *The Books of Enoch: Aramaic Fragments of Qumran Cave 4* (Oxford: Clarendon Press, 1976).

Molenberg, C., *The Interpreter Interpreted: Išo' bar Nun's Selected Questions on the Old Testament* (doctoral thesis, Rijksuniversiteit, Groningen, 1990).

Montefiore, C.G., and H. Loewe, *A Rabbinic Anthology* (London: Macmillan, 1938; repr. New York: Schocken, 1974).

Montgomery, J.A., 'Notes on the Old Testament', *JBL* 31 (1912), pp. 140-49.

Moor, J.C. de, *The Seasonal Pattern in the Ugaritic Myth of Ba'lu: According to the Version of Ilimilku* (AOAT, 16; Neukirchen–Vluyn: Neukirchner Verlag, 1971).

—'The Art of Versification in Ugarit and Israel, II: The Formal Structure', *UF* 10 (1978), pp. 187-217.

Moor, J.C. de, and F. Sepmeijer, 'The Peshitta and the Targum of Joshua', in P.B. Dirksen and A. van der Kooij (eds.), *The Peshitta as a Translation* (MPIL, 8; Leiden: E.J. Brill, 1995), pp. 129-76.

Moore, C.A., *Esther* (AB, 7b; Garden City, NY: Doubleday, 1971).

—'On the Origins of the LXX Additions to the Book of Esther', *JBL* 92 (1973), pp. 382-93.

—*Daniel, Esther and Jeremiah: The Additions* (AB, 44; New York: Doubleday, 1977).

Moorey, P.R.S., *Ancient Mesopotamian Minerals and Industries: The Archaeological Evidence* (Oxford: Clarendon Press, 1994).

Morag, S., *The Vocalization Systems of Arabic, Hebrew and Aramaic* (The Hague: Mouton & Co., 1962).

Moreau, J., 'Le troisième livre des Maccabées', *Chronique d'Egypte* 16 (1941), pp. 111-22.

Morgenstern, J., 'The Loss of Words at the Ends of Lines in Manuscripts of Biblical Poetry', *HUCA* 25 (1954), pp. 41-83.

—'The Book of the Covenant', *HUCA* 5 (1928), pp. 1-151.

—'The Ark, the Ephod, and the Tent of Meeting', *HUCA* 17 (1942–43), pp. 153-265, 18 (1943–44), pp. 1-52.

Morrow, F.J., 'The Text of Isaiah at Qumran' (PhD dissertation, Catholic University of America, Washington, DC, 1973).

Moss, C.B., *Catalogue of Syriac Printed Books and Related Literature in the British Museum* (London: Trustees of the British Museum, 1962).

Motyer, J.A., *The Prophecy of Isaiah* (London: Inter-Varsity Press, 1993).

Mowinckel, S., *He that Cometh* (Oxford: Basil Blackwell, 1959).

Muhly, J.D., *Copper and Tin: The Distribution of Mineral Resources and the Nature of the Metals Trade in the Bronze Age* (New Haven: The Connecticut Academy of Arts and Sciences, 1973).

Mulder, M.J., 'The Use of the Peshitta in Textual Criticism', in N. Fernández Marcos (ed.), *La Septuaginta en la investigacion contemporanea: V Congreso de la International Organization for the Septuagint and Cognate Studies* (Madrid: Instituto 'Arias Montano', 1985), pp. 37-53.

Mulder, M.J. (ed.), *Mikra: Text, Translation, Reading and Interpretation of the Hebrew Bible in Ancient Judaism and Early Christianity* (Assen: Van Gorcum; Philadelphia: Fortress Press, 1988).

Mullen, E.T., *The Divine Council in Canaanite and Early Hebrew Literature* (HSM, 24; Chico, CA: Scholars Press, 1980).

Müller, H.-P., *TLOT*, III, pp. 1112-13.

Nau, F., 'Traduction des lettres XII et XIII de Jacques d'Édesse', *Revue de l'orient chrétien* 10 (1905), pp. 197-208, 258-82.

—*La Second Partie de l'Histoire Ecclesiastique de Barhadbessabba* (PO, 9; Paris: Firmin et Didot, 1913).

Nestle, E., 'Jakob von Edessa über den Schem hammephorasch und andere Gottesnamen. Ein Beitrag zur Geschichte des Tetragrammaton', *ZDMG* 32 (1878), pp. 465-508.

Neubauer, A., *The Book of the Hebrew Roots* (ed. Ibn Janaḥ; Oxford: Oxford University Press, 1875; repr. Amsterdam: Philo Press, 1968).

Neusner, J., *A History of the Jews of Babylonia*, I (Leiden: E.J. Brill, 1969).

Niehr, H., 'Bedeutung und Funktion kanaanäischer Traditionselemente in der Sozialkritik Jesajas', *BZ* NF 28 (1984), pp. 69-81.

Nielsen, K., *There is Hope for a Tree: The Tree as Metaphor in Isaiah* (JSOTSup, 65; Sheffield: JSOT Press, 1989)

Nöldeke, T., *Compendious Syriac Grammar* (London: Williams & Norgate, translated [with the sanction of the author] from the second and improved German edition by J.A. Crighton, 2nd edn, 1904).

North, C.R., *The Second Isaiah: Introduction, Translation and Commentary to Chapters xl–lv* (Oxford: Clarendon Press, 1964).

Nowack, W., *Die kleinen Propheten* (HAT; Göttingen: Vandenhoeck & Ruprecht, 3rd edn, 1922).

Noy, D., *Jewish Inscriptions of Western Europe*, I (Cambridge: Cambridge University Press, 1993).

Oesch, J., *Petucha und Setuma: Untersuchungen zu einer überlieferten Gliederung im hebräischen Text des Alten Testaments* (OBO, 27; Fribourg: Universitatsverlag; Göttingen: Vandenhoeck & Ruprecht, 1979).

Oettli, A., *Amos und Hosea: Zwei Zeugen gegen die Anwendung der Evolutionstheorie und die Religion Israels* (BFCT, 4; Gütersloh, 1901).

Olivier, J.-M., *Diodori Tarsensis Commentarii in Psalmos*, I (CCSG, 6; Turnhout: Brepolis; Leuven: Leuven University Press, 1980).

Olson, D.C., 'Enoch and the Son of Man in the Epilogue of the Parables', *JSP* 18 (1998), pp. 27-38.

Ormerod, H.A., and E.S.G. Robinson, 'Notes and Inscriptions from Pamphylia', *Annual of the British School of Archaeology at Athens* 17 (1910–11), pp. 215-49.

Oswalt, J.N., *The Book of Isaiah, Chapters 1–39* (NICOT; Grand Rapids: Eerdmans, 1986).

Ottley, R.R., *The Book of Isaiah According to the Septuagint (Codex Alexandrinus)*, I, II (Cambridge: Cambridge University Press, 1904, 1906).

Owens, R.J., *The Genesis and Exodus Citations of Aphrahat the Persian Sage* (MPIL, 3; Leiden: E.J. Brill, 1983).

Pardee, D., in W.W. Hallo (ed.), *The Context of Scripture*. I. *Canonical Compositions from the Biblical World* (Leiden: E.J. Brill), pp. 339b, 341a.

Parisot, J. (ed.), *Aphraatis sapientis persae demonstrationes*, I, II (Patrologia Syriaca; Paris: Firmin-Didot, 1894, 1907).

Payne Smith, J., see under Smith, Jessie Payne.

Payne Smith, R., see under Smith, R. Payne.

Peshitta Institute, The, *The Old Testament in Syriac According to the Peshiṭta Version* (Leiden: E.J. Brill, 1962).

Petit, F., *Catenae graecae in Genesim et in Exodum 2: Collectio coisliniana in Genesim* (CCSG, 15; Leuven: Peeters, 1986).

—*La chaîne sur la Genèse: édition intégrale*, I (TEG, 1; Leuven: Peeters, 1992).

—*La chaîne sur la Genèse: édition intégrale*, II (TEG, 2; Leuven: Peeters, 1994).

—*La chaîne sur la Genèse: édition intégrale*, III (TEG, 3; Leuven: Peeters, 1995).

Phillips, G., *Scholia on Passages of the Old Testament, by Mar Jacob, Bishop of Edessa* (London: Williams & Norgate, 1864).

Piovanelli, P., 'Sulla *Vorlage* aramaica dell'Enoch etiopico', *Studi Classici e Orientali* 37 (1987), pp. 545-94.

Ploeg, J.P.M. van der, O.P. van der Woude, A.S. van der Woude and B. Jongeling (eds.), *Le targum de Job de la grotte XI de Qumran* (Leiden: E.J. Brill, 1971).

Porath, R., *Die Sozialkritik im Jesajabuch: Redaktionsgeschichtliche Analyse* (Frankfurt: Peter Lang, 1994).

Prigent, P., *Le Judaïsme et l'image* (TSAJ, 24; Tübingen: Mohr, 1990).

Procksch, O., *Jesaia I* (KAT, 9; Leipzig: A. Deichert, 1930).

Qimron, E., *The Hebrew of the Dead Sea Scrolls* (HSS, 29; Atlanta: Scholars Press, 1986).

Rabin, C. (ed.), *The Zadokite Documents* (Oxford: Clarendon Press, 1954).

Reider, J., 'Substantival 'AL in Biblical Hebrew', *JQR* NS 30 (1940), pp. 263-70.

Rendtorff, R., 'Zur Komposition des Buches Jesaja', *VT* 34 (1984), pp. 295-320.

—*Canon and Theology: Overtures to an Old Testament Theology* (ed. M. Kohl; Edinburgh: T. & T. Clark, 1994).

Rignell, L.G. (ed.), 'Job', in The Peshitta Institute, *The Old Testament in Syriac According to the Peshitta Version* (Leiden: E.J. Brill, 1982).

Rilliet, Frédéric, *Jacques de Saroug: Six homélies festales en prose: Edition critique du texte syriaque, introduction et traduction française* (PO, 43; Turnhout: Brepols, 1986).

Roberts, J.J.M., 'Isaiah in Old Testament Theology', *Int* 36 (1982), pp. 130-43.

Robinson, G.L., *The Book of Isaiah* (Grand Rapids: Baker Book House, rev. edn, 1954).

Rogerson, J.W., and J.D.G. Dunn (eds.), *Commentary 2000* (Grand Rapids: Eerdmans, forthcoming).

—'The Christian Syriac Tradition of Interpretation', in M. Sæbø *et al.* (eds.), *Hebrew Bible/Old Testament. The History of its Interpretation* I. *From the Beginnings to the Middle Ages (until 1300)* 1. *Antiquity* (Göttingen: Vandenhoeck & Ruprecht, 1996), pp. 612-41.

—*Le commentaire sur Genèse–Exode 9,32 du manuscrit (olim) Diyarbakyr 22* (trans.; CSCO, 483, Syr, 205; Leuven: Peeters, 1986).

Rost, L., *Israel bei den Propheten* (BWANT, 71; Stuttgart: Kohlhammer, 1937).

Rothenberg, B., and A. Blanco-Freijeiro, *Studies in Ancient Mining and Metallurgy in South-West Spain* (London: The Institute for Archaeo-Metallurgical Studies, 1981).

Rudolph, W., *Hosea* (KAT, 13/1; Gütersloh: Gerd Mohn, 1966).

Rüger, H.P., *Text und Textform im hebräischen Sirach* (BZAW, 112; Berlin: W. de Gruyter, 1970).

Sabatier, P., *Bibliorum Sacrorum Latinae Versiones antiquae* (Rheims, 1743 [1749]).

Sachs, Michael, *Festgebete der Israeliten* (New Year vol.; Breslau, 23rd edn, 1898).

Saebø, M. (ed.), *Hebrew Bible / Old Testament: The History of its Interpretation. I. From the Beginnings to the Middle Ages (Until 1300); Part 1: Antiquity* (Göttingen: Vandenhoeck & Ruprecht, 1996).

Saley, R.J., *The Samuel Manuscript of Jacob of Edessa: A Study in its Underlying Textual Traditions* (MPIL, 9; Leiden: E.J. Brill, 1998).

Salvesen, A., *Symmachus in the Pentateuch* (JSS Monograph, 15; Manchester: Manchester University Press, 1991).

—'Hexaplaric Readings in Išoʻdad of Merv's Commentary on Genesis', in J. Frishman and L. Van Rompay (eds.), *The Book of Genesis in Jewish and Oriental Christian Interpretation: A Collection of Essays* (TEG, 5; Leuven: Peeters, 1997), pp. 229-52.

—*The Books of Samuel in the Syriac Version of Jacob of Edessa* (MPIL, 10; Leiden: E.J. Brill, 1999).

Samely, A., *The Interpretation of Speech in the Pentateuch Targums: A Study of Method and Presentation in Targumic Exegesis* (TSAJ, 27; Tübingen: J.C.B. Mohr [Paul Siebeck], 1992).

Sanders, J.A., 'Comparative Wisdom: L'Oeuvre Terrien', in J.G. Gammie *et al.* (eds.), *Israelite Wisdom: Theological and Literary Essays in Honour of Samuel Terrien* (New York: Scholars Press for Union Theological Seminary, 1978), pp. 3-14.

Sanders, J.T., 'Ben Sira's Ethics of Caution', *HUCA* 50 (1979), pp. 73-106.

Scher, A., *Theodorus bar Kōnī: Liber Scholiorum 1* (CSCO, 55, Syr, 19; Paris: Imprimerie Nationale, 1910).

Scher, A., and R. Griveau, *Histoire nestorienne (Chronique de Séert)*, II/2 (PO, 13.4; Paris: Firmin-Didot, 1918).

Schiffman, L.H., 'Maccabees, Fourth Book of', in J.H. Hayes (ed.), *Dictionary of Biblical Interpretation* (Nashville: Abingdon Press, 1999), pp. 104-106.

Schleusner, J.F., *Novus thesaurus philologico-criticus, sive lexicon in LXX et reliquos interpretes graecos ac scriptores apocryphos Veteris Testamenti* (3 vols.; Leipzig: Weidmann, 1820–21; 2nd edn, Glasgow: Duncan, 1822 and London: Duncan, 1829; repr. Turnhout: Brepols, 1994).

Schmidt, H., *Die grossen Propheten* (Göttingen: Vandenhoeck & Ruprecht, 2nd edn, 1923).

Schmidt, W.H., 'Wo hat die Aussage: Jahwe "der Heilige" ihren Ursprung?', *ZAW* 74 (1962), pp. 62-66.

—*Alttestamentliche Glaube und seine Umwelt: Zur Geschichte des alttestamentlichen Gottesverständnisses* (Neukirchen–Vluyn: Neukirchener Verlag, 1968) (ET, *The Faith of the Old Testament: A History* [Oxford: Basil Blackwell, 1983]).

Schmitt, J.J., 'The God of Israel and the Holy One', *Hebrew Studies* 24 (1983), pp. 27-31.

Schmuttermayr, G., *Psalm 18 and 2 Samuel 22: Studien zu einem Doppeltext* (SANT, 25; Munich: Kösel, 1971).

Schoettgen, C., *Horae hebraicae et talmudicae*, I (Dresden: C. Hekel, 1733).

Schreiner, J., 'Das Buch jesajanischer Schule', in J. Schreiner (ed.), *Wort und Botschaft: Eine theologische und kritische Einführung in die Probleme des Alten Testaments* (Würzburg: Echter Verlag, 1967), pp. 143-62.

Schürer, E., *The History of the Jewish People in the Time of Jesus Christ* (rev. and ed. G. Vermes, F. Millar and M. Goodman; Edinburgh: T. & T. Clark, 1986).

Schwarzschild, S., and S. Berman, 'Noachide Laws', *EncJud* 12 (1972), pp. 1189-90.

Scoralick, R., *Trishagion und Gottesherrschaft: Psalm 99 als Neuinterpretation von Tora und Propheten* (SBS, 138; Stuttgart: Katholisches Bibelwerk, 1989).

Sebök, M., *Die syrische Übersetzung der zwölf kleinen Propheten* (Breslau, 1887).

Segal, J.B., *The Diacritical Point and the Accents in Syriac* (Oxford: Oxford University Press, 1953).

—'The Jews of Northern Mesopotamia before the Rise of Islam', in J.M. Grintz and J. Liver (eds.), *Studies in the Bible Presented to Professor M.H. Segal* (Jerusalem: Israel Society for Biblical Research by Kiryat Sepher, 1964), pp. 32-63.

Segal, M., and M. Dagut, *English-Hebrew Dictionary* (Jerusalem: Kiriath Sepher, 1977).

Sekine, S., *Die Tritojesajanische Sammlung (Jes 56–66) redaktionsgeschichtlich unter-sucht* (BZAW, 175; Berlin: W. de Gruyter, 1989).

Selms, A. van, 'Isaiah 28 9-13: An Attempt to give a New Interpretation', *ZAW* 85 (1973), pp. 332-39.

—'The Expression "The Holy One of Israel" ', in W.C. Delsman *et al.* (eds.), *Von Kanaan bis Kerala: Festschrift für Prof. Mag. Dr. Dr. J.P.M. van der Ploeg O.P. zur Vollendung des siebzigsten Lebensjahres am 4. Juli 1979* (AOAT, 211; Kevelaer: Butzon & Bercker; Neukirchen–Vluyn: Neukirchener Verlag, 1982), pp. 257-69.

Seow, C.L., 'Ark of the Covenant', *ABD* I (1992), pp. 386-93.

Shepherd, D., 'Translating and Supplementing: A(nother) Look at the Targumic Versions of Genesis 4.3-16', *JAB* 1 (1999), pp. 125-46.

—'Will the Real Targum Please Stand Up? Translation and Coordination in the Ancient Aramaic Versions of Job', *JJS* 51/1 (2000), pp. 88-116.

Shunary, J., 'Avoidance of Anthropomorphism in the Targum of Psalms', *Textus* 5 (1966), pp. 133-44.

Silva, M., 'Bilingualism and the Character of Palestinian Greek', *Bib* 61 (1980), pp. 198-219.

Sirat, C., *Du Scribe au Livre* (Paris: CNRS, 1994).

Skehan, P.W., 'The Text of Isaias at Qumran', *CBQ* 12 (1955), pp. 158-63.

—'Littérature de Qumrân: A) Textes bibliques', *DBSup* IX (1978), pp. 805-22.

Skehan, P.W., and A. Di Lella, *The Wisdom of Ben Sira* (AB, 39; Garden City, NY: Doubleday, 1987).

Skinner, J., *The Book of the Prophet Isaiah: Chapters XL–LXVI* (Cambridge Bible for Schools and Colleges; Cambridge: Cambridge University Press, 2nd edn, 1917).

Smelik, W.F. *The Targum of Judges* (OTS, 36; Leiden: E.J. Brill, 1995).

—'Translation and Commentary in One: The Interplay of Pluses and Substitutions in the Targum of the Prophets', *JSJ* 29 (1998), pp. 245-60.

—'Concordance and Consistency: Translation Studies and Targum Jonathan', *JJS* 49 (1998), pp. 286-305.

Smith, Jessie Payne, *A Compendious Syriac Dictionary* (Oxford: Clarendon Press, 1903) *see also* Margoliouth, J.P.

Smith, M.S., *The Origins and Development of the Waw-Consecutive: Northwest Semitic Evidence from Ugarit to Qumran* (HSS, 39; Atlanta: Scholars Press, 1991).

Smith, P.A., *Rhetoric and Redaction in Trito-Isaiah: The Structure, Growth and Author-ship of Isaiah 56–66* (VTSup, 62; Leiden: E.J. Brill, 1995).

Smith, R. Payne (ed.), *Thesaurus Syriacus* (Oxford: Clarendon Press, 1879–1897).

Smolar, L., and M. Aberbach, *Studies in Targum Jonathan to the Prophets* (Baltimore: Ktav, 1983).

Snaith, N.H., 'Isaiah 40–66: A Study of the Teaching of the Second Isaiah and its Con-sequences', in H.M. Orlinsky and N.H. Snaith, *Studies on the Second Part of the Book of Isaiah* (VTSup, 14; Leiden: E.J. Brill, 1967), pp. 139-46.

Soderlund, S., *The Greek Text of Jeremiah: A Revised Hypothesis* (JSOTSup, 47; Sheffield: JSOT Press, 1985).

Sokoloff, M., *The Targum to Job from the Qumran Cave XI* (Ramat Gan: Bar Ilan Uni-versity Press, 1974).

—*A Dictionary of Jewish Palestinian Aramaic of the Byzantine Period* (Ramat Gan: Bar Ilan University Press, 1990).

Sommer, B.D., *A Prophet Reads Scripture: Allusion in Isaiah 40-66* (Stanford: Stanford University Press, 1998)

Sörries, R., *Die syrische Bibel von Paris. Paris BN syr. 341: Eine frühchristliche Bilderhandschrift aus dem 6. Jahrhundert* (Wiesbaden: Ludwig Reichert, 1991).

Souter, A., *A Glossary of Later Latin to 600 AD* (Oxford: Oxford University Press, 1949).

Sperber, A. (ed.), *The Bible in Aramaic* (5 vols.; Leiden: E.J. Brill, 1959–1973).

Sperber, D., *Material Culture in Eretz-Israel during the Talmudic Period* (Jerusalem: Bar Ilan, 1993).

Staalduine-Sulman, van, E., *Samuel* (A Bilingual Concordance to the Targum of the Prophets, 3; Leiden: E.J. Brill, 1996).

—'Reward and Punishment in the Messianic Age (Targum 2 Sam. 23.1-8)', *JAB* 1 (1999), pp. 273-96.

Stec, D.M. (ed.), *The Text of the Targum of Job: An Introduction and Critical Edition* (AGJU, 20; Leiden: E.J. Brill, 1994).

Steck, O.H., *Studien zu Tritojesaja* (BZAW, 203; Berlin: W. de Gruyter, 1991).

Stern, P., 'The Eighth Century Dating of Psalm 78 Re-argued', *HUCA* 66 (1995), pp. 41-65.

Stevenson, W.B., *Grammar of Palestinian Jewish Aramaic* (Oxford: Clarendon Press, 1924).

Strothmann, W., *Konkordanz zur syrischen Bibel* (14 vols.; Wiesbaden: Otto Harrasowitz, 1984–1995).

Strugnell, J. (ed.), *Qumran Cave XIV* (DJD, 19; Oxford: Clarendon Press, 1995).

Šubḥalmaran, *The Book of Gifts,* British Library Oriental MS 6714 fols 1-73.

Suggs, M.J., 'The Use of Patristic Evidence in the Search for a Primitive New Testament Text', *NTS* 4 (1957–58), pp. 139-47.

Sweeney, M.A., *Isaiah 1–39, with an Introduction to the Prophetic Literature* (FOTL, 16; Grand Rapids: Eerdmans, 1996).

Swete, H.B., *Introduction to the Old Testament in Greek* (Cambridge: Cambridge University Press, 2nd edn, 1914).

Syrén, R., *The Blessings in the Targums: A Study on the Targumic Interpretations of Genesis 49 and Deuteronomy 33* (AAAbo.H, 64/1; Åbo: Åbo Akademie, 1986).

Szpek, H.M., *Translation Technique in the Peshitta to Job* (SBLDS, 137; Atlanta: Scholars Press, 1992).

Tal, A., *The Language of the Targum of the Former Prophets and its Position within the Aramaic Dialects* [Hebrew] (Tel-Aviv: Tel-Aviv University Press, 1975).

Talmon, S., 'The Ancient Hebrew Alphabet and Biblical Text Criticism', in A. Caquot, S. Légasse and M. Tardieu (eds.), *Mélanges bibliques et orientaux en l'honneur de M. Mathias Delcor* (AOAT, 215; Neukirchen–Vluyn: Neukirchener Verlag, 1985), pp. 387-402.

Tanghye, V., 'Dichtung und Ekel in Jesaia xxviii 7-13', *VT* 43 (1953), pp. 235-60.

Tate, M.E., *Psalms 51–100* (WBC, 20; Dallas: Word Books, 1990).

Tcherikover, V.A., 'The Third Book of Maccabees as a Historical Source of Augustus' Time', *Scripta Hierosolymitana* 7 (1961), pp. 1-25 = *Zion* 10 (1944-45), pp. 1-20 [Hebrew].

Terrien, S., *Job* (CAT, 13; Neuchâtel: Delachaux et Niestlé, 1963).

—'The Religion of Israel', in C.M. Laymon (ed.), *The Interpreter's One-Volume Commentary on the Bible* (Nashville: Abingdon Press, 1971; repr. London: Collins, 1972), pp. 1150-58.

—*The Elusive Presence: Toward a New Biblical Theology* (Religious Perspectives, 26; San Francisco: Harper & Row, 1978).

Thomas, D.W., *The Text of the Revised Psalter* (London: SPCK, 1963).

Tiller, P.A., *A Commentary on the Animal Apocalypse of 1 Enoch* (SBL Early Judaism and its Literature, 4; Atlanta: Scholars Press, 1993).

Tondriaux, J., 'Les Thiases dionysiaques royaux de la Cour ptolémaïque', *Chronique d'Egypte* (1946), pp. 149-71.

Torrey, C.C., *The Second Isaiah: A New Interpretation* (Edinburgh: T. & T. Clark, 1928).

Tov, E., 'Lucian and Proto-Lucian', *RB* 79 (1972), pp. 101-13.

—'Some Aspects of the Textual and Literary History of the Book of Jeremiah', in Pierre-Maurice Bogaert (ed.), *Le Livre de Jérémie, le prophète et son milieu, les oracles et leur transmission* (BETL, 54; Leuven: Leuven University Press, 1981), pp. 145-67.

—'The Literary History of the Book of Jeremiah in the Light of its Textual History', in J.H. Tigay (ed.), *Empirical Models for Biblical Criticism* (Philadelphia: University of Pennsylvania Press, 1985), pp. 211-37.

—*Textual Criticism of the Hebrew Bible* (Minneapolis: Fortress Press; Assen: Van Gorcum, 1992).

—'The Significance of the Texts from the Judean Desert for the History of the Text of the Hebrew Bible: A New Synthesis', in F.H. Cryer and T.L. Thompson (eds.), *Qumran between the Old and New Testaments* (JSOTSup, 290; Sheffield: Sheffield Academic Press, 1998), pp. 277-309.

—'Die biblischen Handschriften aus der Wüste Juda—Eine neue Synthese', in U. Dahmen, A. Lange and H. Lichtenberger (eds.), *Die Textfunde vom Toten Meer und der Text der Hebraïschen Bibel* (Neukirchen–Vluyn: Neukirchener Verlag, 2000), pp. 1-34.

Tracy, S., 'III Maccabees and Pseudo-Aristeas', *Yale Classical Studies* 1 (1928), pp. 241-52.

Tur-Sinai, N.H., *The Book of Job: A New Commentary* (Jerusalem: Kiryath Sefer, 1957).

—'ארון', *'Ensiqlopediah miqra'ith* (Jerusalem: Mosad Bialik, 1950), I, pp. 538-50.

Tur-Sinai, N.H., 'ṣaw', in E. Ben Yehuda, *A Complete Dictionary of Ancient and Modern Hebrew*, VI (repr.; New York: Thomas Yoseloff, 1960), p. 5047.

Uhlig, S., *Das äthiopische Henochbuch* (JSHRZ, 5/6; Gütersloh: Gütersloher Verlagshaus Gerd Mohn, 1984).

—*Äthiopische Paläographie* (Äthiopistische Forschungen, 22; Stuttgart: Franz Steiner Verlag, 1988).

Ullendorff, E., 'C'est de l'hébreu pour moi!', *JSS* 13 (1968), pp. 125-35.

Ulrich, E., et al. (eds.), *Qumran Cave 4.X: The Prophets* (DJD, 15; Oxford: Clarendon Press, 1997).

Vandenhoff, B., *Exegesis Psalmorum, imprimis messianicorum, apud Syros Nestorianos e codice adhuc inedito illustrata* (Rheine: Altmeppen, 1899).

VanderKam, J.C., 'Righteous One, Messiah, Chosen One, and Son of Man in 1 Enoch 37–71', in J.H. Charlesworth (ed.), *The Messiah: Developments in Earliest Judaism and Christianity* (Minneapolis: Fortress Press, 1992), pp. 169-91.

Van Rompay, L., *Théodore de Mopsueste: Fragments syriaques du commentaire des Psaumes (Psaume 118 et Psaumes 138–148)* (trans.; CSCO, 436, Syr, 190; Leuven: Peeters, 1982).

Vattioni, F. (ed.), *Ecclesiastico* (Naples: Istituto Orientale di Napoli, 1968).

Vaux, R. de, *Ancient Israel: Its Life and Institutions* (trans. J. McHugh; London: Darton, Longman & Todd, 1961).

Veenhof, K.R., *Aspects of Old Assyrian Trade and its Terminology* (Leiden: E.J. Brill, 1972).

Vermes, G., 'Haggadah in the Onkelos Targum', *JSS* 8 (1963), pp. 159-69.

—*Scripture and Tradition in Judaism: Haggadic Studies* (SPB, 4; Leiden: E.J. Brill, 2nd edn, 1983).

—*The Complete Dead Sea Scrolls in English* (London: Allen Lane, The Penguin Press, 1997).

Vermeylen, J., *Du prophète Isaïe à l'apocalyptique: Isaïe, I–XXXV, miroir d'un demi-millénaire d'experience religieuse en Israël*, II (Paris: J. Gabalda, 1978).

—'Hypothèses sur l'origine d'Isaïe 36–39', in J. van Ruiten and M. Vervenne (eds.), *Studies in the Book of Isaiah: Festschrift Willem A.M. Beuken* (BETL, 132; Leuven: Leuven University Press/Peeters, 1997), pp. 95-118.

Vööbus, A., *The Statutes of the School of Nisibis* (Stockholm, 1961).

—*A History of the School of Nisibis* (CSCO, 226, Subs, 26; Leuven: Peeters, 1965).

—*The Pentateuch in the Version of the Syro-Hexapla: A Fac-simile Edition of a Midyat MS. Discovered 1964* (CSCO, 369, Subs, 45; Leuven: Peeters, 1975).

—*The Lectionary of the Monastery of 'Aziza'el in Tur 'Abdin, Mesopotamia. A Startling Depository of the Syro-Hexapla Texts: A Facsimile Edition of MS. Mardin Orth. 47* (CSCO, 466, Subs, 73; Leuven: Peeters, 1985).

—*A Syriac Lectionary from the Church of the Forty Martyrs in Mardin, Tur 'Abdin, Mesopotamia* (CSCO, 485, Subs, 76; Leuven: Peeters, 1986).

Vosté, J.-M., 'Les citations syro-hexaplaires d'Išo'dad de Merv dans le Commentaire sur les Psaumes', *Bib* 26 (1945), pp. 12-36.

Wallace, S.L., 'Census and Poll Tax in Ptolemaic Egypt', *American Journal of Philology* 59 (1938), pp. 418-42.

Weber, R., *et al.* (eds.), *Biblia Sacra iuxta Vulgatam Versionem*, II (Stuttgart: Württembergische Bibelanstalt, 1969).

Walton, B. (ed.), *Biblia Sacra Polyglotta* (London, 1657).

Wechter, P., *Ibn Barun's Arabic works on Hebrew Grammar and Lexicography* (Philadephia: The Dropsie College for Hebrew and Cognate Learning, 1964).

Weiss, R., *The Aramaic Targum of the Book of Job* [Hebrew] (Tel Aviv: Tel Aviv University Press, 1979).

Weitzman, M.P., 'A Statistical Approach to Textual Criticism, with Special Reference to the Peshitta of the Old Testament' (2 vols., unpublished PhD thesis, University of London, 1974).

—'The Tradition of Manuscripts: A New Approach to the Text of Cyprian: *De Unitate*', *HeyJ* 19 (1978), pp. 28-45.

—'The Analysis of Manuscript Traditions: Isaiah (Peshitta Version) and the Gospel of Matthew', in *Les actes de la deuxième conférence de l'AIBI: Bible et informatique* (Geneva: Slatkine, 1989), pp. 641-52.

—'From Judaism to Christianity: The Syriac Version of the Hebrew Bible', in Judith Lieu, John North and Tessa Rajak (eds.), *The Jews among Pagans and Christians: In the Roman Empire* (London: Routledge, 1992), pp. 147-73.

—'The Interpretative Character of the Syriac Old Testament', in Magne Saebø (ed.), *Hebrew Bible/Old Testament* (Göttingen: Vandenhoeck & Ruprecht, 1996), pp. 587-611 (repr. in A. Rapoport-Albert and G. Greenberg [eds.], *From Judaism to Christianity* [JSSSup, 8; Oxford: Oxford University Press, 1999], pp. 55-89).

—'Is the Peshitta of Chronicles a Targum?', in Paul V.M. Flesher (ed.), *Targum and Peshitta* (Targum Studies, 2, South Florida Studies in the History of Judaism, 165; Atlanta: Scholars Press, 1998), pp. 159-93.

—'The Peshitta Psalter and its Hebrew Vorlage', VT 35 (1985), pp. 341-54, reprinted in A. Rapoport-Albert and G. Greenberg (eds.), *From Judaism to Christianity* (JSSSup, 8; Oxford: Oxford University Press, 1999), pp. 114-29.

—'The Originality of Unique Readings in Peshitta MS 9a1', in P.B. Dirksen and M.J. Mulder (eds.), *The Peshitta: Its Early Text and History* (MPIL, 4; Leiden: E.J. Brill, 1988), pp. 225–258, reprinted in A. Rapoport-Albert and G. Greenberg (eds.), *From Judaism to Christianity* (JSSSup, 8; Oxford: Oxford University Press, 1999), pp. 325-46.

—'Peshitta, Septuagint and Targum', in R. Lavenant (ed.), *Symposium Syriacum VI 1992* (OCA; Rome: PIB, 1994), pp. 51-84, reprinted in A. Rapoport-Albert and G. Greenberg (eds.), *From Judaism to Christianity* (JSSSup, 8; Oxford: Oxford University Press, 1999), pp. 181-216.

—'The Hebrew and Syriac Texts of the Book of Job', in A. Rapoport-Albert and G. Greenberg (eds.), *From Judaism to Christianity* (JSSSup, 8; Oxford: Oxford University Press, 1999), pp. 130-48.

—*The Syriac Version of the Old Testament: An Introduction* (University of Cambridge Oriental Publications, 56; Cambridge: Cambridge University Press, 1999).

Walton, B. (ed.), *Biblia Sacra Polyglotta* (London, 1657).

Wellhausen, J., *Skizzen und Vorarbeiten.* V. *Die kleinen Propheten übersetzt und erklärt* (Berlin: G. Reimer, 3rd edn, 1892; 4th edn, 1898).

Wendt, K., *Das Maṣḥafa Milad (Liber Nativitatis) und Maṣḥafa Sellase (Liber Trinitatis) des Kaisers Zar'a Ya'qob* (4 vols.; CSCO, 221-22, 235-36, Scriptores Aethiopici, 41-44; Louvain: Secrétariat du Corpus SCO, 1962, 1963).

Werner, W., *Studien zur alttestamentlichen Vorstellung vom Plan Jahwes* (BZAW, 173; Berlin: W. de Gruyter, 1988).

Westerholz, J.G., *Images of Inspiration: The Old Testament in Early Christian Art* (Jerusalem: Bible Lands Museum, 2000).

Westermann, C., *Das Buch Jesaja, 40–66* (ATD, 19; Göttingen: Vandenhoeck & Ruprecht, 1966) (ET, *Isaiah 40–66: A Commentary* [OTL; London: SCM Press, 1969]).

White, E., *A Critical Edition of the Targum of Psalms: A Computer Generated Text of Books 1 and 2* (unpublished PhD dissertation, McGill University, Montreal, 1988).

—*Jesaja 1–12* (BKAT, 10/1; Neukirchen–Vluyn: Neukirchener Verlag, 2nd edn, 1980) (ET, *Isaiah 1–12: A Commentary* [Minneapolis: Fortress Press, 1991]).

Wilken, R.L., *John Chrysostom and the Jews* (Berkeley: University of California Press, 1983).

Williamson, H.G.M., *The Book Called Isaiah: Deutero-Isaiah's Role in Composition and Redaction* (Oxford: Clarendon Press, 1994).

—'Relocating Isaiah 1:2-9', in C.C. Broyles and C.A. Evans (eds.), *Writing and Reading the Scroll of Isaiah: Studies of an Interpretive Tradition*, I (VTSup, 50, 1; Leiden: E.J. Brill, 1997), pp. 263-77.

Willrich, H., 'Der historische Kern des III Makkabäerbuches', *Hermes* 39 (1904), pp. 244-58.

Winter, M.M., 'The Origins of Ben Sira in Syriac (Part I)', *VT* 26 (1977), pp. 237-41.

Wordsworth, W.A., *Sawn Asunder: A Study of the Mystery of the Gospel of Isaiah* (London: Alexander Moring, 1927).

Wright, W., 'Two Epistles of Mar Jacob, Bishop of Edessa', *Journal of Sacred Literature and Biblical Record* NS 10 (1867), pp. 430-60.

—*Catalogue of Syriac Manuscripts in the British Museum, Acquired since the Year 1838*, I (London: The Trustees of the British Museum, 1870).

Yadin, Y., *The Ben Sira Scroll from Masada* (Jerusalem: The Israel Exploration Society and The Shrine of the Book, 1965).

Yadin, Y. (ed.), מגילת המקדש, II, *The Temple Scroll* (Jerusalem: Israel Exploration Society, 1983).

Young, E.J., *Who Wrote Isaiah?* (Grand Rapids: Eerdmans, 1958).

Zapff, B.M., *Schriftgelehrte Prophetie—Jes 13 und die Komposition des Jesajabuches: Ein Beitrag zur Erforschung der Redaktionsgeschichte des Jesajabuches* (FzB, 74; Würzburg: Echter Verlag, 1995).

Ziegler, J., *Untersuchungen zur Septuaginta des Buches Isaias* (Alttestamentliche Abhandlungen, 12/3; Münster: Aschendorffsche Verlagsbuchhandlung, 1934).

—*Septuaginta, Vetus Testamentum graecum*, XII/2. *Sapientia Jesu Filii Sirach* (Göttingen: Vandenhoeck & Ruprecht, 1965).

Ziegler, J. (ed.), *Duodecim Prophetae* (Göttingen: Vandenhoeck & Ruprecht, 1967).

Zimmerli, W., 'Zur Sprache Tritojesajas', in *idem, Gottes Offenbarung: Gesammelte Aufsätze zum Alten Testament* (TBü, 19; Munich: Chr. Kaiser Verlag, 1963), pp. 217-33.

Zotenberg, H., *Manuscrits orientaux. Catalogues des manuscrits syriaques et sabéens (Mandaïtes) de la Bibliothèque nationale* (Paris: Imprimerie nationale, 1874).

Zunz, L., *Die gottesdienstlichen Vorträge der Juden historisch entwickelt* (Frankfurt: J. Kaufmann, 2nd edn, 1892).

INDEXES

INDEX OF REFERENCES

OLD TESTAMENT

APOCRYPHA

PSEUDEPIGRAPHA

NEW TESTAMENT

DEAD SEA SCROLLS

Qumran		*4QpIsa(b)*		37.13	289, 293-95
1QH		2.7	314		
1.28-29	47				
		4QpIsa(e)		*4Q375*	117
1QH(a)		5.2	310		
9.28-29	47			*11QT*	
		4QpHab		7.12	117
1QpHab		12.3-4	313		
10.9	46			*CD*	
		11Q10		1.14	46
1QS		5.10	291	4.19	46
7.24-25	172	30.3	292	7.1	46
8.23	172	34.11	287	8.13	46
10.9	47	37.12	296	20.7	172

TARGUMS

Frag. Targ. Gen.		*Sam. Targ. 2 Kgs*		22.21	268
42.23	264	5.23	172	24.18	268
				25.17	262
Genizah frag. Gen.		*Targ. Josh.*		25.25	262
34.15	172	5.7	269	30.22	262
34.22	172	5.8	269		
34.23	172			*Targ. 2 Sam.*	
		Targ. Judg.		2.2	278
Frag. Targ. Exod.		5	262	2.23	269
12.42	264	5.1	256	3.12	269
14.13	264	5.2	256, 277	7.10	269
15.9	270	5.12	266	11.11	275
27.4	174	5.13	276	16.7	262
		5.20	276	19.37	268
Frag. Targ. Lev.		5.31	269	20.1	262
22.27	264	7.21	269	22	245-47, 249, 252, 254, 258, 259, 273, 281
		11.1	278		
Frag. Targ. Deut.		19.22	262		
27.15	264	20.13	262		
				22.1	252, 258, 266, 271
Frag. Targ. 2 Sam.		*Targ. 1 Sam.*		22.2-3	271
22.28	281	1.16	262	22.3	267
		2.1	277	22.4	258, 273, 274
Pal. Targ. 1 Kgs		2.12	262		
16.34	277	10.27	262		
17.1	277	14.9	269		

MIDRASH

OTHER POSTBIBLICAL HEBREW SOURCES

INDEX OF AUTHORS